LAW AND VALUATION
OF LEISURE PROPERTY

LAW AND VALUATION
OF LEISURE PROPERTY
Second Edition

Edited by
HAZEL WILLIAMSON QC MA FCIArba
and
HARVEY MARSHALL BSc FRICS

1996

Estates Gazette

A member of Reed Business Publishing

The Estates Gazette Limited
151 Wardour Street, London W1V 4BN

First published 1994
Second edition 1996

ISBN 0 7282 0275 1

© Note:
For details as to copyright see end of each chapter

**The authors' royalties on the sale of this book have been donated to the
Royal Institution of Chartered Surveyors Benevolent Fund and the
Barristers' Benevolent Fund**

Typeset by Keyword Publishing Services
Printed in Great Britain by The Lavenham Press Ltd, Suffolk

FOREWORD

Sir Colin Marshall, Chairman, British Airways;
President, Confederation of British Industry

Travel and tourism is now the world's largest industry, by virtually every gauge of economic measurement. It is not only set to grow further in the years ahead, but is also widely acknowledged as one of the industries – along with telecommunications – which will become the key drivers of the world economy in the 21st Century.

In Britain alone, travel and tourism now accounts for annual capital investment of more than £12 billion. By the year 2006, according to the World Travel & Tourism Council, industry growth will see that figure almost double, to £22.5 billion. In the process, more than 300,000 new jobs are expected to be created.

The backbone of this important, dynamic industry is formed not by the major travel and tourism companies, such as airlines and hotel groups, but by myriad small and medium sized enterprises committed to serving the booming leisure market.

The very nature of leisure services and facilities means that a substantial part of the industry's increasing level of capital expenditure will go on land and buildings of all kinds, at every level of the property market. In the context of travel and tourism, property is an area of investment with its own, distinct characteristics, which need to be understood fully.

With 'Law and Valuation of Leisure Property', Harvey Marshall and Hazel Williamson bring their combined experience in the property and legal professions, to bear on this intricate subject. Their work is an important contribution to the further, successful development of the travel, tourism and leisure industry in this country.

PREFACE

Even though only just over two years has passed since the first edition was published, it has been surprising how much has changed in the leisure market. This edition reflects the changes that have taken place and are taking place.

Lord Alexander, in the first edition, mentioned how the idea for the book came about as a result of a meeting between a surveyor and Counsel on a particular leisure problem. Since the publication of the first edition the book has become the leading text in the area and had to be re-printed. Owing to the high demand and the many changes that have taken place this new edition will update practitioners. We are also extremely pleased that two new contributors have included sections on golf courses and garden centres.

Sir Colin Marshall, who has written the Foreword to this edition, emphasises the importance of tourism and travel as the world's largest industry. Leisure property forms an important part of this industry and he acknowledges the importance of property to the industry. Only by taking the very best advice and guidance, as is contained in this book, will the operator or investor feel comfortable in being involved in leisure.

Once again, we should like to thank the contributors for the very hard work that they have put into their contributions to the book. Their patience and understanding on the inevitable delays that have taken place during the preparation of the second edition has been tremendous.

HAZEL WILLIAMSON QC MA FCIArb
A Recorder of the South Eastern Circuit
Bencher Gray's Inn
13 Old Square
LONDON WC2

HARVEY MARSHALL BSc FRICS
28 Brook Street
LONDON W1

PREFACE TO THE FIRST EDITION

For most of us there is an involvement with leisure property at some point in our daily lives. Professionally, however, leisure property for the general practitioner in either law or property is a subject that only occasionally passes across the desk. It has, therefore, become a specialist subject, broken down into the particular areas upon which this book is based.

The aim of the book is to assist understanding of the principles of law and valuation touching and affecting various types of leisure property. A word of caution must be given in that, as with any text book, it is dangerous to rely solely upon what one reads without having some practical experience of the matter as well. What this book will do, we hope, is to provide a basis upon which to build ideas and a sound understanding of the law and valuation techniques applicable to leisure property.

As Lord Alexander has mentioned in his foreword, the idea for this book came about as a result of a conference with counsel when the matter of identifying an authoritive book on leisure property was raised. We came to the conclusion that no such book existed – at any rate in a form which drew together the various types and aspects of leisure property and its valuation. This book is not exhaustive and there are several types of leisure property which have not been specifically addressed. There has been a limitation on space in this edition and so we have strived to include in this book the main areas that will be of most use and interest to the general practitioner. Like most books of this type there have been a considerable number of amendments as the book progressed through its various stages. In addition, we live in a very fast and changing world and while we have endeavoured therefore to bring the latest information to the reader's attention, inevitably some of the information will become out of date before long. This particularly applies to the figures used in the various examples of valuations contained within the book.

We should like to thank the contributors to the book whose patience in the preparation and delays that have occurred has been outstanding. We hope that everyone finds the work interesting and informative and we would welcome any observations that you may have upon the content.

HAZEL WILLIAMSON QC MA FCIArb
13 Old Square
Lincoln's Inn
LONDON WC2

HARVEY MARSHALL BSc FRICS
49 Berkeley Square
LONDON W1X 6AL

THE AUTHORS

TABLE OF CASES

TABLE OF STATUTES

Table of Statutes

TABLE OF STATUTORY INSTRUMENTS

CHAPTER 1

Law affecting leisure property

Introduction

Leisure property is a category of real property. There is no legal definition of "leisure property" although the word "leisure" has crept into the Town and Country Planning Use (Classes Order) 1987. Use Class D2 is described as "assembly and leisure". It comprises (a) cinema, (b) concert hall, (c) bingo hall or casino, (d) dance hall, (e) swimming bath, skating rink, gymnasium or other indoor sports or recreation not involving motorised vehicles or firearms.

"Leisure property" in the surveying world is a wider concept, and includes hotels, restaurants and public houses, outdoor sporting and recreational properties such as golf courses, marinas and sports grounds, as well as holiday camps and caravan complexes.

There is no special "law of leisure property", except in the sense that it is often the subject of special regulation in the interests of safety, health, public order and minimising the occasion for crime; the promoting of most leisure activities requires a licence of some sort. The general law relating to real property applies equally to leisure property as to any other property, as do all other principles of general law capable of affecting the activities carried on on leisure property. However, the nature of leisure property means that certain principles of general law assume special importance in a leisure property context.

Leisure property has two features which distinguish it particularly from other commercial property. First and foremost, the value of the property arises from and depends on the value of the business which is being, or which can be, carried on upon it. Second, that business invariably involves members of the public being invited on to the property for the purpose of enjoying some activity, recreation or entertainment, provided by that business.

These features have consequences for the property interest. As value rests upon the success of the business, anything which restricts or interferes with the possibility of profiting from that business will affect the value of the property. These factors may not merely be actual restrictions but potential restrictions which limit or inhibit expansion or change of character. Insofar as they are legal rather than physical restrictions, they may be of a public nature arising from statute (planning control, licensing requirements, safety restrictions, and so on) or they may stem from private relations, such as the terms of a lease, the imposition of restrictive covenants, or the simple common law rights of neighbours.

Since the success of a leisure business will often depend on client loyalty, the business or property reputation, or "goodwill", assumes a greater importance for leisure property than in other property sectors.

The nature of leisure operations is such that the operator frequently has to make a major investment in facilities or equipment. Laying out of grounds, erecting or altering buildings, fitting-out works, the acquisition of gaming machines or equipment for sport, entertainment, hotel or restaurant functions, may be undertaken, depending on the nature of the enterprise. Consequently, and particularly in the case of leasehold property, the law relating to improvements and to fixtures and their ownership is likely to assume a greater importance for leisure property than in other cases.

This chapter does not set out to provide an exhaustive account of all matters of law applicable to leisure property as a sector of property in general. Principles of law of universal application can be found in the standard textbooks such as Megarry and Wade's *Law of Real Property* and Woodfall's *Law of Landlord and Tenant*. Neither is it a manual for leisure property operators. The aim is to provide an indication of the areas of law which either may directly affect or perhaps influence any valuation exercise.

The types of property comprising the description "leisure property" are many and varied, and the section therefore aims to provide a starting point for thought or research in any particular case, just as the valuation sections provide examples of the technique of valuing example types of leisure properties. Insofar as matters affecting the day to day operation of leisure property are dealt with, this is either because they provide an important general knowledge context for the valuation exercise, or because of possible direct implications of those aspects for value.

This chapter is divided into three parts. The first indicates areas of legislative regulation, both by general statutory provision and through control by licensing. The second considers important areas of law governing private relations between the leisure property owner/operator and others. The third looks at legal aspects of valuation situations.

General regulation and licences

General regulation
In addition to general law regulating the state and use of property in general and commercial property in particular, leisure property may be subject to specific regulation according to the nature of the property itself. An example is safety certificates for sports grounds. In addition, the terms of any necessary licences for the conduct of the relevant leisure operation may also impose conditions as to the state of the premises and the facilities provided. Where requirements can be imposed under different statutes (for example, fire safety requirements under general building regulations and under the terms of licences) the legislation will direct which is to prevail. It will usually be the form of regulation made under the statutory system of most recent origin.

The precise basis of regulation may differ according to the location of the property. First, there are still some differences between statutes and regulations applicable in London and in the remainder of the country. These differences arise from the history of building and public health regulation and of the system of local government in the capital and in the rest of England and Wales. Second, there may be other local differences arising, for example, from the existence of local byelaws or Acts of Parliament, or even national policy. Gaming clubs other than bingo halls and bridge and whist clubs are, for example, confined to "permitted areas" under the Gaming Clubs (Permitted Areas) Regulations 1971 (as amended).

It is therefore always important to identify the statutes which are applicable to the particular leisure use in the particular area, both as regards general national legislation and from the specific local perspective.

Public health Leisure property must, naturally, comply with general public health legislation, the code for which is to be found mainly in the Public Health Acts 1936 and 1961 as supplemented by the Clean Air Act 1993, the Health and Safety at Work etc Act 1974, the Control of Pollution Act 1974 and the Environmental Protection Act 1990. The Building Act 1984 and Water Industry Act 1991 Part IV consolidate some of these provisions. Although matters of hygiene, sanitation and building regulation are the general matters of public health most likely to be material to leisure property, other matters covered by the public health code are atmospheric cleanliness, noise pollution, destruction of pests, regulation of sewers and drains and the regulation of dangerous trades. Thus, for example, regulations governing the storage of cine film, being celluloid, were made as part of public health legislation.

Building regulation Building regulation which was previously dealt with in London under the London Building Acts 1930–1939 and regulations made under those Acts, and elsewhere by building regulations under the Public Health Act 1936, has now been largely assimilated across the country, although some provisions of the London Building Acts regarding safety still apply in relation to old or large buildings. Current Building Regulations made generally under the Building Act 1984 (SI 1991/2768, 1992/1180 and 1994/1850) now apply to the whole of England and Wales.

These regulations do not apply to temporary buildings or mobile homes.

Sanitary appliances Apart from general sanitation requirements under building regulation, and the Health and Safety at Work legislation, a local authority is empowered to require the provision of adequate sanitary appliances, suitably positioned, by the owner or occupier of any place normally, or occasionally, used for the holding of any entertainment or sporting event to which the public is admitted either as spectators or participants, or for selling food or drink for consumption on such premises: Local Government Miscellaneous Provisions Act 1976 s 20. Thus, both places of entertainment and restaurants are covered, and the positioning of such appliances would have to accord with building regulations. Such requirement cannot exceed appropriate building regulation standards.

Fire safety Provisions relating to fire safety are complex and vary according to the nature of the property.

Under the Fire Precautions Act 1971, the Secretary of State has power to designate certain classes of use of premises in respect of which to make fire certificates compulsory, and/or to make regulations as to fire precautions. These requirements are imposed on the occupier (and in some cases the owner) of the premises.

The use classes prescribed under Section 1 (2) of the Act include (a) "use . . . for any purpose involving the provision of sleeping accommodation", which thus covers hotels. The Fire Precautions (Hotels and Boarding Houses) Order 1972 (SI 1972/238) was the first to be made. The Fire Precautions (Factories Offices Shops and Railway Premises) Order 1976 (SI 1976/2009) originated after the Health and Safety of Work Act 1974 extended the class of designated uses to "a place of work", and can, therefore, sometimes be applicable to leisure property where office or shop accommodation is included there.

Although "use for the purposes of entertainment, recreation . . . or for the purposes of any club, society or association" and "use for any purpose involving access to the premises by members of the public, whether on payment or otherwise" (Section 1 (2) (c) and (e) of the 1971 Act) are potential classes of leisure property singled out for possible designation, no orders or regulations have yet been made in relation to those classes.

The Fire Safety and Safety of Places of Sport Act 1987 Part I refines the intended scheme of "designation" by making it more flexible, and providing a power for fire authorities to exempt certain premises from fire certificate requirements where appropriate. It also introduces powers of continuing inspection in relation to fire certificate requirements.

Safety certificates in respect of sports grounds and sports stands, under the Fire Safety and Safety of Places of Sport Act 1987 (see below), will include conditions imposed for fire safety reasons.

Where the above statutes do not apply, provision of adequate means of escape in case of fire will be subject to regulation by building regulations, now both within and outside London (see above), by the conditions of particular entertainment licences (see below), by local bye-laws or, in some cases, possibly still under Section 59 of the Public Health Act 1936. This enables the local authority to insist on satisfactory means of ingress to, egress from and passage within buildings of "public resort", including any theatre, hall, or other building used as a place of public resort, any public restaurant in which more than 20 persons are employed, and any club required to be licensed under the Licensing Act 1964. This provision is suspended where any requirements of building regulation, fire certificates or fire precaution regulations or safety certificates for sports ground (see below) come into effect.

Safety at sports grounds Under the Safety of Sports Grounds Act 1975, the Secretary of State is empowered to designate particular sports stadia, having a capacity for 10,000 or more spectators, as requiring a safety certificate, intended to regulate crowd safety and control, which is to be issued by the local authority to a person in a position to secure compliance with its conditions. A general certificate for particular activities or a special certificate for a particular event or events can be issued. Conditions in the certificate will deal with numbers of persons admitted, size and position of exits and their access, both normal and for emergency use, their freedom from obstruction, crush barriers and the like. The police and local building authority must be consulted, and the certificate can require alterations to the stadium. There are provisions for appeals and for variation of certificates, as well as offences.

By the Fire Safety and Safety of Places of Sports Act 1987, the powers under the 1975 Act are extended to all classes of sports ground (the reference to "sports stadium" in the 1975 Act being amended accordingly) with provision for the Secretary of State to designate particular requirements for different classes of sports ground, and to substitute a different figure for the relevant spectator capacity. Certain other minor amendments are made and an emergency procedure, empowering the local authority to serve prohibition notices to prohibit or restrict the admission of spectators until any unacceptable risk to their safety has been remedied, is provided. This is in substitution for the previous procedure by way of application to the court. Relevant regulations have yet to be made.

In addition, however, Part III of the 1987 Act provides for the issue of general and special safety certificates in respect of sports stands at non-designated sports grounds. A "sports stand" is an artificial structure, covered by a roof and providing covered accommodation for spectators at sporting events. Such a stand will be a "regulated stand" if its capacity is more than 500 spectators, and it will require a safety certificate (again, general or special) accordingly. Local authorities have a duty to identify such sports stands within their area and to serve notice which, in effect, will require an application for a safety certificate to be made by the person in control of the stand. Safety certificates will impose appropriate conditions, and where a general certificate is in force, these conditions will override any requirements of, for example, fire certificates, building regulation requirements or requirements of local statutes.

Occupier's liability Consequences of the application of the Occupiers' Liability Act 1957 to leisure property are mentioned below in connection with law governing private relations.

General legislation regulating the workplace and employment Relevant legislation governing the working conditions, such as the requirements of the Health and Safety at Work etc Act 1974 and the Offices, Shops and Railway Premises Act 1963, will apply to leisure property if the qualifying circumstances exist.

Some legislation makes allowance for the special circumstances of leisure activities. However, with the greater freedom as to (for example) shop opening hours and Sunday activities introduced by the Deregulation and Contracting Out Act 1994, the need for such recognition has diminished.

Sunday observance Under the Sunday Observance Act 1780 ss 1 and 2, the holding of any public entertainment in a room, house, or other place (which can include a park: *Culley* v *Harrison* [1956] 2 QB 71) for the payment of admission money, whether charged directly or indirectly (eg by charging a higher price for refreshments) is deemed to be a "disorderly house", and the keeper of it, and any persons managing or advertising it commit offences. However, the Act now no longer applies to any sporting event or activity (Deregulation and Contracting Out Act 1994 s 21), and there are express exceptions for theatrical, cinematograph and music hall entertainments (see the sections below) and also under the Sunday Entertainments Act 1932, in relation to specified entertainments, although these are of a more institutional nature (eg museum, zoological or botanical garden, picture gallery, a lecture or debate).

Planning Planning control applies to leisure property in the same way as to any other property. Under the Town and Country Planning (Use Classes) Order, Class D2 is designated "Assembly and Leisure" and comprises use as (a) a cinema, (b) a concert hall, (c) a bingo hall or casino, (d) a dance hall and (e) a swimming bath, skating rink, gymnasium or other indoor or outdoor sports or recreation not involving motorised vehicles or the use of firearms. However, use as a theatre, or as an amusement arcade or a funfair, is not within any Use Class (Article 3 (6)).

Class C3 comprises use as an hotel, boarding or guest house or as a hostel where, in each case, no significant element of personal care is undertaken.

Restaurant user falls within Class A3.

Caravan parks are a special case, requiring both planning permission and site licences. This is dealt with in the section on Holiday Caravan Parks.

Water The position of leisure property as regards water supply for the normal purposes of drinking, washing and sanitation, is no different from other property, as is the position regarding rights to connect into drains, and obligations regarding pollution.

However, the use of water within or adjoining property for amenity purposes such as fishing, bathing, water sports and boating, or merely as a pleasant setting, is of special importance to leisure property. The law on the use of water for amenity – rights of access, rights of abstraction, fishing rights, bridging rights, right to a level of flow, recreation and navigation rights – is a complex mixture of the private rights of the landowner and the intervention of statute.

Part of the body of law stems from private or public rights deriving from common law. Fishing and navigation rights are two examples. It was only recently established that there is no public right of navigation on a non-tidal river: *Attorney-General (ex rel Yorkshire Derwent Trust Ltd)* v *Brotherton* [1992] 1 AC 425.

Not infrequently rights under private and local Acts of Parliament often deriving from Victorian legislation of the industrial revolution are encountered. The compulsory purchase powers exercised by canal and railway companies often gave rights of access, use and bridging to the dispossessed landowners, which still exist, and assume value as the leisure potential of such waterways begins to be exploited.

In this century, modern public Acts have stepped in more and more, with a dual policy of regulating the supply and use of water as a resource, as well as, latterly, the promotion of the availability of water for sport and recreational purposes. As regards such public legislation, there was a massive consolidation and restructuring in 1991. The Water Industry Act 1991 and the Water Resources Act 1991 are now the main source of relevant legislation.

Thus, by way of example, any major abstraction of water from a flowing or percolating source, however minor, now requires a licence, as does the "impounding" (damming or diverting) of water (Water Resources Act 1991 ss 24–25). These were once entirely common law matters. Water authorities (nowadays the National Rivers Authority and water and sewerage undertakers and drainage boards) have a statutory duty to ensure that their rights to the use of any water or associated lands are exercised so as to make such water and lands available for recreation in the best manner (Water Resources Act 1991 s 16; Water Industry Act 1991 s 3). The powers conferred under this duty can be exercised commercially, for example by leasing or in joint enterprise with an adjoining owner.

It is impossible to provide here a comprehensive overview of the law likely to regulate or affect the use of water for amenity purposes because of the wide variety of circumstances which may apply. These will include the nature of the proposed activity, or the ancillary rights required for it, and the nature of the relevant water feature; natural or artificial, navigable or non-navigable, inland, tidal or coastal, flowing or self-contained. Different authorities may be involved according to the circumstances.

In any instance, therefore, where rights to the use of water for amenity purposes may be of significance to the value of an existing or potential leisure enterprise, resort must be had to the statutes themselves and to specialist works on the subject.

Specific regulation by licensing
Specialist Work; *Paterson's Licensing Acts* (Annual)

Entertainments Places of public entertainment, including theatres, cinemas, places used for public music or public dancing, and also places for sporting entertainments, including certain sports tracks are subject to particular statutory controls regarding their operation and in some cases the state of their structure. This control is exercised by a process of licensing by the relevant local authority. In some cases the system of control may extend beyond public places of entertainment to private entertainments promoted for profit. It may also operate not only under general statute law, but be extended in relation to any particular locality by local Acts, or by local authority bye-laws. It is therefore always necessary to consider and bear in mind any local requirements or regulations which may exist.

The systems for licensing entertainments of all descriptions operate in a broadly similar way, although details will vary as to such matters as the length of notice required for the application, to which additional persons notice may have to be given, the level of fees, the extent of rights of inspection to ensure compliance. Exemptions and exceptions are tailored to particular activities. The following is a general description of the usual scheme.

The licensing authority is the relevant local authority, namely the Council of a London Borough or a District Council.

The procedure is that the applicant, usually an individual, applies for a licence for the holding of the particular kind of entertainment on specified premises. Notice of the application will usually also have to be given to the fire authority (if different) and in some cases also to the police. Regulations as to the provision of information and other matters such as, for example, advertising the application in local newspapers or at the premises, may apply.

Licences are typically granted for a period of a year, but may be granted for occasional events or series of events. They may incorporate restrictions or conditions, which will be aimed at safety, public order and the prevention of nuisance. A modest fee is usually payable (except in some instances of non-commercial use where no fee will be required), and will be fixed by the local authority subject, in some cases, to a statutory maximum.

Licences are generally renewable, transferable to another fit person on application, and devolve on personal representatives subject to restrictions or requirements for prompt transfer to another fit person. They will be revocable on conviction of an offence for contravention of their terms, although actual revocation will be deferred to enable appeal to be made.

Appeals from a decision of the licensing authority as to refusal to grant, renew or transfer a licence, or the imposition of particular conditions, or the revocation of the licence, usually lie to the magistrates court and then to the Crown Court.

Use of premises for a licensable event or activity without the necessary licence is made an offence, as well as committing a breach of the licence conditions. Offences can be committed not only by the organisers and managers of the offending event, but by the owner or occupier of the premises if he, either knowingly or with reasonable grounds for suspicion, allows the premises to be used for an offending event, or lets or makes them available for such use. However, it will generally be a defence for an owner or occupier to prove that the offence occurred despite all reasonable diligence on his part to prevent it.

Police officers and local authority representatives are given powers to enter premises to ensure compliance with licence conditions or otherwise prevent contravention of the licensing rules. Some of these may be exercisable at any time, generally the power to inspect to see that licence conditions are being complied with.

Others will be exercisable only on notice or even only with a magistrates' warrant such as where a power is sought to enter and search premises upon which there is reasonable grounds to suspect an offence is likely to be committed.

The general scheme is related to particular examples below.

In some cases the activity may appear to fall into two categories. For example, the proprietor of a restaurant may wish to provide live musical entertainment, or the operator of a theatre to sell alcoholic drinks. In some cases, two licences will be required; in others the licence for the major activity will cover the secondary one. To take the above examples, the restaurant proprietor may well require a public music/entertainments licence, if the music is a regular and major entertainment, even though the main activity on the premises is the consumption of food (*Hall* v *Green* 1854 9 Exch 247). The theatre proprietor would not require a separate justices' licence unless he proposed to sell liquor outside normal licensing hours; consumption within hours will be covered by a theatre licence provided due notice is given to the clerk to the justices: Licensing Act 1964 s 199 as amended by the Theatres Act 1968.

Theatres Main Statutes: *Theatres Act 1968*; *Sunday Theatre Act 1972*

"Theatre" activities are mostly defined by reference to the performance of a "play", as defined in Theatres Act 1968 s 18 (1). In summary, this means a live or substantially live performance by one or more persons of either (a) a "dramatic piece", ie one performed or substantially performed in speech, singing or acting and involving the playing of a role, or (b) a "ballet".

Broadly, the lawful public performance of a play must be carried out under a theatre licence issued by the local authority for the area. A public performance includes not only performances in any public place, but also performances in a private place to which the public or any section of the public are admitted (and now also non-public performances promoted for "private gain": London Local Authorities Act 1991 s 18). It is not material that admission may be free. Theatres which operated under letters patent from the Crown prior to February 26 1968, may continue to operate without a licence, but the local authority may, by notice, impose similar requirements to those which it could have included in a licence.

The licence is issued to an applicant in respect of specified premises. It may be granted or renewed for a period of up to one year. It can be granted as an occasional licence, and it may be granted provisionally for premises not yet built or converted. The authority must act in a proper and judicial manner in considering the merits of an application or conditions to be imposed. A reasonable fee, fixed by the licensing authority, is payable, unless, in respect of an occasional licence, the authority is satisfied that the performance is for educational, charitable or similar purposes.

The licence is transferable, on application, to another holder, and passes to the personal representatives of a deceased licence holder for a period of three months, after which it will expire unless extended, transferred, cancelled or revoked in the meantime.

Conditions as to the nature and manner of performance of plays may not be imposed except for health and safety reasons, or to prevent demonstrations of hypnotism (which are separately governed by the Hypnotism Act 1952) but otherwise the regulation of performances can be made the subject of conditions. Section 2 of the 1968 Act itself prohibits obscene performances, adopting the common law definition of obscenity as having a "tendency to deprave and corrupt" those likely to attend. The Public Order Act 1986 s 20 prohibits theatrical performances which would have the effect of inciting racial hatred or a breach of the peace.

Applications for the grant, renewal, transfer and variations of licences must be made on the appropriate notice (generally 21 days; 14 days for an occasional licence) and subject to any regulations prescribed by the authority (eg as to advertising). Notice to the police is also required in the case of an application for grant or transfer. The licensing authority's decisions are subject to appeal to the magistrates and then to the Crown Court.

Contravention of the terms of a theatre licence is an offence for which the licence may, upon the holder's conviction, be revoked (subject to deferment to protect rights of appeal). It is also an offence to give a public performance of a play on unlicensed premises; the offence is committed both by those organising the performance and anyone who knowingly, or with reasonable cause for suspicion, allows the premises to be used for the commission of an offence or lets or makes them available. Magistrates may issue warrants enabling the police to enter and inspect premises where there are reasonable grounds to believe that an offence is being or will be committed.

Notwithstanding the Sunday Observance Act 1780, theatres may be licensed to perform on Sundays subject to a restriction on hours, which will generally mean not before 2 pm (Sunday Theatre Act 1972).

Alcoholic liquor can lawfully be sold under a theatre licence provided notice has been given to the licensing justices, but sale is restricted to normal licensing hours. Beyond that, a justices' licence must be obtained, and an extension of hours can only be granted under a justices' licence. Where music is merely part of or accompanies a performance, or is played before, between or after performances for a period not exceeding one quarter of the time taken up on the particular day by such performance(s), a separate music licence is not required (Theatres Act 1968 s 12 (2); Local Government (Miscellaneous Provisions) Act 1982 s 1).

Certain general provisions of statute law are relaxed or varied to accommodate licensed theatres. An example is the requirements for the storage of ice cream under the Food Act 1984.

Cinemas Main Statute: *Cinemas Act 1985*

The Cinemas Act 1985 consolidated the Cinematograph Acts 1909 to 1982. The law is a little more complex than theatre licensing, but similar.

The law is applied by reference to "film exhibitions". A "film exhibition" is an exhibition of moving pictures produced otherwise than through the simultaneous reception and exhibition of programmes included in a "programme service" within the meaning of the Broadcasting Act 1990 (see s 201). It does not cover video amusement games (*British Amusement Catering Trades Association* v *Westminster City Council* [1989] AC 147).

Premises upon which film exhibitions are to be held require to be licensed by the local authority in a similar way to theatres, and must also comply with any regulations made by the Secretary of State. There is a separate licensing scheme for sex cinemas (Local Government (Miscellaneous Provisions) Act 1982 s 2). Special consents are required for film exhibitions specially for children. There are a complicated series of exceptions and exemptions, mainly for occasional, private and/or non-commercial film exhibitions.

As regards relevant regulations, the Secretary of State has made regulations in three main areas. First, there are regulations relating to the keeping and handling of cinema film in general. Second there are wide-ranging health and safety regulations (originating in the Cinematograph (Safety) Regulations 1955 (SI 1955/1129)) governing, for example, exits, seats, staff, the structure of projection rooms and the design of equipment, lighting and electrical installations. Third, there are regulations relating to the health and welfare of children attending film exhibitions, found primarily in the Cinematograph (Children) (No 2) Regulations 1955 (SI 1955/1909), and relating to the admission of young children and the availability of adequate staff at film exhibitions for children.

The licence itself is issued to a fit person in respect of specified premises. It may be granted or renewed for a period of up to one year, and transferred, on application, to another fit person. In Greater London variations of terms may be made, and provisional licences in respect of uncompleted premises can be granted subject to eventual confirmation, but in other parts of the country this is only possible if there is local enabling legislation. Fees fixed by the local authority subject to a maximum fixed by the Secretary of State are payable (currently £600 for the grant of a licence, valid for one year, under SI 1991/2462).

The conditions or restrictions which can be imposed are not limited to matters of safety but may also deal with suitability of the film material, and must deal with the admission of children. Conditions may govern, for example, closing on Sundays and religious holidays. Only if a condition is one which no licensing authority could reasonably have imposed will it be struck down by the court: see *Associated Provincial Picture Houses Ltd* v *Wednesbury Corporation* [1948] 1 KB 223. (This case is the origin of the description "Wednesbury unreasonable" as the test for whether an administrative decision which is not otherwise *ultra vires* is sufficiently wayward that it will be upset by the court.)

If the local authority grants a licence for Sundays it must ensure that employees are not employed on more than 6 days in a week. Similar relaxations to those relating to theatres apply regarding, for example, food legislation.

Applications for the grant, renewal, transfer and variations of licences must be made on not less than 28 days' notice to the local authority, the fire authority (if any and different) and the local chief officer of police. However the local authority has discretion, after appropriate consultations, to grant a licence on shorter notice.

There are complicated provisions for exemption from the requirement of a licence in certain cases, and exceptions to those exemptions. The provisions stem mainly from safety considerations, originating particularly from the notorious fire hazard of ciné film. In relation to leisure property, where film promotions may be used, or where films may be provided as an ancillary facility or entertainment they may require to be considered in detail. The following is a broad general guide.

There are exemptions from the licence requirement for *premises* used only exceptionally for film exhibitions on not more than 6 days in any calendar year, and also for exhibitions on movable premises provided a licence has been obtained in respect of those premises at the owner's base. In each case the exemption from the requirement of a licence is provisional upon notice of the relevant exhibition having been given to the local authority and compliance with their requirements and any applicable regulations made by the Secretary of State.

There are also exemptions for certain film *exhibitions*, such as (a) private film exhibitions (ie given in private dwellinghouses or to which the public is not admitted), (b) free film exhibitions, other than a free children's cinema club, or exhibitions using particular, more hazardous, equipment or (c) exhibitions given by exempt organisations, (ie non-profitmaking organisations which have obtained an exemption certificate from the Secretary of State) provided that no more than three such exempt exhibitions are given in any period of seven days. However, exhibitions made for "private gain" (see Cinemas Act 1985 s 20) are excluded from exemption.

There are a variety of powers of inspection conferred on police and authorised officers of the licensing authority or fire authority to inspect licensed premises, without a warrant, with a view to ensuring that regulations and licence conditions are being complied with, and with a warrant, to enter and search premises in order to prevent offences.

The typical range of offences in relation to the use of unlicensed premises or the contravention of conditions attached to any licence or exemption from licence apply, but there are, additionally, provisions for forfeiture of property involved in the commission of the offence of using any premises without the requisite licence or consent.

Appeals relating to the refusal to grant, renew or transfer a licence, or to the imposition of conditions or the revocation of a licence are made to the Crown Court.

Musical and similar entertainment Main Statutes: *London Government Act 1963* (s 52 and Schedule 12); *Local Government*

(Miscellaneous Provisions) Act 1982; Private Places of Entertainment (Licensing) Act 1967
The use of premises for "public dancing, singing, music or other public entertainment of the like kind" requires a licence. There are technically different régimes relating to Greater London (ie any London Borough or the City of London) and to the rest of the country, although they are substantially similar. In London the licence is a "public music and dancing licence" but elsewhere it may be called an "entertainments licence".

The use of premises for music, dancing or any other entertainment of the like kind which is not a public entertainment but which is promoted for private gain requires a licence if it is carried on within the area of a local authority which has adopted the provisions of the Private Places of Entertainment (Licensing) Act 1967. "Private gain" means, essentially, commercial profit, whether of private individuals or commercial organisations. Where certain other forms of licence are in operation (eg a public entertainment licence, liquor licence, film exhibition licence, theatre licence, etc) or where the premises in question are those of a club registered under the Licensing Act 1964 Part II, no further licence is required for activities which would otherwise need an entertainment licence.

To require a music and dancing licence, the music, singing or dancing must be a substantial part of the event in question, and not merely subsidiary to it, but the premises need not be used exclusively for music and dancing for a licence to be required. A licence is required for occasional events.

Difficulties may arise in interpreting what is "public". Where a "club" is concerned, the test of whether the premises are being used for "public" music and dancing depends not on numbers, but on whether any respectable member of the public, on paying admission, can get in, even though he may then become a "member": *Beynon* v *Lower Caerphilly Licensing Justices* [1970] 1 WLR 369. The test of a bona fide private club is the sufficiency of the degree of selection or segregation for membership, as a matter of impression: *Severn View Social Club and Institute Ltd* v *Chepstow Licensing JJ* [1968] 1 WLR 1512. This case also shows that guests of members of a bona fide club may still not be classified as members of the public.

"Public dancing" includes dancing by members of the public and not merely by professional dancers for entertainment: *Clarke* v *Searle* (1793) 1 Esp 25. However, a bona fide private dancing school would not be "public": *Bellis* v *Burghall* (1799) 2 Esp 722.

There is a relaxation of the entertainment licensing requirements for licensed premises in respect of entertainment by reproduction of radio and television broadcasts or by pre-recorded music or a musical performance by not more than two persons (Licensing Act 1964 s 182 (1)). A special order of exemption extending the hours of a liquor licence may have the effect of extending the hours of any associated entertainment licence without a specific application.

A licensing authority may authorise "musical entertainments" on Sundays but not public dancing: Sunday Entertainments Act 1932 s 3.

London. No premises, public or private (and including even an open space) may be used for public dancing or music or any other entertainment of a like kind (which includes, for example, an exhibition of skating to music) without a public music and dancing licence issued by the local authority as successor to the functions of the Greater London Council. A licence is also required for occasional use.

The requirements and procedures regarding an application for and grant of a music and dancing licence, fees, duration, revocation, offences, powers of entry and appeals are virtually identical to those applicable to theatre licences. Advertisement in a local and a London evening newspaper have been prescribed as requirements on applications for grant of a licence. The former GLC issued "Places of Public Entertainment Technical Regulations" and "Rules of Management" for smaller premises and for other premises which are of general application. A "Code of Practice for Pop Concerts" was also issued. Fire certificates and regulations will override any terms of public music and dancing licences.

Other related forms of licence in respect of which provisions similar to public music and dancing licences apply are "exhibition licences" required for the holding of any public exhibition (excluding boxing, wrestling and film exhibitions, which are separately dealt with) in certain specified major buildings in London (Greater London Council (General Powers) Act 1966 s 21 and Sch 1) and "booking office licences" required by premises operating as independent booking offices (Greater London Council (General Powers) Act 1978 s 5).

Outside London. Outside London, music, singing and dancing entertainment requires an entertainments licence, but the provisions do not apply to music in a place of public religious worship or performed incidentally to a public religious meeting, nor to an entertainment at a "pleasure fair" or to an entertainment held wholly or mainly in the open air.

However, in the last case a licence will be required for a public musical entertainment held on private land if the local authority has so resolved: Local Government (Miscellaneous Provisions) Act 1982 Sch 1 para 4. This provision enables pop concerts to be regulated. There are exceptions for such events as garden fetes, sales of work, sporting or athletic events or displays and similar functions.

The requirements and procedures regarding an application for and grant of an entertainments licence, fees, duration, revocation, offences, powers of entry and appeals are virtually identical to those applicable to cinema licences. Persons providing equipment for unlicensed "acid house" parties have been convicted under Sch 1 para 12(1)(a) of the Act: *Chichester District Council* v *Silvester*, *The Times* May 6 1992.

Non-public entertainment. Licences issued for non-public entertainments promoted for private gain where the Private Places of Entertainment (Licensing) Act 1967 has been applied (see above) operate in a similar way to theatre licences. The fees are now discretionary (London Local Government Act 1991).

Sports entertainment Main statute: *Fire Safety and Safety of Places of Sports Act 1987*

General sporting events A sports entertainment licence is required for the use of any premises for the holding of a sporting event to which the public is invited as spectators. A licence is required for occasional sporting events. "Sport" means any game in which physical skill is the predominant factor or any physical recreation engaged in for the purposes of competition or display except dancing, and a "sporting event" includes both contests and displays.

"Premises" here means a building, including a tent or inflatable building, but not a part of a building unless it is a "sports complex", ie a building which provides for both participation in and spectating of sport and is arranged so that different sports can be engaged in simultaneously in different areas. A licence is not required if the sporting event in question is not the main event for which the building is being used except where the building is a sports complex.

The detailed provisions are assimilated to those relating to public music and dancing licences.

Safety certification of sports grounds and regulated sports stands has been referred to above, in relation to general regulatory legislation.

The Sunday Observance Act 1780 no longer applies to sporting events and activities (Deregulation and Contracting Out Act 1994, s 21).

Boxing and wrestling. Outside Greater London boxing and wrestling fall within the scheme of sports entertainment licensing.

Within Greater London there is a specific system of boxing and wrestling licensing (London Government Act 1963 Sch 12 para 4) which was extended to boxing and wrestling entertainments held wholly or mainly in the open air by the Fire Safety and Safety of Places of Sport Act 1987 Sch 3.

The enforcement provisions in relation to public music, dancing and entertainments licences apply.

Licensing of gambling The regulation of betting, gaming, lotteries, prize competitions and amusements with prizes is governed by various statutes commencing with the Betting, Gaming and Lotteries Act 1963 and the Gaming Act 1968, the latest of which is the Bingo Act 1992. The particular areas of interest as regards leisure property are the licensing of tracks for betting purposes, the system for regulating gaming consisting of the licensing of commercial clubs and the registration of members' clubs (with certain relaxations in relation to bingo), and the restriction on the provision of gaming machines and amusements with prizes in certain circumstances.

It should be noted that commercial gambling incurs duty under various statutes (betting duty, gaming duty, bingo duty, etc).

Licensed race tracks Main Statute: *Betting, Gaming and Lotteries Acts 1963* Part I
Horse racing itself is a lawful game (*Earl of Ellesmere* v *Wallace* [1929] 2 Ch 1) and requires no licence. However, it is unlawful to bet in the street or in any public place and there are statutory restrictions on and regulation of betting at racecourses and the use of any other premises for betting. High street betting offices require to be licensed, with licensing procedures similar to liquor licences, but these are not within the category of leisure property.

Where betting by bookmaking is to take place at any "track" (ie premises on which a race of any description, athletic sports or other sporting events take place), either the occupier of the track must hold a track betting licence from the local authority under Section 6 and Schedule 3 of the 1963 Act, or he must have given due notice to the local chief of police. This can be done for no more than eight separate days between July 1 in one year and July 1 in the next. This requirement does not apply to horserace courses approved and certified by the Horserace Betting Levy Board, although other aspects of regulation of tracks do apply. The Horserace Betting Levy Board's certificate may impose conditions regulating the running of the track and must require a suitable area for bookmaking to be provided.

If unlawful betting takes place on a track an offence is committed both by the bookmaker or totalisator operator and by the owner or occupier of the track, although the latter each has a defence if he can show that the offence took place notwithstanding due diligence by him to prevent it.

Applications for track betting licences are made on two months' notice to the relevant local authority, and also to the planning authority, county council, and local chief of police, accompanied by prescribed information. Advertisements must be placed in local papers. At the time fixed for hearing the application various persons and authorities interested (other than the licensing authority itself) are entitled to be heard, but any objector must have given at least seven days' written notice of his grounds of objection to the applicant and to the licensing authority.

Licences may only be refused in particular circumstances, going to impairment of local amenity (residents, schools, traffic, etc), the bad character of the applicant or the absence of necessary planning consent. A fee is payable both in respect of the application (currently not exceeding £46) and annually (currently not exceeding £464). The licence is for seven years unless revoked or cancelled in the meantime. It can be revoked by the licensing authority for good cause (eg the noisy, improper or unsafe conduct of the track, or the conviction of the operator of an offence of dishonesty) after giving the licensee a proper hearing. An appeal against revocation lies to the Crown Court.

There are restrictions on the amounts the occupier may charge to bookmakers and their assistants for admission to any part of the track, and no occupier of a licensed track, nor his servants, agents, lessees or licensees of any part of the track may engage in bookmaking on the track on their own account.

Pool betting on approved horse races, on and off track, is the statutory monopoly of the Horserace Totalisator Board and those authorised by it. As regards dog racing, the manager of a licensed track may set up a totalisator to be operated in accordance with statutory rules (Betting, Gaming and Lotteries Act 1963 s 16 and Sch 5). However, he must operate it only during dog racing sessions open to the public, and must also admit bookmakers to the track at the same time.

Gaming establishments – Casinos and clubs Main Statute: *Gaming Act 1968*
Gaming is the "playing of games of chance for winnings in money or money's worth". The description "games of chance" nonetheless includes games which also have an element of skill involved.

While gaming is not unlawful at common law, it has been regulated by statute for hundreds of years. This is because of the public policy considerations of containing the perceived evils of gaming; not merely the protection of gamblers from their weakness or from unscrupulous operators, but the public order problems created by the attraction of lucrative gambling operations to undesirable elements in society and its consequent association with crime and vice.

The Act effectively distinguishes three categories of gaming. The first is gaming containing a commercial or profit making element. This is defined as gaming where a player stakes against a bank, or where the chances are not equally favourable to all players or as between all players and any outside person. The effects of Sections 1, 2 and Part II of the 1968 Act are that this type of gaming can only lawfully be carried on on premises licensed for that purpose (casinos and clubs) or on registered premises (members' clubs or miners' welfare institutes). There is an exception for such gaming when purely domestic, and for non-commercial gaming played amongst residents in a hostel or hall of residence.

All other gaming divides into the remaining class of gaming in general, covered by Part I of the Act, and further specific categories of gaming covered by other parts of the Act. These specified categories are (a) gaming by gaming machines governed by Part III of the Act, (b) gaming which constitutes the provision of amusements with prizes under the Lotteries and Amusements Act 1976 and

(c) gaming at entertainments not held for private gain, which is exempted under Section 41 of the 1968 Act.

There are tight restrictions on advertisements for gaming establishments under Section 42 of the Act.

The detailed application of the law to different kinds of gaming in different kinds of premises is complex and reference must be had to the precise terms of the statutes and regulations in question where these are important. The following is a general guide only, to provide the flavour of the legislation, particularly where it may have a financial impact, and to indicate where detailed research may be necessary.

Gaming in general. Where gaming falls under Part I of the Act, it is unlawful to charge for the gaming itself (as opposed to the stake hazarded), whether such charge is made directly or indirectly as, for example, an entrance fee: see Section 3 of the 1968 Act. However, an annual subscription to a bona fide club (ie one which is not itself temporary and of which membership is not temporary) is not treated as a charge for gaming, and genuine members' clubs having at least 25 members and, again, not being of a temporary character, are entitled to charge a nominal entrance fee, subject to regulations made by the Secretary of State. Specific provisions are made to allow higher charges in respect of gaming comprising exclusively bridge and whist (up to £15 under the Gaming (Small Charges) (Amendment) Order 1995 SI 1995/1669).

No levy on winnings may be charged in respect of gaming lawfully carried on on unlicensed or unregistered premises, ie under Part I of the Act.

Gaming on liquor licensed premises. Gaming in any public place, which includes any place to which the public has access whether on payment or otherwise, is unlawful, except that this prohibition does not apply to the playing of dominoes or cribbage on premises with a justices' on-licence. The justices' on-licence may also specifically authorise the playing of other games and may impose conditions, with the aim of ensuring that playing for high stakes is prevented, and that there is no inducement to persons to have resort to the licensed premises for the predominant purpose of gaming (Gaming Act 1968 s 6).

It is an offence for the licensee to suffer gaming on licensed premises in contravention of any statutory or licence restrictions.

These requirements have been strictly construed so that, for example, a licensee who played cards for money privately with friends in his private rooms has been convicted: *Patten* v *Rhymer* (1860) 3 E & E 1. The prohibition on gaming for "money's worth" means that even gaming where the loser buys drinks all round is unlawful if not conducted within the relevant restrictions (*Luff* v *Leaper* (1872) 36 JP 773). It is also an offence to allow anyone under the age of 18 to take part in gaming on licensed premises.

Licensed gaming – casinos and registered clubs. Gaming under Part II of the Act (banker's gaming or games of unequal chance) may only be played on licensed premises or registered premises and subject to the games being conducted in accordance with regulations laid down by the Secretary of State. Roulette, dice, baccarat and blackjack have been so regulated, and pontoon and chemin de fer may be played on registered premises. The restrictions are relaxed in respect of licensed clubs to allow gaming for very small stakes and prizes on certain conditions (see the Gaming Act (Variation of Monetary Limits) Orders made under Section 21(8) of the 1968 Act).

The prohibition on charging for playing and on charging any levy on winnings also applies save insofar as authorised by the Secretary of State in regulations. The maximum amounts and conditions for playing charges and entrance fees are currently laid down in the Gaming Clubs (Hours and Charges) Regulations 1984 SI 1984/248 (but see below for amendment in relation to bingo clubs). Regulations also govern how frequently a gaming charge may be incurred.

There are regulations governing the conduct of licensed club premises as to the provision of credit, the keeping of records, the making and displaying of house rules as to the conduct of games, and the general conduct of licensed premises, such as permitted hours and prohibitions on gratuities. Persons employed in certain capacities have to be approved by the Gaming Board (see below).

Participants in gaming under Part II of the Act must be physically present at the time the gaming takes place. In respect of licensed gaming premises only members of the club specified in the licence, or their bona fide guests, may take part. Neither the licence-holder nor any agent or person employed on the premises may take part in the gaming, although that does not prevent the licence-holder holding the bank. In the case of registered club premises, again, only members and genuine guests may take part and membership must have been held for at least 48 hours. No person under the age of 18 may be present at the time of any such gaming, and there are restrictions on the hours when gaming may take place under gaming licences, gaming on Sundays between the hours of 4am and 2pm being totally excluded.

If any provisions of the Gaming Act or relevant regulations are broken, the licence-holder in respect of licensed premises, and every officer of the relevant club in the case of registered premises, is guilty of an offence. The court convicting any such person may disqualify licensed club premises from holding a licence for a specified period, and may order forfeiture and destruction of property relating to the offence (Gaming Act 1968 ss 24–25).

Licensing/registration procedure. Licensing of premises for gaming is governed by the provisions of Schedule 2 of the 1968 Act, and registration of club premises is governed by Schedule 3. The procedure is similar to that for other justices' licences and hearings are held once each quarter. However, licensing of gaming premises is unique in requiring in effect, dual licensing, both from the Gaming Board as regards the fitness of the applicant to hold the licence for the proposed establishment, and from the licensing authority (here the local licensing justices) in respect of the particular premises. Moreover, a clear segregation is maintained between the licensing of casino-type gambling and that of bingo and other quasi-social card-games.

An applicant for a licence may be either an individual aged over 21 and resident in Great Britain for at least the previous six months, or a corporation registered in Great Britain. The applicant must obtain the prior consent of the Gaming Board to his application. The premises must be identified, and whether the application is in respect of a licence for bingo only or for other gaming must be stated. The Gaming Board will be concerned to see that the applicant is likely to secure compliance with the Gaming Act and to conduct both gaming activity and the premises in general in a fair, proper and orderly way. A Gaming Board certificate of consent will state a time within which the application for a gaming licence must be made.

A certificate of consent may be revoked by the Gaming Board for specified reasons such as discovery of the applicant's lack of qualification, his having given false information, or upon any gaming licence of his being cancelled under a disqualification order (made either by a local authority or the courts), or if it appears that, in fact, some other person who would not be regarded as a fit person is managing the club or it is being carried on for his benefit. If a certificate is revoked, any licence dependent on it falls as well. Where a certificate of consent is issued to a corporation, any change in the identity of the board of directors must be notified to the Gaming Board, and an application for continuance made, in any case other than a bingo licence. The Board may revoke the certificate because of such a change of control.

The form of application for a gaming licence is prescribed by regulations, and must specify the premises and name the club which is intended to use them as well as other prescribed particulars. Within seven days of submitting the application and the certificate of consent to the clerk to the justices, a copy of the application must be sent to the Gaming Board, the chief of police, the local authority, the fire authority and the local Collector of Customs and Excise. Within 14 days a prescribed notice must be placed in a local newspaper inviting any objections to be made to the clerk to the justices. Subject to further time limits, objections are received, and notice of the hearing given to all interested parties. The procedure on renewal of a licence is broadly similar, application being made not more than five nor less than two months before expiration of the existing licence. Time limits and prescribed procedure is strict on an application, see, eg, *R* v *Pontypool Gaming Licensing Committee ex parte Risca Cinemas Ltd* [1970] 3 All ER 241. There may possibly be relaxation in respect of late applications for renewal. Fees are currently £32,030 for grant of a licence and £6,580 for renewal: Gaming Act (Variation of Fees) Order SI 1995/321.

A licence may be granted or renewed without hearing the applicant if there are no objections. Any representations by interested authorities must be heard. Restrictions on hours and on types of gaming may be imposed and where the certificate of consent is limited to a bingo club, the gaming must be so limited. A licence expires after one year if not renewed, subject to earlier cancellation.

A licence may be refused on the grounds of lack of demand or adequate availability of existing facilities. It is largely for this reason that gaming licences are such valuable assets. Other reasons for refusal are unsuitability of premises (by reason of layout, character, condition or location), unfitness of the applicant, or of his apparent principal, a refusal to allow the relevant authorities to inspect or because of arrears of bingo or gaming licence duty.

Pursuant to regulations made by the Secretary of State, a gaming licence must be refused for gaming other than bingo, bridge or whist where the premises are outside specified areas, being central London, county boroughs over a certain size of population and certain other coastal boroughs (Gaming Clubs (Permitted Areas) Regulations 1971 as amended).

A licence may be refused if the premises are accessible, other than in an emergency, from private premises not contained within the licence. Pursuant to regulations, a gaming licence for games other than bingo, bridge and whist must exclude bingo, and must also prohibit the premises from being used for dancing and live performance of musical or other entertainment. A gaming licence may regulate the areas within the premises where gaming takes place.

Renewal of a licence may be refused for lack of demand, because of objectionable aspects of the conduct of the establishment (Gaming Act offences, dishonesty, disorderliness, the presence of criminals or prostitutes, and so on). Renewal must be refused if a disqualification order is in force or if the justices are satisfied that the premises have habitually been used as the resort of criminals or prostitutes.

An application for the transfer of a gaming licence may be made at any time on procedure similar to that for grant and renewal. The transferee must have obtained a certificate of consent. Transfer may only be refused on the grounds that the transferee is not a fit person, or that he has an unfit person as his effective principal, or that gaming licence or bingo duty remains unpaid.

Applications for registration and renewal of registration of club premises are made in a similar way to applications for gaming licences, but on a rather less stringent basis: see Schedule 3 of the 1968 Act as amended by the Gaming (Amendment) Act 1982. For example, a Gaming Board certificate of consent is not required and the special provisions regarding bingo, the requirement to notify the local authority and the fire authority, and to advertise the application at the premises, are omitted. Current registration fee is £190.

Particular grounds for refusal of registration are that the club is not a bona fide permanent club, or has fewer than 25 members, or that the principal purpose of its existence appears to be gaming other than the playing of bridge or whist.

Provisions governing cancellation of registrations are similar to the case of licences. The Gaming Board may apply for the cancellation of a registration. Appeals from the decision of the licensing authority are made to the Crown Court, and either the applicant or the Gaming Board may appeal in the relevant circumstances.

Licensed gaming – bingo clubs. Bingo clubs require gaming licences or registration in exactly the same way as casino gaming, and, in principle, under exactly the same terms. However, because of the completely different market for bingo, there are two forms of both the gaming licence and the required Gaming Board certificate of consent, for bingo on the one hand and for other gaming except bridge and whist on the other. These are mutually exclusive, and in respect of bingo, there are some relaxations of the stringent provisions imposed in relation to casino gaming. The current fee for a bingo club licence (other than multiple bingo) is £2,640.

Special provisions allow bingo to be played via linked premises, despite the general requirement that participants in gaming be present in person, on certain conditions. These require, in effect, that there be a single universal game operated, and they impose limits on stakes and ultimate prize money. Multiple bingo is also authorised under the Gaming (Bingo) Act 1985 to permit the same game to be played simultaneously on several premises, for both local and overall prizes, subject again to monetary limits: Gaming Act (Variation of Monetary Limits) Order 1995 (SI 1995/926). The organisers of multiple bingo require Gaming Board approval.

Membership of any bingo club is required for only 24 hours before participation in gaming takes place, and young persons are not debarred from being present whilst bingo is played, so long as they do not take part. The amount paid out in winnings at bingo in any week may not exceed the total stakes hazarded in that week by more than a fixed sum (£2,500 under SI 1995/926), but any game of multiple bingo or gaming for small prizes under Section 21 of the 1968 Act is excluded from this calculation. Special regulations as to entrance charges (current maximum £6.80) and stakes apply to bingo sessions and games (SI 1984/248 and 1995/927).

A gaming licence limited to bingo may not limit the purposes for which the premises may otherwise be used, whereas in respect of casino gaming, it may do so.

Gaming machines (slot machines) Main Statutes: *Gaming Act 1968* Part III; *Lotteries Act 1975* s 20; *Lotteries and Amusements Act 1976* s 25
Part III of the 1968 Act governs gaming by machines, which the Act

defines, in effect as a coin- or token-operated machine for the playing of a game of chance. Where the "prize" is nothing more than the right to another game free of charge, or the return of the coin or token, the machine is not treated as a regulated gaming machine.

The supply and maintenance of regulated gaming machines to commercial operators requires a permit from the Gaming Board.

Under Sections 30–34 of the Gaming Act 1968, regulated gaming machines can lawfully be used only:

1. on club premises licensed or registered under Part II of the Gaming Act 1968 as gaming premises (s 31), or, as regards members' clubs, on their premises if registered specifically for the purpose of having gaming machines, under Part III of the Act (ss 32 and 34 (1) (b));
2. at non-commercial entertainments (such as sales of work, dinners, sporting events not held for private gain) where they are incidental to the main entertainment and not the main inducement to attend (s 33);
3. for the purposes of amusement, either under permit or as a subsidiary part of a "pleasure fair", when the value of the stakes and prizes is limited by statute (s 34 (1) (a) and (c)).

The number of machines on licensed or registered premises is limited (3–6: Deregulation (Gaming Machines etc) Order 1996 (SI 1996/1359)), the charge for an individual game is limited (currently to 20p: SI 1985/5785), and the prize must be nothing but coins delivered by the machine. Statutory powers exist to limit winnings, but none has yet been imposed. Notices setting out the bases for winning must be displayed. Gaming machines may not be used on licensed or registered club premises at any time when the public has access, whether on payment or otherwise.

Instead of jackpot gaming machines on licensed club premises, the licensee may obtain a licence for a greater number of machines, which can then be used only for small stakes and small prizes under the regulations relating to use of machines for amusement purposes (see below).

Application for registration for gaming machines only, under Part III of the Gaming Act 1968 (s 32), is made to the local licensing justices. Notice must be given to the police. The application must be refused if it appears that the club in question is frequented mainly by persons under 18 years of age and may be refused if the club is not bona fide, or is temporary, or has fewer than 25 members. Renewal may be refused for reasons relating to the conduct of the premises or commission of a Gaming Act offence. A registration can be cancelled on application by the police for any reason justifying refusal to grant or renew a licence.

It is an offence to sell, supply, maintain, or operate gaming machines which contravene the statutory provisions. The removal of money from the machines is regulated, and it is an offence for anyone other than the specified persons to do so.

Gaming machines for amusement purposes may otherwise be operated in premises which carry a permit for such purpose ("amusement machine premises") or as a part of a "pleasure fair" not devoted wholly or substantially to such machines or as part of a "travelling showman's fair" of limited duration and where such machines are not the main inducement to attend.

All gaming machines other than those operating on Part II premises must play for small stakes (currently a maximum of 20p: Gaming Act (Variation of Monetary Limits) (No 2) Order 1989 (SI 1989/2190)) and for small prizes (currently £3 in cash and £6 in kind: Gaming Act (Variation of Monetary Limits) (No 4) Order 1992 (SI 1992/2647)). However, it is not unlawful for prizes to be in "points" capable of being accumulated for a larger money prize: *R* v *Burt & Adams Ltd, The Times* 22 November 1995. See further SI 1996/1359.

Permits for gaming machines are issued by the justices in respect of premises licensed to sell intoxicating liquor and by the local authority in all other cases. The procedure is contained in Schedule 9 of the Gaming Act 1968. The application will be made by the licensee of licensed premises and by the occupier in other cases. The grant of a permit is for a minimum of three years and is always discretionary. However, a permit cannot be granted in respect of licensed gaming premises or registered club premises under Part II of the Act. Justices will have regard to both demand and the possibility of over-provision of gaming machines in the locality when considering applications for permits: *R* v *Chichester Crown Court ex parte Forte, The Times* 9 March 1995; *Matchurban Ltd* v *Kyle and Carrick District Council (No 2)* 1995 SLT 1211.

The renewal of a permit for an amusement arcade (ie where amusement machines are substantially the whole of the business) may only be refused on limited grounds relating to conduct. Where permits are to be granted or renewed for premises other than dedicated amusement arcades, the local authority may limit the number of machines, may resolve not to grant permits for certain classes of premises, and may decline to renew a permit on the grounds of the undesirability of the presence of gaming machines having regard to the type of use of the premises. Appeals against decisions lie to the Crown Court.

A permit is not transferable, but it devolves on the permit-holder's personal representatives for six months and can be extended. If the permit holder ceases to be the occupier of the premises (or the licensee in the case of licensed premises) the permit ceases to have effect.

Offences are laid down in relation to the unlawful provision of gaming machines, and powers of search, under warrant, are provided.

Gaming licence duty now applies to amusement machines (Amusement Machine Licence Duty Regulations 1995 SI 1995/2631).

Lotteries Main Statute: *Lotteries and Amusements Act 1976*
The essence of a lottery is payment by participants for the prospect of obtaining a prize, where the obtaining of the prize depends on pure chance. If merit or skill is involved, it is not a lottery. Where a scheme which would be a lottery is also gaming, it is governed by the Gaming Acts and is not intrinsically unlawful. In principle, all lotteries which are not gaming are unlawful (1976 Act s 1) except for statutory exceptions of which the following may occasionally concern leisure property.

First, small lotteries (Section 3 of the 1976 Act) incidental to "exempt entertainments", ie non-commercial events such as sales of work, fetes, dinners, sporting and athletic events and other entertainments, are lawful provided they comply with certain conditions. They must not be conducted for private gain, they must take place entirely at the event in question, there must be no money prize and they must not be the main inducement to attend. The typical lottery held at a hotel function will be legitimised by this exception; if it were not, the hotelier would be at risk of committing a lottery offence by permitting it.

Second, there are provisions for rendering lawful "society's lotteries" (Section 5 of the 1976 Act). The society must be registered under the Act, its purposes (to which all profits of the lottery must be devoted) must be charitable, sporting, cultural, or otherwise neither commercial nor those of private gain, and the lottery must be conducted in accordance with an approved scheme and either limited to £10,000 in ticket value or registered in advance with the Gaming Board. Further regulations (1993 SI 1993/3222–4) were made under the National Lottery etc Act 1993.

Amusements with prizes Main Statute: *Lotteries and Amusements Act 1976* ss 15–16
Amusements with prizes which are either a lottery, or gaming, or both, but which are neither gaming under Part II of the Gaming Act 1968, nor being provided by way of gaming machines under Part III of that Act may lawfully be provided in two situations only.

The first is in a non-commercial situation, in connection with an "exempt entertainment" (see Lotteries above). The second is where they are provided either in connection with premises operating with a permit for gaming machines, or in connection with a travelling showman's pleasure fair, or, specifically, where a permit under Section 16 of the Lotteries and Amusements Act 1976 itself is obtained.

The scheme relating to such permits operates in the same way as the scheme of permits for gaming machines.

Liquor and catering – Public houses, hotels, restaurants and cafes

Liquor licensing Main Statutes: *Licensing Acts 1964 and 1988; Sporting Events (Control of Alcohol etc) Act 1985*
Textbook: *Underhill's Guide to the Licensing Laws*
The system of liquor licensing will be relatively familiar in general terms if not in detail. It affects all premises where "intoxicating liquor" is to be sold. "Intoxicating liquor" means spirits, wine, beer, cider and any fermented distilled or spiritous liquor. In the leisure property context the licensing system is therefore of importance not only as regards restaurants, hotels and public houses, but also in relation to sale in any shops on caravan sites, or within bar premises in theatres and cinemas or at entertainments venues such as sports grounds.

The whole system of licensing is too detailed for a fully comprehensive account here, because the system of control is very tight but provides for many variations according to circumstances. Reference should be made to specialist works on the subject in relation to any particular aspect. The following provides a general review of the system, but does not consider such ancillary licensing matters as regulation of the delivery and storage of liquor, nor such specialist matters as the licensing of seamen's canteens, all of which are covered by the Acts.

In principle, a justices' licence, which relates to specified premises, is required for the retail sale of intoxicating liquor: s 1 of the 1964 Act. (A manufacturer or wholesale dealer requires an excise licence.) The principle of licensing control is that of prohibiting the sale or supply of intoxicating liquor on licensed premises or its consumption on or removal from those premises outside "permitted hours" (s 59 of the 1964 Act). There are exceptions for such matters as "drinking-up time", sale or supply of liquor to persons residing on the premises and their friends, consumption by employees at the premises, trade sales, etc and so on: s 63 of the 1964 Act. Contravention of the "permitted hours" limits are made criminal offences, and offences in relation to the conduct of licensed premises are also prescribed (eg keeping liquor of a kind not authorised by the licence, selling liquor to persons under 18, permitting drunkenness, permitting prostitutes to assemble, allowing unlawful gaming on the premises: ss 160–178). Powers of entry and search under warrant are conferred on the police for enforcement purposes (ss 186 and 187 of the 1964 Act).

Section 168A of the Licensing Act 1964 (inserted by Section 19 of the Deregulation and Contracting Out Act 1994) now enables children under 14 to be admitted to public bars. A "Children's Certificate" (current fee £6.50: SI 1994/3103) must be obtained and the licensing justices will require that the area is suitable, and that meals and non-alcoholic beverages are also available there.

Specific exemptions from the requirement of a justices' licence relevant to leisure property are exemptions permitting sale under a theatre licence and sale to passengers on pleasure craft (s 199 of the 1964 Act).

Licensed premises in general – public houses. The general licensing procedure is laid down in Part I of the 1964 Act. Licences are granted by a committee of justices for the district (who must be independent of local brewing or selling interests), in their absolute discretion, to a fit and proper individual. Persons of certain professions are disqualified, and persons convicted of certain offences in relation to licensed premises (such as permitting a brothel on licensed premises) are disqualified from holding a licence (ss 9 and 100 of the 1964 Act). Premises may also be disqualified from licensing, the primary grounds for "disqualification" or "prohibition" being the nature of their use (eg as a commercial garage) or previous forfeitures of licences, or the commission of licensing act offences on the premises.

From the above, it will be appreciated that there may be competing interests in the licence between the owner of the premises, and a licensee who is not the owner.

Licences are of two kinds: an "on-licence" where the liquor is sold for consumption on or off the premises, and an "off-licence" where it is sold only for consumption off the premises: s 1 of the 1964 Act. Either form of licence may be for sale of intoxicating liquor of all descriptions or confined to beer, cider and wine only. An on-licence may also be for beer and cider only, cider only or wine only "On-licences" will fall into two classes; general on-licences (mainly public houses), and on-licences for restaurants and guest houses under Part IV of the Act. In addition, bona fide clubs can supply alcoholic liquor to members and their guests within "permitted hours" without a full on-licence if they are registered under Part II of the Act.

An on-licensee (but not an off-licensee) may, on application to the magistrates' court be granted an "occasional licence" under s 180 of the 1964 Act to sell intoxicating liquor to which his licence relates from premises other than his licensed premises for up to three weeks in a year during hours specified in the occasional licence.

Licences used to be granted annually but are now granted on a triennial basis with effect from April 5 1989. A fee of £12.50 is currently payable. The committee will also deal with renewal, transfer (ie a change of individual licensee at the same premises) and removal (ie a change of premises with or without a change of individual licensee). Material alterations to licensed premises also require the justices' consent (in advance: *R v Croydon Crown Ct ex parte Bromley JJ* [1988] 152 JP 245) as well as any other planning or building consents, and upon renewal the justices have powers to require alterations to the premises (ss 19 and 20 of the 1964 Act). A register of licences must be kept. There is now power to revoke a licence (s 20A of the 1964 Act, introduced by the 1988 Act).

A licence may be granted provisionally in respect of premises under construction, subject to later confirmation (s 6 of the 1964 Act).

The justices must hold one general annual licensing meeting in February each year and between four and eight other "sessions" in the year. The sessions are conducted along similar lines to magistrates' court hearings. There are provisions for appeal to the Crown Court against the justices' decisions.

Applications for the grant or renewal of a licence are made on at least 21 days' notice prior to the relevant sessions, to the clerk to the justices, the chief officer of police and the local authority, and in the case of transfer or removal, also notice to the interested parties. Except in the case of transfer, notices on the relevant premises and advertisements in local newspapers 28 days prior to the relevant sessions are also required. The deposit of plans of the premises will also be required. Many licensing committees now issue guidelines to applicants.

A licence can be transferred only to certain persons, being, broadly, the personal representatives or trustee in bankruptcy of a deceased or bankrupt tenant, or a new tenant or occupier of the premises (s 8 of the 1964 Act). A protection order, operating as a kind of temporary licence for either a short period or until superseded by the transfer or removal of the relevant licence, can be obtained by a person intending to apply for a transfer of a licence, or where a licence has been forfeited, by the owner of the licensed premises or his nominee (s 10).

An application for ordinary removal of a licence must be made by the person who will hold the licence after its removal. It may not be granted in the face of an objection of the licence-holder, nor, in the case of an on-licence, of the owner of the premises or any other person whom the justices think has a right to object. Removals can be made to temporary premises, and, in some circumstances, removals can be imposed as "planning removals".

It should be noted that there are provisions giving a greater degree of protection to "old on-licences" and "old beerhouse licences" (broadly, those which have remained in force by renewal, taking no account of transfer, since August 15 1904), as regards renewal, transfer and removal.

Following the Licensing Act 1988 and the Licensing (Sunday Hours) Act 1995, the general licensing hours for on-licence sales are now from 11am to 11pm on weekdays, and on Sundays, Christmas Day or Good Friday from 12noon to 10.30pm but with a break between 3pm and 7pm on Christmas Day (s 60 of the 1964 Act; Sunday opening in Wales is subject to special restrictions: s 66). However, there are many possible variations according to circumstances. A local variation to 10am opening can be adopted. There are provisions for "restriction orders" preventing afternoon opening on weekdays or Sundays, which can be made at the request of certain persons such as the police, local residents or businessmen, and local head teachers (s 67A, introduced by the 1988 Act and amended by the 1995 Act).

A general "exemption order" can be granted for licensed premises or registered clubs situated in the immediate neighbourhood of a marketplace or similar trade place (s 74). A special "exemption order" can be granted for a particular "special occasion" or occasions. Annual occasions such as Christmas Eve, New Year's Eve, Bank Holidays and annual events have been held to qualify as "special occasions" but not regularly recurring events such as market days, or Sundays, or simply days when large custom is expected (*R* v *Cheltenham JJ* (1955) 120 JP 88: shoppers).

"Restaurant extensions" can be granted in respect of alcoholic drinks supplied with "substantial refreshments" in parts of the premises usually set aside for such purpose (an extension to include the time between the two licensing periods on Christmas Day and for an hour after general licensing hours (ss 68–69 of the 1964 Act as amended)). Where there is a restaurant extension in force and the premises are also structurally adapted for the provision of live musical or other entertainment as well as the necessary substantial refreshment, on a habitual basis, an "extended hours order" can be made, extending permitted hours until 1 am on the following morning after a weekday (s 70 of the 1964 Act).

"Special hours" certificates for up to 2am following a weekday, may be granted where there is also a public music and dancing licence in force for licensed or registered club premises, and music and dancing is provided in conjunction with substantial refreshment (ss 76–78 of the 1964 Act). There are provisions for a variety of limitations on such hours: (see ss 78A and 81A, introduced by the 1988 Act).

"Permitted hours" in sports grounds designated by the Secretary of State (notably football grounds) are governed by the Sporting Events (Control of Alcohol etc) Act 1985 which broadly excludes the hours of sporting events from "permitted hours".

The permitted hours for off-licence sales commence at 8am on week days. Permitted hours in registered clubs (see below) on Christmas Day are more limited than under a full on-licence (a maximum of 6.5 hours: see s 62 as amended).

Conditions may be attached by the justices to the grant of new on-licences in the public interest. However, no conditions may be attached to off-licences (although undertakings as to the reasonable and proper use of the off-licence may be required: *R* v *Edmonton Licensing JJ* [1983] 2 All ER 545), and in the case of a wine only on-licence only conditions appropriate to restaurant or residential licences may be attached. In the case of club premises a condition prohibiting sale to non-members may be attached.

Except for temporary buildings in new towns, justices must be satisfied that the premises are structurally adapted to the relevant class of licence. Certain areas (notably Inner London and certain areas which sustained war damage, and new towns) are the subject of systems of licensing planning, exercised by a licensing planning committee with the authority of the Secretary of State. These committees have certain powers in relation to the grant of new on-licences and the surrender or removal of existing on-licences according to the particular circumstances.

Some forms of condition are imposed only at the applicant's request and will also, in general, be revocable on his request. These are: a six day condition (ie, no permitted hours on Sundays), an early-closing condition (ie one hour earlier closing), a seasonal licence condition (ie no permitted hours during a specified part of the year), and an off-sales department condition (ie confining sales in a part of the premises to off-licence sales, with the consequent extension of permitted hours there).

Restaurants and guest houses. "Part IV" licences (s 94 of the 1964 Act) are not full "justices' licences" (see Section 1 and Section 200 (1) of the Act) but are licences for the sale of alcoholic liquor for consumption on premises providing meals with or without board and lodging. A restaurant licence is confined to sale of liquor in bona fide restaurants or cafes, for consumption only with meals. A residential licence is confined to premises providing board and lodging including breakfast and at least one other main meal, and authorises sale only to bona fide residents, and private friends whom they are entertaining, for consumption either on the premises or with a meal supplied on the premises. The two licences can be combined. The general policy of the licensing acts is more favourable to the grant of Part IV licences than a full on-licence.

"Part IV conditions" are imposed at the request of the applicant and are irrevocable. It is a condition of any Part IV licence that other suitable non-alcoholic beverages shall also be available with meals. A mid-day or evening condition may be imposed if the establishment only provides meals at such times, and a "dry room" condition (ie the provision of a dedicated sitting-room where no alcoholic drinks are sold or consumed) will usually be imposed in relation to residential licences. Only certain other conditions, (six day, early-closing, seasonal or sale to club members only) can be imposed, and a Part IV licence cannot be granted by way of removal (s 93 (4) of the 1964 Act).

Justices can only refuse Part IV licences on specified grounds such as the capacity or unsuitability of the applicant, or the premises, the earlier breaking of conditions or refusal to afford inspections, insignificant trade in the provision of meals, the preponderance of unaccompanied young persons frequenting the premises, etc (ss 93 and 98 of the 1964 Act). An applicant who fails to get a full on-licence can ask for the application to be treated as one for a Part IV licence. Conversely there is nothing to prevent a restaurateur or hotelier applying for a full on-licence.

An extension to permitted hours to include the time between the two licensing periods on Christmas Day can be applied: s 68 (1) (a) and s 95 of the 1964 Act as amended.

Registered members' clubs. Part II of the Act (ss 39–58) deals with registration of club premises for the sale of intoxicating liquor. A club becomes registered by obtaining a registration certificate annually from the magistrates court. The club in question must be a bona fide club with at least 25 members and must have at least a 48 hour period before new members may partake of the privileges of membership. Provisions are made to ensure that alcohol is being supplied as a club facility, and not as a disguised commercial enterprise for private gain (s 41).

Generally, provisions are made as to the qualification of clubs for registration (as to which the magistrates will have regard to the rules of the club) inspection of the premises by the local authority before registration, the rights of the fire authority and procedures for grant, renewal, cancellation of registrations, and suchlike. A registered club may sell intoxicating liquor to its members and their guests and, in certain circumstances, to non-members who are members of other clubs (s 49).

Variations of hours by extensions, special hours orders, etc can be applied for in the same way as for fully on-licensed premises.

Other forms of catering

Unlicensed restaurants. In general these require only the appropriate planning consent. If the sitting area is extended on to the pavement outside the premises, a licence from the highway authority will also be required.

Late night refreshment houses – night cafés. Main Statutes *Greater London Council (General Powers) Act 1968 Part VIII; Late Night Refreshment Houses Act 1969; Local Government (Misc. Provs.) Act 1982 s 7; London Local Authorities Act 1990 ss 4–20*

Outside London, under the Late Night Refreshment Houses Acts 1969, a house, room, shop or building kept open for public refreshment resort and entertainment at any time between 10pm and 5am requires a licence, unless it is "exempt licensed premises" (ie licensed premises not kept open for public refreshment, resort and entertainment after their normal licensed closing hours).

The licence is an annual licence taking effect to March 31 in each year, granted by the local authority. It is transmissible on the death of the licence-holder. There is a reduced fee for "beginner's" licences. The local authority may impose conditions as to hours of opening, no charges otherwise than in accordance with a displayed tariff, and prohibiting touting. It is an offence for the keeper of the refreshment house to allow unlawful gaming, thieves, prostitutes or drunken or disorderly persons to come or remain on the premises, and the police must assist in the expulsion of disorderly persons. They have power to enter and inspect at any time.

In London, the former system for registration of "night cafés" which local authorities might previously adopt is being replaced, by a system of night café licensing under the London Local Authorities Act 1990. A licence which is not an occasional licence will normally be in force for 18 months.

Conditions might formerly be imposed on registration as to maintenance of public order and safety, numbers, fire precautions, lighting, sanitation and ventilation, maintenance of means of heating and opening hours. Similar conditions can and no doubt will be imposed in licences. The borough council has power to make standard regulations for all or any particular class of night café licence.

The general structure of the night café licensing system is very similar to that of theatre licensing.

Hotel registration Although provisions exist under the Development of Tourism Act 1969 (s 17) for the introduction of a registration system for hotels and boarding houses with the relevant Tourist Board, no steps have as yet been taken.

Caravan Parks The licensing of Caravan Parks is covered under the specialist section on Holiday Caravan Parks (p. 203).

Leisure property and private relations

The general law of contract and tort (civil wrong) is of more concern for the day to day operation of leisure property than regarding its valuation. However, the valuer will need to be aware of some aspects of these areas of law as part of his understanding of the nature of the business. Some general observations are therefore appropriate, although specific problems must be dealt with by detailed consideration of the principles of general law to be found in the standard textbooks.

Aspects of land law are considered separately.

Contract
Textbook: Cheshire Fifoot & Furmston's *Law of Contract*

Admission contracts Where admission to leisure property is made upon payment of any kind, and whether tickets are issued or not, there is a contract between the proprietor of the business and the member of the public concerned. According to the circumstances of the particular case, the general law of contract will govern the interpretation of the contract, and what constitutes due performance.

For example, a ticket for a specific seat at some play or event may entitle the purchaser to that seat, but not to a different seat. It will not necessarily guarantee that the performance or event will take place. Equally, the contract governs the circumstances in which the organiser may lawfully eject the customer from the premises. Every situation will depend on its facts, and what, on the true view of the bargain, the leisure property operator has undertaken to provide, and, conversely, how the customer has impliedly undertaken to behave.

The general law of contract will also govern whether, for example, terms and conditions printed on the back of a ticket, or referred to in the ticket, will be incorporated into the contract so as to bind the purchaser. This can be of importance where the extent of an operator's liability is sought to be limited by "small print" on the back of a ticket. Unless such terms are adequately brought to the attention of the customer before he purchases admission they cannot form part of the contract.

The safety of persons attending premises may require the installation of expensive safety features. The requirements of fire certification, safety certificates at sports grounds and those of licence conditions have already been noted, but do not necessarily give rise to claims by customers. At common law, where the purpose of a person's entering a premises under a contract is that of watching some sport or show the owner/organiser impliedly warrants in his contract that the premises are reasonably fit for such purpose, having regard to the particular risks of the entertainment. Thus in *Hall v Brooklands Auto-Racing Club* [1933] 1 KB 205, an accident at a motor race occurred, but a spectator who was injured could not recover damages because reasonable and proper safety measures, particularly crash-barriers, had been installed.

Where the injury is the result of an intrinsic risk of the leisure activity itself, as opposed to a defect in the safety of the premises for the event, the owner/organiser will not be liable. The entrant, whether a participant or a spectator, is assumed to accept, voluntarily, the obvious risks of the activity causing an accident, although not the risk that inadequate safety measures have been taken. Thus where a golfer was injured by another player's ball, the golf course itself not being dangerously designed, he did not recover damages against the owners of the club: *Potter v Carlisle and Cliftonville Golf Club Ltd* [1939] NI 114.

Implied contractual duties relating to the conduct of the activities on the premises will be akin to the ordinary common duty of care in negligence. Thus, as regards accidents caused by performers, the owner/organiser will be liable if the performers were his servants and were negligent, or if the entertainment was itself intrinsically dangerous and he did not take adequate steps to ensure safety, such as where a firearm is fired during a play: *Cox v Coulson* [1916] 2 KB 177. However, where the entertainment is not intrinsically dangerous, the owner/organiser will not be liable for unexpected accidents, such as, for example, a heel flying from the shoe of a dancer and causing injury: *Fraser-Wallas v Walters* [1939] 4 All ER 609, or for the acts of persons for whom he is not responsible, such as the negligence of a concessionaire's servant in a side-show: *Sheehan v Dreamland (Margate) Ltd* [1923] 40 TLR 155.

The Occupier's Liability Act 1957 (see below) laid down a general code as regards an occupier's liability to his "lawful visitors", whether present under a contract or not. This is based on a "common duty of care" to take reasonable steps to enable them to be reasonably safe for the purposes for which they are invited or permitted to be on the property. The principles mentioned above would still hold good under the scheme of the Act.

The extent to which the leisure property occupier can reduce or exclude his contractual duty of care to customers by (for example), the terms of the contract or by exhibiting notices, may be a difficult question depending on the facts. In contract, such a limitation of liability might be held to be unreasonable under the Unfair Contract Terms Act 1977, and mere notices would not necessarily be effectively incorporated into the contract.

Hoteliers "Innkeepers" stood in a special position at common law, which has now been codified by the Hotel Proprietors Act 1956. By opening a house as an inn, an innkeeper assumes an obligation to receive guests without favour or discrimination unless he has reasonable excuse for not doing so, such as the hotel being full or the guest being drunk (but not merely being late in arriving, or having an illness short of a "notifiable disease" under the Public Health Acts). He must also receive the guest's goods, his car if possible, and probably his dog. He assumes liability for the safety of the guest and his goods, but the latter can be limited in amount by a statutory notice under the Act, except where the goods are offered for safe deposit, or the loss is caused by the fault of the innkeeper or his staff. In return, he acquires a right of lien and sale against the guest's goods brought on to the premises in respect of unpaid bills.

General Lastly, a general contractual matter of more direct significance to valuation may be the question whether agreements made by one proprietor of a business will bind successors. If the proprietor has made a contract which, in effect, gives the other party an interest in the land, then, subject to general rules of land law regarding registration or notice, the successor will be bound by that contract. Thus, the granting of an exclusive right to occupy a box in a theatre for a period may be held to amount to a lease.

Licences and concessions The distinction between a lease and a licence can be of major significance in the treatment of operating contracts or concessions granted within leisure property. A licence is a mere personal privilege or right to the use of the property or part of it. When granted for payment, it is a contractual licence. A lease or tenancy creates an interest in the land itself. All tenants have "exclusive possession" of the demised premises, meaning that they can exclude anybody, even the landlord (unless he is exercising rights reserved by the lease). A licence may or may not confer "exclusive possession", and whether it does is a question of fact. If, however, an occupier does have exclusive possession, he will have the foundation for an argument that he is, in truth, a tenant and not a mere licensee.

The practical importance of the distinction lies in the very much more limited rights of a licensee when compared with those of a tenant, and hence the greater control and power of the licensor over the property. A licence can be terminated, in accordance with its contractual terms, and the licensee required to leave, or the licence fee increased. A tenant, where there is a business tenancy granted for a sufficient period (see Section 43 (3) of the Landlord and Tenant Act 1954 Part II as amended) acquires security of tenure. So long as the licensor does not break the terms of the licence, he can still make use of the licensed area, either sharing it with the licensee or using the area at other times. (An arrangement under which hours of use are limited is not necessarily a licence; it is possible to construe it as a tenancy with a user restriction.) After some uncertainty, it now seems clear that a mere contractual licence will not bind a successor in title of the licensor; he will not be bound to observe the licence contract, leaving the licensee to any remedy he may have in damages against the licensor. A tenancy, in contrast, will be binding on a successor in title.

For the above reasons, property owners will generally prefer to grant licences. However, the question whether any arrangement is truly a lease or a licence depends on its actual effect, and not on the label the parties may have put upon it: *Addiscombe Garden Estates Ltd* v *Crabbe* [1958] 1 QB 513. Any apparent "licence" arrangements affecting leisure property therefore need to be examined critically, to be confident that they can safely be taken at face value. Whereas a mere contractual licence will not give security of tenure, or bind a successor in title; resulting hardship on the "licensee" in any particular case may incline the court to find the existence of a tenancy if it possibly can.

As regards leisure property, cases relating to the grant of "front of house" rights in theatres illustrate the difficulty of this area of law, and how distinctions may be drawn on fine differences of fact. A grant of the "exclusive" use of theatre refreshment rooms for the purpose of supplying refreshments to visitors has been held to be merely a licence in England (*Clore* v *Theatrical Properties* [1936] 3 All ER 483), whereas in an Australian case, *Radaich* v *Smith* [1959] 101 CLR 209 approved by the House of Lords in *Street* v *Mountford* [1985] AC 809, a very similar arrangement was held to be a tenancy. The true status of the occupier may also be material in relation to the operation of kiosks or similar concessions on other types of leisure property.

The right to erect and maintain advertisements on land will usually be a mere licence: *Kewal Investments Ltd* v *Arthur Maiden Ltd* [1990] 1 EGLR 193. Sporting rights, such as shooting or fishing rights, are potentially more than mere licences, since they confer a right to take away the game or fish, and therefore constitute an interest in the land known as a "profit à prendre". However, such rights have to be properly granted by deed.

Tort

Textbook: Winfield & Jolowicz on *Tort*

The law of tort will affect relations of the owner of leisure property both as regards those who come on to his premises but without a contract, and as regards third parties. The former is governed by principles of negligence, as now largely embodied in statute. Although the law of negligence can arise between the operator/ owner and third parties, it is more likely that the law of nuisance and possibly trespass will be relevant.

Negligence – visitors Persons coming on to the leisure premises for some lawful purpose, but who have not entered under a contract, are "lawful visitors" of the occupier of the property. The duties of care owed by the occupier to such persons used to be governed by the common law as a branch of the law of negligence, but are now governed by the Occupiers' Liability Act 1957. In the result, however, the scope of the implied duties of care in tort and those implied by an admission contract are much the same.

The duty of an occupier of property to anyone coming on to his property lawfully (which means by express or implied invitation or permission) is known as the "common duty of care" under the Act, and is a duty to take such care as is reasonable in all the circumstances to see that the visitor will be reasonably safe in using the premises for the purposes for which the occupier has invited or permitted him to be there (s 2 (2)). Providing adequate lighting and roping-off hazards are obvious precautions which may need to be considered. However a failure to comply with Building Regulations is not decisive evidence of negligence: *Green* v *Building Scene Ltd* [1994] PIQR 259.

Relevant circumstances include the recognition that children will be less careful for themselves than adults (s 2 (3) (a)). The giving of warnings will only absolve the occupier if they would reasonably be enough to enable the visitor to be safe (s 2 (4) (a)). Thus notices saying "danger" are unlikely to suffice if they do not reveal the nature of the danger. However, it is not negligent to fail to provide warnings of obvious dangers: *Cotton* v *Derbyshire Dales D.C.* (CA) *The Times* 20 June 1994 (walker falling over cliff in patently dangerous terrain).

The extent to which an occupier can exclude or reduce this duty of care by notice may, as in the contractual case, be a difficult question of fact, although it is undoubtedly easier than where there is an admission contract. This can be illustrated by the case of *White* v *Blackmore* [1972] 2 QB 651. Safety ropes at a "jalopy racing" event were negligently erected, resulting in their being unexpectedly ripped out and killing a spectator. The spectator was also a competitor and had, as a result, been given free admission. Notices excluding the organisers' liability for any accidents, howsoever caused, had been erected. Lord Denning MR found that the spectator was a contractual visitor and that the notices were not incorporated in the contract, and therefore could not and did not exclude the organisers' liability for their negligence. Buckley and Roskill LJJ found that the spectator was a mere licensee and that they did. The claim for damages therefore failed.

For completeness, it should be mentioned that the Occupiers' Liability Act 1984 lays down a duty of care even towards trespassers on property, but it is again based on reasonableness in all the circumstances (including the fact of the trespass) and is therefore naturally of a lower standard. However, the reasonableness of anticipating the presence of trespassers is a relevant circumstance which will impose a degree of duty to ensure that premises are safe. In the case of some types of leisure property, the likely attraction for child trespassers may therefore impose some degree of duty to take steps to minimise hazards.

Lastly, it should be noted that the Defective Premises Act 1972 (s 4) may in some circumstances impose a liability on landlords who have either an obligation or a right to repair the demised premises, as regards damage caused by the defective state of repair of the premises. Furthermore, the Health and Safety at Work etc Act 1974 imposes duties on employers to persons other than their employees. Such duties would extend to persons using equipment, for example gymnastic apparatus, on leisure premises, with regard to the safety of that apparatus: see *Moualem* v *Carlisle City Council* (1994) 158 JP 1110.

Nuisance – neighbours The law of private nuisance protects an occupier of land in his reasonable enjoyment of his land against unreasonable interference caused by the condition of a neighbour's land, or activities on it. The property does not necessarily have to have a common boundary.

A nuisance may cause encroachment on or physical damage to land or interfere with the comfortable and convenient use of it. It is the last category which may be particularly relevant to the causing of nuisance by some leisure property activities, although instances of physical encroachment can occur, as in *Miller* v *Jackson* [1977] QB 966 (the nuisance lying in the likelihood of errant cricket balls). Making unreasonable noise or causing crowds to collect have been held to be private nuisances.

There are no absolute standards as regards such nuisance; the question is in all cases one of fact. Everyone has to be prepared to put up with a certain degree of inconvenience from the reasonable activities of neighbours. A balance has to be drawn between one party's right to use his property as he chooses and the other party's right to comfortable enjoyment of his own property. In order to establish the permissible limits of inconvenience which may be caused, all the circumstances of the case, and "the ordinary usages of mankind living in the particular society" has been given as a description of the standard in question (*Sedleigh-Denfield* v *O'Callaghan* [1940] AC 880 at 903).

Thus, the standards prevailing in the locality will be relevant: "what would be a nuisance in Belgrave Square would not necessarily be so in Bermondsey": *Sturges* v *Bridgman* (1879) 11 ChD 852, a case which also established that it is no defence to argue that the plaintiff "came to" the nuisance. The frequency or duration of the annoyance, and the severity when it occurs, are also relevant to the balancing exercise. Standards change with the times; prolonged interference with television reception may be held to be a nuisance: *Bridlington Relay* v *Yorkshire Electricity Board* [1965] Ch 436. The mere grant of planning permission for an activity does not authorise the commission of a nuisance by it: *Wheeler* v *JJ Saunders Ltd, The Times* 3 January 1995.

As regards leisure property, it is likely to be the success and hence the continuance or expansion of the activity or entertainment which can begin to cause a nuisance, and hence provoke action to restrain the conduct of the activity. An action of nuisance, by its very nature, is more likely to arise where an activity is prolonged rather than a "one off" event, although in theory such an event could be restrained, in advance, by sufficiently clear evidence of apprehended serious nuisance. Events such as pop concerts are more likely to be restrained in advance by the operation of planning permission and/or licensing requirements, but a private action is still a possibility.

Where there are existing recurrent activities on a leisure property, it can be expansion which causes problems. Noise from entertainments, which local residents can be expected to put up with once a fortnight, may be found to be unreasonable if extended to three evenings a week. Particularly commonplace is nuisance by parking of cars. As a leisure venue grows in popularity the limited parking available results in spectators leaving their cars on, or obstructing, private property, such as the forecourt of a nearby block of flats or business premises. These possible problems are matters which may require consideration when assessing the potential for expanding or maintaining a successful leisure activity.

A landlord may be liable for a nuisance if he has let a tenant into the premises for the known purpose of doing the very act likely to be held to cause an actionable nuisance, but will not otherwise be liable for a nuisance caused by his tenant, as occupier. A licensor may be liable on similar principles: *R* v *Shorrocks* [1993] 3 All ER 917 (obvious likelihood of nuisance from "acid house" party).

A public nuisance is created if there is a nuisance to members of the public exercising rights common to all such persons. Public nuisance is a criminal offence, but in addition any person who suffers individual damage as a result of what would otherwise be a public nuisance has a right of action. Many public nuisances at common law, such as selling food unfit for human consumption or keeping a disorderly house, have been subsequently regulated by statute, such as the Public Health Acts.

The public nuisance most likely to apply to leisure property is in relation to obstruction of the highway. As an example, the causing of queues to gather on the highway thereby obstructing access to other premises has been restrained by injunction: *Lyons, Sons & Co* v *Gulliver* [1914] 1 Ch 681, and it is probable that damages for loss of trade can be recovered. Allowing golf balls to fly dangerously over a public right of way would be an example of another potentially actionable nuisance to the highway.

As regards suffering nuisance, leisure property receives no special protection. A person cannot create an actionable nuisance by carrying on an activity especially susceptible to it. Thus, to be able to restrain an interfering activity, the leisure property owner would have to demonstrate a nuisance by normal standards, rather than by any particular requirements of (say) clean air or quiet which the activities on his premises require.

Lastly, mention must be made here of the rule allied to the law of nuisance known as the "Rule in *Rylands* v *Fletcher*" (1868) LR 3 HL 330. This rule states that the occupier of land who brings on to his property, in the pursuit of any "non-natural" use, a thing liable to do mischief if it escapes, must keep it on his land at his peril, and is strictly liable (ie liable without any negligence) for any damage it does if it escapes.

This rule, which was initially applied in relation to escapes of things such as water, gas, and explosives, has been much reduced in its scope by a general tacit recognition that many one-time "non-natural" uses are in fact highly desirable in modern times. This liability has therefore become narrowed to, broadly, commercial uses with a particularly high danger factor. There are also many defences, such as the unforeseeable acts of strangers, eg vandalism, which have tended to undermine the principle of strict liability as opposed to negligence. However, the rule has been applied, for example, to the escape of a fairground roundabout seat known as a "chair-o'-plane" (*Hale* v *Jennings Bros* [1938] 1 All ER 579).

It is now the better view that people cannot be the "dangerous thing" in question, even though, in *Attorney-General* v Corke [1933] Ch 89 a landowner was held liable under the rule for damage caused by gypsies whom he had licensed to camp on his land. Other bases of liability, such as nuisance, were available in that case (contrast *Page Motors Ltd* v *Epsom & Ewell Borough Council* (1981) 80 LGR 337). It is therefore doubtful whether this rule could be invoked against a landowner in respect of (for example) unruly crowds of spectators going on the rampage after an entertainment. Negligence would have to be proved.

Although the rule has been described as the "wild beast" theory, liability for damage caused by escaping animals is now covered by the *Animals Act* 1971. This would include escaping menagerie animals.

Real property law

Textbook: Megarry and Wade: *Law of Real Property*

English land law is governed largely by statute. Property law was generally revised and consolidated in legislation made in 1925, of which the Law of Property Act 1925 was the main general Act.

Again, there are no special principles applicable to leisure property as such. Nothing need be said, for example, about the general principles of ownership and conveyancing of leisure property, which are those of universal application.

General principles of land law may, however, assume special significance for leisure property in two particular areas.

The first is where they relate to the use to which the property can be put, and hence the extent to which its exploitation for leisure purposes can be exploited or inhibited.

The second is that of the principles governing the relationship between the land itself and any equipment which may be installed, or simply present, upon it in order for the land to be used for the relevant leisure purposes. An understanding of these latter principles is particularly essential for valuation purposes, as a failure to grasp precisely what is (or is not) the legitimate subject matter of a particular valuation can produce a result which is badly adrift.

In the first class, therefore, some pointers on restrictive covenants and easements are considered. These share the attribute that they are rights of one landowner in respect of the land of another, and they therefore affect, and possibly restrict, the use which that other can make of his land. The law of fixtures is considered in the second class.

Matters of importance under leases are then mentioned, with particular reference to the special position of licensed premises.

Restrictive covenants affecting leisure property Restrictive covenants are that species of covenant which "run with the land" outside the relationship of landlord and tenant. By this is meant that they can be enforced against successors in title to the land of the original covenantor (ie the giver of the covenant) even after the freehold of the land is transferred.

To have this enduring quality, such a covenant must, first, be negative in its operation, ie "restrictive", and it must be restrictive of the use of the land. If it does not "touch and concern" land in this way, it may well be construed as a personal covenant only. A covenant may be negative even though framed positively. Thus, a covenant "to use only as a restaurant" is construed as a negative covenant: not to use the premises otherwise than as a restaurant. As an anomalous exception, a covenant to fence land is treated as a negative covenant.

Second, the covenant must benefit land of the recipient of the covenant (ie the covenantee). Benefit to a business carried on on the covenantee's land is treated as benefit to the land itself. Thus, a covenant not to cause any nuisance or annoyance to "the neighbourhood" will not be enforced against a later purchaser if the covenantee has retained no land in "the neighbourhood".

Lastly, to be enforceable against successors, a restrictive covenant must have been duly registered on the register of the covenantor's title at HM Land Registry or (if still applicable) in the Land Charges Register.

If these conditions are not fulfilled, the covenant cannot be directly enforced by injunction against a successor in title to the land.

Restrictive covenants are most likely to affect leisure property by inhibiting the use to which it can be put. Conversely, a leisure property may, of course, have the benefit of a restrictive covenant over another's property, eg a covenant preventing a competing activity. As with any covenant, it is the precise terms of the covenant which must be examined to determine whether or not there is an infringement in any given case. The following points should be borne in mind as guidance when considering whether the exploitation of leisure property may be affected by the terms of any such covenant.

First, the courts will not construe the words of a covenant so strictly as to render its obvious purpose useless. Thus, a covenant that "no hotel, public house or other building for the sale of [alcoholic liquors] shall be built" on the property was held to be infringed when, after a restaurant had been built, the defendants subsequently obtained a justices' on-licence: *Webb* v *Fagotti Bros* [1898] 79 LT 683. The intention of the covenant was that no such building should "be" on the land and hence the word "built" was given a meaning sufficiently wide not to defeat the covenant. Similarly, an undertaking not to permit baccarat to be played on premises was broken by permitting chemin de fer, a species of the same game, to be played (*Jenks* v *Turpin* (1884) 13 QBD 505). On the other hand, the courts will not be astute to extend the scope of the covenant either. A covenant not to use land for a particular purpose is not broken simply by using it as an access to other land where that purpose is lawfully carried on: *Elliott* v *Safeway Stores plc* 1995 1 WLR 1396.

Where the question is whether a particular activity can be carried on in the context of a particular covenant the answer may depend on whether the covenant is directed at laying down the use to which the property can be put or prohibiting its use for a particular purpose. Thus, a covenant to use the premises "only as an hotel" would not prevent the opening of a shopping arcade as an ancillary part of the hotel business, but a covenant "not to use the premises for retail purposes" would do so.

It will, again, be a matter of fact and degree whether the holding of an individual event amounts to a breach of a covenant not to use premises other than for particular specified purposes. In some cases a particular event may legitimately be held as part of and ancillary to the permitted user, but if it is a sufficiently substantial departure from the permitted user, it will be restrained. Thus, it was held in *Seaward* v *Paterson* [1896] 12 TLR, that a covenant to use premises only as a private club would be breached by the holding of a single boxing match to which *ad hoc* members were to be admitted.

Covenants against selling alcoholic liquor and similar trades (eg that of "innkeeper") are common in many differing terms, many of them old-fashioned. They have given rise to many authorities relating to such expressions as "retail of wines spirits and beer", "beer-shop", "the trade of a vintners", both in connection with leisure premises and retail premises generally. In line with general principle, it is no defence to a claim based on a covenant containing a direct prohibition that the relevant activity is being carried out as ancillary to the permitted use. A theatre lessee who maintained a bar in the theatre with no external access was held, nonetheless, to infringe a covenant against use for "the trade of a retailer of wines, spirits and beer", although arguing that such trade was ancillary to use as a theatre.

However, some of the old authorities are of doubtful consistency. Thus, a members' club selling liquor to members has been held not to infringe a prohibition on use for "the sale of liquor" on the grounds that this connoted a sale to members of the public (*Ranken* v *Hunt*

(1894) 10 R 249) whereas in *Devonshire* v *Simmons* (1894) 11 TLR 52 a private hotel selling liquor under licence to hotel guests only, with no members of the public present, appears to have been regarded as a "beer shop" although not a "public house". Care needs to be taken where the effects of any such covenant are critical.

If the terms of a covenant are not sufficiently clear, expert evidence as to their meaning, as terms of art, may be admissible. Thus in *Shaw* v *Applegate* [1977] 1 WLR 970 the term "amusement arcade" was found by the judge, on expert evidence, to be a building with public access and including coin-in-the-slot machines, whether gaming machines or not. (The Court of Appeal was, however, uncertain as to whether or not the expression might not also refer to a place of amusements for children!)

Covenants in more general terms not to permit any activity causing "nuisance" or "annoyance" or "inconvenience" etc, are often found. Such wording will give rise to a breach of covenant at a level of nuisance which is less than that required for the tort of nuisance at common law, even the word "nuisance" itself being given a less strict meaning in this context: see *Ives* v *Brown* [1919] 2 Ch 314. An activity such as a girls' finishing school has been held to amount to such an "annoyance" on the grounds not merely of the noise of the practising of singing and dancing but also because of the continual visiting of relatives and friends: *Kemp* v *Sober* [1851] 1 Sim NS 517. Standards would clearly not be so stringent today!

Lastly, covenants not to do a particular act or carry on a particular activity are not infringed where the covenantor does not, himself or through his agent, offend the prohibition. However, a covenant not to "permit" or "suffer" a particular act or activity can be infringed if the covenantor does not take steps to prevent the prohibited act. Again, the particular covenant and the particular circumstances require careful examination.

Section 84 of the Law of Property Act 1925 gives the Lands Tribunal power to cancel or modify obsolete or unnecessary restrictive covenants in appropriate circumstances.

Easements affecting leisure property An easement is a right enjoyed by one property (the dominant tenement) over another property (the servient tenement) for the benefit of the land comprised in the dominant tenement. A benefit which does not accommodate land is nothing more than a licence. The right must also be of a type which the law recognises as being capable of forming the subject matter of a grant by one owner to another.

The most well known of easements are rights of way (by far the most important), rights of drainage and the passage of service pipes and wires, rights of light (though these have special rules), and rights of support for buildings from other buildings. Other matters can, however, be easements. Rights of storage or car-parking, a right to use a neighbour's chimney or lavatory, a right to pin trees on a neighbour's wall, a right to fetch water from a neighbour's well or stream, have all been held capable of constituting easements.

The law relating to the creation of easements is complicated and, if necessary, reference should be made to specialist text books such as Gale on *Easements*. Broadly, however, an easement may be created by express grant, by implied grant (usually because it is vital to the use of the property in question but has not been expressly stipulated, as where a landlocked plot of land is conveyed) and by prescription. Prescription arises upon the demonstration of uninterrupted user, enjoyed apparently as of right, for at least 20 years. The law will then allow that the right has been acquired, either under statute (the Prescription Act 1832) or because it will presume (although this is a legal fiction) that the right must have been granted by a deed which has been lost.

The existence of easements can affect leisure property either because the leisure use of the property requires the enjoyment of easements over other property or because it will or may interfere with easements enjoyed by others over the property itself.

Difficulties over the adequacy of easements to accommodate the business in question tend to arise when a property is either being acquired for leisure purposes, or the enterprise is being expanded. "Excessive user" is user which increases the burden of the easement upon the servient tenement beyond that which is authorised by the right in question. It can be prevented by the owner of the servient tenement. Rights of way, in particular, are a common source of dispute in this area.

A right of way granted by express grant may be phrased in such wide terms as to cover use in connection with any possible user of the dominant tenement. However, the grant always has to be construed in the context of the surrounding circumstances known to the parties at the time of the grant, so that even a grant "for all purposes" would be limited to all purposes within the reasonable contemplation of the parties at the time of the grant: *Todrick* v

Western National Omnibus Co Ltd [1934] 1 Ch 190. The nature of the dominant tenement and the state and width of the right of way itself at the time may indicate that there are some limitations on the extent of the right.

Thus, a right of way "for all purposes in connection with the cottage known as Whiteacre" may well not authorise use for hotel purposes if Whiteacre is converted into an hotel, and the more alteration that is done to Whiteacre, the more likely that the right of way will be held not to extend to the proposed hotel user. If, however, the words "the cottage known as" were omitted, then the hotel user would be more likely to be held to be covered, on the basis that it was the purposes of the land, rather than the building, to which the grant referred: cf *White* v *Grand Hotel, Eastbourne Ltd* [1913] 1 Ch 113.

Where the right of way is one which has been acquired by prescription (ie by use, rather than actual grant), it will be more strictly defined against the grantee than will an express grant, and it will be limited according to the nature of the use actually made and the circumstances at the time. The purposes for which such a right can be used will therefore be narrowly confined to the purposes for which the right has been prescribed. The dominant owner cannot increase the burden on the servient tenement over which he has obtained a right of way by long use by, for example, building additional buildings on it, nor by improving the right of way (as opposed to repairing it) so as to make it usable in all seasons when it had not previously been: *Mills* v *Silver* [1991] Ch 271. This is explained by the fact that a right acquired by prescription is in the nature of an expropriation of the servient owner's rights, and will therefore be construed in his favour, whereas an express grant will, in principle, be construed against him because he granted it.

Thus, the grantee of a right of way by express grant will be entitled to make up and improve the right of way, and make additional use of it, in the absence of any implied limitation. On the other hand, even a widely worded express grant of a right of way will ultimately have limits. In *Jelbert* v *Davis* [1968] 1 WLR 589 agricultural land was conveyed together with a right of way "at all times and for all purposes" over a driveway "in common with all others entitled to a like right". The Court of Appeal held that although the wide terms of the grant permitted use by forms of transport, namely caravans, not contemplated at the time of the original grant, user of such a degree as would be likely to interfere with use by "all others entitled to the like right" would not have been so contemplated. For that reason, use for access to a 200 unit caravan/camp site proposed for the dominant land would not be permissible.

Again, where a business is to be expanded by the acquisition of further land, it should not be assumed that existing private rights of access will suffice. Where a right of way is granted over a private road to plot A and the owner of plot A subsequently acquires further land behind it, he cannot use the private road for access to the further land: *Bracewell* v *Appleby* [1975] Ch 408.

It should be remembered that the grant of planning permission in no way affects the position as regards private rights such as rights of way, neither conferring them nor extinguishing them. While the presence or absence of such rights may affect the planning authority's attitude to the grant or refusal of permission, it is up to the grantee of the permission to ensure that he has such private rights as are necessary to enable him to implement the permission.

While the above examples relate to rights of way, similar principles will apply where it is desired to exploit other easements. Thus in *Keith* v *Twentieth Century Club Ltd* (1904) 73 LJ Ch 545, the houses round a London garden square each had a right for the owner or his tenants being the occupiers of the house, and his family and friends, to use the square. The defendant company owned several houses which it had converted into a members' club and wished both its resident members and non-resident guests to use the garden. Other occupiers in the square objected. It was held, as a matter of construction of the grant, that resident members of the defendant's club were not within the terms of the grant, being neither tenants nor "friends" of the defendant, and that the grant did not enable the defendant, even as owner, to authorise people to use the square.

Rights to abstract or use water are the subject of complex rules at common law, according to whether the water ran in a defined channel or not, and whether the water was merely diverted or removed. These rules are now of little importance in a commercial context, having been overtaken by statute for all significant purposes: see now the Water Act 1989 and Water Resources Act 1991 and the Water Industry Act 1991: see above (pp. 8–9). Private rights of navigation are similar to rights of way.

The existence of easements over the leisure property itself may inhibit development or expansion. The existence of rights of way may prevent fencing in order to improve an enterprise such as a holiday caravan park or a golf club, unless the dominant owner can be "bought off". Agricultural rights of way may not be regularly used but may cause particular congestion and disturbance in the harvest or breeding season.

Public rights of way, although not strictly easements, can conveniently be mentioned here, as inconveniently placed public footpaths can also make development or expansion projects impractical, whether for reasons of safety or privacy. It is sometimes possible to get these diverted by agreement with the local highway authority, but this is troublesome and time-consuming. In the current general climate such rights tend to be zealously guarded by pressure groups.

In an urban context, rights of escape in case of fire may have been granted which prevent particular alterations of the premises for leisure purposes, or which cause difficulties in fulfilling licence conditions. Every case needs individual examination.

Fixtures and fittings "Fixtures and fittings" are a little considered area of law, but in relation to commercial transactions, the law relating to fixtures can be of importance between landlord and tenant, vendor and purchaser and mortgagor and mortgagee. It is potentially of particular importance regarding leisure property because there is likely to be extensive and valuable investment in construction of appropriate premises, alterations, and the installation of equipment, fixed and unfixed, for use in the leisure activity.

It is a basic rule of land law that anything which is "planted" in the land becomes part of it, and title to the item becomes vested in the owner of the land. Thus a building erected on the land belongs to the owner of the soil, whoever erects it. Any extension to the building similarly adheres to the building, and any item fixed to the fabric of the building similarly becomes part of the real property. All these additions are said to be "annexed" to the land.

If a thing or "chattel", is fixed to the land or the fabric of the building, however lightly, it is *prima facie* a *fixture* and therefore part of the premises (*Holland* v *Hodgson* (1872) LR 7 CP 328 at 335).

However, where the purpose of fixing the chattel to the premises is for the better enjoyment of the chattel itself, rather than the better enjoyment of the land, the chattel retains its legal nature as a chattel. It never becomes part of the premises at all. The classic illustration of this is the fixing of tapestries to the walls of a house by nailing them to moulded frames. The House of Lords held that they remained chattels, removable by the tenant, as they were "never intended to be dedicated to the house" (*Leigh* v *Taylor* [1902] AC 157).

Nowadays the test of whether an item is a fixture or a chattel is more *why* the article was fixed to the premises ("the purpose of annexation") rather than *how* it is fixed ("the degree of annexation"). The mode of fixing may, however, be evidence of the intention behind the affixation. If the article cannot be removed without causing significant damage to either the premises or the article itself, that is strong evidence that it was intended to be annexed to the premises and is therefore a fixture.

Examples of fixtures would be buildings fixed to foundations let into the soil, machinery and plant cemented into the floor, mirrored or panelled wall finishes, stud partitioning, suspended ceilings, heating and air conditioning systems, built-in furniture not removable as a unit, floor finishings including fully fitted carpets, light fittings fixed to the ceiling or walls to take appropriate bulbs (*Young* v *Dalgety plc* [1987] 1 EGLR 116). Occasionally items "fixed" to the soil only by their own weight have been held to be fixtures, but only where they are such a sufficiently integral part of an architectural scheme that they were plainly intended to be permanent.

Examples of non-fixtures, ie items remaining as chattels, would be temporary buildings not affixed to foundations, machines or equipment screwed to the floor solely to keep them steady, mirrors screwed to the wall for support, some kinds of demountable partitioning, pictures screwed to the wall, cupboards and shelves screwed to the wall to keep them in place but removable as units, rugs nailed to the floor to keep them from slipping. It should be noted, however, that in a domestic context, it has been held – perhaps surprisingly – that the category of fixtures extended to co-ordinated curtains and blinds and the "white goods" in a fitted kitchen, even though these items were not physically fixed: *TSB Bank plc* v *Botham* [1995] EGCS 3.

As between vendor and purchaser of land, and mortgagor and mortgagee, the conveyance or mortgage of the land will implicitly include *all* fixtures automatically unless they are expressly excluded.

As between landlord and tenant there is a further distinction between "landlord's fixtures" and "tenant's fixtures". This is as a result of the law's recognition of the hardship on a tenant, if he were obliged to leave behind valuable property which he had affixed to the land in order to use or enjoy the property to the full during his tenancy.

If the fixture is a tenant's fixture, then although it is part of the landlord's property while fixed, the tenant has the right to sever it from the land and treat it as his own property, either during or at the end of the term. He can therefore take it away. He must make good any damage to the premises (eg fill in screw holes).

"Tenant's fixtures" are fixtures installed by the tenant (a) at his own expense, and (b) which fall into one of the categories of trade fixtures, fixtures of ornament and convenience and agricultural fixtures. The latter two categories are mainly relevant to domestic and agricultural properties and therefore have no special significance for leisure property. The first is by far the most important.

"Trade fixtures" comprise all items fixed to the premises by the tenant for the purposes of his trade or manufacture, unless *plainly* intended to become part of the premises as where, for example, their removal would irreparably damage the article itself or cause very substantial damage to the property.

The category will therefore cover almost all items installed by companies. In a leisure context, *New Zealand Government Property Corpn* v *HM&S Ltd* [1982] 2 WLR 837 provides a good illustration of the difference between landlord's and tenant's fixtures. In a theatre, the seats, lights and electrical equipment were held to be tenant's fixtures whereas doors, windows and the safety curtain were held to be landlord's fixtures. In an hotel context, many of the items installed in order to create the desired ambience would be likely to be treated as tenant's fixtures, for example, fitted carpets, ornamental wall finishes capable of removal and re-use, ornamental light fittings and fireplaces, and perhaps the bar and bar fitments. (In a sports hall, fixed sports equipment such as gymnastic apparatus would clearly be a tenant's fixture.)

A fixture can still be a tenant's fixture even if it was installed pursuant to an obligation to the landlord to install it. The obligation to install is a matter of contract only, and does not affect the legal categorisation of the item when installed (*Young* v *Dalgety plc* [1987] 1 EGLR 116). If a tenant replaces a landlord's fixture (ie one provided by the landlord) with one of his own, he is still entitled to remove his own fixture as a "tenant's fixture" but must restore a fixture equivalent to that provided by the landlord (*Martyr* v *Bradley* (1832) 9 Bing 24).

The consequences of an item being a tenant's fixture stem from the tenant's right of removal. First, a covenant to repair the demised premises, without more, does not oblige a tenant to repair tenant's fixtures. Even if the covenant is to repair the demised premises and all fixtures, the tenant can avoid his obligation in respect of tenant's fixtures simply by removing them. This may be a valuable option where fixtures are uneconomic to repair.

Second, the tenant is not obliged to deliver up tenant's fixtures under an ordinary covenant to yield up the demised premises at the end of the term – but neither is he obliged to remove tenant's fixtures unless the covenant to yield up actually requires him to do so.

Third, tenant's fixtures are not part of the "demised premises" for rent review purposes. This is not the consequence of any "disregard" for "tenant's improvements" to the premises; that disregard covers improvements to the demised premises paid for by the tenant but which he could *not* remove, ie landlord's fixtures and alterations and additions to the actual buildings or the land.

Last, ingenious exploitation of these principles may even enable covenants against alterations to be avoided. In one instance known to the author, the tenant of a public house whose lease contained an absolute prohibition on alterations was refused permission to construct a winkle bar in one corner of an up-market public house car park. He therefore had a mobile stall constructed, which was towed into place each weekend, and conducted the desired extension to his business exactly as he wished, but without breaching the covenant.

The term "fittings" has no recognised legal definition as does the term "fixtures" and is often used confusingly. Insofar as it relates to fixed items, it adds nothing to "fixtures". Insofar as it relates to unfixed, free standing items, such as curtains or hanging mirrors, or standard lamps or unfixed equipment, then it means nothing more than "chattels". In such latter cases the expressions "landlord's fittings" or "tenant's fittings" will indicate ownership, but on the basis of the rules of personal property rather than real property.

The implications of these legal differences for valuation situations are mentioned below (pp. 65–6, 74–6).

Leases The important distinction between a lease and a licence has been considered in a leisure property context under contract law (see above).

Where leisure property is leasehold, the terms of the lease are likely to follow those of normal commercial leases. Particular points of interest or difference from the usual commercial property situation are mentioned below.

Benefits in kind. One unusual provision sometimes found in leisure property, arising from the nature of the property itself, is that the landlord may stipulate, in addition to rent in money, for some concessionary treatment as regards admission to the property, eg a certain number of free tickets to a theatre each year, a right to hold a particular annual function in the property, free membership of a golf club or gaming club.

Such a provision might be construed as additional rent. Alternatively the question might arise as to whether it was a covenant which ran with the lease, or was a mere personal covenant by the tenant, unenforceable against assignees without a further direct covenant from them to the landlord. This distinction could be material to value where, for example, the landlord has required accommodation in an hotel to be made available for himself and his friends and this affects the number of available rooms for valuation purposes.

Common covenants. Of the usual clauses appearing in leases, those most likely to have special importance for leisure property will be the following.

(a) *Covenant to observe and comply with the requirements of statutes and authorities.* This common covenant can be particularly onerous in the case of leisure property, given the requirements of licensing and the conditions which will be imposed. Apart from any question of offences committed under the relevant licensing provisions, a breach of such a covenant will give rise to potential forfeiture of the lease. A breach of covenant of this type, if it is notorious or serious enough, may be argued by the landlord to cause a "stigma" on the property, in which case the court may be persuaded to refuse relief from forfeiture to the tenant, notwithstanding the current, reasonably liberal attitude of the court to forfeiture.

(b) *User covenants.* Similar negative covenants are likely to be found in leases to those which have been considered above in relation to freehold properties.

Positive covenants may be found in leases which will be enforceable by reason of privity of estate so long as they concern the land. A "keep open" covenant would fall in this category and may be found in a lease of some kinds of leisure property. Whether a court would enforce such a covenant by injunction is not perfectly clear, Until recently the courts have refused to grant injunctions which have the effect of forcing a person to carry on a business: *Braddon Towers Ltd* v *International Stores Ltd* [1987] 1 EGLR 209. However, the supposed justification for refusing mandatory injunctions (the court's Inability to supervise performance) has been discarded in other cases, such as the enforcement of repairing obligations by injunction, so that this position may change and in *Co-operative Wholesale Society Ltd* v *Argyll Stores (Holdings) Ltd* (CA) [1996] 1 EGLR 71 the Court of Appeal, by a majority, granted such an injunction in relation to a supermarket subject to a 'keep open' clause. Damages for breach of such covenant are certainly available in any event: *Costain Property Developments Ltd* v *Finlay & Co* [1989] 1 EGLR 237.

(c) *Covenants against causing nuisance, annoyance, etc.* This type of covenant will very frequently be encountered in leisure property leases. It has been considered above in relation to restrictive covenants on freehold property, and the principles of construction are the same.

(d) *Alienation.* Licensing requirements and the personal nature of most licenses may well make operation of the alienation covenant more complicated in relation to leisure property leases.

Forfeiture. Section 146 (9) of the Law of Property Act 1925 provides that Section 146 shall not apply to a forfeiture on the bankruptcy (which includes corporate insolvency) of the lessee, or the taking of the lessee's interest in execution in respect of certain classes of lease, including a lease of (c) "a house used or intended to be used as a public house or beer-shop" and (e) "any property with respect to which the personal qualifications of the tenant are of importance to the preservation of the value or character of the property . . .". While the former is easily identifiable, the latter is imprecise and seems scarcely ever to have been invoked. However, given the licensing requirements often applicable to leisure activities, the personal qualifications of the tenant may assume the kind of importance mentioned.

Where Section 146 does not apply, the lessor is not obliged to serve a Section 146 notice prior to effecting a forfeiture, and the right to apply for relief is not available to the tenant under Section 146 (2) (although it is made available to subtenants. and thus to mortgagees, by the Law of Property (Amendment) Act 1929, s 1).

In other cases of forfeiture, the special nature of a leisure property operation may be relevant to the case for or against granting relief from forfeiture.

A further aspect of forfeiture in relation to public house and other licensed premises is worth noting. Many such leases contain "tie clauses" obliging the tenant to purchase supplies from the landlord. When such a lease is forfeited by the landlord, whether for non-payment of rent or for any other cause, the question of the effect of the tie clause arises. Since the covenant in question has been held to "run with the land", it must logically fall with the landlord's election to treat the lease as at an end by service of the forfeiture proceedings. The consequence of this would seem to be that the landlord cannot enforce the purchasing covenant once he has served proceedings, but would, conversely, be entitled to claim mesne profits on the basis of the value of a free house rather than a tied house. If the tenant wished to remain on the premises and sought relief from forfeiture he would, in practice, have to abide by the "tie" clause to demonstrate his good faith.

Law affecting valuations of leisure property

Law affects valuation situations at three points. First, it imposes upon the valuer the duty to value with due skill and care. Second, it will govern what the valuer is to value, since this will depend either on the construction of a document or matters of general legal principle or both. Third, and incidentally to the second, it will provide the process and procedure for the resolution of valuation disputes.

Duty of skill and care in valuing leisure property
Little need be said here on the first point. The valuer's duty to act with the degree of skill and care to be expected of a reasonably competent valuer is well understood, and this whole book is aimed at providing material to assist the valuer of leisure property to provide a skilled valuation. The section on valuation of country hotels provides particularly useful cautionary comment.

From the "duty of care" point of view, the special problems of leisure property lie in the fact that the valuer is evaluating business potential rather than just physical property. This requires a large number of assumptions to be made. The skill of leisure property valuation lies not only in selecting appropriate assumptions, but also in realising where an assumption may have been hidden, and therefore relied upon unconsciously. Any assumption as to continued turnover makes implicit assumptions as to the continuity of the business conditions which produced that turnover. The extent of the hidden assumptions needs to be recognised, so that they too can be examined.

It is worth mentioning here that there is no rule of thumb for determining how far "wrong" a valuation needs to be in order to demonstrate negligence. In *Singer & Friedlander* v *John D Wood & Co* [1977] 2 EGLR 84 the court accepted, without demur, evidence that a margin of 10% on either side of the "right" figure, and in exceptional cases 15%, could reasonably be accounted for by differences of professional opinion without negligence. However, that was simply comment on the particular evidence in that case. It cannot be treated as a rule. A more flexible test was recently put forward in the case of *Mount Banking Corporation Ltd* v *Brian Cooper & Co* [1992] 35 EG 123, namely that the valuer discharges his duty by reaching a figure which is "within the acceptable range of figures that a competent valuer using due skill and care would reach". Since negligence can only be tested in a particular set of circumstances, this is a more helpful, if less precise, approach.

Various possible methods of valuation are referred to in the following sections, where expert valuers have explained their techniques and indicated points of importance which the valuer must be on the look out for in relation to particular types of leisure property. It will have been noted that the particular uniting feature of leisure property valuation is the predominance of the "profits method" as an appropriate approach.

However, while the general law does not dictate to the valuer that this, or indeed any other, approach must be used, a court or other tribunal will often be faced with choosing between the evidence of two valuers who may have adopted different approaches. In such a case, the court will naturally tend to prefer the evidence of the valuer whose approach appears more logical and realistic and therefore more reliable. Furthermore, it would be negligent to adopt an approach which was so inappropriate that it could be said that no reasonably skilful valuer would have used it in that situation although a difference of opinion as to the correct approach amongst respected professionals will be recognised: *Zubaida* v *Hargreaves* [1993] 2 EGLR 170.

However, bearing in mind that most valuation situations involve the estimation of what a hypothetical purchaser or tenant would bid for a property, the valuer must surely be well-advised to approach his task on the same basis as such a bidder would do, in practice. If the hypothetical tenant of a theatre does not calculate his bid simply by thinking of "£X per seat", then the valuer should be wary of doing so, even though this analysis of theatre rents may be a convenient method of comparison for surveyors.

Valuation situations

Lease renewal: Landlord and Tenant Act 1954 Part II The principles of lease renewal of business tenancies under the Landlord and Tenant Act 1954 Part II will be familiar. The basis of assessment of the rent on renewal is contained in Section 34 of the Act. The following aspects may be of special note for leisure property.

"The holding". This comprises the physical premises which are to be the subject matter of the new lease. The exclusion from the physical premises of equipment (whether or not it can be described as "tenant's fittings"), and of tenant's fixtures, properly so called, has been mentioned above under real property law.

In relation to ancillary rights, the court has jurisdiction to include personal rights within the order for a new tenancy if those rights were enjoyed as an adjunct to the old lease such as, for example, a right to maintain an advertisement on land not part of the demise (*Re No 1 Albemarle St* 1959 Ch 531). However, the court has no jurisdiction to extend the property, or ancillary rights such as easements, beyond that which was within the old tenancy.

Disregard of goodwill. Under Section 34 (1) (b) the new rent is to be assessed disregarding "any goodwill attached to the holding by reason of the carrying on thereat of the business of the tenant (whether by him or a predecessor of his in that business)".

"Goodwill" is an elusive concept. It has been described as "the attractive force which brings in custom" or "the expectation that an existing custom or clientele of a business will continue" (*IRC* v *Muller and Co's Margarine* [1901] AC 217). It is thus of major potential importance for leisure property. The key to an understanding of the disregard for goodwill lies in appreciating the distinction between different types of goodwill.

In the first place, there is goodwill attaching to the premises as contrasted with goodwill attaching to the tenant's business. A picturesque description of this was given by Scrutton LJ in *Whiteman Smith Motor Co Ltd* v *Chaplin* [1934] 2 KB 35 at p 42, describing as "cat" goodwill, those customers who will stay with the business at the premises regardless of the fact that the proprietor changes, and as "dog" goodwill, those customers who will follow the business of that tenant to new premises.

Such "dog" goodwill is personal to the tenant and never part of the value of the premises. "Cat" goodwill is part of the value of the premises and would fall to be included in any valuation. However, insofar as it has been created by the presence of the tenant's business, the tenant should not have to pay rent for it, and hence the disregard in Section 34 (1) (b) directs that it should be left out of account.

There is a further refinement, however. Within the value of "cat" goodwill is a further distinction between the value attributable to attraction to customers arising from their knowledge that a business of the general relevant type is carried on there, and the value attributable to the inherent advantages of the premises for the carrying on of such a business. The former is "adherent" goodwill, which adheres as long as the reputation of the premises *as a business* exists, and will evaporate if that kind of business ceases to operate there. The latter is "inherent" goodwill (if, indeed, it is really "goodwill" at all), and is part of the property, not having been created by the carrying on of any business at all. (This may be what Maugham LJ saw as "rabbit" goodwill in the *Whiteman Smith* case, at page 50.) "Inherent goodwill" is thus: site advantages.

To take an illustration from the case of (say) a nightclub, determining the value of the premises by reference to expected rates of custom, any levels of custom apparently attributable to the proprietor's style and personality, and which would therefore tend to go with him if he moved to other premises, is personal goodwill and is never attributable to the property. Levels of custom which are judged to arise because of the known existence of an established nightclub at that address and which will therefore be likely to stay with the premises if such nightclub user continues, are goodwill of the premises. Insofar as this custom arises from the carrying on of the business which the tenant now owns (but not from any independent preceding business, although see below) that is "adherent" goodwill, the value of which is disregarded only because of the direction in Section 34 (1) (b). Insofar as this custom arises because the premises are an obvious place for a nightclub, perhaps being in the heart of the entertainment district of a city, then this value is "inherent" goodwill, attributable to a site advantage, and is not within the terms of the disregard.

Goodwill can still present a problem if the "comparable" method of valuation is used rather than a "profits" method. Comparable open market lettings will inevitably include an element of payment for adherent goodwill unless the letting is of entirely new, untried, premises. This element would have to be identified and stripped out. Comparables which are rent reviews may in theory be on the basis of a disregard for tenant's goodwill. Whether it has been reliably applied is a different matter.

Disregard of effects of tenant's occupation. Section 34 (1) (a) directs a disregard of "any effect on rent of the fact that the tenant has or his predecessors in title have been in occupation of the holding".

Authority on this disregard is rare, mainly because it has little independent scope. It prevents the tenant arguing for a reduction in rent because of the state of repair of the property where it was the tenant's obligation to repair (*Family Management* v *Gray* [1980] 1 EGLR 46). However, the tenant could not take advantage of his own wrong in any event. In practice, the effect of this disregard is probably confined to (a) extending the disregard for "adherent" goodwill to such goodwill as has been created by the independent business of a predecessor in title to the tenancy and (b) directing a disregard of any possible depreciatory effect on rent caused by the nature of the tenant's business (negative goodwill). These possibilities might apply to leisure property in extreme circumstances.

Disregard of "tenant's improvements". Section 34 (1) (c) directs a disregard of "any effect on rent or improvements to which this paragraph applies" and by Section 34 (2) the relevant improvements are, in summary, improvements made by a person who was a tenant at the time, and who made the improvement otherwise than under an obligation to his immediate landlord, and either did so during the current tenancy, or within the previous 21 years so long as there has since been an unbroken succession of protected tenancies renewed under the Act.

The distinction between "tenant's fixtures" and "landlord's fixtures" has been referred to above. "Tenant's fixtures" are never improvements at all; landlord's fixtures and works of alteration are "improvements" the effects of which will be disregarded so long as the relevant conditions are met.

A leisure tenant may make very extensive improvements, such as laying out a golf course (see *Brett* v *Brett Essex Golf Club Ltd* [1986]

1 EGLR 154, itself a rent review case). The question whether improvements will fall to be valued or not on lease renewal or rent review may be of great significance not only to the tenant, but also to a potential assignee of the lease.

Two illustrations will demonstrate the need to consider the facts surrounding improvements carefully, to ensure that there are no unpleasant surprises at a later date. First, the tenant who carries out, or pays for, works to the premises before even an agreement for lease has been entered into may be unable to invoke the disregard: see *Euston Centre Properties* v *H & J Wilson Ltd* [1982] 1 EGLR 57. Second, works of improvement which are carried out pursuant to the requirements of a local authority will not come within this disregard if there is a covenant in the lease that a tenant will comply with all such requirements, thus creating an obligation to the immediate landlord: *Forte & Co Ltd* v *General Accident Life Assurance Ltd* [1986] 2 EGLR 115.

In the context of improvements which *are* carried out in pursuance of an obligation to the landlord, a tenant may undertake to fit out the premises to a stipulated standard but then, for his own reasons, choose to carry out the works to a higher standard or quality. It is an unanswered question whether, in such a case, the landlord could claim a rent based only on the lower standard of improvements, or could argue that the whole of the better works must be treated as carried out pursuant to the relevant obligation.

Lastly, the burden is on the tenant to make out a case that improvements fall to be disregarded. This underlines the need to keep clear records of what works were done, and in what circumstances.

Benefit of on-licence. By Section 34 (1) (d), in the case of property comprising (meaning "including") licensed premises, any addition to value attributable to the licence is to be excluded from account if, in all the circumstances, the court takes the view that the benefit belongs to the tenant (or, if Section 41 relating to tenancies held on trust or Section 42 relating to group companies applies to the relevant beneficiary, or other group company).

Whilst this provision is express in relation to licensed premises, the same result ought to apply, as a matter of logic, in the case of any other form of entertainments licence, or similar, where the personality of the applicant is of importance: compare *Daejan Investments Ltd* v *Cornwall Coast Country Club* [1985] 1 EGLR 77 in a rent review context.

Public houses. Lease renewals of public houses require special mention.

The Landlord and Tenant (Licensed Premises) Act 1990 gradually brought leases of licensed premises which were formerly excluded from security of tenure, into protection, according to the time of the grant of the lease.

Leases granted or agreed to be granted prior to July 11 1989 and not terminated with effect before July 11 1992 continue to be governed by the old law, under which tenancies of licensed premises were excluded from protection with certain exceptions relevant to leisure property. Foremost was the exception of bona fide hotels and restaurants where a substantial proportion of the business comprised transactions other than the sale of alcoholic liquor. A "substantial proportion" may still be less than 50% of turnover (*Ye Olde Cheshire Cheese Ltd* v *The Daily Telegraph plc* [1988] 1 WLR 1173), but not as little as 17–18%, at any rate where the hotel or restaurant transactions are also relatively minor (*Grant* v *Gresham* [1979] 2 EGLR 60). Further exceptions were made for theatres and places of public entertainment, other public places, and similar uses where the holding of a licence is merely ancillary. The exclusion from protection applies only where the tenancy is of licensed premises, so that where the licensed premises were a small part of much larger premises, as within a complex which is the subject of the tenancy, security of tenure still applied.

Leases granted after July 11 1989 or granted before that date but which had not been terminated prior to July 11 1992 came into the protection of Part II of the 1954 Act with effect from July 11 1992.

The terms of Section 34 (1) (d) (disregard of benefit of licence where it belongs to the tenant) will apply

The provisions of the Supply of Beer (Tied Estate) Order 1989 (SI 1989/2390) may also affect the renewal of such leases indirectly. Certain major brewers were directed to reduce the number of licensed premises in which they held interests, and to release tie agreements, in accordance with a formula and provisions in the Order. Furthermore, where a large brewer or brewery group holds more than 2,000 licensed premises in accordance with the Order, unless the lease or licence of the premises was made before December 19 1989, it must now be on tenant's full repairing terms and at a full open market rent (Article 6).

The consequence, in each case, is that such landlords may be unable to grant renewal tenancies on the same terms as to repair as those contained in the previous lease. How these effects will be dealt with in practice remains to be seen.

Procedure. Lease renewals are court cases, and the usual rules of procedure and evidence apply.

Of particular relevance to leisure property will be the question of admissibility of accounts. The landlord is usually anxious to see the tenant's trading accounts to justify an argument based on what the tenant can "afford" to pay. The tenant, unless he is trading badly, will be just as keen to avoid disclosure.

There has been authority in the parallel context of rent review arbitrations, to the following effect. A tenant's trading accounts are admissible evidence where the nature of the premises is such that they ought to be valued on a "profits" basis, but will be confined to those accounts which would be available to the hypothetical tenant in the market, ie the published trading accounts (*Cornwall Coast Country Club* v *Cardgrange Ltd* [1987] 1 EGLR 146). It has been suggested that the exception is also confined to the case where there is no other comparable evidence (*WJ Barton Ltd* v *Long Acre Securities Ltd* [1982] 1 WLR 398) but that case predates any judicial recognition that "profits" valuation is the appropriate method of valuing some types of property (rather than its being always, and only, a second-best to the better known "comparable" method).

Unpublished trading accounts are therefore inadmissible as evidence, on the grounds that they would not be available to the hypothetical willing tenant in the market. They would thus, in theory, suffer not merely from the defect of being irrelevant, but also potentially highly prejudicial. (It is, of course, that very prejudicial effect which makes them appear to be relevant in the first place.)

However, it has also been held that a tenant's unpublished trading accounts may nevertheless be *discoverable*, ie be documents which the tenant is obliged to produce for the landlord's inspection (*Urban Small Space Ltd* v *Burford Investment Co Ltd* [1990] 2 EGLR 120). This is on the grounds that, in accordance with the usual rules as to what documents must be discovered, they may assist the landlord to further his case or to undermine the tenant's. This does not affect the principle that they are inadmissible as evidence. A somewhat illogical situation therefore appears to have been reached.

The implications of the fact that a lease renewal rent will be determined by a judge rather than a surveyor are also worthy of note. The judge will have the training of a lawyer and not a valuer, will probably have little experience of valuation disputes in general, let alone in relation to leisure property. Being a lawyer, the judge will therefore have no "feel" for the right figure against which to measure his reaction to the expert evidence before him for evaluation. His preference of one valuer's evidence to another's will therefore inevitably be dictated only by matters of logic and impression, rather than any underlying intuitive sympathy with the views expressed. Consequently, in a lease renewal situation any shortcomings in the evidence, or any errors made, are unlikely to be "saved" by the fact that the tribunal will accept that the general figures being put forward by one party's valuer "feel right", and will therefore prefer that evidence despite a forensically effective attack on his testimony. This can often happen in arbitrations.

Thus, it is all the more imperative in lease renewal that there are no demonstrable errors or inconsistencies in a valuer's evidence, that the reasoning is lucid and redolent of "common sense" and that evidence is given in a competent professional manner. These points apply to all valuation evidence in court cases, but as leisure property is itself a specialist area of property valuation, the importance of the expert evidence is correspondingly increased.

An alternative which might be adopted would be either for the parties to agree to have the rent determined by arbitration (or even by expert determination) once the terms of the new lease had been settled.

Rent review

General. The basic approach to construing rent review clauses of any type of property is the same. One considers first the effect of any express directions in the rent review clause itself as to the basis for valuation, and these must be applied. Owing to the acknowledged difficulties of valuing leisure property on a direct basis, the rent review may resort to a formula based on some objectively ascertainable fact, such as a percentage of turnover, or the rise in an index, rather than a hypothetical letting.

Where the hypothetical letting basis is prescribed, there may be directions as to the assumed physical state of the property, the assumed lease terms or assumed surrounding circumstances. They will usually be express and direct, but sometimes they will arise as a matter of necessary implication. An example of this is where a property without access other than across existing property of the tenant is directed to be assumed to be "let on the open market"; a disregard of this lack of access will then be implied, since otherwise the express direction cannot be given sensible effect (*Jeffries* v *O'Neill* (1983) 269 EG 131).

The directions for the rent review hypothesis override the real position. Thus, a direction to assume a different user is perfectly valid. Examples would be a direction that a golf course is to be valued on the basis of agricultural land values, or an amusement arcade on the basis of retail use. The effect of such a direction may be to change the nature of the valuation completely, so that it ceases to be a leisure property valuation.

Where there is no clear express or implied direction, so that the rent review provision is silent or ambiguous on a particular point, the "presumption of reality" will apply (*Basingstoke and Deane Borough Council* v *Host Group Ltd* [1988] 1 WLR 348), and the set of circumstances most nearly resembling the situation which is applying, in reality, between the landlord and the tenant for the residue of the term, will form the basis of the rent review assumption.

In the context of leisure property, the courts have warned against making over-elaborate interpretations of rent review provisions. In particular where, as in gaming premises, the available market may be dependent not merely on the existence of potential tenants but on the availability of licences (here, Gaming Board personal approval and a Gaming Act premises licence) it is not legitimate to "pile hypothesis upon hypothesis" in order to support arguments as to the existence – or absence – of a hypothetical tenant capable of taking up the premises: see *Cornwall Coast Country Club* v *Cardgrange* [1987] 1 EGLR 146.

The usual form of rent review clause will postulate a hypothetical letting in a similar way to the basis for determining rent on lease renewal. Although the actual hypotheses laid down on rent reviews are often the same as those in Section 34 of the Landlord and Tenant Act 1954 Part II, it should not be assumed that this is the case, especially when considering reports of cases. For example, in *My Kinda Town Ltd* v *Castlebrook Properties Ltd* [1986] 1 EGLR 121 the discussion of the value of the premises as a successful new restaurant is puzzling in the light of the disregard for goodwill. In fact, the rent review provisions contained no disregard for goodwill but this is not expressly stated in the report of the case.

It should always be borne in mind that express "disregards" are required in order to reproduce the Section 34 position which is so familiar. The importance of checking the legal basis of any rent review used as a "comparable" is also demonstrated.

The lease may use similar, but not exactly the same, wording as Section 34. For example, if only improvements "lawfully" carried out by the tenant are disregarded, the tenant will have to pay rent for any improvements carried out without obtaining the landlord's consent, as required by the lease, and will not be able to rely on an assumption that all covenants in the lease are to be assumed to have been complied with in order to argue that it must be assumed that such consent had in fact been sought and obtained: *Hamish Cathie Travel England Ltd* v *Insight International Tours Ltd* [1986] 1 EGLR 244.

Additional assumptions and disregards will often be written into rent review provisions, over and above the Section 34 position. One which is now commonly found is a direction to assume that the premises are "fit" or "fitted out" for "occupation" or "occupation and use". The purpose of these provisions is generally to prevent a tenant arguing that where rents of "comparables" were agreed along with a rent-free period during which the incoming tenant would have fitted out the premises, the rent for the subject premises must be adjusted downwards to allow for the absence of a rent-free fitting out period in the rent review situation. With leisure property, where a good deal of fitting out can be required, this argument can be of major importance.

It should therefore be noted that "fit" and "fitted out" are not the same thing, "fit" having the connotation merely of "free from disabling disadvantages"; moreover a tenant may "occupy" and "use" premises for the purpose of preparing them for the commencement of trading: see *Pontsarn Investments Ltd* v *Kansallis-Osake-Pankki* [1992] 1 EGLR 148. Thus, the direction of such an assumption does not necessarily mean that no allowance for a fitting out rent-free period can be claimed. Furthermore, even such an assumption as "fitted out for immediate occupation and use" does not, without more, imply that fitting out has been done by and at the expense of the landlord when, in the real world, it has not been and would not be (*London & Leeds Estates Ltd* v *Paribas Ltd* [1993] 2 EGLR 149).

Where the valuable operation of the premises is dependent on the tenant's possession of a licence, difficult questions as to the assumptions required to be made on rent review may well arise, as is illustrated by *Cornwall Coast Country Club* v *Cardgrange Ltd* [1987] 1 EGLR 146 and *Ritz Hotel (London) Ltd* v *Ritz Casino Ltd* [1989] 2 EGLR 135 and *Parkside Clubs (Nottingham) Ltd* v *Armgrade*

Ltd (CA) 1995 2 EGLR 96, where the use of the word "Tenant" rather than "tenant" produced a significantly different valuation scenario.

Procedure In the case of failure to agree, it is the invariable practice for rent reviews to provide for determination by a third party acting either as expert or as arbitrator. The valuation of leisure property is clearly a specialist area and at least one contributor to this book has stated that, as a result, his preference for a third party determination would always be for an expert rather than an arbitrator.

Since rent reviews sometimes offer one party an alternative, and it is always possible, by agreement, to get the third party to change the capacity in which he is determining the rent, it is worth considering the advantages and disadvantages of each form of dispute resolution.

From the parties' point of view, the main advantage of an expert determination as against arbitration will be savings in costs and time; the disadvantage is lack of control.

Arbitration. An arbitration is the equivalent of a private trial with an expert judge for whose services one pays. The rules of evidence apply, and procedures equivalent to procedures in court are broadly made available under the Arbitration Acts 1950–1979. The arbitrator determines the case according to the evidence before him. If he takes into account other evidence without, at any rate, informing the parties, he is guilty of misconduct and his award can be set aside. Naturally, however, he interprets the evidence before him in the light of his own general expert experience; that is the point of his acting. As arbitrator he has jurisdiction to determine all the points necessary in order to enable him to arrive at the determination he is directed to make, including, therefore, points of law arising incidentally.

There is a limited right of appeal under Section 1 of the Arbitration Act 1979 as later interpreted by the courts, especially in *The Nema* [1982] AC 724. An appeal lies only with the leave of the court, where a reasoned award has been requested and made and where the would-be appellant complains of an error of law which would substantially affect the rights of the parties. In the case of a "one off" decision leave will only be granted for an "obvious case of error". In the case of "standard form" contracts where, therefore, the point may arise again, the test is a "strong *prima facie* case of error". A final or single rent review would be a one off situation, whereas a first rent review of several under the lease could be a "standard form" situation: *Ipswich Borough Council* v *Fisons plc* [1990] Ch 709.

Appeals to the Court of Appeal are also subject to restrictions as to leave, and the High Court's certifying that the point is of general public importance: Arbitration Act 1979 s 1 (6).

The parties therefore have some influence over an arbitrator in that they can ensure that they know what evidence he is using, they can ensure that he hears any arguments they wish to advance, and they have a right of appeal, albeit limited.

(See footnote on p. 76 as to the Arbitration Act 1996.)

Experts. An expert operates entirely independently (subject to any constraints in the document under which he is appointed) and exercises a discretion and judgement which need pay no regard to any points the parties might wish to put before him, such as representations or particular pieces of evidence. He is not obliged to inform them of the matters which affect his views of value or of evidence of which he is aware. He does not hold any hearing. There is therefore likely to be a saving in procedural costs and time in comparison to arbitration.

However, there is no appeal from an expert's decision; it is binding, whether it is good or bad. The only way to attack an expert determination is to seek a declaration that it is void. However, that can only be granted on the grounds that the expert answered the wrong question (ie failed to carry out his appointed task at all) and not on the grounds merely that he gave the wrong answer to the right question (ie carried out his appointed task badly).

The stringency of the test is illustrated by a leisure property case, *Nikko Hotels (UK) Ltd v MEPC plc* [1991] 2 EGLR 103, where the expert (an accountant) interpreted the "average room rate" (the average rate at which rooms were made available to members of the general public over a year) as an average based on the published tariff rather than prices actually charged. The tenant sought a declaration that the determination was a nullity for being based on a wrong interpretation of the phrase "average room rate". The court refused the declaration on the grounds that the expert had answered the right question, and, whether or not he had made a mistake of law (which the court declined to decide) the determination was therefore binding.

The method of guarding against such a situation by seeking the court's guidance on points of law which the expert will have to decide in order to make a determination, and, if necessary, persuading (or injuncting) the expert from publishing a determination in the meantime, has now been shown to be of limited use. In *Norwich*

Union Life Insurance Society v *P&O Property Holdings Ltd* [1993] 13 EG 108, it was held by the Court of Appeal that where an expert inevitably had to decide points of law (eg construction of the contract) in order to carry out the task given to him, the parties had confided the determination of such points to the expert alone, and the court would not intervene, even before the expert had made any decision. In that case one party wished the expert to proceed with judicial guidance, and the other did not. It may, however, be possible to obtain guidance for the expert provided both parties are agreed that this should be done.

Apart from the above, an aggrieved party's only recourse is to sue the expert in negligence, and seek to recover from him the damages which the allegedly negligent binding determination has caused to that party in over- or underpayments. However, the prospects of successfully mounting such a claim will be remote, unless the valuation is completely incredible. This is not least because any well-advised expert will not give his reasons.

Where there are no points of law and the field of valuation is as esoteric as many leisure property valuations will be, an expert determination may well be preferable to arbitration on grounds of costs and speed. However, the parties will depend on the quality of the expert for a "right" result.

Freehold interests The valuation of a freehold interest will not usually be governed by complicated directions as to the basis to be adopted, as in lease renewals or rent reviews. The nearest to this is where a valuation is requested upon an "open market" basis or a "forced sale" basis. However, when valuing for mortgage purposes, the extent of the security will be governed by the terms of the mortgage.

The general principles of land law which affect the subject matter of a property transaction, with particular regard to those likely to be specially material to leisure property, have been mentioned above (pp. 48–61) but, the principles of law relating to fixtures and fittings deserve further note here.

In relation to vendor and purchaser of land, these principles will rarely cause problems in practice, since the question of what fixtures or other items are to be included in a sale will usually be considered and recorded between the parties. Only occasionally will resort have to be had to the basic rule that a conveyance carries with it all fixtures, whether in the nature of landlord's or tenant's fixtures.

As regards valuations for mortgage purposes, the question of what items are actually to be included in the security can have great practical significance because of the fact that the value of the leisure property lies in the value of the business being conducted upon it. This can easily be the subject of misunderstanding between client and valuer. Any assumptions made by the valuer as to the inclusion or exclusion of any fixtures or other chattels, or the value being dependent on the continued management of the business, need to be clearly expressed and understood. The following brief summary of the legal background will illustrate why.

As already mentioned, a simple fixed charge by way of legal mortgage will include, automatically, all fixtures. However, it will not cover equipment which is free standing, however vital that may be for the continued running or realisation of the business. Where the borrower is a company, a common form of security which is given, namely a debenture which includes both fixed charges and a floating charge over all the company's assets from time to time, will extend to equipment on the premises so long as it is owned by the company, and it will usually also cover goodwill. In standard forms of debenture, a receiver appointed by the mortgagee will be given wide powers to manage the business. However, in the absence of such a comprehensive charge, and clear powers to continue the business pending sale, it may not be possible to realise the full value of the property as a continuing enterprise.

Where the borrower is an individual and not a company, the problem may be even more acute because an individual cannot give a floating charge. Any attempt to take a charge over chattels will be ineffective unless it complies with the Bills of Sale Acts 1878–82, a procedure which is usually impractical. Without a charge over unattached chattels, the mortgagee or his receiver, on taking possession of the premises, may well find his actions hampered by the presence of items of equipment over which he has no rights but which he cannot sell, or even lawfully throw out. Although the mortgagee who takes possession to enforce his security may, in law, be entitled to "vacant possession" (ie free of such chattels), this right is often beside the point in practice. Many lending institutions therefore have documentation which tries to deal with this difficulty in some way or other.

The above account will demonstrate the importance of the valuer's both recognising any assumptions underlying the valuation and making these clear in the report. In any event, the status of any equipment which is apparently within the scope of a proposed charge needs to be checked, since the continued availability of items held on lease or hire purchase cannot be assumed.

Footnote: At the time of writing the Arbitration Act 1996 has not been brought into force. It will give the arbitrator jurisdiction to decide matters of procedure and evidence where the parties do not agree (s 34). It will limit further the right of appeal to cases where the decision is obviously wrong, or is open to serious doubt on a matter of general public importance, with an overriding requirement that it should be just, in view of the arbitration agreement, that there should be an appeal at all (s 69).

CHAPTER 2

Compulsory purchase and compensation

Introduction

This chapter will deal with two main areas where compensation may be payable to affected persons, these being:

1. The compulsory acquisition of a property in pursuance of statutory powers; and
2. Compensation which may be payable under powers contained in the Town and Country Planning Act, 1990 and the Planning (Listed Buildings and Conservation Areas) Act, 1990.

It is difficult in a single chapter to do more than outline the most important points which need to be considered by businesses, or their advisors, which are affected by either compulsory purchase or compensation matters, but it needs to be recognised that since the completion of the large-scale, post-war road-building schemes and comprehensive redevelopment areas in the 1950s and 1960s, the use of compulsory purchase orders has declined and been limited in recent years to a smaller number of specific projects, of which the M25 motorway may be the best-known national example, with the result that the number of businesses which have suffered the trauma of compulsory purchase have declined.

However, with a move towards a more vigorous replacement of infrastructure by the newly privatised, ex-state owned, industries and the demand for new improved transport routes, the use of compulsory purchase powers is back on the agenda. It is likely that this new wave of compulsory acquisition may involve the increasing use of private Acts of Parliament, whereas in the past, Government departments and local authorities normally used the powers of a Public General Act of Parliament related to a specific compulsory purchase order to identify the affected land. Knowledge of the source of these statutory powers is important since it is these that set the timetable and framework which allow objections to be made to the proposed use of compulsory powers and the claiming of compensation.

It should also be recognised that the private sector is becoming more involved in the new use of compulsory powers to ensure that sites can be assembled to carry out projects in partnership with central or local Government or other bodies possessing compulsory purchase powers and this private/public sector partnership may be expected to impart a vigour into the compulsory purchase process which has not been known in recent years.

The private sector has already used partnerships with public bodies, eg in comprehensive town centre redevelopment schemes, and is aware of the benefits which certainty of acquisition can provide to the programme of the developer or promoter of a scheme.

Compulsory purchase of land and property

The powers of compulsion
As stated above there are two main ways in which statutory bodies may seek to exercise compulsory purchase powers.

Public General Act of Parliament Under this procedure the Act of Parliament authorises the use of compulsory purchase powers to acquire land for a particular purpose, eg Section 226, Town and Country Planning Act, 1990 which allows a local authority to compulsorily acquire land for development and other planning purposes. The Act, therefore, has a general applicability which makes no reference to a particular location, to named persons or to specified land, and therefore, the Act merely settles the principle that compulsory purchase powers may be used to achieve the purpose proposed by the Act of Parliament.

A compulsory purchase order is therefore needed as a second stage to the procedure in order to identify the land needed for a particular scheme and the affected landowners who may object to the proposed compulsory purchase order. If objections are lodged against the compulsory purchase order and are not withdrawn, then the appropriate Secretary of State will hold a public inquiry before deciding whether to confirm the proposed compulsory purchase order. The making and confirmation of a compulsory purchase order is, in almost all cases, governed by the Acquisition of Land Act, 1981 which sets out the procedure for the preparation, making, notification of, objections to and confirmation of the order including the need of a public inquiry. The actual procedure for making a compulsory purchase order is dealt with in more detail later in this chapter.

Private Act of Parliament Before the use of Public General Act of Parliament this was the only real way of obtaining powers of compulsory acquisition and although unlikely to be used by Government Departments or local authorities it is still used by certain bodies when no other powers exist, e.g. London Underground Ltd in respect of the Jubilee line extension and the East–West Crossrail route.

Under this procedure the private bill is presented to Parliament which seeks authority to use compulsory purchase powers to acquire specified land for a stated purpose. The land acquired for the scheme will be specified in a schedule attached to the bill and will also be referred to in deposited plans. The private bill is subject to certain formalities in addition to the usual Parliamentary procedures for considering a bill and the persons affected by the scheme contained in the bill will be notified and they will be able to petition against the bill and if an undertaking is not agreed between the proposers of the scheme contained in a private bill and the petitioner then a select committee will hear those petitions which remain outstanding against the bill.

Although affected persons have the right to petition against a private bill, it should be noted that neither they nor their professional advisors may petition the bill directly since a petition must be lodged by Parliamentary agents and this is an important point to be borne in mind to ensure that a valid petition may be lodged.

It should also be noted that once a bill receives its second reading in Parliament then it is regarded that the principles of the bill have been approved by Parliament and, therefore, petitioners against the bill who appear before the select committee at the committee stage may be limited to presenting objections of a technical nature and be unable to argue against the general principle of the bill. Experience of Private Bills, eg Channel Tunnel Act, 1987, also tends to indicate that there is no certainty that every petitioner who wishes to be heard will be given an opportunity to present their objections, since the select committee may be required to adhere to a strict timetable which may result in some petitioners not being able to present their objections to the committee.

Most modern private bills normally incorporate the provisions of the Compulsory Purchase Act, 1965 and the Land Compensation Acts, 1961 and 1973 by reference, since the former governs the acquisition procedures to be followed in most cases, while the latter set out the rules for the assessment of compensation payable in respect of a compulsory acquisition and their inclusion, therefore, avoids the need to set out these matters in full detail in the private bill.

Whichever method of acquiring compulsory purchase powers is being pursued, the important point for any affected land owner is quickly to consider the implications of the proposed acquisition and its impact on his property, in order to decide whether it is necessary to object to a proposed compulsory purchase order or to petition the private bill and, if so, assess his chances of success.

Making a compulsory purchase order

As stated earlier, where a body is seeking to acquire land by powers contained in a Public General Act of Parliament then a compulsory purchase order needs to be made by the acquiring authority and confirmed by the appropriate Secretary of State to allow the purchase of specified lands to take place.

The making of a compulsory purchase order is now governed by the Acquisition of Land Act, 1981 and this Act sets out the procedures which need to be followed in the preparation, making and confirmation of an order in the majority of cases. Part (II) of the Acquisition of Land Act, 1981 sets out the procedure to be followed when making an order for purchase by a local authority or by other public authorities and Schedule 1 to the 1981 Act sets out the procedure to be followed where the purchase is to be made by the Secretary of State or a Government Department.

Before an acquiring authority may submit the compulsory purchase order for confirmation by the appropriate Secretary of State, part (II) of the 1981 Act requires that certain persons eg owners, lessees and occupiers of affected land must be notified and that certain publicity must be given to the making of the compulsory purchase order, in order that any person may be allowed to make an objection to the order within a specified time limit, but not less than 21 days from the date of the service of the notice. It is not proposed to set out these arrangements in detail since they can be found in Sections 11 and 12 of the 1981 Act.

The procedure for confirming a compulsory purchase order is set out in Section 13 of the 1981 Act and this allows that if no objection is made by any person that is mentioned is Section 12 of the 1981 Act or if all objections which have been made have been withdrawn, then the confirming authority may confirm the order with or without modifications, providing it is satisfied that the proper notices, as required by Sections 11 and 12 of the 1981 Act, have been published and served.

Section 13 also allows that if any objections which have been made are not withdrawn then the confirming authority shall, before confirming the order, either cause a public local inquiry to be held or offer to any person who has made an objection, which has not been withdrawn, an opportunity of appearing before and being heard by a person appointed by the confirming authority for that purpose. After considering the objection and the report of the person who held the inquiry then the confirming authority may confirm the order either with or without modification.

Where it is decided that a public local inquiry is required then the powers and procedures relating to such an inquiry may be found in the Compulsory Purchase by Non-Ministerial Acquiring Authorities (Inquiries Procedure) Rules, 1990 which apply to all cases where the acquisition of land is being proposed by non-ministerial bodies. Again it is not proposed to deal with these matters in detail, since the relevant procedural rules are fully supplied in the appropriate statutory instrument number 512, 1990.

When the compulsory purchase order is confirmed

Once a compulsory purchase order has been confirmed, an acquiring authority then has 3 years in which to exercise the powers of compulsory purchase which have been granted with the 3 years beginning from the date of publication of the Secretary of State's decision to confirm the order.

Before the passing of the Compulsory Purchase (Vesting Declarations) Act, 1981, the first act of an acquiring authority would be to serve a Notice to Treat on affected land owners which requires them to confirm their interest in the property to be acquired and provide details of the claim for compensation within a specified period, normally 3 or 4 weeks. The Notice to Treat also fixes the interest of the claimant which is to be acquired and no claimant can unnecessarily create new interests or carry out building or other works with a view to obtaining compensation where otherwise no compensation would be payable or enhanced compensation in a case where compensation would be payable.

It should also be noted that once a Notice to Treat has been served, then the acquiring authority has the right to take possession of the affected land by issuing Notice of Entry to the claimant and providing that at least 14 days' notice is given before possession is required, then the acquiring authority can enter and take possession of the land, or such part of the affected land as is specified in the Notice of Entry. It can be seen, therefore, that although it may be hoped that an acquiring authority will give as much notice as possible to a displaced claimant, this cannot be guaranteed and again reinforces the need for affected claimants to act swiftly in order to try to mitigate their losses.

Where the Notice to Treat method is used, the eventual outcome is that the title of the land, or the interest in respect of the land which is being acquired, will have to be formally conveyed to the acquiring authority by the land owner. However, the provisions contained in the Compulsory Purchase (Vesting Declarations) Act, 1981 simplify this process since it provides a single procedure, which on a certain date, automatically vests title in the land comprised in the compulsory purchase order, with the acquiring authority.

It is not proposed to set out in detail the procedures detailed in the Compulsory Purchase (Vesting Declarations) Act, 1981, but provided an acquiring authority follows the procedures set down in the Act and legally executes the general vesting declaration, then at the end of a specified period the acquiring authority is regarded as if it had served a Notice to Treat on the date of the declaration and, therefore, on the Vesting Date the land specified in the general vesting declaration, together with the right to enter and take possession of the land, vests with the acquiring authority. The result of this procedure is that an acquiring authority can effectively require claimants to vacate their property when required, although one would hope that an acquiring authority would be sensitive to the need of claimants who were required to relocate as a result of the acquiring authority's scheme.

Section 67 of the Planning and Compensation Act, 1991 has now amended Section 5 of the Compulsory Purchase Act, 1965 to the effect that a Notice to Treat will cease to have effect after 3 years from the date on which it was served, unless:

(a) the compensation has been agreed or awarded, or has been paid or paid into Court;

(b) a general vesting declaration has been executed under Section 4 of the Compulsory Purchase (Vesting Declarations) Act, 1981;

(c) the acquiring authority have entered on and taken possession of the land specified in the notice; or

(d) the question of compensation has been referred to the Lands Tribunal.

Further provisions allow the acquiring authority and the claimant to agree to extend the period of 3 years if they so wish and where an acquiring authority does not continue with the acquisition of a property within the period of 3 years or such other extended period, as may have been agreed with the parties, then the acquiring authority is liable to pay compensation to any person entitled to a notice for any loss or expenses occasioned to him by the giving of the Notice to Treat and its ceasing to have effect.

If the sum of compensation to be paid cannot be agreed, then it may be determined by the Lands Tribunal and any sum of compensation which may be payable, will carry interest at the statutory rate from the date on which the claimant was given notice that the Notice to Treat ceased to have effect, until payment of the compensation is made.

What is acquired

Generally an acquiring authority will seek to acquire the minimum area of land which is needed for the authority's scheme and this, therefore, may in some cases result in a whole property being acquired whereas in other cases the acquiring authority may seek only to acquire part of a claimant's land holding.

However, where only part of a claimant's land holding is proposed to be purchased, provisions are available under Section 8, Compulsory Purchase Act, 1965 in respect of Notice to Treat or Schedule 1, Compulsory Purchase (Vesting Declarations) Act, 1981 where the vesting declaration route is used, which allow the claimant the opportunity to request the acquiring authority to acquire all his land where the part proposed to be acquired cannot be taken without material detriment to a house, building or manufactory.

It should be noted that the procedures included in the 1965 and 1981 Acts differ, with the 1981 Act having a rather more complicated procedure to follow. However, in the final analysis under both procedures, if the claimant and acquiring authority are unable to resolve whether only part or whole of a property needs to be acquired, the dispute will be referred to the Lands Tribunal to determine whether or not there is sufficient material detriment to require the purchase of the whole property rather than merely the part proposed to be acquired by the acquiring authority.

Basis of compensation

Section 5 of the Land Compensation Act, 1961, as amended by the Planning and Compensation Act, 1991 provides the six basic rules for assessing the sum of compensation to be paid and for completeness the rules are set out below:

1. No allowance should be made on account of the acquisition being compulsory.
2. The value of the land shall, subject as hereinafter provided, be taken to be the amount which the land if sold in the open market by a willing seller might be expected to realise.
3. The special suitability or adaptability of the land for any purpose shall not be taken into account if that purpose is a purpose to which it could be applied only in pursuance of statutory powers, or for which there is no particular market apart from the requirements of any authority possessing compulsory purchase powers.
4. Where the value of the land is increased by reason of the use thereof or of any premises thereon in a manner which could be restrained by any court, or is contrary to law, or is detrimental to the health of the occupants of the premises or to the public health, the amount of that increase shall not be taken into account.
5. Where land is, and but for the compulsory acquisition would continue to be, devoted to a purpose of such a nature that there is no general demand or market for land for that purpose, the compensation may, if the Lands Tribunal is satisfied that reinstatement in some other place is bona fide intended, be assessed on the basis of the reasonable cost of equivalent reinstatement.
6. The provisions of rule (2) shall not affect the assessment of compensation of disturbance or any other matter not directly based on the value of the land.

It can be seen, therefore, that the general rule is that a claimant should receive the open market value of the interest which is acquired and in assessing this value, no allowance should be made on account of the acquisition being compulsory and no value should be reflected where such value results from actions which are contrary to law.

In addition, any enhanced value should be disregarded where such value would result only from the use of statutory powers or where there is no market except for the purpose of meeting the needs of any authority possessing compulsory purchase powers.

It can be seen, therefore, that in the majority of cases it is considered that the compensation to be assessed in respect of the "land" element is related to its open market value and not to the loss suffered by the owner. It should also be recognised that in assessing the relevant open market value it is necessary to disregard the effect of the acquiring authority's scheme on the value of the property being acquired.

The basic thrust of these provisions is to ensure that an acquiring authority should not be required to pay for the benefit which the acquiring authority itself creates as a result of its scheme (see Section 6 and Schedule 1 of the Land Compensation Act, 1961), while at the same time ensuring that the claimant should not lose out if the acquiring authority's scheme resulted in the depreciation of the open market value of the claimant's interest (see Section 9, Land Compensation Act, 1961).

The result of these provisions may be best summarised as being that the task of the valuer is to determine the value of the relevant land which is being acquired in the "no scheme" world. The valuer must consider what would have happened to the claimant's property and what development might have been allowed had the acquiring authority's scheme not occurred.

In my view, "the equivalent reinstatement" rule of compensation (Rule 5), may be of particular interest to the valuers of leisure property. This view follows the decision of the House of Lords in the case of *Harrison and Heatherington Ltd* v *Cumbria County Council* (1985), which was a case involving the acquisition of a livestock market. The House of Lords held that, although it was accepted that livestock markets came into the market for sale, they did so rarely, and that a small number of transactions meant that there was a very limited market in such premises and that an intermittent demand, which only occurred when such a property actually came available, was not a general demand as set out in the rule. The fact that a particular property would sell if placed on the market for sale was not, of itself, evidence of a general demand or market for that property and, therefore, latent demand is not evidence of a general demand.

There may well be categories of leisure property which may be capable of being regarded as being marketed in a similar way to livestock markets where, due to their particular characteristics, or due to a small number of operators being in that particular sector of the market, it may be capable of being argued that there is not a general demand or market for such properties. Therefore, it may well be a situation where a case could be made that a property should be compensated on the basis of equivalent reinstatement of the purpose, rather than at the open market value of the property.

In order that compensation may be paid under the "equivalent reinstatement" rule, the following four aspects need to be satisfied:

1. The land must be devoted to a purpose and but for the compulsory purchase would continue to be so devoted to that purpose;
2. The purpose is one for which there is no general demand or market for land for that purpose;
3. There must be a bona fide intention to reinstate on another site;
4. If the previous conditions have been satisfied then the Lands Tribunal must be prepared to exercise reasonable discretion in the favour of the claimant.

It should be noted that in respect of the last point, the discretion will, in practice, first be exercised by the acquiring authorities.

Under the "equivalent reinstatement" rule it is the purpose which is being reinstated and not the building. If, therefore, an ornate Victorian building was being acquired, the acquiring authority would expect to reinstate the purpose carried on within that building in a building of modern design suitable to accommodate the displaced purpose and, therefore, no ornate embellishment would be included in respect of the replacement building and indeed the size of the replacement building may well vary from the size of the original building, dependent on the change in capacity which the purpose now requires when compared to the capacity designed into the original building.

It also needs to be stressed that point (3) above reinforces the fact that the purpose must be reinstated on another site and that there is no option of adopting the compensation under the "equivalent reinstatement" rule to obtain a sum of compensation and then not expend that amount of compensation on a new building to allow the purpose to be reinstated.

Date of assessment of compensation

Having looked at the general basis of assessing the amount of compensation due to a claimant for land which is acquired it is necessary to establish the date at which the sum of compensation is assessed. This date is, in the case of open market value, the earlier of the following:

1. The date at which the compensation is agreed; or
2. The date at which the acquiring authority take entry onto the claimant's land; or
3. The date at which the Lands Tribunal determines the amount of compensation to be paid.

Where an acquiring authority takes entry on to the claimant's land before the sum of compensation has either been agreed with the claimant or determined by the Lands Tribunal, then the sum of compensation which is eventually paid will attract the payment of interest at the statutory rate from the date on which entry onto the claimant's land is taken until the completion of the purchase in the case where possession is taken by way of Notice of Entry.

Where the General Vesting Declaration procedure is used, Section 10 of the Compulsory Purchase (Vesting Declarations) Act, 1981 sets out that interest is payable from the date the land vests in the acquiring authority until the date when compensation is paid by the acquiring authority or determined by the Lands Tribunal.

It should be noted that as a result of the Planning and Compensation Act, 1991 any sum of accrued interest in respect of an amount of compensation may be paid at the same time as the advance payment is paid to the claimant on account of a sum of compensation.

In a case where compensation is being assessed under the "equivalent reinstatement" rule the date for ascertaining the cost of reinstatement is the date when, having regard to all the circumstances, the claimant can reasonably begin replacement.

Cases where part only of claimant's land is required

If it is accepted that part of a claimant's holding may be taken without material detriment to the remainder (see above) then in addition to the sum of compensation due to the claimant in respect of the open market value of the land being acquired, the claimant may also be eligible for further sums of compensation in respect of severance and injurious affection.

Compensation for the severing of a part of a claimant's land holding is not only payable where a claimant's land holding is physically split into two distinct and separate areas by the acquiring authority's scheme, but it may also be payable where an area of land is lost by the claimant to the acquiring authority, and the claimant's retained land remains as a single unit. This is because the loss of the part of the holding acquired by the acquiring authority may depreciate the value of the retained land if it destroys the marriage value that existed in the claimant's original ownership.

Compensation for injurious affection is intended to compensate the claimant who has had land acquired for the subsequent use of the acquiring authority's scheme. An example of this would be a highway scheme where a property may have lost an area of land and as a result the use of the new highway devalues the property which remains due to both visual intrusion of the new highway and also the extra noise, vibration, etc, which may result from the traffic using the highway.

It should be remembered that compensation for both severance and injurious affection relates to the depreciation in the value of land and these items are often assessed together with the value of the land taken rather than as three individual items of compensation by using the "before and after" method of valuation, whereby the value of property is assessed in the absence of the acquiring authority's scheme and is then reassessed with the acquiring authority's scheme built and in use with the amount of compensation under the headings of land taken, severance and injurious affection being the difference between the two valuations.

An acquiring authority may seek to reduce the claim for severance and injurious affection by offering to carry out accommodation works in respect of land retained by a claimant and any agreement entered into will be binding if the authority has the necessary powers and the agreement is supported either by sum consideration or is enacted by deed. However, it should be noted that an acquiring authority cannot normally restrict its statutory powers and duties by way of agreement and it cannot be compelled to provide the accommodation works in the absence of an agreement. Two examples of the types of accommodation works which may be provided by an acquiring authority are listed below:

(a) New access, fencing, gates or walls where land to be acquired has been taken to construct a new or improved road;
(b) Relocation of the water supply or other utility services, pipes, drains, sewers or soakaways.

Since the accommodation works impact on the amount of compensation which may be payable to the claimant, it is usual for these to be negotiated at an early stage, often before the sum of compensation to be paid may be discussed since not only may the accommodation works impact on this sum, but it will also be necessary for an acquiring authority to finalise the relative works as soon as possible, since this may affect the letting of any contracts in respect of the authority's proposed scheme, eg the need to resolve access and boundary treatment works to allow the new or improved highway to be instructed.

Betterment

It can be seen that the majority of this chapter so far has dealt with the situation whereby as a result of an acquiring authority's proposed scheme, compensation is payable to claimants whose position has worsened as a result of the scheme. However, in some cases it may be as a result of the scheme some other land which is owned by the claimant in the same vicinity may be enhanced in value and where this occurs, Section 7 of the Land Compensation Act, 1961 allows for the increase in value in respect of other land owned by the claimant to be set off against the sum of compensation due to the claimant in respect of the land affected by the scheme.

It should be noted that any increase in value in other land owned by the claimant must occur as a direct result of the acquiring authority's scheme and that if, in fact, the enhancement in value actually exceeds the amount of compensation due in respect of the affected land, then no compensation will be payable to the claimant, but the claimant will not be required to pay to the acquiring authority the difference between the enhanced value of the other land over the value of the sum of compensation due in respect of the affected land.

Planning assumptions

So far this chapter has concentrated on looking at the compensation payable to a claimant from a point of view which assumes that its current use is the most valuable in compensation terms However, in a non-compulsory purchase scenario where a property is sold in the open market, purchasers will reflect, when assessing the price to be paid, the value of any existing planning permission or the possibility of obtaining planning permission in the future.

The Land Compensation Act, 1961 contains certain assumptions which may be made in respect of planning permission matters in order to establish the planning background, had the acquiring authority not brought forward their scheme which required the purchase of the affected land. The relevant planning assumptions may be found in Sections 14 to 17 of the 1961 Act and, therefore, it is not proposed to deal with these matters in exceptional detail, but merely to point out the main points to note.

Section 14 of the Act requires that the assumptions mentioned in Sections 15 and 16 are applicable to the whole or any part of the relevant land and shall be taken into account in ascertaining the value of the relevant interest. Planning permission may also be assumed in accordance with provisions of any permission which is valid at the date of Notice to Treat or Vesting and which related to either the whole or part of the land.

Section 14 also states that although it can be assumed that planning permission may be made for a certain development, this does not mean that it needs to be considered that planning permission would be refused for any other form of development, although the likelihood of obtaining permission before any other form of development other than those which may be assumed would have to be assessed. Thus, in effect, the element of hope value would have to be established.

The Planning and Compensation Act, 1991 has extended the provisions to be included under Section 14 of the 1961 Act in respect of acquisitions required for highway schemes which require any planning assumptions to be made or a certificate of appropriate alternative development issued on the basis that it is now required to be assumed that if the required land were not acquired for highway purposes then no highway would be constructed to meet the same, or substantially the same, need as the proposed highway.

Section 15 of the 1961 Act refers to planning assumptions which are not directly derived from development plans and these may be summarised as follows:

1. It may be assumed that planning permission would be forth-coming for the scheme proposed by the acquiring authority.

2. It may be assumed that planning permission would be forthcoming for development contained within Schedule 3 of the Town and Country Planning Act, 1990 unless compensation has already been paid for the refusal of such planning permission.
3. It may be assumed that planning permission would be forthcoming for those uses specified in a certificate of appropriate alternative development provided under Section 17 of the 1961 Act.

Section 16 of the 1961 Act allows that the following assumptions may be made in assessing the sum of compensation to be made:

1. It may be assumed that planning permission would be forthcoming for development of a specified description as defined in the current development plan.
2. It may be assumed that planning permission would be forthcoming for development where land is allocated primarily for a use specified in the current development plan.
3. It may be assumed that planning permission would be forthcoming for development where the land is allocated primarily for a range of two or more uses specified in the current development plan.
4. It may be assumed that planning permission would be forthcoming for development where land is within a comprehensive development area or action area.

In considering these assumptions, it needs to be recognised that they must be related to the claimant's individual land holding, eg a property may be zoned as being in an area of comprehensive redevelopment within a town centre with a proposed use of retail, and it is then necessary for the valuer to decide whether in the "no scheme" world, planning permission for a redevelopment of the claimant's land for retail purposes would have been forthcoming.

As stated earlier, Section 15 of the 1961 Act allows the assumption that planning permission would be forthcoming for uses set out in a certificate of appropriate alternative development issued under Section 17 of that Act.

The Planning and Compensation Act, 1991 has now amended the provisions contained in Section 17 of the 1961 Act and the revised provisions now allow either the claimant or the acquiring authority to apply to the local planning authority for a certificate of appropriate alternative development under Section 17.

A further change introduced by the 1991 Act, allows the local planning authority, when issuing a certificate under Section 17, to issue a certificate stating that permission would be forthcoming for uses other than those specified by the applicant when applying for the certificate.

The 1991 Act now also allows the reasonable expenses incurred by a claimant, in connection with the issue of a Section 17 certificate, including an appeal under Section 18 if necessary, shall be taken into account when the sum of compensation is assessed.

In addition to the amendments made by the Planning and Compensation Act, 1991 detailed above, this Act also revived part (IV) of the Land Compensation Act, 1961 relating to compensation to be paid where provision for additional development is granted after the acquisition of land.

These provisions reintroduce a major area of compensation where an interest in land is acquired and before the expiry of a period of 10 years from the date of completion of the purchase of the acquired land planning permission is granted for the carrying out of additional development and the compensation would have been higher if the planning permission had been granted before the date of Notice to Treat then additional compensation shall be payable to the claimant to make up the shortfall and this additional compensation shall also carry interest at the statutory rate.

Therefore, where a claimant now has an interest purchased by an acquiring authority the claimant has the right to give the acquiring authority his address and the duty is then upon the acquiring authority to give notice to the claimant of any planning permission which will increase the value of the site. The claimant needs to lodge his claim within 6 months of the date of notification or 6 months from the date of the decision to grant planning permission if the claimant does not provide an address for notification.

If the acquiring authority has no interest in the land then the local planning authority has a duty to inform the acquiring authority of any planning permission which may be granted. It should be noted that the following are excluded from these revived provisions:

1. Urban Development Corporations.
2. Highway Authorities operating in urban development areas.
3. Acquisitions under the New Towns Act.
4. Cases where a listed building is being acquired because the property has been allowed to fall into disrepair by its current owners.

Obviously, it is a valuation judgement whether a claimant will receive a greater sum of compensation on the basis of current use value plus disturbance compensation or on the basis of redevelopment. A claimant is not allowed to claim both development value and disturbance compensation, since the Courts have held that it is the purpose of compensation to place the claimant, so far as money can, in the same position as he would have been had no compulsory acquisition taken place and, therefore, it is the view of the Courts that in the "no scheme" world a claimant would have to be disturbed in his occupation of property in order to obtain the benefit of enhanced development value.

Disturbance
All the provisions so far discussed have been based around the open market value of the land to be acquired together with the depreciation caused to the market value of retained land resulting from severance or injurious affection.

The basis of compensation for disturbance is set out in Rule (6) of Section 5 of the Land Compensation Act, 1961, which states that the provisions of Rule (2) (The Open Market Value Rule) shall not affect the assessment of compensation for disturbance or any other matter not directly based on the value of land and, therefore, this preserves the principle that disturbance compensation should be based on the principle of value to owner.

As stated above, the Courts have in previous, although now somewhat dated, decisions held that where development value of a claimant's land is being claimed then disturbance compensation is not payable, since in order to receive the development value in the "no scheme" world, the claimant would as a consequence be naturally disturbed in his occupation.

However, in more recent years notable authorities on compensation such as Barry Denyer-Green have cast doubt on this principle, since in his view, under the current compensation code claimants who are disturbed from possession of their land are entitled to the market value of that land under Rule (2) and also the cost of being disturbed under Rule (6) and it is further suggested that there is nothing in the present Land Compensation Act, 1961 which suggests that an entitlement to disturbance compensation depends on the basis of the valuation of the land taken since even in the "no scheme" world a claimant would be disturbed in his occupation in his land whether he sold it at its current use value or its development value.

In order to lodge a claim for disturbance compensation the claimant must have been the occupier of the property to be acquired and be a person entitled to have received a Notice to Treat, ie either a freeholder or lessee with an unexpired term exceeding a year. The rule that it is only a disturbed occupier who can claim compensation for disturbance has led to problems where ownership and occupation are split between two separate legal entities such as separate limited companies, both of which are nonetheless related in some way, possibly being part of the same group, and in the past the Courts tended to study the relationship of the related companies to determine whether in fact they might be regarded as a single entity.

Where part of a claimant's property is taken for the purpose of the acquiring authority's scheme he will still be entitled to claim disturbance compensation in respect of the land acquired for the scheme. The validity of each item in the disturbance claim must be considered on its merits in relation to the general principles relating to disturbance compensation claims which are considered below.

Before dealing in greater detail with the areas in which a claimant may be able to seek disturbance compensation it is necessary to be aware of the general principles which apply to both the entitlement to and the assessment of the claim for compensation for disturbance.

First, any losses which are claimed must not be too remote and in practice it is considered that a reasonable test of remoteness would be to consider whether a loss flows directly from the dispossession or whether in fact it results from a consequence of a consequence.

Second, a claimant is required to take all reasonable steps in order to mitigate the losses which he may suffer as a result of being disturbed in his occupation of a property. The duty to mitigate normally arises in relation to the need to relocate an affected business at the earliest opportunity, in order to reduce the possible loss of profits.

Decisions of the Lands Tribunal indicate that they also expect the acquiring authority to give a claimant sufficient notice of a need to give up possession of a property in order to allow a claimant to be able to mitigate his losses. If a sufficient period of notice is not given by the acquiring authority, then the Lands Tribunal may consider it is not reasonable to expect a claimant to be able to mitigate his loss.

As a result of these decisions, four rules may be set down to be followed in respect of the need to mitigate the losses.

1. A claimant is required to take all reasonable steps to mitigate the losses suffered by him as a consequence of his eviction and he cannot recover compensation for any loss which may have been avoided.
2. It is for the acquiring authority to prove that a claimant has failed to mitigate his loss having regard to a criterion of reasonableness.
3. The claimant is only required to act reasonably and the standard of reasonableness is held to be not high.
4. A claimant will not be prejudiced if due to his financial inability he is unable to take steps to mitigate his losses.

In the past, being under a duty to mitigate his loss often placed a claimant in a difficult position with regard to intending compulsory purchase since he may in fact maximise the mitigation of his loss by taking action in advance of a Notice to Treat, but for many years the Courts held that only those items of disturbance compensation which were incurred after the date of the Notice to Treat could be included in a valid claim for disturbance compensation.

However, cases heard in both Scotland and England in the early 1980s stated that valid items of claim incurred before the date of the Notice to Treat which served to mitigate the claimant's loss could be regarded as payable provided that a Notice to Treat is ultimately served. It must be stressed that if no Notice to Treat is ultimately served on the claimant, the result is that there is always the risk that costs may be incurred in respect of a proposed acquisition which, ultimately, may not take place and, therefore, no compensation for those costs will be payable.

The final point to be considered with regard to general matters is the principle of value for money. This aspect relates to a situation where a claimant incurs expenditure as a result of a compulsory purchase but for which he receives value for money and if this is the case he cannot then claim compensation for this expenditure. Examples of this may be cited as when a claimant carries out structural alterations to his new premises which constitute improvements or, alternatively, he purchases a property for a higher value than that which was compulsory acquired, but which enjoys better advantages which are, therefore, reflected in the enhanced price which is paid for the new property.

With regard to specific items of disturbance these can be many and varied, but study of case law indicates that the following may be regarded as established items:

Loss of profits The loss of trade profits may either be permanent in the case where a claimant does not seek to reinstate his business in alternative premises or, alternatively, temporary where a claimant does intend to reinstate his business in alternative premises elsewhere.

Provided a claimant acts reasonably then it is his decision as to whether or not the business should be reinstated or not, bearing in mind the need for a claimant to mitigate his loss.

It should also be noted that Section 46 of the Land Compensation Act, 1973 allows any claimant who is aged 60 years or over to claim automatically the right to claim total extinguishment compensation, provided that he gives an undertaking that he will permanently cease trading and that the rateable value of the property being acquired is below the figure of £18,000 rateable value.

The accepted method of assessing the figure to represent the loss of profits due when the business is extinguished is to ascertain the average level of profit achieved over a period of at least 3 years before acquisition, having regard to any upward or downward trend shown in the accounts over this period.

The average net profit is calculated and then needs to be reduced on account of the profit rent where a property is leasehold or the rental value of the premises where it is freehold, the proprietor's remuneration – unless the business is a one man's business – and interest on capital tied up in the business, eg the stock, fixtures and fittings and the cash float.

The resulting figure is then capitalised by the year's purchase, traditionally varying from one to five depending on the trend shown in the accounts, the character of the business and the length of time it has been trading.

Where a business is proposing to relocate in new premises there may well be a temporary loss of profit incurred by the company during the period when the business is preparing for removal from the acquired premises and then building up again at the new premises. However, it could be expected that a business would seek to mitigate its loss during this period of upheaval by building up stocks of its goods before the date of removal to tide it over the period of relocation to the new premises.

In addition to a temporary loss of profits, depending on the circumstances of a removal to new premises and their new location, it may be found that as a result of the relocation there may also be an element of permanent loss of profits suffered by a business.

Loss on forced sale of stock This area of compensation applies mainly to the case of a total extinguishment claim, but in certain circumstances it could also form an item of claim in respect of a business which relocates to smaller premises. Generally, it is usual for this claim to be based on the cost value of the stock which is lost, less amounts which are recovered on the sale of that stock.

Removal of plant and machinery It is usual for the cost of contractors and/or staff wages incurred in the dismantling of any plant and machinery in the premises acquired and its removal and reinstallation in the new premises to be an admissible item of claim. In addition, it is usual to include the cost of connection for any utility services, eg electricity that may be involved in the reinstallation.

Transfer of stock The cost of using contractors and/or the cost of staff wages which are incurred in the removal of stock from the existing to the new premises are an admissible item of claim.

Removal of office furniture and other loose items Again the cost of using contractors and/or the cost of staff wages which are incurred in the removal of these items from the acquired to the new premises form an admissible item of claim.

Fixtures and fittings The cost of adapting the fixtures and fittings for use in the new premises may be allowed or, alternatively, the loss on for sale value may be allowed if the items are left in the acquired premises.

Telephone costs The cost of reconnecting telephone services to the new premises, including intercom systems, telex or fax lines may be allowed, but the claim must exclude any element of betterment in the form of an increased number of lines or extensions.

Changes in stationery The loss due to a value of paper, invoices, order books, visiting cards and any other stationery rendered useless by the change of address, should be allowed as an item of disturbance.

Facia/sign boards The cost of a new sign board or facia board for the new premises, or the removal and adaptation of existing signs may be allowed within the disturbance claim.

Notification of change of address The cost of advertising the change of a business address, telephone and fax number, and the circulation of the same to all existing customers and suppliers should form part of the claim.

Alarm systems The disturbance claim should also include the cost of reinstallation of burglar or fire alarm systems from the existing to the alternative premises, and it should be noted that the acquiring authority will not be prepared to pay for the extra installation costs should a business be moving to larger premises than those which were acquired for the scheme.

Double overheads Obviously, when a business is relocating it may be necessary for the business to maintain two sets of premises for a period of time, and therefore, it is accepted that disturbance compensation will be claimed in respect of rent, rates, electricity and other service costs in respect of the existing premises during the period in which double overheads have to be borne. Furthermore, the cost of any interest paid in respect of bridging loan to finance the removal and relocation should be included in the claim for disturbance compensation.

Directors' staff time Due to the complexity in removing many businesses to new premises it may be that directors and/or senior staff time in the claimant company will be involved in a number of aspects such as searching for and finding alternative premises and also organising and supervising the removal to the new premises and this cost should again be included in the claim for disturbance compensation.

Professional fees The professional fees for both surveyors and solicitors incurred in purchasing suitable alternative premises, will normally be allowed as part of a disturbance claim.

The above list sets down the major areas of disturbance compensation which are generally regarded as being admissible, but it is important to look at each individual case on its merits to ensure that all costs which are incurred by a claimant as a direct result of the acquisition are claimed on behalf of the claimant.

Compensation where no land is acquired

There are basically two sources of compensation which are available to claimants where no land is actually acquired from them for the purpose of an acquiring authority's scheme, these are:

1. Part (I) Land Compensation Act, 1973 – Compensation for the Depreciation Caused by the Use of Public Works; and
2. Section 10, Compulsory Purchase Act, 1965 – Compensation for Injurious Affection Caused by the Execution of Works.

Part (I) Land Compensation Act, 1973 These provisions allow a person to claim compensation for the depreciation in the value of an interest in land due to "physical factors" caused by the use of public works. The "physical factors" are noise, vibration, smell, fumes, smoke and artificial lighting and the discharge onto the land of any solid or liquid substance.

It can be seen that the basis of this provision is basically a claim in lieu of an action for nuisance, since a claim can only be made under the 1973 Act if the authority causing the "physical factors" is immune to an action of nuisance in respect of those factors which may flow from the use of the authority's public works.

However, unlike an action for nuisance, it is not necessary to show an interference with the enjoyment of the property, which is an unreasonable interference, but it is sufficient under the 1973 Act to show that depreciation in value due to the "physical factors" of not less than £50.00 has occurred.

Where a property affected is other than a dwelling then the claimant must have an owner's interest, which means either a legal fee simple or a tenancy for a term of years certain, which at the date of the notice to claim has not less than three years unexpired and it should also be noted that in order to make a claim under the 1973 Act in respect of business premises, the rateable value of the property must not exceed the prescribed amount of £18,000 and it is likely, therefore, that this provision will prevent the majority of commercial business occupiers from being eligible to lodge a claim.

Section 10, Compulsory Purchase Act, 1965 The basis of claim under this Section relates to the right to receive compensation for injurious affection caused by the execution of works and the conditions of bringing forward a claim were set out in *Metropolitan Board of Works* v *McCarthy* (1874) and have become known by the shorthand of the "McCarthy Rules".

It should be noted that it is immaterial whether the works causing the injurious affection are on land which has been compulsorily acquired or acquired by agreement under statutory powers. In order that a satisfactory claim may be lodged the following four rules must be satisfied:

Rule 1: The injury must be done by reason of what has been authorised by Act of Parliament.
Rule 2: The injury must arise from that which would, if done without the authority of Act of Parliament, have been actionable in law.
Rule 3: Damage must arise from a physical interference with some right, public or private, to which the claimant as owner of an interest in property is by law entitled to make use of, in connection with such property, and which gives an additional market value to such property.
Rule 4: The damage must arise from the execution of the works and not by their subsequent use.

Since a claim under this Section is in substitution for an action in law, the rules concerning damages payable in tort are applicable. The damage must be the natural and probable consequence of the execution of the works and must not be too remote. The amount of compensation awarded must, so far as money can, put the claimant in the same position as he would have been had no tort occurred.

The usual measure of compensation is the depreciation in the value of the affected land attributable to the interference or loss of legal right that gave rise to the claim. It should also be noted that the normal rules of compensation for a compulsory acquisition do not apply so, therefore, any betterment of any other land owned by the claimant resulting from the execution of the works does not have to be set off against the compensation due in respect of an affected property owned by the claimant.

Solicitor's and surveyor's fees

The provisions of the compensation code allow a claimant who is affected by compulsory acquisition to be paid his reasonable legal costs and other professional fees incurred in preparing a claim for compensation. In the first instance, an acquiring authority will consider whether or not the fees which are being claimed are reasonable and in respect of surveyor's fees the majority of acquiring authorities assess these in accordance with the provision of Ryde's Scale, 1991.

Conclusions

As stated at the outset, a chapter of this length can only provide a snapshot of the procedural minefield and valuation problems which can flow from the proposed compulsory acquisition of a business and for more detailed reading it is recommended that reference should be made to:

1. *The Encyclopedia of Compulsory Purchase and Compensation* published by Sweet and Maxwell.
2. *Boynton's Guide to Compulsory Purchase and Compensation* by D. J. Hawkins.
3. *Compulsory Purchase and Compensation* by Barry Denyer-Green.

Unlike the other chapters of this book which deal with the methodology of valuation of specific types of leisure properties, the rules and procedures which cover the assessment of compensation do not vary with the type of property to be valued, but remain constant and it is, therefore, the differing methods of valuation which will provide the quantum of compensation to be paid in respect of the various types of property.

As a footnote to this chapter, I propose to comment on the views which the Lands Tribunal have expressed in the past with regard to the methods of valuation which have been adopted in hearings before the Tribunal. The Tribunal has pointed out the generally inherent defects which occur when the residual method of valuation is adopted where the final value of a proposed development is first assessed with the cost of carrying out the development then being deducted with the balance or "residual" sum being the value that can be attributed to the existing property. The Tribunal identifies that the major problem of the residual method of valuation is its susceptibility to marked change as a result of making relatively small adjustments to certain of the factors included in the valuation method.

The Tribunal much prefers to refer to evidence of direct comparable transactions to the property which is being acquired and having these expressed in a format which makes broad comparison relatively easy.

The Tribunal, when it is considering a comparable evidence of sales, also prefers to see a reasoned argument as to the method of comparability which is used between the evidence which is being put forward; it also needs to be recognised that the Lands Tribunal reaches its decisions on the basis of evidence presented to it and the members of the Tribunal seek to weigh the evidence presented to them.

It is, therefore, important to recognise that any evidence which is presented, either to an acquiring authority or, ultimately, the Lands Tribunal, in support of a claim for compensation should be in the form which is generally accepted as being normally acceptable for the type of property under discussion and that any evidence which is produced is presented in the normal analytical method adopted for that type of property, eg barrelage for public houses.

The guiding principle in respect of any compulsory purchase in the final analysis is to ensure that the claimant has, so far as money can, been replaced in the position in which he was before the compulsory acquisition took place.

Compensation under the Town and Country Planning Act and Planning (Listed Buildings and Conservation Areas) Act, 1990

The rights to claim compensation under the Town and Country Planning Act, 1990 are contained in part (IV) of that Act and in addition part (VI) sets out the circumstances in which an owner of land may require the purchase of that interest where the interest is affected by planning decisions or orders, and chapter (II) of part (VI) of the 1990 Act sets out the circumstances in which a blight notice may be served by an owner of the property where the interest has been affected by planning proposals.

The rights to compensation granted under the Planning (Listed Buildings and Conservation Areas) Act, 1990 may be found in chapter (III) of part (I) of the Act and chapter (V) of part (I) of the same Act sets out the circumstances when an authority may use compulsory acquisition to purchase a listed building in need of repair and includes the development proposals for the assessment of compensation in such a case.

Town and Country Planning Act, 1990

If it is considered that the rights to develop or use land are part of the rights of a property owner then, in effect, the Town and Country Planning Act, 1947 revoked these rights as from July 1 1948 since the 1947 Act provided that planning permission was required for the development of land and that if planning permission was refused for any development, other than some minor classes of development known as "existing use development" then no compensation was payable to the landowner. (N.B. The right to compensation in respect of refusals relating to "existing use development" has now been repealed by the Planning and Compensation Act 1991.)

Although the 1947 Act provided that, there is no general entitlement to compensation in respect of planning control and there is no inherent right to develop land unless and until planning permission is granted for the proposed development. However, once permission has been obtained then the right to develop is guaranteed and can be withdrawn only upon payment of compensation.

Section 107 of the Town and Country Planning Act, 1990 sets out the provisions relating to compensation to be paid where planning permission is revoked or modified by the local planning authority and the compensation under this Section is payable in the following

(a) Compensation will be paid in respect of abortive expenditure which includes the preparation of plans for the purposes of work and other similar preparatory matters, but it does not include the cost of any work carried out before the grant of the planning permission which was subsequently revoked or modified by the local planning authority; and

(b) Compensation will also be paid for any other loss or damage which is directly attributable to the revocation or modification of the original planning permission.

This head of claim would also appear to allow a claim in respect of any depreciation in the value of the claimant's interest in land which results from the revocation or modification order and in establishing this depreciation it may be assumed that planning permission would be granted for the development contained within the Third Schedule of the 1990 Act.

Section 117 of the 1990 Act sets out that the rules of compensation contained in Section 5 of the Land Compensation Act, 1961 with any necessary modifications, form the appropriate framework to make the appropriate compensation assessment with regard to depreciation in value.

The phrase "directly attributable" appears to suggest that only losses or damages with a close causal link will be admitted in a compensation claim. However, provided the link is established, the measure of loss may also include any loss of anticipated future business profit likely under a specific contract, but subject to any appropriate deferment if this is required.

A claim of compensation may be made by any person with an interest in the land and the Courts have held that the class of claimant is not limited to persons holding a legal or equitable interest in the land and that an enforceable contractual right to use the land in a way which is then prevented by an order will also suffice. Any person wishing to make a claim under this Section must do so in writing to the local planning authority and serve the claim on the authority by either delivering it at their offices or sending it by prepaid post within 6 months of the date of the decision in respect of which it is made.

Any question of disputed compensation will be referred to the Lands Tribunal for determination and it should also be noted, that where compensation is paid under this Section for depreciation in land value it is potentially recoverable under Section 111 of the 1990 Act if the land is subsequently developed. The sum of compensation paid is also apportioned under Section 109 of the Act if practicable, between the different parts of the land by the local planning authority and notice of the compensation and its apportionment is registered as a local land charge under the provisions of Section 110 of the Act.

Section 108 of the 1990 Act allows for the payment of compensation for the refusal or conditional grant of planning permission formerly granted by development order and such permission may be withdrawn by either:

(a) the revocation or amendment of the development order itself; or
(b) the issue of a direction under the order. Articles 4, 5 and 6 of the Town and Country Planning General Development Order, 1988 make specific provision for the making of directions for the withdrawal of permission granted by Schedule 2 of that order and similar provision is also made by some of the special development orders.

Where permission is withdrawn by one of the methods outlined above, compensation only becomes payable where an application is made for planning permission for development formerly permitted by the development order and this is either refused or granted on conditions which differ from those contained in the development order.

The principles of assessment of compensation are the same as those in relation to revocation or modification orders and it should also be noted that an entitlement to compensation under this Section debars an applicant from lodging a claim for compensation for the depreciation in the value of land under part (IV) of the 1990 Act.

Where a revocation or amendment of the relevant development order occurs the Act requires that the application for planning permission on which the compensation claim is based be made within 12 months of the withdrawal of the relevant permission, and the aim of this period is to allow compensation to be paid to those who were in the process of undertaking a development and who may already have incurred expenditure in reliance on the development order permission. The 12 month time limit on claims does not apply in respect of directions made under Article 4 of the Town and Country Planning General Development Order, 1988.

Section 115 of the 1990 Act allows compensation to be claimed in respect of discontinuance orders made under Section 102 of the 1990 Act. An order made under Section 102 may require the discontinuance of a use of land, impose conditions on the continuation of a use or require specified steps to be taken for the alteration or removal of buildings or works.

A claim for compensation may be made by any person and is not limited only to persons having an interest in the land subject to the order. However, persons who do not have an interest in the land would be entitled only to compensation either in respect of disturbance or for carrying out works in compliance with the order.

The date of assessment of compensation under this Section is the date on which the discontinuance order was confirmed by the Secretary of State and compensation is payable for any damage suffered by any person in consequence of the order in respect of:

(a) depreciation in the value of land;
(b) disturbance;
(c) any expenses reasonably incurred in carrying out works in compliance with the order; and
(d) rehousing.

The Section allows to be deducted from the sum of compensation to be paid to the value to the claimant of any timber, apparatus or other materials removed for the purpose of compliance with the order. It would appear that this deduction can only be made where, and to the extent that, such value was reflected in the compensation and so it may apply where a building whose value was taken into account in determining compensation has been demolished in compliance with the order. However, it may be contended that it would not apply where merely cut timber or apparatus was simply stored on the land and did not form part of the land and was subsequently removed to comply with the order.

Again, a claim for compensation under this Section would be lodged by serving a written claim on the local planning authority by delivery at the offices of the authority or by sending it by prepaid post, with the claim being lodged within a period of 6 months from the date of the discontinuance order.

So far, this part of the chapter has dealt with compensation for the effects of the serving of certain orders which in general serve either to restrict or discontinue development which has already started. However, part (VI) of the 1990 Act sets out the provisions whereby an owner of land may serve a purchase notice on a local planning authority requiring them to acquire land which has become incapable of reasonably beneficial use.

This appears to be a fairly straightforward set of circumstances, but over the years cases have been heard by the Courts which centre on the point as to whether or not the land is incapable of reasonably beneficial use. A purchase notice may only be served in respect of land which has been affected by a planning decision and the decisions which give rise to the right to serve a purchase notice are:

(a) a decision which is a refusal of planning permission or a grant of planning permission subject to conditions;
(b) an order which revokes or modifies a planning permission;
(c) an order requiring the discontinuance of the use of land or imposes conditions of the continuance of the use, or requiring the alteration or removal of any buildings or works;
(d) a decision which is a refusal of listed building consent or the grant of listed building consent subject to conditions, or the modification of a listed building consent.

After the claimant has established that one of the appropriate planning decisions has been made, it is then necessary for the owner to show that the land has become incapable of reasonably beneficial use in its existing state or that where the decision is subject to conditions that the land cannot be rendered capable of reasonably beneficial use by the carrying out of the permitted development in accordance with the conditions.

As stated earlier, these considerations have been the subject of case law in the past and these cases can provide useful guidance in considering whether land is capable of reasonably beneficial use in its existing state.

As a general rule, the Courts have held that where the land is of less value to the owner than it would have been had the planning permission been more favourable is not relevant when considering whether the existing use is reasonably beneficial and, therefore, if it is considered that the existing use is reasonably beneficial then no purchase notice can be served by the claimant.

However, if the existing use is not reasonably beneficial then it is necessary to consider whether some prospective use may be regarded as reasonably beneficial. It is difficult to provide any hard or fast rules with regard to what are and are not reasonably beneficial uses and it is, therefore, necessary to consider each individual case on its merits to determine whether or not this test may be passed in order to allow the serving of a purchase notice to proceed.

The procedure for dealing with the service of a purchase notice may be found in Sections 139–40 of the 1990 Act, and a purchase notice must be served on the local planning authority within 12 months of the date of the planning decision. The local planning authority must then within 3 months of the service of the purchase notice by the claimant serve a counter notice stating:

(a) that the authority is willing to comply with the notice and purchase the land; or
(b) that another specified authority is willing to purchase the land; or
(c) that neither the authority nor any other authority is willing to accept the purchase notice and, therefore, a copy of the purchase notice will be sent to the Secretary of State, together with a copy of the local planning authority's notice expressing unwillingness to accept the purchase notice.

Where (c) above applies, the Secretary of State will then invite representations from the owner, the Council, and where relevant, the County Planning Authority and if the Secretary of State has in mind substituting another specified authority for the local planning authority as the body being required to comply with the purchase notice he will seek their views in addition. If the Secretary of State considers it necessary, he will arrange to hold a hearing or a public local inquiry into the matter.

Having considered the matter, the Secretary of State then has a number of different courses of action which he may follow:

(a) The purchase notice may be confirmed; or
(b) Another specified authority may be substituted for the local planning authority upon whom the purchase notice was originally served; or
(c) Planning permission may be granted for the development which was originally applied for in lieu of confirming the purchase notice or any conditions attached to a planning permission may be varied or revoked with the object of enabling the subject land to be rendered capable of reasonably beneficial use; or
(d) If it is considered that either part or the whole of the land may be rendered capable of reasonably beneficial use, it may be directed that planning permission should be granted for any development which the Secretary of State thinks would achieve this aim in lieu of confirming the purchase notice.

Once a purchase notice has been accepted by the local planning authority, some other authority, or confirmed by the Secretary of State the authority acquiring the land is then deemed to have served Notice to Treat and the procedure from this date onwards, and the compensation to be paid for the land, will be carried out in accordance with the normal rules applicable to a compulsory purchase situation.

Chapter 2 of part (VI) of the Town and Country Planning Act, 1990 includes provisions relating to the service of blight notices where interests are adversely affected by planning proposals. It is not proposed to deal with these provisions in any detail since a blight notice may only be served in respect of a hereditament whose rateable value does not exceed the sum of £18,000 (eighteen thousand pounds) and it is considered unlikely that any of the categories of leisure property considered within this book would fall below this rateable value limit.

Planning (Listed Buildings and Conservation Areas) Act, 1990

This Act of Parliament as its name implies relates specifically to listed buildings and conservation areas and there are provisions contained within the Act which allow for compensation to be paid in certain circumstances that tend to mirror the general compensation provisions contained in the Town and Country Planning Act, 1990.

In particular, compensation may be payable for a refusal of consent to either alter or extend a listed building or, alternatively, if consent is granted subject to conditions.

As in the case of the Town and Country Planning Act 1990, the amount of the claim amounts to the depreciation of the value of the interest of a person in respect of land which results from the refusal of either listed building consent or the granting of consent subject to conditions.

It should be noted that the local planning authority need not pay compensation under Section 27 of the Planning (Listed Buildings and Conservation Areas) Act, 1990 in respect of a building where a building preservation notice is in force, unless and until the building is included in a list compiled or approved by the Secretary of State under Section 1 of the Act, although a claim for such compensation may be made before the building is included on an appropriate list.

Section 28 of the Planning (Listed Buildings and Conservation Areas) Act, 1990 allows for compensation to be paid where listed building consent is revoked or modified by a local planning authority and again the basis of compensation in this case is the same as that provided under the Town and Country Planning Act, 1990 provisions.

Section 29 of the Planning (Listed Buildings and Conservation Areas) Act, 1990 allows compensation to be paid for loss or damage caused by the service of a building preservation notice and the Section allows that the person who has an interest in the building shall be entitled to be paid compensation by the local planning authority in respect of any loss or damage directly attributable to the effect of the building preservation notice which subsequently ceased to have effect without the building having been included in a list compiled or approved by the Secretary of State.

The loss or damage in respect of which compensation is payable may also include the sum payable in respect of any breach of contract caused by the necessity of discontinuing or countermanding any works to the building preservation notice being in force with respect to the building.

Section 31 of the Planning (Listed Buildings and Conservation Areas) Act, 1990 confirms that any compensation which is payable under Sections 27–29 of the Act is in respect of depreciation in the value of an interest in land. The compensation rules are set out in

Section 5 of the Land Compensation Act, 1961 and shall, so far as is applicable and subject to any necessary modifications, have effect for the purpose of assessing compensation for the compulsory acquisition of an interest in land.

Section 32 of the Planning (Listed Buildings and Conservation Areas) Act, 1990 relates to the serving of listed building purchase notices following the refusal or conditional granting of listed building consent and again the provisions which apply mirror those contained in the Town and Country Planning Act, 1990.

Conclusions

The provisions contained within both the Town and Country Planning Act, 1990 and the Planning (Listed Buildings and Conservation Areas) Act, 1990, as amended by the Planning and Compensation Act, 1991, specifically set out the areas where compensation may be payable in respect of decisions which may be made by local planning authorities relating to land or buildings.

In view of this, it is recommended that valuers of leisure property, when considering whether a claim for compensation may be lodged, should always refer back to the relevant Acts of Parliament in order to establish whether the necessary conditions have been fulfilled to allow a valid claim for compensation to be lodged or purchase notice to be served.

It should also be noted that although compensation is available in respect of revocation, modification or discontinuance orders which may be served, a Purchase Notice may be a more appropriate route to follow where it is considered that the serving of such a notice of revocation, modification or discontinuance by the planning authority has made the land incapable of reasonably beneficial use.

It also needs to be recognised that a number of leisure properties, eg cinemas, hotels, public houses, theatres, etc may also be listed buildings and, therefore, reference should always be made to the relevant provisions of the Planning (Listed Buildings and Conservation Areas) Act, 1991 to determine whether compensation may be payable in appropriate circumstances.

However, bearing in mind that a number of leisure properties referred to in this book have their value assessed with regard to the estimated level of profit which the business will make which is then capitalised by an appropriate multiplier, it may prove difficult to prove to an authority's valuer that a depreciation in the value of the owner's interest may have occurred, although it is considered that in situations where adverse planning decisions may not actually affect the level of the profitability of a business from year to year the circumstances may be such as to require an adjustment in the appropriate multiplier in order to reflect the changed circumstances.

It is hoped that this chapter has provided the valuer of leisure property with a number of signposts as to the situations where compensation for various decisions or proposed activities of statutory authorities may be payable and allow the valuer to reflect the requirements of the relevant statutory provisions of compulsory purchase and compensation in his valuation of subject properties in order to establish the sum of compensation, if any, which may be payable to the client.

© Geoffrey Simm, 1996

CHAPTER 3

Valuation of leisure property for rating

Introduction

The basic rules for the valuation of leisure property for rating are the same as those for the valuation of any other class of property. These are laid down in the Local Government Finance Act 1988 (LGFA 1988), the Local Government and Housing Act 1989 (LGHA 1989), and seven later Acts.

The LGFA 1988 is the principal Act covering valuation for rating and is a major departure from the General Rate Act 1967, which covered rating law and practice until April 1 1990, because unlike the 1967 Act it does not purport to include a complete code of law but is an enabling act, giving powers to the Secretary of State to adjust the rules by way of Regulations laid before both Houses of Parliament. Although this may be administratively more convenient, it does lead to greater uncertainty as to the current state of rating law, and inevitably makes it more difficult to provide clients with long-term plans to mitigate their rate liability. This government by regulation is put in context when it is realised that there have been more than 140 sets of regulations since the LGFA 1988, reached the statute book, and in the first four months of 1996 two new acts "The Rating (Caravan and Boats) Act", and the "Non-domestic Rating (Information) Act" reached the statute book.

Rate Liability

1990 changes
A fundamental reform of the rating system took place on April 1 1990, introducing three major changes.

1. Domestic rates were abolished and replaced by the ill-fated Community Charge (or Poll Tax as it is more commonly known). This was itself replaced by the Council Tax on April 1 1993.

2. Locally-fixed rates were abolished and were replaced by the National Non-Domestic Rate (NNDR), which is more commonly called the Uniform Business Rate (UBR). This is fixed nationally, collected by local councils, and paid into separate central pools maintained by the Secretaries of State for the Environment, Scotland and Wales. These pools are then redistributed to local authorities on a basis of the size of their adult population. (The change to UBR took place in Scotland on April 1 1995).

3. All properties in England, Wales and Scotland were reassessed, updating the rental value upon which their rates were charged from April 1 1973 to April 1 1988. A further revaluation of these properties took place on April 1 1995 when the values were again revalued to reflect the level of rents passing on April 1 1993. Legislation requires that future revaluations should take place every five years and the next is scheduled for April 1 2000.

Transitional arrangements

The introduction of changes of this magnitude was inevitably going to cause problems.

The revision of the rental value base after 15 years of major development, and high inflation, coupled with the change from locally-fixed rates which varied from £1.22 in the Royal Borough of Kensington and Chelsea to £3.995 in the City of Sheffield, to a National Rate (in terms of 1973 values) of approximately £2.40, would have caused potential unacceptable increases in liability. These changes would have been particularly hard on the leisure industry, which had changed dramatically in the 15 years from 1988. The industry was, in April 1988, in a bullish mood, and paying very high prices for the right to occupy property. Some London hotels faced increases in their 1990/91 rate liability in excess of four times the level they were paying in the rate year 1989/90. One hotel in the Royal Borough of Kensington faced an increase in its rate bill from £320,000 to £1,244,000. Increases in the provinces were in some cases even higher.

Ministers acknowledged that increases of this magnitude were unacceptable, and introduced transitional arrangements to phase in these increases over as many years as necessary. These regulations were initially self funding, and the relief provided for those who would but for the regulations have paid more was met by imposing on those who should have benefited from the revaluation a premium.

This premium was calculated by restricting the annual percentage by which the liabilities of those who should be better off could fall.

The regulations introduced in 1990 were amended a number of times during their five year life and whilst those relating to properties whose liabilities fell as a result of the revaluation were abolished from April 1 1993, those relating to maximum increases remained in effect with the result that by March 31 1995 some 300,000 properties (many of them leisure properties) remained subject to these rules and were not paying rates in full.

The LGFA 1988 requires Ministers to raise the same total revenue from UBR following a revaluation as was raised in the preceding year, subject only to an adjustment for inflation. The UBR in England rose only by inflation from £0.423 to £0.432, whilst that in Wales fell from £0.448 to £0.39. UBR was introduced in Scotland for the first time in 1995/96 and set at £0.432 in line with UBR in England.

There had, however, been major changes in rental value over the five years from 1988 to 1993. Most property throughout the United Kingdom, other than that in the secondary sector had increased in value, whilst the office market in central London had collapsed. The fall in the office market had been so large that on its own it eliminated almost the entire increase in rental value of property throughout the remainder of England. The total rateable value of England remained unchanged at £13.25 billion. Wales on the other hand saw an increase in its rateable value from £1.259 billion to £1.481 billion.

Ministers decided to continue with the transitional regulations during the 1995 revaluation and introduced a fresh set of rules in the Non-Domestic Rating (Chargeable Amounts) Regulations 1994 SI 1994/3279 and amended by the Non-Domestic Rating (Chargeable Amounts) Regulations 1996 SI 1996/911.

Increases in liability
The calculation of the maximum change in liability starts with the rate liability for the year 1994/95. Any increase in the amount payable was restricted for the 1995/96 year to 10%, after an adjustment for inflation. (Where the 1995 Rateable Value was under £15,000 in London, or £10,000 elsewhere this is reduced to 7.5%. The maximum increase for mixed domestic and non-domestic properties with Rateable Values below these figures was restricted to 5%. The 10% increase was reduced to 7.5%, and the 7.5% to 5% for the 1996/97 year). This calculation is repeated annually until the liability on this basis exceeds that which would be arrived at by multiplying

the 1995 rateable value by the UBR for the year of liability. The Act requires this calculation to be carried out on a daily basis, but for all practical purposes it can be carried out on an annual basis. It must be remembered that this calculation starts with the annual rate liability on March 31 1995. This is, where a property was subject to appeal, the finally agreed rateable value on that day taking into account any transitional relief being received by the property, but ignoring any empty property, charity or discretionary relief which it was receiving.

The effect of these transitional arrangements is the same for all classes of property, but can be demonstrated by looking at the liability of four hotels; two in the provinces, and two in London (see examples, pp. 117–18).

Decreases in liability

Almost all leisure properties are either subject to the ceiling on their rate liability imposed by the transitional regulations or pay rates in full in the normal manner. A few leisure properties would have had substantially reduced liabilities as a result of these changes. These properties are caught by the rules imposing a maximum reduction in liability in any one year.

This transitional floor which restricted the benefit of the 1995 revaluation to those leisure properties who needed it most, was imposed by the Treasury who insist that any relief for those who would otherwise have had to pay more, must be met by restricting any fall in liability for those who would, but for these rules, have paid less. The maximum reduction in liability, in England and Wales, was fixed in 1995/96 and at 5% below the liability in 1994/95 after adding inflation. The same calculation applies in 1996/97. The maximum decrease is increased to 15% in 1997/98 and to 25% for the 1998/99 and 1999/2000 rate years. Inflation is measured having regard to the RPI in September of the preceding year (announced in October), and was 2.2% in 1994 (used in 1995/96 calculation) and 3.9 in 1995 (used in 1996/97 calculation).

Properties with a 1995 rateable value of less than £15,000 in London or £10,000 elsewhere are subject to a maximum fall of 10% in 1995/96 and 1996/97 rising to 20% in 1997/98 and 30% in 1998/99 and 1999/2000.

Qualification for transitional protection

One fundamental difference between the 1990 and 1995 transitional regulations is that the regulations apply to the property and not to the occupier. This means that to determine whether or not a property is subject to the transitional rules one simply has to compare its liability on March 31 1995 with its liability on April 1 that year.

The regulations only relate to the liability of the property occupied on April 1 1995, any increase in rateable value above the figure which was in the list on that day (or which is later substituted for it) is liable to rates in the normal fashion.

Consider a marina which had a value in the rating list on April 1 1995 of £50,000, and where on November 3 1995 construction starts on an extension with the result that the assessment is temporarily reduced to £40,000. Work was completed on May 16 1996, when the assessment was increased to £80,000.

The normal liability for the period April 1 to November 2 1995 is calculated multiplying the RV £50,000 by the UBR 1995/96 of 43.2 p. This is then adjusted for the period to November 2. (Unfortunately 1995/96 was a leap year. The 1995/96 liability must therefore be apportioned using 366 and not 365 days).

A separate calculation of the transitional rate liability must then be carried out. This starts with the 1994/95 rate liability, to which must be added 10% plus inflation at 2.2% to arrive at the maximum liability for the period. The amount payable is then the lower of the two calculations.

Where the assessment of a property, subject to a transitional rate liability is reduced, that liability is reduced in proportion to the reduction in assessment in this case by the factors 40,000/50,000. It should be remembered, however, that the transitional liability for the year 1996/97 starts with the transitional liability for the year 1995/96. This is then increased by 7.5% plus inflation at 3.3% for that year.

The normal calculation of liability for this period must be made; RV, £40,000 × UBR £0.4.49, and the amount payable is the lower of the two figures.

The liability from May 16 1996, must be calculated in two stages. First, the original or first £50,000 of the assessment remains subject to the transitional rules, but adjusted for the balance of the year, and compared with the normal calculation. The lower figure is the amount payable in respect of this £50,000. The increase in the assessment which resulted from the extension to the Marina, (£80,000 − £50,000 = £30,000) is not, however, protected by the transitional regulations and will be subject to rates in full in the conventional manner.

Any property entered in the rating list after April 1 1995 will be subject to rates in the conventional manner, ie Rateable Value × UBR apportioned for the number of days it is occupied in a rate year. Property which is subject to the rules relating to downward transition and which is so altered that it comprises a different property from that which existed prior to the alteration is also exempt from these rules.

This regulation requires the Valuation Officer, if he feels that the property which has been altered is not sufficiently changed to create a different premises, to issue a certificate of the appropriate 1990 rateable value which he believes the premises would have had on March 31 1995 if they had existed on that day. This is a rather unsatisfactory situation and local Valuation Officers have been instructed to hold informal discussions with ratepayers or their agents where it is anticipated that there could be a difficulty. There is a right of appeal against the value in this certificate but not against the issue of a certificate itself.

Example 1   Britannia Hotel, London WC1

Rateable Value 1990 £1,665,000   Rateable Value 1995 £1,665,000
No change in rateable value.

Liability 1994/5 £704,295

Year	Full Liability	Transitional Liability
1995/96	£719,280	£719,280
1996/97	£747,585	£747,585
1997/98	£777,488	£777,488
1998/99	£808,588	£808,588
1999/2000	£840,931	£840,931

Note: This property is not subject to the transitional regulations.

Example 2   Kensington Park Hotel, London W8

Rateable Value 1990 £845,500   Rateable Value 1995 £845,500
No change in rateable value.

Liability 1994/95 £307,683

Year	Full Liability	Transitional Liability
1995/96	£365,256	£345,897
1996/97	£379,630	£379,630
1997/98	£394,815	£394,815
1998/99	£410,607	£410,607
1999/2000	£427,032	£427,033

Note: This property is only subject to transition in 1995/96.

Example 3   Portland Hotel, Manchester

Rateable Value 1990 £340,000   Rateable Value 1995 £265,000

Liability 1994/95   £143,820

Year	Full Liability	Transitional Liability
1995/96	£114,480	£139,635
1996/97	£118,985	£137,827
1997/98	£123,744	£123,744
1998/99	£128,694	£128,694
1999/2000	£133,842	£133,842

Note: This property is subject to downward transition until 1998/1999.

Example 4   Novotel Birmingham Airport

Rateable Value 1990 £240,000   Rateable Value 1995 £338,000

Liability 1994/95   £101,520

Year	Full Liability	Transitional Liability
1995/96	£146,016	£114,129
1996/97	£151,762	£127,473
1997/98	£157,832	£145,829
1998/99	£164,146	£164,146
1999/2000	£170,712	£170,712

Note: This property is subject to upward transition until 1998/1999.
All transitional calculations assume 4% inflation from September 1996 onwards.

Exemption from rates

Domestic property

All domestic property is exempt from the payment of non-domestic rates, by the simple expedient of excluding it from the Rating List (LGFA 1988 section 42(1) as amended). Many leisure properties contain a mixture of domestic and non-domestic (commercial) property, and it is important to consider what is domestic property for the purposes of rating valuation.

Under Section 66(1) property is domestic if:

(a) it is used wholly for the purposes of living accommodation;
(b) it is a yard, garden, outhouse or other appurtenance belonging to or enjoyed with the property falling within paragraph (a) above;

(c) it is a private garage used wholly or mainly for the accommodation of a private motor vehicle; or

(d) it is private storage premises used wholly or mainly for the storage of articles for domestic use.

(2) But property is not domestic if it is wholly or mainly used in the course of a business for the provision of short-stay accommodation, that is to say accommodation:

(a) which is provided for short periods to individuals whose sole or main residence is elsewhere; and

(b) which is not self-contained self-catering accommodation provided commercially.

(2A) Subsection (2) above does not apply if:

(a) it is intended that within the year beginning with the end of the day in relation to which the question is being considered, shortstay accommodation will not be provided within the hereditament for more than six persons simultaneously; and

(b) the person intending to provide such accommodation intends to have his sole or main residence within the hereditament throughout any period when such accommodation is being provided, and that any use of living accommodation within the hereditament which would, apart from this subsection, cause any part of it to be treated as non-domestic, will be subsidiary to the use of the hereditament for, or in connection with, his sole or main residence.

(2B) A building or self-contained part of a building is not domestic property if:

(a) the relevant person intends that, in the year beginning with the end of the day in relation to which the question is being considered, the whole of the building or self-contained part will be available for letting commercially as self-contained accommodation, for short periods totalling 140 days or more; and

(b) on that day his interest in the building or part of the building is such as to enable him to let it for such periods.

(2C) For the purposes of subsection (2B) the relevant person is:

(a) where the property in question is a building and is not subject as a whole to a relevant leasehold interest, the person having the freehold interest in the whole of the building; and

(b) in any other case, any person having a relevant leasehold interest in the building or self-contained part which is not subject (as a whole) to a single relevant leasehold interest.

(2D) Subsection (2B) above does not apply where the building or self-contained part is used as the sole or main residence of any person other than a person who is treated as having such a residence only by virtue of section 2(5A) above and on the day in relation to which the question is being considered is not resident in the building or part.

The LGFA 1988 section 2 (5A) makes the place of residence during term time the sole or main residence of a student undergoing full time education.

Special rules apply to pitches for Caravans and moorings for Boats. The rules set out in LGFA 1988 sections 66 (3) and (4) as amended by the Caravans (Standard Community Charge and Rating Act) 1991 (CCRA 1991) have been replaced by those in the Rating (Caravan and Boats) Act 1996 section 1 (2) (RCBA 1996) and now read as follows:

(3) Subsection (1) above does not apply in the case of a pitch occupied by a caravan, but if in such a case the caravan is the sole or main residence of an individual, the pitch and the caravan, together with any garden, yard, outhouse or other appurtenance belonging to or enjoyed with them, are domestic property.

(4) Subsection (1) above does not apply in the case of a mooring occupied by a boat, but if in such a case the boat is the sole or main residence of an individual, the mooring and the boat, together with any garden, yard, outhouse or other appurtenance belonging to or enjoyed with them, are domestic property.

(4A) Subsection (3) or (4) above does not have effect in the case of a pitch occupied by a caravan, or a mooring occupied by a boat, which is in appurtenance enjoyed with other property to which subsection (1)(a) above applies.

The RCBA 1996 Section 1 (4) makes these amendments to the LGFA 1988 retrospective to April 1 1990, except where a proposal had been made and not withdrawn before 30th January 1995 on the grounds that either the property should not be shown in the rating list or in the case of a composite (mixed domestic and non-domestic) property a proposal had been made on the grounds that the rateable value was too high, and not withdrawn.

(5) Property not in use is domestic if it appears that when next in use it will be domestic.

(6) (Repealed by CCRA 1991.)

(7) Whether anything is a caravan shall be construed in accordance with Part 1 of the Caravan Sites and Control of Development Act 1960.

(8) (Repealed by CCRA 1991.)

(8A) In this section – "business" includes:

(a) any activity carried on by a body of persons, whether corporate or unincorporated; and

(b) any activity carried on by a charity;

"commercially" means on a commercial basis and with the view to the realisation of profits; and

"relevant leasehold interest" means an interest under a lease or underlease which was granted for a term of 6 months or more and conferred the right to exclusive possession throughout the term.

(9) The Secretary of State may by order amend, or substitute another definition for, any definition of domestic property for the time being effective for the purposes of this Part.

It is important to look at LGFA 1988 Section 2 (persons subject to Community Charge now replaced by Council Tax) to decide if the property is the sole or main residence of an individual, however, in so far as leisure property is concerned it is really a matter of common sense.

The most useful part of Section 2 is subsection (4) which states that "if a person's sole or main residence at a particular time consists of premises, and the premises are situated in the areas of two or more authorities, he shall be treated as having his sole or main residence in the area in which the greater or greatest part of the premises is situated."

It follows from this definition that domestic property is exempt from non-domestic rates, and the occupiers are liable for the payment of Council Tax. Community charge (or Poll Tax) was abolished with effect from April 1 1993, and replaced by the Council Tax. This is a tax on the capital value of the property and is explained in more detail in pp 197–8. The boundary, however, between council tax and non-domestic rates remains the same.

Although the definition of domestic property set out in section 66 is fairly self-evident, it is important to consider subsection 66(2) in more detail. Living accommodation is domestic, and exempt from rates although, "property is not domestic if it is wholly or mainly used in the course of a business for the provision of short-stay accommodation, that is to say accommodation:

(a) which is provided for short periods to individuals whose sole or main residence is elsewhere; and

(b) which is not self-contained self-catering accommodation provided commercially."

(These are the main provisions but must be read, as appropriate, with the other provisions set out above.)

It follows from this that most guest accommodation in an hotel, guest house, or activity centre is not domestic (unless it is excluded by the provisions of LGFA 1988 subsections 2A, B, C and D set out above) and is liable to be valued for rating in the normal way. Gentlemen's clubs, some yacht clubs, golf clubs, and many other private members' clubs provide accommodation for their members. There is normally a room charge, but even if the use of these rooms is reflected in the subscription, this accommodation is not domestic.

It is important before leaving this type of property to bear in mind that staff accommodation may be domestic, and therefore exempt from rating. The accommodation must, however, be the sole or main residence of an individual, and not simply a room provided in order to enable him to carry out his duties.

A room in a hotel or club, provided for the manager or secretary when on duty overnight, is not domestic, as it is not his sole or main residence. Some clubs or hotels have stewards or secretaries who live on the premises. Provided that this accommodation is their sole or main residence, then this is domestic and exempt. The fact that they may own a holiday home or a property purchased for their retirement, does not prevent their accommodation within the hotel or club from being domestic. It is possible that some hotels or clubs have "live in" guests, whose occupation of the hotel or club is as their sole or main residence. The Dowager Duchess living in a West End hotel, or the retired Major General in his London club, spring to mind. Provided that their occupation of the accommodation is as their sole or main residence, then that area of the hotel or club is domestic and must be excluded from rating valuation. It is a matter of evidence whether or not the Duchess's occupation of her rooms at the hotel makes this, rather than her family's country estate, her principal residence, and it may prove difficult to convince the VO or the tribunal that these rooms should be treated as domestic, but if, on the facts, the hotel occupation is her principal residence then these rooms are domestic.

General exemptions from rating

Section 51 and Schedule 5 LGFA 1988 provide for a number of general exemptions from rating. These basically replicate the exemptions which have existed for many years, and indeed paragraph 20 allows the Secretary of State by Order to exempt any property which is not included in the current list but which was exempt under previous legislation.

Since some of these exempt properties can be leisure property or part of a leisure property it is important briefly to consider the list. It is not possible in a text book on leisure property to consider all the exemptions in detail, but if a leisure property, or part of a leisure property, would appear to be covered by the list, then the reader is recommended to study the schedule, and to read a rating text book which covers the question of exemption.

The principal properties which are exempt from rates are:

Agricultural premises
Fish farms
Commercial fresh water fishing
Places of public religious worship
Certain property of Trinity House
Sewers
Certain property of Drainage Authorities
Parks
Property used by the disabled
Air-raid protection works
Swinging moorings
Property in enterprise zones.

Some of these are worth further consideration.

Parks A park which is, or that part of it which is, either provided by, or under the management of a County, District, London Borough (including the City of London) the Council of the Isles of Scilly, a Parish or Community Council, or the chairman of a parish meeting, and is available for free and unrestricted use by members of the public is exempt from rates.

A park includes a recreation or pleasure ground, a public walk or an open space within the meaning of the Open Spaces Act 1906, and a playing field provided under the Physical Training and Recreation Act 1937.

The legislation makes it clear that any temporary closure (at night or otherwise) shall be ignored.

It is the policy of most authorities today to lock the changing and pavilion facilities provided for sportsmen when they are not in use. They do so in order to prevent theft and vandalism.

Provided that the accommodation is available for the users of the park when enjoying the sports facilities, then this should not make them rateable. If, however, the accommodation is let out to a local sports club, and they have control over the keys to the accommodation, and lock it in order to restrict the use to their members, then the accommodation is no longer in the control of the authority, and will comprise a separately rateable hereditament in the occupation of the sports club.

Property used by the disabled Property is exempt from rates to the extent that it consists of premises used wholly for any of the following purposes:

(a) the provision of facilities for the training, or keeping suitably occupied, persons who are disabled or who are or have been suffering from an illness;
(b) the provision of welfare services for disabled persons;
(c) the provision of facilities under section 15 of the Disabled Persons (Employment) Act 1944;
(d) the provision of a workshop or of other facilities under section 3(1) of the Disabled Persons (Employment) Act 1958.

A person is disabled if he is blind, deaf or dumb or suffers from mental disorder of any description or is substantially and permanently handicapped by illness, injury, congenital deformity or any other disability for the time being prescribed for the purposes of section 29(1) of the National Assistance Act 1948.

"Illness" has the meaning given by section 128(1) of the National Health Service Act 1977.

"Welfare services for disabled persons" means services or facilities (by whomsoever provided) of a kind which a local authority has power to provide under section 29 of the National Assistance Act 1948.

It is possible that the whole of a property or part of it, in either the control of a local authority, or in private ownership may be exempt rates from under this section.

Some sports clubs may have facilities which have been provided specifically to cater for the disabled, and a whole sports complex could have been provided for the use of the blind. It is exempt from rates to the extent that the accommodation is used wholly for that purpose then.

Air-raid protection works Some older sports facilities may well have part of the property designed originally as part of the air-raid protection for the community.

Provided that they are not being used for any other purpose these facilities are exempt from rates.

Swinging moorings These are exempt provided that they are used or intended to be used by a boat or a ship and are equipped only with a buoy attached to an anchor, weight or other device, which rests on or in the bed of the sea or any river or other waters when in use, and which is designed to be raised from that bed from time to time.

Many marinas have the use of swinging moorings in the waters fronting their premises. Indeed in many rivers trots of swing moorings are common. Provided that they are attached to a buoy, and this is connected to an anchor or other device which is designed to be raised from time to time then these are exempt from rating.

One example of these moorings in a south coast harbour comprises ground tackle provided by an anchor chain from one of Her Majesty's cruisers, laid along the bed of the harbour and which is attached to concrete blocks at each end. Chain pendant moorings are then shackled to the anchor chain with buoys floating on the surface to which yachts are moored. The old cruiser anchor chain is substantial, and is only lifted for inspection approximately once every 20 years, however, after satisfying himself of the facts the Valuation Officer took these moorings out of rating.

It should be remembered under LGFA 1988 section 66(4) that a mooring is domestic if it is occupied by a boat which is the sole or principal residence of an individual.

Property in enterprise zones Property in an enterprise zone is exempt from the payment of rates for ten years from the date when the enterprise zone was first established. The first of these zones, which were established under section 32 of the Local Government, Planning and Land Act 1980, expired in 1990, and the remainder have different unexpired terms.

Although these zones were established to encourage industrial and commercial regeneration within their boundaries, the legislation does not distinguish between classes of property, and all property within the zone is exempt from rates. Many leisure properties are thus exempt. Some indeed actually span the boundary of the zone. Where this occurs the correct procedure while the zone exists is to value the property, and then to apportion the value so as to exclude those parts of the property which are within the zone.

Different rules apply when the zone ceases to exist. (See valuation of former enterprise zone properties, pp. 134–5.)

Since property in an enterprise zone is excluded from liability by not being included in a rating list, it is not when first assessed, subject to the transitional rules because it will not satisfy the requirement of having been in a rating list on March 31 and April 1 1995 (pp. 115–18). Leisure property in a former enterprise zone area will pay rates in full in the normal manner.

Basis of valuation

The law governing the valuation for rating is contained in the Local Government Finance Act 1988, as amended by subsequent legislation and by Regulations made under those acts.

The main body of the law is contained in LGFA 1988 Schedule 6, as amended.

The basic definition of Rateable Value is paragraph 2(1) which reads:

The rateable value of a non-domestic hereditament none of which consists of domestic property and none of which is exempt from local non-domestic rating shall be taken to be an amount equal to the rent at which it is estimated the hereditament might reasonably be expected to let from year to year if the tenant undertook to pay all the usual tenant's rates and taxes and to bear the cost of the repairs and insurance and other expenses (if any) necessary to maintain the hereditament in a state to command that rent.

A hereditament is the unit of valuation for rating purposes.

Rents from year to year or periodic rent reviews

It can be seen from this definition, which is very similar to that under the old rating legislation, that the valuer is required to value the property at a rent which is very close to the traditional full repairing and insuring basis used in institutional leases, subject to the important caveat that the rent is to be from year to year. Courts and tribunals have considered on a number of occasions whether there is any difference between a rent from year to year and a rent fixed for the normal five-year term.

There has not yet been a decision of the Lands Tribunal in respect of an appeal against the 1990 Rating List, which addresses the difference between rents on the basis of the definition of rateable value and those actually negotiated in the open market, although some appeals involving these differences are awaiting a hearing.

The argument is that in times of inflation a landlord and tenant agreeing a rent fixed for five years, would agree a higher rent than if they were negotiating a rent from year to year. Decisions of the Lands Tribunal in the past have all related to valuations carried out in terms of the 1973 market place. This was at a time when not only were negotiations less sophisticated, but when interim rents had not been introduced.

The Lands Tribunal has yet to consider in any detail the market as it existed at April 1 1988 (the valuation date for the 1990 Rating List, or at April 1 1993 (see Antecedent Valuation Date, p. 131)), it has considered, however, what is meant by a rent "from year to year", and has decided that this must be assumed to include the additional words "with a reasonable expectation of continuance" (for details of cases consult Ryde on Rating). It follows that although it is a rent from year to year that the valuer is considering this is not simply a rent for only one year, but rather a lease for at least one year with the expectation of its being renewed annually.

Since in practice most leases have rents fixed for a period of between three and seven years, with five being the most common, the evidence upon which valuers can draw is derived from rents for a fixed term. A valuer who wishes to argue for a discount on the level of rent arrived at as a result of analysing these rents must produce evidence to support any discount.

Interim rents have traditionally been fixed at discounts of around 20% below that which is finally determined, this can not be evidence however of open market transactions, but rather of the development of professional practice under other legislation, which of itself ignores market forces. It is possible to discount evidence deduced from a lease with a five year rent review pattern to bring it into line with a rent from year to year, but it is difficult to prove that the result is accurate, through lack of evidence.

Repair

Leisure properties were valued until March 31 1990, on the assumption that the landlord was responsible for carrying out all repairs to the property, and the courts held that this meant that unless it could be proved that the state of the property was so bad that it would be uneconomical to repair it, the buildings were to be assumed to be in a fit state to command the rent.

The obligation is now on the tenant to repair the property, and valuers must consider the state of repair of the property. It is essential to bear in mind that the rateable value of the property is supposed to be the rent which would be agreed between a reasonable landlord and reasonable tenant on April 1 1993, having regard to the physical state of the property at the date when the proposal is made.

Repair needs to be distinguished from renewal. Whereas the basis of rateable value assumes that the tenant is responsible for all repair, he is not responsible for renewal or any other matter which would improve the state of the property. A swimming bath constructed in the 1930s may still have coal-fired boilers. These are likely to be well worn, and at the end of their useful life. The definition of rateable value would require the tenant to be responsible for repairing these boilers, which may be very expensive, and which would have a substantial effect on the rent he would be prepared to pay in 1993. Although the installation of modern gas-fired boilers might make economic sense, the valuer may not consider such a change as this would amount to renewal or improvement.

When considering whether or not the cost and frequency of repair would affect the rent which a landlord and tenant would agree on April 1 1993, the valuer must decide if the nature and extent of the repair is so substantial that the tenant would demand and the landlord would concede, a reduction in rent. There are five points which a valuer should bear in mind when considering if the state of repair would affect the rent:

1. *The landlord and tenant are reasonably minded people*. The Courts have held that when considering rateable value, the property must be assumed to be vacant and to let (for details of cases consult

Ryde on Rating), and the statutory definition requires the valuer to fix a rent from year to year with a reasonable expectation of continuance. The only way to consider this is to make the further assumption that neither the landlord nor the tenant will assume an intolerant position.

2. *The age of the building.* A modern air conditioned hotel will require far less maintenance than will an old Victorian hotel, even though it provides a similar quality of service. The Intercontinental Hotel at Hyde Park Corner and Claridge's Hotel in Brook Street, London, might be said to compete in the same hotel market, and offer a similar but different service to their potential customers. There is no doubt that the cost of maintaining the fabric and services to Claridge's will be far higher than that at the Intercontinental simply because of the difference in their ages. These additional costs must be taken into account by the valuer.

3. *Locality.* Clearly properties in city centres, or prestige districts, are maintained to higher standards than those in back street locations. A quick look at the difference between public houses or betting shops in these two locations will prove this point. A valuer should only consider the level of repair necessary to maintain the property in a condition consistent with the locality.

4. *Class of tenant of type of property.* Pubs in city centres are maintained to higher standards than are those in decaying residential districts. Modern marinas on the Hamble River are maintained to a standard far in excess of those which dry out alongside muddy backwaters. Where the difference in the level of annual repair can be shown to have a significant effect on the 1993 rental value then it may be taken into account.

5. *The property is maintained in such a way that only an average annual repair bill would be necessary in the future.* Maintenance is normally carried out to a property over a number of years. Some major items are only repaired once every 20 or more years. The lock gates at Brighton Marina might only require major maintenance every 25 years. Decoration is often on a five-year cycle. The valuer is required to consider a rent from year to year with a reasonable expectation of continuance. He must therefore consider these repairs on the basis that they are spread over a number of years and adopt the average cost. This may be more or less than the cost in 1993.

Additional implied covenants
While the definition of rateable value has changed slightly in the LGFA 1988, from that in previous legislation, the changes, other than those

relating to the obligation for repair, are of a minor nature, and it is reasonable to assume that the Lands Tribunal and Higher Courts will require valuers to continue to make the same additional assumptions when valuing property for rating purposes as they have in the past. The main reason for coming to this conclusion is that the rationale behind the decisions which gave rise to these assumptions still holds good.

Vacant and to let
The courts have ruled that in order to determine properly the rent at which it is estimated a property might let, it must be assumed that it is available "vacant and to let" (for details of the cases consult Ryde on Rating).

Hypothetical landlord and tenant
Since it is the property which is to be assessed for rates and not the occupier, the actual landlord and the actual tenant should be ignored, and the rent assessed on the basis of the rent which would be agreed between a willing hypothetical landlord and willing hypothetical tenant.

Alterations and improvements
The courts have decided that it is the property which exists at the date of valuation which is to be assessed, and not the property with the benefit of any planning permission, hope value or other improvement.

The rationale behind this is that rates are a tax on the annual right to occupy property, not upon its capital value, or potential.

Valuers must value property in the physical state it is in on the date that the rating list comes into force, is altered by the valuation officer or when an appeal is lodged. This principle of valuation, which is called valuing the property "Rebus sic Stantibus", means that it is valued in its existing state and no structural alterations can take place to the building. The consequence of this rule is that at the moment when one of these events occurs, the property and its surrounding environment is in effect frozen. This has been likened to taking a photograph of the property at that instant in time.

An example might be an hotel which is undergoing building works to an extension. Some of the bedrooms are incapable of beneficial occupation because their walls are being partly demolished and the plumbing disconnected, and other parts of the hotel are affected by builder's noise, dust and dirt. The valuation under LGFA Schedule 6 must be carried out on the assumption that these works will continue for the duration of the period for which the rent from year to year is being considered.

Date of valuation: Antecedent Valuation Date (AVD)

The Secretary of State is empowered under LGFA 1988 Schedule 6 paragraph (3) (b) to fix an antecedent date by reference to which all valuations under the rating list must be made. This was fixed for the purposes of the 1990 Rating List at April 1 1988, and for the 1995 Rating List at April 1 1993.

Assumptions as to valuation

Sub-paragraphs 4, 5, 6 and 6A require all valuations, whether made in order to prepare the list, to alter it, or to challenge the amount of any assessment in the list, to be made on the assumption that anything other than the matters set out in subparagraph 7 are as they existed or were assumed to be on the AVD (April 1 1988 or 1993 as appropriate).

The matters in sub-paragraph 7 are:

(a)   matters affecting the physical state or physical enjoyment of the hereditament,
(b)   the mode or category of occupation of the hereditament,
(c)   the quantity of minerals or other substances in or extracted from the hereditament.
(cc)* the quantity of refuse or waste material which is brought onto and permanently deposited on the hereditament.
(d)   matters affecting the physical state of the locality in which the hereditament is situated or which though not affecting the physical state of the locality, are nonetheless physically manifest there, and
(e)   the use or occupation of other premises situated in the locality of the hereditament.

The legislation therefore makes it clear that except for the matters set out above everything must be frozen for the life to the Rating List as it was on April 1 1993 (or April 1 for the 1988 List).

It is important to consider these five points when preparing a valuation for rating purposes, whether as VO in preparation or

---

* added by the Local Government and Finance Act 1989.

subsequent alteration of the list, or as an agent in pursuing an appeal against an assessment.

(a) Matters affecting the physical state, or physical enjoyment of the hereditament.

A leisure property must be valued in the physical state that it is in on the date that the Rating List came into force (currently 1st April 1995), when the Valuation Officer alters the list, or that it was in when a proposal was lodged challenging the assessment, but for the life of this Rating List at the level of rent passing on the AVD (1st April 1993).

Imagine a Bingo Club the first floor of which was damaged by fire on 4th June 1996. The fire damage is a matter affecting both the physical state and physical enjoyment of the property and may therefore properly be taken into account when valuing the property, but at the level of rent passing at AVD (1st April 1993). The ground floor of the club may be capable of use, but because the restaurant was on the first floor, and is unusable, and because the overheads of running the Club do not reduce in proportion to the number of seats available for play, is therefore less valuable than it was when it formed part of the entire club.

(b) The mode or category of occupation.

A Leisure Property must be valued for the use to which it is being put at the date when either the Valuation Officer alters the list, or on which a proposal is made to amend the list.

A golf club on the outskirts of a provincial town may have planning permission, and indeed building regulation approval, for the construction of a housing estate on it, however, while it continues to be used as a golf club it must be valued as such, even though its value as a site for housing would be far higher.

The reverse is also true. Imagine an amusement arcade, in a suburban residential street, where, not only has the planning permission expired, and the local planning authority obtained an enforcement notice requiring the property to revert to a store, but the landlord has also obtained a county court order for possession, and as at the valuation date (referred to as the material date) for the appeal the arcade was still trading. It must continue to be valued as an arcade, but at 1993 levels of value.

(c) and (cc) The quantity of minerals or other substances in, or extracted from, the hereditament, and the quantity of refuse or waste material which is brought onto and permanently deposited on the hereditament.

This is unlikely to affect a leisure property, but should a leisure property include activities of this nature, possibly a gravel pit part of which is used for water sports, then it must be remembered that the quantities of minerals extracted from the pit vary annually, and consequently the assessment. The valuation of the minerals or waste must be carried out however, at the level of value they would have achieved on April 1 1993.

(d) Matters relating to the physical state of the locality in which the hereditament is situated or which, though not affecting the physical state of the locality, are nevertheless physically manifest there.

This rule can be divided into two parts. First, anything which affects the physical state of the locality in which the property is located can be taken into account. An example of this might be a marina, which, because of severe silting in the adjoining river, has its access restricted, and can as a consequence only be used by smaller yachts with the result that it becomes less attractive. This would be a matter which affected the physical state of the locality and could be taken into account.

Second, anything which, though not affecting the physical state of the locality, is nonetheless physically manifest there, may also be taken in to account. This is a more difficult concept, but a similar example might be a marina which is located in a major commercial harbour. A change in the nature of the trade in the harbour resulted in its being used by larger and faster commercial ships. These larger vessels make access to the marina more dangerous, with the result that the demand for its berths has reduced. This is a change which though not affecting the physical state of the locality, is nonetheless physically manifest there, and can be taken into account.

(e) The use or occupation of other properties situated in the locality of the hereditament.

The use of other property in the locality must have been changed in a way which would have affected the rental value of the property had that change been in effect on April 1 1993. The opening of a major hotel in a small town, which only had one similar hotel on April 1 1993, might well be a change which could give rise to a reduction in the rateable value of the existing hotel.

Locality

The last two factors both refer to the locality of the hereditament. The locality is of particular importance, when considering leisure property. Locality may be defined as place, situation or district.

The locality of a property has yet to be considered by the tribunals, or the courts, however, it is thought to be broadly the catchment area of the property. Thus for a neighbourhood betting shop it would be a very small area bounded by the local streets, for an established County Golf Club, however, it may well be many hundreds of square miles.

The valuer must look at the property and use his judgement to determine the area that the property would be expected to serve. A change in this locality which was covered by matters in (d) or (e) discussed above can be taken into account, in so far as this would have affected its rental value in 1993.

Properties in former enterprise zone areas

Special rules apply to property located in former enterprise zone areas. It will be remembered that as the enterprise zone status expires, properties located within the former zone become liable to rates in the normal manner (pp. 125–6).

The Valuation for Rating (Former Enterprise Zone) Regulations 1995 (SI 1995/213), apply to these properties when their special status expires. Put simply, these regulations require valuers to value properties within the former zone on the basis that the zone never existed, but at 1993 levels of value.

Consider a cinema located in a former enterprise zone, which competes with a cinema just outside the former zone. It will have to be valued once the status expires at the level of value it would have commanded in 1993, assuming that the zone never existed. It follows from this that it must be valued having regard to the fact that there is another cinema on the edge of the existing zone with which it must compete for business. A straight comparison with the assessment of that cinema would be inappropriate, however, as that property will have been valued on the basis of LGFA 1988 Schedule 6 (set out above) which required the valuation to take into account the existence of the zone, as it had legally been in existence on the AVD (April 1 1993).

The value of the competing cinema would have reflected the fact that the cinema within the zone did not pay rates in 1993 and as a consequence had a commercial advantage being able either to reduce its prices to reflect its rate free position, or to make a greater profit or a combination of both, and following the decision of the House of Lords in *Addis Ltd* v *Clement (VO)* (1988), will have been reduced to the extent that this commercial advantage would have affected the rent.

It follows that the level of assessment of the cinema within the former zone may well be higher than that of its competitor outside the zone.

The abolition of the former enterprise zone is a legal or economic matter, and is not covered by any of the matters set out in paragraph 7 of the 6th Schedule. The competing cinema will continue to enjoy the competitive advantage of a lower rateable value until the new rating list comes into force in 2000.

Where a property spans the boundary of a former enterprise zone, that part of the property within the area of the former zone is to be valued on the assumption that the zone never existed, whereas that part outside the zone is to be valued on the basis that the zone still exists.

It will be remembered (pp. 125–6) that the correct approach to valuing a property which crosses an enterprise zone boundary while the zone still exists is to value the whole property, and then to apportion it between that part within the zone which has to be valued, and the remainder which is exempt.

The correct procedure when the zone expires is to value the whole of the property but in this case on the assumption that the enterprise zone never existed, and then to apportion the value between the area within the former zone and that outside it. The rateable value of a property which straddles the former enterprise zone boundary is then the sum of the rateable value of the property outside the zone as previously determined plus the rateable value of the property within the former enterprise zone. This is not correctly a valuation but the addition of two separate apportionments, however, this is the combined effect of the LGFA 1988 and the Valuation for Rating (Former Enterprise Zones) Regulations 1995.

Alterations and Appeals

Alterations to the rating list and appeals against assessments in the list are governed by Regulations made under the LGFA 1988 Section 55 as amended. The Regulations may at first sight seem daunting.

This is because they had been amended six times before they were codified in a single set of appeal regulations, which has also been amended and which has to be read in conjunction with the Material Day Regulations.

The current regulations are the Non-Domestic Rating (Alteration of Lists and Appeals) Regulations 1993 SI 1993/291, the Non-Domestic Rating (Alteration of Lists and Appeals) (Amendment) Regulations 1994 SI 1994/1809, the Non-Domestic Rating (Alteration of Lists and Appeals) (Amendment) Regulations 1995 SI 1995/609 and the Non-Domestic Rating (Material Day for List Alterations) Regulations 1992 SI 1992/556.

The rating list is now conclusive evidence of most matters relating to rate liability other than the identity of the occupier, or whether the property is in fact occupied rather than empty.

The lists are held by the local VO, and copies are maintained in the office of the local billing authority. These comprise the City of London, the London Boroughs, the former Metropolitan Boroughs, Borough or District Councils, and the Council for the Scilly Isles. Copies of local rating lists can be purchased in microfiche form from the Valuation Office and are available on CD Rom. The current rating lists are also available to subscribers through "Focus".

The local list can be inspected at any time during a normal working day. The list contains the address of the property, together with its assessment number, a brief description, and the rateable value ascribed to it. Where the date from which the rateable value became effective is other than April 1 1990, then that date is shown alongside the property. Any previous effective date is also shown together with the previous assessment. Finally, where the assessment has been determined by either the Valuation and Community Charge Tribunal, or the Lands Tribunal, a letter V or L will appear against the entry.

The VO has a duty to maintain the rating list for the billing authority. He may at any time alter the list, giving a date not earlier than that upon which the change giving rise to his alteration occurred. Where the Valuation Officer becomes aware of an error in the rating list which when corrected will increase its value he can only amend the assessment with effect from the day that he alters the list.

When a proposal is made in response to an alteration of the list by the VO, and it results in a change of assessment, then the alteration will have effect from the day on which the original disputed alteration took place.

A ratepayer may, within six months, request that an alteration be backdated. This provision exists because since the transitional regulations apply only to assessments in the rating list on April 1 1995, it can sometimes be to the ratepayers advantage to have the increased rateable value backdated.

It should be borne in mind that there are two situations in which the VO amends the list. The first is when he chooses of his own volition to alter the list, because for example a property which was in a single assessment is now two separate hereditaments.

The second follows either an agreement between the parties as a result of a proposal to alter the list, or as a result of a decision of the VT requiring the VO to amend the list.

The regulations do not distinguish between the two events. A ratepayer may choose to delay requiring the VO to backdate an alteration in the list until he has either reached agreement with the VO, or had a determination by the Tribunal. This is because valuation is an inexact science and the ratepayer or his valuer cannot be certain of the final value which will be agreed by the parties, or determined by a Tribunal when he initiates an appeal. Although there may be very little doubt in most instances, the ratepayer and his valuer are unlikely to be aware of the strength of the VO's evidence until this has been tested in negotiation.

There is, however, a practical difficulty with an application to have retrospective effect given to an agreement. This is because, although the VO gives formal notice of his initial alteration of the list, he does not give notice of his subsequent alteration of the list following either agreement between the parties or the determination of a tribunal, The VO is required by regulation to alter the list within six weeks of all parties having signed the forms of agreement.

This matter has been discussed informally by the RICS Rating and Local Taxation Group with both the Chief Executive's Office of the Valuation Office (CEO), and the Department of the Environment (DOE). It is understood that Ministers are considering a change in the current regulations, but meanwhile CEO have suggested that a notice in writing served on the local VO at the time that the forms of agreement are signed, or the determination of a tribunal is received should be sufficient.

The Non-Domestic Rating (Material Day) Regulations 1992 (SI 1992/556) deal with six situations where it is necessary to determine the "material day", and they must be read in conjunction with the Appeal Regulations.

(1) Where an alteration is made to correct an inaccuracy in the rating list from the day it came into force (1/4/95), it is 1st April 1995.

(2) Where the material day has to be decided in order to correct an inaccuracy which arose either when the VO made a previous alteration, or as a result of a proposal arising from a previous VO alteration, the material day is the day upon which the matters in sub-paragraph 7 of paragraph 2 to Schedule 6 occurred (see p. 131).

(3) Where the material day has to be established in order to include or delete a hereditament for any of the following reasons, the day upon which that event occurred.

  (a) The hereditament has come into existence or has ceased to exist.

  (b) The hereditament has ceased to be or has become domestic, or exempt.

  (c) The hereditament has ceased to be or is required to be shown in a central non-domestic rating list.

  (d) The hereditament has ceased to be or has become part of an authorities area, as a result of a change in that authorities area.

(4) Where a completion notice has been served, either:

  (a) the date in the notice, or

  (b) the date agreed or determined by the VT.

(5) Where the alteration is to give effect to part of the hereditament becoming or ceasing to be part of a domestic property or exempt, the day on which that change took place.

(6) In all other events the material day is the day upon which the proposal is served on the VO, or the VO alters the list.

References to property which comes into existence or ceases to exist include:

(a) property previously rated as a single hereditament which is now rated in parts;

(b) property previously in different hereditaments now assessed as a single hereditament;

(c) any part of a hereditament becoming part of another hereditament.

The Alterations and Appeal Regulations must be read in conjunction with the Material Day Regulations. An example of how these work might be a golf club where building work commenced on an extension to the club house in May 1995. The work was completed in January 1996, and during a party in mid-February to celebrate the opening of the property the party got out of control and the building caught fire.

The assessment in the rating list on April 1 1995 can be appealed at any time up to March 31 2001. Any appeal against the assessment of the club house on the grounds that part of it is unusable because of building works must be made whilst those works are continuing. It cannot be made either before the work commences or after they have been completed.

The assessment of the club could be increased by the VO following the completion of the extension provided that he had altered the rating list by the date when the fire occurred. The rate payer may appeal against this revised entry. He may also lodge a further appeal against the assessment on the grounds that part of the premises are incapable of occupation because of fire damage. This appeal must be lodged after the fire but before the damage is put right.

The VO is required to advise the person in rateable occupation (or where the property is empty the person entitled to possession), that he has amended the rating list within six weeks of making an alteration to the list. Where he fails to advise the ratepayer within six weeks, this does not make the alteration invalid, but simply delays the start of the period during which appeals against an alteration to the list can be made.

When an appeal may be made

A ratepayer or an interested person may appeal against an assessment by serving a proposal on the Valuation Officer seeking to amend the rating list. An interested person which will include the owner is defined in the Non-Domestic Rating (Alteration of Lists and Appeals) Regulations 1993 (1995 Regs) paragraph 2 (b) as meaning:

(i)   the occupier;
(ii) Any other person (other than a mortgagee not being in possession) having in any part of the hereditament either a legal estate, or an equitable interest such as would entitle him (after the cessation of any prior interest) to possession of the hereditament or any part of it; and
(iii) any person having a qualifying connection with any person described in sub-paragraph (i) or (ii).

Appeals can be made at any time up to and including March 31 2001 (and later in certain circumstances). 1995 Regs paragraph 4A(1).

(a) the rateable value shown in the list for a hereditament was inaccurate on the day it was compiled;

(b) the rateable value shown in the list for a hereditament is inaccurate by reason of a material change of circumstance which occurred on or after the day on which the list was compiled;

(c) the rateable value shown in the list for a hereditament is inaccurate by reason of an alteration made by the valuation officer is or has been inaccurate;

(d) the rateable value or any other information shown in the list for a hereditament is shown, by reason of a decision in relation to another hereditament of a valuation tribunal, the Lands Tribunal or a court determining an appeal or application for review from either such tribunal, to be or to have been inaccurate;

(e) the day from which an alteration is shown in the list as having effect is wrong;

(f) a hereditament not shown in the list ought to be shown in that list;

(g) a hereditament shown in the list ought not to be shown in that list;

(h) the list should show that some part of a hereditament which is shown in the list is domestic property or is exempt from non-domestic rating but does not do so;

(i) the list should show that some part of a hereditament which is shown in the list is domestic or is exempt from non-domestic rating but does so;

(j) property which is shown in the list as more than one hereditament ought to be shown as one or more different hereditaments;

(k) property which is shown in the list as one hereditament ought to be shown as more than one hereditament:

(l) the address shown in the list for a hereditament is wrong;

(m) the description shown in the list for a hereditament is wrong;

(n) any statement required to be made about the hereditament under section 42 of the Local Government Finance Act 1988 has been omitted from the list.

Unlike earlier regulations these restrict proposals to the 14 grounds set out above. A proposal which does not specify one of the grounds (a) to (n) will be invalid.

Regulation 4(5) prevents a further proposal being made under 4(1)(c) when the Valuation Officer alters the list to comply with a determination of a tribunal or court.

Regulation 4(6) prevents a proposal being made other than on the grounds of 1(d) where a tribunal has already considered the same facts in relation to the same hereditament.

There are two situations where the time limit under Regulation

4B(1) of March 31, 2001 can be extended. The first under regulation 4B(2) is where the Valuation Officer amends the list in late 1999 or early 2000 or after it has ceased to have effect, when the time limit is extended to one year after the alteration takes place. The second under regulation 4B(3) is where a tribunal orders the Valuation Officer to alter the rating list either during the last year of the list, or after it has ceased to have effect and the ratepayer believes that as result of this alteration the assessment of his property is wrong. The time limit is extended for one year after the date of the decision of the tribunal.

How to lodge a proposal and make an appeal

An appeal is made by lodging a formal proposal with the Valuation Officer to amend the rating list. It does not need to be made in any particular form, although the Valuation Office will provide a printed form on request. Regulation 5A set out certain requirements which must be satisfied. It must be in writing, however, and served on the Valuation Officer (reg 5A(1)). It must state the name and address of the proposer and the capacity in which he makes the proposal (reg 5(A)(a)). It must identify the property (reg 5A(b)), show the proposed change (reg 5A(c), and include the grounds or circumstances giving rise to the proposal ((a) to (n) above) (reg 5A(1)(d)(i), (ii), or (iii) or under reg 5A(1)(d) (iv)) where the proposal arises as a result of a tribunal or court decision, the identity of the hereditament, the name of the tribunal or court, the date of that decision, why that decision is relevant and the reasons for believing in the light of that decision the rateable value or other information is wrong. Where the effective date is being challenged the date which the proposer is contending should be substituted must be stated (reg 5A(1)(v)).

When a proposal has been served on the Valuation Officer, he has three months in which to decide whether to accept the proposal or agree a compromise with the ratepayer. The Valuation Officer must, at the end of this period – or sooner if he believes agreement cannot be reached with the ratepayer – send the papers relating to the appeal to the Valuation Tribunal. This constitutes an appeal. It is open to the Valuation Officer and the ratepayer to settle the appeal at any time between the service of a proposal and the tribunal hearing. The settlement must be in writing. If the proposal was made by the billing authority, by a previous occupier, or by the owner, then the agreement of the current ratepayer must be obtained to any settlement. Any appeal that is unresolved will be determined by the tribunal.

Billing authority as owner or occupier

Local rating authorities responsible for rate collection were renamed by the LGFA 1988 Charging Authorities. Their name was changed again under the LGFA 1992 to Billing Authorities. Their responsibilities for collection of NNDR are very similar to those of the old rating authorities prior to April 1 1992, except that all the income they receive is payable (with the exception of that collected by the Corporation of London) to the central rate pools maintained by the Department of the Environment and the Welsh Office.

Where a billing authority is an owner or occupier, it has the same rights as any other owner or occupier to appeal in respect of property it owns or occupies. Its right to make a proposal on other grounds are limited under regulation 4A(3) to:

(b) the rateable value shown in the list for a hereditament is inaccurate by reason of a material change of circumstance which occurred on or after the day on which the list was compiled;

(d) the rateable value or any other information shown in the list for a hereditament is shown, by reason of a decision in relation to another hereditament of a valuation tribunal, the Lands Tribunal or a court determining an appeal or application for review from either such tribunal, to be to have been inaccurate;

(f) a hereditament not shown in the list ought to be shown in that list;

(g) a hereditament shown in the list ought not to be shown in that list;

(h) the list should show that some part of a hereditament which is shown in the list is domestic property or is exempt from non-domestic rating but does not do so;

(i) the list should show that some part of a hereditament which is shown in the list is domestic or is exempt from non-domestic rating but does so.

Valuation Tribunals and Lands Tribunal

Unresolved appeals are heard first by the Valuation Tribunal (VT). There is a right of appeal against most decisions of the VT to the Lands Tribunal (LT), which provides a fresh hearing and from which there is only a right of appeal to the Court of Appeal and the House of Lords on matters of law.

A text book on the valuation and law of leisure property is not the place for a detailed explanation of the procedure before the VT or LT, and valuers contemplating taking an appeal to a hearing before either tribunal are recommended to read a rating text book.

Methods of valuation

It will be remembered from an earlier section that the basis of valuation for rating is set out in the LGFA 1988 Schedule 6. The main subparagraph is (2)(1) which reads:

The rateable value of a non-domestic hereditament none of which consists of domestic property and none of which is exempt from local non-domestic rating shall be taken to be an amount equal to the rent at which it is estimated the hereditament might reasonably be expected to let from year to year if the tenant undertook to pay all usual tenant's rates and taxes and to bear the cost of the repairs and insurance and the other expense (if any) necessary to maintain the hereditament in a state to command that rent.

Exceptions to the normal rules
This basis of valuation applies to all classes of property other than those which fall to be valued by statutory formulae (dealt with below), caravan and caravan sites, and land used for the breeding and rearing of horses or ponies, or for marinas for which special rules also apply. These are dealt with on p. 167.

Composite and exempt property
Property which is a mixture of domestic accommodation and non-domestic accommodation (which is referred to as composite property in the legislation), or which is a mixture of non-domestic, or composite property and exempt property, is the subject of special additional rules which must be applied to allow for the fact that part is domestic or exempt. These rules are dealt with on pp. 198–202.

Formulae valuations
Traditionally certain properties primarily occupied by the old statutory undertakers, were valued for rating purposes by reference to a formula. The rationale behind this special legislation would seem to have been that these undertakings were never let in the open market, and were in any case in public ownership, and it was felt therefore that it was reasonable to use a formula to arrive at an assessment upon which rates could be levied.

These ideas have become outdated as a result of the sale of most of the old statutory undertakers into private ownership. Ministers have indicated their intention to return most of the properties currently valued by formulae to conventional rating valuation with effect from the 2000 revaluation. The formulae remain however, by virtue of regulations drawn up under LGFA 1988 Schedule 6 paragraph (1) (9) and if a property is of a class which is covered by the description of the property set out in these regulations then it must be assessed by the rules in that formula. This may result in a higher or a lower level of assessment than would be arrived at had the property been assessed in the normal way. There is no right of appeal against either being assessed by way of a formula, or the rateable value which results, except to argue that the property is not covered by the regulation, and should be assessed in the normal manner.

It may seem unnecessary to include valuation by statutory formula in a text book on leisure property, but some major leisure facilities are valued in this way. Brighton Marina, for instance is assessed under the formula set out in the Docks and Harbours (Rateable Values) (Amendment) Order 1994 SI 1994/3280.

Valuers who have to advise ratepayers who occupy property assessed on a formula are recommended to read the appropriate order very carefully, as it may be possible so to organise the affairs of the ratepayer as to reduce certain figures used in the formula thus keeping the client's liability to a minimum.

Valuation tools

The LGFA 1988 requires Valuation Officers to assess for all property, other than the exceptions set out above, the rent "at which it is estimated the property might reasonably be expected to let" on April 1 1993, on the assumptions set out above and discussed on pp. 126–34. The Act does not attempt to tell the valuer how to set about achieving this requirement. Fortunately valuers have been wrestling with these and similar concepts since rating was established in 1601, and many of the approaches used have been considered in depth, and commented upon by the various courts over the years.

Very few properties were let on leases from year to year from April 1 1993, on the assumptions required by the LGFA 1988 Schedule 6, and as a result valuers have to use an indirect approach to arrive at an assessment which corresponds with the basis of rateable value.

There are three conventional approaches which have been used for many years to achieve these statutory requirements, and which have found favour with the Lands Tribunal and higher courts. These are not, however, set in stone and need constantly to be adjusted to accommodate modern market practice, and changes in both the legislation relating to that particular type of property, and in rating law.

A valuer considering the rating assessment of a leisure property must be familiar with the three conventional approaches to rating valuation which are described later. He should in addition be aware of the way in which the market worked at the AVD (April 1 1993), (as explained on p. 131). Finally he should enquire about any discussions and agreement as to the accepted practice in relation to the valuation for rating of particular classes of property, which may have been entered into by the Chief Executive's Offices (CEO) of the VO, and the Trade Association representing that part of the leisure industry (see p. 162–3).

Valuers should remember that markets are constantly changing, and that what was the normal practice on April 1 1988 (the valuation date for the last rating list) may be very different from what was normal practice in April 1993, and that by April 1998 (the valuation date for the 2000 rating list) it may well have changed again.

The three conventional approaches are as follows:

The rental valuation Some classes of leisure property, particularly in urban areas, let frequently in the open market. These include betting shops, some bingo halls and both fast food and conventional restaurants.

Rating valuers do not create market values nor should they, except in the last resort, set about designing the method by which rents for a class of leisure property should be analysed, and the property valued.

The marketplace determines value, and surveyors practising in that marketplace are in the best place to advise on how rents were fixed. A shop with planning permission for use as a betting shop may or may not, have commanded a premium over other shops in the neighbourhood. This is a matter of evidence.

Where the appeal property is let in the open market, then the rating valuer will have to make the necessary adjustments to the actual rent to allow for the difference between the rent passing and the basis of rateable value. He should then compare the assessment arrived at after making these adjustments with the rent of similar properties in the locality to ensure that the assessment is comparable.

Comparable evidence Although the appeal property may be of a type which normally lets in the open market, the property itself may be freehold or held on a lease which has no relationship to the basis of rateable value. Under these circumstances it is necessary to analyse the assessments of as similar or comparable a property as can be found in order to deduce a basis of valuation which can then be applied to the property to be valued.

The rating valuer should consult his colleagues in the market place, and the trade association representing his client to establish the best method of analysis and the unit of measurement to be applied. He should analyse as many comparable properties as possible. Since valuation is an inexact science he would expect to obtain a variety of results, from which he would hope to deduce a market average which he could then apply to the property he has to value.

The courts have held over the years that it is not the actual rent of the property agreed between the landlord and tenant which is to be assessed, but rather the rent which would be agreed between the hypothetical landlord and hypothetical tenant. It follows, therefore, that the rent at which the actual tenant holds the property is not necessarily the best evidence of the rateable value. The rateable value may be either higher or lower than the actual rent. There is no doubt, however, that the actual rent passing in respect of the property, particularly if it is close to the AVD, and is close to the rateable value definition, is very good evidence of its rateable value, and will require strong conflicting evidence if the tribunal is to be persuaded to disregard it.

Guidance on the market approach is set out in the other sections, and in some of the agreements reached with the Chief Executives Office as set out on pp. 166–97.

It is fundamentally important that the valuer understands the principles behind the method of analysis used, and ensures that whatever method he uses in respect of comparable properties he applies it to the property he is valuing.

Units of comparison can vary enormously. Examples include:

- Prices per square foot in restaurants,
- A zoning approach for some fast food premises,
- A price per barrel of beer sold in public houses,
- A price per foot of usable mooring in a marina,
- A price per table in a snooker hall,
- A price per double room with bath in an hotel.

It must be remembered that any method of valuation is only a tool and that the valuer must stand back and look at the resulting assessment to decide if the figure produced properly reflects the value required by the basis of rateable value. He should make whatever adjustments he believes are necessary to ensure that the valuation corresponds with the statutory basis.

Since the basis of rateable value requires the valuer to provide an estimate of the rent at which the property might reasonably be expected to let, it is not surprising that the Lands Tribunal have time and again preferred valuations arrived at on a rental approach to those deduced by other means.

Some classes of property either never let, or let so infrequently or on terms so far from the basis of rateable value as to be of very little help to the rating surveyor in preparing a valuation in accordance with the basis of rateable value.

Two methods of valuation have been developed to deal with properties which do not normally let in the open market. Both need to be used with skill and adjusted to take into account the particular idiosyncrasies of the particular leisure trade. Guidance on how this may be achieved can be obtained from the agreements reached between the Trade Association and the CEO.

Profits test valuation This is the method used to value properties that generate cash on site, and is the most common approach used to value leisure properties for rating. It has been used in the preparation of valuations for hotels, theatres, golf courses, bingo halls, discotheques and marinas. This valuation technique starts from the premise that there is a relationship between the rent that the hypothetical landlord and tenant of property would be prepared to agree and the income which can be derived from the property.

This technique is used in the marketplace and has been explained in detail in earlier chapters on the valuation of various classes of leisure property. It must be refined slightly when valuing leisure property for rating purposes as what is required is an assessment in terms of rateable value as at the AVD.

A detailed example of a profits valuation of a marina is given later, but the object is to derive a net income from the property (referred to as the divisible balance), after allowing for the normal operating expenses and interest on capital. This divisible balance can then be divided between the entrepreneur (or tenant) as profit and the landlord as rent.

The division between the two will vary according to the level of risk. The riskier the leisure activity, the higher the share of the divisible balance required by the entrepreneur, who it must be remembered is taking the greater risk. Should the leisure activity get into difficulty it is the entrepreneur's profit which will be squeezed first, and it is only when his reserves are exhausted that the landlord will suffer. Figures vary, but the entrepreneur's (tenant's) share is normally in the range of 60–80%.

These percentages have been arrived at by analysing the profits of companies who occupy leisure property on leases which are as close as possible to the basis of rateable value at the AVD. The percentages derived in this manner have to be adjusted when used in individual profits valuations to allow for differences in location, type of property and the potential market which the leisure property will serve. The valuer's skill, experience and judgement have to be used to ensure that the correct percentage is applied.

Example: A profits valuation of a marina

The basic approach to a profits valuation is the same whatever type of leisure property is to be valued. An example of a profits valuation of a marina on the south coast of England demonstrates how the valuation is prepared.

Ideally the valuer will have access to the management accounts for the three years ending, prior to the AVD, and if possible the monthly management accounts for the period from the last year end to the AVD. This is because the valuer must consider the rent at which the property would let at the AVD. The hypothetical landlord and tenant would not have information at the AVD, which has become available as a result of subsequent trading. They would be expected, however, to have the perception of future prospects for trade which were present in the market at that time. (Even if with the benefit of hindsight this perception proved incorrect.)

It may prove necessary to adjust the valuation arrived at by means of the profits test, because the property or its environment had changed physically between April 1988 (AVD), and April 1990, the date when the rating list came into force. This can be achieved by the comparable method of valuation (see below).

Management Accounts

The Management Accounts for a typical marina might look something like this.

Income	Year ending	31/3/91	31/3/92	31/3/93
Receipts		£	£	£
Moorings		605,251	657,271	701,359
Sales of electricity		14,712	17,361	18,702

Brokerage commission	22,070	17,006	23,379
Rents			
Chandlery	30,000	70,000	70,000
Workshops	80,000	80,000	121,600
Gross income	752,033	841,638	935,040
Expenditure			
Wages, NI etc	296,879	331,623	357,359
General insurance	500	575	620
Property insurance	19,700	21,900	22,250
Cleaning	2,000	2,500	3,000
Printing and stationery	1,810	1,020	3,556
Telephone	925	1,076	1,183
Subscriptions	1,100	1,100	1,400
Auditors fees	10,500	20,000	21,000
Repairs and renewals	60,500	50,760	58,470
Legal and professional	3,500	10,175	12,237
Bank charges	22,771	28,000	45,520
Sundry expenses	11,756	18,950	20,071
Rates	31,186	33,712	37,200
Rent for part of river bed	4,000	4,000	6,500
Gross expenditure	470,887	534,491	596,818
Gross profit	281,146	307,147	338,222

A number of adjustments must be made before these accounts can be used to arrive at an assessment of rateable value.

Adjustments Care must be taken where part of the marina is domestic. There are two ways of dealing with this problem. The first is to ensure that both income and expenditure are adjusted to exclude those elements which apply to the domestic portion. The second is to value the whole marina, and then to apportion the assessment between the domestic and non-domestic parts. Properly used, both methods should achieve the same result. The second is, however, probably the safest approach.

It has been assumed for the purposes of this example that none of the marina is domestic.

Income The valuer is only interested in the income generated from the hereditament he is valuing. It follows, therefore, that he should include the income from the moorings as this arises from the hereditament. He should likewise include the income from the sale of electricity, as this is also generated from the marina.

The brokerage commission on the other hand should be ignored because many brokerages are sub let and are separately valued at a price per square metre.

The rents received from the chandlery and the workshops should also be ignored as these will be in a separate occupation and separately assessed.

The valuer must decide what income he would have anticipated that the marina would generate in 1993, in the light of the information he had on the receipts for this property for the preceding three years, his experience of other similar properties and allowing for the perception of the market in late March 1993.

Expenditure The expenditure should be checked to ensure that it does not include any element which would not be incurred by the hypothetical tenant. Examples of such expenditure might include a wife's salary in a privately-owned marina.

All the items shown with the exception of bank charges, and rent for part of the river bed should properly be deducted.

It is important, however, to consider each item and after making any adjustments for the reasons explained above the valuer must calculate the anticipated expenditure for the marina, bearing in mind its past history, and the view which a hypothetical tenant might reasonably arrive at with the knowledge available to him of increases in cost which had already been announced in late March 1993.

The reasons for ignoring bank charges is that a compensating charge is deducted later and is explained under the heading of tenants' capital. The rent of the river bed should be ignored as the purpose of the profits valuation is to arrive at the rent at which the whole marina might let.

It could be argued that the rates should be ignored and an algebraic calculation carried out using the 1995 rateable value which is of course equivalent to the 1993 rent and the UBR in 1995/96. This is, in the author's view, incorrect because despite the advice which they were receiving at the time, marina operators were in 1993 ignoring the potential changes they were going to face in 1995/96. Even if this approach were to be adopted, it would have to be adjusted for the transitional regulations. It is the expenditure in the 1993 year that the valuer must consider, as it is a rent for one year commencing on

April 1 1993 that he is required to assess. The effect of the change in rate liability in 1995/96 may affect the rent in that year, but this is irrelevant for the purposes of fixing the 1993 rental value.

It is a moot point whether there should at this stage be a further deduction to allow for depreciation. The difficulty is that this must to some extent overlap with the deduction for repairs and renewals. The valuer will need to discuss this matter with his client, and then make any appropriate adjustment as necessary.

The adjusted income less the adjusted expenditure will give the "Net profit for Rating Purposes".

The tenant will have invested capital in his marina operation in addition to expenditure on the property. This will include items of plant, furniture and other equipment which he requires to run his business. Whilst the presence of these investments will increase the value of the marina as a business they do not affect the value of the property. He will also have had to inject working capital or cash into the business.

A deduction must be made from this figure to allow for the interest on the capital tied up in the business. Capital comprises three groups of assets.

1. The value of the chattels used in the business, for example a travel hoist, the launch used to move boats around the marina, as well as furniture and typewriters etc.
2. Disposable items used in the business for example stocks of notepaper and items used for repairs.
3. The working capital or cash held in the business. This will as a rule of thumb be equal to around three months' income.

The sum arrived at after deducting the interest on tenant's capital from the net profit for rating purposes is known as the "devisable balance".

This must be divided between rent for the landlord and profit for the entrepreneur. The entrepreneur or tenant will receive the larger share because he is carrying the bigger risk. If things do not go well it is the tenant who is "squeezed" first. The landlord normally only suffers when the tenant's resources are exhausted and he is no longer able to meet the rent.

The division between landlord and tenant depends on how risky the business is. The landlord's share, however, is normally in the range 15–40% depending on risk.

The valuation The valuation may then look something like this:

Anticipated income for year ending 31/3/94

Moorings	£750,000
Sales of electricity	£ 20,000
Gross income	£770,000

Anticipated expenditure for the year ending 31/3/94

Wages, NI etc	£380,000
General insurance	£ 650
Property insurance*	£ 1,875
Light and heat	£ 23,500
Cleaning	£ 3,500
Printing and stationery	£ 2,200
Telephone	£ 1,500
Subscriptions	£ 1,400
Auditors fees	£ 22,500
Repairs and renewals**	£ 30,000
Legal and professional	£ 10,500
Bad debts	£ 3,500
Sundry expenses	£ 22,000
Rates	£ 40,920
Gross expenditure	£544,045
Net trading profit for rating purposes	£225,955

*The property insurance has been adjusted to exclude the costs of insuring those parts of the property which are sublet.
**The repairs and renewals were larger than normal during the last years because of the necessity of carrying out accumulated repairs. The figure used reflects the average annual anticipated cost of future repairs.

Tenant's chattels, travel hoist, tender, furniture etc	£450,000
Stocks of disposable items	£ 9,525
Working capital 3 months' income	£197,500
	£657,025
Say 5% =	£ 32,851
Net trading profit for rating purposes	£225,955
Less interest on capital	£ 32,851

Devisable balance	£193,104
Landlords' share or rent say 30%	£ 57,931
Rateable value say	£ 58,000

Analysis Assume that the marina has a mooring capacity of 798 metres (see basis of valuation agreement on p. 182–3), or 218 berths. The areas of the remaining facilities in square metres are: harbour office, 25.41 showers and WCs, 35.9; open-sided Dutch-barn type building used for winter boat storage, 403.6. There is an area of gravel hard standing which is used for car parking in the summer, but part of which is used for boat storage in winter. This area will park 315 cars. The value of similar offices in this area is £20 per square metre, the Dutch barn £10 and car parking £25 per space.

There is an agreement between CEO and valuers representing the Yacht Harbours Association on the approach to analysing marina assessments (see p. 182–3).

A price per metre of usable mooring can be deduced from the rateable value using the agreed approach.

Rateable value			£58,000
Less – Dutch Barn 403.6 sq m @ £10		£4,036	
– Harbour Master's Office and Shower/WC			
(reflected in berth value)			
– Car Spaces	315		
less			
reflected spaces			
50% of berths	109		
	206 @ £25 = £5,150		£ 9,186
Net value attributable to moorings			£48,814

Total length of usable mooring 798 metres
Value of mooring per metre run = £61.17 (Note 12% of this figure has been agreed by the TYHA and CEO as representing the rental value of the marina).

Comparable valuation It can be seen from this example that having prepared full profits valuations for as many marinas as the valuer has the evidence in terms of full accounts, it is possible to analyse these in terms of prices per metre run of usable moorings, with other values on additional facilities, such as offices, workshops etc, which can then be used to value other marinas in the area where this information is not available.

Despite being part of the Inland Revenue the VO does not have access to detailed accounts, returned to the Inspector of Taxes, relating to individual ratepayers' businesses. He will have access to figures relating to average profits for different classes of leisure property. Although he may have difficulty in using this information in a formal appeal it does help him check the accuracy of information provided to him by ratepayers. Most accounts filed either with the Inspector of Taxes, or at Companies House are, in any case, of little value in preparing a profits valuation as they provide inadequate information, and in any case may cover a group of properties or matters which bear no relation to the operation of the property to be valued. The valuer needs access to the management accounts of the operation.

Forms of return The VO has powers under the LGFA 1988 section 62 – Schedule 9 as amended to require ratepayers to provide information which he believes will assist him in carrying out his functions. (This is dealt with in more detail on p. 159–60.)

Where the VO requires more information he will serve on the ratepayer a special form setting out the information he requires. The powers available to and the extent of the information the VO may request have been substantially increased by the LGFA 1989. These extended powers were not available when most information was being sought for the 1990 revaluation, and to date VO does not appear to have felt it necessary to use his more draconian powers, or to extend the range of information he has required in respect of any class of property.

The special questionnaires sent to occupiers of leisure property require the occupier to provide details of the volume or value of trade carried out at the property over normally the three years preceding the AVD, although forms sent out since then may request more up to date information. The type of question asked might include, for example, the total income of an hotel in terms of food, drink and room hire, or the quantity of beer and spirits sold at a pub.

Receipts or income valuation

The valuation office may use this information on receipts to prepare valuations of individual leisure properties. The method is to value a number of beacon properties, either using a rental approach, or using a full profits valuation. The assessments of these beacon properties are then analysed in terms of their gross income, or the quantity of liquor sold to deduce scales of value which can be used to value other similar properties of the same class.

The difficulty with this approach is that income is only part of the equation, and it is equally important for the valuer to look at expenditure. It is not possible to value a property on the profits basis without looking at both.

The receipts approach is often used by valuers to compare one property with another of a similar class. This technique must, however, be used with great care, because, for example, simply to look at a marina's income is a very inaccurate and dangerous approach.

The level of income which a marina generates depends on its location, and the quality of service it provides. The costs of running the marina, however, depend on geographical factors such as its exposure to the elements, cost of dredging and maintenance of expensive items such as lock gates.

Goodwill

It must be remembered that the basis of rateable value requires the valuer to estimate the rent at which the property might reasonably be expected to let on a rent from year to year at the AVD, and on the other assumptions required by the LGFA 1988 Schedule 6. The Courts have added some additional assumptions to the statutory basis, the more important of which are that the property must be considered to be vacant and to let and that the transaction takes place between a willing hypothetical landlord and a willing hypothetical tenant.

The importance of this is that it is the property not the occupier which is to be valued with all it benefits and disadvantages.

A valuer must ensure that it is the property he is valuing and not the charisma or personal goodwill of the tenant. A public house may be very successful because the licensee is a famous retired sports personality. The valuer should discount the actual trade in this instance to the level he believes would be maintained by the hypothetical tenant. This level of business is referred to as the maintainable trade. This adjustment need not only be made in one direction. Where a valuer believes that the trade is artificially reduced to a level below that which the hypothetical tenant would achieve in the same property, and in the same marketplace, then he may increase it.

Contractor's test valuation

The contractor's test valuation is based broadly on the concept that if the entrepreneur could not rent a property he would have to build it. The method starts with the cost of constructing the property, and after applying a number of safeguards and adjustments, uses these costs to deduce a rent in terms of rateable value.

It is only appropriate to use the contractor's test to value property which is not normally let in the open market, and which does not in itself generate income, which would enable a profits test valuation to be carried out. It will be seen that this method relies on a number of assumptions and as result, even when prepared by experienced valuers, substantial differences in value can result. It has been considered by the Lands Tribunal on a number of occasions, and for this reason has been looked on unfavourably. The Tribunal has made it clear that, given the choice, it prefers a valuation prepared on one of the other approaches. The contractor's test is as a result often referred to as the valuation of last resort. Contractor's test valuations have traditionally been used to prepare valuations of many local authority leisure properties and many have been valued for the 1995 rating list using this approach. The justification for this would appear to be that these properties were almost always owned freehold by the council, and were not run on a commercial basis. This meant that traditionally there was little or no rental evidence and a profits valuation would not provide any meaningful valuation.

It is doubtful whether this argument is sustainable today or indeed was sustainable at the AVD. The advent of major leisure companies covering almost all aspects of the industry, and the move towards compulsory competitive tendering, all cast doubt on the approach. Appeals which should decide the correct method of valuation for major Local Authority leisure property are under appeal to the Lands Tribunal at the time this book is being printed.

There may still be some properties for which there is no market, and the contractor's test is the only method available by which to arrive at a rent in terms of rateable value.

The contractor's test was considered at length by the Lands Tribunal, the Court of Appeal and the House of Lords, in 1986, when hearing the case of *Imperial College of Science and Technology* v *Ebdon (VO) & Westminster City Council*. It was accepted by the Court of Appeal in that case that there are five stages to this method.

Stage 1: Estimate replacement cost

The valuer must estimate the cost of constructing a modern replacement building to provide similar facilities as those which exist in the property to be valued, including any rateable plant and machinery contained within the building as at the AVD.

This means that where a valuer is considering a 1930 leisure centre which contains a swimming pool, four squash courts, an indoor tennis court, and gymnasium, as well as car parking for 25 cars and administrative offices, he needs to calculate the cost of providing the same facilities, ie a swimming pool, four squash courts, the indoor tennis court and the gymnasium as at the AVD. He would have to consider the number of car parking spaces and administrative offices required to run this complex. It would be the cost of constructing this modern complex that he would have to ascertain.

The plant and other rateable equipment contained within the complex, ie boilers, water treatment plant etc would be the state of the art available at the AVD. This will often require the advice of architects and quantity surveyors.

Stage 2: Adjusted replacement cost (or effective capital value)

The valuer must then make appropriate adjustments to the replacement capital cost of the building to allow for its age and obsolescence. This is normally done by way of an end allowance, which is expressed as a percentage. The percentage adjustment can be very high and depend on the type of property, the state of its plant and machinery, and its age.

Stage 3: Capital value of the site

The valuer must then add the value of the land on which the property stands. The value of the land must be that for the purpose for which the property is used and no value relating to an existing planning permission, or hope value for alternative use may be included. The value of the land must be taken as at the AVD.

Stage 4: Annual rental equivalent

The adjusted replacement cost of the land and buildings must be reduced to an annual rental equivalent by applying a decapitalisation rate. This stage in the valuation process was the source of considerable litigation in the past, but for the 1990 Rating List has been fixed by the Non-Domestic Rating (Miscellaneous Provisions) (No. 2) Regulations 1994/3122 at 5.5% (3.67% for educational establishments and hospitals).

Stage 5: The stand back and look stage
The valuer must now consider the resulting value and decide if this is the correct valuation for rating purposes as required by the LGFA 1988 Schedule 6.

This is a most important stage, particularly with leisure property, where local authority leisure properties compete in the market with private facilities. It must be remembered that the property has to be valued vacant and to let at the AVD. There is therefore no assumption that the properly is to be occupied by the local authority. Comparison of the assessments of leisure facilities in the private sector with those in public control often show substantial differences in value. Unless these can be attributed to some feature relating to the age, construction or locality of the property, then there is something wrong with one or both of the valuations.

The fault may lie with either group of valuations or both, however, since the contractor's test valuation normally requires the greatest number adjustments involving valuer's opinion, it is likely that it is this valuation rather than that prepared on another approach which needs further adjustment.

The contractor's test valuation may require adjustment in either direction to bring it into line.

Plant and machinery

Plant and machinery is rateable if it is named in the Valuation for Rating (Plant & Machinery) Regulations 1994 SI 1994/2680. Many items of plant named in these regulations are part and parcel of any building. These relate to the supply of light, power, heating, ventilation and other services to the building, and are reflected in any normal approach to valuation. Indeed to try and value the building without these services would be difficult. Most of the other plant contained within a leisure property is rateable, lifts, hot water boilers, etc.

A text book on the valuation of leisure property is not the place for a detailed explanation of the law and practice relating to the valuation of plant and machinery, and the valuer should consult a specialist text book.

Central discussions with the Chief Executive's Office, Valuation Office Agency Inland Revenue (CEO)

The valuation office is an executive agency of the Inland Revenue and is charged with the responsibility of preparing, maintaining and defending the Rating Lists in England and Wales. The VOA is divided into a regional network of offices, covering the whole of the country. Each office is responsible for one or more billing authority areas. The organisation of the VOA is currently undergoing major reorganisation as it faces the challenges of a changing market and its agency status.

The officer in charge is the valuation officer (VO) for the billing authority areas covered by his office. The VO is a statutory officer appointed by the Commissioners of Inland Revenue under LGFA 1988 Section 61. He is charged under Section 41 of that Act with the responsibility to prepare and maintain both the rating list which came into force on April 1 1990, and new rating lists, including the 1995 list, every five years thereafter.

Local VOs are currently organised on a regional basis, and a region is controlled by a Regional Director. The whole VO network is controlled by the chief executive's office (CEO) based in London.

Preparation for the 1995 rating revaluation

VOs started preparation work on the 1995 rating list in 1992. The details of the terms under which property was leased were obtained by sending, to almost all occupiers of commercial properties, forms requiring the ratepayer to provide information about the tenure of their property. The VO had power to require the provision of this information under Section 82 or 86 of the General Rate Act 1967. The VO is empowered to use the information provided in these forms of return in defence of the Rating List under the LGFA 1988 Section 41(8). His current powers are contained in the LGFA 1988 Section 62 and Schedule 9 paragraphs 5(1)-(4), as amended, which read as follows:

(1)   A VO may serve a notice on a person who is an owner or occupier of a hereditament requesting him to supply to the officer information:
(a) which is specified in the notice, and (b) which the officer reasonably believes will assist him in carrying out functions conferred or imposed on him by or under this Part.

(1A) A notice under this paragraph must state that the officer believes the information requested will assist him carrying out functions conferred or imposed on him by or under this Part.

(2) A person on whom a notice is served under this paragraph shall supply the information requested if it is in his possession or control, and he shall do so in such form and manner as is specified in the notice and within the period of 21 days beginning with the day on which the notice is served.

(3) If a person on whom a notice is served under this paragraph fails without reasonable excuse to comply with subparagraph (2) above, he shall be liable on summary conviction to a fine not exceeding level 2 on the standard scale.

(4) If a notice has been served on a person under this paragraph, and in supplying information in purported compliance with subparagraph (2) above he makes a statement which he knows to be false in a material particular or recklessly makes a statement which is false in a material particular, he shall be liable on summary conviction to imprisonment for a term not exceeding 3 months or to a fine not exceeding level 3 on the standard scale or to both.

These powers which were amended and increased by the LGHA 1989, are more robust than those under the General Rate Act 1967. The 1967 Act powers, and those originally provided by the LGFA 1988, were perfectly adequate to require ratepayers to provide information on the tenure of a property. This enabled local VOs to start preparing the rating list for the more general classes of property (shops, offices, warehouse, and small factories), in their area, which normally let in the open market.

The Non-Domestic Rating (Information) Act 1996, enables local VOs to exchange between themselves and the Regional Assessors who carry out a similar valuation for rating functions in Scotland, information obtained by them under these powers.

Difficulties with the forms sent out by valuation officers
Difficulties very soon arose, however, in respect of those classes of property normally valued on a profits basis (or on a receipts basis, see pp. 154–5).

Ratepayers were reluctant to disclose details of their accounts, receipts, or profits to the valuation office on the forms sent to them. This was not because they were "bloody minded", or because they were prepared to disregard totally the law as it then existed.

There was not only serious concern on the part of the ratepayers about the security, and relevance, of the information that they were being asked to provide, but in addition they were given legal advice that doubts existed over the extent of a VO's power to require the provision of this information.

Security of information

The concern of ratepayers about the security of the information arose because it was thought that the VO would use the returns to build up a library of evidence, which he would use to value that class of property. When the first appeals in respect of that class of property were put down for hearing before a VT, the VO would be required to defend his level of assessment. Since the hereditament would have been valued having regard to its profit, and those of similar properties, he would need to produce evidence not only of the profits of the appeal hereditament, but also those of other similar properties of the same class.

The VO is entitled to rely on information provided in the return and to produce the return in respect of the property and any others he believes to be comparable and which support his level of value at a hearing before either the VT, or the Lands Tribunal (LT). He is given this power by virtue of Regulation 47(3) of the Non-Domestic Rating (Alteration of Lists and Appeals) Regulations 1993. He must give 14 days' notice however, to the ratepayer or his agent, that he intends to use the returns.

Any person on whom notice is served is entitled to call during normal business hours at the valuation office to inspect and take copies of these forms, and to inspect a similar number of forms in relation to other similar properties provided that he gives the VO not less than 24 hours' notice.

It must be remembered that the last ten years have been very volatile in the leisure field. Contested takeovers were not unknown, and most ratepayers were very concerned about the security of information on their receipts and profits. They felt that in the heat of a take-over battle an unscrupulous predator would not hesitate to use this right of inspection if he felt that it would help him obtain confidential trade information to enable him to win the take-over.

Relevance of information requested

The forms of return sent out by the VO, request information on the receipts, sometimes in cash terms, and on others by volume.

Ratepayers and their advisors had, and still have, grave doubts about the relevance of this information, because, for the reasons explained on p. 154, it only provides part of the story. No leisure appeal has to date been determined by the LT, and until the LT has considered the validity of valuations based upon receipts alone, the matter remains unresolved.

Legal doubts

A number of trade associations, including the Brewers' Society, the Hotel and Catering Industry, and the Yacht Harbours Association, took advice about the original powers of the VO to request trade information and were advised that at the very best his power to require this information was marginal.

The Department of the Environment accepted these doubts, and in the LGHA 1989 amended the power of the VO to require information to the basis set out above, and put the matter beyond doubt.

Code of practice on information requested

It was not the wish of the trade associations to thwart the will of Parliament, and they entered into discussions with CEO which resulted in the agreement of codes of practice for most industries. These vary in detail to accommodate differences in trade practice, but the core of the agreement remains constant. The agreed Code of Practice for the Marina Industry, entered into by the Yacht Harbours Association (part of the British Marine Industry Federation), and the CEO is set out on pp 163–6.

Central discussions on valuation practice

The trade associations and their respective advisors were well aware of the difficulty which VO faced in valuing property in the leisure field where few properties are let in the open market, and discussions with CEO have been under way for some time to try and agree the correct valuation practice. Examples of properties subject to central discussion with CEO include pubs, bingo halls and leisure caravans. Where a particular class of leisure property occurs mainly in a single locality, these discussions have taken place with local VOs. Examples of these classes are West End gentlemen's clubs, theatres and casinos.

It has been possible in some cases for a detailed code of valuation practice to be agreed, in others it has been possible to agree how properties should be referenced (measured), but not to settle the basis of valuation. The discussions have proved useful, however, as they have enabled both sides to learn of the difficulties facing the other and to resolve a number of points.

Page 197 lists some of classes of properties where central or local discussions are taking place. Valuers asked to advise upon leisure property should contact the trade association or their appointed advisor.

Details of the approach used in valuing some of the classes of leisure property, and where the code of practice is in the public domain, are set out in pp. 166–97.

Agreement as to the accepted practice at the AVD between the trade association and the CEO cannot be binding upon individual valuers or ratepayers, but an individual who finds these agreements unacceptable faces the added difficulty that the VO will be able to show that he has prepared his evidence and valuation in accordance with the agreed principles of good practice entered into by responsible individuals representing the trade association and advised by professional surveyors experienced in the valuation of this class of leisure property.

It should also be borne in mind that the trade association will have only entered into the agreement after consultation, and consideration of all the evidence it had available, and because it felt the agreement was in the best interests of their members. It is not impossible to persuade the valuation office or the tribunals that the accepted approach is incorrect, but a valuer who intends to try faces a stiff uphill battle.

Example of a Standard Code of Practice as agreed between CEO and a Trade Association
Information required to be supplied to valuation officers
Notice requiring a return for rating purposes
Marinas

This Code of Practice which is being issued as an indication of the general policy of the valuation office supersedes any earlier code of practice and relates to specified information supplied to the valuation officer following a notice served under either Section 82 of the General Rate Act 1967 or paragraph 5 of schedule 9 to the Local Government Finance Act 1988, as amended by paragraph 46 of

Schedule 5 to the Local Government and Housing Act 1989. Such information will have been requested by the valuation officer in the belief that it will assist him/her in carrying out functions conferred or imposed by or under Part III of the 1988 Act (concerning non-domestic rating), including the compilation of a new rating list, or the maintenance of the rating list now in force.

The valuation office acknowledges the wish of members of the Yacht Harbours Association to preserve what they consider to be the confidential nature of trade information supplied to valuation officers in compliance with notices served on them in accordance with the foregoing paragraph.

The Yacht Harbours Association, together with its agents, acknowledges that this Code of Practice is being issued entirely without prejudice to any requirement to disclose the trade information referred to above by law, and to each valuation officer's statutory duty. The valuation officer reserves the right to examine each case on its individual merits.

The information supplied in compliance with such notices will not be disclosed to other government departments, without prejudice to any statutory or other legal requirements to the contrary. Whilst any information supplied to the valuation office will not as a matter of general practice be supplied to other branches of the Inland Revenue no formal restriction can be placed on the use within the Inland Revenue of the returns or the information contained in them.

The following will be the general practice adopted by valuation officers and their staff in dealing with rating cases concerning marinas.

1. Trade information supplied in respect of a hereditament will not be disclosed to any person other than the parties to an appeal in respect of that hereditament without the written consent of the person supplying the information, or the person/body on whose behalf the information was supplied, except in the following circumstances:

   (a) In order to deal with the assertions made by any party in negotiations or prior to the hearing of an appeal in relation to the rating assessment of any similar hereditament, the valuation shall, wherever possible, endeavour to give details of analyses etc which have regard to trade information in such a manner that the trade of a specified hereditament or of an individual cannot be identified.

      If it becomes essential for the valuation officer to refer to the actual trade of a hereditament, that information (or any other information supplied) will be disclosed in confidence only to the parties to an appeal or their professional advisers.

(b) If an appeal cannot be settled by agreement, and it is listed for hearing by the Valuation Tribunal, where the valuation officer considers it necessary to refer to trade information of comparable hereditaments in support of the assessment under appeal he will serve notice in accordance with Regulation 41(2)) of The Non-domestic Rating (Alteration of List and Appeals) Regulations 1993 (SI 1993/291).

Valuation officers undertake to use this procedure judiciously and to limit the number of hereditaments to which the notice relates to those reasonably required to support the level of assessment of the appeal hereditament.

(c) When any person to whom notice has been given in accordance with 1 (b) above serves notice on the valuation officer in accordance with Regulation 39(4), the valuation officer will generally comply provided that he/she intends to support the valuation of the appeal hereditament by reference to trade information and further that he/she is satisfied that the hereditament specified in such a notice is comparable in character or otherwise relevant to the appeal hereditament or that the trade information of the hereditament specified in the notice is directly related to the rating assessment of the appeal hereditament.

The valuation officer may refuse to comply with such notice if he/she is not satisfied that the hereditament is comparable in character or otherwise relevant to the case of the person who served such notice, or to the appeal hereditament, and the valuation officer will not divulge trade information where the assessment of the appeal property falls to be determined solely by reference to rents or cost.

(d) If the person who serves notice under paragraph 1(c) above applies to the Valuation Tribunal or arbitrator under Regulation 42(7) where the valuation officer has refused or failed to comply with the notice or part of it, he/she may defend his/her decision. If the Tribunal or arbitrator is satisfied that it is reasonable to do so, it or he/she may direct the valuation officer to comply with the notice in all or part and in such circumstances the valuation office will, of course, comply subject to any possible appeal.

2. The Yacht Harbours Association will recommend to members that prior to any hearing by the Valuation Tribunal or Lands Tribunal, they, and their professional advisers, should co-operate with valuation officers in the agreement of facts relating to the appeal hereditament, and (so far as they are able) of facts relating to any comparable hereditament to which either side proposes to refer.

3. The valuation officer will not object to a request from any other party under Regulation 40(3) of the aforementioned regulations to the Valuation Tribunal for the case to be heard in camera where trade information is to

be disclosed (but such an arrangement cannot prevail in the event of an appeal to the Lands Tribunal and beyond).
4. Notwithstanding the foregoing, if the Lands Tribunal or a Superior Court make an order for discovery under Rule 40 of the Lands Tribunal Rules 1975 SI 1975/299, the valuation officer will be bound to comply.

Specialist classes of leisure property

Legislation, agreed methods of referencing (measurement) and established valuation practice have resulted in different approaches to the valuation of various classes of leisure property. The range of leisure property is immense and growing all the time. This section sets out to describe the method used to value the more common classes of leisure property.

A valuer asked to advise on a class of property which is not included among those described here is recommended to contact the trade association representing his client and to ask if a surveyor or a firm of surveyors has been retained by that association to advise upon and co-ordinate appeals for that class of property. The valuer might also consider it worthwhile contacting the CEO who may also be able to put him in touch with the surveyor who is coordinating appeals of that class.

Stud farms

The Law LGHA 1989 Schedule 5 Paragraph 38(3) subparagraph 11 amends LGFA 1988 Schedule 6 Paragraph 2(1) by the addition of the following paragraphs:

2A (1) This paragraph applies to a hereditament the whole or any part of which consists in buildings which are:
(a) used for the breeding and rearing of horses or ponies or for either of those purposes; and
(b) are occupied together with any agricultural land or agricultural building.
(2) The rateable value of any hereditament to which this paragraph applies shall be taken to be the amount determined under paragraph 2 above* less whichever is the smaller of the following amounts:
(a) such amount as the Secretary of State may by order specify for the purposes of this paragraph, and
(b) the amount which but for this paragraph would be determined under

paragraph 2 above* in respect of so much of the hereditament as consists of buildings so used and occupied.

(3) In this paragraph:

"agricultural land" means any land of more than two hectares which is agricultural within the meaning of paragraph 2* of Schedule 5 above and is not used exclusively for the pasturing of horses and ponies, and "agricultural buildings" shall be construed in accordance with paragraphs 3 to 7 of that schedule.

The Non-Domestic Rating (Stud Farms) Order 1989 specifies £2,500 as the figure in paragraph 2(A).

Valuation: How the relief operates The valuer must first decide whether the property comprises either in part or as an entirety:

1. of buildings used for the breeding and rearing of horses or ponies, or either of those uses; and which are
2. occupied together with any agricultural land or agricultural buildings. The definitions of these are set out above.

Note: The exemption only applies to "agricultural land" (see the exemptions in LGFA 1988 Schedule 5). Other land which is used as, or as part of, a stud farm cannot have the benefit of this exemption.

It follows that only if the value attributable to that part of the property which is both agricultural and used as a stud farm exceeds £2,500, can the full deduction be made.

Examples

Three examples may help explain this.

1. A stud farm with a total value on the buildings of £6,750.

Value of stud farm	£6,750
Deduct "specified amount"	£2,500
Rateable value of stud farm	£4,250

2. A stud farm which includes a farm shop and repair facilities for non-agricultural motor vehicles. Stud farm RV £1,750, farm shop RV £1,500 and repair facilities RV £3,000. The value of the stud farm in this case is less than the "specified amount", and therefore the maximum sum which can be deducted is the value of the stud farm.

* Author's note: paragraph 2 is the normal basis of valuation.

Value of stud farm	£1,750
Farm shop	£1,500
Vehicle repair facility	£3,000
Total rateable value	£6,250
Deduct value of stud farm	£1,750
Rateable value of stud farm	£4,500

3. A stud farm with a rateable value, before deducting the specified amount, of less than £2,500 and not occupied with other rateable buildings or land, would be entered in the rating list at NIL.

Leisure caravan parks

The law LGFA 1989 Schedule 5 Paragraph 38(3) subparagraph 11 amends LGFA 1988 Schedule 6 Paragraph 2(1) by the addition of the following paragraphs:

2B (1) This paragraph applies where:
  (a) the rateable value of a hereditament consisting of an area of a caravan site is determined with a view to making an alteration to a list which has been compiled (whether or not still in force),
  (b) the area is treated as one hereditament by virtue of regulations under section 64(3)(b).
  [Authors note – these are the powers which allow the Secretary of State to enable the valuation officer to value a property as more than one hereditament, or more than one property as a single hereditament.]
  (c) immediately before the day the alteration is entered in the list or (if the alteration is made in pursuance of a proposal) the day the proposal is made, the list includes a hereditament consisting of an area of a caravan site treated as one hereditament by virtue of such regulations, and
  (d) the area mentioned in paragraph (b) above and the area mentioned in paragraph (c) above are wholly or partly the same.
  (2) In relation to a caravan pitch which is included both in the area mentioned in subparagraph (1)(b) above and in the area mentioned in paragraph 1(c) above, subparagraph (3) below

rather than paragraph 2(6) above (the six matters referred to p. 131) shall apply as respects the matters mentioned in subparagraph (4) below.

(3) The matters mentioned in subparagraph (4) below shall be taken to be as they were assumed to be for the purposes of determining the rateable value of the hereditament mentioned in subparagraph (1)(c) above when the rateable value was last determined.

(4) The matters are:
(a) the nature of the caravan on the pitch, and
(b) the physical state of that caravan.

(5) For the purposes of this paragraph:
"Caravan" has the same meaning as it has for the purposes of Part 1 of the Caravan Sites and Control of Development Act 1960, and "Caravan site" means any land in respect of which a site licence is required under Part I of that Act, or would be so required if paragraph 4 and paragraph 11 of Schedule 1 to the Act (exemption of certain land occupied and supervised by organisations concerned with recreational activities and of land occupied by local authorities) were omitted.

Rating (Caravans and Boats) Act 1996 This Act which has retrospective effect to 1st April 1990 amended the definition of domestic property in LGFA 1988 section 66 subsection 3 to read as follows: "(3) Subsection 1 above does not apply in the case of a pitch occupied by a caravan, but if in such as case the caravan is the sole or main residence of an individual, the pitch and the caravan, together with any garden, yard, outhouse or other appurtenance belonging to or enjoyed with them, are domestic property".

An additional subsection 4A was also added which reads "Subsection (3) or (4) (Author's note, subsection 4 relates to moorings), does not have effect in the case of a pitch occupied by a caravan, or a mooring occupied by a boat, which is an appurtenance enjoyed with other property to which subsection (1)(a) above applies".

The effect of these amendments is to revise the definition of domestic property in so far as caravans (and boats) are concerned with the intention of confirming the existing law as it was earlier understood to be by most professionals dealing with these classes of property.

The Non-Domestic Rating (Caravan Sites) Regulations 1990 SI 673 These regulations which were made under the LGFA 1988, and came into force on April 1 1990 read as follows:

(2) In these regulations:
    (a) "caravan" has the same meaning as it has for the purposes of part 1 of the Caravan Sites and Control of Development Act 1960 (the 1960 Act);
    (b) "Caravan site" means any land in respect of which a site licence is required under part 1 of that Act, or would be so required but for paragraphs 4, 11 and 11A of schedule 1 to that Act (exemption of certain land);
    (c) a caravan pitch is a pitch for a "caravan" if in accordance with any licence or planning permission regulating the use of the caravan site a caravan stationed on the pitch is not allowed to be used for human habitation throughout the year;
    (d) "relevant site" means a caravan site which:
        (i) includes some property which is not domestic, and
        (ii) has an area of 400 square yards or more, and
    (e) "site operator" means the person who is for the purposes of part 1 of the 1960 Act the occupier of the caravan site.

Treatment of pitches etc as one hereditament
(3) (1) Where pitches for caravans on a relevant site separate hereditaments by virtue of their being occupied by persons other than the site operator, those pitches shall, subject to paragraph (2), together with so much of the site as constitutes a hereditament in the occupation of that site operator, be treated as one hereditament and as occupied by that site operator.
    (2) Paragraph (1) does not apply to any pitch which is occupied by a charity or trustees for a charity, and which is wholly or mainly used for charitable purposes (whether of that charity or that and other charities).
    (3) For the purposes of this regulation a caravan pitch, and any area comprising it, shall be taken as including the caravan for the time being on that pitch if apart from this regulation the caravan would be included as part of a rateable hereditament.

Supplementary
(4) (1) Where on the compilation of a local rating list or by virtue of the alteration of such a list there is included in the list a

hereditament which falls to be treated as such solely by virtue of Regulation 3, the VO shall within one month of that compilation or, as the case may be, alteration, inform the site operator in writing that the hereditament is so included, and shall also state in writing

(a) how many caravans stationed on pitches which do not consist of domestic property are included in that hereditament, and

(b) how much (if any) of the rateable value of the hereditament is attributable to those caravans, together with their pitches.

(2) Where it appears to a VO that the information given under paragraph (1) in relation to a hereditament is no longer accurate, but no alteration of the local rating list is required, he shall forthwith inform the site operator of that fact, and shall supply to him a further statement of the matters mentioned in paragraph (1)(a) and (b).

(3) Any person occupying a pitch for a caravan on a relevant site may after giving reasonable notice to the VO at a reasonable time and without payment inspect a copy of any statement supplied to the operator of that site under this regulation.

Valuation It will readily be appreciated that the assessment of rateable value for a leisure caravan site is a long way from the real market.

Every leisure caravan site in excess of 400 square yards must be valued as a single hereditament. The site operator is deemed to be in rateable occupation of the hereditament. Only caravans occupied by a charity will be separately valued.

Unless the site changes in size, the nature of the caravans and their number will remain as they were on April 1 1995.

Inspection The valuer must inspect the site and ask the operator for a sight of the management accounts. He should also ascertain the following information:

1. The number of caravans on the site.
2. The number of caravans whose occupation is domestic for the purposes of the Rating (Caravans and Boats) Bill 1996 (see p 120).
3. The number of caravans occupied by charities or trustees for charities.

4. Are the pitch fees inclusive of rates, water rates, and sewerage or environmental charges. If they are he will require to know:
   (a) The number of caravans authorised by a notice under section 2 of the Rating (Caravan Sites) Act 1976:
   (b) Transitional rate liability for the site in 1993/4.
   (c) The amount of any sewerage rate or environmental charge.
5. Is the use of other facilities included in the pitch fee? Some sites include the use of swimming pools, laundries, and entertainment facilities in the fee, whilst others make an additional charge.

Valuation approach The pitch fees must be adjusted to exclude rates, sewerage charges etc and to exclude any of the facilities which are to be valued separately. Where, however, the operator makes an additional charge for items which would be reflected in the normal pitch rent, for example use of the toilets, or showers, or the cleaning and maintenance of the area around the pitch, then this must be added.

The industry is not consistent in its method of charging for the provision of electricity and insurance. The valuer must ensure that these items have been deducted to arrive at a net site rent.

Some site operators charge van owners for a variety of "extras", these can include for example commission on resale, or sub-letting and club membership. These "extras" form part of the income of the site operator who could as an alternative simply charge a higher site rent. Where such charges exist the pitch fee should be adjusted to reflect their value.

The approach to these charges will vary from site to site, and the valuer must discuss them in detail with the operator to ensure that he is considering a net pitch fee.

The valuer must now consider the net pitch fee in the light of comparable evidence of other similar sites and adjust as appropriate. It must be remembered that the valuation of caravan sites is carried out under special legislation, and that it is inappropriate to compare them with the rents at which chalets and similar properties let, even though the tariffs may appear to be similar. The life expectancy of a caravan can be as low as three years, whereas a chalet may be considered to have a life expectancy of over 50 years.

Banding the caravans The number of caravans on the site must be divided into bands. The valuer should do this with the help of the operator. The bands should be 1–4 years old, 5–10 years old and over

10 years old. They should also be classified as Basic, Standard or Luxury.

The VO has analysed a number of transactions and in their cost guide used to prepare the Rating Lists have used the following figures.

Caravans up to 4 years old

Caravan	Cost	Amortisation	Rateable value
Basic	£5,471	@ 6% for 12 yrs = £651	@ 25% = £163
Standard	£6,500	@ 6% for 12 yrs =£774	@ 25% = £193
Luxury	£9,863	@ 6% for 12 yrs = £1,174	@ 25% = £293

Caravans from 5 to 10 years old

Basic	£3,531	@ 6% for 7 yrs = £630	@ 25% = £157
Standard	£4,124	@ 6% for 7 yrs = £736	@ 25% = £184
Luxury	£6,250	@ 6% for 7 yrs = £1,116	@ 25% = £279

The number of caravans The number of caravans on the site may differ from the number for which the site is licensed. The number is often smaller (unless the site is new and not yet fully occupied). This is because of the tendency towards larger vans and the new fire regulations. The valuer should use the actual number of caravans on site.

It is important to discover if any of the caravans are occupied by charities, as they will have to be separately assessed, and if any are occupied residentially. The latter will be excluded from the valuation, but their occupiers must now pay Council Tax.

Deductions The industry and the VO agreed for the 1990 rating list a number of adjustments. The VO has used different adjustments for the 1995 list. The adjustments are all deductions which must be made from the pitch fees:

Type of adjustment	Agreed 1990 List	VO 1995 List
1. Voids	10%	10%
2. Working expenses	50%	45%
3. Tenant's share	45%	50%
4. Small site (65–99 vans)	5%	5%
5. Under 65 vans	10%	10%

Addition for caravans and age factor The industry and CEO agreed age factors which were applied when preparing the valuation. These factors were a shorthand method of reflecting the age distribution of the caravans on the site. It was agreed that for the purposes of the 1990 Rating List the presence of a caravan aged between 1 and 4 years increased the value of the pitch on which it stood by 50%, whereas one aged between 5 and 10 years increased it by 30% and a van over 10 years old by 10%. This adjustment is inappropriate for the 1995 list since the VO's analyses of costs reflect actual values.

Other parts of the hereditament Many sites include chalets – these should be valued on a price per square metre. However, care should be taken when comparing these with caravan pitch values, because of the great difference in their life expectancy. Profit-earning parts of the site, for example swimming baths, should be valued separately and added to the assessment. Care must be taken to value them at the level of additional value to the site, and not at the level which they might fetch at an off-site location. Other items which should be valued include areas available for tenting, touring and rally caravans. These will be apparent from the site licence.

On-site car parking is reflected, but if the car park is used by casual visitors using off-site facilities then an adjustment may need to be made.

Stand back and look The valuer should consider the resulting valuation to see if it sits comfortably with other similar assessments. If it does not, adjustments may have to be made. He should, however, check to ensure that in preparing his valuation he has not inadvertently double counted any aspect of his valuation, or duplicated any disability factor.

Charity caravans The assessment of charity caravans must be apportioned from the final valuation.

Examples

A site licensed for 310 caravans but with only 300 on site.

These are	Basic	Aged 1–4 years	50	Aged 5–10 years	50
	Standard	Aged 1–4 years	100	Aged 5–10 years	60
	Luxury	Aged 1–4 years	40		

Pitch fees for the 1993 season are £450 excluding rates, water rates and other charges.

Valuation

Net pitch fees 300 x £450	£135,000
Basic 1–4 yrs 50 x £163	£ 8,150
Basic 5–10 yrs 50 x £157	£ 7,850
Standard 1–4 yrs 100 x £193	£ 19,300
Standard 5–10 yrs 60 x £184	£ 11,040
Luxury 1–4 yrs 40 x £293	£ 11,720
Gross enhanced pitch fees	£193,060
Less Pitch fee adjustment	£ 000
Net enhanced pitch fees	£193,060
Less Voids 10%	£ 19,306
	£173,754
Less Working expenses 45%	£ 78,189
	£ 95,565
Less Tenant's share 50%	£ 47,782
Rateable value pitch and van	£ 47,783

Say rateable value £47,750

Notional RV of pitch £47,750 divided by 310 = £154.03

Co-ordination Valuers advising on leisure caravan sites are recommended to contact the National Caravan Council or the surveyors coordinating appeals (see p. 197).

Marinas

The law The rating assessment of a marina is subject to detailed legislation under the LGFA 1988, the LGFA 1992 and to Regulations issued under those acts; principally the Docks and Harbours (Rateable Values) Order 1989 SI 1989/2473, the Docks and Harbours (Rateable Values) (Amendment) Order 1994 SI 1994/3280, and the Non-Domestic Rating (Multiple Moorings) Regulations 1992 SI 1992/557. The Rating (Caravans and Boats) Act 1996 redefines the boundary between domestic and non-domestic property on a marina and its provisions are explained in detail earlier in this chapter (p. 120).

A valuer must first establish whether or not a marina falls to be valued under the Docks and Harbours Order. Paragraph 3(1) of the Order reads:

1. This Order applies, except in the cases described in paragraphs (2) to (4), to any hereditament which consists of a dock or harbour undertaking carried on under authority conferred by or under any enactment.
2. This Order does not apply:
   (a) where the relevant income of the dock or harbour under-taking –
      (i) in any accounting period of twelve months ending during the period beginning on 31st December 1992 and ending with 31st March 1993 or
      (ii) if there was no such accounting period, in the twelve months ending on 31st March 1988, was not more than £50,000; or
   (b) where the persons carrying on the dock or harbour under-taking use the dock or harbour exclusively or mainly for the purpose of bringing or receiving goods –
      (i) manufactured or produced by them; or
      (ii) to be used by them for the manufacture or production of goods or electricity; or
      (iii) to be sold by them; or
      (iv) manufactured or produced by an associated body, and to be sold by that body.
3. For the purposes of paragraph (2)(b), a body shall be treated as the associated body of any person if –
   (a) it is a body corporate in relation to which those persons directly or indirectly own or control not less than 51% of its issued share capital; or
   (b) it is a body corporate in relation to which those persons and any other associated body or bodies of theirs directly or indirectly own or control not less than 51% of its issued share capital.
4. Other than for the purposes of calculating the relevant income this Order does not apply to a hereditament occupied by persons carrying on a dock or harbour undertaking which does not consist exclusively of operational land.
5. In paragraph (4) "Operational Land" means land which is used for the purposes of the carrying on of the undertaking, not being land which, in respect of its nature and situation, is comparable rather with land in general than with land which is used for the purpose of carrying on of statutory undertakings (within the meaning of the Town and Country Planning Act 1971).

Many marinas or, where they have taken over whole docks or harbours, the dock or harbour in which they are located, required a Local Act to enable their construction to take place. An example of this is Brighton Marina, which was constructed and is maintained under the Brighton Marina Act 1967.

Should the marina fall within the definition set out above then its rating assessment is calculated in accordance with the Order, and a valuer should consult the Order to ascertain how the formula works. The resulting assessment may be higher or lower than an assessment arrived at in the normal manner under the LGFA 1988 Schedule 6.

Any swinging moorings are exempt under the LGFA 1988 Schedule 5 paragraph (18) (see p. 125).

The LGFA 1988 Section 66(4) as amended by the RCBA 1996 section 1 (3) reads for subsection (4) of that section (moorings) there shall be substituted Subsection (1)[.......] does not apply in the case of a mooring occupied by a boat, but if in such a case the boat is the sole or main residence of an individual, the mooring and the boat, together with any garden, yard, outhouse or other appurtenance belonging to or enjoyed with them are domestic property.

(4A) Subsection (3) or (4) above does not have effect in the case of a pitch occupied by a caravan, or a mooring occupied by a boat, which is an appurtenance enjoyed with other property to which subsection 1 (a) above applies.

(The question of sole or main residence is dealt with on pp. 121–2.)

The LGFA 1988 Section 42 (contents of local lists) makes it clear that no property which is domestic, nor any part of a composite property which is domestic shall be assessed.

It is not necessary for a mooring to be occupied by a house boat, which has been described as having no engine and potted plants on deck, to be exempt from rating and excluded from the valuation. It is only required that the boat is the sole or principal residence of an individual. That individual need not be the owner. Many large ocean-going yachts have paid crew who live aboard the vessel. The yachts are their sole or principal residence, and therefore the moorings to which they are secured are domestic and exempt from rates.

Since berths in a marina are let out normally on monthly licences, rating law and practice would require each berth to be separately assessed, rather in the way that leased car parking bays are separately assessed. This was administratively time consuming and expensive, and would have created valuation difficulties as the other facilities on the marina, for example car parking spaces, that part of the harbour master's office responsible for the control and security of the marina and the showers and WCs, would have been reflected in the rents paid by the berth occupiers. The Rates Act 1984 Schedule 2 Part 11 allowed VOs to assess as a single hereditament moorings in a Marina.

It was Ministers' intention that these arrangements should be replicated in the 1988 legislation. Unfortunately they were inadvertently omitted from the LGFA 1988, and were dropped from the LGHA 1989 as a result of the guillotine applied during the passage of the Bill. The Government gave an assurance in the House of Lords that the legislation would be replicated at the first opportunity.

This has now been rectified in the LGFA 1992 Schedule 10 paragraph 2 which reads:

(3A) The Secretary of State may make regulations providing that where on any land there are two or more moorings which:
  (a) are owned by the same person
  (b) are not domestic property, and
  (c) are separately occupied, or available for separate occupation, by persons other than that person.

A valuation officer may determine that, for the purposes of the compilation or alteration of a local non-domestic rating list, all or any of the moorings, or all or any of them together with any adjacent moorings or land owned and occupied by that person, shall be treated as one hereditament.

(3B) Regulations under subsection (3A) above may provide that
  (a) where a valuation officer makes a determination as mentioned in that subsection, he shall, if prescribed conditions are fulfilled, supply prescribed persons with prescribed information;
  (b) where such a determination is in force –
    (i) the person who on any day is the owner of the moorings (or the moorings and land) which constitute the hereditament shall be treated for the purposes of sections 43, 44A and 45 above as being in occupation of all of the hereditament on that day; and
    (ii) no other person shall be treated for those purposes as being in occupation of all or any part of the hereditament on that day.

(2) After subsection (11) of that section there shall be inserted the following subsection:
"(12) In subsections (3A) and (3B) above 'owner', in relation to a mooring, means the person who if the mooring is entitled to receive rent, whether on his own account or as agent or trustee for any other person, or (if the mooring is not let) would be so entitled if the mooring were let, and 'owned' shall be construed accordingly."

(3C) Regulations under subsection (3A) above may provide that where a Valuation Officer determines as mentioned in that subsection and prescribed conditions are fulfilled, he shall supply prescribed persons with prescribed information.

The Secretary of State has made regulations under these powers which are set out in the Non-Domestic Rating (Multiple Moorings) Regulations 1992 (SI 1992/557). These read as follows:

Citation, commencement and interpretation
1,–(1) These Regulations may be cited as the Non-Domestic Rating (Multiple Moorings) Regulations 1992 and shall come into force on April 1 1992.
(2) In these Regulations, "the 1988 Act" means the Local Government Finance Act 1988.

Multiple moorings etc treated as one hereditament.

2. Where on any land there are two or more moorings which:
(a) are owned by the same person,
(b) are not domestic property, and
(c) are separately occupied, or available for separate occupation, by persons other than that person,
a valuation officer may determine that, for the purposes of the compilation or alteration of a local non-domestic rating list, all or any of the moorings, or all or any of them together with any adjacent moorings or land owned and occupied by that person, shall be treated as one hereditament.

Occupation of multiple moorings etc.

3. While such a determination as is mentioned in regulation 2 is in force:

(a) the person who on any day is the owner of the moorings (or the moorings and land) which constitute the hereditament shall be treated for the purposes of sections 43, 44A (c) and 45 of the 1988 Act as being in occupation of all of the hereditament on that day; and

(b) no other person shall be treated for those purposes as being in occupation of all or any part of the hereditament on that day.

Information for owners

4.(1) A valuation officer who:

(a) makes such a determination as is mentioned in regulation 2; and

(b) compiles or alters a local non-domestic rating list so as to show as a single hereditament property which, but for the determination, would have been shown in the list as two or more hereditaments, shall supply to the owner of the relevant hereditament the information referred to in paragraph (2).

(2) The information is:

(a) a copy of the information shown in the list in respect of the relevant hereditament; and

(b) if it is not apparent from the information provided under subparagraph (a), a statement of the number of moorings which are not domestic property and which comprise or are included in the relevant hereditament; and

(c) a statement of the amount of the part of the rateable value of the relevant hereditament which, in the opinion of the valuation officer, is attributable to those moorings.

(3) Information required to be given by paragraph (1) shall be supplied within the period of 28 days beginning with the day on which the list was compiled or altered, as the case may be.

(4) Where it appears to a valuation officer that information supplied in accordance with paragraph (1) is no longer accurate but no alteration of the local non-domestic rating list is required, he shall supply to the owner of the relevant hereditament a statement of the matters referred to in subparagraphs 9(a) to (c) of paragraph (2) as soon as reasonably practicable.

(5) In this regulation and regulation 5:

(a) references to the owner of a hereditament are to the person treated, in accordance with regulation 3, as being in occupation of it; and

(b) references to the relevant hereditament are references to the single hereditament to which the determination under regulation 2 relates.

Information for persons other than owners

5(1) Where:
(a) a valuation officer makes such a determination as is mentioned in regulation 2; and
(b) there is served on him by a person to whom paragraph (3) applies a notice requiring him to supply that person with a copy of any statement supplied to the owner of the relevant hereditament under regulation 4, the valuation officer shall supply to that person a copy of the statement supplied or last supplied in accordance with paragraph (1) or (4) of that regulation (as the case may be).

(2) The valuation officer shall comply with such a request as is mentioned in paragraph (1) (b) as soon as reasonably practicable after receipt of the notice.

(3) This paragraph applies to a person who, but for a determination under regulation 2, would on any day have been treated for the purposes of section 43 or 44A or 45 of the 1988 Act as being in occupation of any part of the relevant hereditament on that day.

The Multiple Mooring Regulations have been in force for four years but the author has never heard of an occupier of a marina berth seeking to have his mooring separately assessed. This is not surprising as it is unlikely that the marina would be willing to reduce the charge it was making for the berth, and the occupier would end up paying more.

Difficulties have arisen where marinas have sold berths. These berths are either occupied on their own or with residential accommodation on the marina. Those berths occupied with the residential accommodation may be subject of the same lease or conveyance, or subject to separate documentation.

Where the berths are occupied without any residential occupation in the neighbourhood, then it would seem that they should be assessed separately (subject to the regulations under the LGFA 1992 Schedule 2).

The effect of the RCBA 1996 which amends LGFA 1988 Section 66 reads as follows:

(3) For subsection (4) of that section (moorings) there is substituted:

    (4)   Subsection (1) above does not apply in the case of a mooring occupied by a boat, but if in such a case the boat is the sole or main residence of an individual, the mooring and the boat, together with any garden, yard, outhouse or other appurtenance belonging to or enjoyed with them, are domestic property.

    (4A)   Subsection (3) or (4) above does not have effect in the case of a pitch occupied by a caravan, or a mooring occupied by a boat, which is an appurtenance enjoyed with other property to which subsection (1)(a) above applies.

This Act which has retrospective effect to 1 April 1990 confirms the existing position that moorings enjoyed with other domestic property are exempt from Non-Domestic rating.

It should be noted that where a marina is assessed under the Docks and Harbours Order, these rules do not apply as the marina assessment is calculated on a formula.

Valuation There would appear to be no useful evidence of any marinas let in the open market, at rents which in any way resemble the basis of rateable value. The conventional way to value a marina is on the profits basis (see pp. 148–54).

Agents representing the Yacht Harbours Association held a number of meetings with CEO in 1994 and discussed how the valuations and subsequent appeals in respect of this class of property might best be handled. Agreement was reached on how the property should be referenced (measured), for the purposes of analysing the assessments arrived at on the profits basis, and the subsequent comparison, or valuation on a comparable basis of other marinas.

The full profit and loss accounts of a number of marinas were analysed by both parties and basis of valuation was agreed which uses as its starting point the 1993 tariff for the marina.

Since the marina operation relies upon maximising the space

available, the potential income could be deduced from the capacity of the marina. It was agreed that 12% of net income calculated by multiplying the capacity by the tariff for a 10 metre yacht should produce the 1993 rental value. Since the berthing tariff reflects the quality and other features of the marina the percentage needs only to be adjusted for extraordinary features. 10 metre berths are the most common in UK marinas and their tariff was selected for the purposes of this agreement. Some smaller marinas can not accommodate boats of 10 metres. The calculation must then be carried out using the tariff for the largest vessel which can be accommodated. The VOA used the tariffs shown in the RYA Marina Guide to prepare the 1995 Rating lists. Valuers should check that the tariff published was in fact that in operation at April 1 1993. The figures are exclusive of VAT.

Valuers should be aware of the danger of over counting. This receipts method reflects the presence of boat storage for adequate winter laying-up of yachts, car parking on the basis of one space for two boats, showers, toilets, laundry and administration offices for the marina. Indeed any facility which the yachtsman pays for in the tariff is reflected in the valuation.

Fuel jetties are an additional source of income to the marina and it was agreed that these would be valued by adding 2% to the value of the moorings. This reflected the fact that on the whole the bigger the marina the larger the fuel sales.

Any unusual expenditure, for example excessive dredging or the maintenance of lock gates, would result in an end allowance. It was accepted for this agreement that expenditure on dredging and maintenance of locks would only be excessive if it exceeds 5% of berthing income. It was also agreed that expenditure under these heads should be taken over a number of years.

Referencing It was agreed that it was not necessary to calculate the physical size or number of moorings in the marina. The valuer needs to obtain from the operator the capacity of his marina. This means the number of berths of various sizes. The value of the income derived from these moorings would reflect those aspects of the marina which were necessary to attract people to it. Reflected in the value of the berths would be WCs, showers, harbour master's office and approximately one car space for every two moorings.

Boat workshops, stores, chandlery and brokerage offices together with any additional car parking or land would be measured, valued or analysed separately. These facilities are often "let out" on marinas and separately assessed in any case.

It was agreed that the following factors might be expected to affect the profitability of a marina. It was noted that the suggested factors affecting profitability were generally reflected in the tariff, occupancy rate, and any additional cost of running or maintaining the marina.

Items that are likely to increase the profitability of a marina and therefore its rental value

- Good access by road to large affluent residential areas. It is possible that the residential development around the marina itself may provide the necessary affluent residential area.
- Good quality ancillary accommodation including WCs, showers and shops. Building of a permanent nature rather than of a temporary construction.
- Good quality club rooms/bars/social facilities.
- Adequate good quality laying-up facilities and workshops.
- Good quality pontoons with easy access of land and full services available to each berth.
- Good standard chandlers and brokerage available.
- Deep water. A minimum of 1.50–2.00 m depth at low water spring tides both at the moorings and in the access channels and marina entrance.
- Access by water at all states of the tide for deep keel craft.
- Direct access to open water without passing through a lock.
- Moorings and channels which either do not need dredging or only need infrequent dredging.
- Sheltered harbour.
- Within easy sailing distance of other good quality harbours or marinas.
- Local sailing in area with an attractive coastline, or in pleasant countryside, with access to large rivers or the canal network.
- Marinas with full occupancy.
- Marinas of regular shape.
- These marinas are unlikely to have swinging moorings or houseboats.

Items that are likely to reduce the profitability of a marina and therefore its rental value

- Poor access by road, or isolated and distant from residential areas, particularly affluent residential areas. No good quality residential accommodation within the complex.

- Inadequate or poor parking.
- Poor ancillary accommodation, often in temporary buildings.
- Either poor quality social facilities or none available.
- Inadequate laying-up facilities, poor workshops etc.
- Poor quality pontoons, which are old or in a poor state of repair, with difficult access to the land.
- Either no chandlers or brokerage or only those of a poor quality.
- Limited depth. Marina only capable of taking craft which dry out.
- Access by water restricted to certain states of the tide.
- Access to open water through a lock.
- Frequent dredging required.
- Exposed harbour.
- Isolated from other marinas or harbours. Located on unattractive coastline or in dull countryside.
- Limited access to rivers or canal network.
- The presence of houseboats.

Example
See pp. 148–54 for an example of a full profits valuation of a marina.

Co-ordination Valuers involved with marina assessments are advised to contact the Yacht Harbours Association, or the valuer coordinating rating appeals in respect of marinas (see pp. 163–6).

Hotels

The law There are no special legal provisions in rating law which apply to hotels. The valuer must however exercise special care to ensure that any part of the hotel which is residential is excluded from the assessment. A property which includes both domestic and non-domestic parts is called composite. Composite properties are dealt with in detail on pp. 198–202. Where the VO believes a property to be composite he will have described it in the rating list with the addition of the word "part" in brackets. Thus a composite hotel should appear in the rating list with the description Hotel and Premises (Part).

Valuation Very few hotels let in the open market at rents which resemble the basis of rateable value. Where they do exist valuers should use the normal adjustments to bring the rent into line with a rent in terms of rateable value.

A valuer who has a client with an hotel which is let in the open market should endeavour to obtain copies of his client's management accounts and then carry out a full profits valuation. This should enable him to check the split of the devisable balance between tenant's share and landlord's share. He should also compare the rent in terms of rateable value with the result that he would have arrived at using one of the two shorthand methods explained below.

Profits test valuation Where the valuer can obtain copies of the management accounts, he should carry out a full profits test valuation, following the principles set out on pp. 148–54. Unfortunately, however, it has proved extremely difficult for the VO to obtain copies of management accounts, and it is in practice extremely difficult for agents to persuade their clients to release this information to them even though they are retained to ensure that the rate liability of the hotel is kept to a minimum. A valuer should treat the results of a single profits test valuation with caution. He needs to examine the results of a number of hotel profit test valuations to identify a consistent basis of valuation.

Shorthand valuation methods Two shorthand valuation methods have been devised to enable surveyors to value hotels. They are both derived from those few hotels where it has proved possible to carry out full profits test valuations. The problem of confidentiality has meant, however, that neither the VO nor private practice will identify the hotels from which they obtained their data. Clearly if a major hotel proceeds to a hearing before the Lands Tribunal, either this difficulty will be resolved by agreement of facts before the hearing or both sides will have to identify, and allow the other side to examine critically their basic evidence.

The two shorthand approaches used by surveyors dealing with hotels are either to value using a comparative room basis, or to take a percentage of the hotel's gross income.

Comparative room basis This is a valuation using the "comparability" approach, which is explained on pp. 145–7. It uses as its yardstick the number of double bed units (DBU) in the hotel. A number of other yardsticks have been used in the past, but since most hotels seek to achieve as many double bedrooms with en suite bathrooms as possible, this is the most reliable method of comparison in the current market.

Conversion to Double Bed Units Since not all hotels comprise double rooms with en suite facilities, adjustments must be made to other rooms to calculate the number of equivalent DBUs. No agreement has been reached between the VO and surveyors advising the hotel industry but the multipliers which should be applied to each type of room to calculate the number of DBUs in a hotel are in the author's opinion as follows:

Single	Single en suite	Double	Double en suite
Provincial non-tourist hotel below 3 star			
45%	50%	75%	100%
3 star and above (assuming all rooms are en suite)			
—	50%	—	100%
Provincial tourist areas 3 star and above			
—	50%	—	100%
London below 3 star			
—	55%	—	100%
London 3 star and above			
—	70%	—	100%

Items reflected in the DBU rate The following items within the hotel are normally reflected in the value applied to the DBU, since they are reflected in the room tariff and are enjoyed by the hotel guests:

Any room which is required by the guest to enjoy his stay, for example the dining room, and the residents' bar and lounge. Accommodation which has to be provided to service the guest during his stay is also reflected, for example the kitchen, serveries, management offices, linen stores and larders.

The public rooms required by the hotel's guests, for example the residents' lounges, dining rooms and reception areas. Where the hotel has a licence only to sell liquor to the guests then this would be reflected in the DBU rate.

Hotels are assumed to have adequate lifts, and it is only where either the hotel is undergoing refurbishment or of less than 3-star status that these will not be present. Where there is no adequate lift an adjustment would have to be made, and the discount to be applied can probably be identified by comparing the tariffs for each floor. A rule of thumb is to deduct 10% from the DBU rate and a further 5% for each floor above first floor.

It should be remembered that resident staff accommodation, and proprietor's accommodation is domestic, and must be excluded from the valuation.

Items excluded from the DBU rate and valued separately The value applied to DBUs is intended to reflect the items which the hotel guest would expect when hiring a room. It follows that other items such as restaurants and bars for non-residents, ballrooms and conference facilities are valued separately and added to the assessment. Modern hotels often offer additional facilities to residents and non-residents for example health facilities such as jacuzzis, exercise rooms, swimming pools and saunas. Although these may be free to guests they are not as yet the norm in hotels and should be valued as an addition to the value arrived at using DBUs.

Public houses and nightclubs attached to an hotel should be valued separately, even if they share the hotel entrance.

Most hotels either do not have car parking, or the car parking is inadequate. The car parking where it exists should be added to the value of the hotel at the local rate.

Tariffs and DBUs It is possible to compare 1993 tariffs for double rooms with en suite facilities, with DBU prices, but this should only be used as a check, since the tariff makes no allowance for different costs of operating the hotel (see pp. 128–9).

The relationship between 1993 tariffs and DBU rates in a provincial town might be as follows:

Tariff 1993 en suite bath	DBU
Up to £ 20	£ 225
£ 21–£ 25	£ 325
£ 26–£ 30	£ 425
£ 31–£ 35	£ 525
£ 36–£ 40	£ 625
£ 41–£ 45	£ 725
£ 46–£ 50	£ 850
£ 51–£ 60	£1,000
£ 61–£ 70	£1,150
£ 71–£ 80	£1,325
£ 81–£ 90	£1,500
£ 91–£100	£1,650
£101–£120	£1,825
From £121	£2,000

Percentage of gross income The second shorthand approach used by valuers to arrive at the rateable value of hotels is to consider the gross income of the hotel and to take a percentage of this figure. This method simplifies the full profits valuation, but must be used with discretion because it ignores entirely the differences in the operating costs (see pp. 128–9).

It is used extensively, and provided that the valuer is aware of its shortcomings and makes the appropriate adjustments to allow for them, it can be used to overcome the absence of full accounts.

The income received from the hotel can normally be divided into four types:

Income from the hire of rooms.
Income from the sale of food.
Income from the sale of liquor.
Other income for example use of leisure facilities, profit on currency exchange and profit on telephone calls.

The percentage of gross income (excluding VAT) varies but as a guide can be taken as:

Hire of rooms	(normally approx. 40% of total income)	7.5%–9.0%
Sale of food	(normally approx. 30% of total income)	6.0%–8.0%
Sale of liquor	(normally approx. 25% of total income)	7.0%–8.5%
Other Income	(normally approx. 5% of total income)	6.0%–12.0%*

(*Depending upon services provided.)

The figures provided by the hotel should not be taken at their face value, however, as they may need adjustment. Private provincial hotels have been known to run outside catering. The income from the sale of food and drink must be reduced to reflect any extraneous matters such as external catering receipts.

A simpler approach is to look at the total income from the hotel and to consider the percentage of this income which would reflect the landlord's share of the rateable value. Appeals against the assessments of provincial hotels have been settled on the 1990 rating list at a percentage of gross income in the order of 8%. Valuers must treat percentages with care, however, as the balance of business within the hotel will affect the overall value.

Example
A 150-bedroom 4-star hotel in a city centre with 100 double bedrooms and 50 single all with en suite facilities. The hotel has a ballroom and bar with a total area of 375 sq. metres, which is used for conference facilities, and 150 car parking spaces. April 1993 tariff: double room with continental breakfast £130; single room with continental breakfast £90. Car parking spaces in the area are assessed at £500 per space, Local restaurants and other entertainment facilities are assessed at between £45 (poor) to £70 (best).

The total income of the hotel for the year ending March 31 1993 was £4,502,234, which can be divided into income from rooms £1,806,550; food £1,340,725; liquor £136,559; and ancillary income £218,400.

DBU valuation

Rooms		*DBUs*
Double rooms en suite	100 @ 100% =	100
Single rooms en suite	50 @ 70% =	35
Total DBUs		135

Value of rooms		
	135 DBUs @ £2,000 =	£ 270,000

Add value of ancillaries		
Ballroom/conference area	375 sq. m @ £ 60 =	£ 22,500
Car parking	150 spaces @ £ 500 =	£ 75,000
	Rateable value	£ 367,500

Percentage of gross income (excluding VAT)		
Income from hotel		£4,502,234
Landlord's share	@ 8%	
	Rateable value	£ 360,178

Percentage based upon division of takings		
Hire of rooms	£1,806,550 @ 9.0% =	£ 162,589
Sale of food	£1,340,725 @ 7.0% =	£ 93,851
Sale of liquor	£1,136,559 @ 8.0% =	£ 90,925
Ancillary income	£218,400 @ 8.5% =	£ 18,564
	Rateable value	£ 365,929

Co-ordination Valuers advising upon hotel assessments are recommended to consult with the surveyors advising the hotel industry before discussing any appeals with the VO.

Public concert halls

The law There is no special rating legislation covering this type of property.

Valuation Traditionally most of these halls have been owned by local authorities and have been valued on the contractor's test. Some have been valued on the profits test. There is evidence of open market rental transactions, and where these exist they should be used as better evidence than that which will be derived from the profits test. Care should be taken, however, to ensure that the rental evidence is an arm's length transaction. (For further comment on the contractor's test valuation see pp. 155–8.)

Co-ordination Appeals against assessments of this type are being coordinated and agents are recommended to consult the surveyors coordinating these appeals (see p. 197).

Cinemas

The law There is no special rating legislation covering this type of property.

Valuation There has been very little evidence of open market rental transactions in respect of cinemas for some years, however the revival of the cinema business in the late 1980s has continued into the 1990s. Admissions have increased from 75 million in 1988 to an estimated 112 million in 1993 producing more evidence than was available in 1988. It is still difficult to ascertain a pattern of values.

This class of property has always been valued on a profits or profits-related basis. It is often difficult for a valuer to obtain full accounts in respect of his client's property, and almost always impossible to do so in respect of comparable property. The practice has grown up of comparing cinemas on a percentage of gross take.

A general guide to the percentage of the level of receipts to rateable value excluding multiplex cinemas is in the following range:

Income per seat	*% of Gross Receipts to RV*
Under £ 249	5%
£ 250–£ 599	5%–7%
£ 600–£ 999	7%–8%
£1,000–£1,374	8%–9%
£1,375–£1,749	9%–10%
Over £1,750	10%

Multiplex cinemas are normally valued on a straight price per seat and as a general guide values are in the following range.

Income per seat	*RV per seat*
Under £ 600	£ 60
£ 700	£ 75
£ 800	£ 90
£1,000	£125
£1,200	£160
Over £1,300	£175

Co-ordination Appeals against assessments of this type are being coordinated and agents are recommended to consult the surveyors coordinating these appeals (see p. 197).

Theatres

The law There is no special rating legislation covering this type of property.

Types of theatre The type of theatre, the reason for their construction, and the very cause of their continued existence, are so varied that with the possible exception of central London theatres, each has to be treated as almost unique.

It is possible broadly to group theatres into the following groups

1. *Central London Theatres:* these are run as commercial enterprises without subsidy, and depend for their continued existence on producing successful plays.
2. *Large traditional theatres in the provinces:* these are often in buildings of unique architectural value, but suffer from immense cost of upkeep. Examples of theatres of this type are the Opera House in Manchester and the Theatre Royal in Brighton.
3. *Modem post-war theatres:* these were constructed where there was a perceived need. They are more efficient to run and less costly in upkeep. An example of this type is the Festival Theatre in Chichester.
4. *Small theatres in provincial towns:* provided that there is not too much competition, these survive with the help of grants.
5. *Theatres in holiday resorts:* these form part of the entertainment complex of the resort, and their success is dependent on the prosperity of the town and its ability to attract visitors. The Blackpool theatres are an example.
6. *Purpose-built civic theatres:* these were almost always constructed because of a perceived civic or cultural need. They were constructed in the full knowledge that they would only survive if supported by generous civic grants.
7. *Small playhouse theatres:* these are the traditional home of the amateur dramatic company. They often occupy converted buildings. Some have freehold premises, whereas others occupy on leases. The property is normally too small to be of interest to the professional theatre company.

Valuation Theatres are difficult to value as they are rarely let in the open market, and are traditionally subsidised by way of grants, from local and central government and from industry and commerce.

Theatres are built from time to time, but normally the motive for construction is either civic aggrandisement, or more often these days the belief that there is a social need.

The income derived from a theatre depends more on the play or show running in the theatre than upon its location, size or age.

Lack of useful rental evidence has resulted in valuations being carried out in a variety of ways.

Full profits valuation It is difficult to carry out a conventional full profits valuation of a theatre because most are supported by grant, and even in central London, the income from a theatre is dependent far more on the play that is running than on the shape, age, locality or number of seats in the actual theatre.

Price per seat This is the method which has traditionally been used in central London, but requires an in-depth knowledge of the theatre to make it work properly. Theatres in central London are at around £100 per seat whereas those in the provinces between £20 and £40.

It can be used outside the capital but because of the variety of theatres will only provide a rough check.

Percentage of receipts This method has been used extensively outside London in the past, and is still probably the most reliable method of valuation even if it has a number of obvious drawbacks. Percentages of between 2% and 5% of gross take (excluding VAT) would seem to arrive at acceptable results.

The gross take is from ticket sales, and should ignore any grant or subsidy. Many local authorities provide grants to the theatre at the end of their financial year to "balance the books".

The object of the assessment is to arrive at the rental value of the theatre where grants may not necessarily be available to the hypothetical tenant.

Contractor's test It is possible to value a theatre on the contractor's test. It is difficult to do so accurately, however, as most theatres are either old and expensive to maintain or have been constructed for non-profit-making motives. This means that the valuer must either apply very substantial allowances for age and obsolescence, or make large discretionary adjustments at the "stand back and look" stage. The result is a valuation which is based more upon valuer's opinion than upon a foundation of fact.

Co-ordination Appeals against assessments of this type are being coordinated and agents are recommended to consult the surveyors coordinating these appeals (see p. 197).

Bingo Halls

The law There is no special rating legislation covering this type of property.

Valuation Traditionally bingo halls have been valued having regard to the receipts. This almost certainly arose because in 1973, there was very little evidence of open market rental transactions. The market has changed dramatically since then with the increased presence of large public companies in the bingo market and the replacement of the converted cinema by purpose-built bingo halls with up to 11,000 seats, occupying converted warehouse accommodation on industrial estates. These new clubs are intended to be social centres, closer to a traditional social club than to the regimented classroom atmosphere of the converted cinema.

There are two schools of thought on the way to value bingo clubs: the traditional followed by the VO, and by part of the industry, and the modern followed by the remainder of the industry. Agreement has been reached between the VOA and agents acting for the industry that the traditional profits-related approach should be used to settle the 1990 appeals, but it is likely that part of the industry at least will argue for the modern approach for the 1995 revaluation.

The traditional approach This is a profits-related approach, and is based on a percentage of gross receipts.

The VOA and agents analysed the available evidence and the following conclusions were reached:

1. The evidence showed that regional variations existed in the relativities between gross receipts and rental values. Rents in the south east of England reflected a higher percentage of rental value than elsewhere in the country.

2. It was agreed that for the purposes of the analysis the counties of Bedfordshire, Berkshire, Buckinghamshire, East Sussex, Essex, Greater London, Hampshire, Hertfordshire, Kent, Oxfordshire, Surrey and West Sussex comprise the "South East".

3. It was recognised that the percentage of rental value to gross receipts was 1% higher in the South East than elsewhere in England and Wales. There was also evidence that rents in coastal holiday resorts from the north coast of Devon in the West to Essex in the East might show a further small increase in the percentage rents to gross receipts.

4. The percentages to be applied varied from 6% to 12% depending upon the location, property and size of the turnover.

The gross receipts were defined as including all receipts, including:

1. admission money;
2. gross takings from bars, restaurants, etc,
3. income from car parks,
4. participation fees; and
5. income from gaming machines.

These figures are exclusive of VAT.

Ancillary accommodation This approach values all ancillary accommodation which is used in connection with the club, for example, car parks, stores, staff rest rooms and management offices.

The modern approach A significant section of the bingo industry finds the receipts basis unacceptable as it penalises good management. The receipts basis works on the principle that the level of receipts equates to the income that the hypothetical tenant would generate, but in effect values the business and not the property.

There was so little rental evidence in the market in 1973, that this was the only method available to valuers. Today there is a considerable library of rental evidence with rents per square metre ranging from £12.25 to £33.67. The difference can be accounted for by location and type of property. Converted cinemas had been valued with circle seating areas at between 10% and 25% of ground floor depending upon demand.

Co-ordination Appeals against assessments of this type are being coordinated and agents are recommended to consult the surveyor coordinating these appeals (see p. 197).

Casinos

The law There is no special rating legislation covering this type of property.

Valuation The normal approach to the valuation of casinos is on either a direct rental method or on a comparative value approach based upon other casinos valued by the direct rental method. It is normal to analyse casino rents and assessments by applying a higher value to the gaming rooms than to the dining areas. The support areas are then valued at an even lower rate.

Co-ordination Casinos are a particularly difficult class of property to value, and an agent asked to advise upon a casino should immediately contact the surveyors coordinating casino appeals (see p. 197).

Golf courses

The law There is no special rating legislation covering this type of property.

Classification of golf courses
Golf courses can be conveniently classified into four classes:
1. Local authority or poor courses.
2. The average well-established course.
3. The very good club course often used for county matches such as the West Sussex course.
4. The top class prestige courses used for championship events such as the Royal Birkdale.

Immature courses, which have recently been laid out or extended may need to be either downgraded or given a temporary reduction until they reach maturity.

Valuation There is market evidence of rents paid for golf clubs. It is not possible to value these at so much per hole, or in relation to the club house, as almost all clubs provide the same basic facilities.

The accepted method of valuation currently depends on the rental evidence and the valuers' judgement.

Co-ordination Appeals against assessments of this type are being coordinated and agents are recommended to consult the surveyors coordinating these appeals (see below).

Surveyors coordinating appeals

Property type	*Lead agent(s)*
Stud farms	Unknown
Leisure caravan parks	Fleury Manico & Charles F. Jones
Marinas	Lambert Smith Hampton & Gerald Eve
Hotels	Lambert Smith Hampton & Gerald Eve
Public concert halls	Wilkes Head & Eve
Cinemas	Gerald Eve
Theatres	Colliers Erdman Lewis Rating
Bingo halls	Gerald Eve & Lambert Smith Hampton
Casinos	Colliers Erdman Lewis Rating
Golf courses	Gerald Eve

Council tax

The system under which tax was raised on domestic property was changed from April 1 1990 in England and Wales (1989 in Scotland), by the abolition of domestic rates, a tax on property, and its replacement by a tax on people, the Community Charge or Poll Tax. This tax was abolished April 1 1992, and replaced by the Council Tax. This is a tax on property, which assumes that each property is occupied by two adults, unless the occupier proves that he or she is the sole occupant of the property, in which case the tax rate is reduced by 25%.

All domestic property is assessed for Council Tax purposes by the VO, who must consider the capital value of the freehold interest in the property as at April 1 1991, or where the property is leasehold, the capital value of a 99-year lease of the property on the basis that the tenant is responsible for all repairs, insurance and at a peppercorn rent. The VO is required to place every property in one of eight predetermined bands of value. The upper level of each band is as follows:

Band	England	Scotland	Wales
A	£ 40,000	£ 27,000	£ 30,000
B	£ 52,000	£ 35,000	£ 39,000
C	£ 68,000	£ 45,000	£ 51,000
D	£ 88,000	£ 58,000	£ 66,000
E	£120,000	£ 80,000	£ 90,000
F	£160,000	£106,000	£120,000
G	£320,000	£212,000	£240,000
H	+£320,000	+£212,000	+£240,000

Many leisure properties include domestic accommodation within their boundary. This accommodation is exempt from non-domestic rating and has to be included in the local valuation list. This is a separate list from the rating list which contains details of the non-domestic rating assessments.

Valuers advising on the rating assessment of property which comprises a mixture of domestic and non-domestic property, must ensure that the VO has excluded all domestic property from the non-domestic rating assessment.

It is likely that most staff accommodation within leisure property will be assessed in bands A–C, although owners' accommodation could in some private hotels, for example, be assessed in a higher band.

Level of council tax
Under the council tax the local authority, as the billing authority, fix the level of tax for band D, and the level of tax in the other bands is a fixed percentage of this tax for this band:

Band A   67%
Band B   78%
Band C   89%
Band D   100%
Band E   122%
Band F   144%
Band G   167%
Band H   200%

Composite property

Valuation of composite property for non-domestic rating
A hereditament which comprises both domestic and non-domestic

property is a "Composite Property" for rating valuation. The simplest form of composite property is the shop with flat above which is not self-contained. The shopkeeper is responsible for paying UBR in respect of his shop, and council tax in respect of his flat.

The range of composite properties is vast and includes flats in golf clubs, domestic accommodation in pubs and hotels, staff accommodation at a tennis centre, residential caravans on an otherwise non-domestic park, and residential moorings in a marina.

Non-domestic properties which the VO believes are composite are identified in the rating list by the addition of "(part)" after their description.

The LGFA 1988 and subsequent legislation does not lay down rules for the valuation of composite properties, other than for caravan sites, probably because the draftsmen realised that the variety of composite property was so great, that any rule which fitted one case would not necessarily be appropriate to another type of property.

There seems however, to be two principal ways in which the valuer can approach the problem of valuing a composite property. Clearly he is required to value the whole property with the benefit or burden of the residential part and then to exclude the residential element.

Consider the leisure centre which has a caretaker's flat above without its own independent access. The valuer will be able to use his own judgement to arrive at a value of the leisure centre based upon its receipts, contractor's test, or comparison with other centres. He must then consider whether the value he has arrived at requires adjustment to allow for the burden or benefit of the caretaker's flat. This is, in effect, the additional or reduced price which the hypothetical tenant would pay for the right to run the centre with the flat as part of the complex.

The property might, for example, be more secure with a caretaker in residence, or the fact that the caretaker and his family have to traverse the bar or lounge to gain access to their flat could possibly detract from its value. The valuer must not, however, attribute any value to the flat itself.

The same approach can be used in valuing a marina which includes moorings occupied by boats which are the sole or main residence of an individual. Marinas are normally valued by reference to profits or takings. Clearly, these will include income from those moorings which are domestic. It is possible to value the marina and then to apportion the value arrived at excluding those moorings which are domestic. Many marinas actively discourage residential boats as they make greater demands upon their facilities and are a source of dirt, noise and disruption. The valuer may wish to adjust the value arrived at for the non-domestic part of the marina for the disability of having shared moorings with residential occupiers.

Other property does not lend itself to this method of valuation. Consider a traditional hotel. The hotel is likely to provide accommodation for the manager and domestic staff in addition to rooms and facilities for guests. Although the manager may have accommodation elsewhere, it is common for the staff to live on the premises. Often, they have their own staff canteen and rest room in the basement and their bedrooms in the roof space, using accommodation which is unsuitable for letting to guests. Where the presence of live-in staff adds to the service provided and the value of the hotel it must be taken into consideration when valuing the hereditament. The rooms occupied by the staff must then be excluded from the valuation as must those facilities used by the residential staff – rest rooms, dining rooms etc – but not where the rooms are also used by domestic staff who live out. Rooms which are used by both "live-in" and "live-out" staff must have their value apportioned between the two types of staff.

It follows that the whole of every hereditament comprising composite property must be valued with all its benefits and burdens and then the resulting valuation adjusted to exclude the domestic element contained within the hereditament. Just how this is to be achieved is left to valuation judgement.

Valuation of composite property for council tax
The same principle of valuation judgement applies when valuing the domestic accommodation of a composite hereditament for council tax. The basis is contained in the Council Tax (Situation and Valuation of Dwellings) Regulations 1992. These regulations provide that the band ascribed to a composite dwelling is to be determined on the basis of the value of the whole hereditament on the normal valuation basis for council tax, and then apportioning a value to the domestic element only. This means that the whole hereditament, both domestic and commercial, must be valued on the following assumptions:

1. A sale with vacant possession;
2. The interest sold is freehold or long leasehold;

3. The property is in a reasonable state of repair;
4. The valuation date is April 1 1991.

The capital value is then apportioned to determine the council tax band into which the domestic dwelling should fall.

The council tax valuation for some properties will be relatively straightforward. The flat above an amusement arcade which has been built in a former shop unit will be valued as one entity using comparable evidence. It is a matter of valuation judgement as to the proportion that is attributable to the domestic use. Many high street retailers consider a flat above a shop, which is not self-contained, to be a liability rather than a benefit and the value of the flat will be low.

Not all composite properties are as straightforward. Many contain not just one residential unit but several. A country club may have staff houses, flats and staff bed-sitting rooms, whereas an hotel might have staff bedrooms, as well as staff flats and houses. The Council Tax (Chargeable Dwellings) Order 1992 (SI 1992/549) makes special provision for this class of hereditament. The rule is that where a single property contains more than one self-contained unit, the property shall be treated as comprising as many dwellings as there are units. The capital value of the whole property must be apportioned in a fair manner between the commercial area and each separate dwelling.

This is simpler to say than to put into practice. It is doubtful whether the valuation officer approached the valuation of the many complex composite properties by valuing the whole complex on the open market as at April 1 1991, and then apportioning the value between the domestic and non-domestic parts of the property. Instead he is likely to have started by considering the value at which the residential unit might have sold in the open market. This approach will almost certainly have resulted in a level of value which is too high.

A valuer must tackle the statutory valuation assumptions in order to value a composite property correctly for council tax purposes. The valuation of a country park, a marina, or an hotel is not easy and is subject to wide variations. Some of these properties rarely sell in the open market. The value of such properties should be arrived at using depreciated replacement cost. This is a method which is in itself open to interpretation and argument.

Not only is there limited comparable evidence as to the open market value of many classes of composite property, but there are no regulations or market evidence as to how the apportionment between the domestic and non-domestic elements of the valuation should be carried out. It is left to valuation judgement, negotiation and if this fails to the common sense of the Valuation Tribunal from which there is no right of appeal on valuation matters.

CHAPTER 4

Holiday caravan parks

This chapter concentrates on the valuation and law affecting holiday caravan parks. This covers touring caravan parks (ie parks accommodating towed caravans and motorised caravans) and static holiday caravan parks (ie parks accommodating caravans sited throughout the year, but let for holidays, or used as holiday homes). It does not cover caravan parks used residentially (mobile home parks) or sites for gypsies.

Before attempting a valuation, a knowledge of the legal and planning framework is essential. Therefore the first part of this chapter concentrates on some of the legal, planning and site licensing aspects, before moving to the valuation techniques.

The law

Caravan parks are unique among leisure property in being controlled by special legislation. The main statutes are the Caravan Sites and Control of Development Act 1960, the Caravan Sites Act 1968 and the Mobile Homes Act 1983. Caravan parks are of course affected directly and indirectly by many other more general Acts and by an array of regulations, statutory instruments, and circulars.

The purpose of this section is to review the law affecting caravan parks in relation to their valuation. It is not intended to be an authoritative work on the case and statute law affecting caravan parks. Instead, it attempts to guide the valuer through the more important aspects of the law which affect the running and development of parks and, consequently, their value.

What is a caravan?

First, the valuer has to be clear as to what is meant by "caravan". Section 29 of the Caravan Sites and Control of Development Act 1960 defines a caravan as:

. . . any structure designed or adapted for human habitation which is capable of being moved from one place to another (whether by being towed, or by being transported on a motor vehicle or trailer) and any motor vehicle so designed or adapted, but does not include –

(a) any railway rolling stock which is for the time being on rails forming part of a railway system, or

(b) any tent:

The all-important term "caravan site" is described in section 1(4) of the Act as meaning:

land on which a caravan is stationed for the purposes of human habitation and land which is used in conjunction with land on which a caravan is so stationed.

It will be noticed from section 29 that:

(a) The requirement is that the structure is capable of "being *moved* from one place to another". It does not have to be capable of being towed, nor indeed does it have to have wheels.

(b) The definition does not include any limitation on the period during which the structure is used.

(c) There are no criteria as to design, or materials used in construction, other than that the structure must be designed or adapted for human habitation and it must not be a tent or comprise "railway rolling stock which is for the time being on rails forming part of a railway system". Clearly from this, railway rolling stock *not* on rails etc could come within the definition of a caravan if it were adapted for human habitation. This illustrates the very wide number of structures that can be termed "caravans". Also of interest is the inclusion in the definition of a motor vehicle designed or adapted for human habitation.

(d) There are no size limits (other than capacity to be towed or transported on a motor vehicle or trailer).

It should be noted from section 1 that the expression "caravan site" relates to the *use* of land. When considering planning implications it is important to appreciate that a caravan site is a use of land only. What is important is the stationing of caravans on that land. For the purposes of the 1960 Act, the land has to be used for the stationing of caravans "for human habitation". Land used for the storage of caravans, therefore, or for the display of caravans for sale, is excluded from the provisions of this Act.

The definition of caravan is extended by section 13(1) of the

Caravan Sites Act 1968. By the curious use of a double negative ("shall not be treated as not being . . . a caravan") this section extends the definition to include twin-unit caravans. Since 1968 a caravan can include a structure designed and adapted for human habitation and which:

(a) is composed of not more than two sections separately constructed and designed to be assembled on a site by means of bolts, clamps or other devices; and
(b) is, when assembled, physically capable of being moved by road from one place to another (whether by being towed or by being transported on a motor vehicle or trailer).

The section goes on to provide that the structure will not be excluded from the definition of caravan merely because it cannot lawfully be moved on a highway when assembled.

The effect of the use of the double negative is to avoid making "two sections" the maximum number of assembly sections for the structure to come within the definition of "caravan". Assembly in more than two sections is not necessarily fatal if the structure complies with the definition in all other respects.

Section 13(2) then provides maximum dimensions for twin-unit caravans as being:

(a) length (exclusive of any drawbar): 60 feet (18.288 metres);
(b) width – 20 feet (6.096 metres)
(c) overall height of living accommodation (measured internally from the floor at the lowest level to the ceiling at the highest level): 10 feet (3.048 metres).

These maximum dimensions apply only to twin-unit caravans covered by section 13(1)(*a*) and (*b*) of the 1968 Act, summarised above. They do not relate back to the definition of caravan in section 29 of the 1960 Act. It would appear, therefore, that there are still no dimensional limits on single-structure caravans, providing they comply with section 29.

The grant of consent for holiday caravans will permit the stationing of any structure within the statutory definition of "caravan", unless the consent contains conditions to the contrary. This has been established by the case of *Wyre Forest District Council* v *Secretary of State for the Environment* [1990] 2 PLR 95. This House of Lords decision, overturning an earlier Court of Appeal decision, decided that the term "caravan" contained in a planning consent granted after the commencement of the 1960 Act, should have its statutory meaning. In this particular case, the owners of a park with consent granted in 1961 for "holiday caravans" were allowed to site twin-unit Cosalt holiday homes.

Section 13 of the 1968 Act gives the minister power to make statutory instruments to vary the maximum dimensions. This power has not yet been exercised. Unfortunately, neither section 13, nor regulations, set out the way in which the maximum dimensions are to be measured. For instance, does the 20ft maximum width relate to the distance between the main sides of the unit measured externally, or does it relate to the distance between eaves where there is a pitched and overhanging roof? Should projecting porches be included or excluded from the measurement? In practice, these questions have created substantial difficulties for local authorities, park owners and manufacturers.

While the questions have not been resolved through the courts, considerable help is provided by a planning appeal decision in October 1991. The appeal was by Allied Care Initiative Ltd and related to the Pines Caravan Park, Anglesey (P45/1093–1165; P45/1184). *Inter alia*, the inspector decided:

(a) The correct method of measurement for the purposes of section 13(2)(*b*) of the 1968 Act should be between the exterior surfaces of the structure's side elevations.

(b) Width measurements should exclude projections such as eaves and guttering.

(c) A marginal excess in width of 1 or 2 ins should be regarded as *de minimis* and is not sufficient to bring structures outside the definition.

(d) Open type porches, of the type envisaged by the 1989 Model Site Licence Standards, should be treated as "projections" and not be included in the width measurement for definition purposes.

An indication of the limits of the definition of caravan, is given by another planning appeal decision. This decision, dated April 1991, concerned Mr and Mrs Short and their appeal in respect of Stour Hill Farm, Dorset (APP/C/89/N1215/1,2,4,5). Here it was contended that the existence of planning consent for residential caravans permitted the erection of structures known as "Permohomes". The inspector held that these were outside the statutory definition of "caravans" because, *inter alia*:

(a) The Permohomes had the appearance of bungalows.

(b) The movement of them was impractical.

(c) To accord with manufacturer's recommendations, Permo-homes required the support of brick plinths on permanent strip foundations, incorporating damp-proof courses and internal piers.

(d) The roofing of the Permohomes was undertaken after the structures had been put in place, involving felting, boarding and tiling which amounted to "building operations" well in excess of assembly "by means of bolts, clamps or other devices" specified in section 13(1)(a) of the 1968 Act.

The Pines Caravan Park appeal was heard after the result of the Stour Hill Farm appeal. The appellant's submissions in the *Pines* case contrasted the normal "skirting" around the base of caravans and mobile homes, with the structurally significant plinth and support to Permohomes. They also contrasted the practice of sometimes adding roof parts *in situ* to mobile homes, with the conventional tiling and other roofing work needed to Permohomes. These contrasts seem to have been accepted by the inspector in the *Pines* case.

More recent guidance has been provided by the case of *Carter* v *Secretary of State for the Environment* (1 WLR 1212), decided by the Court of Appeal in March 1994. The case concerned a structure consisting of four prefabricated panels brought to the site by lorry. The panels were bolted together on site and then dragged into position by a mechanical digger. The structure had no chassis, and rested on concrete blocks on a concrete base. Evidence had been given that the structure had not been designed to be moved as a single structure, and could be removed from the site only if it was dismantled. The Court held that to comply with the legal definition of "a caravan" a structure had to be capable of being moved as a single unit.

To qualify as "a caravan" it is essential that a structure has been *designed or adapted* for human habitation. It is not sufficient that a structure happens to be lived in. In the case of *Backer* v *Secretary of State for the Environment* (1983 1 WLR 1485) it was held that a Comer van, which was being used for human habitation, was not "a caravan" because it had not been physically altered for the purpose of habitation.

It is clear that the definition of caravan relates to the nature of the structure and the purpose for which it is designed or adapted. The definition does not concern itself with the use to which it is actually put. The term "caravan", therefore, will embrace equally:

(a) a small touring caravan towed to a site at holiday times and for the rest of the time parked in its owner's driveway,

(b) a dormobile (motorised caravan),

(c) a luxury 12ft-wide holiday caravan left on its pitch throughout the year and connected directly to mains water, electricity, gas and drainage, and

(d) a 1,200 sq ft mobile home occupied as a residence and complete with central heating and double glazing.

All legally are caravans. Equally, all land used for the stationing of such structures comprise "caravan sites" if the structures are so stationed for the purposes of habitation.

Questions of the type and length of use of caravan sites will depend on conditions contained in the authorising planning consents and site licences. Whether they are to be used residentially or for holidays, whether they can remain on site throughout the year or for short periods only, whether they can be occupied throughout the year or for part of the year only. All these are matters which are controlled by express conditions. In the absence of such conditions, the site owner will have complete freedom of choice as to the size and use of the structures on his site, providing they comply with the definition of "caravan".

Caravan Sites and Control of Development Act 1960

Apart from defining "a caravan", this Act introduced a special form of control of caravan sites by means of site licences. For caravans this replaced the more general powers of control for "moveable dwellings" contained in section 269 of the Public Health Act 1936. Henceforward, caravan parks were subject to dual control under planning and licensing regulations. It must be appreciated that a caravan site today must have *both* consents. Planning consents and site licence consents are not alternatives.

As a use of land, caravan sites constitute a form of development. As such, since the introduction of the Town and Country Planning Act 1947, they have required planning consent. Failure to obtain consent gives rise to the same powers of enforcement under the Town and Country Planning Acts as any other form of unauthorised development.

Since 1960, no land may be used as a caravan site unless the occupier holds a current site licence under Part I of the Caravan Sites and Control of Development Act 1960. Contravention of this requirement is an offence for which the occupier can be fined on conviction. Enforcement, therefore, is through the courts rather than through the planning mechanism set up by the Town and Country Planning Acts. The 1960 Act, and subsequent regulations, lay down the timetable for the application for, and grant of, site licences, and the form which applications must take. Special provisions were made for dealing with land already in use as a caravan site when the Act came into effect.

Before a site licence can be issued, the occupier of the land *must* have the benefit of a specific planning consent. Section 3(3) of the Act is very emphatic on this point:

A local authority may on an application under this section issue a site licence in respect of the land if, *and only if*, the applicant is, at the time when the site licence is issued, entitled to the benefit of a permission for the use of the land as a caravan site granted under Part III of the Act of 1947. . . .

This has created a serious anomaly in relation to Established Use Certificates which are referred to later in this chapter.

The local authority is empowered to impose conditions in a site licence and these powers are very wide. Section 5(1) authorises such conditions as the local authority may think "necessary or desirable to impose on the occupier of the land in the interests of persons dwelling thereon in caravans, or of any other class of persons, or of the public at large". In particular, the conditions may:

(a) Restrict the occasions on which caravans are stationed on the land or the number of caravans which may be stationed at any one time.

(b) Control the types of caravan which may be stationed on the land.

(c) Regulate the positions in which caravans may be stationed on the land, and restrict or regulate the stationing on the land, at any time when caravans are so stationed, of structures, vehicles and tents.

(d) Secure steps to preserve or enhance the amenity of the land, including planting and replanting with trees and bushes.

(e) Secure that when caravans are stationed on the land, proper measures are taken to prevent and detect fire and that adequate means of fire fighting are provided and maintained.

(f) Secure that adequate sanitary facilities, services and equipment are provided for the use of persons dwelling on the land in caravans, and that such facilities are properly maintained.

The original intention was that planning control should determine whether the principle of using land as a caravan site was acceptable. In other words, it should determine the principle in relation to policy, amenity and highway considerations. All other matters of layout, type, length of use, facilities, etc. should be controlled through the site licence. The situation was summarised in Para 6 of Development Control Policy Note Number 8 entitled *Caravan sites*, issued in 1969. Para 6 has now been withdrawn by PPG3 (Housing) 1992. However, Para 10, which relates to holiday caravans, remains in force and refers back to the parts of former Para 6 which dealt with planning conditions. The following extract from former Para 6 therefore remains helpful when considering what matters normally should be covered by planning conditions and what matters by site licence conditions.

Planning permission will normally be required for the change of use of the land involved in stationing caravans upon it, rather than the site works and services. Caravan sites (with certain exceptions) also have to be licensed under the Caravan Sites and Control of Development Act 1960 and such matters as services, equipment and living conditions on the site are regulated by the terms of the site licence. Any ancillary development required by the site licence has a general permission under the Town and Country Planning General Development Order so that any conditions attached to the planning permission will normally be concerned with the land use aspects and not with matters which can more properly be dealt with by a site licence. The distinction is broadly between the external effects of the project, ie the impact of the site on its surroundings. and the internal conditions or matters which affect only the caravans. There may, however, be circumstances in which it would be right for the planning permission to regulate a matter which is normally left to the site licence. For example, it may sometimes be necessary for amenity reasons to limit the number of caravans on a site or to control the layout, design or siting of ancillary buildings more strictly than would be necessary for licensing purposes.

From the outset, however, it was common for the planning consent to include conditions determining the *type* of site (eg residential, static holiday, touring). Steadily, the trend has grown for planning consents to include conditions controlling a number of other aspects of the use and development of caravan sites, in particular as to numbers, length of season and landscaping. There is now much duplication between planning conditions and site licence conditions. Policy varies widely between different local authorities. Some authorities still control only the type of park through planning conditions. Others, at the other extreme, impose conditions reserving to the local planning authority the right to approve detailed layouts, roads and parking arrangements and buildings required with the development.

The extent of licence conditions is governed by section 5 of the 1960 Act. It used to be believed that licence conditions could not relate to matters which strictly were of a *planning* nature rather than of a public health nature. Recently, the position has been clarified by the Court of Appeal decision in the case of *Babbage* v *North Norfolk District Council* [1990] 1 PLR 65.

This case related to the physical removal of static holiday caravans during the winter months. This was not required by planning conditions, but was required by site licence conditions. It was decided that this was an invalid licence condition which "took away" from the grant of planning consent. It was decided that the condition was directed to the improvement of visual amenity during the winter, not to the site as a caravan site. From the text of the decision it seems that site licence conditions can deal validly with matters which come both within normal "planning" considerations and within normal "site licence" considerations, but they cannot deal validly with matters which come *solely* within normal "planning" considerations.

Section 5(6) of the 1960 Act authorises the minister to specify model standards to cover layout and the provision of facilities, services and equipment. The original model standards were issued in 1960 and have since been revised. The current model standards are contained in Circular 23/83 – *Caravan Sites and Control of Development Act 1960* – for touring caravan parks, and in Circular 14/89 – *Caravan Sites and Control of Development Act 1960* – *Model Standards* – for static holiday parks and residential parks. The 1960 Act requires that the local authority "shall have regard to any standards so specified", but the authority has discretion to vary or supplement the standard conditions. In the event of an applicant being dissatisfied with imposed licence conditions, there is a right of appeal to the magistrates' court. The local authority has the right to vary conditions at any time. Equally, the occupier can apply for a variation at any time.

Exemptions from planning and site licence control

Exemptions from site licensing Schedule 1 to the Caravan Sites and Control of Development Act 1960 lists 11 situations where land may be used as a caravan site without a licence. Briefly, these may be summarised as follows:

1. Use of land within the curtilage of a dwelling house if the use is incidental to the enjoyment of that dwelling house.
2. Use of land by a person travelling with a caravan for a period including not more than two nights, providing:
   (a) that only one caravan is stationed on the land at any one time; and
   (b) the number of days during which caravans are stationed on the land does not exceed 28 in total in any one year.
3. Use of land with an area of not less than 5 acres, for a maximum of three caravans at any one time, for a maximum of 28 days in total in any one year.
4. Use of land occupied by an exempted organisation (ie an organisation holding a certificate of exemption under para 12, Schedule 1 to the 1960 Act). The use must be for the purposes of recreation and must be under the supervision of the organisation.
5. Use of land approved by an exempted organisation for up to five caravans at any one time provided that the stationing of caravans is for the recreational use of the members of that organisation.
6. Use of land for meetings (rallies) of members of an exempted organisation, providing the meetings are supervised by that organisation and last for not more than five days.
7 and 8. Use of land for the accommodation of seasonal agricultural and forestry workers during the season that those workers are employed in agriculture or forestry work, on land in the same occupation.
9. Use of land part of, or adjoining, a building site for the accommodation of persons connected with the building work.
10. Use of land by travelling showmen, provided that the showman is a member of an organisation of travelling showmen holding a current certificate from the minister, and that either the showman is travelling for the purposes of business or has taken up winter quarters on the land during the period October 1 to March 1.
11. Use of land occupied by the local authority in whose area the land is situated.

Exemptions from planning control The Town and Country Planning (General Permitted Development) Order 1995 includes two specific categories for caravan sites, under which development is permitted, subject to any restriction imposed by a direction under article 4 of the order.

Schedule 2, Part 5, Class A treats as permitted development most of the uses of land as a caravan site, which are exempt from the need for a site licence under the Caravan Sites and Control of Development Act 1960. These are the circumstances listed in Schedule 1 to the Act and already summarised. The circumstances listed in Schedule 1 and which are *not* covered by this part of the general development order as permitted development are:

1. Use of land within the curtilage of a dwelling (this use is already covered by the more general category of permitted development in Part 1 in Schedule 2 to the order).
2. Use of land by a travelling showman for his winter quarters (however, use by a travelling showman while travelling for the purpose of his business is included as permitted development).

Schedule 2, Part 5, Class B treats as permitted development any development required by the conditions of a current site licence under the 1960 Act.

This is a most important concession for caravan sites and avoids the necessity of obtaining planning consent for a very wide range of work which has to be undertaken when a caravan site is developed. Having obtained planning consent for the *use* of land as a caravan site, and having obtained a site licence to lay out the site in a certain way, no further planning consent is needed for the works required by that site licence, even though these works may amount to development involving building or engineering works. However, consent under the building regulations will still be required in certain circumstances.

It has to be noted that to come within Class B, the development must be *required* by the site licence. Other development will still require planning consent, even though it may represent an improvement on the minimum standards required by the site licence. For instance, a site licence condition requiring the provision of a facilities block to provide communal toilet, washing and shower facilities for a holiday park, will not cover the alternative of providing direct drain connections to individual caravans.

The detailed requirements of site licences vary between different authorities and different types of sites. However, a licence following the 1989 model standards would include the following main categories of development which become permitted development under Class B:

- toilet and shower blocks
- roads
- parking facilities
- hard standings
- fire and water points
- sewage treatment facilities (where mains sewerage is not available).

Special planning considerations

The valuer should be aware of two planning considerations which may have an important impact on the use and value of certain parks. These relate to Established Use Certificates & Certificates of Lawful Use or Development (Town and Country Planning Act 1990, as amended) and Deemed Planning Consents (Caravan Sites and Control of Development Act 1960).

Certificates of Established Use/Lawful Use

A use of land for caravans, without planning consent, may be "established" if the use commenced prior to the end of 1963 and has been continuous since. An Established Use Certificate could be obtained under section 192 of the Town and Country Planning Act 1990. However an Established Use Certificate itself will not legally entitle the owner to use the land as a caravan site, since a site licence will also be needed. Under the 1960 Act a licence can be granted only if planning consent exists. An Established Use Certificate does not amount to the grant of planning consent. It merely protects the owner from enforcement action by the local authority. Holding a certificate therefore does not entitle the owner to the vital site licence.

Since July 1992 the provisions for Established Use Certificates have been replaced by provisions for Certificates of Lawful Use or Development (section 10, Planning and Compensation Act 1991), For the purposes of obtaining a caravan site licence under the Caravan Site and Control of Development Act 1960, a Certificate of Lawful Use or Development will have the same effect as the grant of planning consent. To qualify for a Certificate of Lawful Use, the applicant must be able to prove the continuation of use for at least

10 years prior to the date of the application. Holders of Established Use Certificates may apply for their "conversion" to Certificates of Lawful Use.

Deemed Planning Consents

Deemed planning consents may arise from the detailed timetable for licence applications and decisions laid down in the 1960 Act. Section 3 provides for the issue of a licence only where land has a specific planning consent. In 1960 many caravan parks existed, which had grown up in the past without any specific planning consent. Section 17, therefore, dealing with those "existing sites" provided that an application for a site licence should also be treated as an application for planning consent. This applied where site licence applications were made within two months of the commencement date of the Act (August 29, 1960), or within such longer periods as the local authority allowed.

From the date of the licence application the local planning authority had a period of six months within which either:

(a) to grant planning consent, with or without conditions; or

(b) to serve an enforcement notice.

If the planning authority failed to take either of those steps within the six-month period, then consent was deemed to be granted "without condition or limitation".

Where deemed consents apply (in practice many have been found in the past and even now – 35 years later – the occasional "new discovery" is still made), it is important to realise that there is no planning limitation on the type of caravan, on the number of caravans, or on the method of use of caravans. The only control will be through site licence conditions. Whatever may be its present use, therefore, a park with a deemed planning consent can be available for mobile homes, static holiday caravans or touring caravans, to the maximum density allowed under site licence conditions. The significance of such flexibility on the valuation of a caravan park can be substantial, especially for a holiday park in an area with a high demand for mobile homes.

Methods of valuation

General considerations

A characteristic which holiday caravan parks share with other forms of leisure property, is that they are essentially *businesses*. When deciding what purchase price or rent to pay, the prospective purchaser or tenant will be concerned with the direct financial rewards. The vital question is that of profitability. How much profit can be generated? Out of that profit how much can be afforded in the form of rent? What capital cost will be supported by that profit? Are present trading results reliable? Do they reflect the true potential or are there other factors which have not yet been realised? Can the profit level be sustained – have there been changes in trading conditions or are there special factors (such as sales of caravans) which may not be repeated?

Holiday caravan parks share the characteristic of other leisure properties, that in almost all cases value will reflect a business which is already trading. Rarely will the valuer be faced with an empty disused property to be valued. Normally the business will be up and running – even if it is badly run – and the valuation will reflect not only the "bricks and mortar of the property" but also the reputation which has been built up for the property, and the established trading, supported by records and other systems. Usually the property will be transferred with the benefit of trade equipment and furnishings, in addition to the customary "landlord's fixtures and fittings". Frequently the purchase of a caravan park will include the value of a number of sited caravans, complete with their equipment.

On the face of it, it should be possible to separate the value of equipment and furnishings from the value of the freehold property. In practice this does not work if one is taking over a trading business. How does one continue to run a club for instance without the necessary furniture and equipment? The cost of replacing existing furniture and equipment may be out of all proportion to the value of the existing items as part of the going concern.

More difficult still is the attempt to separate goodwill. On a small park the length of season and number of repeat bookings frequently is influenced by the personality of the owner. However, this is not likely to evaporate immediately on change of ownership. The benefit would be lost only if the new owner showed a totally different attitude. Most of the goodwill therefore will attach to the name of the property, rather than the name of the owner, and will automatically transfer to the purchaser. This is not something which the vendor can "detach and take away with him".

Much of the business generated by a park will be due to its location rather than to its management. This part of the business is sometimes referred to as "inherent goodwill". This is business that has been built up due to the location of the park (eg its proximity to the beach) rather than to the personality of its owner. Clearly this cannot be separated from the park.

A different situation arises where several parks are owned and run under a well-known "brand name". Because of the way holiday-makers may have been persuaded to associate that brand name with quality of service, quality of facilities etc, the loss of the use of the brand name (and of the corporate advertising that goes with it) could well be a serious loss to the business. For such parks, being sold or let separately and privately, the capital or rental value could well be less than is indicated by its trading results whilst part of the original group.

When valuing caravan parks therefore it is usual to value them inclusive of goodwill. If, for accountancy purposes, a split is required this will be an "artificial" apportionment only – a fact which should be made clear in any report.

Since, with a holiday caravan park, the prime concern will be with actual or potential profit, all valuations will include an assessment of profit. Where reliable trading accounts are available these will form the basis of the "profits method" of valuation These will be subject to a number of adjustments referred to later. Where reliable trading accounts are not available, the valuer will need to produce an assessment of available trading to produce a predicted profit level. Such an assessment will in any event be needed to check the "reality" of any disclosed accounts.

In valuations, the use of trading accounts, and of profit and loss predictions, can be taken only so far. The valuation of a caravan park still depends on the analysis of known market results and the use of that information in assessing the value of the subject property. Even though the final assessment may result largely or entirely from a consideration of profit potential, it still has to relate back to the reality of the market place. One cannot assume for instance that the yield required from a caravan park will be the same as a yield required from a retail shop, from an investment with a building society, or from an investment in an amusement arcade. The valuation of a caravan park still has to follow the market, not seek to lead it.

To adopt an accounts basis with any confidence one has first to analyse known market results in relation to the trading achieved on those parks, or the predicted trading on those parks. Only in that way will one be able to judge the yield that the market would require from its investment. Equally one has to assess how to treat the "add ons" such as bar and amusement facilities, shop, playground and swimming facilities and living accommodation. A valuation based on trading potential can be built up for most of these elements, but only if the figures are based on the analysis of known market results.

In practice, rarely will a valuation be completed solely on the accounts basis. Normally this basis will run side by side with a direct physical comparison, each basis acting as a check on the other. The weight to be given to each will depend largely on the strength of evidence available. If the best evidence available produces a comparison on a physical basis, then this will be the method to be adopted first. Such information as is available on actual or estimated trading, will then be used as a check. Equally, if physical comparison evidence is very limited, but there is good information on financial results, then it is the trading basis which will be looked to first and the physical comparison used as a check.

One method used without the other is extremely dangerous. A set of accounts produced by a highly successful operator may suggest a value, seen to be unrealistically high when checked on a physical comparison basis. Equally, a valuation on the physical comparison basis may seem realistic until one considers the actual trading results. These may indicate that the figure is too high and could never be supported by the available profit.

A third check is sometimes provided by looking at development costs (ie the contractors' test). This may occasionally be of help, particularly with an undeveloped park. However, while it may seem logical to approach valuation on the basis of basic land values plus cost of development, what matters at the end of the day is not how much the development will cost, but how much profit can be generated from it. It is that, and only that, which will determine the proper value.

In practice of course rarely does a comparison of the financial and physical methods of valuation produce a neat and consistent answer. The actual market place will include prospective purchasers who take a subjective view of the property. This may be because they like the view, or the locality, or the living accommodation. There will be prospective purchasers who are over optimistic (or over pessimistic) on the results they can achieve, and purchasers with special needs (such as purchasers looking for roll-over relief from taxation, and owners of existing groups wishing to expand). Such influences can distort market evidence but cannot be ignored.

These influences will be greater with the smaller parks and less with the larger parks. Purchasers of large parks will tend to be established businessmen or company groups, who will take a hard view on potential profit. Individuals, supported by lending organisations, again will be forced to take a hard view on likely profits. The individual buying a small park, however, with all or most of the money available without having to borrow, will be heavily influenced by the "way of life" attitude. He or she will certainly be influenced by the part of the country and the quality of the living accommodation. For many such purchasers it is less a question of the "proper value" and more a question of whether he or she has sufficient money to buy the proposed property.

However much care is taken in comparing one property with another, and however much care is taken in checking and analysing accounts, inevitably at the end of the day the final value will depend very much on the valuer's "instinct", gained from experience in the industry and from a detailed knowledge of the current market conditions. This is an essential ingredient which must always be added to the "mathematical" valuations based on direct comparisons, and accounts.

Factors influencing value

It is impossible to provide an exhaustive list of all the factors that have to be borne in mind when preparing a valuation of a holiday caravan park. However there are some prime factors which will apply to all parks.

Location As with all property, the fundamental factor is that of location. This is particularly important for holiday caravan parks. Location is vital in a national sense and in a local sense.

Nationally, location is vital in determining whether the park is in an area for which there is a demand, and is in an area accessible to the source of that demand. Also whether the location is "fashionable". As an example of the last, parts of Wales and the West Country historically were pre-eminent in attracting the family tourist – ie those looking for fresh air, freedom from congestion and areas of unspoilt coastline, particularly sandy beaches. With the advent of the packaged foreign holiday, and the availability of inexpensive holidays on the sunny beaches of Spain and elsewhere, much of that trade has moved abroad, leaving park owners in those areas looking for alternative holiday outlets.

At the same time increased emphasis on leisure activities and the shortening of the average working week, has increased the demand for short second holidays, for weekend breaks and for the ownership of holiday "cottages". For these, the factor of prime importance is proximity both to attractive parts of the countryside and to the source of demand. For weekend use, it is essential to be able to reach the accommodation during a Friday evening and to return on a Sunday evening or early Monday morning. This has boosted the value of parks within easy access, via the motorway network, of centres such as London, Birmingham and Manchester. Largely because of this Hampshire and East Dorset have become "fashionable" and high-demand areas.

Local location is also of great importance. This will include proximity to centres of interest (eg historic towns, historic houses, etc), proximity to National Parks and areas of high landscape value (the New Forest and the Lake District are obvious examples). Above all, proximity to the coast.

Local factors of increasing importance, following the rapid increase in interest in "activity" holidays, is accessibility to pursuits such as water sports, fishing and riding. Some of these factors can be created "artificially" (eg it may be possible to start a new riding centre). In other cases availability of the activity depends entirely on the proximity to the right physical assets (eg a large lake for water sports).

Planning and site licence Not only does the valuer have to be sure that current planning and site licence consents exist, he will also have to check:

(a) If the consents are time-limited or permanent (in this connection it should be noted that a site licence can be for a period only as long as the planning consent).

(b) If the consent covers the whole area to be valued.

(c) What conditions are imposed in the consents, particularly as to the type of use permitted (eg static holiday caravans or touring caravans) and the number of caravans permitted and the length of season.

(d) To what extent conditions have been complied with.

Points (a) and (b) above are self evident. In relation to (c) (planning conditions) the valuer needs to consider:

(i) to what extent can the numbers be increased;

(ii) to what extent can the area be increased;

(iii) to what extent can the length of season be increased; and

(iv) can the permitted numbers physically be accommodated?

With the recent increase in the size of the average holiday caravan, on many occasions one now finds holiday parks where physically one cannot accommodate the total number of caravans permitted by the planning consent and site licence.

The extent to which conditions have been complied with (d) is particularly important in connection with the site licence. Are the roads of adequate width? Is there adequate distance between caravans, between caravans and the road and between caravans and the site boundary? Where central toilet facilities are involved, are there any caravans that are too far away? Is the number of communal facilities adequate? Are the fire points sufficient in number and specification? All these questions will require a detailed understanding of site licence conditions and the extent to which they can be "negotiated". For instance, the purchaser who buys on the basis of the existing number of caravan pitches, could find that this number dwindles, and that high cost is incurred, if subsequently caravans have to be moved wider apart.

On touring parks, over the last few years there has been an increasing tendency to refer to "touring units", instead of to touring caravans or to tents. A "touring unit" will now normally mean a towed caravan, a motorised caravan, or a tent. The caravans may be with or without awnings. A park with consent for "touring units" therefore will give the park owner flexibility as to the type of units which he accommodates and in what proportion.

This flexibility is important because demand for the three types of unit fluctuates from year to year and from one part of a year to another. Frequently tourers arrive in groups – families or friends often with a combination of towed caravan and tent. These expect not only to be accommodated on the same park, but also to be able to place the caravan and tent next to each other. There is an increasing difficulty in distinguishing between some types of caravans and tents – collapsible caravans and trailer tents are good examples. Also a combination of motorised caravan and tent gives rise to the question – is the motorised caravan used as a conveyance only (in which case legally it can be accommodated on a tent-only park); or is it used partially as living accommodation (in which case legally it cannot be accommodated on a tent-only park).

Quite apart from investigating the permitted number of units therefore it is important to check if these units relate only to caravans, or only to tents, or to a combination of the two. If it is to a combination, is there any restriction on which parts of the park can be used for each, or on the numerical proportions of each?

A further point that should be remembered in this connection is that whereas touring caravans and motorised caravans are licensed under the Caravan Sites and Control Development Act 1960, tents are still licensed under the Public Health Act 1936. Strictly speaking therefore a park with planning consent for say 100 "touring units" will need one 1960 Act licence for 100 caravans and one 1936 Act licence for 100 tents. To the unwary, this could well indicate a park with consent for 100 caravans plus 100 tents – ie a park with consent for 200 touring units. This is the stuff that negligence claims are made of!

Tenure Is the interest to be valued freehold or leasehold? If the latter what are the terms of the lease? How long has the lease to run, when is the next review, what is the basis for review, is the rent intended to cover everything or are there substantial tenants' improvements to be disregarded? A number of caravan parks have been developed by a tenant on someone else's land, on the basis that on review the value of tenants' improvements is ignored (ie essentially rent is paid on the land value only). These may be for a term as short as 21 or 25 years. Towards the end of the term therefore the rent may look modest in relation to the overall value of the improved park, and the profit-rent element will be high. However, apart from fears that the lease may not be renewed at the end of the term, one also has to remember that the rent under a renewed lease may be able to reflect the value of the improved park. I have come across more than one hapless tenant who could not believe that a landlord was entitled to charge a rent substantially higher than the equivalent value of the rent when he purchased the lease.

Whether the interest is freehold or leasehold one has to be aware of encumbrances – particulary easements, rights of way and public footpaths. I know of at least one case of a park subject to a right of way to a local farm which created no difficulty while the farmer used the right as an occasional alternative access for his tractors and wagons at hay making time. The position changed dramatically when the right became regularly (and lawfully) used for the twice daily passage of a large milking herd to a newly constructed milking parlour! Similarly with public rights of way. If a park is to be upgraded to provide a secluded holiday park with expensive units and a high level of facilities, the value will not be enhanced if members of the general public have the right to cross over it between the village and the beach.

Also under this heading, the valuer must be very clear as to the extent of any tenancies or licences. A long lease, for instance, of the club complex could well inhibit redevelopment plans, or the wish to run the park in a different way. Licences may be genuine licences or they may turn out to have the legal effect of tenancies, with disastrous results on the purchaser's development and management plans.

Pitch fees The level of pitch fee is most important and provides a valuable guide to the relative value of parks. The level of fee will have to be competitive with nearby and similar parks. For static caravans it may be difficult to raise immediately the level of fees which traditionally has been set at a low level. There may be agreements which prevent this. Even if legally the fees can be increased, it may not be possible to achieve this in the immediate future without totally disrupting the park and risking a high level of vacancies.

Length of season The length of season is most important, particulary for static parks with "hire fleet" caravans, and on touring parks. An apparently attractive high level of tariff will not help if it is acting as a deterrent and can be achieved only during a few weeks of the year. The need increasingly is to expand the use of the park over a longer period of the year and to even out the peaks and troughs.

Level of competition in the area The level of competition in the area is of obvious importance. However, special considerations apply to parks which include pitches for tents. In popular touring areas, many farms take in tents under the 28-day rule. For this neither planning consent nor a site licence is required. (Town and Country Planning General Development Order 1988, Schedule 2, Part 4, Class B.) Consequently, the facilities offered can be extremely limited. Because of this the costs to the farm owners are low. They can afford to under-cut the charge from owners of nearby licensed sites where much higher overheads have to be carried. In many areas this right of 28-day camping has been restricted or removed by the introduction of an article 4 direction. Where such directions exist, a site with planning consent for tents will have something of a "monopoly" situation and will be able to charge high prices, and secure a good occupancy rate. In areas where directions do not exist, competition from unlicensed sites will reduce occupancy rates and limit the fee charged, especially during the peak period when the 28-day rights are normally exercised.

Similar situations may arise with competition from nearby touring caravan parks operated privately as parks approved by an exempted organisation, or parks run directly by an exempted organisation. In each case the parks will be outside both planning and site licence control (paras 4 and 5, of Schedule 1, Caravan Sites and Control of Development Act 1960).

Pitch licence agreements On static holiday parks inquiry has to be made as to the existence of pitch agreements. There is a code of practice for the sale and siting of holiday caravans which has been drawn up by the British Holiday & Home Parks Association Ltd and the National Caravan Council in conjunction with the Office of Fair Trading. Pitch agreements provided in accordance with this code provide, *inter alia*, a measure of security to the caravan owner, and a limitation on the amount of annual pitch fee increases. This will be most important where the level of fees appears to be low and one is considering potential income. Where these agreements exist it will be important to know the date when the agreements were issued and the age of caravans. This will determine how soon caravan owners could be required to remove their caravans, opening the door to profit on the sale of new caravans, and the adjustment of the level of pitch fees.

Other general factors Other factors of vital importance, but more self evident, include:
- the standard of development and the condition of the park and its buildings
- the extent and quality of central facilities (eg covered swimming pool, bar and restaurant, amusement arcade)
- the availability of services
- the quality of living accommodation and, on larger parks, staff accommodation
- The trading records.

Direct physical comparison
This is the method used for most forms of non-leisure property and is the simplest to understand. Essentially it is based on a direct

physical comparison between the park being valued, and one or more similar parks which have recently been sold or let. In other words, with other parks for which the current open market capital or rental value is known.

For such a system to be used, there are two requirements:
1. reliable open-market evidence
2. a reliable form of analysis.

1. Reliable market evidence To be reliable, this evidence must be:
- recent
- comparable
- arms length.

The result will be only as good as the quality of the evidence. The evidence used must be as close as possible in time to the date of the valuation exercise. The recent economic recession and down-turn in property values makes the bulk of earlier evidence of little value for current valuations. Details of a sale of a holiday caravan park in 1988, for instance, when the market was strong, will be of very little help when valuing a park early in 1993, when the market was weak. This is true however similar the parks may have been in other ways. If evidence of value has to be adjusted for substantial fluctuations in market conditions, then those adjustments will be subject to judgement, and will make the exercise unreliable.

The property must be similar in type. While analysis will iron out a number of differences between comparable properties (referred to later) it still relies on comparing like with like. The analysed sale for instance of a touring caravan or tenting park, will be of limited value when trying to value a static holiday caravan or chalet park. Similarly, the analysis of the sale of a 50-pitch static park without facilities but with a pleasant house, may be very misleading when used to help value a large commercial park of say 1,000 pitches, fully equipped with dance hall, swimming pool and amusement arcade.

The comparables must be similar in terms of location. In practice, in most cases the valuer will have to cope with locational adjustments, since a holiday caravan park relies so much on its precise location. Rarely will the valuer have the luxury of valuing a park, knowing the market price paid for a similar park almost next door. There will be marked differences in value resulting from a comparatively small physical distance. Obvious examples will be proximity to the sea, to inland water, to hillside views and so on. Whatever system of valuation is used, the valuer must be able to adjust to reflect differences in the immediate situation. Some help in dealing with this will be provided by the comparative level of pitch fees.

As the degree of separation increases however so does the difficulty of adjustment. There then come into question not only differences of situation within a particular area, but also differences between the areas themselves. As has already been explained some areas are fashionable, some are not – due to a number of factors such as proximity to centres of population, ease of access, and climate. Whilst it is possible to adjust for variations between a park, say, overlooking the sea at Torbay, and one situated slightly further inland, it is much more difficult to adjust for differences of situation between, say, the area of Torbay (an area traditionally popular with holiday-makers) and an area in the Midlands which will rely on totally different demands.

While evidence of sales and lettings in different areas can provide a helpful guide sometimes, the amount of adjustment (even reflecting differences in pitch fees) is so great that the evidence relies more on judgement than on the actual transaction. One is left relying on instinct and judgement rather than on market evidence. At the best, such comparisons can give an indication of the sort of bracket of value one would expect; as a basis for an accurate valuation they are useless. Such evidence from different areas should only be used as an indicator, to check a valuation based on another method (or based on more reliable physical evidence). It should not be used as the basis itself.

The need for evidence to be "arms length" speaks for itself. The valuer is seeking to determine open-market value, assuming full exposure of the property to the market and assuming a willing buyer and willing seller. Inter company transactions, and inter family transactions, will not have tested the market, and will be unreliable as evidence. At best the prices will merely reflect the opinion of the advisors concerned. There are many reasons why the parties may have preferred the transaction to be high or low.

A similar problem will arise with evidence obtained from transactions involving special circumstances. The purchase of a park by an adjoining park owner may be influenced by the wish to cut costs by the economy of scale, or to secure the shared use of central facilities. There may be a premium involved in putting the two parks together – as a result the purchaser may be prepared to pay a higher price. This will still be an arms-length transaction, but it will provide a misleading picture if used for the valuation of a park in more normal circumstances.

It follows that the valuer must know something of the background to transactions to be used as comparables, as well as the financial details of those transactions.

Method of analysis – touring caravan parks

Basic pitch analysis Just like most forms of non-leisure property, caravan parks have their own normal form of analysis. Farms are compared on an acreage basis, offices and warehouses on a square foot or metre basis, and shops on a zoned-square-foot or metre basis. Caravan parks are normally compared on a pitch basis. The business generated by caravan parks will depend largely on the number of caravans which it can accommodate. The number of pitches will be controlled partly by the planning consent, partly by the site licence and partly by physical considerations. Analysis on a pitch basis therefore is far more reliable than one on an area basis.

Looked at at its simplest, if a touring park with 100 developed pitches and no buildings other than the communal toilet/shower blocks, is sold for £250,000, then this would analyse at £2,500 per developed pitch. That value per pitch would then be applied to the property to be valued, with adjustment as necessary to reflect differences in situation. The analysis normally assumes that items of development on the park which are essential for the proper running of the park, but which do not themselves produce income, are reflected in the pitch fee. In this example, therefore, the analysis of £2,500 per pitch will reflect the value of the infrastructure on the park (eg roads, services, standpipes, fire points and electrical hook-ups). It will also include the buildings necessary for the running of the park, and which in the main are required by the site licence. This will cover principally the communal showers, toilets, washing and laundry facilities.

Adjustment for general facilities There is some argument as to whether a launderette, fitted with modern coin-operated machines, should be included in the value of the pitch or valued separately. My own view is that except on a very large commercial park with access to custom from outside, a launderette is never likely to make any significant profit. It is really provided as a facility on the park. However, the method does not greatly matter, as long as one is careful to use the same method for valuing as one does for the analysis (ie if the pitch analysis includes the value of the launderette, the same approach must be adopted when applying the pitch value to the park being valued).

Some doubt arises as to the treatment of ancillary buildings which are not income producing, but which are not a requirement of the site licence. Examples would be a reception office, an administrative office, workshops and stores. If these are on a scale commensurate with the type of park, then my view is that they should be reflected in the pitch value. It is only if they are out of scale, or if they have some alternative commercial use, that they should be valued separately. Again it is a question of valuing and devaluing on the same basis. In practice one tries to reflect in the pitch fee what one would normally expect to find on the park and then to adjust for the exception, rather than the other way round.

In making use of the analysed pitch value, clearly one must bear in mind the standard of development of the park analysed. While one should include within the pitch value items such as roads, services, and communal facilities, one must still reflect the fact that a park with a high standard of development and facilities will be worth more than one with a poor standard. Holiday-makers are going to be more attracted to a park with communal facilities with modern fittings, hot-air dryers and tiled floors and walls, than they would be to a park with what used to be the traditional toilet block constructed of corrugated-asbestos roof and concrete-block limewashed walls! This greater attractiveness will either enable the owner to charge a higher pitch fee, or to fill his park for a longer period of the year (ie achieve a higher occupancy rate), or to keep his park in use for a longer season. Possibly a combination of all three. Turnover, and profit-ability, will thus be higher, and the resultant capital or rental value higher. Some indication of the adjustment necessary will be given by a comparison of the nightly pitch fees. A far better guide will be provided by combining the comparison of pitch fees with a comparison of occupancy rates achieved. This will enable the annual turnover per pitch to be compared, providing a much more reliable guide on comparative values.

Similar adjustments will be needed where the park includes a swimming pool. Normally the pool will be available for use by holiday-makers on the park only. It will usually be used by them free of charge. Normally therefore the value of this would reflect in the pitch fee, although clearly that resultant pitch value will be substantially more than for an equivalent park without a pool. As with the above example of standard of communal facilities, the presence of a pool will normally make the park more attractive to holiday-makers. The need for, and the approach to, pitch value adjustments is the same.

Adjustment for pitch services One also has to differentiate between pitches with electrical hook-ups and those without. To readers not used to touring caravans, an "electrical hook-up" is an electrical point on or close to the pitch to which the caravan can be connected to provide electricity for lighting, refrigerator and television. Commonly these hook-ups come in "banks" of four, one unit servicing four pitches. There is usually an additional charge for an electrical hook-up (commonly the tariff will quote the price for a standard pitch and then quote the extra charge for a pitch with a hook-up). Clearly, a pitch with hook-up facilities will be capable of generating more income and consequently have a higher capital or rental value than an equivalent pitch without.

The provision of services to touring pitches is still developing. The majority of touring parks now have at least some of their pitches provided with electrical hook-ups. An increasing number of parks are also providing either direct water connections, or standpipes and drains serving one or a small group of caravans (the standard site licence condition merely provides for every caravan to be not further than 90 m from a standpipe). There is a growing tendency for parks to provide pitches with their own personal group of services – electricity, water (with or without pipe connection) and drain (usually for basin and sink waste only).

The norm in America, and an increasing tendency on the continent, is to go one step further than this – to provide touring pitches with water, electricity and combined water/foul sewage drainage facilities. Normally this is coupled with providing a hardened base for use by large four-wheeled trailer caravans. These come equipped with toilet and shower facilities as well as the normal sink and wash basin. They provide "self contained" holiday units. On arrival they connect to the water, electricity and drainage connections and are then used very much like a serviced holiday static caravan, until they are disconnected and move on. So far only a minority of parks in the UK have been developed in this way, but undoubtedly this is a trend that will develop. When analysing sales therefore it is essential to understand what type of services can be provided and what are provided, and to adjust as necessary when comparing with the park to be valued.

A final word on adjustments for pitch services. The example so far has assumed 100 developed pitches. I mentioned adjustments for whether hook-ups and other services exist. There will of course be situations where a park includes all developed pitches, but some with hook-ups, some without. In analysing a sale of such a park one either has to analyse on the basis of unserviced pitches and then reflect the increased value of the services, or vice versa. What one should *not* do is to analyse by dividing the sale price by the number of pitches, without reflecting the difference in value of the serviced and non-serviced pitches.

Adjustments for partial development Greater disparities will be produced on parks where the number of developed pitches is less than the number permitted by the planning consent and site licence. Assume for example a park with consent for 150 touring pitches, but where only 100 pitches so far have been developed. The land available for the balance of the 50 pitches may be used for recreational or other purposes, or may be used as an occasional over-spill area. Clearly the right to develop the extra 50 pitches will have a value (unless the demand in that area is totally saturated) but this value will be less than the value of the developed pitches. The difference will depend on the amount of work that is needed to complete the development of the additional pitches. If it involves merely the extension of a roadway, or the provision of a few standpipes and firepoints, then the difference in value will be small. If on the other hand the use of the extra 50 pitches involves the construction of a new toilet block, then the difference in value will be substantial. This is one of the few situations where the "contractor's" method of valuation is used. Commonly the difference in value is calculated by reference to the capital cost of completing the development.

When analysing the sale of a park which is partially developed, the difference between developed and undeveloped pitches *must* be reflected. Taking the example of a permitted 150 pitches, but with only 100 developed, a straight division of the sale price by 150 clearly would produce too low a value for developed pitches when applied elsewhere. Similarly, a division by 100 would produce too high a value per pitch when used elsewhere. The analysis therefore must produce one figure for the developed pitches and one figure for the undeveloped pitches.

One further word of warning, using the same example. Substantial expenditure may be needed to bring into use the remaining 50 pitches – because of the need for extra roads, toilet block etc. However, the remaining 50 pitches will still benefit from *some* of the existing development of the park. It will use the same main-road entrance, the same service connections, the same reception office, possibly the same swimming pool and ancillary building. This compares starkly with the situation of land elsewhere with consent for 50 pitches, where the owner would have to start from scratch. The result of the analysis of the 50 "undeveloped" pitches in the example therefore could not be used to calculate the value of a "green field site" for a new touring park.

Adjustment for living accommodation Living accommodation can present a problem for analysis. Most parks will include at least one unit of living accommodation for the owner or manager. Some parks may include more. The accommodation may vary from a large luxury modern bungalow to a second-hand mobile home. Clearly the more valuable the living accommodation and the smaller the park, the greater will be the proportionate value of the living accommodation, and the more difficult will be the reliable analysis of the sale price.

Some valuers analyse sales to include living accommodation. My view is that this is too dangerous and difficult. I prefer instead, first to deduct from the known sale price the assumed value of the living accommodation and then to analyse the residue. When using this information in a valuation, one works in reverse, valuing first the pitches, and then adding on the value of the living accommodation.

Assessing the value of the living accommodation, either for analysis or valuation, is not easy. Hopefully, within the area, there will be evidence of value of similar types of living accommodation. However, that is only the beginning. One has to consider first that the living accommodation will normally adjoin the holiday park, and frequently be an integral part of it. This may make it less desirable as a private residence and the value will have to be adjusted accordingly. Also one needs to check carefully the planning consent to see if there are conditions included which limit the use of the living accommodation to someone involved with the management of the park. This is quite common with purpose-built dwellings on caravan parks. If the living accommodation is an integral part of the park then there may be no real difference in value. If on the other hand the living accommodation adjoins the park, but physically could be sold off separately, then the difference in value may be considerable.

Having assessed the value of the living accommodation (with adjustments as necessary) one then has to consider whether this value is supportable with the nature of the park. For a normal bungalow or house on a medium or large park, there should be no difficulty. That value of accommodation will probably be needed. However, if it is a luxury property on a small park, then assessment is more difficult. As already mentioned, a small park may appeal to a new entrant into the holiday park business. Typically that will be someone with a house or small business to sell. He will wish to invest the proceeds in a park and to borrow the difference between the sale proceeds and the price of the park. He will wish to buy as large a park as his available capital will allow. Consequently, that purchaser will normally prefer to invest the maximum amount of his capital in the productive part of the park (ie pitches and income-producing facilities) and the minimum in living accommodation. He may well prefer to live in a small bungalow or mobile home if this enables him to acquire a larger park. While on the face of it therefore the presence of a luxury house may appear an attraction, in reality it may prove an obstacle to purchase because of the disproportionate amount of capital to be invested in the living accommodation as opposed to the productive park. That factor has to be reflected both in analysis and valuation.

Illustration of analysis/valuation of touring parks At the end of this chapter example 1 illustrates the analysis of a straightforward 100-pitch touring park, with owner's living accommodation, and a proportion of pitches with hook-ups. Example 2 shows the use of this analysis in valuing a 100-pitch park with scope for further development. For reasons of simplicity it has been assumed that basic pitch values are the same for the park analysed and the park being valued.

Adjustment for revenue-producing buildings Revenue-producing buildings will include such items as a shop, a licensed bar, a restaurant, an amusement arcade and a take-away. On larger parks facilities may also include items such as sports facilities, keep-fit clubs and so on. These certainly have to be treated separately and should never be included within the analysis of pitch value. As with the method of dealing with living accommodation, when analysing a known sale the value of such income-producing buildings has to be first deducted, before the balance is analysed into a value per pitch. In valuing a property, the value of the pitches is first calculated and the value of the buildings then added.

The value of income-producing facilities will vary enormously with the type and size of the park, the availability of outside custom and the scale, standard and condition of the facilities.

The first two of these factors are linked. As with the valuation of the park itself, the true value of the buildings will relate back to the income they are capable of generating. This in turn will depend on the available custom. In most cases this custom will come from within the park itself, so that income produced will vary directly with the number of people accommodated on the park and the length of season. It is important to emphasise here that the determining factor will be the number of people, not the number of pitches. With touring parks, average occupancy per caravan varies quite widely. Commercially run coastal sites will attract caravans with a greater number of occupants than will quieter, inland sites. The annual number of holiday-makers per pitch will depend on the average occupancy per pitch, the occupancy rate for the park (ie the average to which the park is used to capacity) and the length of the season during which the park is open.

The takings from the facilities, and consequently their value, will also vary with available custom from outside. Also with the extent of outside competition. A shop on a park, selling groceries and other everyday items, may have the ability to attract custom from an adjoining park or from an adjoining town, as well as from its own residents. Equally however this may mean that there are competing alternative facilities in the town. It is quite common for park residents to use the park shop for basic everyday needs (or forgotten items), but to do the bulk of their shopping in the nearby town's supermarkets. On the other hand, a shop on a park "in the middle of nowhere" may have to rely solely on the park residents for its custom. However, in the absence of alternative facilities within easy driving distance, the park residents will provide a "captive market".

Shops are probably the most extreme variable in this sense, although a similar situation will apply to licensed bars, restaurants and amusement arcades where facilities can benefit very greatly from custom outside the park, but equally may lose from competition. In considering this question of licensed bars it is necessary to find out the details of the type of licence. Commonly the facilities are limited to use by people resident on the park. In some cases the bar facilities have a full "on" licence enabling general members of the public to be catered for, like any other public house.

Finally, an increasing number of parks are now developing entertainment, club, sports and health facilities to a size and standard which can be "hired out" outside the main holiday season. Frequently these facilities are available only for park users during the main season, but can then be used for outside functions (conferences, weddings, receptions) outside the season. This can be a very valuable source of extra income and will increase substantially the value to be placed on those buildings.

So how does one value the central income-producing facilities in order to analyse sales of parks?

This can be done in one of two ways:

(a) capitalised rental value
(b) capitalised profit.

(a) Capitalised rental value This is the conventional approach to valuing buildings, depending on an assessment of net rental value (clear of costs of repairs, insurance and services). Rental value is then capitalised to reflect the return required for the investment. Rental evidence is available from actual lettings on parks, although arrangements more usually involve licences or concessions, rather than leases. Licence or concession income will need to be adjusted to reflect the services etc provided by the owner – also to reflect the seasonal nature of the occupancy. "Rental value" essentially will reflect a proportion of the potential profit to be derived from the building.

For the reasons already explained, income from park facilities will depend mainly on the number of park residents – not on floor area. Direct comparison from one park to another therefore is very difficult. In practice rental value usually has to be assessed for an individual park calculated from known or estimated profits. Analysis of known transactions will provide valuable evidence on likely profitability per customer and the percentage of profit which a tenant is prepared to pay as rent. Normally this method of valuation will be used only where buildings are in fact occupied under lease licence or concession.

(b) Capitalised profit In most cases the only safe way is to value the buildings on a profits basis (explained below) – ideally based on actual detailed accounts; failing that based on estimated accounts.

To that extent it converts the direct comparison method of valuation to a "hybrid" valuation – ie part physical comparison, part accounts.

Method of analysis – static holiday caravan parks

General principles Most of the principles referred to in connection with touring parks will apply equally to the analysis and valuation of static holiday parks. It is just that with static parks the problems tend to be greater!

As with touring parks, we will consider a straightforward situation of 100 developed pitches. A park of 100 developed pitches without any living accommodation or central facilities might sell for £400,000. That produces a very simple analysis of £4,000 per pitch. As with touring caravans this figure normally will include the infrastructure (roads and services) and any non-income-producing buildings needed for the running of the park (eg reception office, administration office, workshops and stores). The same exceptions also will apply. Similar treatment will be needed for swimming pools, owner's accommodation and income-producing buildings. Precisely the same criteria apply whether it be static holiday caravans or touring caravans.

The main differences arise with the adjustments needed to pitch values, and in the treatment of the caravans themselves.

Pitch values First the pitches. Pitch values will vary even more widely than for touring pitches. This is because of the greater variation possible in the standard of services, and the implication that this has for future sales.

Originally, all static holiday parks comprised small caravans parked on grass with virtually no facilities inside. Lighting and cooking was by bottled gas; water came from standpipes; communal buildings provided toilet, shower, washing and laundry facilities. This still applies to some holiday parks although the great majority of parks now provide at least some direct services to their pitches. On the up to date parks, all the caravans are large modern units including toilet, bath or shower, sink and wash basin facilities. These have water, electricity and foul drainage connected. Gas either is provided in "bottles", or is directly connected, either from the gas-mains supply, or from a bulk-gas supply from within the park itself. Usually these caravans have concrete bases. Until recently most of these holiday caravans were 10ft wide; a growing proportion are now

12ft wide. A number of parks accommodate "twin units" (units bolted together on site giving accommodation 20 ft wide by anything up to 60ft long). The difference in value is substantial. So is the difference in pitch fees available, and/or income available from letting "hire fleet" units.

Some years ago, on a large proportion of static holiday parks all or most of the caravans were owned by the park owner. These were let out for holidays and were known as the owner's "hire fleet". This is still the case with some parks – particularly parks owned by the large companies, owning more than one park, and managing the parks and letting the caravans on a group basis. The pitches on the majority of private parks, however, are now offered out for privately-owned caravans with only a small proportion of pitches occupied by caravans owned by the park owner. For those owners, the main source of income is pitch fees and commissions on sales, plus of course income from any central facilities.

Pitches for privately-owned caravans – sales income In valuing caravan parks it is essential to understand how this system of management works. When a pitch is available, it is offered out to someone who wishes to place a caravan on it. Almost invariably the private individual wanting to use that pitch will have to purchase the caravan through the park operator. In some cases the park operator will already have placed the caravan upon the pitch and the caravan will then be offered for sale with the benefit of its siting and its connection to the services. The initial profit to the park owner will be the difference between the cost of developing the pitch, purchasing the caravan and connecting it to services, and the sale price he receives. His margin will depend entirely on the attractiveness of the park and the degree to which cheaper alternatives are available from his competitors. This is essentially a question of supply and demand. The margin can range from anything from a few hundred pounds to several thousand pounds.

The alternative is for the pitch to be developed with concrete base, and services provided, and for purchasers then to buy a caravan through one of the agencies stipulated by the park owner. The park owner will then site the caravan and connect it to the services. In return for this, the park owner will normally receive a discount from the caravan manufacturer or distributor (ie the purchaser will pay the list price and the park owner will pay a price usually between 20% and 30% less). Frequently a "siting fee" is charged to the caravan purchaser, which will cover the physical cost of positioning the caravan and connecting it to services and may leave a balance to the park owner. In effect this balance provides an element of "key money" to get onto the park. The profits from the siting fee and commission combined will often equate to the profit available through selling the caravan on pitch.

On purchasing the caravan the purchaser will also be granted an annual licence to use the pitch. Historically these licences have been subject to cancellation at the end of the season and the caravan owners have been vulnerable to park owners wishing to secure another sale or to increase pitch fees. Now that more expensive caravans are involved an increasing number of parks provide longer-term agreements. These give a measure of security (usually between five and 10 years), and limit the extent of pitch fee increases. Provision is made for the caravan owner to sell on site. Reference has already been made to the BH&HPA/NCC code of practice.

Pitches for privately-owned caravans – fee income Having purchased a caravan, the purchaser will pay to the park owner a pitch fee – in effect an annual rent for the use of the pitch. This used to be an inclusive fee, but on modern parks now normally covers the use of the pitch only. The caravan owner is then charged with a proportion of rates and services.

Rates are assessed on the park as a whole (including the value of the caravans). Normally this is apportioned roughly in accordance with numbers (after excluding any element of rates relating to central facilities) and recharged to the caravan owner at cost. Electricity is normally recharged through a private meter. A margin of profit is allowed on the recovery of electricity consumed. Gas supplied from bulk storage also normally is recharged through a private meter. In the case of mains gas, it is charged direct by the Gas Board to the caravan owner. Water and drainage commonly still are covered by the pitch fee although there is a growing tendency to exclude these also, the park owner paying the total costs for the park initially and then apportioning this between individual pitches. With the advent of measured sewage charges, and with the rapid increase in water charges since the privatisation of water companies, water and drainage charges are representing a significant cost to the park owner. The tendency will grow for these to be charged as an extra to the pitch fee.

In comparing pitch fees therefore the valuer has to be very clear as to the extent to which the pitch fees represent "net" income to the park owner, or include the cost of services paid for by him. Pitch fees are also now subject to VAT and again the valuer needs to be sure that the figure he is using is net of VAT.

Comparative value of serviced/unserviced pitches An apparent anomaly can arise with the relative values of serviced and unserviced pitches. As with touring parks, a serviced static pitch will normally be worth more than an unserviced static pitch, and this has to be reflected both in the analysis of sales, and in a valuation. However this is not always the case. With a park in a popular area, if there are unserviced pitches which can be made available (because either they are vacant or because there are old caravans which can be removed), then there may be potential to service those pitches and then to sell caravans on them producing a profit *greater* than the cost of development. In those circumstances, if occupation of the serviced pitches was secured by agreement to 5–10 years (ie where the prospect of profit on resale is deferred for that period), then the value of the immediately available unserviced pitches could be greater than the value of the occupied serviced pitches.

Valuation of caravans Where a park includes "hire fleet" caravans then these normally will be included in the valuation. The value of the caravans must be allowed for in addition to the pitch value. The "hire fleet" caravans will normally be valued with the benefit of existing furnishing and equipment – in other words on a going concern basis including everything in the caravan necessary to allow it to be let.

There is a *Glass's Guide* issued several times a year which lists the second-hand value of caravans. This is commonly used to establish the value of caravans for analysis and valuation. This will usually produce the minimum value – ie the use of the guide will indicate the value of the caravans if sold off separately. However, the cost of siting the caravans and connecting them to services has already been covered. Also, for the reasons explained above, the sited caravan may well have a value significantly higher than the combined second-hand value of the caravan, plus the average value of the pitch. This therefore has to be allowed for, usually by valuing the pitch and caravan as one unit. Normally, of course, the total value of these "units", when included in the overall value of the park, will be less than the multiple of the individual sale values of the "units".

This is necessary to reflect the time, effort, risk and advertising cost to the park owner of securing those sales; plus his expected share of profit. However, the potential is very real and must be reflected in both valuation and analysis.

Profits

It has already been emphasised that a caravan park essentially is a business, normally bought and sold as a going concern. The prime concern of anyone buying or leasing a park therefore is the profit that the business of that park can generate. This therefore comes down to the real fundamentals of valuation. What profit will the business generate, and how much of that profit is needed to reflect the purchaser's or tenant's risk, enterprise and management skills? For a rental valuation, the prime concern will be "divisible profit" (ie the profit left after taking out expenses before rent). This is the balance available to provide the landlord with payment for the use of his property and the tenant for his enterprise management and risk. The proportion in which this balance has to be divided, will vary with the nature and size of the business, the security of the income, and the scope for increasing income.

Where a calculation of capital value is concerned, then the question will be the relation of net profit to purchase price – ie the percentage return yielded by the investment. Again the percentage return required will vary with the type and size of business, the security of the income, and the scope for increasing income (and/or capital value).

Before explaining how accounts and predictions are used, it must be emphasised again that the profits method of valuation has to be related to the reality of the market place. The profits method is a means of calculating what a willing and properly-advised tenant or purchaser would pay for a property. Unlike the direct physical comparison method, the use of accounts and predictions will to some extent "create" market value. This is the way in which the prospective tenant or purchaser will assess what they can afford to pay. However, market forces will dictate the degree to which a tenant or purchaser is cautious or optimistic in treating trends in lettings and sales. More fundamentally, only the market can determine what an actual tenant or an actual purchaser will be prepared to accept as their part of the "divisible balance of profit" or as a return on capital invested. These percentages are absolutely fundamental to a valuation and only a small variation will make a very significant difference to the outcome. The percentages will fluctuate with market conditions. Clearly, in a strong growth market, a tenant will be prepared to accept a lower proportion of divisible profit and a purchaser will accept a lower return. Conversely, in a stagnant market the expected proportion of divisible profit will be higher and the return will be higher.

The profits method will be applied either to actual accounts, or to financial predictions, or possibly to a combination of the two.

The preference will be to use actual accounts, since these provide firm evidence of what actually can be achieved from a particular park. Ideally one looks at accounts over the immediately preceding three years and then takes either the average, or the most recent year. This will depend upon the trend which has been shown during the three years, and upon the valuer's view of future prospects. A number of adjustments have to be made which will be dealt with later.

Unfortunately, accounts are not always available. Sometimes prospective vendors refuse to disclose them. The vendor may have been trading from that park for a short time only. The vendor may be behind with his accounting, and the most recent available accounts may be two years "out of date". The park may be newly developed and trading only just started. In those circumstances the valuer using the profits method will have to predict the likely income and expenditure. Again this is dealt with in detail later.

The valuer may be provided with some actual accounts, which include information which the valuer feels is unreliable on which to base a valuation. This may be because they are out of date, or the valuer has reason to believe that the park has been either under-trading or over-trading. In these circumstances the valuer may be able to use some of the basic information provided by the accounts, but have to use his own knowledge and experience to adjust the figures to reflect what he feels should be achievable from the park.

Valuations based on actual accounts Even when apparently reliable accounts are available, it is essential for the valuer first to consider whether or not they show results which are likely to continue. There are many reasons why accounts may show results lower or higher than one would expect for the future. A park may be building up business and still not have realised its full potential. Developments may be underway increasing potential income, but which have not yet "shown through" in the accounts. Extra pitches may be being developed. For personal reasons the owner may have been reluctant to increase charges to their full potential, resulting in charges on the park below the going rate. In all these cases adjustments are needed to the accounts to reflect true potential.

On the other side of the coin, the park may have formed part of a larger group and have benefited from wide-spread corporate advertising. Receipts may have been boosted by a large number of sales of caravans during development or refurbishment, which will not be repeated to the same scale in future years. In these cases adjustment to income will be needed to reflect reasonable expectations.

Assuming however that the accounts do show a realistic picture of the park's potential, the profits method of valuation is essentially a question of calculating the profit figure, clear of rent or similar property charges. To achieve the profit figure that is needed, most accounts require a number of adjustments, particularly to the expenditure.

Adjustments to expenditure. The accounts frequently will include an item for interest on mortgage or bank loan. This has to be excluded since it is a cost related to buying the business, rather than to running it. However, when excluding this, care must be taken to leave in any bank charges which relate to the running of the business. Equally, the business may need working capital which either will be provided by the owner from funds elsewhere, or borrowed from the bank. This again is a business expense unrelated to the capital value of the property itself and needs to be left in the expenses. If the working capital is introduced from the owner's own resources then interest may need to be added to the expenditure in the accounts.

A frequent difficulty is the treatment of depreciation. Invariably this will have been included in the accounts. Normally it will cover the writing down of value of furniture, equipment, vehicles etc. Depending on whether the accounts are for a company or an individual, the depreciation may also cover the writing down of the cost of improvements, or the value of leasehold property.

There is some disagreement on the treatment of depreciation. Some valuers prefer to exclude it from the accounts altogether. In my opinion, if the depreciation genuinely reflects the annual cost of providing items of equipment, then this should remain in the accounts valuation, as reflecting the true cost of running the business. I refer in particular to such items as "hire fleet" caravans where substantial investment in caravans and equipment has to be written down over a comparatively short period of time. Not to allow for this would provide a distorted picture.

Depreciation on the cost of improvements, on the other hand, should always be excluded. These are long-term expenditure items, which in practice will be kept in repair. The true running cost should be the cost of maintenance, rather than an artificial depreciation allowance. My preference therefore is to apportion the depreciation allowance and to include an allowance which realistically reflects the cost to the business. The percentage to be used may not be the same as the percentage used by the accountants, which will be determined by the maximum allowance permitted by the Inland Revenue. Whichever way depreciation is treated, it is imperative to adopt the same policy for analysing accounts of known sales, and for valuing a park.

Parks may be improved or developed by "ploughing back" profits. There are tax advantages in treating as much as possible of this expenditure as "income expenditure" rather than as "capital expenditure". This however will result in an accounts profit figure below the true potential profit. The accounts figure for "repairs and maintenance" therefore should always be carefully considered and adjusted if necessary.

Finally, company accounts may show directors' fees, and partnership accounts may show drawings. Any payments made to the owner in respect of his own management should be excluded for valuation purposes since his management share will come from the divisible profit at the end. However on small parks, where the owner undertakes direct physical functions, such as grass cutting, manning the reception office, cleaning caravans etc, it may be reasonable to make some allowance for this in the accounts. Practice on this varies. Frequently these costs are ignored where the park is small and where one would expect these functions to be carried out by the owner. Again it is a question of comparing like with like. On large parks it is normal to employ a site manager to run the park. If this function is performed by the park owner, over and above the overall management of the business, then again it may be appropriate to include the cost of this in the accounts.

Having adjusted the accounts, the resulting profit has to be multiplied to reflect the yield required. This is illustrated in example 3 at the end of the chapter.

Additions to profits valuation. Having completed the profits valuation the valuer then has to consider whether there are any other elements that have to be added. The accounts-based valuation will reflect all the items on the park which contribute towards the financial results – it will not cover anything else. There are two main examples of further items.

The first of these is living accommodation. On most parks there will be living accommodation for the owner in one form or another. The size, quality and value in practice varies enormously. In analysing known sales on an accounts basis, one could analyse the entire sale price, including living accommodation. Obviously this could produce a lower yield. There is considerable logic in adopting this approach because it can be argued that at least one unit of living accommodation is essential on any park and that a purchaser is buying the park as a whole, not in bits. To that extent it is artificial to differentiate between the income-producing parts and the living accommodation. There may even be examples where the living accommodation forms an integral part of the income-producing buildings. Living accommodation for instance may be a flat over the club.

The problem with this approach is that the rate of yield will be affected, quite dramatically in the case of high-quality accommodation on a small park. First, this will make it difficult to relate yields to those expected from other leisure properties. Second, it will require a judgement adjustment of yield to reflect different qualities of accommodation. This becomes an impossible exercise to undertake with any accuracy and confidence. One has to remember that the adjustment would have to reflect not only difference in quality, but also difference in size of park. The smaller the park the greater will be the impact of the living accommodation and vice versa.

A better approach is to exclude any living accommodation from the initial valuation. In analysing a known sale, the value of the living accommodation will first be assessed (in exactly the same way as explained for the physical comparison method). The balance of the purchase price will then be compared with the profits achieved, in order to arrive at the required yield. In the valuation exercise, the actual or assessed profit will be multiplied to provide the necessary yield, and the value of any living accommodation then added afterwards.

Whilst living accommodation should be excluded from the income calculation, *all* items contributing to the running of the park should be included. This of course will include both items which directly produce income (such as caravan pitches, shop, restaurant, etc) and also items which do not directly produce income (for instance a swimming pool freely available to the users of the park, reception office, stores and workshops). The reason for this is that the non-productive items are actually used in the running of the park. They therefore will affect both the overall income (eg the existence of a swimming pool may increase pitch fee income) and the overall costs (eg a reception office will have to be kept in repair).

The only exceptions to this would be buildings with potential for income production that is not already reflected in the accounts. A large workshop for instance may be more than is needed for the running of the park, and could produce a commercial rent for storage, quite unconnected with the running of the park. There are two ways of dealing with such buildings. The potential income from letting can be included in the predicted income from the park (and thus increase the profit calculation), or the capital value can be added at the end of the valuation. The method will depend on the degree to which the building in reality can be separated from the park, and how immediate is the opportunity to secure rental income. While a measure of "hybrid valuation" is inevitable with living accommodation, it is preferable to limit the number of "hybrid" items. Where possible, items of potential income should be dealt with within the profits calculation.

The second main example of end adjustments, will be for additional land, or for potential for changes in planning consent. There may be situations where pitches have been recently developed but where the benefit is not yet reflected in the accounts. These can readily be allowed for by including potential income in the predictions or adjusted accounts. However, this will be appropriate only if the new income is immediate. I have illustrated the valuation of a touring park, using the direct comparison method. I referred to adjoining land with planning consent for touring pitches, but not yet fully developed and brought into use. Clearly the income from these pitches will not reflect in the actual accounts for the park. Neither will that income be available until development work is completed. This therefore has to be dealt with by an end addition to the main valuation, the addition reflecting the value of this extra land with its potential for caravan pitches. The calculation of that addition of course may itself be dealt with on a profits basis, by:

(a) predicting potential income and expenditure;
(b) capitalising to reflect the required yield;

(c) deducting as appropriate the likely cost of development; and
(d) possibly deferring all or part of the resulting figure to reflect the time it may take to bring the extra part into use.

A similar approach should be used for any other form of property owned with the park, but which is not used with the business. The caravan park may form part of an agricultural holding. The remaining farm would be valued on a normal agricultural basis, reflecting as appropriate any "hope value" for future development.

When considering the method of valuing the "additions," it is also appropriate to consider the yield to be expected. For the profits calculation on the park itself, we already know that the yield will be affected by the security of the income and the risk that is being taken by the purchaser. The greater the risk or uncertainty, the higher will be the yield required. This will also apply when valuing additions on a profits basis, where the potential profits will be based on predictions. Profits from the "additions" may be more speculative than those from the established park. Consequently a higher yield may be appropriate for the valuation of the additions, compared with the valuation of the basic park.

Potential for changes in planning consent on the park itself may need different treatment. If the potential is for an extra building, or for extra pitches, then this can be allowed for in the same way as additional land with planning consent. A planning consent to change the nature of the park however will require a different approach. An example would be consent to convert a touring park into a static holiday park. Here one must start from scratch, estimating the income and expenditure from the new type of park and calculating eventual value from the predicted net profit. The percentage yield to be allowed will have to reflect the unproven nature of the profit (ie a higher yield will be required, compared with that for an established business). Allowances will also have to be made for any delay in bringing the park into full use. This can be allowed for either by deferring value for the period of development or by allowing in the profits prediction for a phased increase in income over the first few years of the park's use. From this value will have to be deducted the cost of development, allowing for the owner's involvement and for interest on initial capital.

The principles of an accounts-based valuation are illustrated in example 3.

Valuations based on predicted accounts The principles when using predicted accounts are precisely the same as those when using actual accounts. One is deducting estimated expenditure from estimated income, to produce a profit which is then multiplied to produce capital value, the multiple reflecting the required yield.

The difference of course is that the valuer has to use his own knowledge in order to prepare a hypothetical set of accounts, instead of being able to use the actual accounts. However this difference is less than it may appear. No valuer should ever use actual accounts unless, first, he is capable of checking for himself whether those accounts show a realistic picture and, second, he has gone through this exercise and adjusted the accounts as necessary. As with the valuation of any other form of leisure business, one cannot produce a mathematical formula which automatically will produce the right answer from any given set of accounts. As has already been explained, accounts may show too high or too low a result, for many reasons.

Sources of income – pitch fees and hire fleet. The preparation of predicted accounts, or the checking and adjustment of existing accounts, will require careful consideration of the sources of income. For caravan pitches, the most straightforward source is pitch-fee income, where pitches are occupied by privately-owned caravans. There will be a need to ensure that this fee income is net (ie that any included payments for rates or services are deducted) and that the figures are net of VAT. It will also be necessary to check that the level of fee is in line with that charged for other similar parks in the area. It will be necessary to assess demand in the area to decide whether the park is likely to be completely full, or whether there are likely to be empty pitches. If the latter, then a void allowance will have to be made from the theoretical total pitch-fee income, produced by multiplying the number of pitches by the net annual pitch fee.

Income from hire fleet static holiday caravans is more difficult, since the income will reflect the size of caravan, the extent of services in the caravan, the period of the year and the occupancy rate (ie the total number of weeks in the year when the average caravan is in use). Unless the valuer is looking at an entirely new park, the park records will normally give guidance as to likely occupancy rates. However, the valuer will need to be able to assess whether these rates reflect the park's potential, and how they compare with the achievement of nearby parks. Almost always there will be a tariff, which will give the weekly charges for the different types of caravan. These charges will vary with the time of year.

For touring caravan pitches, again the income will fluctuate with the time of year (the highest charge will normally be in the peak period of mid July to the first week of September). The actual annual income will depend on the occupancy rate. Calculating likely income from touring pitches, even with the benefit of an actual tariff, can be quite complex. One has to exclude VAT and then consider what is the likely average combination for the pitch. Some tariffs may be straightforward with a set charge for caravan awning and car, regardless of the number of people using the caravan. More usually however there are at least some variables, depending on whether or not an awning is used, or how many people occupy the caravan. The most difficult tariffs are those which set out the price per pitch to cover the caravan and car, and then add separately for:

(a) number of adults
(b) number of children
(c) number of dogs
(d) use of awning
(e) use of hook-up
(f) parking for extra car.

Usually park records will give a guide as to the normal average pitch fee. Otherwise the valuer can only work out the most likely combination and calculate the average fee accordingly.

Calculating the occupancy rate of touring pitches can be difficult. The actual rate will fluctuate from one year to another. It will be influenced by weather conditions. This will apply particularly to parks including tent pitches. Again the valuer will have to use his general experience of the area to supplement information available from the park records.

Sources of income – sales. An important source of income on caravan parks, and one difficult to deal with, is the profit on sale of static holiday caravans.

The way in which income initially is achieved has already been explained in some detail. Obviously the figure to be included as income will be the "gross profit" from the sale of caravans – ie the difference between sale price and purchase price. However, this must not be confused with net profit. Unless paid for separately through a siting fee, the sale of a caravan on its pitch will involve cost to the park owner in siting and connecting to services. This either needs to be allowed for within the expenses section, or deducted when calculating the gross profit. On most parks there will also be promotional expenses which will reflect in the figure for advertising in the expenses section. Larger parks employ a sales staff and sometimes have a showroom. These will all increase the appropriate costs in the expenses section.

Profit from sales of caravans is a continuing process since they "wear out". They have to be replaced either when too old, or in accordance with the park rules or park agreements. The normal "allowed" life is between five and 10 years. In assessing income, one has to allow for this continuous process. However, there is a danger of double counting. With an established park with a normal renewal programme, it will be sufficient to allow for profit per pitch, divided by the number of years in the allowed "cycle". Where, however, new pitches have been developed, or a park is due for refurbishment, there may be a large number of initial sales available in the first or second year. These will be in addition to the normal cycle of sales, but are obviously "one-off" additions. Consequently they cannot be included in the general predicted income.

In such circumstances it is normal to add this at the end of the accounts-based valuation, reflecting the number of potential initial sales and the potential profit. However this potential will have to be apportioned between seller and buyer. The park purchaser will not pay the full equivalent profit potential from all these initial sales. He will need to share in that profit and also to be covered for cost of sales, delay and uncertainty. One also has to be aware of the possible effect that these potential initial sales may have on the normal cycle of subsequent sales. If one assumes a 10-year regular cycle, this will require a mature park programmed in that way. Clearly a large number of immediate sales will produce an immediate increase in profit but on those pitches subsequent sales will be deferred until the end of the "cycle".

A similar warning applies to a park where the vendor has just sold a large number of new caravans. This will "artificially" inflate his profit in the last year of ownership, while at the same time delaying potential profit from subsequent sales.

In addition to the normal renewal cycle, there are also likely to be sales of caravans on site. Private owners may wish to resell because of ill health, death, a wish to move elsewhere etc. Frequently the park owner allows sales on pitch to an approved purchaser, but subject to a commission paid to the park owner, commonly 15%. In assessing potential income from sales therefore one needs to make some allowance for this potential source of income.

Income from amenity buildings. The other main sources of income will be from profit-producing buildings such as bar, restaurant, and shop. These may be:

- separately leased
- held under licence
- held under concession
- or run directly by the park owner.

If the last then one will have regard either to actual income, or to assessed income. One will of course be looking to gross profit rather than to total turnover. If one of the first three categories, then normally one will allow for the income actually being produced. However, as with all property valuations, it will be necessary to check the terms to see which party is responsible for repairs, insurance, rates and services. Even with known returns, the valuer will still have to assess the extent to which the returns are realistic and maintainable. As examples of the need for this:

(a) A concessionaire may have over-assessed potential income from an amusement arcade, and may not be prepared to continue at the same level in the following year.
(b) There may be historic licences at considerations which are now too low.
(c) A lease of the bar may be at a historically low figure, and fall for renewal next year. This may allow a substantial increase in rent, or it may allow the park owner to take the bar back into his own management.

For the assessment of value of ancillary buildings, there will usually be some help from the park records or accounts. Failing that, the valuer has to use his experience of similar buildings elsewhere and to analyse known results and relate them to the park in question. Occasionally analysis on a square-foot basis is used, but normally this has little bearing on the actual income-producing capacity. A more normal basis of comparison is on the potential number of people likely to use the park. Comment has already been made on the need to reflect the type of licence for the bar, and the availability of custom or competition elsewhere.

Miscellaneous sources of income. Income may be achieved from commissions on the subletting of privately-owned caravans. The policy varies enormously. Some parks allow subletting in return for a small commission being paid to the park owner. Some park owners run a letting service and insist that sublettings are made only through that service. Commission in return for this service commonly ranges between 10% and 20%. When allowing for this source of income, one must remember to allow additional costs to the park owner, for instance for advertising, office staffing, printing, telephone and postage. Other sources will include:

- sales of bottled gas
- profit on coin telephones
- profit on resale of electricity
- commissions received from nearby attractions and entertainments, receiving custom from bookings through the park
- charges for use of peripheral facilities such as tennis courts, crazy golf etc
- concessions for use of part buildings – eg a coach company
- concessions for use of land – eg riding lessons.

Predicted costs

Little more need be said about the calculation of costs. With most purchases there will be some information available from the accounts, even if it has to be adjusted. In the absence of help from the accounts, then the valuer will have to go through the laborious process of building up an expenses schedule item by item, relying on the analysis of accounts of sales elsewhere. Alternatively he may assess costs as a percentage of turnover. However this can vary enormously and much will depend on the type and size of park. A calculation assessing costs as a proportion of turnover therefore should be used only as a rough check on some other basis of calculation (for instance a direct physical comparison). It should never be relied on on its own.

It is profit which will determine value, and profit can be influenced just as much by the level of expenses as it can by the level of income. To take an obvious example. The easiest to run holiday park will be one with all static pitches, where all the pitches are occupied by privately-owned caravans with pitch fees paid net, annually in advance, and where there are no profit-producing buildings. On such a park profit can be a high proportion of total turnover. At the other extreme, the most expensive type of park to run will be one with a hire fleet of static holiday caravans, with touring pitches and with a wide range of commercial central facilities. Pitch for pitch, turnover is likely to be substantially higher for the second example than for the first example. However, expenses will also be substantially higher. The resultant net profit may well be less.

Stock and equipment

As a going concern valuation, the valuation of a caravan park will normally include the fixtures and equipment necessary for the running of the business. Apart from normal landlords' fixtures, this will include such items as tables and chairs in the restaurant, bedding and crockery in the caravans (if used as a hire fleet) and the stock of brochures, booking charts and records in the office. In analysing and valuing it is normal to assume adequate equipment for the proper running of the park. If the equipment is deficient (for instance if all the tables and chairs in the restaurant are old and need renewal) then that will be allowed for as a deduction from the valuation.

Frequently a sale will include items of equipment such as motor vehicles and grass cutting machinery. Whilst it could be argued that these are necessary "for the proper running of the business", value and type will vary greatly. Normal practice therefore is to exclude these items from analysis and valuation, either describing the valuation as being exclusive of such items, or adding the value of the items at the end of the calculation.

Stock, in the form of food, drink, cleaning materials etc, is usually treated separately. An inventory is taken at the date of completion and the items valued separately from the agreed price of the park.

Seasonal adjustments

Traditionally, holiday parks were sold outside the normal holiday season. However, with the recent expansion of the season, this is becoming more difficult. In many cases sales now have to be completed during the trading season. This will involve adjustments for costs incurred and income received prior to completion, but relating, at least in part, to post completion. Deposits received for future holiday accommodation are an example. This is something which normally is dealt with by the accountants, although sometimes the valuer may be involved.

In this connection particular attention has to be given to the treatment of pitch fees on static holiday parks with privately-owned caravans. Traditionally the season ends at the end of October or November and at that time caravan owners are invited to renew for another year. Often pitch fees are paid annually in advance. As a result, a sale completed for instance in January, which on the face of it would avoid most adjustments necessary during a mid-season purchase, may need substantial adjustment. Otherwise the vendor will have received all the pitch fee income for the coming year, leaving the purchaser with just the season's expenses! It is certainly an aspect of which the valuer should be well aware.

Purchase of parks by shares

This chapter has concentrated on the methods of valuation of *property*. An increasing number of parks are now conveyed by means of acquiring the shares in the owning company, rather than by purchasing the property. Normally the valuer will be required to value the asset itself, leaving to the accountants the task of calculating the adjustments to reflect the other assets and liabilities of the company. There can be substantial tax implications involved in the purchase of company shares rather than the asset, but these are beyond the scope of this chapter.

Examples

Examples 1 and 2 illustrate the analysis of a touring park and the use of that analysis in the valuation of a touring park. Example 3 illustrates the use of the accounts basis, applied to the same park as in example 2. To give a touch of reality, the two different bases in examples 2 and 3 do not produce the same answer! Faced with this situation the valuer will be guided by the strength of evidence available to support each of the two bases, to help decide which is the more reliable calculation. He will be guided also by his own experience and "instinct".

The examples are intentionally simple, to illustrate the method of valuation without confusing the picture with excessive detail.

Example 1

Analysis of sale price of touring caravan park

Assumed details
Freehold site of 4 acres
Sold with vacant possession for £300,000
Planning and site licence consent for 100 touring caravans
Developed for 100 touring pitches with electrical hook-ups to 40
Site includes a three-bedroom modern bungalow
Tariff indicates a 15% premium for the pitches with hook-ups.

Analysis		
Sale price		£300,000
Less value of bungalow		£75,000
Value attributable to pitches		£225,000
60 unserviced pitches @ 1 unit of value	=	60 units
40 pitches with hook-ups @ 1.15 unit of value		
(ie in this example hook-ups are assumed to have		
a premium value of 15% above the basic)	=	46 units
		106 units
Value per unit (i.e. 225,000 ÷ 106 units)	=	£2,123
		say £2,125

Final analysis:		
Bungalow		£75,000
60 unserviced pitches @ £2,125		£127,500
40 pitches with hook-ups @ £2,125 + 15% (= £2,443)		
say £2,445	=	£97,800
		£300,300

Example 2

Valuation of touring park using analysis from example 1

Assumed details
Freehold site of 6 acres
Vacant possession
Planning and site licence consent for 150 touring pitches
4 acres developed with 80 serviced pitches and 20 unserviced pitches
2 acres ready for use after extension of roads and services and
enlargement of toilet block (total cost estimated at £100,000).

Park includes:
- Mobile home used by owner
- Swimming pool (assumed to increase pitch values by 10%)
- Shop (valued at £10,000)
- Small reception office.

Valuation

Developed 4 acres – 80 serviced pitches	
@ £2,445 + 10% = £2,689 say £2,690	£215,200
20 unserviced pitches @ £2,125 + 10% = £2,337 say £2,340	£46,800
	£262,000
Partially developed 2 acres	
Potential 50 serviced pitches @ £2,690 = £134,500	
Less: cost of development £100,000	£34,500
	£296,500
Mobile home, say	£25,000
Shop	£10,000
Reception office (reflected in value of pitches)	N/A
Total value	£331,500
Say	£330,000

Example 3

Profits valuation of park described in example 2

Developed 4 acres

Income as annual accounts:		
Income from pitches		£80,000
Gross profit from shop		£5,000
Sales of gas and miscellaneous items		£2,000
Total gross income		£87,000
Costs, as per annual accounts		£65,000
		£22,000
Add back from accounts:		
Mortgage interest	£15,000	
Depreciation	£5,000	£20,000
Adjusted profit		£42,000
YP @ 15% (secure, established business)		6.67
		£280,140

Partially developed 2 acres

Predicted extra income	£35,000	
Less predicted extra costs	£12,000	
	£23,000	
YP @ 17.5% (reflecting delay and less certainty)	5.71	
	£131,330	
Less actual costs of development	£100,000	£31,330
		£311,470
Additional items:		
Mobile home		£25,000
Shop (included in the profits valuation of the 4 acre part)		N/A
Reception office and swimming pool (reflected in the income from the park)		N/A
		£336,470
Say		£335,000

© John Ridgwell, 1996

CHAPTER 5

Urban leisure: cinemas, bingo clubs, discotheques and nightclubs, ten pin bowling centres

Method of valuation

Trading potential

The underlying method of valuation of properties in the urban leisure field is the same as for other types of leisure property which is by reference to trading potential, commonly called the profits method.

A valuation is by definition an estimate of the best price that a property would achieve in the open market. To make that assessment the valuer must adopt an approach or method which reflects that used in the market. The market approach is based on an assessment of trading potential and therefore all valuations of leisure properties require an assessment of maintainable profit. The profit and loss account is one of the principal tools of the trade for the leisure valuer who should be able to interpret and make adjustments, if appropriate, for the purpose of the valuation. If trading information is not available the valuer must have the experience to make an assessment of the trading potential and make a projection of income and costs to form a profit and loss account. For valuations of proposed ventures, business projections are provided and the valuer must be able to recognise whether or not those projections both as to income and costs are reasonably attainable and must not blindly value on the basis of those projections. Nor must actual accounts be followed blindly as the history may not give an accurate trend of future performance for a number of reasons. The acounts for each business must be assessed in the light of knowledge of the sector generally and measured against other similar properties.

Comparisons

There is often more evidence of single transactions at the lower end of the market than at the top end and there are different valuation considerations to the two ends of the market because the buyers in the respective markets have different financial considerations. Even if there were sufficient information to analyse a transaction relating to many properties with some degree of accuracy, it is by no means certain that information could then automatically be applied because a large transaction could have the effect of adjusting market values in the future. In certain fields the entry into or departure from the market of just one or two active players can have a marked effect on values. It would therefore be inappropriate to apply comparables in a market which had shifted from the date of the comparable. Knowledge of comparables cannot be applied without a knowledge of the market.

The introduction to SAVP 12 makes the point that that particular SAVP is required because of the difficulty in interpreting information on transactions which relate to the transfer of a business. Often there is insufficient or uncorroborated information as to tenure and other necessary details of the properties and business. Additionally there will be matters relating to staff salaries, pensions and benefits, redundancies, apportionments between the value of the property, goodwill and trade contents which can affect VAT, stamp duty, capital gains tax, etc and therefore the eventual price; some of these considerations would not be present in the sale with vacant possession of an individual property.

The difficulty in analysing transactions is compounded by the absence of a meaningful unit of comparison in certain sectors. Although it may be possible to produce a basis for a sector such as snooker clubs by value per table other sectors provide problems. For example a twin cinema of 750 seats could be more profitable than a single-auditorium 1,500 seat cinema because it has a wider choice of films and lower operating costs. There will be valuation considerations of greater importance than the number of seats. Having evolved from purpose-built cinemas, bingo provides the problem of how the circle seating, mechanised cash bingo and prize bingo units may be brought into a unit of comparison. Without a meaningful unit of comparison there can be little assistance obtained from comparables in many cases and the principal method of valuation will be the profits method.

Planning the valuation

Generally, but especially in the case of the valuation of a large portfolio, it is very important to prepare thoroughly and carefully prior to setting out on inspections which can often cover a very large part of the country. The Red Book sets out clearly the necessity for the valuer to state the content and source of the information relied on for the valuation. An information pack on which the valuation will be based should provide a comprehensive schedule of the properties to be valued set out in the following categories:

Occupied by the company
Not occupied by the company
In course of development
Held for development
Held as investment
Surplus to requirements.

The following information is required for each property:

Property records providing information as to tenure
Reports on title if available
Site plans
Floor plans
Profit and loss accounts for the last 3 years plus latest period to date
Capital expenditure details, past and proposed
Copies of licences and certificates.

It is important to have the opportunity to study this information prior to inspection and ensure complete familiarity with the basis and terminology used in company accounts. Site plans, floor plans and licences should be checked before the inspection but it is particularly important to ensure that a senior member of local management is available during the inspection and is able to discuss matters freely relating to the property to be valued and local competition.

A proforma on which required details of the property and location can be entered is important in ensuring a standard procedure and a final page check list should ensure all essential details and questions are covered. The proforma should be designed to cater for the leisure sector which is the subject of the valuation.

Capital valuation: Cinemas

The film industry has a basic similarity with other businesses which are made up of manufacturing, wholesaling and retailing. The corresponding functions are production, distribution and exhibition. The parallel is not quite the same as other businesses for various reasons but perhaps the main difference is that film distribution plays a more commercially active role than would normally be attributed to a wholesaler. The relationship between these elements has had an important bearing on cinema exhibition and, therefore, the valuation of cinemas has certain historic factors which are of importance even in the present ever-changing scene. Although it is not within the scope of this chapter to cover such a large topic in detail a brief sketch of some of the main historic and contemporary features may be of interest and help to understand the valuation process.

Cinema progressed from its infancy in booths as part of a travelling show to converted existing buildings for showing films in the early years of the century. Following a number of tragedies caused by the flammable film used in those days the Cinematograph Act 1909 was brought in to govern the safety of cinemas by means of an annual cinematograph licence issued by local authorities, which is a system that has endured until today under the Cinemas Act 1985 and the Cinema Safety Regulations 1955. In those early days there was a considerable export trade in English films to America but the First World War curtailed English film-making and brought about the American dominance of the industry. Various attempts have been made to counter this American dominance starting with a statutory quota system in 1927 requiring 5% of films shown to be British made. The Cinematograph Films Act 1938 applied to both distributors and exhibitors and established an escalating quota for ten years starting at 12.5% in 1938 increasing to 25% in 1947. In 1949 came the National Film Finance Corporation which became funded in 1957 by the British Film Fund Agency by way of a tax called the Eady Levy of about 8% of box office receipts. The idea was that the levy would subsidise the specific production which raised the tax but that meant that successful British films, like the James Bond series, were major recipients and British films were funded by American producers who were then entitled to the Eady Levy provided by the British cinema-goers. The scheme was abandoned in favour of a voluntary scheme, but the British film industry still provides a small proportion of the films shown in this country.

During the period between the wars the cinema industry boomed. In Britain the two major circuits, Rank (Odeon) and Associated British Picture Corporation (ABC) were formed and prospered with vertical integration of production, distribution and exhibition. Early links called the "alliance" with major American producer/distributor companies were forged. Rank with Paramount, Universal, Twentieth Century Fox and Walt Disney; ABC with Warner Brothers, Columbia and MGM. The two major cinema chains controlled which films were given a general release and the independent exhibitors were obliged to keep with one or other circuit. This block booking led to "barring" which meant in effect that a cinema barred its neighbouring cinemas from showing a certain film at the same time. Those cinemas showing the films first were called "first run" cinemas. Although at the end of the war the two major circuits together owned only about 20% of the country's cinemas and perhaps about a third of the seating capacity, their control through the alignment system enabled them to control distribution to the smaller circuits and independents so that the other cinemas booked either the Rank or ABC "stream of release" and did not switch between the two.

The large measure of control of the industry by the duopoly has been the subject of two reports by the Monopolies Commission. The first in 1966, although finding in general terms that the degree and form of control was monopolistic and contrary to the public interest, did little or nothing to change the situation. By that time the cinema industry was suffering the effects of television and was about to embark on a costly programme of converting the single auditorium cinemas into two or more auditoria with a view to reviving interest and increasing admissions by providing a wider choice at the cinema complex. The degree to which the cinema business declined in the 20 years after the Second World War and in the wake of the increasing popularity of television is shown by the figures in Table 5.1.

Despite the conversion programme the next 20 years was much the same uphill battle against falling attendances as is illustrated in Table 5.2. It will be clear from these figures that by the time the Monopolies Commission made its second report in 1984 the problem of the industry was that of survival and again nothing was done in the way of enforcement to change the system. In addition, there was added competition; this time from home videos. In 1984 the situation was nothing short of disastrous and the future was looking very bleak. However, as in all the best scripts, rescue was at hand just over the horizon. At a place called Milton Keynes!

Table 5.1. Decline in the cinema business, 1946–1966

	1946	1966	Variance
Cinemas	4,700	1,850	−60%
Admissions (millions)	1,650	290	−82%
Average seat price	4.5p	20p	345%

Table 5.2.

	1975	1985	Variance
Cinemas	1,100	660	−40%
Admissions (millions)	124	53	−57%
Average seat price	60p	195p	325%

For some years cinema exhibitors in the United States had largely abandoned the conversion of old downtown cinemas in favour of building new cinemas out of town, the main feature of which was a number of small auditoria built on relatively cheap land with good access by car and ample surface parking close to the building. Further features were large confectionery sales kiosks and associated fast food restaurants. In 1984 when admissions in this country reached their lowest level ever but were about to start a recovery, admissions in the United States which had been increasing with the building of multiplex cinemas had peaked and started to decline. There was a view by the larger American exhibitors that without an increase in the cinema-going rate cinema building in the United States had reached saturation point and their eyes turned towards Europe and Britain in particular where admissions per capita had sunk to about one per year.

In November 1985 The Point at Milton Keynes was opened by American MultiCinema (AMC) which one year later was able to announce one million admissions in its first year. Just in time for the opening by Cannon of the country's second multiplex at Salford Quays, Manchester. The multiplex cinema had arrived and so, slowly at first, the race began with new entrants CIC (later with United Artists to acquire the AMC Multiplexes and become United Cinema International – UCI), National Amusements (Showcase cinemas), Warner Brothers, Cineplex Odeon of Canada, named Gallery Cinemas in this country to avoid confusion with the long-standing Odeon name and in turn to be acquired by Cannon, itself now named Metro Goldwyn Mayer Cinemas (MGM) and Rank the only wholly British Company. The rate of growth showing the number built in each year is in Table 5.3.

Table 5.3. Increase in the number of multiplex cinemas in the UK, 1985–1991

Year	Cinemas	Screens
1985	1	10
1986	1	8
1987	3	26
1988	9	93
1989	15	145
1990	12	102
1991	13	103
Totals	54	487

I think it true to say that the American companies who have committed such effort into the building of multiplexes were disappointed on two counts. First, it took far longer than expected to find sites and obtain planning and other consents and second, the cost of construction was about twice what they had expected. The figures in Table 5.3 indicate that the rate of building has not slackened and is perhaps continuing at the same rate. However, I do not believe that to be the case and think that a number of the cinemas built in the last two years followed contractual commitments which had been made in earlier years. In fact, as far as sentiment is concerned the boom probably peaked in 1989 when the company which built the largest multiplex decided quite shortly to scale-down the size of future projects. Another company which opened a number of multiplexes in 1989 has opened only one in the last two years. It is most unlikely that multiplex cinemas will be built in the future at the rate we have seen over the last few years but there are still a number of locations in the country which for site finding or planning delay reasons do not have a multiplex and those locations are still likely targets.

Although multiplexes comprise only 10% of the number of cinemas they may account for up to 40% of admissions. As must be expected in any business which is revolutionised and expanded at such a pace mistakes were made but the concept itself was right for the time and successful. In a relatively brief period the multiplex phenomenon has transformed the face of cinema exhibition in this country. The transformation is not merely physical because neither barring nor the traditional distribution pattern apply so that all films on current release are shown at the multiplex.

Factors affecting value

Competition Each cinema will be either first or second run which is the principal factor and take either the Rank or Cannon film release. However, following the closure of such a large number of cinemas it has become more common for towns to have one main cinema which has become entitled to both streams of release and is termed "a solo situation". Of more significance is the proximity of an existing or proposed multiplex cinema.

Quality and comfort For adult cinema-goers these factors are of utmost importance, and lack of adequate standards will deter cinema-goers irrespective of the quality of the film, especially now that release on video and television follows relatively quickly after general release at the cinema. Quality and comfort relates not only to the decor and seating but the sound and picture quality, space heating and cooling.

State of repair Most cinemas were built before the Second World War and are now over 50 years old. Because cinemas are large buildings, repairs are costly and with admissions reducing over many years, much patching has been carried out rather than costly full repair. The most familiar and costly item of repair is the asbestos roof which has exceeded the expected life span by many years. In some parts of the country in particular on older converted theatres, roofs were slated and have been patched and "turnerised" to extend the useful life. Parapet walls and copings and rainwater gullies have been neglected leading to rainwater penetration which affects the steel frame causing fracturing of the brickwork in the main walls.

Equipment The cinematograph licence requires a current test certificate for electrical installation. Rewiring a large cinema is likely to cost up to £50,000 and such a requirement by the licensing authority has often been the final straw which has led to closure of a number of cinemas. A ceiling certificate is also required, usually every five years. Ceilings are another critical part of the building as much of the decorative fibrous plaster has deteriorated. A few years ago one of the gimmicks to entice back the dwindling cinema audience was a sound system called "Sensurround", devised to accompany a film entitled "Earthquake". A special ceiling certificate was required for the sound system and several failed. There should be evidence of regular maintenance on heating and plenum plant and servicing the secondary lighting battery system.

Sales kiosk Sale of confectionery, ice cream and drinks has always been a traditional part of cinema going and an important, not to say vital, part of cinema viability. Although no longer the case, at one time a sizeable proportion of ice cream sold in this country was at the cinema. As so called "dark sales", that is selling ice cream from a tray during the performance, have reduced so the importance of the size and location of the kiosk has increased. The importance of theatre sales is shown by the size and prominence of the kiosk in multiplex cinemas where sales per admission is sometimes double that achieved in traditional cinemas.

Auditorium size The size of individual auditoria and the mix of sizes in either a converted pre-War cinema or a multiplex may affect admissions particularly where there is a choice of cinema. In traditional and multiplex cinemas the size of the screen is governed by the size of the auditorium and cinema-goers may feel that a small auditorium with a seating capacity of perhaps only 100 seats does not do justice to the film they wish to see. The size of the auditorium and the business that it is capable of generating may not warrant the expense of the best projection and sound systems which are provided in a larger auditorium. To take a very simple example, in the case of a cinema with 1,000 seats the proportions in individual auditoria of 500:350:150 is generally preferable to 800:100:100.

Goodwill There is little or no personal goodwill to be disregarded as it is the status of the cinema and not the proprietor which dictates whether or not the cinema is solo, first run or second run. There are many good cinema proprietors and managers and it would be wrong to disregard as ineffective the sometimes considerable time, ingenuity and hard work spent in booking the film they think their local customers would want to see and promoting that film, but taking a longer view I believe that at the end of the day it is the public by word of mouth which decides the success or otherwise of the film on current release and on which cinemas rely for their profit.

London's West End is a different market where there are a number of cinemas owned ultimately by major producers and those cinemas are used to show their own films. There are West End cinemas which trade at a level which is enhanced by personal goodwill.

Admissions An accurate estimate of admissions is all important and the ability to do so requires experience and continuous contact with those in the industry and study of trade journals. Box office receipts on a film by film basis are published weekly for cinemas in the West End which is a useful check on the general level of current business and the health of the industry. The annual business monitor publication by the Government's Statistical Office on the cinema industry ceased publication a few years ago and that in-depth survey information is no longer available from another single source. Fortunately, monthly admission figures for Britain are collated on behalf of the Cinema Advertising Association and published in the trade press.

Cinema valuation: Example 1
For this example I have selected a typical pre-War cinema built in the mid-1930s in a large, possibly county town almost anywhere in the country. Originally the cinema had a total of 1,800 seats which was typical if not the optimum size for cinemas of the period and arranged with 1,200 seats in the stalls and 600 in the circle. Around 1975 the cinema was converted to a triple auditorium complex with the circle left intact with 600 seats and two auditoria constructed in the stalls of 450 and 300 seats making 1,350 in all. At one time this cinema was one of about two dozen in the town centre and surrounding suburbs but now only two cinemas remain. The other cinema is also a typical mid-1930s cinema which has been converted into a three-screen cinema so each cinema in the town is first run and each takes the film release of one or other of the two major circuits.

The interior has been well cared for with carpet, seating and decor all to a reasonably good standard. The projection equipment is modern and the two largest auditoria have the latest sound equipment. There is a car park at the rear of the cinema for about 50 cars which is licensed on a monthly basis to local business people and on Saturday the car park is used as a market and occasionally on a Sunday there is a car boot sale. However, the car park surface requires attention. The building had a new roof about ten years ago and is in good condition but some severe fracturing of the brickwork to the scenery fly tower above the old stage area is evident and it is necessary to remove several feet of the fly tower, which of course is now redundant, and re-roof. Planning enquiries reveal nothing adverse in the way of proposals which would affect the property. The location is slightly away from the best of the commercial centre, but it is in a good location and would be suitable for redevelopment at some appropriate time in the future. There is no multiplex cinema in or close to the town but it is known that the major multiplex operators had been seeking a suitable site. Nothing has emerged to date nor are there any current planning applications but the town is a possible target for the future as multiplexes have been built in towns of similar size and strategic location.

Estimating income and costs For the purpose of the valuation weekly admissions are estimated at 5,000. Based on the total seating capacity of 1,350 seats this represents about 3.7 "capacities" or "fills" per week against 21 performances made up of three on weekdays and two on Sundays with a late show on Fridays.

A weekly capacity figure can be a useful method of comparison and assist with estimating admissions. Seat prices are largely a matter of fact presuming the present operator has judged the pricing correctly and had regard to the competition prices. The prices include VAT which must be deducted and there must be an estimate based on experience of the ratio between adult and child prices to arrive at an average net seat price. The sale of confectionery, drinks and ice cream must be estimated normally as an average spend per admission. Screen advertising rates escalate with admissions.

Film hire rates are negotiated film by film for each cinema and naturally the distributor will expect a higher rate for films which have been successful in the USA and strongly promoted. The film hire rate starts at a low level for the exhibitors and increases to a higher level or levels with increased takings. The takings figure at which the rate increases is known as a "break figure". The film hire rates will obviously be higher for first run than for second run cinemas. In general, the lower the level of business, the lower will be the film hire rate.

The estimate of costs derives from knowledge of cinemas of similar size and admission levels, the main items of which are fairly obvious. Miscellaneous costs would cover such matters as film transport, post, telephone, licences, Performing Rights Society, cleaning materials, uniforms, etc.

The basic information and assumptions may now be set out in table form followed by a projected profit and loss account to arrive at the maintainable profit.

Seating capacity	1: 600
	2: 450
	3: 300
Total	1, 350

Weekly admissions	5,000
Annual admissions	260,000
Weekly capacities	3.7
Seat price adult	£3.20 (£2.72 net)
Seat price child	£1.70 (£1.36 net)
Average net seat price	£2.20

Projected Profit and Loss Account

Income

Box Office receipts	£572,000	
Confectionery sales	£130,000	
Screen Advertising	£ 25,000	
Car Park Income	£ 23,000	
		£750,000

Costs

Film Hire (40%)	£230,000	
Confectionery purchases (50%)	£ 65,000	
Salaries (23%)	£175,000	
Rates	£ 35,000	
Heat and power	£ 25,000	
Repairs and maintenance	£ 25,000	
Insurance	£ 10,000	
Publicity	£ 25,000	
Miscellaneous	£ 20,000	
		£610,000
	Profit	£140,000 (18.7%)

Capital Valuation

Estimated maintainable profit	£140,000
YP in perpetuity 25%	4
	£560,000

Less cost of car park and fly tower repair		£ 60,000
	Capital Value	£500,000

Cinema valuation: Example 2

The second cinema example is a modern multiplex cinema located in a retail park, close to a town of some regional importance and with a catchment population of about 800,000. There is good surface car parking provision. The site is held on a lease for 125 years at a peppercorn rent. There are no onerous covenants as to use and alienation so the title is virtually freehold from a valuation point of view.

The principles which applied to the converted pre-War cinema in example 1 apply to the multiplex but the cinema trades more intensively and has more late night shows at weekends. Certain facts and estimates are set out as in example 1 followed by the projected profit and loss account and capital valuation. It will be noted that the multiplex trades a higher number of capacities per week and sales per admission are higher and show a slightly better mark-up. The kiosk is large and centrally placed with sufficient sales points to avoid queuing. Attention to layout, trading up in size in confectionery and post-mix drinks dispensing all assist in boosting sales per admission.

Seating capacity	2,000
Auditoria	8
Weekly admissions	15,000
Annual admissions	832,000
Weekly capacities	8 approximately
Seat price adult	£3.50 (£2.98 net)
Seat price child	£2.00 (£1.70 net)
Average net seat price	£2.50

Projected Profit and Loss Account

Income

Box Office receipts	£2,080,000
Confectionery sales (85 pence)	£ 707,000
Screen Advertising	£ 70,000
	£2,857,000

Costs

Film Hire (42%)	£	875,000
Confectionery purchases (45%)	£	320,000
Salaries (15%)	£	425,000
Rates	£	100,000
Heat and power	£	50,000
Repairs and maintenance	£	40,000
Service charge – car park, security etc	£	20,000
Insurance	£	15,000
Publicity	£	75,000
Miscellaneous	£	25,000

£1,945,000

Profit £ 912,000 (32%)

Capital valuation This multiplex trades at a good level of business and subject to the right films coming along in suitable numbers will continue to trade well as there is now little likelihood of another multiplex which would encroach on its catchment area. At today's building and equipment prices this cinema would cost between £5m and £6m.

Estimated maintainable profit	£ 900,000
YP	5.5

£4,950,000

Capital value £5,000,000

Bingo clubs

Commercial bingo started in the 1950s, becoming increasingly popular in the 1960s and conveniently occupying the large number of cinemas which were closing at that time. It is a comparatively recent leisure pursuit but even in that short time the business has changed considerably. To begin with it was often the smaller cinemas in small towns, villages or suburban locations which closed first and it was therefore into these preponderantly smaller buildings in secondary locations where bingo started to take hold. The rate of growth was quite dramatic but had probably peaked by the mid-1970s when annual admissions were approaching 300m in about 1,600 clubs. This rapid expansion was certainly made possible by the ready supply of redundant cinemas and quite obviously commercial bingo was fulfilling a largely unsatisfied demand for a leisure pursuit outside the home for the patrons who were predominantly female and middle-aged to elderly. The main reason, however, for the rapid expansion was that the operators found they had a money spinner often in relatively inexpensive accommodation and with very little initial outlay. In the early days the cinema was used as it stood complete with raked floor and tip-up seats. Subsequently the floors were made level and banquette seating in units of four to a table replaced the cinema tip-up seats. Because of the far steeper rake in the circle, cinema seats remained.

During the ten years from the mid-1970s to the mid-1980s the industry contracted from about 1,600 clubs to around 1,000 clubs and admissions reduced from close on 300m to about 175m. The industry clearly had a problem, but it was one that it had recognised and had concerned it for some time; namely that the membership, made up principally of the middle-aged and elderly, was declining with the passage of the years and the lost membership was not being replaced with new and younger members. From the mid-1980s in an effort to revive the industry there has been a sustained and costly refurbishment programme on the larger and more successful clubs with £750,000 and sometimes more being spent on refurbishment of the large clubs. The motivators and principal participants in this concerted effort to raise the image of bingo were the four major companies, Bass, Granada, Mecca and Rank who together owned about 40% of the total number of clubs and probably a higher percentage of admissions. These changes have given the clubs a more polished appearance which is hopefully more inviting and capable of attracting new members. At the same time the earning potential of the clubs improved by the introduction of mechanised cash bingo, the National Game, the substitution of the two permitted jackpot machines with a large number of amusement-with-prizes machines and more recently the maximum stake for gaming machines has been increased from 10p to 20p. It may be that as a result of this effort and investment particularly by the larger companies, the decline has slowed considerably. From the latest report from the Gaming Board it is interesting to see that the number of clubs in England and Wales had not reduced in the 12 months covered by the report and in Scotland the reduction was only five clubs. During the first three years of the 1980s the rate of closure averaged 90 clubs per year. Although the slower rate of closure indicates greater stability in the industry and there is now a substantial core of large expensively refurbished clubs there is still a good percentage of clubs which have low and declining admission figures and which struggle to remain viable.

The market

Over the past few years the market has been dominated by deals involving clubs at the lower end of the market which the larger companies wish to shed in order to concentrate on larger clubs worthy of investment. There has been a number of freehold and leasehold transactions. In addition the four major companies have purchased single properties and smaller chains such as Essoldo, Kingsway, Zetters and Strettons at reported prices which reflected what was often a multiplier in excess of ten times actual profit. During 1990/91 the number of large companies in the industry has reduced from four to two. First, Rank Organisation acquired Mecca by company takeover in August 1990 and then in May 1991 Bass purchased the Granada bingo clubs at a reported price which reflected an average of £2m per club. The combined Bass and Granada clubs are being relaunched under the new name of Gala, the publicity for which states that the Company proposes spending £20m over a 12-month period. The commitment to bingo by these two very large companies indicates that they see bingo as a worthwhile and solid investment and the indications from annual reports are that bingo has weathered the current economic recession better than other sectors in the leisure industry. This is borne out in the latest report of the Gaming Board which shows a total amount staked of £614m at September 1990, an increase of 4.6% over the previous 12 months. During the last two or three years there has been a small number of newly built out-of-town bingo clubs. There is a view that, although redundant cinemas particularly those with a large auditorium, have enabled the growth of the bingo industry, cinema buildings are often far from ideal in a number of respects. For that reason I think that further new out-of-town bingo developments are likely and although initially they may have to be supported by considerable bussing where the sites are remote from the town centre, the incidence of travel by public transport will surely decrease if the industry attracts the younger generation who are more likely to be car drivers.

The larger companies consider that the real growth which can only come from enlarging the percentage of the population which wishes to play bingo is inhibited by the public perception of bingo. Research indicates that there is a very negative impression of bingo from people who had never been to a bingo club and would doubtless be surprised at the appearance of the modern bingo clubs. Research also indicates that some 70% of the industry's target audience has never been to a bingo club and are unlikely to do so because of the unfavourable image. Bingo itself, as a game, can of course be advertised but a section of the industry has long felt that the image of the game will be altered only when people have experienced the atmosphere at a bingo club and that is unlikely to be achieved without the ability to advertise particular clubs. At present that is not possible as it is unlawful to advertise premises at which gaming is the principal event. The major clubs are concentrating more on the provision of cabaret type entertainment and the social side of clubs generally. Although the same attitude may not be shared unanimously by the operators of smaller bingo clubs the industry has been seeking to persuade the Gaming Board for some years that the inability to advertise bingo clubs is an unnecessary protection of the public against soft gambling and insufficient weight is given to the benefits provided by the social atmosphere and activities.

Legislation

Before turning to valuation it is necessary to understand the legislation and other controls which affect bingo and the various activities which make up the business.

Bingo is gaming although it is termed "soft" gaming as distinct from "hard" gaming at casinos. The principal legislation governing bingo is the Gaming Act 1968, three subsequent amending acts of 1973, 1980 and 1982 and the Gaming (Bingo) Act 1985 together with regulations introduced from time to time by statutory instrument. Bingo is controlled by the Gaming Board for Great Britain which was established by the 1968 Act which aimed to separate bingo from other forms of commercial gambling and restrict it to a neighbourly form of gaming for modest prizes played in a social atmosphere. The Gaming Board seeks to ensure that bingo club proprietors keep both to the letter and the spirit of the Act.

Under the terms of this legislation a person or company wishing to operate a bingo club must first apply to the Gaming Board for a certificate of consent and the Board will satisfy itself that the applicant is fit and proper to be a proprietor. Once obtained, a certificate of consent enables the holder to apply within a specified period to the gaming licensing committee in the area for a licence to operate bingo at specified premises and to play the games specified in the certificate of consent. Obtaining a bingo licence for new premises requires the applicant to provide proof of need to satisfy unstimulated demand which is no easy matter and it is fairly common for the proprietors of bingo clubs in the locality to oppose a fresh licence by providing evidence of sufficient or over-supply of bingo provision. A certificate of consent is not transferable and a bingo licence is transferable only between parties and cannot be transferred from one property to another. The Gaming Board is enpowered to revoke a certificate of consent in which case the bingo licence automatically ceases to have effect. The Gaming Board undertakes its control function by means of inspectors in regions covering the country and where necessary calls on the assistance of the police.

A manager of a bingo club requires a certificate of approval from the Gaming Board who will ensure by means of a written test and interview that the manager is suitable generally and has sufficient knowledge of the law relating to gaming and lotteries in general and bingo in particular and has a knowledge of the proper conduct of the main game and ancillary games which make up a bingo session. Admissions are restricted to club members and bona-fide guests all of whom must be over 18 years old. A session of bingo must last at least two hours and it is common practice to run two sessions together particularly in the evening. The amounts paid by members for admission, participation and stake money must be clearly displayed and all stake money less gaming duty is returned to the players as prize money. The main game is therefore non profit-making and the operator obtains his profit from admission money, participation fees, interval games, gaming machines, bar and buffet/restaurant. It is necessary to understand the nature of these different profit centres which go to make up the bingo business.

These various aspects of the business are dealt with in turn.

Admission and participation fee There should be a clear notice for members stating the times for the charging period or session, admission price and participation fees for the games to be played. There is a maximum charge for admission and participation which is amended from time to time in regulations made under the Gaming Act. It is presently £5.70 plus VAT.

Linked bingo Linked bingo is simply a small number of clubs which join together through a video or sound link-up and aggregate their stake to play a game of bingo. About three quarters of bingo clubs play linked bingo. The maximum total weekly prize allowed at present, is £4,500 to be shared between the clubs in the link.

The National Game The National Game is a game of bingo run by a company set up for that purpose and is available to member clubs who pay an annual fee. About two-thirds of the clubs are members. The game is played every evening and additionally, as a more recent innovation, on Saturday afternoon for a maximum national prize of £50,000 and ten regional prizes each of £5,000 ie up to a total of £100,000 per game. Although the National Game was introduced in June 1986 it had been mooted for some years previously as one way in which to generate interest which was flagging at that time. In its first five years it has paid out £147m in prize money; averaging about £80,000 every day. The National Game is a good example of how a sector of the leisure industry has made use of modern technology which has enabled some 650 bingo clubs throughout the land to play a game of bingo together through a computerised control centre.

Interval games The ancillary games is another area where modern technology has played a part in changing the type and pace of interval games, principally prize bingo and mini cash bingo. The days of the stake of threepenny pieces placed on playing cards and the speed of the game dependent on the card handling skill of the operator has given way to computerised table top mini cash bingo equipment (mechanised cash bingo) which provides instant information on the number of participants, participation fee, stake money and prize money. Each game is limited to 200 players.

Added prize money Proprietors are permitted to add their own money to the stake in order to increase the prize. This enables for example the proprietor to guarantee a certain level of prize even if that amount is not covered by the stake. The extent of the use of added prize money and the reasons for its use or lack of use has a very important bearing on the success and profitability of a bingo club. The amount which may be spent in this way is presently limited to £2,000 per week.

Gaming machines Gaming machines are a further important part of a bingo club's financial make-up providing an alternative to interval games. Some years ago larger clubs faced with the problem created by the limit of only two jackpot machines started to introduce amusement with prizes (AWP) machines. There is a threshold produced by the number of admissions and the cost of licences which influences the small clubs to continue with the two permitted jackpot machines. There has recently been an attempt to obtain regislation to increase the permitted number of jackpot machines to four. The present annual licence fee for a jackpot machine is £960 and for an AWP £375. The maximum prize for a jackpot machine is £150 and for the AWP is £2.40 cash or non-monetary prize of £4.80 In value provided in tokens exchangeable for merchandise on display.

Bar and buffet Food and drink is an increasingly important profit centre and more and more attention is being given to this aspect of the business which is capable of making a substantial contribution to total profit. Although invariably licensed it is clear that bingo players are generally not hard drinkers.

Factors affecting value
With an understanding of the nature of the industry, the legislation which controls it and the various individual profit centres during a bingo session attention may now be given to valuation considerations.

Location It is important that the area generally should be non-threatening. Other important features are proximity to bus services which are reliable and cater for at least the close of the early evening session. Car parking should be close at hand, safe and well lit. A club which is not close to the centre of town where bus services converge will have to provide transport on a regular basis, the full cost of which may not be recoverable from the patrons.

Competition Competition not only dilutes the available admissions but promotions to gain a larger share, or keep an existing market share, lead to the greater use of added prize money and restrict ability to increase admission charges.

The property The preference is for ground floor level with the minimum amount of stairs and all seating on one level for the required seating capacity. The larger clubs have separate bar and restaurant areas. For many years the industry considered the adverse elements of weather to be ice, snow and gales but with three hot summers in succession which have had an effect on admissions more attention is being given to air cooling. In the right location with a substantial catchment area size is vital because apart from linked games and the National Game the amount of prize money is dependent on the stake provided by those at the session.

The equipment The modern equipment for random number selection and computerised display board enable the game to be conducted at the required pace and information relayed immediately and clearly for all to see. The table-top mechanised cash bingo also provides speed and clarity and this game has become more popular as an alternative to prize bingo.

Audience profile It is well recorded that the leisure industry is increasingly aware of and targeting the more mature section of the community which has become more affluent at a time of life when financial commitments by way of mortgage payments and child rearing are reducing. This is the bingo audience and it is a large part of the strength of the industry provided it can renew the natural decline in its audience with the following generation.

Industry profile The industry has invested in its buildings and equipment and is now working at transforming its traditional image to attract a wider audience. Its present audience has increasing disposable income and is generally committed to bingo on a regular basis. Growth may not be dramatic but the business is more predictable and less affected by fashion as is the case of night clubs, nor does it fluctuate due to variable product as in cinemas and theatres. There may be no bonanzas but far fewer disappointments. The major factor for the future is the prospect of at least some relaxation on advertising which is dependent initially on the attitude of the Gaming Board and then on Parliament providing the amending legislation.

Bingo valuation: Example 1

The first bingo club is a typical former cinema well located in a town centre close to the main shopping area and a bus station. There are other clubs in the town centre and suburbs. The club has 950 seats in the former stalls, 200 of which are equipped with table-top mechanised cash bingo units.

There is a 100 prize bingo unit and 40 AWPs. The circle accommodates 400 cinema tip-up seats which are used on busy nights. The club was refurbished to a good standard about a year ago and is therefore in a good state of decoration and repair. The property is held freehold. Annual admissions are estimated at 200,000 a year averaging around 4,000 a week and total retained spend per head is £4.50 as shown in the profit and loss projection. The proportions of the total income will depend very largely on the facilities at the club, management philosophy and preferences of the members.

Profit and loss projection

Income	£	£
Admission charge	90,000	
Participation fees	180,000	
AWP	270,000	
Prize bingo	100,000	
MCB	125,000	
Bar/buffet	135,000	
Total income		900,000
Costs		
Wages	150,000	
Cost of prizes	60,000	
Cost of bar/buffet	90,000	
Bingo books	10,000	
Added prize money	50,000	
Licences	10,000	
Buses	10,000	
Telephone, post, stationery	20,000	
Repair, maintenance	25,000	
Rates, water	50,000	
Heat, light	25,000	
Insurance	10,000	
Miscellaneous	60,000	
		570,000
Profit (36%)		330,000

Capital valuation This club has reasonably good admissions but the spend per head is capable of being improved and the capacity would allow improved admissions. The combination of the recent refurbishment and scope for improvement of the business justifies a relatively high YP.

Maintainable Profit	£	330,000
YP		6
Capital Value		£1,980,000
Say		£2,000,000

Bingo valuation: Example 2

The second bingo club is in a small country town and is located in a converted cinema but smaller than the first example. It is the only commercial bingo club in the town but of course bingo is played in other establishments. The competition comes from bingo clubs in a larger town about ten miles away, the largest of which has fairly recently had a major refurbishment and is now being aggressively promoted. In particular the large town club provides free bus transport which reduces potential admissions at our example club. In the former stalls there are 400 seats, an 80 place prize bingo unit, 20 AWP machines and a small bar/buffet. In the circle there are 300 tip-up seats but there is not much call for these to be used. It is some years since the club was reseated and carpeted although some decoration has been carried out more recently. Considering the lack of any major improvement the overall appearance is reasonable. The level of business would not justify major investment. Annual admissions are estimated at 65,000 averaging around 1,250 per week but have been declining steadily in recent years. The retained spend per head is estimated at £4.

Profit and loss projection

Income	£	£
Admission charge	25,000	
Participation fees	65,000	
AWP	85,000	
Prize bingo	20,000	
MCB	25,000	
Bar/buffet	40,000	
Total income		260,000
Costs		
Wages	80,000	
Cost of prizes	10,000	
Cost of bar/buffet	25,000	
Bingo books	3,000	
Added prize money	25,000	
Licences	2,000	
Buses	2,000	
Telephone, post, stationery	3,000	
Repair, maintenance	5,000	
Rates, water	10,000	
Heat, light	10,000	
Miscellaneous	20,000	
		195,000
Profit (25%)		65,000

Capital valuation The club is making a reasonable profit at the moment but there is steady loss in the membership. The younger potential members prefer the larger newly refurbished club in the nearby town for which there is a bus provided. More members visit the example club occasionally in the afternoon which is convenient but prefer the competition club in the evening. Even so, admissions in the afternoon are sometimes very low and it may be better to open on only one weekday and Saturday afternoon. It seems inevitable that admissions and profit will decline and it is appropriate to adjust for maintainable profit and apply a conservative multiplier to ensure a reasonable and quicker pay back.

Maintainable Profit	£ 50,000
YP in perpetuity	3.5
	£175,000

Dance halls, discotheques and nightclubs

Public dance halls or "Palais de Dance" became popular in the 1920s catering for the contemporary taste in popular music which was being made more readily available through the radio and gramophone records. Although the sound of the music and the form of dancing has changed over the years the industry has hardly looked back since those days. In recent years, the most obvious changes have been the proliferation of smaller discotheques in the 1960s and 1970s, the replacement of dance bands with recorded music and disc jockeys and the importance of lighting systems. More recently theme bars, fun pubs, karaoke and the rave scene have been competition for the nightclub business. As with other leisure uses nightclubs have been built out of town with licensed capacities of up to 2,000. One of the advantages of moving out of town is that it helps to avoid some of the problems associated with rowdyism and violence when nightclubs are in town centres and/or close to residential areas.

It is necessary to understand the importance of licensing in this sector. Nightclubs and discotheques require an alcohol licence granted by local licensing justices and since the Licensing Act 1988 this licence is valid for three years (although it is subject to revocation). The public entertainment licence for music and dancing is now granted annually by the local authority in place of the licensing justices and some local authorities have used these new powers to impose conditions in the licence which have a material effect on the style of business and profit potential of the nightclub. Such conditions have required entry to members only, a lower age limit for males and females and no admission after a certain hour. The proprietor may be required to keep membership records for inspection by the council. A special hours certificate is also required from the licensing justices to extend the licensing hours normally to 2 am although there are towns where an earlier or later hour applies or an earlier hour may be applied specifically to certain premises. A club cannot trade to its full profit potential if handicapped with restricted hours and/or limited access by the public generally.

A feature of the nightclub industry is that clubs often follow a business cycle and it is important for the valuer to be able to interpret the trading information to the familiar life cycle pattern.

Stage 1

This life cycle begins with the opening or re-opening of a club with maximum promotion and advertising. Refurbishment may cost £750,000 for a medium size club and £2m for a large club incorporating a themed feeder bar. The principal characteristics for the initial two years are:

High admissions, trading to capacity on Fridays and Saturdays and at a good level on two other evenings.
High admission prices with little discounting.
High bar take at high margin.
High salary costs.
Strict door policy on age and dress standard.
Tight security.
High promotion costs.
Low repairs charge.
High depreciation.

Caution must be exercised regarding over-trading in the period of peak demand not only because it distorts the lawful trading potential but also jeopardises the licence. It is also necessary to consider under-trading and the valuer must decide whether a higher turnover and maintainable profit could be achieved by another operator.

Stage 2

In the middle of the cycle, years three and four, the following characteristics are often evident if investment has not been made to maintain the initial high standards:

Admissions slightly reduced but fairly stable due to relaxing door policy on age and dress standard.
Take per head reducing through greater use of time split pricing (eg £1 before 10 pm and £3 after) and concessionary ticketing.
Bar take per head being maintained but lower margin.
The club shows signs of wear and tear.

During this stage the reduction in admission numbers, door take and bar margin leading to lower profits is being countered by cutting costs on staff, promotion and maintenance in an effort to keep to the profit target. Without investment at this stage that profit will be short-lived and the club may become vulnerable to competition.

Stage 3

During the last stage at around year five onwards the club is likely to display the following main characteristics:

Admissions much reduced.
Admission prices reduced.
Bar prices reduced to encourage admissions.
Little pretence at door policy and now trading to the younger age group with minimum dress standard imposed.
The club appears very worn.

During this stage profit will be at a very low ebb. Rowdyism inside and outside the club requiring the attention of the police is occurring increasingly which threatens renewal of the licence or conditions which would restrict the business and profit potential. The future without substantial refurbishment and a relaunch is very uncertain and the valuer must assess the likely cost and potential of refurbishment. At this stage the club is very vulnerable to competition.

Factors affecting value

Location Public transport is less of a consideration because people rely on cars and taxis so car parking facilities at the premises or in close proximity is therefore of greater importance. The success of out-of-town locations, provided there is ample car parking, indicates that a town centre site is not essential. The age profile of the catchment area is important as is the presence of university or college. The particular importance of large academic centres is that they often provide a well supported week-day by means of a student's evening where admission prices are reduced and dress standard suitably relaxed.

Competition Some competition is almost inevitable but it is the amount of competition in relation to the catchment population which is important. Of major importance is a large capacity club existing or proposed which can make a substantial impact on the trading potential of existing clubs. In larger towns or cities a number of clubs may trade together in a complementary fashion by catering to different ages and music tastes. There is a tendency for people to be attracted to a new or refurbished club, which is usually heavily promoted, to sample the new decor and atmosphere. That success often lasts only until the next club has a refurbishment and relaunch to win back its previous market share.

The premises It is difficult to be precise as to what characteristics make a satisfactory discotheque or nightclub because they have been converted from such a variety of original buildings, such as theatres, cinemas, factories, warehouses, churches, tram sheds etc, that it seems that almost any shape or size can lend itself to this use.

Equipment Good and modern sound and lighting systems are fundamental and have become increasingly sophisticated, elaborate and expensive. It is in the nature of the industry that only the latest and best will do and a valuer will be aware that the cost is not always justified in being fully reflected in the value of the business.

Business profile There may be doubts about the staying power of some sectors in the leisure industry but it is difficult to foresee in our present society a leisure industry where music and dancing does not play a major part. What is difficult to predict is the form that it will take. The vitality of the industry almost dictates that it will be susceptible to changes in fashion. A manifestation of this is the re-introduction of the large capacity nightclub at the expense of smaller discotheques. In short the underlying demand for music and dancing is lasting but the industry is fashion led and constantly changing.

Customer profile The majority of demand is from the 18–25-year-old age group. Many clubs run a mid-week over-25 night which is a way of obtaining mid-week business but the necessity to make the distinction is an indication that the main stream of the business is targeted at the under-25s. All demographic forecasts indicate a decrease in the population in this age range which inevitably will reduce total spend in the industry in the next few years. The industry is made up of a very wide range in the scale of operation and the operators range from large companies controlling a chain of generally medium to high capacity clubs to sole operators who run a single nightclub sometimes as a side line to their main business activity. It is an industry which attracts people from various other unassociated businesses who wish to invest in owning and running a nightclub. This aspect is far more marked than in other urban leisure sectors and perhaps explains the fairly regular high turnover in the market.

Capital valuation
Because of the wide variety in the size and other aspects of the discotheque and nightclub business three examples have been selected which hopefully will illustrate some of the earlier points. All are freehold.

Example 1
This is a large nightclub with a licensed capacity of 1,500 in a large town with university. The club has had a substantial refurbishment to a high standard within the last 12 months so although there is competition from other nightclubs our example has average admissions of 3,300 per week; 170,000 per year. The town and general catchment area is fairly affluent and the standard of club allows it to charge £6 for admission at weekends and full bar prices. Total average take per head is over £7.

Projected profit and loss account

Income	£	£
Box office	550,000	
Miscellaneous income	35,000	
Bar income	610,000	
Food income	40,000	
Total income		1,235,000
Costs		
Wages	225,000	
Catering cost of sales	190,000	
Promotion/DJ/bands	60,000	
Heat and light	50,000	
Miscellaneous costs	110,000	635,000
Net profit	(48%)	600,000

Valuation The net profit should be adjusted to provide annual expenditure over and above basic actual repairs at an amount sufficient to keep the club at a standard which will maintain the present level of business. With regular reinvestment and good promotion the club should remain as profitable for some years and should increase when the economy and general level of employment improve. A 20% return on capital is considered appropriate for this established nightclub.

Net profit	£ 600,000
Refurbishment allowance	£ 100,000
Maintainable profit	£ 500,000
YP	5
Capital value	£2,500,000

Example 2

This club with a licensed capacity of 1,000 is located in a large, perhaps county, town in the middle of England and there is a good catchment area. The club is located in the town centre but because of the size of the town there are several other clubs of comparative size in competition. There has been no refurbishment for four years and the club is looking tired. The equipment does not need replacement but attention is required to carpets, upholstery, and bars. The club could be transformed for £250,000. Two of the comparable sized clubs in competition have had refurbishments in the last two years. Admission price at the weekend is £4 but there are a number of concessions particularly free admission for ladies before 10.30pm. Bar prices are slightly above public house prices. In the face of the competition admissions are averaging slightly less than 3,000 per week; around 150,000 per year. The total average take per head is £5.

Projected profit and loss account

Income	£	£
Box office	300,000	
Miscellaneous income	25,000	
Bar income	345,000	
Food income	80,000	
Total income		750,000
Costs		
Wages	235,000	
Catering cost of sales	160,000	
Promotion/DJ/bands	40,000	
Heat and light	15,000	
Miscellaneous costs	80,000	530,000
Net profit	(29%)	220,000

Valuation The valuation must address the problems encountered in this critical mid-stage of the cycle. An initial increase in market share by re-establishing former levels of admissions and pricing can be achieved by an initial refurbishment to halt the potential further decline. Maintainable profit must be adjusted to reflect better business but also increased operating costs to maintain that business and provide for annual reinvestment out of operating profit.

Maintainable profit	£ 250,000
YP 25%	4
	£1,000,000
Immediate refurbishment	£ 250,000
Capital value	£ 750,000

Example 3

The third example is a smaller club with a licensed capacity of 800 in a medium-sized town. There is no university or major college from which to draw admissions and the competition is from other small discotheques and public houses. Annual admissions are averaging 1,450 per week, an annual level of 75,000. It is five years since refurbishment and admissions are reducing. To counter this, admission prices at the weekend are £3 on Saturday, £2.50 on Friday but only £1 before 10.30pm. Drink prices have been reduced to the same level as public houses. The total average take per head is £4.

Projected profit and loss account

Income	£	£
Box office	130,000	
Miscellaneous income	15,000	
Bar income	150,000	
Food income	5,000	
Total income		300,000
Costs		
Wages	70,000	
Catering cost of sales	65,000	
Promotion/DJ/band	20,000	
Heat and light	10,000	
Miscellaneous costs	60,000	225,000
Net profit	(25%)	75,000

Valuation In this example the business has been eroded by failure to reinvest and maintain standards by refurbishment to equip the club to a standard to recover its market share from the two main competitors. There may be too much competition and it is considered that the proper value for this club is based on comparable sales of other similar run-down clubs. There is a value in the "opportunity to trade" even to the lower end of the market for which there is a demand.

Maintainable profit	£ 75,000
YP	3
Capital value	£225,000

Ten pin bowling

Recent history
The ten pin bowling boom which started in the mid-1980s was rather unexpected as it was a comparatively short time since the bowling alley boom of the 1960s which was noticeably short lived. The recent boom was driven by a small number of companies some of which had no previous experience in ten pin bowling. On the face of it there was initially little reason to suppose that what can only be described as a leisure sector failure should be successful about 25 years later on. However, there are several important differences starting with the amount of disposable income enjoyed by the younger age range which is mainly attracted to ten pin bowling.

In the 1960s the development followed very closely the American industry, the main feature of which is that 75% of play is derived from leagues and only 25% by members of the general public; known as open play. In America with something like 8,000 bowls the dominance of league players was not a problem but in this country where about 200 bowls were built the near monopoly by leagues and clubs left insufficient capacity for casual players who were obliged to wait a long time to get a game or leave without playing. Also, the complex scoring cards deterred the beginners and although this may seem a fairly inconsequential point I believe that the introduction into the new bowling centres of the graphic computerised score and display system has added considerably to the ease with which beginners can take to and enjoy the game. The emphasis today is on entertainment rather than sport and open play accounts for around 75% of total play. There are bowling centres where leagues are not allowed and all lanes are available for open play.

Various other reasons are given for the failure of the early bowling alleys including the suggestion that the properties were made valuable redevelopment sites in the property boom of the 1960s. That is not my recollection of the situation as many were in converted cinemas in poor locations and other purpose-built bowls were either part of a building at basement or first floor level. Others were elevated on piers to enable car parking requirement below the bowling alley. Many such bowls were problem disposals and remained vacant for some years. There were obviously a number of related reasons for the failure of bowling in the 1960s which do not apply today. In my experience the modern bowling centres have a brighter atmosphere and are altogether more attractive places to visit than those in the 1960s.

Out of the 200 bowls built in the 1960s only about 35 survived into the 1980s and they were kept profitable by the league players often prepared to travel some distance to the nearest remaining bowl. Although profit was not exciting, inflation took care of return on capital because historic building cost was in the region of £100,000. The time came when the bowls became so worn that some refurbishment had to be carried out even if on a tight budget. The refurbishment justified increased prices and fortunately admissions increased in response to the refurbishment. AMF who operate bowls in this country but are best known as international suppliers of bowling equipment introduced the computerised scoring display system which was the innovation which provided a breakthrough and a new boom was under way.

Factors affecting value

Location Prime locations for bowling centres are out-of-town retail/leisure parks with complementary leisure uses and ample car parking in a catchment population of around 250,000 representing around 7,500 per lane.

Competition In situations where the number of bowling centres exceeds what will be supported by the reasonable catchment criterion and competing centres are within a fifteen or twenty minute drive time the bowling centres will not trade to their full potential.

Valuation example

This modern ten pin bowling centre was built about two years ago and is located on a retail and leisure park on the edge of a large town. The catchment population within a ten mile radius is 300,000 and access by motorway and trunk road is excellent. The centre has 30 lanes, a licensed bar and restaurant, a shop, shoe hire facility, and a room with pool tables, amusement and gaming machines. The interior is of typical high quality with computerised scoring. There is no ten pin bowling centre in the same town, the nearest competition being some 30 miles away and there are no known proposals for a further bowling centre in the locality. There is ample car parking provision. The site is held by a lease for 125 years at a peppercorn and there are no onerous restrictions or covenants.

Estimate of turnover is usually by reference to "lineage" which is the average number of games per lane per day multiplied by the income from all sources per game. This is a very popular bowling centre and the lineage is assessed at 45. The total income per game is estimated at £2.45 net of VAT. An estimate of turnover may be achieved using the lineage rule of thumb as follows:

45 × £2.45 × 30 lanes × 52 weeks × 7 days = £1,203,930.

Profit and loss projection

Income

Admissions	£ 60,000	
Bowling income	£660,000	
Licensed bar	£160,000	
Catering	£170,000	
Shoe hire	£ 70,000	
Shop	£ 7,000	
Machines	£ 60,000	
Sundry items	£ 13,000	
		£1,200,000

Costs

Wages	£300,000	
Operating costs	£250,000	
Bar	£ 60,000	
Catering	£ 90,000	
		£ 700,000
Net profit		£ 500,000 (42%)

Capital valuation This is a successful business which would be attractive to existing operators and those wishing to join the field. The companies engaged in the ten pin bowling centre development are looking for a minimum 25% return from new developments and that is an appropriate rate to apply for this established business.

Estimated maintainable profit	£ 500,000
YP in perpetuity 25%	4
Capital value	£2,000,000

Rental valuation

The principles contained in SAVP 12 apply equally to rental valuation and in particular the problems relating to the lack of comparable evidence and where available the ability to analyse the evidence. For other commercial property comparable evidence will usually be drawn from nearby premises often the same high street, office building or industrial estate. Invariably that will not be the case with leisure property because there may be little or no rental evidence in the vicinity or same town and if there is there may be no generally accepted basis of analysis because of the difficulty for some sectors in providing a meaningful unit of comparison. By that is meant a reliable rent per sq ft on a zoning basis with generally accepted lower rates for basement and upper floor sales and stocks space as used for the rental valuation of shops.

There are sectors where the use of comparables is generally accepted and the most easily recognisable is snooker. The snooker business expanded very rapidly in the early 1980s often in leasehold premises in fringe commercial locations and in accommodation of marginal value at basement or first floor in high street, retail or office premises. Because of the number of snooker clubs in any sizeable town and in the suburbs of larger towns and cities there is fairly readily available market evidence which shows a pattern of a rent per table or a rent per square foot provided there is a reasonably economic layout. A relatively clear pattern of rental values simply reflects the degree of uniformity in the size of club, pricing policy, average hours of operation and consequent profit potential; the income and operating costs providing little scope for major varia-tions. The same degree of uniformity in trading pattern coupled with a convenient unit of comparison would apply to squash clubs and ten pin bowling, but in the case of squash clubs there is lack of market evidence although there is ample rental evidence of ten pin bowling rents. Night-clubs and discotheques are another sector where for entirely different reasons the use of comparables on a rent per square foot are widely used The reasons for this may be the opposite to those which apply to snooker clubs because the cost of fitting out and regular refurbishment and volatility of the business generally dictate that although the value of the business may vary from time to time in line with a number of factors the value of the building is a more constant factor. The type of building whether purpose-built or converted from a range of other commercial uses does not appear to be a significant influence on value. The licensed capacity will have a bearing because premises of equal size may not have the same licensed capacity which may be limited by considerations, such as emergency exit facilities, inherent in a property.

In the case of cinemas a rent per seat might provide a useful unit of comparison if there were sufficient rental evidence available. The rent per seat basis is made more complicated by the variety in the sizes of auditoria with barring being the most significant valuation factor of all.

In the case of bingo clubs, because they are predominantly converted from purpose-built cinemas they have literally a two tier seating system. Although the stalls have usually been converted to banquette seating around tables, the circle remains in its original form with steep rake and tip-up seats. The remoteness of the circle from the main game, machines and interval games makes these seats difficult to quantify as a unit of comparison. In some clubs they are in constant use having been respaced with side tables and cash bingo units and in other clubs there is little or no demand. In comparing similar-sized clubs quite wide variations may arise in take per head due to the locality and the influence of competition. Similar admission figures may, therefore, produce considerably different profit.

The general point to bear in mind when considering the use and reliability of comparables is that if the market estimates rental value by the profits method it is questionable whether an artificial or contrived system of analysis by a valuer will achieve the correct answer.

Subject to the above comments on comparable evidence, the assessment of rental value starts with the estimation of maintainable profit and is therefore precisely the same process as required for a capital valuation. The rental value is the proportion of the maintainable profit which a tenant would pay by way of rent and is commonly called the "tenant's bid". The proportion is normally between 25% and 50% according to the degree of risk in the particular leisure sector, quality of the earnings and the scale of the operation. The market's perception of the degree of risk in the various leisure sectors is the first consideration and will normally establish a narrower band within the broad band of 25% to 50%. In certain cases the percentage may even be outside the broad band. If bingo is used as an example it will be noted from what has been said earlier that it is a sector which has certain areas of difficulty such as increasing potential audience awareness and age profile but the problems are recognised and being addressed by the industry leaders. The positive aspects are lack of volatility, increasing prosperity of the main customer base and that the sector appears to withstand recession better than other sectors. For properties of the optimum seating capacity and layout the sector should bid in the upper half of the broad band.

Keeping with the gaming industry, casinos, especially in London, provide an example of the lower end of the broad band. It is known from the latest report of the Gaming Board that in the year to March 31 1991 there were 119 casinos outside London and 21 casinos in the London area. The total drop (money exchanged for chips) in casinos in Great Britain was £1,936m of which £1,199m (62% of the total) was in London. The average amount retained by casinos (house win) was 18% (a consistent figure over the past three years) indicating a national house win of £350m for the year. So, although it is clearly a business with extremely high turnover, there are two aspects of the casino business which set it apart from other sectors in the leisure industry. First, the percentage of operating costs to turnover is exceptionally high and difficult to reduce in line with turn-over. Second, in the high staking casinos the drop often fluctuates depending on a handful of high rollers which may give rise to a house win percentage considerably different from the average house percentage win. It is inherent in the nature of the business that substantial losses, perhaps only short term, are a distinct possibility and this very high degree of risk may put the tenant's bid below the broad band particularly in times of recession and other world events which can influence the industry.

The impact of scale on the level of the tenant's bid is perhaps also best illustrated by taking examples at the extremes. In the case of a small business capable, because of its size and location, of producing a maintainable profit of just £50,000, even a marginal decline would erode the profit before rent down to a level where the risk would hardly be worthwhile. In such cases the tenant's bid will be at the lower end of the broad band. On the other hand where a business is capable of a very high profit some reduction, even if sizeable in pure money terms, will still leave a substantial profit after rent although the tenant's share is reduced as a percentage of profit. There are also those locations which are so sought after, such as the West End of London, where competition for properties produces a premium value and for that reason the tenant's bid may be above the broad band.

Considerations at rent review

"Rent review clauses seem unhappily to vary almost infinitely in their terms." So said Mr Justice Vinelott in giving judgment in the case of *Ritz Hotel (London) Ltd* v *Ritz Casino Ltd* [1989] 2 EGLR 135 which was an application under the Arbitration Act for the determination of questions arising in a rent review arbitration. Within the last few years there have been four cases which examine in detail the interpretation of rent review provisions in certain London casinos. Apart from the Ritz case mentioned above, the other cases which also arose out of rent review arbitrations are:

Daejan Investments Ltd v *Cornwall Coast Country Club* [1985] 1 EGLR 77; (1984) 273 EG 1122
Cornwall Coast Country Club v *Cardgrange Ltd* [1987] 1 EGLR 146; (1987) 282 EG 1664
Electricity Supply Nominees Ltd v *London Clubs Ltd* [1988] 2 EGLR 152; [1988] 34 EG 71

These cases should be studied carefully as they deal with rent review considerations similar to those which are incorporated in leases of leisure properties and many points are of general or further application and not relevant only to casinos. It so happens that the rents of London casinos are high and differences in interpretation take on greater significance in the rental valuation. In one of the Crockfords cases the rents submitted by the parties' expert valuers were £180,000 p.a. and £3,000,000 p.a. respectively. It is hardly surprising that those sums and the amount of difference concentrates the mind and litigation results.

Although the basic initial approach to rental value for rent review is usually the same as for capital and rental valuation for a fully equipped operational business, rent reviews often provide particular problem areas. To help illustrate the point Guidance Notes 4 and 7 from SAVP 12 are set out below.

4. The operational entity includes, besides the land and buildings, items such as fixtures, furniture, goodwill and stock at valuation.
7. Certain operations can only be carried on under statutory consents, permits and licences and their continuance is an assumption which should be specifically stated in the Valuation Certificate.

These Guidance Notes give valuers a clear instruction of what is to be taken into account and incorporated in a capital valuation but at rent review the terms of the lease, the description of the premises, the assumptions and disregards may call for an entirely different valuation. Sometimes what is to be valued is insufficiently described even where there are licences for alterations because of lack of drawings and specifications or schedules of works. The assumptions and disregards or their absence may not provide a complete picture and may even be contradictory. What is certain is that, perhaps because by comparison with general commercial property, leisure property is rarely dealt with, which results in the rent review provisions containing matters or failing to include matters which necessitate a more eccentric valuation process not always envisaged by the parties. The amount of variation in leases seems limitless but the following are some general observations on matters which often require attention.

The premises Deciding what is to be valued requires close examination not only of the description of the premises in the lease but any prior agreement for lease and subsequent licences for alteration and deeds of variation. Whether or not alterations and/or improvements or their effect on value are to be disregarded will have a very significant effect on value.

The state and condition of the premises to be valued commonly falls into one of three categories although there can of course be any number of variations from these three categories evident from the lease and other documents.

1. The bare building shell.
2. The building as brought forward complete with services, electrics, plumbing, air conditioning and finishes to walls, floors and ceilings and landlords' fixtures and fittings.
3. Fully fitted, equipped and ready to trade.

Although neither case relates to properties in leisure use the cases of *GREA Real Property Investments Ltd* v *Williams* [1979] 1 EGLR 121 and *Estate Projects Ltd* v *Greenwich London Borough* (1979) 251 EG 851 help in establishing that when faced with the valuation of a shell building the approach should follow as closely as possible the approach of hypothetical tenants likely to be in the market. The usual approach for leisure properties, namely the profits method, and the reasons for it has been discussed earlier and I believe it follows that a similar approach would be used by the market in assessing rental value of a shell building. Leisure operators will normally estimate the likely profit from the fully fitted and equipped trading operation and the percentage of that which should be paid as rent. The annualised cost of bringing forward and fitting out is deducted from the rental value of the fully fitted operation to provide rental value as building shell. A simple example is as follows:

Maintainable profit		£600,000
Tenant's bid @ 40%		0.4
ERV fully fitted		£250,000 p.a.
Costs	£835,000	
Annualised 15%	6.67	£125,000 p.a.
ERV shell		£125,000 p.a.

A disregard of the effect on value of trade fixtures and fittings may justify a different approach but again this depends on the approach followed by the market. There are instances where those in the market would invariably refit so the presence and quality of existing trade fixtures and fittings may have little relevance to value if they would be discarded by a hypothetical tenant. The equipment in certain leisure uses such as cinema and bingo clubs is quite long-lived and is likely to be taken into account by a hypothetical tenant. Nightclubs would be an example of where much of the trade fixtures and fittings are relatively short-lived and the hypothetical tenant is more than likely to bring in its own style of operation.

As in all residual valuations caution must be exercised in the use of estimated cost figures which if exaggerated will distort the true rental value. However where the valuation results in a low rental value for the shell this may well be due, especially at the first rent review, to the tenant's over-ambitious profit projection and cost estimate.

User It is not unusual to find the assumption as to user at rent review different from the permitted user in the lease. The landlord's intention is to ensure rental growth and this reflects the landlord's doubts about rental growth in the leisure industry and perhaps lack of knowledge of the basis of valuation. Alternatively there may be a wide range of permitted uses including commercial uses such as retail or offices in the hope that a wide selection of uses will provide the best opportunity for rental growth. It is important to distinguish between these two situations. In the first instance where the assumption as to user for valuation purposes is clearly defined in the rent review clause it is of no relevance that such use is not permitted by the lease and does not have planning or other consents which would enable that use to be carried on from the premises. The case of *Bovis Group Pension Fund Ltd* v *GC Flooring & Furnishing Ltd* [1984] 1 EGLR 23 established this principle quite clearly. In the second of these circumstances where the user for valuation purposes is intended to relate to the highest of a number of permitted commercial or leisure uses the situation is not so certain because although a use may be permitted by the lease whether or not that use would obtain planning and other consents is a material valuation consideration. Leases invariably contain a covenant by the tenant to comply with current legislation and, by inference or specifically, planning legislation. In such cases it is necessary to investigate the adopted and proposed planning policy relating to the location of the property and to judge to what extent, if at all, the relevant alternative use would be likely to obtain planning consent. There is sometimes a policy to retain existing leisure uses and any application for change of use would be resisted by the planning authority. A further planning-related point is that many properties in leisure use have been constructed as part of a larger development either in town centres or out-of-town retail and leisure schemes where the retention of the leisure element which had been included as planning gain is established in a Section 106 Agreement. In those particular cases the rental valuation cannot have regard to a use which would not comply with the terms of the Section 106 Agreement. The cases of *Compton Group Ltd* v *Estates Gazette Ltd* and *6th Centre Ltd* v *Guildville Ltd* indicate that the valuer must exclude from consideration the value of any use of the premises which would be in breach of planning control although the valuer may have regard to hope value according to the prospects of obtaining planning consent. Where hope value may apply there may be costs of conversion to take into account and the cost of additional parking provision or payment in lieu according to the planning authority's parking standards.

Term of years The term of years to be assumed may have an important bearing on the rental value where the assumed term is significantly either longer or shorter than the term acceptable in the market. The term of years takes on greater significance when related to other covenants and rent review assumptions. An obvious case is where the rent review is to the value of the bare building shell and the assumption as to the term is a short period of perhaps only five or ten years and where the permitted user would require major expense to bring forward and fit out. In such cases the rental value at the rent review date may be below the rent passing. The assumption of a long term of say 35 or 40 years can be equally significant if there is an absolute user clause restricting the use to, for example, live theatre or a small cinema faced with a new multiplex as competition. In such cases although there may be a market for a short-term or annual tenancy there may be little or no market on the assumption of a long term of years.

The case of *Ritz Hotel (London) Ltd* v *Ritz Casino Ltd* included among a number of interesting points a decision relating to the term of years to be assumed. The relevant phrase in the rent review clause was: "for a term equivalent to the term hereby granted". It was held that the hypothetical term to be assumed at the rent review date would be equal to the then unexpired residue of the actual term.

Tenant's goodwill and previous occupation Goodwill may arise from personal ability and reputation or a well known brand or theme identity. Of all the valuation considerations goodwill is the most difficult to quantify. Valuers are not alone in finding goodwill a problem area because for some time the accountancy profession has been debating the principle of introducing into company balance sheets a separate value attributed to intangible assets such as product brand names and a fuller disclosure of the treatment of goodwill particularly following the sale of a business. That certain brand names are saleable is difficult to question but problems arise over quantification and possible double counting. Similar considerations apply in the valuation of leisure property and the specific valuation problem is highlighted and stated in SAVP 12 at Guidance Note 9.

Problems can be encountered in differentiating between the value of the trading potential which runs with the property and the value of the goodwill which has been created by the present owner and which may be transferable to other properties in the event of the subject property being sold. In such cases the Valuer when assessing future trading potential should exclude any turnover which would only be available to the present owner and/or management, but reflect any trading potential that might be realised in the hands of a more efficient operator.

In rent review negotiations most leisure operators will say that they operate their business with more efficiency and style than their competitors and therefore resent paying for what they regard as their personal goodwill. Such claims are often exaggerated and are not borne out by an impartial assessment which indicates a level of business more attributable to objective factors relating to the premises and their location. The perception of those in the market of their ability to trade at an equal or better level than others in the market indicates at times that in an open market situation the market is prepared to pay for its own goodwill and/or that of the vendor. When the proprietor of a business which he claims to have built up through personal goodwill becomes a vendor he will rarely suggest that the price should be reduced because his personal goodwill is being removed The price required will reflect fully any element in the value attributable to personal goodwill and in a good market it is likely that the vendor will not be disappointed.

However, there is no doubt that personal goodwill does exist and obvious examples would be West End theatres whose proprietor has the ability to write hit musical shows or cinemas ultimately owned by a major American film production company which consistently makes popular films. With such notable exceptions goodwill is often more imaginary than real and where it exists it is often disregarded by the market.

The two consequences of the disregard of the tenant's previous occupation and use of the premises is first that it implies a disregard of tenant's goodwill, even if that is not explicit. The second effect on value is that it may not be assumed that a tenant would bid above the market to ensure continuity of an existing business.

The benefit of a licence I believe that there is a consensus among valuers that the disregard of a licence does not mean that the premises will not have the benefit of a licence throughout the assumed term but although the tenant will not have a licence on the commencement date of the hypothetical lease he would expect to be able to obtain one. It should follow that a willing tenant will have the experience to predict the risk, cost and time required to obtain a licence and unless those predictions were satisfactory he would not be a willing tenant. Whether or not the tenant would temper his rental offer, and if so by how much, will depend on the circumstances. The degree of risk in obtaining any licence will depend on the nature of the licence and premises and any known attitude of the licensing authority. If obtaining a licence is little more than routine little would turn on this disregard in the valuation. The exception to this is the casino market. In recent reports the Gaming Board has reported its objections to new licences in the provinces and in the case of London has been on record for some years that in its opinion there are already sufficient casinos and the Board formally opposes applications for new licences. The implications on value will therefore depend on the particular circumstances and the type of licence.

Summary

The desired results of achieving a fair open market rent between the parties and in accordance with their intentions is often not a question of value but the interpretation of assumptions and disregards which often impinge in a manner not envisaged by the parties. This may often occur through the failure of the parties to take expert legal and valuation advice when the lease is drafted and agreed. However, it is invariably time and effort well spent if it avoids serious errors and unfairness at rent review. Because of the specialised nature of the valuation of leisure property I would invariably advise that the third party independent surveyor should act as an expert rather than an arbitrator. Following the ruling in *Cornwall Coast Country Club* v *Cardgrange Ltd* that only trading information which would be available in the market at the relevant time should be admissible as evidence there is a difficulty in submitting useful evidence to an arbitrator. A less-favoured alternative to reference to an expert surveyor would be provision for the arbitrator to be provided with trading information following the lines of *Electricity Supply Nominees Ltd* v *London Clubs Ltd.*

CHAPTER 6

City centre hotels

Introduction

This chapter is aimed primarily at city and other major centre hotels and the valuation thereof. It is principally directed at the valuation of hotels in the United Kingdom; the principles may also be used in the valuation of prime centre hotels in Europe and the rest of the world, but each individual country has particular practices and laws which impact on the valuation approach for hotels and other businesses. It would be dangerous for any valuer to proceed to value an hotel outside the United Kingdom purely on the basis of the contents of this chapter, without a thorough working knowledge of the country in which the subject property is located, indeed the *RICS Appraisal and Valuation Manual* ("The Red Book") is particularly specific with regard to valuers undertaking work outside their particular sphere of knowledge.

Unlike other commercial property where a valuer commences with the superficial area, either gross or net internal, of a property, and applies the appropriate rent to that building either overall or based on the type of space available, followed by an appropriate multiplier to arrive at the capital value, hotels and their values are driven by the generation of profit and without an existing profit or the potentiality of a profit the hotel will have no value (other than for some alternative use). No valuer should ignore the possibility that the hotel could have an alternative value, which is higher than that resulting from the capitalisation of the profit level.

As will have been demonstrated in the chapter relating to provincial and country house hotels/public houses, hotels and their profit generation is a very personalised affair; whilst all companies and/or general managers will claim that their particular company or unit is the best in the market, the ability of the company to market itself and the ability of the general manager to project himself into the local market will have a significant bearing on the capability of the individual unit to generate the necessary profits. No valuation of an hotel can be carried out without an understanding of the ability of the operating company and/or the manager in that particular market.

In order for the valuation of an hotel to be undertaken in accordance with the *RICS Appraisal and Valuation Manual* and to accurately reflect the property and its business the appointed valuer must be fully cognizant of the following three aspects:

1. the hotel business, the sources of demand and the ability of that source to generate occupancy;
2. the ability to understand and interpret the accounts provided and to adapt the accounts as appropriate;
3. a working knowledge of the property, construction and their relevance to the hotel industry.

The hotel industry is a cyclical and volatile market which can be easily upset by events outside *its* particular sector such as:

1. currency fluctuations – this has the effect of increasing or decreasing the flow of visitors – the dollar and the yen are two particularly influential currencies, not only in relation to business travel but also to the tourist sector;
2. external political decisions – the bombing of Libya by the United States and the Gulf War;
3. external ecological events – the Chernobyl disaster;
4. economic growth or recession in various parts of the world.

History

A brief overview of the growth of hotels will provide a useful backdrop to this chapter.

The development of hotels or overnight accommodation commenced through the necessity for overnight stay during the horse-drawn period; this developed through the coffee houses and clubs, more particularly in London and spread throughout the provinces with the development of coaching inns in the county towns.

Hotels, in the sense that we understand at present, started to become known in the 1800s as the industrial revolution gathered pace and more overnight accommodation was required.

London developed hotels during the 1800s and more particularly in the second half of the century, when the construction of a number of "luxury" hotels occurred, such as the Langham and the Ritz as well as other hotels which have now disappeared from the face of London.

Significant growth of hotels during the 19th century also came as a result of the development of the railway network and each railway company developed hotels at the various termini; London naturally became the focus for this particular development – Great Western Hotel, Paddington; Great Central Hotel, Marylebone; Great Eastern Hotel, Liverpool Street, etc.

In the early 1900s and before World War II there were few significant hotel groups as we understand hotel groups at the present time. Hotel companies such as Trust Houses and Fredricks existed but did not have the same impact on the market as their successors.

After nationalisation of the railway industry the railway hotels in the early 1950s were formed into British Transport Hotels and BTH became one of the early powerful hotel companies.

The 1950s and the early 1960s saw the start of hotel development, particularly in London with hotels such as the Royal Garden Hotel and the Royal Lancaster Hotel being funded by pension funds.

The 1970s saw very substantial growth in hotels, particularly in London. This development phase was accelerated by the grant system initiated by the Government in the late 1960s and which ran until 1973, whereby a grant of £1,000 was given for every bedroom constructed. Whilst this generated a large development boom in hotels it is now cursed by many hoteliers since the form of construction was poor (cheap) and the size of many rooms is, in *current* terms, extremely poor and small. At that stage many of the developers were supported by pension funds and the insurance companies. The growth in hotels was immediately followed by the recession between 1974 and 1975 and the crash in the property market. The recession impacted upon the profitability of the hotels and this coupled with falling property values impacted on the return to the funds. It is considered by many experts in the hotel industry that the current reluctance of many of the insurance companies, pension funds etc to provide finance to the hotel industry is a direct result of the effects of their entry into the hotel business in the early 1970s.

The late 1960s and early 1970s saw the arrival in Europe and in the United Kingdom (London) of many of the United States and overseas hotel companies. Their expansion into the remainder of the United Kingdom was gradual and even today is extremely limited.

During this period many of the current hotel companies expanded or merged to provide the conglomerates known today – Forte Plc (now owned by Granada Plc), Grand Metropolitan (now Inter-Continental Hotels), Queens Moat Plc etc.

The 1980s started with a recession and very limited development. Commonwealth Holiday Inns of Canada (as they were known then) were one of the first companies to enter into a drop lock scheme for development and financing of their hotels. London during this period saw very little development of new hotels due to the restrictive attitude of two of the main Local Authorities, namely Westminster City Council and the Royal Borough of Kensington and Chelsea.

The late 1980s saw the dramatic growth of hotels and hotel companies throughout the United Kingdom – Crest (now part of Forte), Thistle (now part of Mount Charlotte), Mount Charlotte, Baron Group (no longer in existence). The late 1980s saw also the further expansion in the United Kingdom of the overseas groups and either their entry or noticeable expansion into the provincial cities of the United Kingdom – Marriott, Ramada, Campanile, Novotel etc.

The growth of some of the large hotel companies at the end of the 1980s was by merger and acquisition rather than the development of individual units, e.g. Queens Moat, Mount Charlotte, Forte Plc.

The growth of budget hotels particularly in the provinces has been significant in the last few years, led by Granada, Travel Lodge and Travel Inns, together with a limited number of overseas companies. It can reasonably be expected to continue to be a growth market.

During the later 1980s profit and capital gain drove the hotel market. The economic recession, compounded by the Gulf War in 1991/92 saw a major reversal in the fortunes of hotel companies and many either went into receivership or experienced severe financial difficulties (a similar situation to 1974/75 and 1980/81, but with greater impact). The valuation of hotels reverted to a basis of net cash flow and adequate returns thereon.

Since 1993 London in particular has seen a return to performance related growth and demand for ownership from Far East companies.

Recent changes have seen the take-over of Forte Plc by Granada; the acquisition of the Copthorne Group by CDL of Singapore; the expansion of Whitbread in the hotel sector.

Type of hotel

Generally city centre and provincial hotels can be divided into very simple bands of hotels.

The luxury hotels ie 5 star. Until recently there were a very limited number of these hotels outside London eg Gleneagles, Caledonian in Edinburgh etc. However, more recently a number of new "5 star" hotels have been constructed in city centres outside London and a number of refurbished hotels are attaining 5 star ratings.

The bulk of the business hotels in London and the provinces is in the 3/4 star market.

A recent growth has been in the budget hotels sector, which, nominally have a 1 or 2 star category. They often provide a more comfortable and functional bedroom and en-suite facility than is normally associated with the traditional 2 star market; most hotel guides have introduced a new category to cover this type of hotel.

The "bijou" hotel has now established itself in the market and it provides a very high quality of accommodation with personalised service, but with very limited additional service ie virtually no food and beverage facility. A further growth is in "all-suite hotels", a category that mainly is derived from the United States and is now beginning to be seen in London eg the Conrad at Chelsea Harbour, 47 Park Street etc.

The last sector which is starting to grow is the 'serviced apartment'.

The last category is the guesthouse/bed and breakfast accommodation which is primarily family run. This category is, in fact, the bulk of the UK accommodation.

Unlike most European countries and many other countries around the world the United Kingdom has no official hotel grading standard. The most commonly known grading organisations are those of the Automobile Association and the Royal Automobile Club of Great Britain; the English, Welsh and Scottish Tourist Boards also have the crown system of grading, although this has been subject to change and also criticism over the last few years, and certainly in the higher category hotels is deemed by many to be irrelevant. Several hotel companies internally grade their hotels.

Some guides include 'service' with the appropriate judgement factors rather than just facilities.

Reasons for valuation

Although in many minds there are a multitude of reasons for having a valuation, they can, in fact, be broken down into four very simple categories:

1. the sale or purchase of the property;
2. accounts purposes ie balance sheet, corporate accounts etc;
3. financial purposes – either the raising of finance, or for the review of the security provided to the lending institution;
4. for internal advice for the owner/corporate company etc.

Type of valuation

A detailed exposé of the new *RICS Appraisal and Valuation Manual*, in force since January 1996, is provided elsewhere in the book and it is, therefore, not the intention of this chapter to repeat those definitions. It is sufficient to refer to three particular aspects:

1. a reasonable marketing period;
2. willing seller;
3. the exclusion of a special purchaser.

While in general terms there are a multitude of valuations that can be undertaken, the root of each valuation is the same ie the ability or otherwise of the property to generate profits.

Since the issue of the new RICS Manual the following valuations may normally be anticipated:

1. "Open market value" for sale or purchase, for finance purposes, for accounts etc. Irrespective of the reason for the valuation open market value must mean the price which that particular property could obtain at the date of valuation in an open market situation. Open market value must mean open market value.
2. "Estimated Realisation Price" (ERP) – this new definition is principally the same as "open market value" except that it anticipates that the sale will take place at a date in the future which is to be specified by the valuer. In other words the valuer now has to decide on the length of the potential marketing period and try to anticipate market movements.

3. "Estimated Restricted Realisation Price" – this in effect replaces the valuation in the event of default. It starts from the basis of ERP, but presumes a restricted marketing period and a number of other restrictions.
4. Bricks and mortar value – sometimes referred to as land and buildings, this is a hypothetical valuation and is a mathematical apportionment of open market value. In essence it means the valuation of the hotel assuming that there is no goodwill, no furniture or loose equipment and that the new operator will have to generate profits; it does however assume the benefit of existing licences. Any valuation report which refers to a valuation in this category should be very specific in indicating the root of the valuation. This valuation should also not be confused with the valuation for insurance purposes, which is principally a valuation or assessment of the cost to replace the property in the event of its destruction and does not include any element for land.

Within the above types of valuation, valuations may also be required for development purposes ie the site value or the value of the property assuming that development has been carried out.

No valuation should be undertaken in any of the above categories without also considering the possibility of the property having a higher alternative use value.

Within the various categories detailed above ownership/title of the hotel will guide the type of valuation being undertaken.

1. freehold value with vacant possession;
2. leasehold value with vacant possession;
3. investment value for a freehold or leasehold property
   – subject to a lease
   – subject to a management contract with an operating company
   – a franchise agreement;
4. the value of a management contract.

A valuer may be asked to ascribe the value to a particular brand name. This has been the subject of correspondence, publication etc both by the Royal Institution of Chartered Surveyors and the Institute of Chartered Accountants and should be approached with extreme care and caution by any valuer.

The valuation process

In undertaking this particular section of the chapter, it has been assumed that the student/reader of this chapter has a basic property and business knowledge. It is, therefore, intended to provide a synopsis of the various aspects which should be taken into consideration when undertaking a valuation of an hotel, but this list should not be assumed to be exhaustive nor taken as gospel. Any valuer proceeding to undertake a valuation should assume that this could be a useful check list, but conversely should not assume that simply answering or providing the answers to each of the points set out below, gives an automatic right to assume that everything has been covered and that, therefore, the valuation has taken into account all factors affecting its determination. An understanding of property and more particularly the business derived from that property is not only vital but without such knowledge it could lead to a negligent valuation.

The valuer is advised to be familiar with the Appraisal Manual and the valuation check lists contained therein.

Title

The freehold In most valuations it is assumed that when the client/instructing party states that the property is held freehold the property is free from any restriction or encumbrance. Whilst in general terms this may be correct a physical inspection of the property may indicate certain rights of way or other restrictions affecting it. In addition an inspection of the accounts may throw up other particular aspects.

Restrictive covenants, easements, public rights of way, could impact upon the ability of the property to generate full profit levels.

The author is aware of two particular instances where the blind assumption that the title was clear would have produced a negligent valuation.

- The reference in the accounts to rent, ultimately produced a situation where investigation showed that half of the property was held leasehold with only 15 years to run at a low rent; furthermore the demarkation line ran through the middle of the reception, restaurants, kitchen etc. together with bedrooms on the upper floors.
- At another property an enquiry on another item resulted in the production of the Land Registry document which referred to a brewery restriction and the inability of that hotel to sell alcohol.

It should be remembered that Scotland and European countries permit the concept of flying freeholds and also shared maintenance, rights of support etc which are important.

The lease A detailed review of the lease and its clauses is essential. The application of the rent review clause and its impact on profits will be dealt with later in this chapter. In particular the following clauses should be noted and, more particularly, certain sectors thereof.

1. The demise – what are the boundaries of the property, is the property demised unfurnished, in shell condition or fully furnished.
2. The term – is it a short term or long term lease.
3. Repair – is it held on full repairing covenants; what impact does this have on the hotel's repair and maintenance programme and, in particular, the correlation of the redecoration clause; does the clause require the hotel company to rebuild at any particular time; dependent upon the length of the clause, or length of the lease and the phraseology of the repairing clause the case of the *Norwich Union Life Insurance Society* v *British Railways Board* could be important ie what impact does the requirement to rebuild the hotel have on value if held on a long lease.
4. Alienation – can the lessee assign or sublet, with or without consent, is consent not to be unreasonably withheld, and does this prohibit a company sale. In addition, does the clause permit the granting of concessions particularly in the various shop units, showcases etc.

    If a lease is unassignable the property will only have value to the occupying company, unless a share transfer can take place, and any valuation should provide the appropriate caveat. The "Landlord & Tenant (Covenants) Act 1995" and its effect on assignments etc. may be relevant in consideration of any new leases.
5. The rent review clause –
    (a) What is the review pattern – if over 7 years the general property approach is to add a premium to the assessed rent to reflect the long review clause; whilst this is acceptable in normal property terms, the impact on profitability of the hotel can be significant in the first few years.
    (b) Further items that need to be analysed are those factors that need to be disregarded in the calculation of rent. These include disregarding any goodwill, the effect of occupation by

the lessee, any improvements which have been carried out, other than an obligation under the lease. Also of importance is whether the property is to be considered with vacant possession – if this is the case it can be argued that since it takes several years before an hotel is achieving a full turnover and profit level that an allowance should be made in the calculation of the rental value for the build-up period to full profitability.

6. User – many user clauses refer to the use of the premises as "a high class or high quality hotel" or an hotel of a particular category. When a category is defined there is no problem in allocating the hotel to that particular standard; however there does not appear to be any defined interpretation of high quality hotel and, therefore, in this instance commonsense and practical knowledge must apply. This definition can cause problems since a "high quality hotel" some 10 or 15 years previously may no longer be a high quality hotel, as a result of changing standards, and current requirements of guests. Dispute is certain to arise as to whether certain items of capital expenditure on the property are deemed as falling under the repairing liability, improvements by the tenant, or necessary works to comply with the user and other clauses within the lease.

It must be remembered that in Scotland legal interpretation of leases is sometimes different to that in England and Wales.

Management contracts When considering whether a management contract can be valued careful discussion with the company's accountants is advised since in general terms there is no property element to the evaluation, but purely an appraisal of the business and the rights of occupation and operation of the business. In addition, the value of the contract often lies with the particular company and any transfer of the contract could diminish the value (if permitted under the contract).

In considering a management contract it is essential to take careful cognisance of the following:

- The term of the contract – which is normally for a period of 10, 15 or 20 years with the operator's right to renew for periods of 5 or 10 years.
- Analysis must be made to see whether any equity input was provided with the management contract by the operator.

- Historic management contracts rarely allowed for the owner to terminate the contract except under very specific terms. More modern contracts allow for termination if the operator fails to meet certain budgetary targets or in the event that the owner wishes to sell his particular interest. In the latter case, compensation is usually payable on a predefined formula, which is often a multiple of a number of years average profit fees.
- Many new management contracts provide minimum guaranteed returns (MGR). Whilst there may be an MGR it must be related to the ability of that particular unit to perform even though there may be a corporate guarantee. At the same time as considering the MGR it is important to verify the ultimate guarantor in order to ensure that the guarantee is enforceable. This is particularly important where guarantees are provided by US companies, where it is vital to check that the contract can be enforceable in the particular State in which the guarantor's head office lies. It is rare under a management contract (or even a lease as above) for the company in the document to be other than a specifically set up subsidiary or company.
- Other factors which need to be considered are whether there is a fee for the membership of marketing organisations and the fees pertaining thereto; provision is usually made for a percentage of turnover to be allocated for maintenance and repairs and renewal; certain management contracts if related to a major corporate company will provide for compliance with that particular company's code of operation.
- Whilst the calculation of the base fee is usually a percentage of turnover and is, therefore, relatively simple to calculate, the incentive fee calculation must be considered very carefully since the profit line at which the incentive fee is calculated often varies between management contracts.
- In the majority of management contracts the responsibility for all the staff lies with the owning company and it is rare for any member of staff other than the general manager and certain other heads of department to remain the responsibility and in the employment of the operating company.

Licences/certificates

Operating licences It is not intended to detail the various reasons or rights under the licences that may be required for an hotel, but merely to list those licences that could be applicable and any valuer should ensure that the relevant licences are valid.

1. Justices-on-licence
2. Restaurant licence
3. Public entertainments licence
4. Supper hours
5. Performing Rights Society
6. Radio paging

Certificates (i) The principal certificate that is required for an hotel in the United Kingdom is the Fire Certificate. This certificate is issued by the Fire Officer in accordance with the Fire Precautions Act 1971, together with any statutory amendments or bye-laws. It should be verified that an up-to-date certificate is available, that the Fire Officer has made a recent inspection and most importantly the valuer should check what alterations have taken place since the last issue of the fire certificate and whether Fire Officer approval has been obtained in writing for these alterations.

Each country has a different code of practice relating to fire precautions and those in the United States are far more stringent than those currently in practice in the United Kingdom and more particularly in Europe. No valuer should assume that an hotel complying with one set of fire regulations would comply with another country's requirements. When valuing for a United States company the valuer must be careful in handling the demands under fire precautions by a United States company against those that might be required for another company bidding for the same property in the open market. Whilst the US company may require additional precautions to be installed and would reflect the cost thereof in any bid, the valuer must remember that he is providing an open market value and should differentiate between that and the value of the property to the US bidding company.

(ii) Other certificates – whilst in general terms no other certificates are required in the United Kingdom, hotels on the continent will require opening licences, tourism certificates etc. and any valuer should check these are valid.

Local authority enquiries
Due to the structure of local authorities it is accepted that, in many instances, it is impossible to obtain written confirmation of enquiries

made of the local authority in time for the submission of a report. In addition, it is usually the case that no party wishes to incur the cost of making a formal search or enquiry until such time as formal legal enquiries are made. It has been a practice of many valuers to make purely telephone enquiries of the local authority – it is considered that this is an extremely dangerous practice, since the valuer has no way of verifying the information and in most instances the authority only replies to the specific question posed. The valuer also has no means of checking that the relevant officer has appreciated the extent of the property and may, therefore, inadvertently be giving erroneous answers.

The following is a schedule, but not an exhaustive schedule, of various enquiries that should be made.

1. Notices – has the property ever been the subject of a dangerous structure notice, has any notice under the Health and Safety Acts been issued and has the Environmental Health Officer (EHO) made a recent inspection and issued a cautionary letter. In this instance all valuers should be aware of the new EHO rules with regard to food preparation and the Food Safety Acts.

2. Rating enquiries should be made – the regulations relating to transitional relief often alter under the annual Finance Act and the valuer should ensure that the correct amount is shown in the actual and budget forecasts for the hotel.

Some hotels have staff accommodation either attached to the property or in a separate location. The valuer should verify this fact and ascertain whether the community charge is being paid by the occupants, or whether a separate assessment is being raised.

3. Planning – enquiries should be made, an inspection undertaken of the planning register to check that the hotel has the relevant consents and that all conditions pertaining to such consents have been complied with or are in force. If a refusal has been issued on the hotel the reasons should be analysed. Other enquiries should be made as to whether the property is listed as being of special architectural or historic importance, whether the property lies within a conservation area and whether the grounds are affected by any tree preservation orders.

Equally important, enquiries should be made with regard to the surrounding area since new developments, new roads etc could have a material effect on the current and future business of the hotel. Consents for new hotels in the area could have a major impact.

Consideration should also be given as to whether there is an alternative use for the property, since open market value could be higher in certain circumstances i.e. office development. Additional enquiries will be needed if the property either is within or close to an Enterprise Zone, assisted status area etc.

In the event that a valuation is undertaken prior to a formal search being made by solicitors acting on behalf of a company, the valuer should reserve the right to reconsider his valuation subsequent upon the formal search being available.

The inspection

As mentioned at the outset, the valuer should not only have a detailed knowledge of the property industry, but should also have a detailed working knowledge of the hotel industry and the rules attaining thereto. Any inspection of the property must encompass both disciplines.

Each valuer will have his own system for inspecting and recording details of the property and the information below is, therefore, only to be used as a cross-check. It is relevant to note the comments in two court cases with regard to inspections:

1. "the written report is only as good as the inspection" – *Summers* v *Congreve Horner* – 1991;

2. "the reason that the defendant failed to observe these important matters is because he did not carry out his inspection with the reasonable skill and care that was required. He was negligent in the way in which he carried out his inspection" – *Henley* v *Cloake & Sons* – 1991.

The new Appraisal Manual sets out a suggested check list of matters for inspection and enquiry.

When undertaking the inspection and writing the notes the valuer should always remember that it may be necessary for another person, not necessarily within the same practice, to refer to the notes and the file, and must, therefore, be able to follow the notes in a clear, precise and logical fashion.

A general review of the structure, its repair and decorative order is a fundamental issue. Two particular categories should be taken into account, general repair and maintenance and items requiring a major capital injection, as a one-off item.

The rooms – any inspection of the rooms should take into account the size, the quality of the room, the age of the fittings and furniture and its decorative repair. In addition details should be taken of the facilities in the bathroom, the general amenities provided ie hair-dryers, trouser press. In relation to the above the requirements of the Housing Act with regard to minimum sizes/capacity of rooms must be acknowledged particularly in the lower category hotels within city centres. Whilst it would appear not to be generally enforced, local authorities have the powers to close a number of rooms, or reduce the number of beds should they not meet the minimum area categories set out in the Housing Acts. The AA and RAC have particular requirements as to the size and quality of the furniture, facilities within each room, relating to each individual category. Many of the guides now include comment and category for service and facilities.

Food and beverage – food and beverage outlets, in particular hygiene and the ability to serve from the kitchen and other areas should be carefully considered. The capacity of the various outlets should also be noted.

Health clubs – is the facility purely for the hotel resident or is it open to general membership, and if so what is the catchment area and the facilities provided. The availability of health clubs and leisure centres is always an area of discussion and disagreement between hoteliers. Particularly outside London, it is argued that an hotel must have a health facility even if the numbers using the facility are extremely small since guests are prone to prefer an hotel with a leisure facility even if they have no intention of using the same.

The kitchen – this is becoming more of an important area to be considered, taking into account the new requirements of the Environmental Health Officer and the requirements of the Food Safety Acts. In particular the following should be considered – division of use, access, cleanliness and repair and age of equipment, loading etc.

General – other areas to be considered are business facilities, conference and banqueting rooms, parking facilities, casinos, and the ease of servicing the various areas.

The valuer when looking at the hotel must primarily consider himself in the position of a client in the hotel and consider whether the facilities meet the category of the hotel and current requirements. It is said in the industry that the best way for a general manager to obtain an impression of his hotel is to stay in one of the rooms and be considered as a guest; it is also said that the best place to check the cleanliness of the room is from the bath. A valuer could, therefore, do no better than stay in the hotel having checked in anonymously the day before and only announcing his presence after having experienced the facilities.

When in the hotel the valuer must consider the quality/repair of the fixtures, furniture and equipment, the repair of the property and the general layout.

An item that may be considered as rather simple and of no great importance is "the room count". Even in the smallest hotel it is often surprising the different numbers of rooms that can be obtained from enquiry. It is the writers experience of having checked a London hotel in finding 80% of the rooms visited not complying with the designation of the front office printout. It is, therefore, essential that the source of the room count is identified and where possible cross referenced.

In addition confusion can often arise when an hotel will refer to rooms as the number of keys and vice versa. Care must, therefore, be taken; a suite which has two bedrooms may have two rooms, but be considered as "one key". Each hotel will also have a multitude of different categories of rooms and, therefore, these should be understood – twins, doubles, king size beds, queen size beds etc.

Another item of importance which must be identified in the general inspection is the service element in the hotel i.e. the plant and equipment. The replacement of such equipment can be extremely expensive not only in the price of the individual item, but more importantly the effect on rooms being taken out of commission during the repair work, with a subsequent loss of profit and disruption to business.

As well as inspecting the property itself and the grounds, the valuer should undertake a review of the surrounding area and the competition to the property and business.

The business

As indicated above a knowledge of accounts and the business is essential when reviewing the ability of an hotel to perform in its market segment or its ability to move to alternative segments and provide a better bottom line.

Most international and group hoteliers follow a system of accounting and reporting method known as "the uniform system of accounting" or a variation thereof. The uniform system basically originated from the United States and is in its eighth edition (there are discussions currently taking place with regard to a new edition). The uniform system is a standard form of reporting overall results for management purposes and also deals with a reporting system for each individual department or cost centre. Many hotels or companies (and more particularly individuals) adapt this to suit their own particular requirements, although the principles may be basically similar. It must, however, be remembered that the management accounts provided to a valuer will most likely not have been audited and, therefore, must be considered carefully.

When the valuer is considering an hotel that is currently trading and is being invited to do so by the existing management or with the co-operation of the existing management, then availability of past and current management accounts should be no problem and most hotels will also have budgets prepared. It is often helpful, if obtainable, to compare the actual results with the previous year's budget forecast; this will enable the valuer to compare the accuracy of the company's budgeting process.

However, the valuer may be required to appraise an hotel for a new purchaser or in the course of development and will, therefore, be only provided, at best, with budgets or forecast cash flows. Many of the 1990/1991 problems in the hotel industry arose from the preparation of these business forecasts and their blind acceptance by valuers in earlier years. No budget or forecast should be accepted without careful analysis and questioning particularly of the source of these forecasts and the reason for their preparation. Budgets submitted to financiers are likely to be of an optimistic nature since finance is being sought and the most optimistic light will be shed on the forecasts. Unless a valuer has either market knowledge or a comprehensive database within the office, it will be extremely difficult for that valuer to make adequate and accurate analysis of any forecast. During the course of his business the valuer will have access to accounts from various sources and whilst the valuer must treat this information as highly confidential, not only for the protection of his own reputation, the protection of the providing source, and also under the auspices of Data Protection Act, the valuer will be able to use the knowledge of these other accounts in a comparative format. He will, therefore, be able to analyse the margins and see how they compare with the competition in the area, and to be able to consider whether the hotel should move up or down into a new business sector. He will also be able to decide whether any improvements to the property will provide sufficient profit to justify the cost and result in an increase in value.

The valuer must take into consideration the grading requirements of organisations such as the AA, RAC and ETB when comparing current business with future business. Should the hotel be regraded up or down business and performance could be affected.

The ability of an hotel to perform in its particular market can be affected if it is part of a chain – it will benefit from cross purchasing, cross marketing and the corporate name. An open market valuation must consider the position of the hotel outside that particular chain, although its acquisition by another corporate chain may not change its overall position.

An hotel in private ownership or with a personality manager/owner may be able to justify a different turnover and net cash flow situation as a result of its individuality. Business may continue in the short term as a result of the previous ownership/management but consideration should be taken of the effect on cash flow after the benefits from the personality manager/owner have dissipated.

Ultimately the valuer is attempting to analyse the accounts in order to consider what the hypothetically average/reasonable operator could achieve in that situation; the ability of a particular individual or company to perform over and above that level would enable the bidding company to offer a price higher than all its competitors or obtain a better return on capital invested.

Definitions It is not intended to set out a full explanation of each definition or lines within the uniform system of accounting:

1. *Rack rates* – these are the published tariffs and often include breakfast, VAT and sometimes dinner. There is usually a multiplicity of rack rates ie full rate, corporate rate, weekend rate and so on. There may also be special rates for air crew etc.

2. *Occupancy* – either provided as the occupancy per room or occupancy per bed night. In comparing the two it would be possible to provide the percentage double occupancy achieved by any hotel. A valuer must be careful not to confuse the two, since hotels do not always specify how occupancy is calculated. The lower category hotels are more likely to use bednights.

3. *Average room rate* – the rate achieved by each room net of breakfast, VAT and after discounts etc.

4. *Yield per room* – the average rate is usually struck before application of the occupancy and, therefore, does not accurately reflect the actual monies being achieved per customer or room at the hotel. The trend is, therefore, now to consider the yield per room ie reflecting the actual performance of the overall hotel.

5. *POMEC* – this line primarily covers property operations i.e. maintenance and repair, and energy. Energy efficiency is an important factor in this particular line.

6. *Direct costs* – these costs are the costs relating specifically to each individual income producing source and those costs that can be directly attributed thereto.

7. *Gross profit* – this line is normally struck after deduction of the direct costs from the total revenue.

8. *Unallocated costs* – these costs are those particular costs that cannot be directly attributed to each separate income producing source ie administration and general expenses, sales and marketing, repair and maintenance, POMEC (see above) etc.

9. *IBFC* – income before fixed charges; fixed charges are normally defined as rates, insurance, replacements and renewals allowance. It is, also, before depreciation, finance charges etc.

Set out in example A is a typical layout for a management accounts system adopting the uniform system of accounts – applied against each line are average percentages to show the relativity of each section. The reader must not adopt these percentages as gospel as they will vary according to individual circumstances, including location, amount of conference business, popularity of restaurants, bars, etc.

Example A

Number of rooms
Occupancy per room
AARR

Revenue	%
Rooms	60
Food	21
Beverage	10
Telephones	6
Other	3
Total revenue	100

Expenditure	
Direct costs	
Rooms	60
F&B	80
Telephones	80
Other	–
Total direct costs	46
Gross profit	54

Undistributed costs

Admin and general	8
Sales and marketing	4
Energy	3
Repairs and maintenance	4
Total undistributed	19
IBFC	35

Note: the example does not show rates, insurance, management fees or replacement reserve.

The market No valuer can proceed to his appraisal without undertaking a general review of the market place in which the hotel is located. Consideration must be given as to where the business is coming from, the trends in the industry in general and the particular locality. An hotel which relies on one particular contract for a large percentage of its business would be dangerously exposed to any variations in market conditions eg the hotel with 70% American tourists would be exposed to variations in the dollar/sterling ratio; an hotel relying on one particular industry on its doorstep for 80% of its business (corporate bednights and conferences for example) would be exposed to variations in the business ability of its major customer.

Each hotel will have varying sources of business and the valuer must understand the source and characteristics of demand for accommodation – this includes: commercial, conference, tourists, incentives, air-crew etc. The time when accommodation is required, length of stay and amount available for such accommodation will vary between each group.

Any possibility of new competition coming on stream could have an impact on turnover and thus on profitability. In addition new road systems, rail systems, airports etc. could also impact on profitability eg the new Heathrow/Paddington link could provide hotel business for the Marylebone/Paddington area; a new motorway or trunk road bypassing many provincial towns could have a detrimental effect on overnight business, since it would be possible for travellers, representatives etc to cover further distances in a shorter space of time and thereby eliminating the need for an overnight stay. This effect was noticeably demonstrated when the M4 and M5 were constructed bypassing many of the towns between London and Bristol and London and Exeter.

Leased equipment Many hotels lease or rent or hold on hire purchase certain equipment and a valuer must obtain information thereon. It has been known for hotels to have leased on finance agreements such capital items as air-conditioning, all furniture and soft furnishings, and in one instance even the floor boards! It is normal practice for a valuation to take into account items that are on a rental agreement ie telephones, televisions etc but to assume that leased items ie plant and equipment are in fact owned by the hotel. The valuer should discuss these particular points and in particular the leased items with the directors particularly if the valuation is for accounts purposes, but also with the accountants and auditors in order to ensure that there is no double counting. A purchaser would also need to reflect the capital effect in any offer.

However, whatever is the final outcome of the discussions, the valuer should make his assumptions clear in the body of his report.

Evidence

No valuation should be undertaken without analysis of recent market evidence, firstly for providing support to the trends and business levels and secondly as to the price that is applicable to the individual unit. In the 1973 Court case of *Corisand Investments Ltd* v *Druce & Co*, the Judge indicated that the valuer should be able to also judge future trends in business and the property market. This comment is now particularly pertinent to the definition "estimated realisation price".

Unlike other commercial property where specification and location can be almost identical, no two hotels are identical, except in the circumstance of a standard chain construction i.e. Travel Lodge. Even so a Travel Lodge in the suburbs of London may charge the same room rate as a Travel Lodge in Scotland, but the ability to provide the same bottom line may not be identical and, therefore, the value will be different.

Unlike many countries in Europe and the United States in particular, the United Kingdom does not have a publicly available system of recording sales and their details. The collation of comparable evidence, therefore, is extremely restrictive and, therefore, in-house data and careful research is of prime importance. Obviously in-house data is the most reliable indicator and care must be taken in the analysis of published data since only a limited amount of information eg price and number of rooms may be available and, therefore, the true circumstances behind each transaction may not be known ie planning consents, leased equipment, bad debts etc. Evidence may be analysed on a price per room, a multiple to turnover or a multiple to net operating profit. Extreme caution must, therefore, be placed on using uncorroborated evidence, particularly on a per room basis.

The other major difficulty in obtaining transaction evidence in the United Kingdom and in the hotel business is the fact that many transactions take place at a corporate level and involve company sales. The prices attached to individual hotels are, therefore, not available.

Whilst the hotel business is a sector on its own, no valuer should ignore trends in other property sectors with regard to movements in yields etc. These trends may give indications as to a forthcoming recession or boom. Also a lack of transactions can possibly be indicative as to a change in market trends. Lastly, the most dangerous form of evidence is hearsay evidence particularly if it is third hand.

The valuation

General principles
It is assumed that all valuers are fully conversant with the conditions attached to the *RICS Appraisal and Valuation Manual* and therefore only certain general principles are set out below. Compliance with the new "Red Book" is mandatory in most circumstances and it would therefore be prudent practice to adopt the principles and guidelines in all circumstances.

1. The purpose and date of the valuation should be made extremely clear in any report; a valuation that states that it is to current open market value and is undated could lead to very dangerous assumptions being made; any valuation carried out immediately before the Gulf conflict could have been materially different to a valuation say one month after the Gulf conflict commenced.

"Open market value" assumes that a sale is completed at that date and it therefore follows that the requisite marketing process has already been completed. "Estimated realisation price" assumes a sale in the future and that marketing is due to commence – obviously it is impossible to predict events such as the Gulf Conflict and IRA bombs, but some consideration of economic trends will be necessary.

2. Any valuation must take into account the economic and political trends in the relevant country – the Court case of *Corisand* v *Druce & Co* stated that a valuer must reflect economic trends and any changes in the market which could be reasonably anticipated. (See comment also in (1) above.)

3. Any valuation that is based specifically on information and figures provided by another party must be made clear, particularly where they are being relied upon in their totality.

4. In general terms all valuations should be provided in present day terms/values and not upon future values (ie inflation included). Where instructions request the valuation to indicate likely future values this should either be resisted by the valuer or the assumptions and the precise inflation percentages should be clearly set out not only at the beginning of the report but also in the valuation paragraph, at the same time emphasising that the valuation reported has had regard to current market and economic conditions and that the valuer cannot predict the changes in value that might follow if these were to alter.

5. Any other assumptions made by the valuer should be clearly stated in the report and reasons for making such assumptions should be clearly set down (the new Red Book is particularly relevant). Obviously the timescale available for carrying out a valuation and the information provided to the valuer will dictate the number of assumptions made, but in general terms the fewer assumptions made the more reliable the valuation.

The valuation process The problems in the hotel property market following the boom in 1988/89 period when capital appreciation and speculation was behind the dramatic increase in hotel values have been well documented.

Valuations and market transactions are now based upon net cash flow, rather than speculation or calculated purely on a price per bedroom. Net cash flow is derived from the total revenue achievable by the hotel and the subsequent profit available. Demand from potential purchasers may lower the acceptable return on net cash flow, but the root of the calculation remains net cash flow.

The profit available for capitalisation must reflect various factors amongst which are:

- Is the hotel performing to its optimum capability and if not how many years are required for such profit level to be achieved.
- Turnover should be net of VAT and in some European countries bed tax is also to be deducted. Likewise expenditure should also be on a net basis.
- Personality managers or special circumstances should be discounted to arrive at the profit level attainable by "the market efficient" operating company.
- Accounts may need to be adjusted to reflect future competition or improvements in infrastructure which may have a positive or negative effect on cash flow in the short to medium term.
- If in the valuers opinion the profitability of the hotel could be improved by either carrying out improvements or by altering its market position, this should be reflected in the valuation; the valuer should not forget to deduct any improvement costs relevant to the adjustment in net cash flow and any adjustment to market positioning may also require an adjustment upwards or downwards in the resultant capitaliser.

All accounts should be brought to the consistent line of "income before fixed charges" (IBFC). All income and expenditure above this line is purely derived from the ability of the hotel operation to perform in its market segment. Certain accounts will include above the IBFC line an item for management fee. The management fee at this level is normally the base fee in any management contract; whilst in undertaking a valuation for vacant possession purposes the management fee deduction should be added back to the calculation of IBFC, care should be taken to ensure that items such as sales and marketing, administration and general expenses adequately reflect the expenditure that would be incurred in the event that the hotel was liable for all of its own expenditure under sales and administration, which would otherwise be incurred by the management company through head office.

It is necessary to ensure that "head office charges" are adequately reflected where those charges more particularly relate to the hotel performance itself. Corporate or group franchise charges should also be taken into account.

Example B sets out the deductions that will be made from the income before fixed charges prior to capitalisation. These include where appropriate rates payable, insurance liability and for leasehold properties the rent payable.

Example B

		£	
Income before fixed charges			£A
		£	
Less	Rates	£B	
	Insurance	£C	
	Rent	£D	
	Repairs/renewals	£E	
Net cash flow			£X

Many accounts also show deductions post IBFC for the following items – depreciation, taxation, finance charges, VAT and renewals/replacements. With the exception of renewals and replacement the net cash flow available for capitalisation should be struck before deduction of any of the above items. It is arguable whether net cash flow should be after renewals and replacement reserve provisions. There are no set rules regarding this particular line; however, provided the capitaliser reflects the different approach the resultant value should be identical.

There are circumstances where the hotel receives a significant amount of income (rent) from shops, casinos and other non-hotel related sources. Dependent upon the quantum of income and the possibility of being able to sell this income stream separately in the open market it may be appropriate to separate the income from the hotel valuation *per se* and value the income separately using an investment return relevant to the particular circumstances.

Valuations should not include an allowance for loose stock/perishables nor cash balances in hand since these vary on a daily basis.

In certain circumstances hotels may have significant numbers of antiques/memorabilia. It is generally advisable that these are valued as separate items by a chattels valuer and an allowance is made against the main property valuation for the replacement of such antiques by similar quality reproduction items.

However, in this particular instance it is not expected that items such as special panelling or wall coverings etc. would fall within this category.

Within any valuation there are basically three elements of goodwill (and is referred to in the RICS valuation notes):

1. locational goodwill – this attaches to the property;
2. operational goodwill – this attaches to the property and reflects licences, the furnishings, management etc;

3. personal goodwill – this may or may not disappear on change of
   ownership.

Capitalisation factor
In arriving at the appropriate capitaliser for the property the valuer
should take careful consideration of the following:

- the yields applied to other market transactions ie the return on
  other hotel or leisure property sales;
- yields applicable to Government stocks ie what are the redemption
  yields and returns on dividends applicable to Government dated
  stock;
- the PE ratios applicable to quoted hotel and leisure companies,
  not only on the main market but also on the secondary markets;
- the returns applicable to other types of property ie offices, shops
  and industrial.

During the "boom" period of 1988/1989 returns in the Park Lane/
Mayfair area could have dropped as low as 3%–4%, although this
was never proved by open market evidence. In the depressed 1991/
92 period the view was that returns had increased to 5%–6%, but
again with no evidence.

Other prime city returns for hotels were in the range of 7%–10%,
compared with the returns on provincial hotels of 11%–13%.

Other considerations
The general principles above can be distorted as a result of the
following and any one of these would not reflect "open market
value", but rather special circumstances.

- the acquisition of a trophy building eg the development of a luxury
  hotel at the former St Georges Hospital on Hyde Park Corner;
- a strategic corporate acquisition where the multi-national or
  international company requires an hotel in a specific location in
  order to complete a particular marketing network and may be
  prepared to pay in excess of market norms in order to guarantee
  such acquisition;
- the late 1980s included a particular distortion where many
  acquisitions were purely calculated on the basis of speculation and
  hope value, assuming that capital appreciation will occur in excess
  of inflation;

- lastly the intervention of a special purchaser eg an adjoining owner may be prepared to pay in excess of "the open market value" for expansion or other purposes; and a freeholder or leaseholder may acquire another interest in the same property releasing some of the latent value and would pay a price to reflect some of the "merger or marriage value".

Rental valuation

There is extremely limited evidence of rental comparables for hotels above the 3 star category in the United Kingdom provincial and London market compared with other types of commercial property. There are few, if any, examples of hotels of 3 star or above being offered on the open market on a purely rental basis. The majority of instances where new rentals are quoted relate to financing or leasing arrangements, which have particular tax driven benefits. Other "new lettings" in fact relate to lease renewals between the existing parties. Under the section on the lease earlier, certain items which need to be considered in analysing the relevant lease were detailed.

1. Repair – the matter of the repairing covenants and any possible liability for rebuilding must be considered.
2. Alienation – can assignment or subletting take place.
3. The review clause – what is the length of the lease.
4. Alterations – what are the landlord and tenant rights with regard to this; this can be an extremely vexed subject and there is ample case law on the subject. If improvements have to be ignored it is possible that the valuer is confronted by the need to consider a property which no longer complies with modern day requirements and will, therefore, not only have a different turnover and profit line, but may not comply with the user clause if a category is referred to.
5. The valuer will need to consider whether the demise is of a property fully furnished or in shell condition.
6. In certain rent review clauses provision is made for the landlord and his advisors to be provided with copies of the actual trading accounts of the hotel. In all other circumstances the valuer to the landlord will either have to rely on information available at Companies House or other sources or provide his own proforma accounts.

Valuers should be cautioned, however, when considering the actual trading accounts into carefully reflecting whether the accounts reflect certain special abilities of the operator or whether on the contrary the hotel is not performing to its maximum ability. A rental bid must reflect the open market and what a prospective tenant considers he could achieve when operating the property.

Example C sets out below the workings of a typical rental valuation calculation. It will be noted that the calculation starts from income before fixed charges from which deductions are made for rating liability, insurance, allowance for tenants working capital, and if appropriate an allowance to reflect the annual equivalent of furnishing the hotel, if committed by the tenant. A renewals allowance is also included. In the example, the divisible balance has been divided in equal portions between the landlord and tenant, although the division may range between 45% and 60% depending upon the unit, its location and its general attractiveness in the market.

Example C

Income before fixed charges			£2,000,000
Less Rates		£250,000	
Insurance		£ 40,000	
Less (a) Working capital		£ 40,000	
(b) Return on FF&E			
200 rooms @ £9,500 @ 15%		£285,000	
(c) R & R			
3% of turnover (say)		£170,000	
			£785,000
Divisible balance			£1,215,000
50%/50%			
Rental value			£607,500

The valuer must not forget to take account of any income derived from sublettings such as casinos, car parking, shopping etc. Care must be taken to ensure that double counting does not occur as this element of income may already appear under "other income" in the accounts.

In the author's experience rent reviews are extremely difficult due to the subjective nature and impact of the review – the landlord will be claiming that the prospective tenant would take an optimistic view of his bid, while the encumbant tenant will be arguing that his hotel is already performing to its maximum and that he can, therefore, afford to pay no more than currently payable! In many instances the rent is ultimately settled on a direct principal to principal basis.

Reference has already been made to a percentage premium being added to reflect the benefit to the tenant of a long period between reviews ie greater than 5 years. Although commercial property now appears to have established a regular pattern this does not seem to be the case for hotels and they are, therefore, argued on an individual basis.

Freehold/leasehold valuation possession

Set out in Example D is the standard valuation of a freehold or leasehold hotel being offered with vacant possession. As previously detailed the calculation will start with the net cash flow situation or income before fixed charges. In Example D a capitaliser is provided to the income before fixed charges after deduction for rates and insurance.

Example D

Income before fixed charges		£2,000,000	
Less Rates	£250,000		
Insurance	£ 40,000	£290,000	
NOP		£1,710,000	
Years Purchase @ 10%		10	
Capital value			£17,100,000
Say			£17,000,000

Example E is an alternative approach which should provide a result which is not substantially different to Example D above. This method is rarely used. It will be noted that this example is broken into three sectors:

1. dividing the income before fixed charges into a rental proportion and capitalising the rent;

2. the addition of a capital cost for furnishing the hotel. In most instances a precise figure will not be available and, therefore, a sum per room will be applied. The quantum of the price per room will vary according to the category of hotel and quality of the fittings;

3. the remaining calculation is a derivative from (1) and (2) above. The rental figure, together with the annualised cost of the FF&E figure is deducted from the total profit. The resultant net figure is deemed the profit to the operator and is capitalised on a goodwill/profit factor (between 0.5 and 5).

Example E

A.	Income before fixed charges		£2,000,000	
	Less Rates	£250,000		
	Insurance	£40,000		
	NOP		£1,710,000	
	@ 50% to rent		£855,000	
	Years purchase @ 7%		14.28	
	Capital value			£12,214,285
B.	Furniture etc			
	200 rooms @ £9,500 per room			£1,900,000
C.	Operators Profit		£1,710,000	
	Less Rent	£855,000		
	Return on			
	FF&E 10%	£190,000		
			£665,000	
	At years purchase		3.5	
				£2,327,500
	Gross capital value			£16,441,786
	Say			£16,500,000

Since each hotel is completely different it is dangerous and is **not** recommended practice to purely apply a price per room in order to arrive at the capital valuation. Obviously, the valuers research into the price being paid for hotels in order to support the level of his valuation will provide a valid cross-check to his principal route of valuation; it should not be relied on as the sole method. As a further cross-check the valuer may wish to apply a multiplier to the gross turnover again using market evidence.

The "income approach" is in the view of the author and many other authorities the only method which can and should be utilised.

Many of the United States Banks wish to see a valuation report supported by the figures and calculations, not only on the income approach, but also on the comparable approach and the contractors method. The contractors method is certainly not applicable in the United Kingdom city centre market. There is little or no comparable evidence of city centre transactions for sites and the purely comparable approach of price per room is also unreliable.

There are many instances when a valuer is asked to provide the open market value of an hotel that has not yet opened or has only been trading for a limited period. In those instances there is either no track record or a very limited track record. The valuer should be very specific in the assumptions that he makes, but should take allowance of the lack of established or any goodwill and the risk element that a purchaser will incur by acquiring the hotel still requiring business improvement. The valuer should reflect these in his calculation by a discount on the gross price as calculated previously, and should also reflect the "loss in profits" ie the profit not being achieved in comparison with a stabilised business, and these should be deducted from the value.

As mentioned previously a "bricks and mortar" valuation is a hypothetical mathematical apportionment of an open market valuation and deducts therefrom the "goodwill" element, the cost of all furniture and fittings which are deemed movable and any profit element; it does however assume the property has a licence.

Estimated restricted realisation price (often called a "forced" sale valuation) assumes an unreasonable time period in which to affect a sale, and this can vary from property to property and location to location; it may assume that the hotel has been closed and almost certainly assumes that there is little or no goodwill attaching to the hotel. Difficulties can arise where the hotel itself is profitable but has gone into receivership as a result of problems elsewhere in the company.

The application of discounted cash flows is moving towards being the "recommended method" and an example is set out in example F of the application of a discounted cash flow. The use of the DCF has been the subject of debate between the RICS and the British Association of Hotel Accountants (BAHA).

The discounted cash flow (DCF) approach to valuing a hotel is similar in principle to valuing any other form of investment property by this method. The basic approach is to identify an anticipated future cash flow which has been prepared using explicit assumptions as to variables such as inflation/growth rate. This cash flow is then discounted at a rate representing the total return an investor might expect from this type of investment, to bring the cash flow back to present values.

The cash flow needs to be run for a finite number of periods, which can be monthly, quarterly or annually, as long as the discount rate adopted reflects this frequency, for example 15% annually or 3.75% quarterly. Generally, the longer the cash flow is run the more accurate will be the result, although periods too far into the future become so heavily discounted that they have little effect on the final present value figure. Since it is difficult to predict with any accuracy assumptions such as growth, costs, state of the building and the market, it is generally accepted that 10 years is a reasonable period over which to run a DCF.

If, as in most instances, income will continue to be received beyond the finite period of the DCF, then this must be represented at the end of the cash flow, when one must assume that a "notional sale" takes place. Depending upon the discount rate adopted and the term of the DCF, this residual value at the end of the cash flow period can have a profound affect on the investment value in present day terms, especially where a low percentage discount rate has been adopted, or for shorter analysis periods.

The net cash flow arrived at must be discounted by an appropriate factor, to bring the projected, future values back to present day terms. The discount rate adopted should reflect the total return expected by an investor, which is often taken as a sufficient margin above the return on government stock to reflect additional risk.

It is possible in DCF calculations to allow for rent reviews, potential capital expenditure etc. at any date during the period of the cash flow.

Example F has been shortened to a 5-year period for simplification, although normally a longer period would provide a more realistic result.

The analysis to arrive at the income before fixed charges is relatively straightforward in the example. It is assumed that the only variables are the room rate and the occupancy rate (with inflation applied as appropriate), whereas in practice there could be many other variables. The net IBFC is carried down into a cash flow line, to which is added a sum representing the residual value of the hotel at the end of the period, which is arrived at by capitalising the income at that point by an appropriate capitalisation rate, in this case 10%.

The projected cash flow is then discounted at a rate of 15% per annum by multiplying by a present value of £1. This DCF line representing each of the future anticipated receipts discounted to a present value is then summated to arrive at a total present value of £8,750,000. For comparison purposes, this reflects a straight capitaliser of just under 7%.

Example F

Year	1	2	3	4	5	End
Rooms	100	100	100	100	100	100
AARR	£50	£60	£70	£75	£80	£85
Occ. Rate	55%	65%	70%	70%	70%	70%
TR	£2,007,500	£2,847,000	£3,577,000	£3,832,500	£4,088,000	£4,343,500
Net Cash Flow*	£ 602,250	£ 854,100	£1,073,100	£1,149,750	£1,226,400	£1,303,050
Projected Cash Flow	£ 602,250	£ 854,100	£1,073,100	£1,149,750	£1,226,400	£13,030,500
PV @ £1	0.8695	0.7561	0.6575	0.5718	0.4972	0.4323
DCF @ 15%	£ 523,656	£ 645,785	£ 705,563	£ 657,427	£ 609,766	£5,633,085
Present value =	£8,775,282					
Say	£8,750,000					

* @ 30% to allow for rates and insurance – at this line rent and replacement reserve can be incorporated if appropriate.

Investment valuations

The valuation of a freehold or leasehold investment, assuming that the rent is fixed, will follow the normal principles of an investment valuation, ie a return applied to the rent. As with other investments the valuer should check on the ability of the hotel to pay the rent.

Where an investment has its rent geared to turnover or profit, then the rent is liable to fluctuate in line with the business performance of the hotel and the return required by the investor will reflect such risk.

Where a valuer is faced with considering an investment, subject to a management agreement, the valuer must take care to ensure that all the clauses in the management agreement are fully reflected in his calculation of capitalisable net cash flow ie after repairs and renewals replacement, marketing costs, working capital etc. The calculation of the management fees will be of critical importance.

Overseas valuations

It is not the intention of the current chapter to set out all the principles and provide guidance to valuations outside the United Kingdom; however, certain cautionary notes are set out below should a valuer be tempted to undertake a valuation outside the United Kingdom and outside his particular sphere of knowledge.

- *The RICS Appraisal and Valuation Manual* is particularly categoric on limiting a valuer to his sphere of knowledge and experience.
- Ownership of properties, particularly in Europe, is governed by Roman law rather than Canon law and factors such as flying freeholds can be common. In addition, the law relating to leases, security of tenure and calculation of rental values is approached in a completely different way. In most countries the repairing liabilities on owners and occupiers is also different to that in the United Kingdom.
- Dependent upon the purpose of the valuation and the addressee of the valuation it may be necessary for the valuer to be licensed to undertake such valuations in the particular country.
- Until such time as there is harmonisation in the EU, employment laws can be different in each country and the impact upon profitability will compound on the income available for capitalisation ie in many countries the wage costs are substantially higher than in the United Kingdom.

- In certain countries the Governments or regional authorities will provide grants for improvements or new construction and may, therefore, diminish the value of existing properties.
- Each country has different licensing requirements with regard to opening licences, liquor licences etc.
- Structural control and design techniques are different in each country and often depend upon the sophistication or otherwise of the building industry in that country.

Report writing

"The written report is only as good as the inspection" (*Summers* v *Congreve Horner* – 1991).

The RICS Appraisal and Valuation Manual and the *Stock Exchange Yellow Book* are extremely specific in the way that reports and in particular valuation certificates are written and phrased. Valuers should refer to both documents for details.

As indicated earlier in the chapter, it is essential that each report clearly sets out the basis of valuation, the source or otherwise of the accounts utilised in the valuation and the reasoning behind any adjustments thereto, and any assumptions made or unverified information relied upon should be clearly stated.

As a result of a number of poor valuations and badly written reports prepared during the late 1980s, the valuing fraternity has been required to improve their report presentation and the recipients of valuation reports now require far greater detail and justification.

Each client has a different requirement as to the reporting format and, therefore, each valuer should check with the client prior to submitting a report. Dependent upon the timescale available and the particular client, a draft report can form the basis of a discussion document, firstly to ensure it covers all the client's requirements and secondly as a means of verifying some of the facts.

CHAPTER 7

Garden centres

General garden retail market

The term garden centre is loosely applied to a host of outlets selling a range of garden related products and includes the small, rural retail nursery, as well as the garden section enclosed within DIY superstores, through to the modern, large garden retail centre.

In wider terms, it can also include water gardens and aquaria, and retail and bulk pet supplies.

The traditional garden centre has typically grown from its origins as a nursery into a more sophisticated shopping experience, providing an extensive range of traditional horticultural products, as well as supplementary products and services.

It is the supplementary areas that differentiate the new concept of garden centres, from the smaller, traditional garden centres/retail nurseries and these areas include coffee shops, pet centres, greenhouses and garden building displays, swimming pools, garden furniture, garden machinery and aquatics operations.

The growth of garden centre retailing has come through satisfying the needs of the active gardener, by offering extensive ranges of plants, coupled with advice based on horticultural knowledge. Consumers have grown to accept garden centres as attractive places to visit, especially at weekends.

Gardening has always been a great British passion, and throughout the last ten years has become one of the most popular leisure interests, which has largely been driven by a much improved consumer knowledge and improved garden retailing.

The garden retail market, which includes sales of all plants, sundries, machinery, furniture and usual garden centre items is estimated to have grown by 60% in value terms between 1986 and 1993, representing real growth of around 25%.

Various sources, Mintel, Promosalons and ADAS estimate the UK garden retail market value to reach around £3.0 billion (retail prices) in 1995, an increase over 1990 of 20% at current prices, which ranks it favourably with other retail sectors being considerably larger than the UK records/cd/tape retail market for example. This market value converts to an average spend per household of around £95 per annum which is considerably less than is spent in Germany and France, and considerable potential therefore exists to increase the size of the market.

This estimate of market value does not include the pets market, or many of the supplementary areas, such as swimming pools etc. Specialist garden centres face increasing competition from garden departments attached to DIY stores, especially in product ranges, such as garden tools, including lawn mowers and the bottom end of the garden furniture range, and garden fertilisers/composts. In these outlets manufacturers brands are purchased and displayed in large quantities at highly competitive prices.

The largest of the six product sectors comprising the garden product market is growing stock, more than twice any other at £1.15 billion including house plants, representing nearly 40% of the total garden products market, an improvement on its 35% share in 1990.

The structure of the UK garden retail market has changed rapidly in the last 10 years. Garden centres have significantly increased market share and have laterally been matched in growth rates by the main DIY multiples. The market share splits for the garden retail market between 1985 and 1995 are shown in Table 7.1.

During this same period, the number of garden centres has substantially increased and it is estimated (difficult to be precise due to the grey area between retail nurseries and garden centres) that there are approximately 2,000 garden centres/retail plant centres within the United Kingdom.

Table 7.1 *(per cent of value)*

	1985	1991	1993	1995
Garden centres	20	37	37	36
DIY multiples	17	19	21	25
Hardware shops	14	10	10	9
Grocery supermarkets	13	10	10	9
Florists/garden shops	10	5	4	4
Mail Order	9	12	12	11
Variety/department stores	5	3	2	2
Woolworths	5	2	2	2
Others	7	2	2	2

The DIY multiples led by B & Q and Texas (now Homebase) have largely competed on price and convenience, but have latterly improved their staff product knowledge and range to compete more directly with garden centres. The DIY multiples' action have undoubtedly stimulated growth in the overall market by increasing consumer familiarity with plant products.

The key external factors affecting the garden market and garden centre visiting are: home, garden and car ownership, the weather and levels of PDI. Home owners spend more on their gardens than those who rent, and this is exacerbated by the fact that a higher proportion of rented accommodation do not have gardens. The number of owner occupied dwellings is forecast to increase by over 10% between 1994 and 1999, which means that 72% of all dwellings will be owner occupied by the end of the century.

Car ownership is critical, particularly as garden centre customers place a high priority on the availability of parking spaces. Car ownership in 1994 stood at 74% of households, and is forecast to continue to rise.

Traditional garden centres have maintained competitive advantage because of the following key areas:

- Excellent product range, especially plants.
- Excellent consumer service and staff product knowledge.
- Building on ancillary retail/leisure areas to give a "day out".
- Stocking good quality plants.

Mintel commissioned a survey which asked "which of the following attributes do you consider important when visiting a garden centre or nursery", and the findings are shown in Fig. 7.1.

A typical garden centre would generate around 50% of sales from plants (shrubs, bedding and house plants) with the remaining proportion depending heavily on product mix. There is a tremendous variation in product lines between centres, whether they are in house or concessioned out, and often this is dependent upon planning.

The trend for modern garden centres is to be developed close to areas of high catchment population, but in out of town locations.

The majority of modern garden centres do not grow plants themselves, but rely upon specialist nurseries which supply on a wholesale basis only, not selling to the customer directly.

UK garden centres typically have a catchment population covering a 20 minute drive time from the site. A 1988 survey showed that 75%

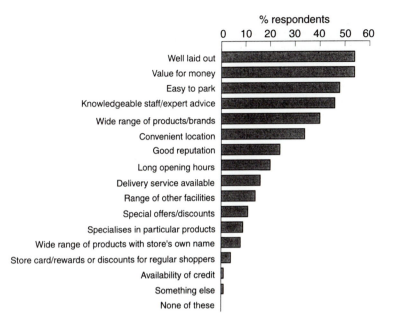

% respondents

Well laid out
Value for money
Easy to park
Knowledgeable staff/expert advice
Wide range of products/brands
Convenient location
Good reputation
Long opening hours
Delivery service available
Range of other facilities
Special offers/discounts
Specialises in particular products
Wide range of products with store's own name
Store card/rewards or discounts for regular shoppers
Availability of credit
Something else
None of these

Fig. 7.1

of customers came from a 10 mile radius and that garden centres have increased product range by attracting concessions to their sites. This gives smaller businesses low cost retail space and gives garden centre owners/occupiers valuable income. Some national high street retailers are keen to develop concessions on larger garden sites and Edinburgh Woollen Mills and Neal's Yard Whole-foods for example are already on or have purchased garden centres.

The financial performance of UK garden centres has been strong throughout the recession of the first half of the 1990s, and they have certainly faired better than high street retailers, however, although performance has been consistent it has not been stunning.

Table 7.2 shows the financial performance of sixty three UK garden centres across a spectrum of sizes and locations, taken from a trade association performance scheme covering the 1994 sales season. The best financial performers are those centres which are able to combine high average spend with high stock turnover and high customer throughput. It is the interaction of these three areas in terms of professionalism of retailing which offer the industry most scope for improvement.

Table 7.2

	Average	Maximum	Minimum
Sales per customer	£9.13	£19.55	£5.23
Sales per sq ft	£21.53	£67.27	£5.21
Sales per employee	£60,659	£115,756	£25,169
Stockturn	4.4	14.8	1
Net profit (%)	8.8%	27%	−8%

The clear differential between traditional garden centres and the DIY/food multiples relates to the stockturn, with an average for garden centres of 4.4 times, with the multiples towards 20 and Marks and Spencer at 23. This is also mirrored by much lower customer spend and sales per sq ft than many high street retailers.

Clearly if as a business you are turning stock over five times more readily, with better margins due to increased buying power, there will be a substantial differential between rental levels that can be paid.

The types of operators within the market

The UK garden centre market can be segmented into the following broad sectors.

Chains
These are largely regional with only Wyevale Garden Centres PLC (50) getting anywhere near a national presence, with only fourteen companies operating five or more garden centres, a total of 104.

These are six companies operating four garden centres, seven companies operating three garden centres or retail nurseries and circa eleven companies operating two garden centres. Therefore only circa 111 garden centres are operated as non-solus sites.

The larger operators, those with five or more garden centres, tend to have more sites with a lower average turnover than the best independents, say in the region of £750,000 to £1m.

Wyevale are funded on the unlisted securities market, Country Gardens have joined the Alternative Investment Market (AIM) as well as a BES scheme in common with Capital Gardens PLC. The majority of the other companies are family owned and operated, some for more than two generations.

Independent garden centres

The leading independents occupy larger garden centre sites, and tend to be well established businesses. They offer the day out approach, and very professional retailing, but there are only a handful with turnovers in excess of £4 m.

Over 90% of garden centres within this country are single site operations and the majority of these will be in the £250,000–£750,000 turnover band.

Specialist plant centres

These centres offer a very high plant focus (up to 80% of sales) and are often combined with a production nursery, and appeal to the connoisseur gardener. Their stock performance is much lower although high average prices mean that profit performance is often better than garden centres. However, there are few that turnover more than £500,000 and their infrastructure tends to be converted production glass and thus of lower value.

Blooms of Bressingham are the only specialist operators opening new purpose built plant centres with limited covered areas, and a tea room and their customer base is backed up by an existing well established mail order business.

In conclusion there are estimated to be around 1,200 chain and independent garden centres largely represented by the membership of the Horticultural Trades Association, the industry's lead body, and the Garden Centre Association.

In addition, we estimate that there are in the region of 800 quasi-garden centres/retail nurseries (although this is a grey area depending upon the town planning or other definition).

DIY multiples

We are not including within this chapter the valuation of DIY multiples or the garden centres attached thereto, but on the basis of the growth of market share that this sector has captured, we believe that it is relevant to mention

The DIY multiple garden centre operators are as set out in Table 7.3.

The average garden centre related turnover per DIY store is in the region of £240,000, net of VAT, and it is interesting to note that Homebase, the most upmarket of the DIY chains, and the only one to have the word garden in their title, has turnover in excess of 50% more than the average at £370,000 per store. This is backed up by

Table 7.3

DIY store	GC sites	% with GC	GC sq ft *	Estimated GC sales	Average garden turnover per site
B & Q PLC	256	92%	8,000	£55,000,000	£215,000
Texas †	164	69%	4,000	£40,000,000	£243,000
Homebase	83	100%	12,000	£30,000,000	£370,000
Do It All	193	50%	5,000	£25,000,000	£130,000
Great Mills	90	95%	10,000	£20,000,000	£230,000
Focus	60	90%	10,000	£15,000,000	£250,000

* Based on estimates from Verdict Market Research.
† Acquired by Homebase in 1995.

research that indicates that it is the ABC 1's who spend more money in garden centres than the rest of the population.

Other types of operators within the sector
There are a wide range of related operators within the garden centre sector to include pets operators, aquatics operators, garden machinery sales and repair, swimming pools, garden buildings, greenhouses, conservatories, hardlandscaping and others. The vast majority of companies who operate these types of businesses on garden centres are single site operators.

Due to the problems with needing direct access to car parks, pet outlets are not as prevalent on garden centres as aquatics outlets, and it is probably partly due to the reason of access that out of town pet superstores are beginning to make an impact with almost 10% of the market, but they are as yet relatively few in number and according to Mintel's consumer research they are not yet regarded as a prime source of purchase.

Four groups have emerged, Pets at Home has twelve stores, mainly in the north; Pet World which has two stores in London; Jollye's has thirteen stores and a broad geographic spread from Eastbourne to Newcastle, including Northern Ireland and are the only one to take outlets on garden centres, and Pet City, the largest chain, with twenty one stores in the Midlands to the south of England. A fifth group, Pet Depot, opened its first store in South London in Spring 1995.

These outlets have more space to expand their interests and stock holdings than the traditional pet shop. We believe that the bigger garden centres will ensure that suitably, well located accommodation is made available to attract these newer, larger operations.

In the aquatics side of the business there are a number of specialist water garden/aquatic operators within this country, these are mainly single site operations, many of which are located in or adjacent to garden centres, the majority being aquatic operators selling tropical and cold water fish and accessories.

The division in the market is shown in Fig. 7.2.

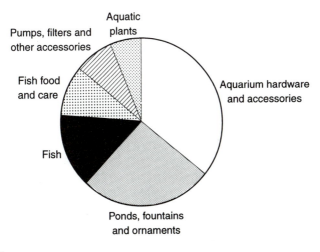

Fig. 7.2.

True water gardening outlets are still relatively rare. The market leader is World of Water, where a high degree of practical advice is available as well as a broader range of products that can normally be found on garden centres.

World of Water has 13 outlets which makes it larger than all but three of the garden centre groups. A number of their outlets are standalone water garden centres, but many of them are self-contained units adjacent to (or within the curtilage of) existing garden centres, rather than more traditional aquatics concessions, which occupy a partitioned area within a garden centre's main covered retail area.

The types of garden centres and sizes thereof

Garden centres can be divided into four broad bands:

1. Regional garden centres occupying sites in excess of five acres, turning over in excess of £3,000,000, offering a wide range of products and customer attractions and catering for a half to a full day visit.

    Examples such as these would be Bridgemere Garden World in Cheshire, Van Hages Garden Centre in Hertfordshire, Burford Garden Centre in Oxfordshire, Cadbury Garden Centre in Avon.
2. The good chain, and independent garden centre, with a site of 4–5 acres usually in a main road location, covered retail area 1,400–1,900 sq. m (15,000–20,000 sq. ft). Turnover £750,000–£1,250,000. Modern or well refurbished, traditional garden centre buildings with a coffee shop and an average range of concessions normally to include garden buildings/conservatories, aquatics and one or two others.
3. The traditional, local garden centre/retail plant centre on a site of between 2 and 4 acres, usually secondary location, smaller and/or poorer quality buildings, often converted production glass.

    Only 50% would have a coffee shop, many would have no concessions. Turning over £250,000–£750,000. The stand alone water garden centres would normally fall into this category.
4. Urban garden centres. These would normally be on sites of under 1 acre with limited car parking, relatively high covered area, circa 1,000 sq m, would not have a coffee shop and are unlikely to have concessions. Would be heavily plant based and cater for the quick turn around garden products shopping.

What determines value

There are numerous factors to be taken into consideration, when considering value.

Geographical location

That is, the area of the country in which the business is, the competition within the area, and the demand from purchasers to buy a garden centre within the area. Nationally garden centres are concentrated in the south of the country, particularly the London/TVS region. The larger garden centre chains generally establish themselves in one area and then grow throughout the region by developing new sites or acquiring existing garden centres.

Country Gardens probably have the best locations, being concentrated in central, southern England, from the south west Midlands, to the south coast.

Wyevale Garden Centres PLC were traditionally on the west, but they merged with Cramphorns who are traditionally on the east and now have the greatest national presence, excluding Scotland.

At the present time, only four of the groups seek to purchase in the north of England and Scotland.

Table 7.4 shows the regional distribution of garden centres and adult population.

Table 7.4

	Garden centre (%)	Adult population (%)
London & Meridian	40	31
Harlech/HTV	22	28
Anglia/Central	14	30
Granada	11	20
Yorkshire/Tyne Tees	10	14
Scotland	3	10
TOTAL	100	116

Adult population does not equal 100% due to the regional overlap.

Specific location

Main road, road system, catchment population, socio-economic demographics, competition in the area. On the basis that most people will only drive 20 minutes to visit a garden centre – this will begin to establish turnover potential.

Secondary characteristics relating to specific locations are local/regional weather trends, ie higher than average rainfall or shorter season in Scotland, and tourist population.

The site

The size and topography of the site and whether there are any advantageous or damaging features. For example, on a large site a prominent water feature would be an advantage, on a small site it restricts the retail area.

The presence of a residential dwelling can be an advantage, but

not if it is located within the centre of the site, and is unable to be sub-
divided unless the building is capable of economic conversion to
alternative uses, such as coffee shop, concession operators with
perhaps manager's flat on first floor.

On a larger garden centre some slight variation of levels can be an
advantage. However, steep slopes on garden centres are generally
a disadvantage due to the additional costs of terracing and creating
pedestrian walkways, capable of taking disabled people to all parts
of the garden centre.

It is important to assess the site in terms of the existing and
potential turnover.

What is the size of the formal and overspill car parking areas, is
there an appropriate goods yard, or if not could one be created
keeping delivery vehicles away from the car park, and retail areas?

Does the configuration of the site and buildings allow for
appropriate additional buildings to be constructed, cost effectively,
for the planteria to be increased in size etc?

Is there an opportunity to purchase additional, adjacent land?

The buildings

Most garden centre buildings are not constructed to the same
standard as conventional high street/out of town retail environments.
They largely fall into three categories as follows:

1. Former horticultural glasshouses converted for retail use. These
   are not the most desirable retail covering for customer safety or
   for an aethistic and appealing environment.

   Many of these buildings have now had the glass removed from
   the roof and replaced by polycarbonate, but in general terms the
   structures are old and they leak.
2. Steel framed buildings with polycarbonate roof. It is the steel
   framed polycarbonate buildings that offer best value for money at
   circa £20.00 per sq ft, construction costs to include the installation
   of services which offer the most attractive and appealing retailing
   environment and thus add most value.

   These buildings, albeit occasionally with brick front elevations,
   are the most commonly used by modern bespoke garden centres.
3. Brick built conventional portal frame buildings. These buildings do
   not engender the advantages that one would imagine. They
   normally have a restrictive planning consent to garden centre
   use, and therefore cannot be used for alternative uses. They have

a higher capital cost to build, have higher running costs, particularly rates, and they do not appear to encourage higher turnover than other garden centres.

The construction, condition and size of the buildings is important both in regard to the cost of maintenance and estimated replacement date and whether the size allows scope for increased turnover and the bringing on of concessions over and above what may already be there.

Fixtures and fittings

At the present time all the fixtures and fittings within garden centres are included within the value of the physical asset, the land, buildings and infrastructure.

The value of internal shelving and display units and the commonly seen movable, tiered wooden display units in planterias can be considerable, but these are generally not paid for in addition, such as stock at valuation.

Additional buildings

On some garden centres ancillary buildings can be found, for example old farm/storage buildings, pine log cabins, Nissen huts etc.

These buildings add value, if:

(a) They are, or can be made, presentable.
(b) They are suitably located within the site.
(c) If they can be used for retail by concessions, or by an area of business that can benefit from being outside the main garden centre retail area, for example farm shop or landscape design business, or if they can be used for storage and free-up covered area that could be used for retailing elsewhere on the site.

Residential dwellings

The presence of a residential dwelling on site can be an advantage, but not if the property is located within the centre of the site, and is incapable of sub-division or if the dwelling is too large and prestigious.

Modest three bedroom, detached houses/bungalows located on the edge of the site, whether tied or untied to horticulture are normally an advantage. They can be lived in by owner/occupiers or by managers. Too often, however, we find that the owners who occupied a small dwelling when first buying the site have extended the property to a substantial size, so that it becomes inappropriate for any new purchaser, mainly due to its capital cost.

The main garden centre groups do not wish to tie up capital in the purchase of residential dwellings unless they are capable of economic conversion to alternative uses, such as coffee shop/retail areas for concessions, with perhaps manager's flat or garden centre offices and staff facilities on the first floor.

Where there is a large house on site that is either tied to horticulture or is in the centre of the garden centre and cannot be sold the combined value of the garden centre and the house is usually quite substantially reduced, due to the fact that:

(a) The groups are not interested in purchasing the house and
(b) The majority of owner/occupiers are unable to raise the necessary finance to purchase both at appropriate levels, due to the fact that the garden centre does not provide sufficient profit to fund the capital borrowings required.

Conversely, where there is an appropriate sized house, although the combined values would not increase, many purchasers would find funding easier to obtain.

In general terms, when valuing residential dwellings on garden centres one would arrive at a value of a comparable property, a similar sized house, number of reception rooms, bedrooms, similar sized garden, then discount as appropriate, if the quiet enjoyment of the dwelling suffers from being too close to the garden centre or if there is shared access etc, and then if the property is tied, and more often than not it is, we would normally affect a reduction of circa 35%.

Tied houses such as we see in this country do not occur in Europe and there is a school of thought that as we move towards one market, ties within Britain will become lifted, which will have two effects:

1. The values of these residential dwellings will increase, and
2a. The dwellings could be sold off so long as physical separation can occur without detriment to the garden centre, which in certain instances would increase the value of the garden centre, or
2b. Upon retirement the owners could remain living in the house and lease the garden centre to generate rental income.

Town planning consent

The detailed wording of the consent is vital to value. It is essential the consent allows an operator to sell the full range of garden centre products and sundries. Many garden centres have evolved from wholesale nurseries, who started by selling what they grew and then added sundries and slowly expanded to the full garden centre product range.

In these instances, it is general to find that when they need to submit a planning application for redevelopment, they either have an unrestricted garden centre consent on the whole site, or they have no formal planning consent at all. In the latter circumstances, we recommend that they immediately apply for a Certificate of Lawful Established Use and Development (CLEUD). This can usually be obtained on the basis that the operator can prove that they have been selling their existing range of products for at least ten years.

A garden centre town planning consent is *sui generis* and its scope has not been fully tested, with many centres widening the range of goods sold.

Since it became apparent that garden centres comprise substantial out of town businesses with the potential for enormous traffic generation, particularly on holiday weekends, new town planning consents are generally restricted by Section 106 Agreements. In many cases they will comprise two sheets of paper listing all of the products that can be sold. These will be product specific, either listing those items which can only be sold, or alternatively, and arguably less restrictive, those items which cannot be sold.

We cannot stress enough the importance of instructing appropriate town planning consultants with good experience of obtaining garden centre consents. The precise wording of a town planning consent has a material effect on value.

Where no house exists on site, and where there is sufficient site area for the construction of a dwelling, town planning authorities generally are unable to resist an application for a tied property due to the advantages of an owner/occupier or manager living on site, in regard to theft and service failure, ie the heating failing during the winter and green goods being lost.

In many instances, the obtaining of a planning consent for a house on site adds more value pro-rata than having an existing dwelling.

Development potential

Alternative use value needs to be considered on part or all of garden centre sites, as depending on site size and usage, it can be possible to obtain town planning consents for residential, retail and roadside uses such as petrol filling stations, fast food restaurants and travel hotels.

Concessions

Consideration should be given to the concession operators on site. In particular, the strength of the operation, the product they are selling, the terms of the lease or licence, and the level of rental income.

The majority of concessions on garden centres are "men of straw". There are few multi-located well run companies, albeit one or two within the aquatics field, one within pet foods and garden building sectors.

Since the recession, conservatories and swimming pool concession operators are rare, and the ones that remain tend to be good, well run, single site operations.

Hardlandscape and garden machinery offer very low margins, and do not appear attractive and accordingly there are few good operators in these fields. Garden machinery operators in particular have been hit hard because of the hot summers.

Our experience indicates that many of the smaller concession operators come and go and although concession rents are holding up, many operators are preferring turnover based rents or low rents with turnover top-up, on a fully inclusive basis. In our experience, when the true costs of occupation are calculated some garden centres are leasing quality accommodation at cost.

Generally, concession operators consider garden centres a low occupational cost option, as compared to high street, or standalone operations.

In our experience the better the garden centre the better the concessions that are located thereon, and this is due in the main to the fact that individual concession operators cannot operate stand-alone businesses, and therefore do better when there is a higher customer throughput to the garden centre. This will be particularly true of those concessions located within the garden centre, such as a coffee shop.

Financial performance

When considering accounts it is important to see not only the last three years audited accounts, but the current management accounts, and projections for the following year. The garden centre industry is a cash business and accordingly it is not always the level of profit that is of paramount importance. Having said that, profit has to be considered mainly in regard to how the purchase of a particular garden centre is going to be funded, ie if funds need to be borrowed from a lending institution, then there either needs to be a good profit performance, good cash surpluses or a strongly improving performance trend to be able to fund an acquisition.

The areas to focus on in the accounts are as follows:

Level of turnover Considering the size of site and buildings, age of buildings, and feel for the product range of the particular garden centre.

When considering turnover it is helpful if it is broken down into monthly amounts. The three best months in the year (depending upon location) are likely to be May, April/June and December, (assuming that the garden centre concentrates on Christmas). It is also helpful to see the turnover divided into product range, for example it is usually easier for a garden centre to increase turnover if their plant sales are a low percentage, rather than if they are high.

It should be noted if substantial turnover is coming from items that in many garden centres are concessioned, for example garden buildings, garden machinery, pets, aquatics etc. There are good reasons for this. Taking conservatories, they are high value items with a low margin and many garden centre operators would not wish to sell them direct, therefore this would cease when the garden centre was sold, and in the current economic climate it might prove difficult to find a suitable concession to take over this area of operation.

Garden machinery has low margins and generally only works well when retailing is linked with repair and service and many operators, particularly the garden centre chains, do not sell garden machinery and therefore discount this area of turnover prior to purchase.

Hardlandscaping materials are a product most garden centres offer, but they are low margin, with little scope for improvement.

Aquatics and pets need to be considered because they are specialist areas and need specialist staff if they are being run by the owners of the garden centre. It may well be that any new purchasers will not have the capability to continue running them to the same standard.

Another area to be considered is that of the coffee shop, as poor coffee shops can be a liability, good coffee shops a considerable asset. However, average coffee shops on garden centres make little profit and their profitability rarely justifies the capital costs of installing them, although the profitability of the overall garden centre does. Accordingly, this area of turnover also needs to be identified, as apart from the whole. At least one operator discounts the entire coffee shop turnover from their valuation and adds back a capital sum for the estimated discounted cost of installing the coffee shop.

Where a coffee shop/restaurant on a garden centre is being run to a very high standard, particularly if it is done so in house, then the majority of purchasers, to include the garden centre chains, would still discount the turnover from their valuations on the basis that it is highly unlikely they would be able to continue to run the coffee shop/restaurant to the same standards.

Therefore, if a garden centre is turning over say £1.5 m with half this amount coming from the above areas, rather than traditional products, this will have a considerable impact on value.

For example, we are aware of one garden centre turning over circa £1.25 m where £250,000 was coming purely from hardlandscaping products, with little or no profit being made, and interested parties discounted this area of turnover almost entirely from their calculations.

Gross margin The industry average is 38/39% although plant orientated centres should be higher than this, as are the majority of the larger chains due to their increased buying power and better quality systems, relating to wastage and theft.

When valuing a garden centre, it is most important to look at the trend in gross margin. Over the past few years, many garden centres have had a drop in gross margin, ie reduced prices and thus increased (bought) turnover which is usually a regressive step. Conversely if turnover is remaining static but gross margins are increasing, this is considered an improving trend, and generates a higher element of goodwill.

Beware, changing stock levels can have a dramatic effect on gross margin, and can occur when a garden centre has not had a stock take (or has only had internal stock takings) for some time.

Profit/contribution The industry involves a lot of cash and thus the profits shown by many independents may not be a true reflection.

The majority of independent garden centres have grown by expanding infrastructure, buildings and stock levels through utilising cash surpluses. Some of the larger independents are family businesses and run a number of prestigious cars and incur far higher levels of expenditure in regard to directors salaries, pensions expenses, than would be occurred once the property was bought by one of the garden centre chains.

A knowledge of industry norms is therefore necessary. The level of profit or cash surpluses or potential profit or cash surpluses is important if funding is likely to be required by a purchaser.

Most chains look at contribution, as they buy centrally, and thus individual centres are often more profitable to them than to independents. Accordingly, in some circumstances there can be a twin level market, ie a different value to one of the major chains than to another independent purchaser.

Ratios and percentages Key ratios to look at are the percentage of staff costs to turnover, normally 15–17%, the percentage of marketing costs, normally 2–3%, whether a notional rent is being paid, or the level of borrowings and how the interest payments relate to a notional rent. As a general rule of thumb rental values would normally be between 4% and 6.5% of turnover, the former for poor quality garden centres, the larger being for the state of the art, modern, low maintenance garden centres.

Concession income Concession income will add value, but again there are many points to consider, for example Wyevale Garden Centres plc now undertake their own pets and aquatics business, and if there is one on site, they are likely to end the occupation at the earliest opportunity.

Some garden centre operators allow concessions on site who offer no synergy to the garden centre operation, for example bathrooms, kitchens, double glazing, and many new purchasers would consider this detrimental to the unique retailing atmosphere of a garden centre and thus would not require them to remain on site and so would discount the income currently being generated.

The majority of garden centre operators are "men of straw", they come and they go. The majority, even if they are "offering guarantees", by influence of having the lease or licence in their own name are not worth suing if they default on their rental payments.

Only successful garden centres generally find it easy to generate concessionary income from reasonable tenants, and in some circumstances even the best garden centres find it difficult to offer the full range of concessionary services, due to the lack of appropriate operators.

In general, the majority of concession operators operate on leases outside of The Landlord and Tenant Act, or licences of between one and five years, and this appears to suit the majority of operators.

Except in exceptional circumstances, security of tenure should be excluded as cases have been known where often substantial offers have been made for a garden centre for alternative development such as food retailing and there has been a concession operator located centrally within the site with security of tenure, who has been able to ransom the vendor for a sum of money substantially more than the theoretical value.

The more substantial concession operators will invest considerable sums of money into the site in shop fittings, equipment etc, and therefore often require a longer lease and may try to insist upon security of tenure. When this occurs, capital value is added, but care should be given to the location of the operator within the site, and we would suggest that a development break-clause with a landlords penalty should be inserted within the legal document.

Other information If we can obtain additional information, then we would consider other ratios compared to industry norms, such as occupancy costs as a percentage of turnover, average stock levels, stock turnover, sales per sq ft etc.

Summary Once one has considered the above points, there are three basic areas of value:

1. *The physical asset.* The land, the buildings, the infrastructure, where an appropriate rent and yield has to be applied.
2. *The concessionary income.* Where appropriate investment yields have to be applied.
3. *The trading potential/goodwill of the business* Where the accounts have to be adjusted, taking into account the areas set out above and the appropriate profit multiplier used.

Once these have been added together, and even on the basis that valuations of garden centres are usually plus stock at valuation, one should consider the stock, the split of product lines, the split between green and dry goods, the division of the bigger items, as for example after a bad summer, there could be a surplus of bar-b-cues and garden furniture, which will not sell for a further nine/ten months. Plant stock could be "old and leggy", past its best and retailing under glass often means that the packaging of the dry goods is faded.

There may be surpluses of unusual items and certainly if one is going to sell to one of the groups who have standardised stock ranges, it may well be that a fair proportion, say 25% for example, might not be appropriate and therefore would not be purchased by them. Comments like this are valued by those seeking garden centre valuations and can have a material effect on agency transactions because a vendor tends to look at the total figure that he will obtain. If a substantial amount of stock is to be dropped, this could jeopardise a transaction.

Finally, one has arrived at a value, but this is not the end of the valuation. Next one has to consider comparable evidence in regard to what garden centres sell for, and the reason they achieved this which means that detailed knowledge of garden centre transactions is essential, eg special purchaser, strategic location.

Then one has to consider who is in the market to purchase any given garden centre, and this will depend upon its location, its size, its potential and its immediate competitors. For example, take the hypothetical disposal of a sizeable garden centre in the North of England with a turnover in excess of £1,000,000. Within this area, both the groups who may be interested are already represented and the garden centre is too close to one other major potential purchaser.

The north of the country is not currently of interest to most of the main garden centre groups, and accordingly it would be necessary to seek a local purchaser, and we are aware that there are not that many companies or individuals within the industry with the inclination and financial resources or business experience to purchase a garden centre business of this size.

However, we are aware that there is one operator within the locality who has agreed to sell their substantial centre for alternative development and accordingly he is likely to have a "rollover" problem and this garden centre is ideally situated for his company.

Accordingly, it may be that we are able to sell this garden centre to a special purchaser quickly and for a good price. Alternatively, we would be searching for a local entrepreneur who may, or may not, pay what we believe is open market value, as they will have their own opinion of value as a business man, ie what it is worth to them depending upon their circumstances and inclination and accordingly, our valuation needs to be prudent, substantiated by the use of comparable evidence, stipulating the range of values that may be achieved within the body of the report and the reasons why this could occur.

Greenfield sites

Greenfield sites are currently very difficult to value as there has been little demand and thus little comparable evidence. Traditionally in the late 1980s, other than certain exceptions, prices of circa £50,000 per acre were being achieved for sites of 4 to 5 acres. Current values per acre are generally lower than this and some bare sites are virtually unsaleable.

Another reason the market for greenfield sites has been depressed for a number of years and continues to be depressed is because of the availability of established garden centres at prices that mean purchasers cannot justify a site and new build cost in the region of £1,000,000, prior to fitting out and stocking, with the inherent losses that will almost inevitably incur in the first one or two years.

As garden centre site values are lower than almost any other form of development, few land owners try to obtain planning consent for garden centre use other than as a preliminary planning consent as a pre-cursor for more valuable uses.

Lastly, only the major groups or those with a strong established track record can obtain funding for greenfield sites, as the majority of banks are not keen to lend money for this type of project.

Freehold versus leasehold: a two tier market

Leasehold garden centres are disliked or misunderstood by all but the main groups who tend to look at the contribution that an individual garden centre will make to the group under their method of operation and value it accordingly.

Leasehold garden centres offer the ability for rapid expansion without large capital costs. As long as contributions are generated after occupational costs, the premium can be paid back in relatively few years, and thus the chains see leaseholds as a rapid and cheap way of expansion.

The question of the way chains view acquisitions on a contribution basis leads us to a potential situation in the market where leasehold centres are worth more to the chains than to the independents, as they can afford to pay back more quickly on contribution than independents can regardless of turnover or margin performance. In addition, the main clearing banks have a tendency to refuse to lend on leases of under twenty five years.

In regard to lease terms, we tend to recommend that clients take as long a lease as they can, twenty five years plus, for two main reasons:

1. There is the opportunity to depreciate the cost of the buildings twice during the period, as it is our experience that typical garden centre building structures need substantial refurbishment after twenty years, and
2. The majority of independent operators are seeking to create a capital asset in addition to income and short leases, even with security of tenure, will have an effect on asset value.

Due to the reasons set out above, valuing such properties is becoming more difficult, as the difference between what the two operator types can pay is substantial and we may be moving into a two tier market for £1,000,000+ turnover leasehold garden centres.

In certain instances, we see highly profitable leasehold garden centres achieving prices similar to smaller sized, but less profitable, freehold centres.

In our experience leasehold garden centres tend to comprise one of two types:

1. Small garden centres both in terms of site area and turnover, which is taken leasehold by the operator because it is the only way into the industry working for themselves.
2. Garden centres turning over or capable of turning over £1,000,000 plus generally operated by one of the groups.

The RICS red book

When undertaking valuations of operating garden centres, it is imperative that valuers refer to the new RICS Appraisal and Guidance Manual Note 7, relating to trading and related valuations and goodwill. The notes are not directly concerned with valuation methods, but with the practical approach to the assembly and interpretation of relevant information.

Guidance Note 7.2 relates to the valuation of property fully equipped as an operational entity and valued having regard to trading potential and includes:

(a) The land and buildings.
(b) Trade fixtures, fittings, furniture, furnishings and equipment.
(c) The market's perception of the trading potential excluding personal goodwill.

Consumable stock should be excluded from the valuation.

The notes are generally common sense, and in general terms follow the approach set out in earlier chapters, as follows:

The valuation method adopted by the valuer should reflect the approach generally used by the market for the particular type of property.

The valuer should analyse and review the trading accounts for the current and previous years and projections for future years, where these are available, and form an opinion by reference to analysis of trading accounts and comparable properties as to the future trading performance, and fair, maintainable operating profit likely to be achieved by an operator taking over the existing business at the date of valuation.

Alternative uses should also be considered.

Consideration should be given to the annual cost of repairing and maintaining the property and its fixtures and fittings.

Head office costs must be understood and due allowance made for them, where appropriate.

The accounts of a particular property will only show how that property is trading under the particular management at that time. The task of the valuer is to assess the fair maintainable level of trade and future profitability that can be achieved by an operator of the business upon which a potential purchaser would be likely to base his offer. The trading potential must be carefully differentiated from personal goodwill, which is that which has been created in the business by the present owner or management which is not expected to remain with the business in the event of the subject property being sold.

The determination of the capitalisation multiplier with a discount rate to be applied in arriving at the capital value of the property relies upon the experience and judgement of the valuer. It should reflect the valuer's opinion of the perception of the risk and security associated with the subject property and its current and future trading potential, taking into account all available market evidence, and economic market factors, such as interest rates and inflation.

In conclusion, therefore, a detailed knowledge of the trading patterns of garden centres is required by valuers to undertake valuations to include trading potential, and even with this knowledge if detailed knowledge of market demand is not also to hand, substantial mistakes can be made due to the very localised demand that exists in many parts of the United Kingdom and the difficulties that many purchasers face in the raising of capital sums to purchase the property and working capital to buy the stock and run the business.

Example valuations

Set out below are four hypothetical examples of garden centres valuations:

Example 1
Example 1 is a large garden centre located in the north of England on a site of 6.5 acres with good access onto one side of a fast dual carriageway in open countryside close to one major town. The garden centre has grown over twenty years through cashflow with extensions being built and added as money has allowed, and consequently some areas of the garden centre, both internal and external, are in need of refurbishment and upgrading.

There is 3,030 sq. m (32,615 sq. ft) of covered, heated accommodation and 701.4 sq. m (7,550 sq. ft) of canopy, excluding concession buildings.

There is substantial concessionary income on site from seven separate concession operators, and there is a four-bedroom, detached, residential dwelling tied to horticulture.

	1992/93	1993/94	1994/95
Turnover	£2.05 million	£2.26 million	£2.45 million
Gross margin	39.4%	40.6%	42.7%
Operating margin	6.9%	4.8%	8.6%
Net margin	5.7%	4.0%	7.8%
Concessionary income	£57,125	£70,170	£59,976
Number of concessions	7	8	7

Running costs of the business are as follows:

Wages and National Insurance	£440,239	18%	high
Rent, rates, lighting and heat	£ 92,595	3.8%	low
Advertising	£107,449	4.4%	average
Printing, stationery, telephones	£ 23,638	–	–
Repairs and renewal	£ 48,286	–	low
General expenses	£ 84,970	–	–
Bad debts	£ 6,639	–	–
Bank charges and interest	£ 25,458	1%	low

TOTAL RUNNING COSTS   £829,274 excluding Director's remuneration.

Valuation

Land and buildings

Turnover	£2,450,000	
Rental value say 5% £122,500 YP and perp – 10%		£1,225,000
Operating profit 8.6% £210,700 YP times 3		£ 632,100
Concessionary income Total £59,976 On long lease £37,500 YP 6.5		£ 243,750
Annual licence £22,476 YP 3		£ 67,428
House value of £80,000, less 35% due to tie		£ 55,000
Total		£2,223,278
Less £225,000 estimated cost to be spent by one of the groups to refurbish the buildings externally to include re-roofing, upgrade the areas that need upgrading internally and re-do the planteria.	——————	(£ 225,000)
FINAL TOTAL		£1,998,278
	say	£2,000,000

Example 2

A small freehold garden centre on 2.5 acres, with 761 sq. m (8,194 sq. ft) covered area, 227.6 sq. m (2,988 sq. ft) canopy, located off a main road in a rural area, but on a tourist route in the southern half of England.

The garden centre is hard to find and there is substantial competition in the area.

The buildings are unusual, car parking is well spread out and there are no concessions and little potential for them.

The garden centre is family run and as part of the group there is a nursery which supplies a fair amount of plants.

	1993	1994	1995
Turnover	£690,000	£735,000	£737,500
Gross margin	34%	32%	33%
Operating margin	21.7%	16.1%	15.5%
Net margin	Not provided	Not provided	Not provided
Concessionary income	Not provided	Not provided	Not provided
Number of concessions	Not provided	Not provided	Not provided

As this garden centre was run as part of a large nursery plus a further retail plant centre, we only received limited financial information as follows:

Wages and National Insurance	£ 66,680	9%	low
Rates, lighting and heating	£ 17,491	2.4%	low
Advertising	£ 23,703	3.2%	low
Printing, stationery, telephone	£ 1,302	–	low
Repairs and renewal	£ 6,456	–	low
General expenses	£ 13,484	1.8%	low
Bad debts	No information		
Bank charges and interest	No information		
Depreciation	No information		
Total costs	£129,066		
Operating profit	£114,312	15.5%	

The gross margin is too low and any purchaser would look to increase it to at least 36% initially which should reduce turnover to circa £675,000. Accordingly, operating costs have been adjusted on this assumption.

Accordingly, we would adjust the operating profit as follows:

Add in rent/cost of servicing capital say 4% of turnover	£ 27,000
Increase wages by 5% of turnover to take 9% to 14%	£ 27,820

Increase other expenses to 3.5% of turnover to include bad debts	£ 10,141	
Allow 1% bank charges and interest	£ 6,750	
Additional costs	£ 71,882	
This leaves an operating profit	£ 42,430	
Turnover therefore say	£675,000	

Rental 5% say £33,750
YP 12.5% 8   £270,000

Profit £42,430
YP 3   £137,400

                                                                             £407,400

                                                              Say   £410,000

Example 3

A small, freehold garden centre, bought out of receivership three years ago, located in a rural position, but close to substantial areas of population and to the main motorway network.

The site extends to approximately 3 acres, has 914.4 sq. m of horticultural glass and 373.4 sq. m of Nicotarp open protected area.

There is a mobile home on site, but planning consent for a house tied to horticulture is being resisted.

	1993	1994	1995
Turnover	Not trading	£280,723	£441,765
Gross margin	,,	29%	33%
Operating margin	,,	− (17%)	− (2%)
Net margin	,,	− (19%)	− (6.6%)
Concessionary income	,,	−	−
Number of concessions	,,	−	−

Operating costs

Wages and National Insurance	£ 58,223	13%	average
Rent, rates, light and heating	£ 6,858	1.6%	low
Advertising	£ 12,637	2.8%	low
Printing, stationery, telephones	£ 6,818	−	−
Repairs and renewal	£ 5,780	−	low
General expenses	£ 51,591	11.6%	high
Bad debts	−	38%	−
Bank charges, interest	£ 9,237	−	−

Accordingly, an operating loss of £29,000 was made

Accordingly, we looked at the budgets for next year, 1996, which showed turnover increasing to	£576,000	
Gross margin increasing to 39%		
Overheads increasing to	£196,500	
Showing a net operating profit of 7%, and a net profit of 4%	£ 40,320	
Increasing thereafter in 1997 and 1998	£ 23,040	

Valuation

Land and buildings rental value estimated at	£25,000	
YP and perp 12.5% 8		£200,000
Estimated operating profit 1996	£40,000	
YP 2.5%		£100,000
Mobile home and plot say		£ 25,000
Valuation		£325,000

Our advice in this instance would be that this is a theoretical value and that it would be very difficult to sell at the present time due to the fact that there are only two years trading accounts, following the property being bought out of receivership and the fact that losses have been made, and it will be very difficult, if not impossible, for a purchaser to borrow against the current trading accounts, and that to ensure a sale in the current market, other than to a cash purchaser, a figure of nearer £250,000 would be more likely.

Out of interest, the property was bought out of receivership two and a half years earlier in the sum of £165,000, to include the stock and business assets, since when capital improvements such as the Nicotarp have been made.

Example 4

A leasehold garden centre on a small site of two acres with additional shared car parking with 1,117 sq. m (12,020 sq. ft) of covered area situated on the edge of a prosperous and well known market town.

The lease has security of tenure, with 10.5 years unexpired, and a rent passing of £41,500 with four yearly rent reviews, the next review due 1997.

There are two concessions generating £19,000 income gross.

	1993	1994	1995
Turnover	£1,175,000	£1,183,000	£1,178,000
Gross margin	38.4%	38.3%	40.8%
Operating margin	17%	13%	15.1%
Net margin	–	–	–
Concessionary income	£18,400	£18,700	£19,000
Number of concessions	2	2	2

General expenses

Wages and National Insurance	£164,316	14%	low
Rent, rates, heating and lighting	£ 65,340	5.5%	average
Advertising	£ 29,230	2.5%	average
Printing and stationery, telephones	£ 7,916		
Repairs and renewal	£ 3,450		
General expenses	£ 32,494		

Total cost	£302,746
Operating profit	£177,878

Valuation

Land and buildings, rent review in one year's time	Nil value	
Operating profit	£177,878	
YP 2		£355,756
Concession income on annual licences £19,000		
YP 2		£ 38,000
Total		£393,756
	Say	£395,000

This garden centre would appear to be at maximum turnover and with gross margins increasing to 40.8% there is little scope for any increases here, and with only ten years to go, only the groups would have the financial ability and inclination to purchase this property, particularly on the basis that there is security of tenure and it would not appear that the landlords are likely to re-occupy.

If a new twenty five year lease was granted, we would expect the value to increase substantially on the basis that the groups can buy turnover on a well, but tightly, run garden centre.

Conclusion

The valuation of garden centres without reference to direct comparable evidence and without detailed knowledge of supply and demand relating to specific operators within the industry is a very inaccurate science, with detailed market knowledge it becomes an art.

© Simon E Quinton Smith, 1996

CHAPTER 8

Golf courses

In this chapter I will examine the capital valuation of golf courses in the UK. In order to understand the method of valuation of golf courses, it is necessary to explain about the type of golf courses operating in the UK and also to give an overview and background to the market over the last few years.

Types of golf course

Before attempting to value UK golf courses, it is necessary to have an understanding of the structure of the UK golf industry. Broadly speaking, the types of golf course that the valuer is likely to come across in the course of this work can be summarised as; private members clubs, municipal golf courses, proprietary owned golf courses and country clubs.

A private members' club will be operated by its members, for the benefit of those members and will not aim to make a profit after meeting outgoings. There may be a surplus built up over a number of years for the future development of the course, ie new clubhouse or extra nine holes, but this is unlikely to reach very high levels or the members would complain they were being overcharged. A private members' golf club is not usually open to the public but would allow member's guests, golf societies and green fee payers with a handicap to play the course usually mid-week only. However, in recent times, many private members' clubs have begun to take a higher level of green fee players as a result of decreasing membership numbers and in some cases where the club rents the golf course from a landlord, considerably higher rental payments.

A municipal golf course is operated by the local authority for the benefit of the community and as such will probably have no membership and will charge discounted playing fees to the market average. However, there has been a trend in recent times under compulsory competitive tendering for municipal golf courses to become operated by commercial profit earning companies. However, these are still in the minority and in many cases still restricted by the green fees they are able to charge.

The proprietary club is the one most valuers will meet in the course of their business and this can either be pay and play or membership. This is run commercially for the benefit of the owner and will be expected to make a commercial profit in the normal way to give the owner a proper return on their investment. Country clubs are an offshoot of the proprietary golf club and are generally defined as having a large income from non-golf activities such as food and beverage, conference and function trade.

Within the types of golf courses outlined above, there will be sub-categories, depending on the facilities provided. For example, a pay and play course aimed at the beginners or players without a handicap is likely to consist of nine holes, a floodlit driving range and clubhouse with a well stocked pro-shop. The country club on the other hand, is likely to have a much larger clubhouse to accommodate the various function and conference facilities, together with between 18 and 36 holes of golf constructed to a high and challenging standard.

It is important that the valuer has an understanding of the type of golf course they are considering and the market segment that the golf course is aimed at, since this will impact on the level of green fee and membership attainable and the total revenue generated from the whole complex.

Background and overview of the market

In order to understand the methods of valuing today, I believe it is important for the valuer to have an understanding of the golf course market and how it has changed in recent years.

The golf boom in the late 1980s was fuelled by the success of the European Ryder Cup Team at the Belfry in 1985. Furthermore, a report by the Royal & Ancient in 1989 concluded that the UK required 700 new courses to meet existing demand by the year 2000. This report coincided with the Government urging farmers to diversify into uses other than agriculture. The result of these various factors was an explosion in golf development, increasingly fuelled by the buoyant UK and overseas economies.

Since 1989, there have been more new courses constructed than in total over the previous 20 years. Bank and institutional finance was easy for developers to obtain and this increased demand and consequently values of golf development projects. Japanese companies were also desperate to invest in the UK property market and saw UK golf as being cheap and under utilised compared with the market in Japan.

These factors contributed to rising capital values in both existing golf facilities and green field development sites. Because of these rising values and the expectation in the hotel and other property market segments, that values would continue to rise, the type of development tended to be towards "high quality exclusive clubs". These were typified by large clubhouses with lavish interiors and "signature" design golf courses. As well as a rise in capital values, courses were constructed on the basis that pure ownerships and shares could be sold in line with American and Japanese price levels. £15,000 to £25,000 per share/membership were not uncommon levels to find around the M25.

Then came the downturn in the UK economy, high interest rates, and a realisation that golf courses, like any other business, needed to produce an income to not only service debt levels but to pay the owner a satisfactory return on his capital.

Method of valuation – factors for the valuer to consider

General

As with most other leisure businesses, golf courses are in general valued by the profits method. This is then checked against the valuer's own knowledge of direct comparables in the market place.

When deciding what purchase price to pay a prospective purchaser will in general be concerned with the direct financial rewards he can obtain from the trading business. In assessing this he will consider the current trading and how this can improve or more importantly be sustained.

It may be the case that this requires further capital expenditure, ie the construction of a new maintenance facility, purchase of new green keeping equipment or refurbishment of an existing club room. Depending on the amount of expenditure required the purchaser is likely to discount this from the capital value to allow for these improvements not having been made.

Where there is a perceived increase in trading at the golf course, the purchaser will have to assess how much of this additional income they are prepared to pay the current owner for. This is likely to vary depending upon general market conditions and also the position of the vendor. In a market where there is high demand for golf facilities the whole or most of this "hope" value is likely to be included in the value. However, in a market with fewer purchasers this will become more heavily discounted and in the case of a forced seller, ie a property in receivership, the value may reflect little or no additional trading potential.

"Trophy and lifestyle" properties

Whilst profitability of the golf business must be paramount in the valuer's mind when assessing a property, the golf market can be distorted by "trophy" products and "lifestyle" purchasers.

The former tend to be well located facilities in areas of high population which have a name or branding in the golf market. This is likely in most cases to have been built up over a number of years most likely through the hosting of a regional or national tournament. The most obvious example of this is Wentworth in Surrey, but there are many lesser "trophy" products. The key characteristics in these golf courses is the likely attraction to overseas purchasers if they were to be sold. The widening of the market onto an international basis means demand tends to be higher and consequently values follow suit. The companies/individuals are in general buying for the prestige of owning the property rather than a specific return on capital.

With the latter − "lifestyle" purchasers − the purchase of the golf business is only one of a number of factors affecting their decision to buy. Quality of the facility, availability of high class living accommodation and location in the country will all influence this type of purchaser. Whilst they will not necessarily disregard a return on capital completely, they may be prepared to accept a lower return than other commercial operators in the market place.

It is primarily because of these two types of purchaser that the valuer cannot rely entirely on the profits method. Consideration must be given to direct comparable transactions in the market place alongside the conclusions drawn from the profits method. The valuer must distinguish between different types of golf facility in order to assess which is the most appropriate method to use. However, as in most cases, it will usually be a combination of the two methods, each acting as a check for major disparities from the other.

Goodwill

One of the key considerations for the valuer when assessing golf course values is the element of goodwill which should or should not be discounted. With larger golf complexes which have many staff, it is unlikely that the ultimate owner has worked up much personal goodwill. The operator may have increased trading at the facility but this is a very different matter to personal goodwill. Should the operator sell the complex, it is highly unlikely that many of his members would follow him unless he was to purchase a new golf facility in the immediate catchment area.

However, should a chain of golf properties be built up by one or more companies, there may well be an element of goodwill attached to all the properties, because of the perceived quality and stability of the clubs. Normally when a golf property changes hands it would be likely that the purchaser would insert a clause in the contract that the vendor could not trade within a certain radius of the golf course. Where the golf course is a small family run concern, there may be members who belong because of the type of atmosphere at the club. If the golf course was taken over by a larger organisation, then it could be argued that some of those members would not wish to remain at the facility. However, I believe that so long as the incoming operator is as good a manager and the facilities remain to the same standard or better, it is unlikely that there is much true personal goodwill.

Particular factors influencing value

Many of the factors which influence the value of golf courses are comparable with other types of leisure businesses and indeed other types of property generally. Below I have attempted to summarise some of the factors which are important for the valuer to consider when assessing the value of a golf facility:

Location

An obvious one perhaps, but you would not necessarily think so when you see some of the golf facilities which have been developed in outlying locations and which are now for all intents and purposes in receivership. Whether the new course will be all members or pay and play, the key criterion is number of people within 20 and 30 minute drive times. For country clubs and golf/hotels, these drive times might extend further and for starter courses and driving ranges, the drive times may be less than 20 minutes. The valuer should remember that not only is the number of people within the drive times important but also the profile of those people.

From the valuer's point of view, the results of a population survey are important, since if a facility is trading well but there are relatively few people within the 20 and 30 minute drive times, it should make them aware that the complex is probably open to declining trade should a new competitor open in the area.

Planning

Planning conditions and Section 106 Agreements may influence the value and the valuer should check the relevant documents carefully. Road improvements which are subject to Section 106 Agreements and which have not been implemented, will have a capital cost and therefore an affect on value. Equally the valuer should be aware of any planning conditions which have not been fulfilled such as landscaping or the tarmacadam of the car park and could have an impact on value.

Tenure

At the moment valuers should be aware that there is a substantial change occurring within the rent review market in relation to golf courses. There is a very large upward trend in golf rental values currently and this will obviously have an effect on the ultimate profitability of the complex and therefore its value. For the larger complexes long leases (35 years plus) are unlikely to deter bigger operators or multiple golf course owners. However, properties which may attract overseas or lifestyle purchasers, as described earlier, could have a detrimental effect on value if they are leasehold. The valuer therefore should be aware of this effect and in some cases make allowance for the possibility of the purchase of the freehold land if they feel this is possible.

Fees

The level of membership subscription and green fees charged are important indicators to the valuer. If the charges are too low the margins may decrease to a level which makes it unattractive for a potential purchaser. In addition if a facility starts low it is not an indication that it will be able to raise its prices back up to the level of other competitors, since there is a general reluctance for golfers to pay higher increased prices at the current facility that they use.

Competition

Competition is not just a matter of how many other facilities there are in the area although obviously the valuer should take this into account. More importantly the valuer must assess which segment of the market those current facilities are aiming at and whether they are in direct competition with the golf course being valued. The valuer should also be aware that many traditional members' clubs which have had long waiting lists and restrictive green fee times are now opening their doors more freely to the public. This may mean that a public golf course suddenly finds it has a lot of further competition, as private members' clubs open their doors.

Licences

The type of licence that the golf club has for its bar, restaurant and function facilities will obviously have an effect on value. However, the fact that the facility does not have a Justice full-on licence, would not necessarily be detrimental if for example the club was to be operated as a members only facility. A public pay and play facility which did not have a Justices full-on licence, for example, could be viewed as restrictive. Once again, the valuer must decide on the segment of the market the golf course is aiming at and the appropriate licence that should be in place.

Construction of the golf course

Long dry summers and very wet winters soon begin to separate the well constructed golf courses from the badly constructed ones. Therefore the valuer should take into account the construction of the tees and greens, irrigation facilities and drainage.

Quality of the golf course

Many of the farmers' fields with their cut grass and a few holes pinpointed in them, attracted players whilst there was a low level of supply. Now that supply has increased, golfers have become more concerned with the type of facility they are able to play at.

However, again the valuer should not be preconceived about such matters as the length of the course and number of water features, since these will vary according to the market segment the golf course is aimed at. A pay and play facility expecting to play 35,000 to 40,000 rounds per annum, will need to be relatively short, ie 6,000 yards and free of areas of rough or else the majority of players will take too long to get round the course. If the facility is aimed at handicapped members paying membership fees of £1,000 per annum the standard and maturity of the course including trees and water features will be expected to be much higher.

Valuation methods

Market evidence/direct comparables
The general physical factors affecting the value of a golf course when looking at market evidence and using direct comparables, has more or less been covered in the information on factors influencing value. As far as the valuer is concerned, the main use of direct comparables will be as back-up to any analysis of the trading accounts. More particularly, it is especially useful where the complex may have gone into receivership before being completed, or in a few rare instances, a valuation of a completed complex with no trading.

The final situation that valuers may find themselves relying on direct market evidence could be in the event of a course they feel suitable for purchase by the international market. This type of course described earlier as a possible "trophy" course is likely to change hands with much less emphasis on its trading than a lesser known competitor.

In this instance it would be necessary for the valuer to look at other golf courses of a similar stature which have been sold to the international community and to compare them with the course being valued. However, it is fair to say that the international market has not been at all active in the golf market in the last three or four years and as a result, the number of properties which the valuer should decide falls into this category are likely to be very few and far between.

One of the fundamental difficulties for the valuer in using direct comparison of market transactions is the general complexity which always seems to surround the sale of the golf course. I have already considered the enormous number of factors influencing the value of the golf course and clearly unless the valuer has an understanding of all those factors in the relevant transaction, they may find it very difficult to analyse the transaction well enough for it to be of use to them. Apportionment of memberships, taking over of the leases of machinery, deferred payments and further payments relating to the success of the operation, will all have influenced the end price paid by a purchaser. Consequently, the valuer must be very careful when using market evidence and ensure that the facts reported are the facts in the transaction.

Profits method using actual and predicted accounts

Actual accounts When valuing the property, it is useful for the valuer to have two years' mature trading accounts plus up to date management information for the year in progress. Unfortunately, it is rare for the valuer to receive this type of information when asked to consider a golf operation.

In reality the valuer will be lucky to receive much more than 1–2 year's accounts which give a true trading picture. In most cases the valuer will have to construct accounts for the business and this is dealt with later.

When considering actual accounts the valuer must make assumptions and adjustments in order to achieve a normalised operating profit. Firstly, the normalised operating profit should be expressed before bank/directors loan charges, HP payments on machinery and interest. In most cases it will also be pre-depreciation.

In analysing the turnover for the business, the valuer should be aware of any one-off income items which an incoming operator could not rely upon in the year to year trading. These may be the sale of life memberships, income from joining fees or, in some cases, income from outside sources such as set-a-side payments or tipping rights. Clearly in any trading year there will be some element of joining fees but the valuer must be especially careful when a course is in its first/ second year of trading and there is likely to be a large proportion of joining fees.

In analysing the expenditure part of the accounts the valuer must consider any unusual elements. Particular areas to be watched are director's/manager's salaries and items of maintenance which would be more appropriately described as capital expenditure. With director's/manager's salaries the valuer must decide what level of remuneration the manager/director should be paid for the size of the facility being operated. In some cases the figure in the accounts will be much higher and should be adjusted downwards. Sometimes the valuer will be given a set of accounts with no manager's salary and in this case a figure will need to be inserted.

Predicted accounts If there are no accounts available as in a receivership or in the case of newly opened facilities, the valuer will have to construct normalised profit and loss accounts using a working knowledge of the courses in the same market segment. It is therefore necessary to gauge some potential turnover for the complex and to apply the necessary gross profit margins that the expenditure is likely to allow.

This will also be the case where the valuer is provided with projections by an operator. In this case these will need to be analysed to see if they match those expected by the valuer.

It should always be made expressly clear in the valuation report, backed up by detailed notes on the valuer's file, what trading figures have been relied upon, where the data has been supplied from and what, if any, assumptions the valuer made to reach the conclusions regarding predicted trading potential.

Other factors for the valuer to consider

Stock and equipment
Stock, as with most leisure facilities is normally transferred at cost on completion. Whilst this may be usual for the food and beverage side of the golf business, many incoming purchasers do not wish to take on a large sum of stock in the professional shop. Therefore in some circumstances it may be necessary for the valuer to make an allowance for this in the valuation. As far as machinery for green keeping is concerned, this would usually be included within a valuation and assumed to be unencumbered from lease payments. Since the golf course could not operate without this equipment it would be wrong for the valuer to exclude or assume it has not been paid for.

Joining fees and debentures
When valuing golf courses the valuer must be aware of the potential effect that joining fees, debentures and share issues could have.

Joining fees, as mentioned previously, must be considered carefully by the valuer especially in the first couple of years of trading. During this time there will be a large income from joining fees with new members joining a new club. Consequently in general those joining fees taken at this stage should be discounted for the purposes of the profit and loss accounts. The valuer will have to decide how many more memberships the club can sell before it reaches its optimum level. Thereafter the valuer should allow for a small percentage of joining fees, new members replacing those who drop out each year.

Debentures

These need to be considered carefully by the valuer and treated in a similar way to joining fees. However, in many cases debentures are technically redeemable at a given date and therefore, may constitute a liability. The valuer must be aware of this potential liability in addition to the other considerations outlined for joining fees above, when assessing a club's maintainable profit.

Example 1

This example deals with a provincial golf course operating on a pay and play basis, with the food and professional's shop franchised out. The profit and loss account is likely to be as follows:

Provincial pay and play

Income	Green fees	£340K
	Driving range	£ 30K
	Bar	£ 55K
	Other	£ 20K
	Total	£445K
Overheads	Bar purchases	£ 40K
	Salaries	£108K
	Rates	£ 13K
	Course maintenance	£ 14K
	Repairs	£ 30K
	Running costs	£ 25K
	Other	£ 20K
	Bank interest	£ 25K
	Depreciation	£ 15K
	Total	£290K
	Operating profit	£155K

Having considered the accounts, the valuer decides to make the following adjustments:

(a) Income – remove £10,000 of income from the "other" section which related to an insurance claim.
(b) Overheads – remove bank interest and depreciation. In addition there is no manager's salary in the salaries so the valuer decides to add an additional £20,000 for this item.

Taking these adjustments into account, the valuer arrives at an adjusted operating profit of £165,000.

To this adjusted operating profit the valuer applies a multiple of 6.5 × (approximately 15.5% return) reflecting the provincial nature of the property but also the high level of golf income:

£165,000 × 6.6 YP = £1,089,000 – say £1.1 million.

Example 2

This deals with a London pay and play golf course on lease from the local authority. The Pro Shop is operated by a third party. There are 50 years remaining on the lease and the rent is fixed at 25% of turnover.

Income		*Overheads*	
Green fees	£450K	Salaries and wages	£130K
Bar and food sales	£170K	National Insurance costs	£ 12K
		Staff pension scheme	£ 4K
	£620K	Postage and stationery	£ 4K
		Telephone charges	£ 2K
Cost of sales	£140K	Insurances	£ 2K
		Rent	£150K
Gross profit	£480K	Rates and water	£ 20K
		Lighting and heating	£ 17K
		Property maintenance	£ 6K
		Bank charges	£ 7K
		Professional fees	£ 12K
		Management charges	£110K
		Auditor's remuneration	£ 3K
		Total	£479K
		Operating profit – £1	

The valuer makes the following adjustments

(a) Income – none.
(b) Expenses – removes professional fees (one-off charges) and reduces management charge to £30,000 to reflect a more realistic salary.

Therefore adjusted operating profit will be £80,000. To this a multiplier 6.3 × is applied reflecting a 15% return and a sinking fund of 3.5%. Whilst the location and trading are good and could reflect a lower yield, the high rent payable (25% of turnover) makes the property less attractive.

£80,000 x 6.3 YP = £500,000.

Example 3

This gives an outline of a modern, well constructed London golf club with a large element of food and beverage trade from functions and the owner operates the professional shop. The club operates primarily as a proprietary members club.

Income		*Administration overheads*	
Subscriptions	£490K	Rates	£ 30K
Locker rental	£ 6K	Heat and light	£ 25K
Pro shop sales	£ 45K	Insurance	£ 9K
Buggy/range hire	£ 18K	Maintenance	£ 65K
Green fees	£ 45K	Salaries	£ 60K
Bar sales	£190K	Motor expenses	£ 6K
Food sales	£ 80K	Telephone/fax	£ 6K
Societies	£ 70K	Advertising	£ 30K
Joining fees	£ 50K	Postage/stationery	£ 18K
	———	Security costs	£ 17K
	£994K	Office equipment	£ 8K
	———	Audit/accountancy	£ 7K
Cost of Sales		Consultancy fees	£ 10K
		Legal fees	£ 3K
Pro shop	£ 55K	Uniforms/cleaning	£ 10K
Food/functions	£ 75K		
Bar	£ 95K	Total admin expenses	£304K
Direct wages	£240K		
	———	Operating profit	£225K
	£465K		

In this case the valuer makes the following adjustments:

(a) Income – golf course is only in its second year of trading and therefore there is still a high element of joining fees. Valuer estimates in normal year 50 new members paying £500 – joining fee income = £25,000.
(b) Overheads – valuer makes an adjustment to consultancy fees, office equipment (both one-off charges) and removes £20,000 from salaries to give manager's salary of £40K which is more appropriate than £60K.

This gives an adjusted operating profit of £238,000. To this the valuer applies a multiplier of 8 × (12.5% return reflecting the quality nature of the golf course and its location).

£238,000 × 8YP = £1.9m

© Andrew Hillier, 1996

CHAPTER 9

Provincial hotels

The valuer of provincial hotels needs to rely more on judgement and experience than on complicated mathematical formulae and this chapter is written as a practical guide to assist the professional or lay person in the principles involved. The detailed application of these principles requires knowledge of the hotel industry and an up to date understanding of latest changes and trends. In particular allowance needs to be made for the cyclical nature of the market for all types of leisure property.

Post-war history

The hotel industry was one of the last to recover after the war. Even after food and petrol rationing ended in the early 1950s people continued to lead lives of austerity. Tourism outside the resorts was primitive and travel was slow. Car ownership was still the prerogative of the fairly well off and the M1 motorway only opened in 1959.

In those days service industries were looked on as poor relations contributing little to the nation's wealth, so much so that in the 1960s selective employment tax was levied on all workers not regarded as producing actual goods. The British have always had difficulty appreciating the value and status of service and the hotel trade in particular was regarded as a Cinderella. There was little training outside some of the larger hotels in London and some provincial cities. Indeed the ultimate reference for an aspiring hotelier was that he had been trained at a British Transport Hotel, nationalised along with the railways in 1946.

With so little expertise available it was not surprising that most privately-owned hotels were operated by enthusiastic amateurs on a wing and a prayer and with the aid of unskilled staff, if, indeed, any could be found. There was little corporate ownership apart from Trust Houses, which were genuinely represented right across the country, but which were smaller units by far than today's group-owned hotels, albeit aspiring to a good, if unexciting, standard of facilities. There were also a small number of groups operating in the seaside resorts, but most other hotels were privately owned and offered basic facilities and simple food, with beer still forming the bulk of liquor sales.

Most people were content with one or two weeks' holiday, often returning to the same establishment in the same week year after year. Pubs were yet to realise their potential for selling food. Women were discouraged from bars. Private bathrooms were the exception.

In the mid 1960s standards of living started to rise. Cheaper foreign travel raised people's expectations of food and service. Motorways and better communications gave flexibility to the tourist, who became more mobile. People booked less far ahead and stayed for shorter periods.

In 1971 grants were made available for hotel bedrooms in order to stimulate the home tourist industry, with mixed results. The grant was the lesser of £1,000 per bedroom or 50% of cost. Bedrooms were often built where none were needed, schemes were hurriedly put together to meet the grant deadline, and the sudden flush of bedrooms created a glut in some areas which contributed to the mid-1970s collapse of the hotel market. Grant-aided bedroom wings can still be found in provincial hotels. Cheaply built, they are frequently of indifferent standard.

The advent of cheap foreign travel in the 1960s and 1970s eroded the business of Britain's holiday resorts, and this gradual decline continues. Some resorts have been able to adapt to other industries and have successfully fought back by improving their conference facilities, or by providing attractions for coach tours, but the location of others has made it difficult to maintain a viable tourist trade.

At the same time the congestion of inner cities and the improvements to bypasses led to the appearance of out-of-town hotels, served by main roads and on large sites, landscaped to provide car parking and a degree of peace and quiet. Group-owned "bedroom factories", offering few dining or bar facilities, but catering for the businessman, appeared outside many towns and yielded considerable profits.

Increasing sophistication led to a growth of wine sales, at the expense of beer, and to more health awareness towards diet. The large brewers grew by takeover, and then expanded into the hotel scene, competing with the established hotel groups for the bigger hotels. Fast food and franchising led to the appearance of theme pubs and restaurant chains.

The prosperity of the 1980s, augmented by lower taxes on higher incomes, led to a leap in spending at luxury level and there was rapid growth in the development of country house hotels, followed in the late 1980s by sudden interest in golf hotels. The boom continued into 1989 when the English Tourist Board reported a record year for tourist investment in England, 70% up on 1988, with 96 new hotels under construction in December.

As corporate profits rose in the 1980s, the hotel industry experienced its full share of company takeover and acquisition, and it seemed that, as fast as hotels could be enlarged or built they were acquired by groups large and small. One of the largest takeovers, Mount Charlotte's acquisition of Scottish & Newcastle's Thistle Hotel Group for £645m, took place just before it became apparent that the boom was over.

It was not until the early 1990s, however, that the full implications of the inevitable collapse in values became fully apparent. To any detached observer of the hotel market it was obvious that values could not long continue to rise at the rate maintained in the late 1980s, and that the speculative market must end. There had been a short sharp boom in 1972/73, and a lesser one in 1988/89, but in neither case was the speculative market so long-lived, or the price/earnings ratio so high. A material drop in values was predictable in the light of the experience of the two previous cycles, even without anticipating the depth of the economic recession of the early 1990s.

When the recession hit the economy, spending on non-essentials like hotels and leisure declined rapidly coinciding with the imposition of high interest rates on borrowings which were in many cases excessive. Tariff cutting in the fight to maintain room occupancies further eroded profits, and the collapse of the property market in other sectors affected the value of hotel freeholds. Hotels and hotel groups were soon in trouble, with widespread reductions in share prices and many receiverships and closures. The fall in hotel values varied widely between different regions and the different categories of hotel, as banks realised that profitability and not asset value should be the basic lending criterion.

By the end of 1993, however, it was apparent that the worst was over, and 1994 saw an average rise of operating profit for UK hotels of 17.1% (Source: *Pannell Kerr Forster Associates' Statistical Report Outlook: UK Trends* 1995 Edition). Room occupancy rose to 69.8 per cent, against 64.7 per cent in 1993 for the total sample. Average room rate increased by just under £2 to reach £56.31. In London the rise in average room rate was twice the UK average. It is anticipated that 1995 and 1996 will see an acceleration of this recovery.

As the industry moves forward it will become ever more sophisticated. Branding and group marketing muscle have made economies of scale increasingly important. Leisure facilities are a useful marketing tool, if not always operating at a departmental profit. Most hotels in public companies are three, four or five star, and many hotel companies are affiliated to groups which are subsidiaries of larger companies, such as brewers or leisure or property companies. New budget hotels represent the fastest expanding part of the UK hotel industry.

Individually-owned hotels and small groups have responded to group pressure by joining buying and marketing consortia. This American concept has been adopted by hotels operating at different levels, some, like Pride of Britain, aiming to provide exclusivity and luxury, whereas others operate in the economy market. Members of Best Western have the right of veto to new members in their own area. Regional consortia like Welsh Rarebits combine to attract trade to their region.

Individually-owned hotels also rely on the guide books for promotion. Ashley Courtenay's *Let's Halt Awhile* led the way in the 1930s, and was followed by others. Few of the books can survive solely on sales revenue, and whereas some require a subscription from the hotels listed, others seek sponsorship or advertising or are owned by a larger organisation such as the AA, whose star ratings are still more widely recognised than the crown ratings of the Tourist Board.

Good food and individual service is the third weapon in the small hotel's armoury against the major groups. There always will be demand by the discerning for a change from the facilities offered in the large hotels, which can seem impersonal no matter how well run. Demand for personal service and individual attention in privately-run hotels, restaurants, and inns or wine bars will grow with other types of spending on leisure. Nevertheless the main future trend will be the continuing growth of the corporate market.

Big company activity can have a major influence on consumer choice, leading in turn to greater profit, investment growth and further expansion. The corporate structure stimulates the development of new brands, new products, and new hotel building. An important growth area is budget hotels, which generally have between 20 and 50 rooms, and have benefited during the recession from trading down by customers. New units can be built rapidly and cheaply on or near motorways and bypasses.

Recent trends in the industry

The holiday market
Travel for pleasure and holidays makes up two-thirds to three-quarters of all world travel by volume. Our climate militates against us, however, and the British penchant for travelling abroad gives the UK an adverse balance on tourism. Nevertheless tourism employed 1.5 million people in the UK in 1995 (Department of National Heritage).

Demographic changes will increase demand for facilities suited to people in older age groups who look for greater comfort and peace and quiet. They are less likely to travel abroad, leading to a partial reversal to be anticipated in the trend towards foreign holidays.

The short-break market
Patterns of home tourism are also changing. Whilst long home holidays decline, the short-break market grows. The weekend originated in London when, in 1732, the statesman Sir Robert Walpole persuaded the Commons to abandon its Saturday sittings so that he "might secure at least one day's hunting a week". The idea has caught on, and home tourism is a major industry, which has had its share of disappointment in the recession, with a substantial drop in occupancies and a tendency for those holidaying at home to economise by staying with relatives or friends for at least part of the time. However, 1995 saw an improvement, due partly no doubt to the hot summer, and there may be a further recovery as the economy recovers from the recession.

The short-break market has its own profile, career couples and middle-aged or retired people forming the major part. The most popular periods are the shoulder months – Easter/May and August/October. The most visited regions are the North West, West Country, London, Yorkshire and Humberside. 130 miles was the average distance between home and hotel, and trips were planned at short notice, two-thirds being booked within a month. Requirements are for good hotel accommodation, peace and quiet, variety of things to do in all weathers, and countryside. (Source: The Central Statistical Office.)

International travel
International travel is one of the world's biggest growth industries, and in 1994 expenditure within Britain by overseas visitors was £9.8 billion, a record year, with a further increase anticipated for 1995 (Source: *The Central Statistical Office*). However the adverse UK balance of payments for tourism worsened to an estimated £3.9 billion. The industry has to endure wide and unpredictable fluctuations brought on by such factors as the vagaries of British summer weather, hostilities such as The Gulf War and terrorism, and fluctuations in the respective value of currencies. The first five months of 1995, for example, showed a 10% increase in visitors from abroad as compared with the same period in 1994 (Source: *The Central Statistical Office*), partly because of a drop in value of the pound.

The business sector
Although growth in tourism is widespread in all categories, it is the business sector which has shown the greatest increase in the last two decades. This increase in business trade is of importance to the hotel industry, because business clientele are usually better spenders than private clientele. Not surprisingly business nights relate to economic activity. Improved motorways and telecommunications reduce the necessity for business nights, but growth in exhibitions, seminars and conferences can boost trade at appropriately located hotels considerably.

Conferences
The importance of training staff in modern business techniques has been recognised for some time. As the recession started to bite there was a flurry of demand for hotel conference facilities as companies sought to fight its adverse effect on profits, followed by an even bigger fall in demand as they cut overheads in the struggle for survival. Along with other sectors there has been some recovery in the early 1990s, but bookings are selective and cost conscious, and frequently left until the last minute. Since conferences are held throughout most of the year except in holiday periods they are a valuable source of trade to the industry.

Budget hotels

An important trend in Britain is the growth in number of budget hotels. The basic components of a budget hotel are low price, standardised format, high throughput, 2 star standard en suite bedrooms, and brand marketing. They generally have between 20 and 50 rooms, and should achieve an average room rate of £29 at 1995 values with an 80% occupancy. The AA recognised the trend by introducing the "Lodge" category in its listings in the 1980s. Developed separately in France and the USA, budget hotels were introduced to Britain initially by the French with such names as Accor's Ibis chain, Campanile, and others. British companies have followed suit with Forte's Travelodge, Granada's Motorlodge, Whitbread Travel Inns, and others, while American names like Holiday Inn Express and Marriott Courtyard have also arrived. One of the advantages to large companies lies in their suitability for franchising or management contracts, and in offering inexpensive facilities in times of economic recession. The opening of a budget hotel can affect trade and profits of existing hotels in the vicinity, with a consequent reduction in value.

Golf hotels

The 1989 estimate by The Royal and Ancient at St Andrews that there was a need for a further 700 golf courses in addition to the existing 1,900 led to a surge of interest which has included the creation of golf hotels. The high cost of developing golf courses, with or without hotels, led to excessive borrowings for golf course developments in the 1980s, and an excess of courses on the market in ensuing years. Viability of new developments has to be evaluated with caution, and the cost of creating a new golf course can exceed values at mid-1990s prices. Experience shows that viability of golf depends upon close proximity to major and well to do population centres, although there are some successful destination courses, usually in exceptionally attractive surroundings. Golf can also be subsidised by the sale of debentures to members, or by support from other parts of a development, to which it provides an amenity enhancement in return. Hotels are an example of such a development.

Agriculture relies heavily on EC subsidies, and value of farmland varies with changes in the Common Agricultural Policy as regards grants, loans, and set-aside etc. More farmland becomes available at lower prices for alternative uses such as golf when agricultural subsidies fall, but an over-riding factor is likely to be a shortage of suitably attractive and well-located sites, which are also acceptable to planners and environmentalists. Reluctance to see farmland converted to golf is likely to limit the numbers of new golf hotel developments in Britain, although some growth can be anticipated.

The Monopolies and Mergers Commission (MMC) Report
Somewhat more marginal to the hotel scene are the after-effects of the 1989 MMC report *Supply of Beer*. The Government's ensuing directives required the brewers to reduce their tied house estates by November 1992. A large number of pubs were offered coincidental with the property recession, helping thereby to depress pub values further, and hence the value of all licensed property, hotels included. There were closures, together with a major restructuring of the companies owning both breweries and tied estates. The limitation to 2,000 tied outlets per brewery (with the requirement that half of those in excess of this figure must be free of tie) means that brewers now seek to hold fewer but larger outlets. The possibility that the 1997 European Commission review of the block exemption for the beer tie may impose further restrictions on tied house ownership could lead to further major redeployment of pubs thereafter, with possible repurcussions on licensed and leisure property values generally.

Categories of hotel

Provincial hotels take their characteristics and style of operation first from whether they are group or privately owned and whether they are fully licensed or have a restricted licence, usually restaurant/residential.

They may be purpose built, including modern hotels to serve motorways, bypasses, airports, ski or holiday resorts and conference centres. The 19th century saw hotels built to serve spas, seaside resorts and railways. Before then inns and hostelries developed to serve the mail coaches, or grew up in towns and villages.

In more modern times hotels have been developed from a variety of redundant buildings, including the country and town houses of the rich, mills, forts and others.

Hotels are inclined to specialise, depending on the facilities they offer. Good modern facilities and a suitable location enable an hotel to charge high tariffs in a commercial letting trade. Attractive and quieter surroundings lead to up-market exclusivity combined with service and haute cuisine. Competition can lead an hotel to market itself by offering leisure facilities. Other hotels have been developed for functions and weddings. Conference facilities help to fill bedrooms. Golf and sporting hotels are developed wherever people come to follow a pastime.

Regional variations

The value of hotel property in the regions reflects local prosperity and commercial property values generally. There is a premium on hotels located in areas which are seen as being desirable on the grounds of amenity or fashion. Many corporate hoteliers feel that seasonal areas generally offer less scope for profit than do those which provide a dependable trade year round, with a consequent reduction in values.

As would be expected, London and the south-east of England normally attract the highest prices, followed by the Midlands where access to the NEC and the International Convention Centre is an important consideration. By and large the further north and west the location the more can be bought for a given sum in the way of property and trading (rather than profit) capacity. London and the south-east respond most quickly to value fluctuations, the outer provinces following the trends after some delay, which has the effect of reducing the differentials in the peaks and troughs of value.

Certain areas have traditionally been priced in relation to the rest of the region. The South Hams in Devon, the Cotswolds, parts of Yorkshire, the Lake District and Perthshire are examples of high-amenity areas each of which commands a premium. Cardiff and the M4 corridor in South Wales are favoured in relation to the rest of Wales where hotel values have trailed behind those in England increasingly since the 1960s. Short tourist seasons in north Norfolk, north Devon, parts of Lancashire and north-east Scotland restrict trading performance and hence sale value. Narrow coastal strips with moor or hill inland may look attractive, but suffer from lack of accessible populations, examples being between the Bristol Channel and Exmoor, North Northumberland between the North Sea and the Cheviots and the west coast of Cumbria.

Coastal regions also suffer because much of the potential catchment radius is inundated by the sea. The larger the marine sector the worse the effect. Local economies on headlands like east

Kent, south-west Cornwall, the Lleyn Peninsula and isolated parts of the Scottish coastline suffer from being cut off by the sea from a number of sides, and local hotel values suffer with them. On the other hand, hotels on the Channel Islands and the Isle of Man offer a better post-tax return on profits in times of high taxation.

The hotel valuer should also bear in mind the regional differences in value not only between property values but also between values of turnover. Tariffs and menu prices of food and drink vary according to the ability of local people to pay. While staff costs also vary considerably with the regions, other overheads remain more constant. High-volume sales in Scotland, where gross profits may be low and overheads may be high due to the remoteness of the outlet, obviously have less profit potential than a similar sales volume in a region where the operator can shop around for supplies and services.

Seasonal differences

The most marked seasonal variation in hotel values applies to holiday hotels in resort areas, where the value of seasonal cash flow is understood on the local hotel market. If an hotel's profitable occupancy ends in October for the season, the owner will have to fund borrowings until cash flow starts again when the hotel opens at the beginning of the following season, which may be five or six months away.

Naturally most purchasers are reluctant to take up borrowings to complete a purchase as far ahead as this. Similarly, vendors who have defrayed the cost of borrowing and other winter outgoings become increasingly reluctant sellers as spring approaches. It is not unusual for some vendors to withdraw their hotels from the market if a sale has not been achieved by early spring on the grounds that it is now too late to reinvest in time for the season. The combined effect of this behaviour by buyers and sellers is to lead to a slack market in autumn, with prices rising and deals going through more quickly and easily as the spring approaches.

This effect is mitigated to some extent by the need for some buyers to take possession of the property sufficiently early to enable them to prepare for the coming season. Such preparations can include attending to repairs or alterations and advance marketing. For this reason the most pronounced seasonal variation occurs with the smaller owner-operated units. Larger hotels with a more complex business plan usually need a longer lead-in period, particularly if group-owned, so the spring premium may be less noticeable in such cases.

Even non-seasonal hotels can experience seasonal fluctuations in price. People feel more optimistic in the spring and more inclined to launch forth on new ventures. There is increasing impatience to go out and buy properties which are looking better with the sun shining on garden flowers than they looked on a rainy day in January.

It is not possible to quantify with any scientific accuracy how much the value of an hotel may vary seasonally, but it can be by a material amount and is unlikely to be less than 10% in the case of hotels in holiday areas.

Categories of purchaser

The hotel market divides into corporate and private, each with its own criteria and motives. The RICS 1995 Red Book states in the Guidance Notes for Valuers (GN 7.2.11) that "With most types of hotel, leisure and licensed property it is particularly important to be able to identify closely the type of person or entity which constitutes a potential purchaser of such a property (excluding a "special purchaser"). . . . Consequently it is essential for the valuer to have detailed knowledge of current trends and experience of purchasers' requirements in that particular market." This applies equally to both the corporate and the private sectors.

Motives for acquiring hotels

Profits
Hotels are usually valued on the profits method, and profits are, or should be, the principal motive for acquiring an hotel. Most corporate operators are motivated almost entirely by profit potential.

Development potential
All purchasers, whether corporate or private, prefer to think that a site offers some scope for expansion or development, and units which are fully developed have less appeal, particularly to private buyers. Development potential is, however, of marginal value only,

since the increase in value of adding on a wing of bedrooms or an extension to public areas is by no means certain to add value in excess of cost, at any rate in real terms. Except on exceptional sites like, for example, motorway junctions, airports and the like, the value of an hotel planning consent, whether as a start up venture or an extension to an existing unit, can be disappointing.

Speculative gain

The chance of a capital gain, either because of a rising market, or by means of entrepreneurial development of property or business with gainful sale in mind, plays a large part in the minds of many hotel buyers, particularly private entrepreneurial operators, rather than corporate.

Retail outlets

Brewers have a history of holding licensed property with a view to tying it to the sale of their products. Following the 1990 MMC Report the larger brewery estates are having to be reduced in size, but larger units of good quality where volume liquor sales can be achieved will always be of interest to brewers. The pub chains formed to acquire post-MMC brewery disposals have established a lively market for both managed and tenanted pubs, whether singly or in groups.

Status

The desire to own an attractive hotel property for its own sake is understandable. Country house hotels have the most obvious appeal to status seekers, but the acquisition of the leading hotel in a community can confer on those who value these things the status of being recognised by a large number of people as having made good. Hotel groups will on occasion aspire to raise corporate status by the acquisition of trophy properties. Hotels conferring status always value at a lower return than those which do not.

Tax-free living benefits

In times of high income tax the cash advantages to private operators of living in an hotel have considerable value. The smaller the hotel the greater the proportion of its value can be ascribed to living benefits to a resident proprietor. Hotels vary as to the quality of the private accommodation, but the opportunity to set family living costs against profits in return for a relatively modest charge from the Inland Revenue has strong appeal to many.

Independence

As people grow older they find it harder to be told what to do, particularly after being made redundant or reaching the highest level of promotion within their own organisation. To such people the appeal of being one's own boss is considerable. 45% of UK hotels generated sales of less than £100,000 a year in 1994 (Source: *"Hotels" by Key Note*). This report goes on to explain that many of the smaller units are in traditional holiday resorts. Although the total number of units is falling (14,410 in 1990 to 12,994 in 1994, largely as a result of recession) there is still a large market for small units for private operation by people seeking semi-retirement or a change in career.

From the foregoing it will be seen that there is a strong "human element" to the valuation of small rather than corporate provincial hotels. The analysis of recent comparable sales can on occasion be the most reliable method of valuing small hotels which can be identified as appealing to purchasers of this type.

General considerations

Location

"The three most important factors affecting the success of an hotel are location, location and location". This cliché has been ascribed to a number of successful hoteliers. No other factor affects so deeply the success, and therefore the value, of an hotel. Hotel locations are chosen for their perceived attraction to potential clientele and sources of business. The availability of suitable staff can also be a factor. In considering location it is advisable to check that the hotel is not to be bypassed by new road schemes, or threatened by new hotel developments, or the possible loss of an important company client.

The site

An hotel site should ideally provide it with some amenity, or at least car parking. Town-centre hotels lacking car-park facilities operate at a disadvantage, and values are reduced if such facilities are lacking.

Most purchasers like to buy an hotel with a site large enough to increase the accommodation, even if they have no intention of building extensions themselves. They seek growth potential, whether short or long term. An hotel which has been developed to occupy its site fully will therefore appeal to fewer buyers than one which can be extended.

Hotels on restricted sites in town centres or resorts frequently cannot by their nature be extended, so this stricture applies less to them, but an out-of-town hotel property can be expected to command a better price if the site is large enough to take an extension and the extra car-parking spaces which would be required to go with it.

Local planning
Plans for major local development can affect an hotel's value by bringing employment to the area or clientele to the door. New roads and bypasses can bring new trade, or take existing trade away.

Hotels and inns which draw the bulk of their business from the main road can suffer loss of value if bypassed. If located near to alternative sources of trade their value can also be enhanced if a bypass removes heavy traffic allowing the business to attract a better class of local trade.

Compatibility
Corporates usually make the strongest sector of the hotel market, and the valuer needs to understand the requirements of the main players in the field. Many but not all hotels of sufficient capacity can be identified as fitting in with one or more corporate brands. If by reason of some defect of character or location a large hotel does not fit in with the requirements of any corporate buyers its value may be low, particularly if no alternative use can be identified.

Town planning and planning consents
As in all types of property an hotel's use must conform with all planning requirements.

Planning consents can add value to hotel premises in times of boom, or if there is a perceived shortage of hotel facilities in the area, plus a shortage of consents to correct the problem.

This does not happen often in provincial areas, unless a site has an outstanding location on main road intersections or at airports, exhibition centres, or other positions which enable the operator to gain definite advantage over the competition.

Many local authorities are keen to see hotel facilities increased in their areas, because they are regarded as bringing an attractive amenity and a spending clientele into the community. Planning consents will normally be restricted to sites which do not harm local amenities, but there are sufficient opportunities for hotel development in most provincial areas of planning sensitivity for scarcity value to develop only rarely.

Furthermore, the cost of building a new bedroom wing or restaurant extension will not necessarily enhance value much beyond the cost of the work. Frequently the cost will be more than the increase in value.

For these reasons planning consent will not necessarily increase the value of an hotel, although it may make it more attractive in the eyes of a purchaser who takes comfort from the fact that, even if he does not want to develop the site himself, he may one day be able to sell on to someone who does.

Most finance sources for hotels and leisure are more concerned with ensuring that their loans or equity are serviced adequately by short-term cash flow than in development propositions. Purchasers depending on debt or equity finance will be unable to pay a high premium for a planning consent therefore, unless they have a successful track record of similar developments, or perhaps unless the project is in some way exceptional.

Value during and after construction or extension
Most categories of commercial property reach maximum value when construction and landscaping works are completed and they are ready for occupation.

Since hotels are valued by reference to profits, however, it follows that newly-built hotels do not reach their full value until they have been trading long enough for their trading accounts to prove their success and value in the market. The same applies to the value of hotels which have been extended.

The charts show the difference between hotels and other types of property. In the case of hotels there is a period of perhaps two or three years (see Figs 9.1 and 9.2) when the cost of the new hotel, or an extension to an existing hotel, exceeds its sale value.

Condition of property
While a valuation does not include a structural survey unless specifically requested, the hotel valuer's eye should be trained for symptoms of structural defects, just as it would be in valuing any other kind of property, and make an appropriate adjustment to his valuation to allow for making good perceived structural defects, or backlog of repairs.

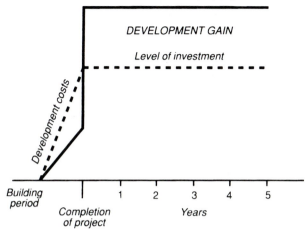

Fig. 9.1. Pattern of increasing values following development of offices, shops, factories and houses. (Inflation discounted.) *Source*: Robert Barry & Co.

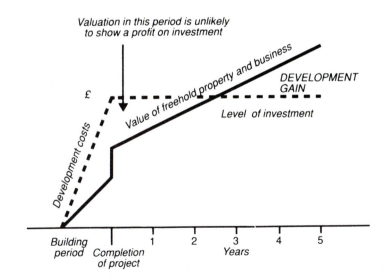

Fig 9.2. Pattern of increasing values following development of hotels and licensed property. (Inflation discounted.) *Source*: Robert Barry & Co.

If in any doubt the valuer should recommend a purchaser to take the appropriate advice as to structural condition and to make an appropriate discount thereafter. Wear and tear on fixtures and fittings and decorations is especially heavy in licensed property and maintenance expenditure has to be maintained constantly if there is not to be a rapid deterioration.

Competition

New competition from a modern hotel with superior location and appointments or from a budget hotel with competitive tariffs can have a serious effect on trading performance and value of an existing business. The valuer should be aware of this risk. Likewise, good food establishments are at risk from new and enthusiastic competitors setting up and undercutting prices. For this reason hotels and restaurants relying on good food are regarded as vulnerable investments and valued accordingly.

There can be occasions when the arrival of new hotels can help to make a venue more attractive to the public. The development of ski resorts in the Scottish Highlands of necessity includes new hotel development, for example. Existing hotels, particularly those offering personalised service, can benefit more from the influx of visitors than they lost to the new competition.

Clientele

No operator wants trouble with his clientele. Young people can be tough and difficult to work with. Sophisticated high spenders can be demanding and threatening to those lacking the social skills to handle them. All classes of trade require special skills in handling people in outlets with a heavy consumption of alcohol. Such considerations will be important in the eyes of many buyers and affect value.

The prudent purchaser also hesitates to buy an hotel which is reliant on a small number of customers. Some towns rely on one major employer, and all tradesmen there are at risk if that employer cuts back. A proportion of hotels relies on substantial bookings from a limited number of company clients. The prudent operator avoids over-dependence on one source of trade and purchasers should discount their bidding accordingly.

Standard and condition of contents

It takes a trained eye to assess the standard and condition of the inventory in an hotel. The skilled operator does not waste money on over-capitalisation of plant and equipment and a casual inspection can be deceived by cosmetic presentation of the business to purchaser or valuer. Skills have to be developed in assessing the quality and condition of the hotel's contents, including, for example, catering and storage equipment, furniture, furnishings, bar fittings, carpets, crockery and other sundries. Domestic-grade equipment and furnishings, however new at the time of inspection, have a short working life in commercial use and staff can be persuaded to make do with defective equipment which collapses immediately after the hotel changes hands. While a valuer cannot be expected to test any items of equipment, it is important to bear in mind the variation in price that can be paid because an hotel's appointments are above or below what might otherwise be anticipated.

The provisions of The Health and Safety at Work Act 1974 make it a matter of diligence for the proprietor of licensed premises to ensure that equipment is safe, rather than requiring him to carry out actual tests, but a valuer acting for a purchaser cannot place a value on equipment which is faulty. If a client wants an inventory valued separately his valuer should require him to arrange for all working equipment to be tested and certified before it is valued.

Most privately-owned and many group-owned hotels reflect the inclinations of their proprietors in the standard of their appointments. The retired engineer's hotel may be beautifully equipped behind the scenes, with the latest technology in central heating plant or heat-saving insulation, while lacking style and flair in decor. On the other hand, the ex-marketing man's hotel may have all the latest in drapes and design, with a leaking roof and neglected drains. If inadequately advised, the unwary may pay a high price for either, but the valuer has the responsibility of identifying the defects and quantifying them.

Gradings and guide book entries

An important part of the goodwill of an individually-operated hotel lies in its gradings and listings in hotels and gastronomic guides. These come in two main categories – those which require a payment from the hotelier for inclusion and those which are financed by other means such as book sales, sponsorship, advertising and subscription.

Few of the guides are commercially viable without financial support to supplement book sales revenue and they vary in status and circulation. Some are exclusive, aiming at a sophisticated clientele prepared to pay high tariffs. The best known gradings are the AA and RAC star systems, some hotels depending heavily on the business resulting while others find it irrelevant. The nearest Britain comes to a universal star system is the Tourist Board rating of one to five crowns, but, unlike in some countries abroad, there are no rules fixing tariffs, charges, or number of staff to be employed to the number of crowns awarded.

Special accolades are usually awarded to the operator, so they lapse when the business changes hands, being restored when the purchaser can convince a visiting inspector that the new management merit a similar award. Despite this automatic loss of listing, there is a time-lag between a sale and the production of the next issue of the guides. It can be unfortunate if a listing is cancelled following a sale and the new book goes to print before the inspector has had time to visit the hotel.

Some accolades are of more value than others. Awards which relate to the standard of letting bedrooms, for example, are less ephemeral than those which are in recognition of the catering skills of a chef proprietor, who takes his following with him when he quits.

Exceptionally high awards can also be a deterrent to prospective purchasers who may doubt, often correctly, that they have the skills to follow a vendor who is more competent than they are. This is of particular concern in a "restaurant avec chambres" where the vendor has also been doing the cooking. Difficult though they are to achieve, therefore, top accolades can on occasion make a catering business more difficult to sell than otherwise, with an effect on value that is not always beneficial.

The valuer also needs to recognise the situation where top accolades are received by an hotel at the expense of profitability. Attempts to give good value for food and service may lead to operators charging prices which do not leave adequate margins to lead to a satisfactory trading profit. Similarly, to upgrade an hotel from three to four stars can on occasion lead to an increase in service overheads which largely cancels out the benefit of the higher tariffs. In such cases an increase in turnover does not necessarily lead to growth in value.

The loss of accolades and listings, for whatever reason, is likely to lead to a reduction in the trade associated with them and this will result in a fall in the value of an hotel. Similarly a newly-developed hotel business will often make slow progress, particularly if it is a little off the beaten track, until it has attracted favourable comments in the guides and books. A valuer should be aware of these influences on sale value and make adjustments to his appraisal accordingly.

As public expectations grow and as hoteliers compete for custom, hotel appointments constantly improve, encouraged by ever more demanding requirements from the motoring organisations and the Tourist Boards in respect of any given star or crown rating. The required standard of bedroom appointments and minimum dimensions are increased periodically for each rating. The valuer needs to be alert to the fact that an hotel may be on the verge of losing one of its AA or RAC stars because new regulations require standards such as room sizes which it may be too expensive or too difficult to meet, with the consequent loss of star or crown.

It should also be borne in mind that an hotel will not necessarily do better by achieving an extra star if by doing so it puts off its regular clientele who may fear that it is now too expensive, particularly if the hotel's status does not suit it to the higher rating. It is better to operate a good 3 star hotel, appointed perhaps to 4 star standards, than to claim four stars when the hotel's status does not merit them.

Layout and construction

The layout of a well-planned hotel can greatly enhance ease of operation, with scope for reduced overheads and enhanced sales if properly planned. Apart from purchases, staff costs are the highest single outgoing so a well-planned modern hotel is designed for economy of staffing. Domestic areas need specialist planning and points of sale should be reduced to the minimum, with bar serveries, reception desks and other manned stations being placed together so that two or more can be covered by one person when business is quiet. Old-fashioned properties, especially fully-licensed coaching inns, inherit layouts designed in times when labour was cheap, and can be difficult to operate under modern conditions. Converted terraced houses frequently suffer from a multiplicity of staircases and inadequate horizontal communications on upper landings, especially where different levels make it difficult to break through from one former house to the next.

Modern construction and up-to-date fittings can also save overheads such as fuel costs by means of insulation, secondary and double glazing, economy lighting and modern heating systems. Maintenance-free roof coverings, surfaces and windows help save maintenance costs. Appropriate planning can also enhance turnover, especially at points of high-volume sales like bar serveries.

Customer satisfaction responds to a well-planned layout, starting with easy vehicular access and delivery of passengers to reception.

The reception area should be uncongested and welcoming, stairs easily negotiable, and corridors short. Sales frequently increase after internal partitions are removed and bars and restaurant areas made open plan, but care is needed to divide up large areas with screens and similar fittings to combine some privacy with a feeling of space. The AA and the Tourist Boards require ever larger bedroom dimensions and appointments if existing gradings are to be retained. Bedrooms should have a pleasant outlook, be well lit, warmed and ventilated, and free from noise from hotel plant, traffic or guests, especially late at night.

Proprietor amenity and status

Amenity and status account for a good part of the variations between yield and capital value that can be found between different types of hotel, and between different hotels of the same type, particularly for small to medium-sized units.

Resident proprietors (as opposed to corporate purchasers and those who propose to live off-site) will pay better prices for hotels which offer them superior facilities. These include living accommodation, which may be a bed-sitter overlooking a noisy street at one extreme, or a private house in its own garden at the other. Other amenities may include a yacht mooring, riding facilities, shooting or fishing rights, or the opportunity to entertain in a prestigious restaurant. Status of ownership has strong appeal to those who aspire to a mediaeval castle or an 18th century manor.

Even a small guest house contains a residential element in its market value. A purchaser knows that to acquire and live in a flat will cost a substantial amount in annual outgoings, including mortgage interest, heat, light, food and drink. An hotel offers all these facilities plus a contribution towards such outgoings as motoring, telephone and marketing trips abroad. The capital value of such amenities is never easy to estimate, but plays a large, if subjective, part in a private purchaser's assessment of an hotel's value to him.

Availability of suitable staff

Staff shortages can create problems for hotel management, with a consequent effect on trading performance and hence of value. Resort hotels are dependent on staff many of whom change each year, have limited loyalties and can be difficult to train as a reliable and efficient team in time for each season. Regions with full employment, where demand for hotel facilities is strongest, may offer the local work-force jobs at wage levels above those normally paid to hotel staff, particularly in times of prosperity and economic growth. Rural areas may lack the leisure opportunities desired by sophisticated catering staff who have to be lured by tempting salary levels, with the additional requirement of living-in accommodation to add further to costs and management time.

On the other hand, hotels located near to population centres can sometimes draw on a locally-based pool of labour which, if offered reasonable pay and conditions, will assist good management to operate at satisfactory margins.

The Food Safety Act 1990
The Act came into force on January 1 1991. It is largely an "enabling act", subject to regulations, of which the Food Hygiene (Amendment) Regulations 1990 are relevant to hotels. The legislation empowers magistrates' courts to impose heavy penalties and fines. The regulations are tough and are inclined to affect the viability of certain types of food retail outlets. The legislation is enforced by enforcement officers (formerly environmental health officers), who decide if premises conform with the regulations. While no valuer can be expected to advise on detail, he needs to be aware of the risk involved in operating with substandard equipment and arrangements.

Transfer of undertakings regulations
Provisions relating to employment rights on the transfer of a business such as an hotel are contained in the Transfer of Undertakings (Protection of Employment) Regulations 1981, as amended by the Transfer of Undertakings (Protection of Employment) (Amendment) Regulations 1987. The regulations do not cover sales effected by share transfers where there is technically no change of employer.

In asset sales, however, the main effect of the 1981 regulations is that in acquiring a business a new employer inherits the contracts of employment of the persons employed in it. Any such employee who is dismissed by his new employer merely because of the transfer of ownership may present a complaint of unfair dismissal to an industrial tribunal.

The Department of Employment's leaflet PL699 explains the legislation in detail.

A vendor operating an over-staffed business may be requested by a purchaser to meet him over the cost of compensation to staff entitled to claim under the legislation.

Items on hire purchase, lease, etc.
Most hotels operate with at least some items of equipment on hire purchase or hire. The most common examples are television and radio sets, telephones, microwaves, fire-precaution equipment and food refrigerating and freezing plant etc.

Items on hire purchase or lease purchase are deemed to be the property of the vendor, who is required to redeem the HP agreement and include the items on the inventory.

Items on hire or lease are frequently taken over by the purchaser, unless he objects that the terms of the hire agreement are unreasonable or too expensive, or that he does not want the equipment. In such a case a vendor may be left with heavy costs in buying himself out of the contract.

To cover this point the valuer needs to know if there are items on hire or lease which would normally be owned and the value adjusted accordingly. If, for example, it transpires that the bar fitting, carpets and furniture in the bar are all on lease, as can happen on occasion, an appropriate reduction in value should be made.

Licences
The valuer needs a basic understanding of the different kinds of liquor licence as set out in chapter 1. There are differences between England and Scotland and also local variations as to the application of the law.

A full on-licence (a public house licence or an hotel licence in Scotland) permits consumption of alcohol without the need by the customer to eat or sleep on the premises. It is the typical pub licence, but is also usual in town-centre hotels and indeed in any sizeable hotel which offers a full service to the public. It can be a useful attribute not only in boosting liquor sales but also in marketing, as a potential customer can more easily investigate an hotel with future patronage in mind if he can pop in for a drink, or he may be introduced to it by a friend, who would not have been able to take him for a drink at premises with a restricted licence.

A restaurant licence, as its name implies, gives a restaurateur the right to serve alcohol to diners, but he has to turn away custom from those who are not eating. A residential licence (restricted hotel licence in Scotland) enables a resident to drink without eating. Many small hotels operate with restaurant and residential licences, which require less in the way of bar facilities and regulations from the licensing authorities, and also enable the proprietor to turn away custom he does not want. This can be important if he is aiming for exclusivity in bar and restaurant.

A restaurant certificate (or supper hour certificate) is needed by a fully-licensed establishment to enable diners to drink for up to an hour after pub licensing hours have ended.

Public entertainment licences are required for places and occasions when people come for entertainment. Special hours certificates are for late night functions and occasional licences for a licensee who wishes to sell liquor from a location other than his own premises eg village fetes, race meetings, etc. An off-licence permits the sale of liquor for consumption off the premises.

In addition to liquor licences, The Marriage Act 1994 enables hotels and other venues to apply for a licence for marriages to take place on the premises.

A licence confers a degree of monopoly in many trading situations, conferring a value which can be regarded as part of the value of the goodwill. The loss of a licence for any reason, if only temporary, obviously leads to a rapid loss in trade, goodwill and value.

Fire precautions

Fire precaution work is needed for all commercial premises. Under the Fire Precautions Act 1971 the Fire Precautions (Hotels and Boarding Houses) Order 1972 requires that a fire certificate be obtained for any premises used as an hotel or guest house if sleeping accommodation is provided for more than six persons (whether guests or staff) or there is some sleeping accommodation above the first floor or below the ground floor. The owner must notify the fire authority of any proposed material alterations to premises with a fire certificate. The valuer needs to establish that there is a valid fire certificate at the time of valuation, or to mention in his valuation if he has not inspected it.

Tourist Board grants

In England these are normally repayable if the hotel is sold within 10 years of the receipt of the grant. This has not always been the case, but the administration of the regulations was tightened in 1989, so that it is now more difficult to get this requirement waived than used to be the case. Vendors who have received grants should be warned that, unless they are very persuasive, they will be required by the Tourist Board to repay some or all of the grants within 10 years on sales other than company sales. Vendors who can argue that they are retiring for health reasons or with retirement in view can sometimes negotiate a waiver of the repayment requirement. Grants ceased to be available in 1988 so the requirement to repay on a sale within ten years is now met less frequently.

In Scotland, Tourist Board grants are not repayable even on a sale provided the conditions under which the grant was made are met, such conditions typically including a requirement that the premises continue to be used as an hotel.

Restrictive covenants

Many properties still have restrictive covenants on the sale of liquor dating from the days of temperance movements and brewery sales. Unless such covenants can be lifted they are a risk to the value of premises as licensed outlets.

Brewer's tie

When an hotel is subject to a brewer's tie, the operator is restricted in his ability to offer choice of liquor to his clientele, and also negotiate discounts from his suppliers. The result of such constraints will show in the trading accounts and should be taken into account in preparing trading projections.

There were two orders following the MMC report – Supply of Beer (Tied Estate) Order 1989 and Supply of Beer (Loan, Ties, Licensed Premises and Wholesale Prices) Order 1989. These have led to the relaxation of the system of brewers' ties, and purchasers and lenders are now inclined to take a less concerned view than used to be the case. Nevertheless, a freehold or a leasehold with a tie to a brewery may need to be appropriately discounted in value to take account of any reductions in profits resulting.

A tie agreed by a proprietor in return for a brewery loan will normally be discharged on repayment of the loan, so should not need to be regarded as a valuation factor.

Uniform business rates

In assessing profitability by reference to existing trading accounts the valuer should adjust the charge for UBR to take account of any variation in rates payable in current and future years taking into account the phasing procedures involved in the application of transitional relief.

Group hotels

The value of hotels sold as part of a homogeneous group is enhanced in recognition of the advantages conferred by the economies of scale and the benefits of branding and group marketing. Similarly, if an hotel is sold out of a group the valuer needs to recognise that trading performance is likely to suffer when it can no longer enjoy these benefits.

Principles of valuation: the profits method

Hotels are valued freehold or leasehold and complete with goodwill and trade contents. The lump-sum figure excludes wet and dry stock (food, liquor, fuel and consumables) and personal items of furniture etc, which can be claimed as personal property by the vendor.

Such items can be a cause of dispute when being used by the vendor of businesses, and purchasers sometimes insist on appropriate replacements. Items of ornament such as clocks and pictures are more often removed by vendors, at any rate in privately-owned hotels. There is a story that the purchaser of a group-owned hotel found a Greek vase in it, which he sold for more than the price he paid for the hotel, so vendors with a genuine claim to personal items can have an equitable case.

It is usual for an inventory of movables to be attached to the contract for sale. There can be differences between the parties as to whether antiques in an up-market hotel are part of the business and compromise may be needed on occasion. Glasses in use are normally included in the inventory. Glass, cutlery, crockery and other items not yet in use but still in the packing cases in which they were delivered are valued as stock. Brochures are valued as stock unless they are branded.

Stock is valued on completion day by a stock-taker acting independently between the parties, unless there is a large stock or one which contains special wines in which case a stock-taker may act for each party with provision for an umpire in the event of disagreement.

The cost method

In parts of the world where land is cheap and planning consent easily obtained, the cost of acquiring a site and building a new hotel can be used as a means of valuing existing hotels. In the UK such a method is unlikely to yield an accurate assessment of market value.

Market comparables

In times of a stable and healthy market, evidence of recent comparable transactions can be a reliable method of valuation, if sufficient comparables are available. This may indeed happen if the subject property is in a city or large resort where genuine comparables are known. Comparables are not often available, however, for most provincial hotels.

In times of recession sale prices may drop below what a prudent purchaser will pay and bargains can be picked up by a well-advised entrepreneur in hotel property. Likewise evidence of recent sales in times of boom can be a dangerous method of valuation, as in *Corisand*, p. 425 ff. In these circumstances, hotels are best assessed by reference to their potential yields. If, after being advised of commercial value, the purchaser wishes to pay over the odds for speculative or other reasons, or a bank wishes to lend in order to compete in the market, they may feel free to do so, but at their own risk.

There will always be a substantial minority of hotels where the comparable method is the most appropriate because the commercial element is only a small part of value. For example, an elegant Queen Anne house in its own grounds overlooking a Cornish estuary may only have a turnover of £70,000 pa as a licensed country hotel, but could sell for £250,000 to a rat-race escaper, who has sold a modest house in a London suburb for more than that. The valuer in the non-commercial sector of the hotel market will therefore rely on comparables for properties which are operated on a relatively non-commercial basis. The more commercial the operation the more appropriate the profits method becomes.

A commonly applied rule of thumb is value per bedroom, and this can be a helpful if superficial check when comparing similar hotels with each other, for example in resorts or large towns. It has to be remembered that bedrooms are one of many criteria in hotel valuations, so the hotels being compared have to be similar in other characteristics, including location and trading performance, if value per bedroom is to be valid.

The profits method

Hotels are specialised buildings which cannot easily be adapted for other purposes. Furthermore, it is relatively unusual for hotels to be let at a rack-rent. For these reasons hotels are traditionally valued by reference to perceived trading capacity and likely profitability.

Few hoteliers provide their own finance. Most private purchasers gear themselves up with loans of 50% or more, and corporate buyers are usually financed by the City. The hotel vendor needs to convince not only the purchaser and his advisors, but also the prospective financier, as to the value of the business and its ability to service typical gearing.

Trading projections are therefore required to finance a sale, and market values follow from these projections which should preferably be based on actual performance, if possible over a period of years. Whereas three or four years' trading accounts may be available for larger outlets, it frequently happens with smaller units that there has been a change of ownership within that time. Since most hotel owner-operators lack formal hotel or business training, hotel accounts frequently show unexpected results. Accounts for group-owned hotels may also exclude some overheads such as marketing on the grounds that they are picked up by the group itself. The hotel valuer needs an understanding of the trade in arriving at a true identification of profit. If the business has not been run properly he needs to form a view as to how a purchaser can put things to rights, at what cost and over what time-scale.

Viability in hotels is largely governed by size. All businesses benefit from the economies of scale, but hotels in particular show better profit margins if they are over a certain size. This is because all hotels carry certain fixed overheads, many of which are not greatly increased by adding more bedrooms. The cost of maintaining parking facilities for 50 bedrooms, for example, is not much greater than for 25. One receptionist can service a reception desk for 50 bedrooms as effectively as for 10 for most of the day. If these considerations are taken right through the hotel the economies of scale are substantial. Increasing letting capacity by 30% can double profits, provided, of course, that the hotel's restaurant, bar and other facilities have the extra capacity.

Viability is also enhanced by group purchasing, branding and marketing. An hotel being offered for sale out of a group is likely to suffer a reduction in performance at least temporarily and the valuer needs to discount the sales and profit figures accordingly. For these reasons hotels are frequently worth more if sold as part of a compatible group than if sold off singly.

Care is also needed where an hotel's sales are derived from one particular source, as for example a major local employer, particularly if there are few others, or from a single tour operator. Return on investment should be higher in such cases, and even more so if the source of trade has a finite life, as in an oil town.

To be of assistance to a valuer, hotel trading accounts need to apportion sales as between food, drink, accommodation and sundries, all net of VAT. They should show the cost of food, drink, wages and all other outgoings in detail.

Before considering examples of trading accounts, it should be remembered that not all operators show their trading figures to best advantage. They may wish, quite legally, to reduce income tax. Many fail to operate to maximum efficiency. Others take long holidays, or are prey to pilferage. The following examples show a greater level of profits than is often shown in trading accounts, but lower than can be found on occasion. They are intended to show the likely pattern of income and expenditure which might be achieved by reasonably efficient operators in normal circumstances. In practice the variations in performance can be extreme.

The correct way of calculating operating profits also needs to be understood. Operating profit is net profit which has been adjusted by appropriate additions and subtractions. Rather than take one year in isolation, the valuer should take into account performance in other recent years as a check to ensure that the most recent year is representative of the hotel's current capacity.

Additions to net profit to arrive at operating profit include interest charges, rent (where it is a paper transaction), depreciation, amortisation, directors' fees and pensions, salaries paid to the proprietors and losses incurred in the disposal of non-trading assets such as cars. They may also include items charged to the business which are not strictly business outgoings such as a proportion of motoring (where the proprietor includes the cost of his two Rolls Royces in overheads!), and excess professional or legal fees (for the establishment of a new company for example). Gross profits can be adjusted if it is apparent that the operator is not achieving accepted levels for the type of business. Legitimate add-backs also include excess repairs and renewals where a major back-log is paid for in one year, or where repairs have a material element of improvement, excess wages where the owner is operating with wasteful staff levels and other overheads incurred needlessly or on a one-off or non-recurring basis.

Deductions from net profit to arrive at operating profit include those cases where the owners' family are doing a lot of work for little pay, adjustment for variation in uniform business rates to take into account the phasing procedures involved in the application of transitional relief, interest credited to the profit and loss account from bank deposits, profit on sale of motor vehicles or other non-trading assets, and a more appropriate allowance for repairs and renewals or other overheads where it is apparent that they have been skimped or not fully declared.

In the five examples of freehold hotels given below space does not permit a breakdown of overheads. Leasehold hotels are covered on p. 435 ff. Experience of hotel profit and loss accounts enables a valuer to cast an eye down trading accounts and projections to ensure that they do not contain any unusual items or exceptional levels of overhead. If they do, due adjustment should be made.

The first four examples below take four provincial hotels of different types but all trading at £650,000 pa net of VAT, in order to show how the results from any given turnover can vary. The exercise highlights the imprudence of using turnover or number of bedrooms as anything more than a very rough rule of thumb as a valuation tool. In each case the trading accounts compare with those of the previous two to three years, showing a steady level of trade.

It should be noted that there are regional differences both to trading patterns and to valuation multiples. Thus gross profits and overheads vary with the regions for all types of licensed property. Likewise, the valuer needs to draw on experience in arriving at an appropriate investment yield for each region.

Example 1

A 3 star fully licensed hotel, well placed on a good road serving a reasonably well to do community in the south of England, with 30 letting rooms plus a management flat and adequate bar, restaurant, function and parking facilities, might show a trading pattern as follows:

	Sales £	Gross profit %	£
Accommodation	220,000	100	220,000
Food	250,000	63	157,000
Drink	160,000	54	87,000
Sundries	20,000	100	20,000
Total sales	650,000	74	484,000
Wages	26%	£169,000	
Overheads	22%	£143,000	312,000
Net operating profit	26.3%		172,000

(Note: Gross profits are arrived at after adjusting for opening and closing stock.)

In this hotel there is a healthy balance of sales between the various departments, with a good gross profit achieved to reflect the quality of the hotel's facilities. It would appeal to a variety of buyers, including perhaps a small hotel group, a business wishing to diversify, or to an owner-operator. Disregarding elements of development potential offered by the site, or status which might accrue to a proprietor and therefore enhance sale value, the business value of such an hotel could be simply evaluated on the basis, say, of a 12.5% return.

Valuation

	£
Net operating profit	172,000
YP in perpetuity @ 12.5%	8
	1,376,000
say	1.4m

12.5% is appropriate for this hotel, well located as it is in southern England. A similar location in other regions could lead to a higher yield – say 18% in favoured parts of Scotland; even more in less well-favoured areas. Likewise regional variations in overhead percentages need to be taken into account in checking accounts or preparing projections.

Note:
The percentage yields in all the examples given in this section are arrived at by reference to average conditions observed in the economic cycles which took place in the thirty years following the late 1960s. Yields on all commercial property vary with the times and hotels are no exception. The hotel valuer has to take account of such market fluctuations and to distinguish between genuine changes in investment climate and the intrusion of the speculative element.

This valuation would need to be adjusted upwards in respect of any development or status value and downwards to take account of liabilities such as those enumerated above.

A very different value might be placed on the same turnover, but with a different type of hotel, as in the next example.

Example 2

This is a 2 star fully licensed hotel, converted from a former roadside inn, with 12 letting bedrooms, a luxury private flat and banqueting facilities for 600 and a large beer garden. The trade is essentially volume sales at the competitive prices which go with functions and family meals. Bedroom sales are low, reflecting the small size of the rooms, which are old fashioned and suffer from noise during functions and from the car park at night.

	Sales	Gross profit	
	£	%	£
Accommodation	65,000	100	65,000
Food	335,000	55	184,000
Drink	240,000	50	120,000
Sundries	10,000	100	10,000
Total sales	650,000	58	379,000
Wages	20%	£130,000	
Overheads	17%	£110,000	240,000
Net operating profit	21.4%		139,000

The valuation of a fully-licensed functions centre is never easy, depending very much on the location and style of the premises. This one will appeal to those attracted by turnover rather than profits, by the chance for cash takings on the door, and a large cash flow. They are in fact hard work, with long unsocial hours, and competitive in the sense that anyone booking a large wedding or hunt ball can make a substantial saving on the total cost by ringing round to obtain alternative prices – far more so than when ordering a family dinner or business lunch. If situated near to a large industrial town the clientele may be tough and the way of life demanding. As seen from the example above, trading margins can be low.

The figures show a low gross profit reflecting the need to cut prices to maintain sales. The apportionment of sales is poor, with low bedroom sales, so overall gross profit is low, but people do not want to sleep above a dance floor. Wages percentage is low, however, since the standard of service is not high and the meals are served plated up. General overheads are also low in relation to turnover as the premises are not extensive and high standards of furnishing and decor are not expected. It is the low gross profit on food and drink which is the main obstacle to increasing profits.

Since it is of more appeal to an owner-operator a business of this kind is more likely to have a luxury private flat, and this amenity, together with the appeal of the high turnover in relation to floor area, will encourage bidding at quite low returns. Here again regional variation will be wide – say 12.5% in an up-market part of the Cotswolds, 15% in parts of the north of England or Scotland, or maybe as much as 20% in northern Scotland (where, however, ratios of gross profits and wages can be somewhat different).

Valuation

	£
Operating profit	139,000
YP in perpetuity @ 12.5%	8
	1,112,000
say	1.1m

		£
Operating profit		139,000
YP in perpetuity @ 15%		6.7
		931,300
	say	900,000
Operating profit		139,000
YP in perpetuity @ 20%		5
		695,000
	say	700,000

Once again the yield will fluctuate widely depending on the date of valuation in the economic cycle.

This valuation, as in example 1, needs adjustment up or down as appropriate to take account of regional variations. Consideration also needs to be taken account of whether one of the pub groups would pay more for this site if it could be acquired for incorporation into a themed outlet or franchise, in which case comparable sales may be more appropriate than the profit method in assessing value.

Similar turnover might be found in an up-market country house hotel specialising in good food, as in the next example.

Example 3

An attractive, period house in a few acres in southern England, accessible to main roads, population centres and suitable attractions; it has 18 luxury letting bedrooms and suites, a lounge, a restaurant, and a small indoor swimming pool. It is not of outstanding architectural appeal (which would have enhanced value for non-commercial reasons), but the owners operate as a family partnership and two cottages have been created from the outbuildings for them. Neither is suitable for selling off separately, so the valuation is simply for hotel use. Because the owners aim for exclusivity they operate with a restaurant/residential licence only. Prices and tariffs are high, and the hotel has achieved top accolades in the guides and three red stars AA.

	Sales	*Gross profit*	
	£	%	£
Accommodation	290,000	100	290,000
Food	225,000	65	146,000
Drink	115,000	60	69,000
Sundries	20,000	100	20,000
Total sales	650,000	81	525,000
Wages	31%	£201,000	
Overheads	31%	£201,000	402,000
Net operating profit	18.9%		123,000

Despite high food prices, cost of exotic food is high and waste is inevitable, so food gross profits are not as high as might be imagined. The ability to charge top prices for wines outside London is limited, but the guests expect good wine, so again gross profit suffers. Room tariffs are good, however, so 81% overall gross profit is achieved, but sophisticated staff and high staff levels are needed to achieve top standards of service, so wages are also high. The cost of maintaining and running a large old house and grounds also leads to high overheads, so the net operating profit is disappointing.

Such units appealed more to the optimism of the 1980s than to the more austere life-styles more usually followed in the 1990s. On the other hand the status of owning and operating at the top of this exclusive market is still very real and the market will bid accordingly in times of optimism, provided the prospect of rising rates of income tax does not threaten to annihilate the spending power of the better paid.

Valuation

	£
Operating profit	123,000
YP in perpetuity @ 8%	12.5
	1,537,500
say	1.5 m

It goes without saying that the high prices and tariffs payable in accessible parts of southern England cannot be achieved in the less prosperous regions, and tariffs and values in Scotland, for example, are likely to be considerably lower. On the other hand top class sporting hotels in Scotland or elsewhere, when operating in the international market, can and do command appropriately high tariffs, and may attract rich purchasers from abroad who will pay prices related more to status than to investment value. Here again recent comparables may be a more reliable guide than the profits method of valuation.

The list of examples of different patterns of trade on turnover £650,000 are endless, but a fourth may be useful in helping to show how values can vary for different hotels all taking the same amount, and for different reasons.

Example 4

A 60-bedroom, 3 star, fully-licensed hotel with better than average leisure facilities in a favoured resort, on the sea front and convenient for central attractions. It dates from the turn of the century and the public rooms are spacious if somewhat dated. The fully-licensed bars are patronised by hotel guests, but there is little local bar trade other than some casual meals and drinks sold to holidaymakers during the summer season. It is open all year, the bulk of the trade being done in seven to eight months. Holiday clientele is supplemented by conferences, a few local functions and limited coach tours which are deliberately restricted to early and late (in the shoulder months).

	Sales £	Gross profit %	£
Accommodation	250,000	100	250,000
Food	250,000	65	162,000
Drink	130,000	50	65,000
Sundries	20,000	100	20,000
Total sales	650,000	76	497,000
Wages	27%	£175,000	
Overheads	20%	£130,000	305,000
Net operating profit	29.5%		192,000

Food gross profit is high in relation to the quality of the food because much of the restaurant trade is standard *table d'hôte* and pre-booked to known quantities. Room occupancy and conferences depend on forceful marketing. Profitability is better in resorts which have a better climate, status, or amenities, allowing higher tariffs and a longer season.

Returns vary considerably depending on the resort. Well-favoured resorts like Bournemouth in the South, Blackpool and Scarborough in the North, and Oban in Scotland, offer better long-term security than those in the outer provinces.

There is so much variation that specialist up to date experience is needed to assess appropriate return, which, however, usually falls between 15% and 20% for the larger hotels. This range indicates the varying appeal offered by the different resorts to operators in this sector. Bournemouth in particular can offer low yields, although increasing competition from foreign holiday venues, modern conference hotels near large towns and motorways, and a growing variety of hotels with leisure facilities such as golf has steadily eroded confidence in Britain's resorts and their hotels.

It will be seen, therefore, that valuation factors vary between one resort and another. The hotel in this example could sell for as much as £1.3 million in a favoured resort, and for under £1 million in a resort where the supply of hotels exceeds demand.

Example 5

This is a modern 100-bedroom provincial hotel, 4 star, well located for conferences and business clientele, with a large site and car parking, and modern leisure facilities including indoor swimming pool, fitness centre, sauna, solarium, hairdressers, boutiques, etc. There are several large conference and function rooms, well planned for flexibility of operation, lifts to all floors and ample offices for the administrative and sales teams. Its location and character are such that it will appeal to hotel groups.

	Income		*Gross profit*	
	%	£	%	£
Rooms	51.2	1,100,000	100.0	1,100,000
Food	32.6	700,000	64.0	450,000
Liquor	13.9	300,000	60.0	180,000
Sundries	2.3	50,000	100.0	50,000
Total	100.0	2,150,000	82.8	1,780,000

Less	%	£		
Wages:				
Rooms	16.0	176,000		
Food	37.0	259,000		
Liquor	15.0	45,000		
Management	3.5	75,000		
Total wages	25.8	555,000		
Operating and establishment expenses	22.0	473,000		1,028,000
Net operating profit	35.0			752,000

This hotel shows a healthy apportionment of sales, with over 50% on room sales where the greatest profit lies. Costs in all departments are under firm control, but not to the detriment of maintaining standards. The modern construction and layout facilitates economies on maintenance and overheads.

Valuation

	£
Net operating profit	752,000
YP in perpetuity @ 9%	11
	8,272,000
say	8.25m

There are two potential factors which would encourage suitably positioned hotel groups to bid higher prices for an hotel of this category. If offered as part of a group of hotels with which it is compatible, its price as part of a package could be enhanced considerably. Similarly, an expanding hotel group in need of another outlet of this type or location should be prepared to offer more if it calculates that it could enhance performance without the injection of large further sums on improvements but by means of bringing into play its own group marketing or branding.

As detailed above, not only is there a wide variety of types of hotel, but each unit incorporates a different blend of the various types of trade available, leading to endless permutations of how the trade is made up, the levels of gross profit which can be achieved in each department, and a requirement for different standards of staffing and other overheads. Provided the requirements of each outlet are understood, however, and the principles of valuation applied correctly, accurate valuation of the commercial value of each hotel can be achieved.

This value then has to be adjusted upwards and downwards. Upwards to take account of development value, status of ownership, or the inclusion of assets which are not fully employed in the business – a private house, for example, a valuable inventory, sporting rights on hill or stream, or unexploited trading potential which can be tapped by a purchaser without the need for substantial capital expenditure.

On the down side the items listed above need to be remembered – structural problems for example, a loss of AA rating, the departure of personal goodwill with a high-profile vendor, the risk of closure of the main company client, a worn out inventory or too many items on hire or lease. There should also be suitable private and management or staff accommodation on site or available to suit the style of the business, and the price should be discounted appropriately in its absence.

The principals to the deal may be allowed the luxury of buying or selling because of their likes and dislikes. The valuer has to detach himself from his own sentiments, and remember that all that glisters is not gold, and also that even the least prepossessing places will appeal to someone.

Discounted Cash Flow (DCF)

A lively controversy followed the promotion of discounted cash flow (DCF) by The British Association of Hotel Accountants (BAHA) in 1993 as a method of valuing hotels and similar businesses as an alternative to the profits method, but there is no need to regard the two methods as alternatives. Instead they should be used to complement one another, whilst bearing in mind the reason why the client needs the valuation, and the purpose to which it is to be put.

DCF has been used by hotel companies for decades to evaluate acquisitions and to rank portfolios of hotels in terms of performance and hence their respective value to the individual companies. The BAHA Report was an attempt to avoid the propensity for valuers to yield to pressure to permit their valuations to follow the short term property cycle by extending the period to up to ten years over which profits and cash flow have to be evaluated.

Rather than applying a rate of return "in perpetuity" to an hotel's recent profit performance and projections, the DCF valuer applies it to cash flow discounted from one to ten years ahead. The future projections should normally be adjusted for inflation. The discount rate is the Government discount rate plus an appropriate risk rate. The total of the ten years' discounted figure equates to DCF value.

Subjective judgment is applied by a valuer viewing a business from the point of view of an individual client. A valuer appraising a unit in order to arrive at market value has to select a discount rate which seems to him to equate to a discount rate which will be acceptable to a willing purchaser who is acting "prudently and without compulsion" and has no "special interest". as in the RICS Red Book's definition of "market value".

Small hotels which are likely to appeal to private and less sophisticated purchasers may not be appropriate for DCF calculations. The valuer should look at the unit from the point of view of the hypothetical buyer, and if he is unlikely to understand DCF, its use may not be appropriate, other than as a theoretical check in marginal cases.

A criticism of DCF might be that no appraiser can forecast a hotel's performance ten years ahead. Even five years is too long for more than inspired guesswork. However, the calculations are more sensitive about the assumptions applying to the early rather than the later years, so reliance is not too heavily placed upon the expectation that the valuer can see many years ahead.

The subjectivity which has to be exercised in selecting the discount rate is still one opportunity for the client to apply pressure to the valuer to respond to short term market trends. If deals start to go through at ever lower yields in a property boom the DCF valuer needs to be no less aware of the dangers of valuing in a speculative market than he does when using other methods.

Comparing the results of different methods of valuation

It is unlikely that a valuer using comparables, the profits method, and DCF will arrive at the same valuation figure for all three methods, but they should be similar. If very different figures result the calculations should be checked for error of judgement. To select the method on the basis of whichever result best suits the requirements of one of the parties to a valuation will lead to error.

Hotel groups

The convenience of buying or selling a group of hotels in one deal as opposed to individual ones is very considerable. If the hotels are in one ownership the purchasers will acquire an existing management team, with marketing arrangements already in place. The lenders will find it easier to collate the information they require for the finance package if it is derived from a single source. Legal costs for a single sale will be lower, less complicated and less time consuming.

For these reasons it is recognised that a group of hotels, provided they are reasonably homogeneous, are likely to fetch a better price if sold together rather than separately.

The vendors will also be better suited by a single sale. It enables the vendor to be rid of the less attractive units in the group by using the more appealing ones to attract buyers. Hotels sold out of a group may also suffer a loss of trade once excluded from group marketing. Furthermore, staff will become demoralised if they see hotels being sold out of the group, fearing for their own future, and this unease may spread also to clientele; both eventualities can damage trade and hence value.

Group value is recognised as leading to prices which are higher than could be justified by valuations of the hotels individually. The actual amount of extra value will vary considerably, depending on the number of units involved and how well they go together as regards location, size, character, class and achieved profits.

Assessing existing accounts and preparing trading projections

The hotel valuer needs to be able to assess trading accounts and to prepare realistic projections if none are available. He also needs to be able to form a view on the validity of projections prepared by others.

Fig 9.3 is a sample trading and profit and loss account. Turnover is shown net of VAT and is apportioned between the three principal departments and sundries. The cost of food and drink deducted from sales gives gross profit. Operating overheads are divided between wages, operating expenses, and establishment expenses, and, when deducted from gross profit, leave the net operating profit. Financial expenses, depreciation and directors' emoluments (if any) are deducted from NOP to give net profit.

Sales		£1,100,000
Food		700,000
Liquor		300,000
Sundries		50,000
TOTAL SALES		2,150,000
Cost of sales		
Food	£250,000	
Drink	120,000	370,000
Gross profit		1,780,000
Wages and staff costs		555,000
		1,225,000
Other expenses		
Laundry	45,000	
Cleaning	20,000	
Gas and electricity	50,000	
Printing, stationery	15,000	
Telephone and postage	10,000	
Entertainment	8,000	
Property maintenance	40,000	
Repairs and renewals – equipment	47,000	
Staff training and recruitment	20,000	
Sundries	10,000	
Commission and discounts	60,000	
Bad debts	15,000	
Establishment expenses		
Rates and water	72,000	
Insurance	20,000	
Bank charges	3,000	
Equipment hire	20,000	
Audit and accountancy	10,000	
Legal fees	3,000	
Stocktakings	1,000	
Subscriptions	4,000	473,000
NET OPERATING PROFIT		752,000
Financial expenses		
Bank overdraft interest	30,000	
Mortgage interest	280,000	
Hire purchase interest	14,000	
Depreciation	40,000	£364,000
NET PROFIT		**£388,000**

Fig. 9.3 Sample trading and profit and loss account

The purchaser's financier will prefer actual trading records and may look askance at projections, so the finance available for the purchase will probably be less if the purchaser's loan application is based only on projections than would have been offered for the hotel had trading accounts been available. This is one of the reasons why newly built hotels, or hotels with new extensions or improvements, are likely to fetch materially lower prices on sale than they would have done had they been traded on for an appropriate period before being sold. Nevertheless, a valuer should be able to prepare and analyse trading projections.

Bar and restaurant sales have to be forecast in the light of knowledge of similar operations. Room sales have to be assessed in the light of achieved tariffs excluding VAT and breakfast, rather than those that are quoted in the hotel brochure or tariff sheet, taking due cognisance of group discounts, bargain breaks etc. Room occupancies vary by region and season and are published by various bodies including the tourist authorities.

Gross profits vary according to region and class of trade. They are likely to be higher in establishments offering good food and service, but wages and other overheads are likely to be higher too. In regions where cheap labour is available prices and gross profits can afford to be lower.

Maintenance and establishment expenses will be high in proportion to turnover in hotels where a relatively low-volume trade is carried on in a large property. Future contingencies should be allowed for in respect of property maintenance. The liability for uniform business rates should be checked, since the rates payable will rise on change of ownership if the vendor has been claiming transitional relief.

Marketing expenses must be adequately provided for. Items on hire purchase should be redeemed by the vendor, but the purchaser may be required to take over agreements for hire or lease of equipment, and these can be onerous.

Value, price and worth

There can be confusion between these three concepts. "Worth" is probably best defined as the subjective value to an individual or organisation of an interest judged against defined criteria. Assets are frequently "worth" more to the present owner than to the hypothetical purchaser.

"Value" is defined at length in the RICS 1995 Red Book.

The Royal Institution of Chartered Surveyors Appraisal and Valuation Manual (The 1995 Red Book)

Following considerable criticism of valuation methods after the property boom of 1972 and the bust of 1973, it became clear that there was a need for valuation standards in order to protect the public from misleading valuations. In 1976 the RICS responded by publishing the Red Book (initially entitled 'Guidance Notes on the Valuation of Assets' and in 1990 retitled 'Statements of Asset Valuation Practice and Guidance Notes'). It was concerned mainly with published valuations and in February 1991 it achieved mandatory status.

The White Book ('Manual of Valuation Guidance Notes') was published in 1980 to complement the Red Book. Whereas the Red Book is principally concerned with which basis of valuation to adopt in particular cases, the White Book deals with good practice in undertaking valuations. Although not mandatory, the importance of the White Book increased in recent years as the RICS expanded it to include guidance on best practice for undertaking valuations for loan security purposes.

The existence of two books was confusing clients, the courts and the media and inevitably led to some duplication of material.

There was also, following the publication of the highly influential Mallinson Report in 1994, pressure for making some fundamental changes to valuation practice generally, including consideration of the concept of "worth".

The new Red Book ('RICS Appraisal and Valuation Manual') was published in September 1995, although certain sections, notably the Guidance Note on Environmental Factors, are still being prepared at the time of going to press.

The 1995 Red Book merged, and in some cases revised, the contents of the old Red Book and the White Book. Whilst the two books continued as sources of best practice until the end of 1995, the new Red Book applies to valuations reported after 1st January 1996.

The 1995 Red Book prescribes certain requirements as mandatory (subject to a right to justify departure) in respect of valuations over a much wider range of services than those to which the old Red Book applies. It also incorporates about 60% of the recommendations of the Mallinson Committee.

In providing a valuation for secured lending purposes, the appropriate bases are:

1. *Open market value (OMV)*

   This basis assumes completion of a sale at the valuation date, the property having already been marketed openly for sale for an appropriate period. The 1995 Red Book Definition defines OMV in PS 4.2:

   "An opinion of the best price at which the sale of an interest in property would have been completed unconditionally for cash consideration on the date of valuation, assuming:

   (a) a willing seller;
   (b) that, prior to the date of valuation, there had been a reasonable period (having regard to the nature of the property and the state of the market) for the proper marketing of the interest, for the agreement of the price and terms and for the completion of the sale;
   (c) that the state of the market, level of values and other circumstances were, on any earlier assumed date of exchange of contracts, the same as on the date of valuation;
   (d) that no account is taken of any additional bid by a prospective purchaser with a special interest; and
   (e) that both parties to the transaction had acted knowledgeably, prudently and without compulsion".

   The only difference introduced by the 1995 Red Book is (e) which it is to be hoped may curb some of the excesses of valuations supporting excessive bids in competitive situations.

2. *Market value (MV)* (PS 4.1).

   This is an entirely new definition which is essentially the same as OMV, which it may gradually supersede:

   "The estimated amount for which an asset should exchange on the date of valuation between a willing buyer and a willing seller in an arm's length transaction after proper marketing wherein the parties had each acted knowledgeably, prudently and without compulsion".

3. *Estimated realisation price (ERP)*

   This assumes the same basis of sale (ie completion), but that the marketing period starts on the valuation date and the valuer provides an estimate of the price likely to be realised at some specified future date following marketing and taking into account likely changes – to the market, the property and the business – during this period.

   The 1995 Red Book defines ERP in PS 4.5:

   "An opinion as to the amount of cash consideration before deduction of costs of sale which the valuer considers, on the date of valuation can reasonably be expected to be obtained on future completion of an unconditional sale of the interest in the subject property assuming:

(a) a willing seller;
(b) that completion will take place on a future date specified by the valuer to allow a reasonable period for the proper marketing (having regard to the nature of the property and the state of the market);
(c) that no account is taken of any additional bid by a prospective purchaser with a special interest; and
(d) that both parties will act knowledgeably, prudently and without compulsion".

1995 Red Book definitions of value in distressed circumstances are dealt with on p. 434 ff.

The Guidance Note on Trading-Related Valuations (GN 7) now explicitly states what is required of a valuer in this sector of the market. Amongst other things the valuer should:

1. "have detailed knowledge of current trends and experience of purchasers' requirements in that particular market".
2. be able to "compare trading profitability with similar types and styles of operation" and have "a proper understanding of the profit potential of the relevant sector of the market".
3. "be aware of the impact of current levels of competition and, if he anticipates a significant change from existing levels, he should clearly identify such change in his report and the general impact it might have on profitability and value".
4. provide an opinion, when valuing for loan security "as to the sustainability of the type of business carried out within the property, and possible future fluctuations in its status as a security".

GN 7 summarises all matters relating to trading-related valuations. With regard to methodology GN 7.2.2 confirms that "different methods, including the profits method, discounted cash flow (DCF), analysis of comparable transactions, or a combination of these will be appropriate for different types and sizes of property".

PS 1.3 lists valuation and other matters to which The Red Book does not apply. The list is lengthy, and covers a large part of valuation work. Nevertheless, the valuer who follows its requirements, stating that he does so, has the advantage that there is no doubt where he stands.

(It is worth noting in passing that PS 12.6.2 and GN 7.3.1 both make it clear that the term "going concern value" must not be attributed to "land and buildings fully equipped as an operational entity and valued having regard to trading potential". "Going Concern relates to the net value of a company, not a trading property".)

The "speculative" element in "commercial" valuations

Cecil Graham: What is a cynic?
Lord Darlington: A man who knows the price of everything and the value of nothing.

Lady Windermere's Fan, Oscar Wilde

The changing fortunes of the hotel industry can in times of economic expansion attract speculative buyers intent as much on capital gains as on investment return, although a return to the speculative conditions of the 1980s is unlikely to occur for a while. Nevertheless the problems caused by that boom continue to rumble on and are worth further consideration.

Oscar Wilde knew that price and value are not necessarily the same and the hotel valuer needs to take extra care to acquaint himself of the difference, and not merely to follow the fashion of the moment.

The hotel trade is speculative because profitability can change more rapidly than for other sectors for two reasons:

1. In times of prosperity people spend more on luxuries. In recession they cut back on non-essentials like eating out and holidays. The hospitality and leisure industries therefore experience greater swings of turnover between boom and recession than most.

2. Hotel operating profits accrue after meeting all overheads, a large proportion of which are fixed. Once the fixed overheads are paid for, virtually all room sales are profit, and nearly half of food and drink sales should be too (after paying for variable costs such as food, drink and a proportion of wages, etc). Above a certain level of sales the proportion of turnover which ends up on the bottom line can therefore be very large, and the effect on hotel profits when turnover is high is dramatic.

Such prospects will attract a Klondike-style rush of speculators in time of economic boom. A shortage of commercial property investments and development opportunities in times of boom attracts property people to acquire hotels on returns which appear to be more attractive than those offered by other types of property. They do not always appreciate the significance of the difference between rents on the one hand and profits which require specialist hotel operating skills, and which are also more vulnerable to economic fluctuations, on the other. Speculation in hotel property is well documented as a problem for the hotel industry, including operators, financiers, and the valuers who serve both.

The recent history of the UK hotel trade provides three examples of hotel property boom – in 1972–73, 1979–80 and 1988–89. Fig 9.4 shows the historical trend in average hotel prices between January 1970 and early 1996. The most recent of these surges in value is a good example of how economic, political and fiscal changes can create sudden change in the financial environment in which hotels operate.

The decrease in the top rate of British income tax from 83 pence in the pound (98 pence on "unearned" income) in the 1970s to 40 pence in the late 1980s coincided with a period of economic prosperity to contribute to a massive increase in the spending power of the better paid. Hotels designed to cater for high spenders proliferated rapidly in the 1980s as a result, but their flowering was short-lived in many cases and when the boom ended those who had evaluated them only on the evidence of prices paid during boom conditions were quickly proved to have been mistaken.

Hotels, like most businesses, should be regarded as medium- to long-term investments. The establishment of an hotel business, from acquisition, planning, development, staffing, marketing, and the build-up of goodwill takes years. To rely too heavily on recent comparable sales in arriving at values is likely, therefore, to lead to disappointment following an acquisition in times of boom, and to a failure to make a good quality investment in times of slump.

The loss of opportunity for a good investment may be fortunate for the investor, but the consequences of a heavily-geared purchase at an excessive price can be tragic for all concerned if a forced sale ensues. The investor ranks after the unsecured creditors in receiving his share of the sale proceeds and may be left with nothing if the sale price is materially less than what he paid for the hotel initially. The creditors likewise may lose much if not all of what they are owed,

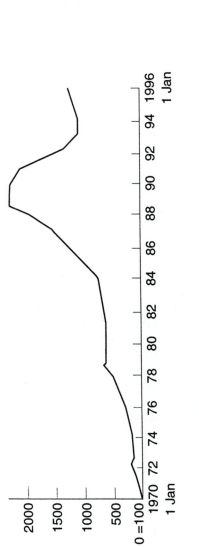

Fig. 9.4. Historical trend in provincial hotel prices: January 1970 to December 1995. Average values in southern England. *Source:* Robert Barry & Co.

depending on the terms of the loan. The valuer thus has a serious responsibility to many people for a valuation which leads to a purchase at a price which cannot be justified in commercial (rather than speculative) terms.

Corisand

It is outside the scope of the RICS Red Book to address the speculative problems of a specialist corner of the property market or to draw attention to the "commercial" and "speculative" elements of value in times of boom. However, the problem is not new and has been dealt with adequately in the courts. The case of *Corisand Investments Ltd* v *Druce & Co* (1978) concerned a valuation of a medium sized hotel in North London prepared for mortgage purposes in September 1973. As reported in the *Estates Gazette* in 1978 (Vol. 248 *et seq.*) "this valuation was relied upon by the plaintiffs, a firm of moneylenders, who advanced on a second mortgage a sum sufficient to increase the total amount secured on the property to 70 per cent of its stated value. When, shortly afterwards, the hotel market crashed, the borrowers were unable to repay the loan, and the plaintiffs suffered substantial loss".

Mr Justice Gibson found against the valuers on a number of counts, and they were obliged to pay damages. In his summing up the judge said that the valuer regarded it as "essential to value in accordance with market conditions at the precise moment of the date of the valuation". The judge understood that "the valuation was based upon his [the valuer's] opinion that the market was still in boom condition, with purchasers eager to pay more . . . than any ordinary calculation of investment return could justify, and his valuation reflected what he judged could at that time be immediately realised at auction on that hotel".

Gibson J made the point in passing that there can "be no answer of general principle . . . as to the need or obligation of a valuer to make any specific deduction from his open market valuation, in any particular amount or any proportion, in order properly to determine a valuation for mortgage purposes", as opposed to a valuation for any other purpose.

However, the "valuer must, in valuing" for mortgage purposes, exclude from his valuation any apparent asset or valuable content of the hotel as a saleable property which will not be, or may well not be, available for sale by the mortgagee when he attempts to realise the sale of the security. That sale price which the valuer must try to estimate for the guidance of the intending lender is that sale price which the property is likely to fetch – as the valuer can judge it – at the time relevant to the possible realisation of the security and in the circumstances then relevant.

It follows that, if the current open market value price which the valuer judges would be realised at auction at the time of the valuation is based upon a market which the valuer knows to be "high", and supported by speculative buyers apparently willing to pay prices not justified by ordinary principles of investment return, then such content of the market price so estimated as depends upon the market being in that state (which I shall call the "speculative element") should either not be included in a valuation for mortgage purposes, or should be identified as such, and so included, for the guidance of the lender, if at the time of valuation there is substantial ground for the valuer to know that the speculative content of his estimated market price will not or may well not be maintained in the future . . .

The need to discount the speculative element from value

The judge was quite specific on the fact that a valuer must either discount from his valuation the speculative content altogether, or else include it as an identifiable and separate amount. The valuer has a duty to know the hotel market sufficiently well to differentiate between Oscar Wilde's cynic's knowledge of the price the speculator will pay, and the prudent investor's understanding of commercial value, and to define it, in his valuation.

The judge went on to say that the valuer "cannot be expected to peer very far ahead" into the future, but that he "can reasonably be required to be aware that the market is 'high', or unusually buoyant, when such are the circumstances, and to guard against over-confidence in such market conditions. He can reasonably be required to consider what the position of the property may well be in circumstances of forced sale within 6 to 12 months of his valuation".

A hotel valuer, therefore, needs to understand the hotel industry in order to recognise trends within it sufficiently well to be able to see which way this specialised investment market is moving at the time of his valuation.

Gibson J stresses the need for this in-depth understanding:

I do not of course . . . thereby decide that in valuing for mortgage purposes any particular percentage of what is thought to be the current market price in a high or speculative market must be deducted from that market price. The nature of the process is such that in every case the valuer must be free to apply the clear principles of his discipline . . .

The judge was also helpful in defining "speculative". "The concept of a speculator's price, as I understand it, is to pay more for a property than other buyers are then willing to pay on ordinary principles of investment return in the belief that the market will rise to and overtake the price so paid."

He found that, at the date of the valuation in September 1973, it had not been proved to him that "a competent valuer should have known that the boom in the property market was then coming to an end, in the sense that he should have known that a drop in prices was about to happen". He goes further by saying that "I am quite sure that [such] a valuer was not negligent because he did not them anticipate or suspect the impending collapse of the property market".

Although the judge did not expect the gift of prophecy he did expect due recognition of the speculative element in the valuation.

I therefore conclude . . . that by reason of their breach of duty in failing to allow for the speculative content in their open market price in advising for mortgage purposes the defendants put forward a valuation which was by at least £55,000 more than any competent valuer could or should have put forward. If, instead of reducing their figures to allow for the speculative content, the defendants had chosen to make adequate reference in their report to the fact that their open market valuation was based upon [a] view of the market which necessarily caused there to be within it a substantial speculative element, I have no doubt whatever . . . that the plaintiffs would have insisted upon having advice from the defendants as to a sensible deduction to be made in respect of it before making any loan.

Conclusions

1. The judge was clear in a lengthy and detailed judgement that the valuation of hotels, if not of other types of property, entails more than a reference to current market prices and recent comparable sales.

2. The judge did not expect a valuer to foresee future market trends. Although at least some hotel valuers were aware of a collapsing hotel market well before September 1973 the judge did not find negligence in failing to recognise the impending collapse.

3. Although some speculators and sources of finance contribute to the boom in property cycles by bidding and lending recklessly, this does not exonerate the valuer from pointing out the speculative element in hotel valuation. Those relying on the valuation, whether as client or third party, may not be aware of the size of the risks involved, and are entitled to expect appropriate advice.

Factors which stimulate speculation in hotel property

Hotel property may be unique, or at any rate requiring of special consideration, in this respect. The market for hotels differs from other types of property in ways which require the valuer to be specially vigilant. These differences include the following:

1. Hotels are specialist buildings, not always easily convertible to other use, for which planning consent might in any case be refused if the local and planning authorities wish to see the hotel retained as such. It is difficult, therefore, to check hotel value against alternative use value.

2. The varied characteristics of hotels as regards standards, size, location and performance means that there are few comparables for a purchaser to consider at any one time.

3. The far-flung locations of hotels, whether nationally or inter-nationally, makes it hard for an operator to acquire detailed knowledge of local conditions for every purchase, so a percentage of transactions will be based on mistaken assumptions as to the local trading potential. This applies less to city hotels (where there may be comparables) than to the "provincial hotels" which are the subject of this chapter. Some apparently comparable transactions are based on mistaken judgement as to the strength of local opportunities, and should not be used for valuation comparisons.

4. Investors in other types of commercial property have a wide database of investment properties to work on. Any town of any size has recognised local values for shops, offices, and factories, etc. in every street or road. Hotel buyers have access to no such local data.

5. Whereas a substantial proportion of commercial property is owned by investors and leased to tenants, hotels are more usually owner-operated. This means that whereas the market for shops, offices and industrial properties is informed and led by sophisticated specialists in property investment, which set a market in each locality at a reasonable level, provincial hotels are often bought by individual hoteliers or hotel groups whose understanding of property matters may be limited. Such purchasers cannot draw on the specialist example of those investing objectively in property for its own sake, but only from other potential operators, who are at risk of taking a more subjective view, and who are likely to bid more erratically as a result.

6. The wide swing in profitability experienced by hotels and leisure between periods of prosperity and slump attract speculative buyers when the market is seen to be rising, thus forcing prices up still further.

7. When yields on commercial properties fall to low levels, shortage of opportunity tempts investors to switch to hotels where yields (based on profits) can look tempting.

These factors combine to provide perfect conditions for speculation in hotels, and are further augmented by the attraction which cash businesses hold for people with a propensity for risk taking. This propensity is increased when capital gains are taxed at a lower level than income.

These considerations explain Mr Justice Gibson's concern in *Corisand* that a valuer of hotels should recognise and evaluate the speculative element in value.

The difference between "commercial" and "speculative" values
Although this is fine in theory, the valuer on the ground does have practical difficulties in differentiating between speculative value and commercial value, especially when there are many buyers prepared to join in the speculative bidding. When does sheer force of numbers convert a speculative bid into open market value by means of evidence of comparable sales?

The answer to the hotel valuer's dilemma is first to ascertain commercial value by means of the profits method of valuation, as detailed elsewhere in this chapter. The profits method of arriving at commercial value is the result of the need for the hotel operator to receive a sufficient profit margin after servicing a normal level of borrowing to ensure the healthy survival of the business. Commercial value will not exceed a price at which borrowings of say 50–70% will place such a heavy burden on cash flow that viability is threatened.

Nevertheless, commercial value will fluctuate with the market to a certain extent. In times of optimism investors of all kinds are content with a lower yield. Their very optimism encourages them to permit a smaller safety margin. Likewise an appropriate year's purchase of profits is lower for valuation purposes in recession than it is in boom conditions, because investors take a more cautious view.

Having arrived at a commercial valuation appropriate to the phase in the economic cycle by the profits method, the valuer can then consider market evidence, and arrive at current speculative value. If the purchaser is prepared, for reasons of his own, to pay this price after being advised of its excess over commercial value then he is clearly free to do so. Banks lending in a competitive market may feel compelled to proceed regardless likewise. In either case the valuer ought to point out the existence of the speculative content in the value, and attempt to quantify it if asked to do so, if his knowledge of the market leads him to think that those placing reliance on his valuation are likely to be at risk if he does not.

Apportionment of value and requests for "bricks and mortar" valuation or "security on land and buildings only"

Hotel values need to be apportioned for contracts of sale, for balance sheets, and for the purposes of distributing sale proceeds between creditors who have loans secured respectively on the property and on the contents.

This apportionment splits the value between the freehold or leasehold element, goodwill, and trade contents or movables.

The apportionment for a sale is required mainly for taxation purposes. Trade movables do not attract stamp duty, so if the contents receive a generous apportionment as to value the purchaser is spared some expense. Furthermore, the higher the value of the contents the more he will be able to depreciate against income tax under Section 19 of the Capital Allowances Act 1990. For these reasons it is usually in the purchaser's interest to see movables apportioned high.

Vendors, on the other hand, pay income tax at the top applicable rate on a balancing charge calculated by deducting the written down value of the movables from the price achieved for them. Capital gains tax is paid on the increase in value of property and goodwill which make up the remainder of the price, less allowable deductions and the agreed value of the owners' private accommodation.

While capital gains tax and the top rate of income tax are charged at the same rate the vendor can afford to take a relaxed view of the apportionment, but in times when income tax is higher he is likely to want to see the movables apportioned low.

Therefore, a realistic compromise is required between the parties and the agent needs to be able to advise informally as to a sensible apportionment.

As mentioned on pp. 443–444 valuations of movables are needed from time to time, most usually for liquidations and receiverships when different creditors' security is pledged respectively on property and movables. Experience of such valuations is usually sufficient to enable an agent to advise as to an appropriate apportionment, without the need to put the parties to the expense of a valuation.

Likewise an apportionment to be ascribed to goodwill can be arrived at either from previous experience or by agreement on an equitable compromise between the parties.

It should be remembered that an apportionment is not a valuation. An hotel may be sold to one purchaser at a certain price, and the apportionment agreed prior to exchange of contracts. If the sale falls through and is negotiated with a second buyer at a lower price, the apportionment of all three elements at the new price will be lower overall, but may not necessarily be in the same proportion. Neither the higher nor the lower set of figures can be regarded as an indication of actual value of any of the elements.

If the movables are regarded as security for creditors then a formal valuation of the movables will be needed. In such a case the mortgagee on the property will have less security as the overall price comes down, while the interest of the creditors secured on the movables at valuation will remain unchanged. Under no circumstances, therefore, should an interested party place reliance on a mere apportionment as an indication of value.

The Red Book PS 2.7.5 covers this point. It states that whilst an apportionment "is possible as a hypothetical exercise, the valuer must emphasise to the client and in his report, that the resultant figures are informal apportionments and that the individual figures do not themselves represent the open market value of the elements involved, since the true valuation can only be the figures taken as a whole. The valuer may be asked to refer to the open market value for alternative use for vacant possession".

Alternatively, a valuer being asked for a "bricks and mortar" valuation by a lender may point out that estimated restricted realisation price for the existing use as an operational entity having regard to trading potential (ERRPEU) as defined in PS 4.7 is appropriate for lending purposes.

Goodwill

"There are two kinds of goodwill" he declared, topping up his glass as he passed the optic. "Dog goodwill, and cat goodwill. Dog goodwill leaves with the owner when he moves away. Cat goodwill stays on at the property."

Those who have built up trade by means of a high profile personality behind the bar, in the restaurant, or by brilliant cooking, or by achieving top accolades in the guides, will have less goodwill to sell than those who achieve their profits without such measures.

Goodwill can be defined as the difference in sale value between the hotel freehold, complete with trade contents, and what it might sell for if closed, but with the contents *in situ*. The margin can add up to a large sum.

And rightly so. The cost of getting a business going from scratch, recruiting staff, training and assembling a harmonious and productive team, and then accumulating a reliable clientele with profitable bookings from good payers is enormous, and can take years. In the meantime all establishment, fixed, and borrowing costs have to be met, leading in the initial period to negative cash flow, thus adding substantially to the capital cost of the project. The difference in value between a newly built hotel and one which has been operating for a few years can be large, and that difference is the price of goodwill.

A rule of thumb, which is no more reliable than any other, and needs to be treated with the utmost caution, is that goodwill is worth around one year's purchase of the operating profit which the purchaser reckons he will inherit on acquiring the hotel. This is likely to be less than the above-mentioned difference in value as between the business open and the same business closed. An experienced hotelier will be less inclined to pay for goodwill than a buyer who lacks the self-confidence in his own ability to get a business going. A purchaser cannot be expected to pay for trading potential which he has to develop or generate himself.

Steaming up a business to enhance goodwill value can be overdone. A purchaser will complete a deal only if he thinks he can do better than the vendor, or at least no worse. If the vendor appears to have exploited every last bit of potential, and produced profits at the expense of maintenance, the purchaser will discount the value of the goodwill. Goodwill is also more valuable if it is related to profits earned on a trade which does not require special skills or undue application from the proprietor.

Whole treatises have been written about goodwill, and it is a field in which everyone can safely hold his own opinion. The RICS Red Book makes no attempt to define its value, although pointing out the difference between personal goodwill and goodwill which passes with the property, and reminding of the need to value assets accordingly. Hotels are sold at an inclusive price, including freehold, contents, and goodwill as a single figure, so the valuer does not need to arrive at an accurate assessment of the value of goodwill as such when advising the principals in a sale. However, opinions on the subject are needed when it comes to apportioning the values on sale, or in advising mortgagees as to the value of their freehold security, and in advising as to the value of a premium for a new lease.

Valuation of contents and movables

Hotels are usually sold for a price which includes the freehold or leasehold property, goodwill and trade contents, excluding personal items and trading stock.

Under normal circumstances no formal valuation of the contents takes place, the advisors to the parties arriving at an equitable apportionment between the three elements by negotiation. The apportionment will be likely to take into account the requirements of the parties for tax purposes, and the assistance of a valuer may be sought only if the parties fail to agree.

On such an occasion the valuer is required to arrive at an equitable *"in situ"* value of the contents, or their value to the business as a going concern.

This *"in situ"* value will be below the cost of replacing the inventory with new items, which would obviously be very expensive, and above the likely value for sale if disposed of by auction or other sale from the premises. Such a value would be inequitably low.

An inventory and valuations of the contents or "movables" will also be required on most occasions when a property or business comes into the hands of an Administrative or Law of Property Act Receiver, or a Liquidator.

The need for inventory and separate valuation of movables is occasioned by the different classes of creditor seeking payment on their security. The situation varies as to whether or not the property is owned by a company. If this is the case and the bank has a debenture then both the freehold/leasehold interest and the contents and stock will be covered by the fixed and floating charge to the bank. The fixed charge covers the freehold; the floating charge covers the other items and the proceeds of sale of these are paid to the bank after the preferential debts (government and employees) are settled. In such cases an Administrative Receiver is the usual form of appointment.

When the bank has a fixed charge over the company's freehold/ leasehold property only, or where no company is involved, then it is likely that a Receiver will be appointed under the Law of Property Act.

Thus valuations of the contents will normally be required whenever an Insolvency Practitioner is appointed, and the apportionment of the price on the contract for a subsequent sale will have to be backed up by the valuations. On such occasions the valuer is likely to be asked to provide two valuations, ie "*in situ*" value and disposal value off the premises by auction or by similar means.

Valuation in distressed circumstances

The 1995 RICS Red Book replaces "Valuation in the Event of Default" with "Estimated Restricted Realisation Price for the Existing Use as an operational entity having regard to trading potential (ERRPEU)."

This variation of estimated realisation price provides an indication of value in distressed circumstances and requires the valuer to agree with the lender certain assumptions such as the time limit in which the property is to be sold, whether or not the business is still trading and the availability of trading records.

The 1995 Red Book definition of ERRPEU is to be found in PS 4.7. It is the same as ERP, except that (b) is amended and an extra paragraph (e) is added as follows:

(b) that completion will take place on a future date specified by the Client (and recorded in the Valuer's Report) which does not allow a reasonable period for proper marketing (having regard to the nature of the property and the state of the market);

(e) such of the following as the Client requires (and the Valuer shall state in the Report):
  (i) accounts or records of trade would not be available to or relied upon by a prospective purchaser;
  (ii) the business is open for trade;
  (iii) the business is closed;
  (iv) the inventory has been removed;
  (v) the Justices' or other licences, consents, certificates and/or permits are lost or are in jeopardy; and
  (vi) the property has been vandalised to a defined extent.

There will be a substantial difference in value for any individual unit according to which of the foregoing sub-sections (i) to (vi) are applied. All parties concerned should understand the implications of these different levels of value, and creditors should be advised to take no action which forces closure unless absolutely necessary. If the parties do deem closure or the removal of the contents necessary, it should be understood that the capital value will suffer an immediate and substantial reduction.

Valuation in the event of default (VED), the distressed equivalent of open market value, has been excluded from the 1995 Red Book, although a valuation on this basis can effectively still be provided by valuing on the basis of OMV subject to appropriate special assumptions (as defined in the 1995 Red Book) which equate to the various qualifications to OMV stated in the definition of VED. Alternatively an ERRPEU valuation, which requires the valuer to make similar assumptions, can be provided.

Contents as security

Mortgages secured on property are therefore at risk if the action by a creditor in removing contents from an hotel leads to its closure. Receivers will save mortgagees and other creditors large sums, therefore, if they can ensure that this does not happen, and that the contents are left in the premises to allow the business to continue to trade. Banks can protect their own position by stipulating from the start that mortgagors do not offer hotel contents as security for loans. In those cases where the loan is to a hotel company, rather than a trading individual or partnership, the lender can and should insist on a fixed and floating charge on the contents.

Leasehold hotels

Leasehold licensed property gives purchasers with low capital resources the opportunity to mount the bottom rung of the ladder as self-employed proprietors. Quite a low capital sum can secure a business with a substantial cash flow. Many a hotel millionaire started with a short lease, and there is a growing practice world wide, as property investment becomes more sophisticated, for the ownership of hotel property to be separated from hotel operation by means of leasing or franchising.

As in freehold values, leasehold prices are split three ways. There is a premium or "key money", the value of the goodwill, and the "*in situ*" value of the inventory. Trading stock is taken over at valuation. The longer the lease and the higher the profit rent the more valuable the premium element.

A major restriction on value is the attitude of banks and other lenders to the limited security offered by a leasehold interest. Financiers need to lend in order to stay in business, but many of the conventional sources of commercial borrowing take a cautious view on leaseholds, particularly if they have not many years to run. The shorter the lease the lower the lending, and this affects sale value. The fact that a lessee may be able to claim protection of Landlord and Tenant legislation does not reassure prospective lenders, who are aware that landlords may on occasion obtain possession for the purposes stipulated in Section 30 of the Landlord and Tenant Act 1954.

To be saleable a lease should contain no unusual or onerous clauses. Modern leases are usually on full repairing and insuring terms, requiring the lessee to maintain the property, to pay the landlord's insurance premiums, to use the premises only for existing or similar use, not to part with possession of part of the property, and to assign only with the consent of the landlord. The landlord usually has the right to foreclose if the lessee goes bankrupt or compounds with his creditors, which gives an incentive to mortgagees to restrict their level of lending to allow the borrower an ample trading margin, and not to enforce the debt too stringently should there be cash flow problems. Rent reviews are usually at three to five year intervals, and are to open market rent or to some formula designed to achieve open market rent incorporating "disregards" similar to those set out in Section 34 of the Landlord and Tenant Act 1954. These include briefly the effect on rent of the tenant's occupation, tenant's goodwill, tenant's improvements, and liquor licence if the court considers that the benefit of the licence belongs to the tenant.

Leases which do not follow this general pattern need to be studied with care to ensure that sale value is not adversely affected as a result. For example, furniture may be included in the demise, or rent reviews may be at unusual intervals, or subject to unusual methods of assessment or review.

The assessment of actual sale value of leasehold hotels requires specialist expertise in view of the immense variation and variety in the relevant terms. A 999-year ground lease at a nominal fixed rent will have a value equating to freehold for all practical purposes, whereas a lease with no profit rent and only a few years to run may have a negative value.

The nature of the landlord can also affect the value of the lease. Some landlords are more likely than others to want to repossess the property at the end of the lease under Section 30 of the 1954 Act. Brewers in particular may claim possession for purposes of their own. They may also require a whole or partial tie, thus reducing profitability and value. If the whole or part of an hotel is held on lease from the owner-occupiers of adjoining property whose business is expanding the landlords may wish to take their property back for their own occupation when the lease expires. Purchasers of leases with such characteristics would be advised to take a cautious view if they hope to claim an extension under the Act, and their valuers should discount their valuations accordingly.

Other landlords may be more favourable than the norm, provided the lessees confirm to their requirements. The owner of a country house, for example, may not require it for his own occupation for the foreseeable future. His first priority may be maintenance of the fabric and preservation of architectural integrity rather than the best possible rent. Likewise the owner of a country estate may be more concerned that the residential inn in the village should be kept traditional, and he may be prepared to agree favourable terms on the understanding that it is not commercialised, or modernised unsympathetically. Such leases can look attractive and command good prices.

The RICS Background Paper no. BP6 deals with negative values of leases, pointing out that these can occur "when the rent received under the lease exceeds the open market value and/or there are onerous covenants on the lessee's part". The Paper goes on to say that to report the value of such an interest as "nil" does not correctly indicate the true position. Negative value should thus be quantified as to the extent of the net liability when possible.

The private market in leasehold licensed property is unsophisticated, and objective assessment of value can be overtaken by competitive bidders who lack professional advice, particularly at the cheaper end. Comparables of short lease sales can be found, and valuations can usually be arrived at by reference to recent transactions.

The market for brewers' leases, which was originally spearheaded by Grand Metropolitan's Inntrepreneur leases, and has now been imitated in one form or another by other brewers, is covered in greater detail in chapter 4.

Demand for leases among private buyers declines above a certain price level, this level again depending on the phase of the economic cycle. If a purchaser can afford to pay the freehold price for a small but viable business he or she will probably elect to do so, rather than pay a similar sum for a business which, although more profitable, can only offer leasehold tenure.

Leasehold values show even more fluctuation in value than freehold values during economic cycles. When confidence in property is high, and freehold commercial opportunities hard to find, operators will bid and banks will lend well on leaseholds. When the property market is down purchasers can pick and choose, and lenders likewise, so leaseholds, which offer less security and scope for capital growth, lose value rapidly.

It will be seen, therefore, that set levels of investment return are harder to lay down than for freeholds. Nevertheless, lack of comparables at the top end of the market means that the profits method of valuation has to be adopted. The yield is calculated on the operating profit after rent (no such deduction from profits being appropriate for freeholds). To this post-rent operating profit on a lease on conventional terms and reasonable length (say 20–25 years) is applied a yield in perpetuity of around double that which would have been applied had the property been freehold. As mentioned above, however, the yields fluctuate more widely between periods of property boom and recession than they do for freeholds.

Rental valuations

Comparable evidence of rental values for provincial hotels is even harder to find than sale comparables. Relatively few hotels (as opposed to pubs and inns) are let, if only because of the risks involved to a landlord that an ineffectual lessee or his assignee may allow the business to deteriorate and then use the reduction in trade as an argument against rent increases. The hotel industry is traditionally vertically integrated, with the hotel groups owning the majority of the hotels they run, although the signs are that this may change in time.

As in capital values, hotel rents are related to trading performance. Although due care has to be taken not to penalise a lessee by making him pay a higher rent if the business does well, lack of valid comparables means that hotel rents are usually valued by the profits method.

The calculations as to open market rental value start with the preparation of a trading and profit and loss account. In those cases in which the valuer is provided with actual figures by the operator, he should check the accounts just as he would for valuing the assets.

Taking the modern 100 bedroom hotel in example 5 on pp. 412–413 the calculation would be as follows:

Turnover net of VAT					£2,150,000
Net profit as calculated previously					752,000
Less	Interest on tenant's investment:				
	(a)	Value of tenant's inventory	550,000		
	(b)	Wet and dry stock	10,000		
	(c)	The value of tenant's improvements as agreed and approved by the landlord, including professional fees where appropriate	230,000		
	(d)	Working capital	20,000		
Interest on			810,000	@ 12%	97,200
Divisible balance					654,800
Rental value @ 50%					£327,400

Due allowance should be made for overage where rent reviews are infrequent.

Not all of the foregoing items will be readily agreed between the parties. The figure for working capital is not related to the value of the lease, but to the need for a business of this size to be able to draw on immediate reserves which will form part of the usual borrowing facility from the bank. The value of the other items on which interest is allowable is not necessarily related to cost. The interest rate to which the tenant may be regarded as being entitled is also open for discussion, and should be a fair median rate likely to be encountered for the period up to the next rent review.

An apportionment has to be assessed between landlord and tenant for the "divisible balance" of profit. The landlord's share is usually reckoned to be between 40% and 60% of the divisible balance, depending on the aspects of the case. If the hotel is particularly desirable, easy to let, operate and maintain, then the landlord can look for a larger share. If, however, the lessee is having to operate at some disadvantage, with old structure, inconvenient layout, or secondary location, it is equitable to allow him a larger share of profit.

In the event of a dispute between the parties the matter may have to be referred to an arbitrator or a surveyor acting as an expert, in which case one of the parties may claim that the lessee's trading accounts should not be taken as evidence of profit potential for purposes of assessing rental value. The ground for such a claim is that a hypothetical prospective lessee would not have access to the outgoing lessee's trading accounts and would have to arrive at his own assessment of trading potential without the use of such evidence. The counter argument, which can prevail in certain cases, is that each hotel is unique and comparables are misleading, while theoretical trading projections may be inaccurate and potentially inequitable, so the best guide as to potential performance is the existing accounts, adjusted to take account of the special circumstances which may apply to the sitting tenant.

Further reading

RICS Statements of Asset Valuation Practice and Guidance Notes.
Hattersley W.M. *Valuation: Principles into Practice* 1988.
Corisand Investments Ltd v Druce & Co. (1978) 248 E.G. 315.
Westbrook R.W. *The Valuation of Licensed Premises* 1983.

CHAPTER 10

Public houses

Present market

For many years, in particular since the Second World War, the brewing industry, while being a very powerful lobby, has managed to keep a low profile. Although there have been various reports into how the industry operates and the ramifications of the monopoly situation, it was the Monopolies and Mergers Commission Report "The Supply of Beer" (the MMC Report), presented to Parliament in March 1989, that resulted in a major upheaval to the industry. Not only with regard to its structure but also, as a result of the legislation that ensued, the valuation of freehold and leasehold public houses has been affected.

The history of the public house dates back many centuries, to before Roman times. The true beginnings of the public house probably date back to when the first licences were granted, in the mid 16th century. Since the 19th century the public house, or more probably a local ale house, displayed two criteria which are still very evident today. Not only did it require a licence to trade but it was vertically integrated with regard to the products it sold. In addition to the houses that brewed beer on site there were wholesale brewers, operating in a fashion similar to present day brewers, who brewed at one main outlet and distributed to various retail public houses. During the 19th century the "tied house" system began to emerge whereby the brewers made loans to publicans in return for a tie whereby the outlet stocked the brewer's beer exclusively. From then onwards the number of brewers began to decrease as beer consumption started to decline which, coupled with more restrictive licensing requirements, saw them acquiring individual and small brewery estates to safeguard and extend their market shares. The demise of the horse drawn dray in favour of the dray powered by the internal combustion engine improved and increased the area of distribution.

This general pattern of events has carried on to the MMC Report and subject to a few minor variations it has resulted in the emergence of four main categories of public houses. The first two are brewery owned, or the holding company will have a substantial shareholding owned by a brewer, or a brewer will have a supply agreement with the holding company.

Managed Houses. The owning company has the right to nominate all products sold through the outlet including beers, lagers, ciders, wines, spirits, minerals, tobaccos and all sundry supplies. All outgoings are borne by the operating company, including the salary of the manager who is an employee of that company. In some instances the manager might well pay a catering rent to the owner in return for operating the food franchise. On average, managed houses are the most profitable public houses and have the highest capital values. The majority of managed houses are targeted at specific segments of the market. The key elements of a managed house are a high level of retail profit in either actual or percentage terms coupled with a high barrelage throughput. More often than not a high proportion of the bottom line net profit will be attributable to machine income.

Tenanted Houses. These have identical ownership to managed houses, the public house is let to a tenant. The terms of occupation, historically, have been a short-term agreement, normally an annual agreement subject to three-yearly rent reviews. In recent years longer leases have been introduced and at the present time 6, 9, 10, 15, 20, 21 and 35-year leases are on offer by the brewers and operating companies. The tenancy agreement or lease will deter-mine a specific rent or alternatively a mechanism, such as with a turnover lease, as to the amount of rent to be paid. There will be specific purchasing and stocking obligations, particularly with regard to beer purchases. Unlike the manager the tenant has a financial stake. He will own the inventory of contents comprising tenant's furniture and fittings, together with the stock. Also possibly certain of the trade fixtures, such as the bar, backfittings, urinals, may be owned by the tenant. The tenant is responsible for the viability of the business and it is up to him to produce the business plan, the pricing structure and the style of the operation. His remuneration is the income that is left after meeting the various fixed and variable costs of the business such as the rent, purchases, rates, energy, staff and other outgoings.

Free Houses. Independently owned and not tied to any specified brewer or supplier in respect of liquor supplies. Such properties can be either individually owned or form part of the assets of a multiple company. If the latter then they will operate with a manager employed by the multiple company.

Loan Tied Free Houses. Similar to the above category. To a greater or lesser extent the owner, in return for financial support or other capital sum, undertakes to purchase minimum purchasing obligations in respect of liquor supplies from a nominated supplier in the form of a brewer.

With regard to the total number of public houses in the United Kingdom the most relevant statistics are published by the Brewers and Licensed Retailers Association (formerly the Brewers Society) (Table 8.1). In respect of the last full year, 1992, the total number of public houses was estimated at 83,300. This figure includes all licensed premises, including hotels and the other categories which hold on-licences.

Table 8.1. Number of licensed premises in the UK (excluding off-licences)

	Full on-licence	Restricted on-licence	Licensed and registered clubs	Total
1969	73,900	9,800	27,800	111,500
1983	78,600	25,300	33,900	137,800
1985	79,700	27,000	33,700	140,400
1988	81,200	30,400	33,400	145,000
1989	82,000	31,400	33,300	147,000
1990	82,800	32,300	32,700	147,800
1991	83,600	33,200	32,200	149,000
1992	83,300	31,800	32,100	147,200

Source: The BLRA Statistical Handbook 1995 Edition.

As can be seen from the statistics the number of full on-licences has grown relatively modestly over the last 20 years, approximately 6.0%.

The trend in the brewers' ownership of on-licensed premises is also demonstrated by other statistics produced by the BLRA (Table 8.2).

Table 8.2. Ownership of licensed premises in the UK

	Managed on-licences	Tenanted on-licences	Managed and tenanted sub-total	Free on-licences	Total
1983	13,000	34,400	47,400	31,500	78,900
1985	12,900	33,600	46,500	46,700	80,300
1988	12,900	32,300	45,200	36,900	82,100
1989	13,500	30,500	44,000	39,000	83,000
1990	13,500	29,800	43,300	(No figures available)	
1991	13,000	25,100	38,100		
1992	12,000	19,100	31,100		
1993	12,000	18,600	30,600		
1994	11,700	18,600	30,300		

Source: The BLRA Statistical Handbook 1995 Edition

Between 1983 and 1989 the total number of on-licences increased by 5.2% compared to a 23.8% increase in free on-licences. In contrast the number of brewery on-licences declined, a decline still evident in 1990; however, the subsequent change in the structure of the brewery estates can be clearly seen. Since 1990 the Brewers have had to comply with the MMC Report. There has been a decline of over 34% in total ownership to 30,300. It should be noted that in 1990 the higher value managed houses comprised 31.1% of the total, compared to 38.6% in 1994. This trend should continue.

There has also been a downturn in the percentage of beer sales to total sales, although beer sales still account for the major proportion of sales. Table 8.3 (reproduced from the MMC Report) is based on sales in respect of managed houses owned by five of the major national brewers. The decline in beer sales as a percentage of sales contrasts with the growth in food.

Table 8.3. Estimated percentage of non-beer sales in the managed houses of the national brewers, 1986–1995*

	1986	1987	1988	1989	1995 (Est)
Beer	56	53	54	52	38
Other beverages	25	24	24	24	30
Food	12	16	16	19	20
Other**	7	6	6	6	12
Total	100	100	100	100	100

Source: MMC Study.
 * Percentages may not sum to 100 because of rounding.
** Including income arising from amusement machines.

Beer supply

Although there have been quite significant changes in the total number and make-up of the number of licensed premises there are substantially different patterns which emerge with regard to the demand for beer. In the last 20 years there has been relatively little movement (Table 8.4).

As shown in Table 8.4 consumption reached a peak of 40.7 million barrels in 1980. The growth of lager from only a nominal market penetration in the 1960s can be clearly identified. As a result of the heavy promotion since the 1970s it has now captured over 50% of the market. In the last few years growth has slowed and realistically it would seem that it would peak out at around 55% of the market but nevertheless there are some estimates which put total market penetration at 75%. The growth of draught beer consumption appears to have reached its peak in 1980, since when it has declined steadily, the shortfall being taken up by packaged beers. Packaged beers fall into two categories: returnables which are in decline, and non-returnable bottles and cans both of which are on the increase with the sale of canned beer currently out-selling non-returnable bottles by almost 4 to 1. This major growth area has been in the take-home trade rather than in public houses. It is evidence of the

Table 8.4. Beer: UK market by type and package

| | | By type* | | By container* | |
	Consumption** (Million barrels)	Ale*** (%)	Lager (%)	Draught*** (%)	Other (%)
1960	27.6	99.0	1.0	64.0	36.0
1970	35.0	93.0	7.0	73.0	27.0
1980	40.7	69.3	30.7	78.9	21.1
1985	37.7	59.1	40.9	77.2	22.8
1986	37.8	56.6	43.4	75.8	24.2
1987	38.6	53.4	46.6	74.4	25.7
1988	39.7	51.4	48.6	73.4	26.7
1989	39.9	49.7	50.3	72.6	27.3
1990	39.8	48.6	51.4	71.6	28.3
1991	38.5	48.9	51.1	70.5	29.5
1992	37.2	48.6	51.4	69.4	30.6
1993	35.9	48.0	52.0	68.1	31.9
1994	36.5	46.9	53.1	66.7	33.3

Source: The BLRA Statistical Handbook 1995 Edition
   *Percentages may not sum to 100 because of rounding.
  ** Defined as production plus imports less exports.
*** Includes stout.

purchasing power in particular of the supermarket chains who command substantial discounts.

The definition of "real ale" has been quite hotly debated in recent years, the brewers would contend that all beer they brew is real. Nevertheless, the expression "real ale" is generally understood to mean cask-conditioned beer which undergoes fermentation in the container from which it is served for consumption and at present it comprises about 20% of all draught beers sold. Finally the other entry to the market in recent years has been non-alcohol and low-alcohol beers, commonly referred to as Nab/Labs. "No alcohol" beers are those whose alcoholic strength does not exceed 0.05% alcohol by volume. "Low alcohol" beers have a strength exceeding 0.05% but not exceeding 1.2% alcohol by volume. Although a growth area, Brewers' Society estimates suggest that they only account for about 1.5% of the total market.

Following the acquisition of the brewing interests of Grand Metropolitan plc by Courage Ltd (a wholly owned subsidiary of Elders IXL Ltd) in 1989, the big six national brewers were reduced to five, the remainder being Allied Lyons Breweries plc, Bass plc, Whitbread and Company plc and Scottish & Newcastle Breweries plc. Between them they accounted for some 77% of all beer sold in the UK in 1989 which equates to almost four out of every five barrels sold.

In 1995 Scottish & Newcastle acquired Courage for £425 million. The remaining national brewers now number four, Scottish-Courage, Whitbread, Carlsberg Tetley and Bass, with every indication that the number will be reduced to three within the near future.

Monopolies and Mergers Commission report "The supply of beer"

Of all the reports into the brewing industry it is this one, presented in March 1989, that has had the most far-reaching effects. The terminology adopted was "A report on the supply of beer for retail sale in the United Kingdom".

The overall effect on the industry is still not clear. However, there are immediate ramifications for the valuer involved in licensed property. Firstly, in the field of agency – some 11,000 public houses will have to be released from the tie either by the sale of the freehold or long-term leases free of tie (or perhaps by the brewers closing public houses); secondly, valuation – the creation of long leases either free or tied will result in tenants requiring specialist advice not only on rent but on all the other terms of the lease; thirdly, as a direct result of public houses being afforded the protection of the security provisions of Part II of the Landlord and Tenant Act 1954 by the repeal of Section 43(1)(d) there will be a substantial increase in rent review negotiations.

It is important therefore to look briefly at this, the MMC Report, which was a very comprehensive and detailed study, running to 501 pages. The view of the MMC Report was that there was a complex monopoly situation at all levels existing in favour of the brewers, which operated to the detriment of the public interest. In summary their conclusions were:

- the price of a pint of beer in a public house had risen too fast in the last few years;

- the high price of lager was not justified by the cost of producing it;
- the variation in wholesale prices between regions of the country was excessive;
- consumer choice was restricted because one brewer does not usually allow another brewer's beer to be sold in the outlets which he owns; this restriction often happens in loan-tied outlets as well;
- consumer choice was further restricted because of brewers' efforts to ensure that their own brands of cider and soft drinks were sold in their outlets;
- tenants were unable to play a full part in meeting consumer preferences, both because of the tie and because the tenant's bargaining position was so much weaker than his landlord's; and
- independent manufacturers and wholesalers of beer and other drinks were allowed only limited access to the on-licence market.

The original recommendations of the MMC Report were somewhat radical and following strong representations from the brewers, on July 10 1989 the Secretary of State for Industry introduced two Orders, "The Supply of Beer (Loan Ties, Licensed Premises and Wholesale Prices) Order 1989" and "The Supply of Beer (Tied Estate) Order 1989".

The Tied Estate Order includes the following provisions:

- It applies to any brewing company or group, including any company which holds at least 15% of a brewer;
- Article 2 requires that the half-excess of the brewers' estates over 2,000 premises must be untied altogether by November 1 1992 either by sale or by letting on full repairing leases at open market rents.
- Brewers who own more than 2,000 full on-licence premises must allow their tied customers (whether tenants, loan-tied or tied in any other way) to be free from May 1 1990 to buy at least one brand of cask-conditioned beer from another supplier and end all ties on wines, spirits, cider, soft drinks and non- and low-alcohol beers.

The Loan Ties Order applies to all brewers, regardless of the size of their tied estate to enable recipients of brewers' loans to end the arrangements at three months' notice without penalty, to publish wholesale price lists for their beer, showing maximum prices for different categories of customer, though they are allowed to offer special discounts, brewers may not withhold wholesale beer supplies, except under certain circumstances, and they may not impose any restrictions on the use of premises as licensed premises when they dispose of them.

The MMC Report also recommended that tenancies of all on-licensed premises should be brought within the provisions of the Landlord and Tenant Act 1954 Part II. The Landlord and Tenant (Licensed Premises) Act 1990 ("the 1990 Act") repeals Section 43(i)(d) of the 1954 Act which had excluded licensed premises from security of tenure. The ramifications of the 1990 Act are considered elsewhere in this chapter.

Whereas the recommendations of the MMC Report provided for some 22,000 public houses to be divested by the national brewers, the Orders as enacted will result in some 11,000 public houses being released from the tie.

The strategies of most of the national and major regional brewers have been clarified. There have been some major policy decisions that have been implemented. These are mainly concerned with traditional brewers divesting themselves of their production facility to concentrate on public house ownership. In September 1989 The Boddington Group plc sold its brewing division to Whitbread, in order to concentrate on the development of its public house and retail estates. Subsequently The Greenall Group plc which was formerly the largest of the regional brewers, has followed a similar route and will be placing contracts with various brewers, in particular Allied Lyons. In November 1995 Greenalls acquired Boddingtons resulting in a total estate of 2,430 houses. One of the largest transactions involved Grand Metropolitan plc and Fosters Brewing Group Ltd whereby Grand Metropolitan sold its UK brewing operations to Courage Group plc, the UK brewing subsidiary of Fosters. The second arm of the transaction was that the whole estate of Courage and the tenanted estate of Grand Metropolitan is merged into the portfolio of a new company, Inntrepreneur Estates, which will initially comprise some 7,500 public houses subject to a seven year supply agreement with Courage to purchase the whole of their beer requirements other than "guest" beers, no-alcohol and low-alcohol drinks.

The company has recently been re-named the Inntrepreneur Pub Company and the number of houses in the estate reduced to 4,330.

The estates of the four national brewers have changed in accordance with the following table.

Table 8.5

	Prior to 1989	January 1996	Tenanted Lease	Managed
Carlsberg-Tetley	6,678	4,065	1,780	2,285
Bass	7,492	4,156	1,478	2,678
Scottish-Courage	2,354	2,700	779	1,921
Whitbread	6,628	3,750	2,100	1,650

Source: S.G. Warburg Securities & Publican

In the wake of this disinvestment a completely new sector has emerged, generally referred to as Multiple Pub Companies. There are some 155–160 Companies with a total estate of around 10,500–11,000 houses. Many have estates in single figures only, the larger number several hundreds.

In addition to the MMC Report, which will be subject to a review by the Office of Fair Trading, European Community law might well also play a major role in a further restructuring of the industry. The block exemption with regard to Article 85 of the Treaty of Rome and EC Regulation 1984/83 expires in 1997 and will be fully reviewed before that date. The block exemption allows the continuation of the tied house system for the present; however, it is not known what the Commission's review will recommend.

Office of Fair Trading Enquiry into Brewers' Wholesale Pricing Policy – May 1995

This enquiry focused on the question whether tenants of tied pubs pay more for beer than their competitors in the free trade, and, if so, whether any action was justified under UK competition legislation.

The conclusion was that although a minority of tied tenants on long leases had experienced some hardship, the differential in wholesale pricing policy had not placed the tied trade at a disadvantage to free houses, and there were insufficient grounds to refer the issue to the Monopolies and Mergers Commission.

Certain other findings were highlighted:

1. Free houses, on average, bought lager at a price of 19% lower than tied tenants. The margin for bitter was 13%. In 1991 the differentials were 14% and 12% respectively.

2. Tied tenants benefited from lower rents compared to free houses, amounting to 2 to 3 percentage points of turnover.
3. Tied tenants benefited from a range of support from their landlord, including for example rent concessions, buying discounts (for items other than beer), training and promotional support.

Valuation considerations: Referencing: Factors affecting value

The modern method of valuing a public house is undertaken by adopting what is known as a Profits Valuation. This involves the assessment of a fair maintainable level of trade for the particular business assuming a competent operator and properly maintained premises. From this the gross profit and net profit for the business can be calculated.

The general approach to referencing a public house is no different to the majority of other classifications of property and the format as set out in the RICS Appraisal and Valuation Manual (the "Red Book") provides a good guideline.

As important as the property itself, is the locality in which it is situated and the competition in the immediate area. It must be remembered that the valuer is trying to ascertain the fair maintainable level of trade. Besides the valuer's knowledge of the area the licensee will probably be the most obvious source of information with regard to competing houses. For example, if the house concerned is a large managed house with a high barrelage of say 800 barrels in the middle of a sprawling 1960s council estate, there would be concern over the security of the trade of the house if a working men's or a British Legion club was to be opened in the vicinity. They would be competing for the same trade ie high barrelage volumes, but the club would normally sell liquor with a lower tariff structure, as it is not highly profit motivated, which would impact quite severely on the trade of the managed house.

Although the managed house in question might not be the valuer's idea of what a "local" should be, nevertheless it is this type of house which usually commands the highest capital value, although evidence of market value is limited as they are rarely traded.

In contrast there is the typical "roses around the door" free house, where quality of life and the appeal of the building is of greater importance than profitability. The valuer will soon form a general classification of public houses. There is no common classification and various brewers and valuers tend to adopt their own in-house categories. For example, one of the national brewers has recently identified a series of market segments into which its pubs should fit.

Town taverns – urban outlets offering a range of products and services including food.

Country taverns – broadly similar but in a rural setting and therefore with a different type of product.

Pub bars – essentially urban and heavily skewed towards drink only.

Venues – mostly urban but with the prime attraction being facilities other than just food and drink, ranging from full blown entertainment to simple convenience of location.

Local community – these are the true community pubs, meeting places for a neighbourhood either rural or suburban but unlikely to be town centre.

It is not uncommon for brewers to have an assessment form to assist in analysing competing houses. The following is typical:

Type

Managed	Tenanted	
Food	Hot table	
	Snack catering	
	Good wholesome food	
	Sandwiches	
	Nil	

Seasonal	Year Round	
Broad Based Local	Quality Traditional Wet	
Local Community	Quality Traditional Dry	
Urban Drinking		City
Other		

Interior

Decorations	Good	Average	Poor
F&F	Good	Average	Poor

No. of bars
No. of serveries
Function Room
No. of toilets   Upgraded and Modern
No. of AWPs
Services

Exterior

Building Fabric	Good	Average	Poor	
Decorations	Good	Average	Poor	
Signage	Good	Average	Poor	Corporate
Car Park	None	5–10	11–20	20–30	30+
Garden	sq ft			

The individual valuer will soon determine how sophisticated and comprehensive the assessment form or check list needs to be.

The pub market like most other markets is constantly changing to adapt to public demands. Sometimes legislation can affect values. For example, the proliferation of rural free houses offering a wide range of real ales with good car parking facilities, for a period from the late 1970s to the early 1980s, enjoyed a distinct advantage. However, the level of trade in certain circumstances has been affected by the breathalyser. The number of people convicted for drinking and driving has almost doubled to over 100,000 persons per annum between 1975 and 1990. The number has gradually decreased since to just over 80,000 persons per annum. Also the additional trade that was attributable to the free house cachet has been reduced over the last few years, more recently with the introduction of the guest beer provisions but also with the reciprocal beer agreements between the brewers to allow greater choice of beers in their managed houses, which effectively allows many of them to trade as free outlets.

The age, appearance and construction are of course relevant as are the standard of fixtures and fittings and services. If any are deficient and repairs and decoration are required an end deduction will have to be made in respect of the capital expenditure from the valuation. In particular, overdue external redecorations, poor inadequate signage and lighting, will not only require a capital sum to put right but probably will also have resulted in a lower recent historical level of trade than would normally be expected.

It does not follow that the size of the public house is directly related to the level of trade and/or value. The house has to offer sufficient drinking space to allow for the full potential of the site to be exploited, but over and above that the additional space will probably tend to lower the licensed value. Up to the 1930s size was probably a good indicator of trade and value, but the beer volumes achieved in that period have generally not been sustained. It is therefore not appropriate to measure the property unless the instruction includes a valuation for reinstatement purposes. There have at times been attempts to reconcile the valuation of a pub to size and trading areas but the results are inconclusive and unless a lot more detailed investigation is undertaken in this area, the method for the present should not be considered to be either accurate or realistic.

In considering the physical size of the public house, the typical large 1930s house will only have additional value if there is a potential use that can exploit the space. For example, in particular, a themed operation such as an entertainment venue, or alternatively it might be appropriate for a food operation.

The existing layout and configuration of the bars and serveries has to be considered, but the valuer should always have an open mind as to whether the removal of an internal wall or the relocation of the serveries would result in a more efficient operation and therefore increase the potential profit of the house. Alternatively the erection of a conservatory over a courtyard or part of a garden is a relatively low-cost option to substantially increase the drinking area if it is required. In addition to the ambience, style and furnishing and decoration of the bars, particularly important are the state of repair and condition of the toilets, kitchens and cellars. On a square foot basis the reconstruction costs of toilet and kitchen accommodation is generally higher than the bar area. Obviously end allowances must be made for external substandard toilet accommodation. It is also becoming very rare, other than where the house is essentially appealing to a 100% male orientated liquor trade, for a public house not to have a fully equipped catering kitchen and preparation area. Food income as a percentage of total income is now far higher than it was 10–20 years ago. The size and sophistication of the kitchen needs to be matched to the demands that are likely. Quite frequently this is not the case, in particular with some free houses where the personality of the licensee and facilities offered have resulted in far greater food trade than originally envisaged. This situation can be compared to a modern purpose-built managed house with first class kitchens which are rarely used to their full potential, because there is little incentive for the manager to fully exploit this segment of the trade. As with the liquor trade the valuer is trying to assess the fair maintainable level of food income that should be achieved. It should be noted that when there is a trade kitchen fitted and equipped to the required standards, in addition there should by law be a separate domestic kitchen within the residential area.

The traditional location of the beer store or cellar was in the basement. The reason was the requirement for the draught beer to be kept at a constant temperature of approximately 53°–57°F, and the most stable conditions were to be found in the basement. Also, when the vast majority of public houses were constructed, excavation was not a particularly expensive item. Nowadays it is the exception rather than the rule for the cellar not to be mechanically cooled. Temperature tends to be slightly lower as a result of the volume of lager sold and most modern public houses are constructed with cellars on the ground floor. In addition to being adequately insulated the cold room and associated cellar areas need to have sound floors, walls that can be easily cleansed, with provision for drainage, adequate working height and good access for deliveries.

The kitchen and the cellar share one factor, they should be capable of being easily worked. For example, the kitchen should be located to the rear of the bar servery or adjoining the food servery or the point of dispense. Similarly good access is required to the cellar not only for delivery vehicles but also for the staff. Access to many cellars is still via a flap behind the bar servery which can be of considerable inconvenience and disruption to the bar staff when casks and kegs have to be changed during opening hours. These are small points but ones which the valuer needs to be aware of.

The residential element of the building, as long as it provides adequate self-contained accommodation in good repair and condition, with modern fixtures and fittings in the bathroom and kitchen, is secondary in valuation terms to the other criteria considered. Primarily a public house is bought as a business and not a home. Additional residential accommodation can be an asset if it is utilised either for staff or letting accommodation. Too much ancillary accommodation, which is prevalent in many traditional public houses, tends to fall into disrepair. It results in higher outgoings with regard to power and maintenance, which reduce net profit. These comments remain good for the majority of managed, tenanted and free properties. The only exceptions are free houses with a low volume trade which the owner has probably acquired as part business, part home possibly with retirement in mind, where good spacious residential accommodation will be an asset. On a profits basis of valuation the public house will only be marginal and will rely on a strong underlying residential value to underpin the figures.

Detailed consideration of the various statutes, rules and regulations which govern the conduct of the business in a public house, including Environmental Health, Safety at Work, Customs and Excise, Food Hygiene Regulations, Customs and Excise Acts, Fire Precautions Act, Gaming and Licensing Acts, Transfer of Undertakings Regulations are outside the scope of consideration of this chapter. They are, nevertheless, integral factors of a public house valuation.

Particular note should be made of the tariffs in respect of liquor. It is not necessary to take note of the complete bar tariffs; however, specific prices need to be noted. The valuer should compare differences between the tariffs in the bars, if any, and, for the purposes of referencing and comparison, should endeavour to always try and take the tariffs of certain common drinks that are likely to be found in most public houses. For example, best bitter, session lager, premium lager, half pint bottle light ale and the house pouring whisky and gin.

These are examples and a different product range could be chosen. However, it is important that the valuer should remain consistent so that the overall level of gross profit that is being earned at the particular public house can be quickly ascertained.

It should also be noted that prices can affect volumes. If prices are substantially above those of comparable competing outlets, the level of trade might well be below potential, and vice versa.

Similarly the bar food tariff needs to be noted and if there is a restaurant it is usual to obtain a copy of the menu which will include the wine list and prices. If there is a restaurant, then a note of the number of covers should be taken.

Particular attention must be paid to the number of gaming machines (AWPs, amusement with prizes) and any other machines such as videos, and pool tables.

Additional sources of income will be from tobacco, sundries such as crisps and peanuts, and door money if an entertainment venue. Outside of the bar areas additional income might well accrue from letting accommodation, car parking, garaging, caravans, fishing rights, etc.

It is important for the valuer to assess how well the particular licensee is operating the business – is he personable, well presented and tidy? Does his wife support him in the running of the business? Is the housekeeping not only in the public but private areas to a good level? Are there darts and pool teams or association with other sporting activities? The licensee should be engaged in conversation as he is a relevant source of information as to what is happening or not happening at the house at that particular time.

Following the inspection of the subject premises, locally competing houses and of the customer drawing area the valuer will have formed his own views as to the nature of the trade of the house, its profitability, any opposition, and will endeavour to arrive at the fair level of maintainable trade that the house should achieve.

More often than not the valuer will be provided with, or have access to some extent to, the level of trade that is being achieved. For example, if valuing for a brewery with a managed house, details of the liquor throughput and the trading and profit and loss account should be available. If it is tenanted there will be details of the basis of the letting together with the rent and details of the liquor throughput, which will probably not be as comprehensive as with a managed house. Depending on the terms of the agreement the tenant to some extent will usually have freedom to purchase certain of his supplies from other than the brewery. The Tied Estate Orders which apply to those brewers with an interest in more than 2,000 pubs, require their tenants to have freedom with regard to one cask-conditioned beer and they are free as to where they purchase all wines, spirits, cider, soft drinks and non- and low-alcoholic beers. Any information supplied from a brewer which falls within these categories is therefore of limited importance and must be treated with caution. If a free house is involved then the valuation will be on behalf of the purchaser or the owner, in connection with probable finance requirements or a sale and it will be unusual if the vendor has not supplied the accounts of the business.

One of the areas where direct trading information is rarely available is to the valuer acting on behalf of a landlord in a rent review or lease renewal situation. Discovery of trading accounts is considered elsewhere in this chapter, however, in such circumstances the valuer usually has to draw on his knowledge of the trade of comparable public houses.

The valuer should also reflect again on the Red Book requirements as to an "asset valuer", reference PS 5.1.1(a) "has, in respect of the particular type of property, sufficient current local, national and international (as appropriate) knowledge of the particular market and the skills and understanding necessary to undertake the valuation competently". Furthermore PS 5.1.2 adds the following: "it is essential that any valuer undertaking a valuation based on accounts has a sound knowledge and understanding of the type of business carried on".

In addition therefore to whatever trading information the valuer will have at the subject property, he should also have a good working knowledge of the trade that is being achieved in the competing houses in the vicinity.

Valuers can attempt to assess the level of throughput by counting the number of casks or kegs in the cellar at the time of the inspection. Even for experienced licensed property valuers this is a task fraught with problems. It is essential to know the capacity of the individual containers. It is a common misconception but most people assume that a cask and barrel have the same meaning. A barrel is a specific measure of 36 gallons.

The traditional beer measures that are in regular use are:

Pin	4.5 gallons
Firkin	9 gallons
Kilderkin	18 gallons
Barrel	36 gallons
Hogs Head	54 gallons

Although it is very rare to see a Hogs Head.

In addition there are metal containers – kegs which come in a variety of sizes, 4.5, 5, 9, 10, 11, 18, 22 and 36 gallons. The historic terms are tending to become a thing of the past. After ascertaining the size of the individual casks and containers it is then necessary to ascertain used and unused stock, the number of deliveries per week and from what source. If it is possible to ascertain these facts other enquiries still have to be made. For example, the licensee might have overstocked as a result of a special promotion, alternatively there might be a bank holiday in the offing, or perhaps he is awaiting a delivery. The task with bottled beer is even harder as it can be located throughout the majority of the cellar areas as well as of course on the shelves and cold shelves in the serveries. A very imprecise approach, which is not recommended, and should only be considered if there is no alternative.

It is the valuer's objective to assess the fair maintainable level of trade. An example of overtrading is where a licensee, through his personality, has established special goodwill. This could well be by the style of operation, a live music venue or good quality food at close to cost price. The valuer would be unwise to value on these levels as the licensee will most probably take this element of trade, or personal goodwill with him to another property. Alternatively a brewery-owned tenanted house might have a licensee whose family have run the house for several generations and as a result of the bad publicity that might otherwise ensue, the brewery have allowed the tenant to continue trading at a very low level of barrelage and probably rent. Often as a result of the lack of capital and revenue expenditure a house will be substantially undertrading and it is necessary for the valuer to assess the capital sum that it will be necessary to spend to achieve a fair level of trade or perhaps there might be further potential which could be exploited by an extension or substantial development.

Although the basis of valuation will normally be on a fully operational basis for the existing use, the valuer will be negligent if he is of the opinion that there is an alternative higher use value and he does not include within his report a note to the effect that there is a possible higher alternative use value. The Town and Country Planning (Use Classes) Order 1972 did not include any prescribed use class for public houses. In effect they stood apart and this demonstrates to some extent how compatible and ancillary a public house is to almost every other land use. The Use Classes Order 1987 included public houses within Class A3 which also includes restaurants, cafes, wine bars and shops for the sale of hot food. Inclusion within Class A3 will immediately make the valuer's task easier to ascertain if there is a higher use value that would appertain if one of the other uses in that class were a relevant and viable alternative.

Often, as already mentioned, public houses have far too much ancillary accommodation with regard to the residential element. In this case the valuer can consider a break-up valuation of perhaps self-contained flats on the upper floors with a lock-up public house or wine bar on the ground floor. Similarly, in rural areas, the potential for a housing plot on garden land or the conversion of redundant garaging and stabling blocks into alternative uses might be relevant, perhaps in addition to or in substitution for the existing public house.

A recent Act of Parliament might well prove to be an indirect factor influencing the value of a particular segment of the market. The Finance Act 1989 introduced an extension in the application of VAT. With regard to existing commercial property, including public houses, owners ie brewers, have the option to elect to charge VAT on rent. Many have done so. This election not only covers rent but is also charged on the sale of the property. VAT is not charged on the domestic part of the public house, which is excluded, and the general deduction is 10% of the whole. The purchaser can set off the VAT paid against VAT paid on purchases, however, there is a period of delay in recouping the total outlay. At the lower end of the market, if there is an over supply of public houses for sale coupled with a period of recession and high interest rates, making it difficult to secure finance for the purchase of a property, this incidence of VAT could well depress capital values.

The Licensing Act 1988 among other provisions allowed for flexible licensing hours. The MMC Report commented:

The introduction of flexible licensing hours was too recent to allow accurate assessment of its results. Preliminary indications pointed to no major increase in sales as a whole but to seasonal increases in specific, particularly tourist, areas. The change should be set in the context of a general increase in consumer demand for the provision in public houses of food, coffee, soft drinks, facilities for children and an ambience attractive for women and families generally. In that context the change was likely to benefit the public house in capturing trade from other eating and drinking outlets and from the off-trade but it was too early to say this with any certainty.

All day opening has not been the elixir that the industry had hoped for. Many houses that originally opened throughout the day soon found that the increased overhead costs with regard to staff, light, heat and power were not offset by a corresponding increase in trade and they were losing money by staying open. The only houses that are likely to have benefited in terms of increased trade are, as the MMC Report indicated, those where the location attracts a reasonable amount of tourist trade. This is of course not limited to the traditional holiday and seaside resorts but also major city centres which have attractions for both United Kingdom and foreign tourists. The only other houses that are likely to have increased trade are those that are well located to prime retail locations.

The Deregulation and Contracting Out Act 1994 introduced the concept of Children's Certificates. A certificate will allow children into a designated area, accompanied by an adult, where meals and non-intoxicating beverages must be available. The certificate will normally operate until 9.00 pm. There is an opinion that Children's Certificates are somewhat restrictive and will be of little benefit to the trading pattern.

Profits – Accounts method of valuation

To trade as a public house a Justices' licence is required. The licence is granted to a person, but it requires premises to which it is attached. It is not an interest in the land, however, for the purposes of valuation the premises and the benefit of the licence are considered as one. A brief description of the various types of licence is included in Chapter 2.

The prerequisite of a licence to carry on a trade in any field creates a monopoly situation. As far as public houses are concerned the monopoly situation has been guarded jealously, in particular by the brewers, the various licensed trade protection associations and free house owners. Although there are still certain areas where it is notoriously difficult to obtain the grant of a new Justices' on-licence, overall it is now a somewhat easier task. For example, certain very successful multiple companies, although owning a relatively small number of pubs, have been able to assemble their estates by finding suitable retail outlets, obtaining change of use and a new Justices' on-licence. The situation will probably continue to ease, as a result of the large number of houses that the brewers have to free of tie. Some of the lower barrelage outlets will be uneconomic and their use will be higher on a de-licensed alternative use value. The Brewers' Society together with the brewers and the trade protection associations are also far less active in pursuing and sustaining objections to the grant of new provisional on-licences. Not only is the cost a deterrent but also the political ramifications in the wake of the MMC Report tend to indicate a more liberal approach as to whom should own public houses and that there should be much more competition generally.

The traditional methods of public house valuation date back to certain cases in the early part of this century. In particular *Ashby's Cobham Brewery Co. Ltd* Re *'The Hand & Spear' Woking* [1906] 2 KB 754. This case dealt with compensation in respect of the loss of an old on-licence. Kennedy J in his judgment set down the basis of valuation. Essentially this was to capitalise the brewer's tied rent and wholesale profit, subject to various adjustments and deductions. This method still forms the basis of valuation of a traditional brewery tied outlet at the present time. The majority of other case law established over the years is in connection with either compensation or rating, in particular the latter. Common to both methods was the establishment of analysing the trade of the house in terms of converted barrels. A converted barrel was either one barrel of beer (either bottled or draught), a barrel of cider, or three gallons of wines and spirits. The reason behind this last calculation was that it was generally accepted that the profit on the sale of three gallons of wines and spirits was equivalent to that of one barrel of beer. For example, a house which traded at 300 beer barrels, 20 barrels of cider, 20 barrels of bottled beer and 300 gallons of wines and spirits would have a beer barrelage trade of 320 and a converted barrelage of 440. Using this system it was then possible to equate not only rents but capital values expressed in terms of barrelage or converted barrelage. This method of analysis had a number of shortcomings. In particular it was difficult to value free houses on this basis, where it was unusual to find that the proprietor kept his records in terms of barrelage and gallonage. Instead the trade was represented by the trading and profit and loss account.

This system was first affected by the majority of the brewers releasing the wines and spirits tie, in whole or part. More recently the MMC Report, which has imposed additional restrictions on the tie that the major brewers can impose on their tenants renders this system less effective as a method of either analysis or valuation.

Valuations arrived at on either a barrelage or converted barrelage basis as a direct method in most instances will be based on unreliable information as the brewer will not be able to ascertain accurately how much their supplies comprise of the total throughput of the particular house. Certain of the small provincial brewers still impose a full tie, and therefore this system should only be utilised as a check or form of analysis in certain circumstances but not as a direct method of valuation.

There are other reasons why this method should be downgraded.

The system was originally a reasonably accurate method when the majority of the liquor throughput of a public house was almost exclusively beer. This is no longer the situation and in the present market total turnover will probably consist of the sale of many other items, such as food, minerals, letting accommodation, tobacco, crisps, peanuts, sundries, etc. These additional sources of income all tend to make an analysis by this method less reliable.

Common to all three broad classifications of public houses, managed, tenanted and free, either independent or loan tied, is the trading and profit and loss account. It is the valuer's task to assess the fair maintainable level of trade for the particular house and the most reliable source is for the valuer to prepare a hypothetical trading and profit and loss account for the house. Once turnover, gross and net profit have been ascertained the profits valuation can be undertaken.

In the case of a free house, either free or loan tied, the capital or rental value is relatively straightforward once the maintainable level of profit is assessed. With regard to brewery-owned assets the approach is slightly different as the majority of the brewery outlets are likely to be let on some form of tenancy, thus the asset is a form of investment. Obviously managed houses are valued as though they are free houses as immediate vacant possession would be available to a prospective purchaser.

It is necessary to appreciate that although the house may fall into the category of a free house or tenancy this factor alone does not automatically determine the format of the valuation. It might well be necessary to value on several alternative bases to ascertain the highest value and the most likely purchaser.

Where the property is let it is necessary to assess the nature of the letting and the rights of the tenant. Historically brewers adopted annual agreements with an understanding with the tenant that his rent would only be reviewed at every third anniversary. In reality these were no more than tenancies at will. Although "The Brewers' Society Code of Practice on Tenants' Security" gave some protection to tenants, nevertheless it was not legally enforceable. In particular the MMC Report with regard to rent under such agreements commented as follows:

But if a tenant underperforms against the expectations of his landlord, he may find that the new rent proposed at the time of his rent review is raised to a level which makes his overall business unprofitable. Alternatively he may have his tenancy terminated. If, on the other hand between rent reviews the tenant's business results are somewhat better than his landlord had expected, at the next rent review the tenant can expect the rent to be additionally increased to a level which reflects the enhanced level of business. Arbitration is available to resolve disputes over rent levels but we believe many tenants are not willing to take this course, because of the possible consequences of doing so on the relationship with their brewer/landlord. The NLVA has also confirmed that many tenants are unwilling to go to arbitration.

In recent years there has been experimentation by various brewers with five- and six-year leases; 10-year leases, with both fixed rentals and turnover rental provisions; turnover-related agreements; where tenants have invested heavily in refurbishment or improvements 15- and 20-year leases; and occasionally long-term ground rents where the brewer has sold a long lease at a peppercorn to raise finance but at the same time retained a tie. In all these cases the valuer has to value the asset as an investment, reflecting the tenant's right of occupation.

The advent of the modern commercial brewery long lease, the first of which was Grand Metropolitan's 20-year Inntrepreneur Lease, together with the other leases that have followed are considered in a separate section.

In the examples in this chapter, although reference is made to a specific style of house, nevertheless, as will be appreciated, the variables in a profits valuation can arise at every line of the calculation and they can all tend to magnify differences. The tariffs, product splits, gross profit percentages that have been adopted are all realistic possibilities in certain instances, however, it is the knowledge and expertise of the valuer who will determine the ratios, turnover profit percentages, etc in each instance.

The example valuations are to demonstrate principles of valuation. The house in example 1 is located within a city centre in the South East. The tariffs, product mix and volumes, gross and net profits would vary quite substantially if compared to, say, a physically identical house within a city centre in the North West.

Example 1

- Major brewery who has to comply with the Tied Estate Order.
- Provincial city centre house in the South East, no car parking or land or potential to extend.
- 1930s traditional style house in good internal and external state of repair and decoration, no capital expenditure required.
- Single bar operation, good all year round trade, generally quieter in the evenings and at weekends.
- At present run under annual tied tenancy.

- Trade steady and secure, details have been supplied by the brewery and the volumes adopted represent fair maintainable levels of trade.
- Lunchtime bar food operation.
- Brewery requires two capital valuations:
  - (a) let on a long lease for 15 years subject to five-yearly rent reviews to open market value. Full repairing and insuring. Beer tie except one cask-conditioned "guest beer", beers below 1.2% alcohol, minimum purchasing obligation in respect of beers with penalty provision and/or incentive scheme to guarantee barrelage, free for machines; and
  - (b) retained as a managed house (see example 2).

Example 1

Product	Volume	Tariff		£
Bitter	75 Barrels	1.35p per pint	× 288	29,160
Premium Bitter	55 Barrels	1.55p per pint	× 288	24,552
Mild	0			0
Lager	80 Barrels	1.52p per pint	× 288	35,020
Premium Lager	60 Barrels	1.70p per pint	× 288	29,376
Stout	20 Barrels	1.55p per pint	× 288	8,928
Cider	20 Barrels	1.45p per pint	× 288	8,352
Packaged Beer	25 Barrels	1.20p per ½ pint	× 288 × 2	17,280
Wine Table	500 litres	1.25p per 125ml glass	× 8	5,000
Wine Fortified	675 litres	1.05p per 50ml glass	× 20	14,175
Spirit	800 litres	1.05p per 25ml glass	× 40	33,600
				205,443

Less VAT @ 17.5% $\left(£205,443 \times \dfrac{100}{117.5} \right)$ 174,845

Gross profit   × 50%

87,422

Minerals, Sundries and Tobacco
Adopt 40% of net turnover of wines and spirits, say,   18,000

$£5,000 + £14,175 + £33,600 \times \dfrac{100}{117.5} \times 40\%$

Gross profit   × 50%

9,000

Other Income

Catering £100 per day × 5.5 days × 52 weeks   28,600

Less VAT @ 17.5% $\left(£28,600 \times \dfrac{100}{117.5} \right)$ 24,340

Gross profit	× 55%
	13,387
Machine Income (Net of rental and duty)	7,500
Gross profit	117,309
	(52.2%)

(N.B. Turnover

Liquor	174,845	
Minerals, Sundries and Tobacco	18,000	
Other Income	24,340	
	217,185	
Machine Income	7,500	
Total turnover	£224,685	
Gross profit	117,309)	

Less

Wages and NHI (Approx 13% of T/O)	29,000
Energy	£5,000
General and Water Rates, Community Charge	7,000
Insurances	2,500
Licence Duty, Permits, TV, Sound, Performing Rights and Fees	700
Repairs	6,000
Renewals	3,000
Telephone	750
Cleaning Materials and Laundry	1,000
Professional Fees	1,500
Entertainment and Discretionary	750
Rentals and Maintenance Contracts	1,000
Sundries	2,000
	60,200
Net Profit	57,109 (25.4%)

Less Interest on Tenant's Capital

Inventory	20,000		
Stock (approx 2 weeks)	4,000		
Working Capital	4,000		
	28,000		
Interest @	× 15%		
		−4,200	
Divisible Balance		52,909	
Rental Bid		× 50%	
ERV			26,454
			26,454

Wholesale	Volume		
Bitter	75 Barrels × 75%	56.25	
Premium Bitter	55 Barrels × 100%	55	
Mild	0		
Lager	80 Barrels × 100%	80	
Premium Lager	60 Barrels × 100%	60	
Stout	20 Barrels × 100%	20	
Cider	20 Barrels × 0%		
Packaged Beer	25 Barrels × 80%	20	
Wine	1175 Litres × 0%		
Spirit	800 Litres × 0%		
		291.25	
Wholesale contribution per barrel		× £50	
			14,562
			41,016
			× 8YP
Capital Value, Say			£328,100

Analysis

$$\frac{\text{C.V.}}{\text{T.O.}} \quad \frac{328,100}{224,685} = 1.46 \times \text{T/O}$$

$$\frac{\text{Rent}}{\text{T.O.}} \quad \frac{26{,}454 \times 100}{224{,}685} = 11.77\% \text{ of T/O}$$

The first stage of the valuation is to calculate turnover from the various sources of sales income.

The product mix displays general trends. Lager volumes are slightly in excess of bitter sales, no mild sold, both stout and cider represent a small element of the turnover, as does the packaged beer. Wines and spirits throughput is at a reasonably high level and reflects the city centre location. To simplify the example, this is a single bar house, if there are two bars or more and there is a different tariff, allowances will have to be made. The price per pint has been multiplied by 288 which is the number of pints in a barrel. If there was a very high volume of cask-conditioned beer where there is a certain amount of wastage, an allowance might be considered as appropriate. It is necessary to differentiate between table and fortified wine. A glass of wine has been taken at 125 ml which represents 8 glasses to the litre. Unlike beer and spirits, there is no statutory or recognised measure for wine. Fortified wine has been taken at a measure of 50 ml. Spirits have been taken at the standard measure of 25 ml which represents 40 measures per litre.

VAT is deducted at the prevailing rate.

At this stage gross profit would normally be calculated by deducting the cost of the purchases from sales. This is a lengthy detailed calculation and is considered inappropriate to include within the examples. There are various factors other than the purchase and sale price which affect the gross turnover and profit. For example discounts at times will be given on certain lines, or perhaps the licensee might operate a happy hour with discounted prices. In this example there is a straight deduction to gross profit of 50%. This figure has wide variations, a higher barrelage house with a preponderance of low gravity beers such as mild and session bitter, and with lagers comprising say 40% of throughput coupled with a low gallonage of wines and spirits could have a liquor gross profit closer to 40%. On the other hand a higher percentage of lagers, premium bitters and spirits could increase the gross profit to 55% or more.

Minerals, sundries and tobacco income is normally arrived at as a percentage of wines and spirits turnover, however, there are various other rule of thumb measures. It is to be noted that as gross profit on tobacco is very low often it will be sold through vending machines to prevent pilferage. Other income has to be taken into account.

Catering is the most common, but there might be additional income as already mentioned from letting accommodation, fishing rights, caravan site rentals, etc.

Machine income comprises an important element of net profit. Machine income includes not only amusement with prize income (AWPs) but also income from video and other machines such as pool tables.

With regard to outgoings, there is no standard format or recognised schedule of allowable deductions in respect of a public house valuation, unlike the Uniform System of Accounting for Hotels.

The outgoings cover the main areas of expenditure and each will vary on every line from house to house.

It is not intended to consider in detail outgoings, which in general can be classified as either fixed or variable. It is for the valuer to assess the fair annual average level that is appropriate. There may well be exceptionally high levels from time to time, particularly with regard to repairs, which tend to be on a five-year rather than an annual cycle.

Normally the largest outgoing in percentage terms is staff wages which can vary enormously with a wide range from perhaps less than 10% to more than 30% of turnover in exceptional circumstances.

As with gross profit the net profit percentage has a wide variation from as low as 15% to in excess of 30% for a managed house with a high percentage of income from machines; or a free house with a high barrelage and good levels of discount.

From the net profit, which in this example is 25.4%, it is necessary to deduct interest on the tenant's capital employed, the currently accepted rate is 15%. For a tenanted house the tenant's normal capital outlay will be in the inventory, stock and working capital.

The divisible balance is available for distribution between the tenant as a return to him in operating the business, and to the landlord in respect of rent.

The percentage of the divisible balance that a lessee is prepared to pay to the lessor depends on many factors, however, it is essentially linked to the risk factor in earning the money, the ease with which it can be earned, the volume of the divisible balance and the terms of the lease. It is generally accepted that a rent bid in the region of between 45% and 55% can be expected.

In addition to the rent the brewer will receive wholesale benefits from the tie provisions.

In this example the hypothetical lease terms provide for only certain products to be purchased from the brewery. The wholesale contribution that the brewer will be in receipt of has therefore to be considered. The tenant is free to purchase a guest cask-conditioned beer, this is provided for by allowing 75% of the purchases of bitter only. Similarly the lessee is not tied with regard to cider. Packaged beer includes low-alcohol and no-alcohol beers which the lessee is free to buy from other sources. Sales of these beers are still relatively low, to reflect this an allowance of 20% has been made.

Although it is not unusual for a lease of this type to specify certain brands of wines and spirits to be stocked, this lease does not include a tie with regard to wines and spirits purchases. The brewery cannot be guaranteed any wholesale contribution therefore from wines and spirits.

The total tied volume is 291.25 beer barrels.

The wholesale profit that brewers make is still one of the most closely guarded secrets in the whole of the industry. This is quite understandable, and is prevalent in many other manufacturing industries. For example, it would be most unusual to see a motor manufacturer publish the net profit it makes on each different model line.

Not only do wholesale prices differ between the same brewer on a regional basis and from brewer to brewer, but their level of wholesale profit will also differ. Excise duty is levied on the strength of beer and at January 1 1995 the amount of duty at average strength per pint was calculated at 24.59p (source: HM Customs & Excise). In general terms the higher the gravity the higher the wholesale profit, however, this is not necessarily so with lager where strengths roughly equate with bitter beers and wholesale margins are higher. One of the main conclusions of the MMC Report was that the high price of lager was not justified by the cost of producing it.

Although it would be possible to determine the approximate wholesale profits that individual brewers made on each product line, the results of such an investigation would not be that material to the particular property being valued. It is not the value that accrues to that particular brewery owner, whether or not he makes more or less wholesale profit per barrel than other brewers, it is more the average wholesale profit that the valuer is seeking to arrive at. It is open market value, not deprival value or value to the brewery, that is to be considered.

A general range of wholesale profits is reasonably reflected by the following:

	Wholesale profit (£ per barrel)
Session bitter	60
Best bitter	65
Premium bitter	75
Session lager	75
Best lager	80
Premium lager	90
Stout	45
Packaged beer	100
Packaged lager (own)	120
Packaged lager (foreign)	60

The valuer could apply the relevant wholesale profit to the individual product lines. However, for the reasons already explained with regard to the wide variations, it is more common to look at the overall product mix and volume and to apply one wholesale figure to the whole of the barrelage.

It is also important to consider the importance of the value of the "marginal barrel". A brewer has high fixed costs. Capital is invested in the brewery, wholesaling and distribution facilities. Any spare or additional capacity that can be taken up can be done so at very little cost and is mainly attributable to the additional raw materials, slightly higher distribution costs and of course additional excise duty. The profit on a marginal barrel of beer will therefore be considerably in excess of those indicated above.

An indication of the level of marginal wholesale profit can be given by reference to the penalty shortfall payments that feature in some long leases when barrelage targets are not met. A figure in the region of £70 per barrel at the present would not be unusual, however, one brewery in the Midlands has a shortfall payment of only £35 per barrel.

It is for this reason that a brewer can often carry out an extension to a property that otherwise would not show a realistic return. The brewer is also in a position to acquire new outlets, either existing operations or green-field sites, by outbidding a free house operator quite substantially if the marginal value is adopted in the calculation. In reality, however, the brewer would only seek to make one bid better than the market value in order to secure the opportunity. That market may or may not include other brewers with different levels of marginal wholesale profit.

It follows, therefore, that if the house, subject to the valuation, would appeal strongly to a brewer as a result of high beer volumes, then it could be valued on the marginal value basis. To some extent this is reflected by the valuer when considering the volume of throughput. A brewer will be far more interested in acquiring a high than a low barrelage house and in the same way that the valuer tends to adopt a single wholesale profit figure depending on the product mix, he will also adjust this figure by reference to the volume throughput.

A system of banding is therefore appropriate, one on the following lines might not be unrealistic:

Beer barrels per annum	Wholesale Profit per barrel
Up to 200	£45
200–300	£45–£50
300–600	£50–£70
600 +	£75

The lower volume houses will generally be located in rural areas of low population density and the increased distribution costs are reflected in part in the lower wholesale profit figures.

The combined return to the brewery of rent and wholesale profit is capitalised in this example by adopting the same yield of 12.5%.

A traditional tied house valuation on these lines quite frequently adopted a different yield for rent and wholesale profit. The yields were generally at a much lower level and it would not be uncommon to see 12YP being used as the multiplier on the rent and 8–9YP on the wholesale profit. The main reason that differing YPs were necessary was that the level of tied rents that appertained (and still do appertain at the present time with some traditional brewers annual agreements subject to three-yearly reviews) were at substantially lower levels than a brewer will achieve with some form of a modern long lease. The rent was therefore very secure and bore more resemblance to a ground rent than a market rent.

It is still relevant to adopt differing yields if there is a substantial degree of insecurity with regard to the receipt of the rent or wholesale profit, for example, in considering a long lease where the brewer has relinquished his right to be in possession for a long period. Unlike an annual agreement where he can to some extent retrieve the situation if barrelage falls substantially by reletting the house to a new tenant, this is not the situation with a long lease. With the long lease, therefore, it is sensible to build in safeguards either by way of minimum purchasing obligations on the tenant with penalty barrelage shortfall payments if they are not met. Alternatively, rather than implementing a minimum purchasing obligation, consideration can be given to a barrelage volume incentive scheme. Put simply, barrelage discount after target or minimum purchase obligation figures are achieved.

The capital value of £328,100 can be analysed most directly by comparison with turnover, the factor is 1.46 × T/O. A similar analysis is appropriate with regard to the rent which equates to 11.77% of turnover.

As already noted, the traditional methods of analysis of comparing capital and rental value to either beer barrels or converted barrels will result in inaccurate and misleading figures. First, the lessee will be free for wines and spirits purchases and once the lease has been granted the brewery will not have any accurate records of the throughput. Similar provisions apply to cider and of course the guest beer and non- and low-alcohol beers. The traditional method of analysis is still appropriate in certain instances, for example with regard to a managed house where the brewery has the option of specifying 100% of the liquor supplies. Also those breweries that have fewer than 2,000 outlets are in a position to impose more stringent liquor ties, but it could not be said that they all adopt the same policy.

For these reasons it would be prudent for the valuer, who will not be valuing exclusively for one client, to adopt a method of analysis and comparison which will be relevant to all public house valuations whether managed, tied or free. At the present, turnover is the most obvious and logical criterion for both capital and rental values.

It should be stressed that this is a method of analysis for purposes of comparison. Neither method of analysis should be adopted as a direct method of valuation. It is prudent and should be regarded as best practice to undertake a full profits valuation for capital and rental valuations.

Example 2
Same house as in Example 1: capital value if retained and run as a managed house for purposes of comparison.

		£
Gross Profit		117,309
Less		
Outgoings	60,200	
Manager's Salary, NHI		
and Bonus	18,000	
		78,200
Retail Profit		39,109 (17.4%)
		4.5 YP
		175,990

Wholesale	Volume		
Bitter	75 Barrels		
Premium Bitter	55 Barrels		
Mild	0 Barrels		
Lager	80 Barrels		
Premium Lager	60 Barrels	} × 100%	
Stout	20 Barrels		
Cider	20 Barrels		
Packaged Beer	25 Barrels		
	335		

Wholesale contribution per barrel		335 × £50	
		16,750	
Wine	1175 Litres		
Spirits	800		
Discount per gallon		1975 × £1	
			1,975
			18,752 × 7.5 YP
			40,437
			316,427
Less Inventory			20,000
			296,427
		Say	£296,400

Analysis

$$\frac{\text{C.V.}}{\text{T.O.}} \quad \frac{296,400}{224,685} = 1.31 \times \text{T/O}$$

It is assumed that the turnover and gross profit are maintained at the same levels as in example 1.

Outgoings have also been assumed to be identical subject to an increase in respect of the manager's salary, National Health and Insurance contributions and bonus. It is not unknown for additional outgoings such as depreciation and head office charges to be shown on some managed house trading and profit and loss accounts. These are not acceptable deductions as the amounts that will be shown will only be relevant to that individual managed house company and will depend on their particular accounting policies. The retail profit of a managed house is a higher risk receipt in terms of income than rent. The vulnerability of the income is reflected in the yield and the general range at present is between 14% and 25%, ie 4–7YP.

The determination of the yield will depend not only on the risk but also on the volume of net profit element. It is not uncommon with the majority of managed houses for the machine income to form a high percentage of the total net profit. Machine income has at times been capitalised independently, however, it is such an important component of the managed house profit that it is now generally included in the overall figure. The volume of net profit is the other factor. In this instance the amount of the net profit is very small in relation to turnover, 17.4%. Any decline in turnover will immediately impact on the gross profit and as the overheads are relatively fixed the profit could be reduced substantially to only a nominal sum. Managed house profits will rarely drift below 15% unless the low level of profit is compensated by a very high barrelage. At the top end the premier flagship managed houses will make in excess of 30% net profit.

The YP in this example is 4.5 reflecting the low volume and profit percentage of retail profit and its vulnerability.

The calculation of the wholesale contribution differs from example 1, in this example the brewery will enjoy 100% of the liquor supplies. Not calculated will be the additional profit from minerals and sundry supplies that will be sold. This is rarely shown as a wholesale income to the individual property, it is more common for the brewery-managed house company to receive a royalty payment direct from the various nominated suppliers.

It is not normal for any allowance to be made in respect of the capital the managed house company have tied up in respect of stock and working capital, by comparison with the tenanted valuation in example 1.

The YP used to capitalise the wholesale contribution is slightly less than with example 1 (7.5YP compared to 8YP), although the barrelage remains the same. The lessee in example 1 will have the benefit of a long lease, it is his business and he will be tied in to either penalty barrelage commitments or incentive barrelage schemes to ensure that his barrelage purchases are kept on target. These incentives are not there to the same degree with a manager, the volume throughput, although initially the same, will be more vulnerable in the medium to long term and if this is the case it should be reflected in a higher yield.

With a managed house the valuation is similar to a free house in that it includes the value of the inventory. For a direct comparison with example 1, £328,100, the capital value as a managed house is £276,400 (£296,400 − £20,000).

If the property were currently vacant this does not mean that it has a different value according to the method used. It means that it is more than likely it will be purchased by a company favouring the grant of 15-year tied leases because they can afford to pay more than a company favouring directly managed houses.

Conclusions

In this example the brewery would be advised that they would have a higher value asset if they leased the house than operated it under direct management.

The total barrelage of 335 (including cider) coupled with the very low amount of machine income, £7,500, and a total overall retail profit of £39,109, is too low to support a managed house operation, which unlike the long lease will still require a substantial head office back-up facility with regard to district managers, surveyors and accountants, etc. It would not be appropriate to value this as a managed house using the marginal wholesale rate (of say £70 wholesale profit per barrel) as it is extremely unlikely that any brewery would regard 335 barrels as a valuable incremental increase in their managed house estate.

Example 3

- Freehold free house, licensee is owner-operator.
- Located within densely populated housing estate on the periphery of the same city as the house in example 1.
- Constructed in the 1960s, typical two-storey brick with pitched roof, half acre site, car parking for 30 vehicles.

- Large two bar operation including games area, adequate three bedroom self-contained accommodation on first floor.
- Predominantly local trade, male orientated, mainly evening and weekend trade.
- Trading at full potential, no passing trade, little demand for food.
- In good internal and external state of repair and decoration, no capital expenditure required, adequate additional land available for extension, but not warranted.
- The licensee owner-operator requires two capital valuations:

  (a) the open market value of the freehold with vacant possession, and
  (b) he has been approached by a major regional brewer who has little representation in the area and is seeking to expand, what could he realistically expect that brewer to bid?

Example 3

Product	Volume	Tariff		£
Bitter	250 Barrels	1.30p per pint	× 288	93,600
Premium Bitter	25 Barrels	1.50p per pint	× 288	10,800
Mild	20 Barrels	1.25p per pint	× 288	7,200
Lager	220 Barrels	1.45p per pint	× 288	91,872
Premium Lager	100 Barrels	1.65p per pint	× 288	47,520
Stout	40 Barrels	1.55p per pint	× 288	17,856
Cider	40 Barrels	1.45p per pint	× 288	16,704
Packaged Beer	50 Barrels	1.20p per ½ pint	× 288 × 2	34,560
Wine – Table	100 litres	1.20p per 125ml glass	× 8	960
Wine – Fortified	675 litres	1.00p per 50ml meas.	× 20	13,500
Spirits	1250 litres	1.00p per 25ml meas.	× 40	50,000

	384,572
Less VAT @ 17.5%	327,295
Gross Profit	× 45%

	147,282

Minerals, Sundries and Tobacco net of VAT	22,000
Gross Profit	× 50%

	11,000

Other Income
Catering – nominal £150 per week × 52	7,800
Less VAT @ 17.5%	6,638
Gross Profit	× 20%

	1,327

Machine Income (net of rental and duty) incl. Video and Pool Tables		20,000
Discounts		
Total barrelage (incl. cider)		745
Average discount per barrel		× £45
		29,800
Gross Profit		209,409
		(55.7%)
(N.B. Turnover		
Liquor	327,295	
Minerals, Sundries and Tobacco	22,000	
Other Income	6,638	
	355,933	
Machine Income	20,000	
Total Turnover	375,933	
Gross Profit	209,409)	
		209,409
Less		
Wages and NHI (12% of T/O excl. MI)	43,000	
Energy	7,000	
Gen. and Water Rates, Community Charge	12,000	
Insurances	3,500	
Licence Duty, Permits, T.V., Sound and Performing Rights and Fees	700	
Repairs	7,000	
Renewals	4,000	
Telephone	750	
Cleaning Materials and Laundry	1,000	
Professional Fees	1,500	
Entertainment and Discretionary	1,000	
Rentals and Maintenance	1,200	
Sundries	2,500	
Loan Interest	30,000	
Motor Expenses	2,500	
Depreciation	10,000	
Owner's Drawings	40,000	
		167,650
Net Profit		41,759

Add back		
Loan Interest	30,000	
Motor Expenses	2,500	
Depreciation	10,000	
Owner's Drawings	40,000	
	82,500	
Adjusted Net Profit	124,259	
Less		
Allowance for Manager's Salary, Pension, NHI and Bonus	22,500	
	101,759	
Adjusted Net Profit	× 7YP	
	712,313	
Less		
Inventory	35,000	
		677,313
	Say	677,000

$$\frac{\text{C.V.}}{\text{T.O.}} \quad \frac{677,000}{375,933} = 1.80 \times \text{T/O}$$

The valuer would normally be provided with the trading and profit and loss account from the free house owner. They would represent figures showing turnover less purchases and an opening and closing stock and VAT, resulting in a straight deduction to gross profit. For example purposes, however, an extended valuation similar to example 1 has been produced to demonstrate certain differences.

The volume of the beer throughput is substantially higher and there is a higher percentage of lager sales. As to wines and spirits, although the throughput of 2,025 litres is similar (compared to 1,975 litres), the house in example 3 has a far higher spirits turnover and a very low percentage of table to fortified wine. There is a lower tariff of approximately 5p per pint. The gross profit at 45% is slightly lower.

The free house owner is not tied with regard to purchases. The beers sold in this house are predominantly keg, there is little demand for cask-conditioned beer and he takes his supplies from two whole-salers, the average discount per barrel per annum achieved is £40.

The owner has in part funded the free house by a bank loan rather than a "soft loan" from a brewer in return for a tie on barrelage.

Wines and spirits purchases are direct from wholesalers and cash and carry stores by the licensee, therefore there is no discount. Catering income is nominal and will make a small loss in net profit terms, however, the amount of these sales in overall terms is very small.

Machine income over the last few years shows relatively little fluctuation in percentage terms and even though running at a relatively high level of £20,000 per annum still only comprises a minor percentage of the overall net profit.

The outgoings adopted in examples 1 and 2 are to be regarded as specimens and equate to realistic percentages. However, with example 3 which is in respect of a free house, consideration is now given to the amount and accuracy of outgoings and whether they represent realistic annual deductions.

For example, if an owner spends most of his time on the trade side of the bar wages might be particularly high. Similarly repairs need to be carefully considered, they might be particularly high for individual years as the repairs sum includes an element of capital expenditure. There are then individual outgoings particular to that house which have to be added back. In this instance loan interest, motor expenses, depreciation and owner's drawings have been added back.

In this example the licensee is the owner-operator, he lives in the house and therefore as he is a full-time employee in the business a further adjustment has to be made to allow for a manager's salary.

For the purposes of analysis a sum has been deducted in respect of the value of the tenant's inventory.

The yield to be adopted on a free house depends not only on the financial circumstances that appertain at the date of the valuation, in particular the rate of interest and the availability of finance, but also on the nature of the trade and ambience of the free house and the accommodation offered. This example is a modern, high barrelage free house with adequate living accommodation, situated in the middle of a modern council housing estate. It is unlikely therefore that any purchaser would acquire this property other than by a decision based purely on a financial appraisal to show an adequate rate of return. By way of contrast different criteria would apply to the valuation of a thatched timber-framed free house with a luxury flat set within two acres in the Home Counties.

Example 4
The same house as in example 3: likely value that a brewer will bid to, to acquire the property.

Example 4

Gross Profit		209,409	

Less

Barrelage Discounts		29,800	
Adjusted Gross Profit		179,609	

Less

Outgoings		167,650	
Loan Interest	30,000		
Motor Expenses	2,500		
Depreciation	10,000		
Owner's Drawings	40,000	−82,500	
		−85,150	
		94,459	

Less

Manager's Salary, Pension, NHI and Bonus	22,500	
	71,959	
	6YP	
		431,754

Wholesale		
Total Beer Barrels	705	
Marginal contribution per barrel	× £70	
		49,350
Cider Barrels	40	
Wholesale contribution per barrel	× £50	
		2,000

Wines and Spirits Litres	2,025			
Wholesale discount per Litre	× £1			
		2,025		
		53,375		
		× 8YP		
			427,000	
			858,754	

Less
Inventory   35,000

                                                                                                823,754

                                                            Say   823,700

Analysis

$$\frac{\text{C.V.}}{\text{T.O.}} \quad \frac{823,700}{375,933} = 2.19 \times \text{T/O}$$

An analysis of the product mix of beers and lagers shows that there is no particularly strong local preference, there is not a wide range of cask-conditioned beers and the brewer will be expected to replace the present product list exclusively with his own brands and not lose any volume trade.

The gross profit has to be adjusted in respect of the barrelage discounts (a brewery will receive wholesale profit and not discounts) and similarly adjustments are made to the outgoings as with example 3.

The brewery do not have any other representation in this area and therefore all of the barrelage that they obtain will be additional, and will not be at the expense of a loss in any of their other houses. For this reason the marginal wholesale profit per barrel is adopted.

Different yields are adopted in respect of the retail profit and the wholesale profit. The level of fair maintainable trade that has been adopted should be sustainable in volume terms. Although machine income at £20,000 represents some 28% of the overall net profit of £71,959, the profit as a result of the lack of control over outgoings is nevertheless at higher risk and this is reflected in adopting a different yield.

In these particular circumstances the brewer could therefore bid up to £823,700, net of the tenant's inventory, however, it is unlikely that they would pay more than 10% in excess of the freehouse value, £745,000, unless they were in competition with another brewer who had adopted similar criteria in their approach to the valuation.

Low barrelage and low value houses

A profits valuation can in certain circumstances with houses that have a low barrelage or a low level of turnover and net profit, become somewhat academic as there is insufficient profit to capitalise at the relevant prevailing yields to deduce a value which equates to the market value of the house.

The two types of houses most commonly encountered in this area are the rural free house, the typical roses round the door style of property, with a trade of £50,000 per annum or less, which has been acquired by the owner for reasons other than a straightforward business, and disposals by the breweries.

With the free house, in particular those in the more remote rural areas, it is not uncommon for at least 50% of the trade volume to be attributable to non-liquor sales, mainly catering. It is the exception rather than the rule for the trading accounts of the low turnover free house to show a net profit that accords with the profit that the valuer is trying to ascertain, which is the fair maintainable level. There might be a number of reasons for this, the owner might be achieving a higher level of trade than the valuer would expect as a result of his or her personality. If so, this has to be discounted. Alternatively the owner might perceive the business as secondary to his or her requirement to own and live in the property for his or her retirement. Perhaps the licensee may have an alternative employment as the main source of income leaving the running of the business throughout the daytime to his or her partner. In this instance the house most probably will be undertrading. As considered elsewhere in this chapter, it is necessary therefore for the valuer to adjust both turnover and net profit to what is regarded as the fair maintainable level.

A typical example of this type of property might well have a maintainable turnover of £50,000 per annum and a maintainable net profit of 16%. A profits valuation on the traditional basis, adopting an abbreviated form, would be on the following lines.

Example 5

Turnover	£50,000
Adjusted net profit @ 16%	£8,000
	× 8YP
Capital value	£64,000

If the valuer is aware that a three-bedroom detached house in the village is worth £120,000, then it is obvious that this method of valuation is inappropriate.

In the case of brewery disposals, as has been demonstrated in Table 8.2, the brewers have been pursuing a policy of disposing of low barrelage houses. The basic criterion adopted is barrelage and the benchmark originally adopted was a minimum of 100 beer barrels in the early 1960s. During the last five years or so this threshold has risen to 150 barrels and with regard to urban and inner city locations a realistic threshold at the present time is probably at least 200 barrels. However, these approximate levels of threshold apply to the major brewers, and it is still feasible for the provincial brewers and smaller independent companies that have been formed in the wake of the MMC Report, to acquire provincial houses that are trading at approximately 150–175 barrels.

The valuation of brewery houses which are to be considered for disposal tend to be in the main by direct comparison with other sales. This does not mean that the profits valuation should be abandoned, but it is unlikely to provide the correct valuation. The valuer will not necessarily be in possession of the whole of the liquor supplies to the property from the brewer. Neither will he be in possession of the trading accounts of the tenant as he is not involved in either valuing or selling the tenant's interest. Brewery disposals within inner city and urban areas tend to be arrived at by the valuer by direct comparison with other disposals. Normally the actual barrelage will be of secondary importance and perhaps two almost identical houses, one with an average trade of 100 barrels per annum and the other of 150 barrels per annum, although owned and let by the brewery, might well achieve the same value in the open market as it is the purchaser who will ultimately determine open market value from his perception as to what level of trade and profit he can achieve at the property.

With the rural, village and peripheral town free house, in addition to direct comparable evidence, the valuer can arrive at a valuation by considering the individual components of the valuation. These are:

1. The value of the property, either freehold or leasehold, on a de-licensed basis for alternative use.
2. The trade contents.
3. Goodwill.

More often than not the most relevant alternative use value for such type of houses is the underlying residential value. If there happens to be a higher alternative value for commercial use, or alternatively a break-up value, then the valuer can go direct to this value. It has to be remembered that the conversion of the property to residential use is an integral part of the valuation process, not only internally with regard to the bars and toilets, but externally car parks, the facia and signing will have to be removed and made good. A deduction from the residential value will have to be made for these conversion works.

The value of the trade contents has to be considered. When a brewer's tenancy changes hands it is normal practice for the outgoing and ingoing licensee to each appoint their own chattels valuer whose task is to agree the valuation between them. There is normally a contract between the parties and if the valuers are unable to agree, then there is provision for recourse to an umpire. In this example, however, it would be unusual for the valuer to go to the expense of involving a chattels valuer, usually he would adopt a "spot figure" in respect of the value of the contents.

The value that is to be considered is the "*in situ*" value of the trade contents that are used and necessary for the trade of the house. It is not the depreciated replacement cost, neither is it the value that the items would achieve if removed from the house and sold individually either by private treaty or auction.

The last component of the valuation is goodwill. Goodwill is deduced by adopting a year's purchase on the adjusted maintainable net profit, the range is normally between 1 and 3YP. The relevant year's purchase adopted depends on various factors such as the actual volume of the net profit, the ease with which it is earned, the nature of the clientele of the house, and the overall potential of the business. For example, with regard to the house mentioned above with a turnover of £50,000 and an adjusted net profit of £8,000, this is a very marginal sum by way of return to the owner. Assuming this house was in a pleasant location and was unopposed with some potential, this would be reflected by increasing the YP to, say, 2–3YP. Alternatively, if it were one of say four houses all with almost identical trade, in a small village all competing for a finite amount of trade, the net profit is therefore more vulnerable and a lower year's purchase of say 1YP might well be more appropriate for the valuer to adopt.

This type of valuation should only be considered relevant for low turnover and low profit houses where it is apparent to the valuer that on his initial appraisal of the house on a traditional profits basis of valuation, the resultant figure falls far short of the inherent underlying value of the property.

Often the valuer will undertake this style of valuation in connection with a possible agency instruction. Quite frequently it might be for security purposes, where the valuer will be expected to have regard to the Red Book, in particular P.S. 2.7.4. This deals with a request for "bricks and mortar valuation" or "security on land and buildings only". The valuer can apportion the open market value to its constituent parts, but, as with the above example, it is a hypothetical exercise and the valuer is under a duty to emphasise that the individual figures are informal apportionments only and they do not represent the individual open market value of the elements involved, since the true valuation can only be the figure taken as a whole.

Portfolio valuations

It cannot be stressed too strongly that in addition to being recognised as a specialist licensed property valuer if the valuer intends to embark on a portfolio valuation of licensed premises it is essential that the valuer has a detailed knowledge of the Red Book.

The same principles apply when approaching a portfolio valuation as to whether the estate comprises a relatively small number of outlets, perhaps between 10 and 20, or alternatively when dealing with a major client involving in excess of several thousand outlets.

It is not intended to deal with referencing or the approach to the physical task of the valuation of a portfolio of public houses, as the valuer if attempting such an instruction should have formulated his own pro forma with regard to inspection notes and the form of the valuation itself. This section is concerned with the Red Book requirements and attempts to consider some of the difficulties that can arise in the commissioning of a portfolio valuation.

G.N. 7.1 is in respect of Trading-Related Valuations and Goodwill. The valuer requires a sound knowledge of this Guidance Note, it details the general approach of the valuation of licensed premises.

P.S. 12.6 "Land and buildings fully equipped as an operational entity and valued having regard to trading potential" – The normal basis is EUV, however, where licensed premises owned by brewers and other pub-owning groups are let on a tied basis for the benefit of the continuing business, the valuation will generally be on the EUV basis, although vacant possession is not assumed.

It is at this stage that the valuer depending on the size of the portfolio will have to consider in conjunction with the client what departures and special assumptions are to be included, if any. Departures will probably be essential if the portfolio consists of more than about 100 properties, and special assumptions will depend on the client's instructions.

Common departures that might have to be considered are as follows:

1. *Description and age.* This should be included within the schedule appended to the valuation certificate. If the valuer agrees with the client that as a result of the number of properties involved in the valuation no details are given under this heading, the departure must be stated and the valuer might consider further qualifications and state that he has also not given any details of the service installations or the state of repair.

2. *Tenure.* It might well be agreed with the client that details of the tenure are inappropriate and that the properties are identified only as freehold, long leasehold or short leasehold. This might well arise as the information could be construed as being commercially sensitive. Similarly for this reason it might be agreed that no details are given of the leases or tenancies that the brewer has granted.

3. In all probability if a tenanted estate is involved, the properties will not be owner occupied. If so it will be necessary to include wording to such effect, see PS 12.6.3.

4. *Higher alternative use value.* Although the valuer is not valuing on this basis, nevertheless if it is apparent that there is the possibility of a higher alternative use value then it would be prudent to state that the valuer has identified these to the client and made them the subject of a separate report.

It is also a requirement to state if any Special Assumptions are relevant.

With regard to a portfolio valuation of trading properties such as public houses, there are certain economies of scale that result from owning and running groups or chains of public houses in regions. Such a group might well attract a premium, i.e. a sum in excess of the aggregate of the individual values if sold as one lot. On the other hand it might well be that a group of say ten low barrelage houses within a small geographic area of a depressed inner city if considered for sale as one lot, might well sell at less than the aggregate value of the individual properties.

This Special Assumption is considered in G.N. 1.15.

Depending on market circumstances at the time, the valuation of a portfolio as a whole or in parts may produce a greater or a lesser figure than the aggregate value of the separate properties it contains. It would be entirely appropriate for a Valuer to comment on such a situation. It is suggested that valuers consider the implications closely with their clients before expressing such comments on portfolios in their reports.

There is no doubt that as a result of the vertical integration of the brewing industry where a brewer or an owner can be in receipt of not only rent but also wholesale contribution as a result of the tie or other such provisions, to a greater or lesser extent, there are benefits in acquiring relevantly lotted groups of public houses.

This is a complex issue which depends not only on the quantity, the quality and the regional distribution of the portfolio and the relevant lotting or groups that the valuer is to consider, but also perhaps on other extraneous factors.

It should be noted that if a premium in respect of lotting is reported, it is not accepted accounting practice for the additional premium to be allocated on an individual basis to the properties. This is particularly important if the valuation is for incorporation in company accounts.

There may be various other special assumptions and departures that are to be considered with the client and it is important to stress that these should be highlighted within the valuation certificate, and preferably be included immediately following the basis and the definition of the valuation.

G.N. 7.2 is concerned in part with fixtures and fittings. It is important for the valuer, if he is valuing a mixed portfolio of managed and tenanted houses, to be quite clear what his valuation includes and excludes. For example, it would normally include landlord's fixtures and fittings. If it is a managed house it will probably also include the "tenant's" inventory of fittings, furniture and chattels. Quite often, however, after discussion with the client it might transpire that these are included elsewhere in the balance sheet and are depreciated separately and should be excluded from the valuation figure reported, otherwise there will be an element of double counting. Normally with most houses that are leased or let on agreements the valuation will exclude the tenant's inventory items. It is also important to state that trading stock has been excluded from the valuation.

G.N. 7.4 deals with goodwill which has been created in the business by the present owner, as distinct from the trading potential which runs with the property. The certificate might well incorporate the following wording so that there can be no doubt that if there is any personal goodwill which might be capable of being transferred to other properties that it is excluded, as follows: "The valuations ignore any value attributable to goodwill other than that which is reflected in the trading potential which attaches to and runs with the property."

G.N. 7.8.3 deals with the verification of trading information. The trading figures that are adopted by the valuer form the basis of the valuation. Particular regard should be had to this very important guidance note.

With a portfolio of a reasonable size, in all probability on the relevant valuation date one or more properties will be the subject of a major redevelopment or refurbishment. P.S. 3.3.1 deals with non-specialised properties in the course of development and sets out two bases which may be adopted according to the circumstances. Unfortunately whatever basis is adopted with regard to a public house which is undergoing a substantial refurbishment at the date of valuation, depending on the state of the development, an artificially low valuation can often result. Reference is made within the chapter dealing with Provincial Hotels on value during and after construction or extension. The same principle applies to public houses. For example, consider a high barrelage managed house on a large site which the brewery propose to redevelop into a branded restaurant with capital expenditure of say £500,000. If the valuation date is two weeks after the initial demolition works have commenced and at the date of inspection and valuation the property is no more than a non-operational shell or perhaps only one bar remains trading, capital value will have been lost, and until the new unit is fully operational in its new form with a proven profits record, the valuer will have no alternative but to heavily discount the value of the property. It is suggested that properties that fall within this category are discussed with the client and reported under a separate heading. It is accepted practice with certain brewers and hotel companies that where a property has been subject to major capital expenditure, that it is excluded from an open market valuation for at least a year or perhaps two years until it has reached full potential or a relevant trading pattern has emerged.

Negative values are not unusual in a portfolio valuation. Public houses are not an exception to the rule. If there is a negative value it should be reported separately and not set off against positive values of other property. (See P.S. 3.7, 7.4.12.) Quite frequently a negative value will apply with a short leasehold and reference therefore needs to be made to P.S. 12.5.1 where it is quite usual with a large portfolio for short leasehold interests to be omitted. If this is agreed with the directors, reference needs to be included within the valuation certificate as to the reason for their omission.

Restrictions on assignment are considered in P.S. 12.5.2. It is not uncommon to find prohibitions against alienation in leases of public houses. The advice is that these assets can be valued, "subject to adequate potential profitability of the business". The valuer should draw attention to the fact that these assets only have value to the business.

In the case of an extended portfolio, the valuer should state whether the whole portfolio has been valued or alternatively state known admissions and why. For example, short leaseholds with less than 10 years might have been excluded by agreement with the directors.

The above comprise some, but not an exhaustive list, of the various matters that have to be addressed with particular attention to the valuation of a portfolio of public houses.

The alternative to a portfolio valuation is some form of sampling exercise. It is accepted practice that once a portfolio has been valued in its entirety, an annual sample valuation can be undertaken. Realistically such an exercise can only be undertaken for a limited number of years. If this is the case, then it is preferable that the sample is provided by the client's auditors in conjunction with statisticians to ensure that the sample is representative. It will be the valuer's role to revalue the individual sample properties. The auditors' duty, in association with the statistician, will be to ensure that the sample is representative and to determine the basis and accuracy of the extrapolation exercise and finally the tolerances of the degree of accuracy of the value of the entire portfolio.

Long leases

The legislative changes following the MMC Report have forced the brewing industry to consider carefully the future style of their estates, in particular with regard to leasing. Although a generalisation, and referred to elsewhere in this chapter, the traditional letting arrangement was the annual brewery agreement subject to a three-yearly rent review, which essentially was little more than a tenancy at will. In March 1988 Grand Metropolitan launched its Inntrepreneur scheme which was the forerunner in the field of the long brewery commercial lease. This was of course before the MMC Report, but, following the report nearly all the national and provincial brewers are now offering long leases on varying terms and conditions.The main advantages of the lease as propounded by Grand Metropolitan were to the landlord:

- a higher and more secure rental stream;
- a simpler relationship between lessor and lessee, ie a commercial landlord and tenant relationship;
- lower administration costs;

and to the tenant:

- guaranteed security to the tenant;
- the tenant as a result of security would have the confidence and motivation to invest in the outlet;
- independence;
- the ability to assign his interest and thus capitalise on the goodwill he had built into the property.

As the Inntrepreneur lease was the first in the field and some 3,000 have now been completed, it is considered appropriate to set out a summary of the standard terms of the original lease, although longer leases are now on offer.

Inntrepreneur lease – main terms

Length of term:	20 years.
Premium:	No premium on the grant of lease.
Permitted use:	Fully licensed public house with catering facilities and other sources of ancillary income, eg letting bedrooms.
Assignment/Alienation:	Assignment after an initial agreed period, normally two years, but negotiable down to six months.
Ability to charge lease:	Lease is chargeable as security to raise finance.
Rent:	Best open market rent reflecting trading tie to the nominated supplier. Reviews at five-yearly intervals upwards-only to open market rent. Interim reviews may be triggered by landlord or statute if the tie is reduced or eliminated.
Repairs:	Obligation on lessee to put and keep in good repair, decorations on a three-yearly cycle.
Improvements:	Structural improvements require prior consent of landlord, at rent review voluntary improvements excluded from review assumptions. On reversion improvements become landlord's without payment of compensation, no obligation on the lessee to reinstate.
External signing:	Lessee free to determine the trading image subject to advertising of other brewers' brands limited to those which may be purchased outside the tie. Landlord has right to affix advertising hoardings.
Fixtures and fittings:	Landlord's revert to the landlord at the end of lease at no cost. Loose trade inventory – landlord has the option to purchase at valuation at the end of lease.
Insurance:	Building and landlord's fixtures and fittings – landlord will insure and recharge premium to lessee, including three years loss of rent and licence.

Beer tie:	Full tie for all beers excluding low- and no-alcohol beers and guest beer subject to a minimum purchase obligation, subject to a shortfall payment adjusted annually.
Other drinks:	Lessee is free with regard to the purchase of cider, soft drinks and wines and spirits. There is a stocking obligation with regard to certain brands of spirits, liquors and vermouths irrespective of source of supply.
Machines:	All income to the lessee who is free to select the supplier and either rent or purchase the machines.
Legal fees:	All legal fees payable by the lessee.

The Inntrepreneur lease as described above is in a standard form, however, there are two main variations, the "B" and "C" style leases which differ and are as follows:

"B":	The lessee is under an obligation to effect essential agreed repairs.
"C":	Houses with development potential where the lessee is under an obligation to effect agreed alterations.

Other leases

The MMC Report also appears to have had another side effect on the brewers. For once they appear to have addressed a major issue such as the decision to grant long leases from totally independent viewpoints, with the end result that there is little uniformity in the form of leases that are emerging. The main terms of the leases on offer from the major brewers are considered briefly together with a few of the independents.

Allied Lyons – the Vanguard lease. Ten-year term, full repairing and insuring, annual rent indexation, five-yearly rent review, EC style of tie/stocking agreement, no minimum purchasing obligation or penalty, composite barrelage volume incentive scheme. Conditions on machines. Assignable after two or three years, landlord has right of pre-emption.

Bass – Bass Leasing Company. A variety of short-term leases, long leases of 10, 15 or 20 years, full repairing and insuring, five-yearly rent reviews and penultimate day. EC style of tie/stocking agreement, no minimum purchasing obligations or penalties, all machine income to tenant. Assignment after two years, landlord has right of pre-emption.

Whitbread – Whitbread Pub Partnership. Twenty years, full repairing and insuring. Three-yearly rent reviews and penultimate day. EC style of tie/stocking agreement, no minimum purchasing obligation or penalties, all machine income to tenant, machine to be supplied by Whitbread. Assignment after three years, landlord has right of pre-emption.

Gibbs Mew – Twenty years, full repairing and insuring (landlord to put in full repair at outset), five-yearly rent reviews, full tie including wines and spirits, minimum purchasing obligation, all machine income to tenant.

Morland – Pub Master. Twenty-one years, full repairing and insuring, three-yearly rent reviews, beer, wines and spirits and soft drinks tie, minimum purchasing obligation on beers and cider, all machine income to tenant. Assignment after two years, landlord has right of pre-emption.

No doubt various of the above terms will be amended in due course (and perhaps by the time of publication) but they serve to demonstrate the very wide range of leases now on offer.

Valuation of long leases

With regard to both the landlord's and the tenant's interest, the market is imperfect as a result of lack of comparable evidence.

As to the valuation of the interest of the landlord, there is little market evidence of any of the brewers disposing of a property at arms-length with a modern commercial long lease in place. Until such time as the market in long brewery leases has settled and rent reviews have taken place and the majority of the national and provincial brewers' estates have been transferred to the new forms of letting on offer, it would seem that the proper approach for valuers is to adopt the traditional method based entirely on previous working practices and accepted methods of valuation.

Turning to consideration of the value of the lessee's interest, the majority of the market evidence is with regard to the sales of

Inntrepreneur leases that have taken place. An analysis of premiums achieved shows quite a wide variation, not only as a result of the imperfections in the market, but more importantly those leases that have come to the market have tended to do so in a period of severe recession in property values. It would be unwise therefore to attempt at this stage to formulate a hard and fast set of rules for the valuation of the lessee's interest but on a traditional approach of a year's purchase multiplier on the fair maintainable level of net profit, on average the premiums being achieved, including the value of the lessee's inventory, equate to approximately 1½–2YP.

Landlord and Tenant (Licensed Premises) Act 1990

The purpose of this Act, which received Royal Assent on November 1 1990, was to repeal Section 43(1)(d) of Part II of the Landlord and Tenant Act 1954 which excluded public houses from the protection afforded by the Act. The relevant section is:

43. – (1) This part of the Act does not apply –
    (d) To a tenancy of premises licensed for the sale of intoxicating liquor for consumption on the premises, other than –
    (i) Premises which are structurally adapted to be used and are bona fide used, for a business which comprises one or both of the following, namely, the reception of guests and travellers desiring to sleep on the premises and the carrying on of a restaurant, being a business a substantial proportion of which consists of transactions other than the sale of intoxicating liquor.

The subsequent sections (ii) and (iii) specify other categories of premises similarly exempted.

The exemption was repealed by a transitionary period being provided from July 11 1989 to July 11 1992.

All tenancies granted on or after July 11 1989, unless entered into in pursuance of a contract before that date, are given full protection.

Tenancies entered into before July 11 1989 or after that date in pursuance of a contract made before that date would not be given protection unless the tenancy continues up to or beyond July 11 1992.

In passing, mention should also be made of an additional bill that was introduced at the same time to extend the compensation provisions with regard to licensed premises. "The Landlord and Tenant (Licensed Premises) (No 2) Bill" provided for additional compensation to be payable when the landlord was successful on preventing a new lease being granted when he depended on the ground specified on Section 30(1)(g) of the 1954 Act which is where the landlord wishes to use the premises for his own use and occupation. The Bill was read for a third time in the House of Lords and sent to the Commons but ran out of time and is therefore dead. It is not known at the present time if the Bill will be re-introduced.

It will be appreciated that the Landlord and Tenant Act 1954 (Part II) will therefore be relevant in the future with regard to the terms of a new lease of a public house. The general principles and case law that has been established will now apply from the end of the transitionary period, July 11 1992. If the terms in respect of the new lease are not agreed by negotiation between the parties, then it will be up to the court to decide in the normal way what the relevant terms are to be. As is well known, with regard to the duration, it will be "As determined by the court to be reasonable in all the circumstances . . . not exceeding 14 years." The other terms will be those agreed between the parties or "Determined by the court and in determining those terms the court shall have regard to the terms of the current tenancy and to all relevant circumstances."

This will no doubt prove to be a very fertile field, not only for the legal profession but also for any valuer specialising in licensed property.

The rent, of course, cannot be ascertained until the other terms of the lease are resolved. The rent will be determined in accordance with Section 34 of the Landlord and Tenant Act 1954 Part II (as amended).

The wording adopted in this section, to a greater or lesser extent, is normally found in the rent review provisions in most modern commercial leases. The disregards are the tenant's (a) occupation, (b) goodwill, (c) improvements, and (d) the value attributable to the licence if it appears the benefit of the licence belongs to the tenant.

The terms of the tenancy, and the disregards, have to be considered when formulating a rental valuation as set out in example 1. The basis of the valuation is to assess the fair maintainable level of trade. If the valuer achieves this he will have complied with the disregards (a) and (b).

As has been mentioned earlier, the most frequent instance when the valuer is not in receipt of at least some of the trade of the house is when acting for a landlord at review, and the question of the discovery of the trading accounts might be a relevant issue.

There is a considerable amount of case law, the majority of which can be referred to in *Handbook of Rent Review* and the matter is dealt with at 7–23. The general rule would appear to be that if the lessee's trading accounts are available in the open market, for example by way of a search at Companies House, then they are admissible as far as the valuation of a public house is concerned. The authors of the *Handbook of Rent Review*, however, put forward a very interesting hypothesis:

The Authors suggest that, as a result of these decisions, the rule as to the admissibility of trading accounts is precisely the opposite of what it should be. Accounts which would have been available to the hypothetical lessee should not be admitted because to do so would fail to give effect to the usual requirement to "disregard the effect on rent of . . . the occupation of the tenant". If the tenant had not been in occupation, there would have been no published accounts available to the hypothetical lessee and the disregard requires that any effect which such accounts would have had on the mind of the hypothetical tenant, and thus on the market, must be ignored. Yet the same criticism cannot be made of accounts which were not public and thus could not directly have affected the market. Such accounts should be admitted because, without infringing the disregard, they bear direct relevance to the central question in a notional profits valuation, namely what is the profit-earning potential of the premises. The proposition can be illustrated by an example: in the rent review of a casino, both landlord and tenant might adopt the notional profits method. The landlord might allege that a casino of the quality and in the location of the subject premises might be expected to achieve a turnover of £4 million per annum. The tenant might assert that a properly-run casino of that size in that location could only be expected to achieve a turnover of £1 million. In deciding who was right, surely the arbitrator ought to be entitled to receive evidence as to the actual turnover achieved by the tenant over the previous five years. If he had in fact been turning over some £4 million then, in the absence of some good explanation, the arbitrator would be justified in treating the tenant's case with some scepticism.

Looking at the issue from the practical viewpoint of the valuer when acting for either the landlord or tenant, it is preferable that the rental valuation should, in the first instance, be approached from a position which is as unbiased and unfettered as possible, ie without the benefit of the actual trading accounts. In more cases than not a tenant or his valuer will be more forthcoming with the trading accounts when they are aware that they are underperforming the market.

Improvements (c) that fall to be disregarded need to be agreed between the parties. There is often some debate as to what are classified as improvements. Often they are no more than the tenant is obliged to undertake in accordance with the repairing and decorating covenants. It is normal practice for the property to be valued in its existing state with the benefit of the improvements, the reason being that it is a more feasible and realistic exercise to value the actual building rather than a hypothetical building which does not exist any more. A figure representing the current cost of the improvements requires to be agreed between the valuers and the total amount of the capital expenditure is allowed for in the profits valuation as a tenant's capital sum which includes the inventory, stock and working capital. With reference to example 1, if the profits valuation had been for a rental valuation and tenant's improvements were agreed at £20,000 the valuation is as follows:

Example 5

		£
Net Profit		**57,109 (25.4%)**

Less Interest on Tenant's Capital and Improvements

Inventory	20,000	
Stock (approx 2 weeks)	4,000	
Working Capital	4,000	
Improvements	20,000	
	48,000	
Interest @	× 15%	
		−7,200
Divisible Balance		49,909
Rental Bid		× 50%
		24,954
E.R.V.		Say £25,000 pa.

In the above example interest has been allowed on the cost of improvements at the rate of 15%. Often a lower rate of say, 10%, will be adopted in respect of the element of improvements.

It is extremely rare for the fourth disregard (d) with regard to the value of the licence to form part of the rental negotiation. The reason is that most leases contain a provision for the Justices' Licence on the determination of the lease to revert to the landlord or a nominee. It should also be noted that if the licence belongs to the tenant it is not necessary to disregard the existence of the licence and the effect that that would have on the rent but merely the addition (if any) to the value of the holding. As far as case law or precedent is concerned there does not appear to be any guidance on how this disregard, if it is relevant, should be reflected in the rental value.

© John Nicholl, 1996

CHAPTER 11

Restaurants

Introduction and brief history

Restaurants are now fully established as a totally independent and specialised sector of the property market. This sector itself is broken down into numerous types of restaurants, many of which differ in terms of location, size, demand, concept and most importantly in the approach to be adopted for capital and rental valuation purposes. It is estimated that in 1994 £15 billion of food was eaten outside of the home, an increase of 250% in ten years. Of this, approximately £4.5 billion related to pub catering, and approximately £5 billion to fast food with the residue being attributable to traditional restaurants and other outlets.

This sector has evolved dramatically over the last three decades and continues to grow. It has attracted some of the most important tenants and valuable sites to be found not only in retail locations, but in all types of locations throughout the United Kingdom.

Sizes of restaurants now range from small kiosks to units over 20,000 sq.ft. and fitting out costs can now run into millions of pounds. Catering tenants traditionally scorned by landlords are now well received by investors, landlords and developers. The dynamic emergence of the catering market in the form that is now recognised can be traced to the beginning of the 1960s. Throughout the United Kingdom for centuries, inns, taverns, hostelries and public houses had traditionally formed the hard-core of the venues in which the general public and especially the traveller could meet, eat and drink and indeed to this day those establishments hold their own special position in the catering marketplace, whether it be for simple bar food, or the comprehensive catering of the major steak house brands.

Until the latter part of the 19th century, restaurants in town centres, especially in prime positions, were the exclusive domain of the higher classes. The middle classes drank or ate in the taverns and the working class would tuck into cheaper fare at the local eel and pie shop, chippy or working man's eating room.

The latter part of the 19th century and the early 20th century saw the establishment of the middle of the road eating places in central London and other major cities throughout the country catering for the tremendous influx of visitors into the capital and Great Britain in general as the Empire reached its peak of importance and as the cities expanded to produce more housing, offices and industrial content.

At the forefront of the expansion into popular catering was J. Lyons & Co Ltd with their tea-shops – in their day, revolutionary in their style of operation. They anticipated a great number of the trends that are now established as acceptable features in most popular restaurants. Self-service with a long counter, a cashier and meals being taken by the customer to their selected tables. Trays were placed in stacks in the restaurant and waitresses cleared up after the customer departed. Not generally different from today's motorway or hamburger restaurant.

Other brands including Tea Importers, Carwadines, Express Dairies, Black & White Milk Bars, Kardomah and Fortes, all expanded within London and major cities throughout the country, and together with the fish and chip shops, pubs and local individually owner-run restaurants, they formed the basic foundation of catering throughout the UK until the early 1950s.

After the war, we saw the advent of milk bars and coffee bars, with the first Wimpy Bars appearing in the 1950s, again under the J. Lyons banner and subsequently through franchising. Indeed, Wimpy and Golden Egg were the forerunners of today's catering franchise world and many major operators evolved from those small beginnings as franchisees of Lyons.

The 1950s and 1960s also saw the expansion of the Italian Trattoria, and growth in the Chinese restaurant and Indian restaurant sector, mainly in sit-down restaurants, but with the take-away concept to follow.

The concept of over the counter and take away was not the creation of the Americans. In the UK, there had been bakers selling hot food, fish and chip shops, eel and pie shops and Chinese and Indian restaurants for many years, all dealing in their own form of counter service and take-away for a long time before anyone ever sold a Big Mac. In the mid-1960s we saw the first major American caterer, Kentucky Fried Chicken appear in the high streets. They had dynamic expansion, mainly through master franchisees and they were followed in 1970 by many popular caterers and indeed the approach to catering for many popular caterers and indeed the eating habits of the general public throughout the United Kingdom.

The 1970s also saw the expansion of Pizzaland, Pizza Hut, Strikes and Garfunkels as well as numerous brands controlled by major brewers. By the beginning of the 1970s, therefore, the traditional UK catering locations had many newcomers from overseas and homegrown. Indeed for a couple of years, expansion in any location but especially in the high streets was relatively easy. But from 1972, the criteria that had created the marketplace began to change so that by the present day, there has been a complete juxtaposition of those criteria.

The main aspects of change over the last two decades are as follows:

Planning

The Local Authority had very little part to play in the control of the expansion of restaurants into Class 1 retail premises, as no planning consent was required to open a restaurant in a retail location until October 23 1972. On that date, the Town and Country Planning (Use Classes) Order 1972 came into operation and became the single most important factor contributing to the growth in rentals and capital values associated with the sector thereafter. From this date, Class 1 retail use excluded "a shop for the sale of hot food". With this particular statutory instrument in hand, the local authorities had the ammunition to restrict the dynamic expansion of the catering sector in the high streets of the UK. Planning refusals became common-place and it soon became apparent that certain local authorities were taking very bigoted views indeed over the possible appearance of a restaurant on their doorstep.

Some local authorities blatantly refused to give any planning consent for catering in their shopping centres and others placed restrictions on take away use and opening hours, even Sunday trading.

The 1980s saw the marketplace reaching very competitive levels with premiums and rents generally reaching their peak in 1988/1989.

This demand was further enhanced by the provisions of the Town and Country Planning (Use Classes) Order 1987 which amalgamated restaurants, cafes, public houses, wine bars and hot food take aways into one Use Class known as A3, covering food and drink. This was followed hot on its heels by the Town and Country Planning General Development Order 1988 and this permitted, among other use changes, the ability for a restaurant to interchange not only with the uses within its own class order but also between A2 and A1 use, although the inverse did not apply. From that date, in October 1988, estate agents, banks, betting offices, building societies, and other financial professional services, all of whom had had great difficulty in obtaining their own consent in prime retail positions, now looked to the A3 sector to achieve their ends. As a result the marketplace became even more congested with higher than ever demand in all locations for a wide range of restaurant concepts and sizes.

Attitudes of landlords

Before 1972 the major problem in acquiring catering units lay solely with the attitude of landlords who did not wish to have caterers as tenants because of the detrimental effect they had on the interests of good estate management and investment value. Those landlords displayed, sometimes justified but more often than not prejudiced, attitudes towards the possible bad effects that restaurant smells, refuse, effluent and disturbances would have on their property.

This attitude had a major effect on the restaurant market and catering investments tended to have two or three points knocked off their yields, in comparison to a retailer in a similar location. This negative attitude of landlords led to further shortages and higher rentals and premiums even in those early days in comparison to shop properties.

In the 1980s, public expenditure in the sector led to an increase in operator demand, rental growth, higher standards of shopfitting and greater tenant quality coming into the marketplace. This changed the attitude of many landlords and the caterer is now seen as one of the most sought after and active tenants. Investment yields have begun to almost reach parity with retail investment yields. It is far easier today to obtain landlords' consent for change of use than it was say 20 years ago, especially in the current marketplace where retailers have suffered, generally, to a greater extent than caterers.

Changes in attitude to unit size

Another major metamorphosis in the marketplace has occurred over the last 20 years in many catering locations. There has been a dramatic change in the criteria of size of the units taken by caterers.

When J. Lyons were taking their tea shops the average size of their units in the high streets were in the region of 3,000–4,000 sq.ft. All of their units were split up and sold in the early 1970s and although some of them were passed to caterers, the majority were actually sold to retailers due to the fact that the early expansion of the restaurant groups in the 1960s and 1970s seemed to polarise around a unit size of about 1,500 sq.ft. It was not unusual for units of 1,000 sq.ft or sometimes even less, to be acquired by the main groups, especially Kentucky Fried Chicken and some Wimpy franchisees. Certainly the early Pizzaland units had an average size of around 1,250 sq ft with some ancillary storage.

McDonalds led the way in increasing the size of trading units with their minimum area being around 2,500 sq.ft from the earliest stage and larger sizes subsequently.

With the growth of awareness of the general public in popular catering coupled with their increasing affluence, all types of caterers began to appreciate that the cardinal sin was to turn away customers at peak hours. As a result, in order to satisfy the higher volumes, it made a great deal of sense to increase unit size.

In addition, with the benefit of economies of scale, the large units produced a greater degree of net profit and unit size increased to 2,000 sq.ft on average in the early 1970s and units in excess of 10,000 sq.ft have been very much in demand in city centres and tourist locations. Currently, most major caterers need a minimum of 2,500 sq.ft gross in city centres and roadside locations, although there are obviously exceptions to this rule.

At the other end of the scale it is not unusual to have demands for units in excess of 20,000 sq.ft and currently up to 70,000 sq.ft in the centre of major conurbations from international operators such as Planet Hollywood, Hard Rock Cafe, Dave & Buster's and numerous other concepts coming from various parts of the world.

However, most catering agents find that the greatest number of instructions which return to them for resale are units of less than 1,750 sq.ft gross, where it is far harder to make profits due to the restriction on the maximum turnover on a unit of this size. The major growth in prices and rents is now for the larger unit with an ever-increasing gap between the values of units of less than 1,500 sq.ft and larger units over 2,500 sq.ft in most locations.

Changes in siting policy

In the early 1980s, retailers played a major part in increasing rentals and premiums in competition with the caterer in the high streets and traditional restaurant locations around town centres. Coupled with the fact that planning was a problem and the acquisition of existing restaurants highly expensive, with fewer sites remaining, the need to find different marketplaces and locations was imperative if many of the newly formed catering groups were to survive and expand.

The first dynamic move was to the periphery of the town centres close to entertainment, transport and social venues. Parking was far easier as was access for loading and servicing and trading was possible for far longer hours normally for every day of the week. The safety of customers was also better protected on the periphery than in what had become fairly dangerous town centres in the early 1980s.

In high density cities and tourist locations, destination restaurants became more popular with increasingly larger units being located in obscure positions depending upon the goodwill of the tenant to draw custom from a wide area.

The roadside marketplace also evolved with many of the brands such as Kentucky Fried Chicken, McDonald's, Pizza Hut and Wimpy beginning to take up roadside positions on trunk roads and important inner city roads for drive-to and drive-through operations in competition with the brewers who had always been established in that location. In addition, the home delivery market evolved with many pizza operators taking tertiary positions in high density residential areas through the country for their particular style of operation.

Accordingly, in the last two decades we have seen the marketplace expand into new areas of operations as demand increases for units throughout the sector.

Licensing

The Justices' attitude to restricting licences favourably changed during the 1980s and as a result the incidence of a Justices' full on licence, not only permitting the sale of alcoholic drink to customers eating a meal, but also to others not wishing to eat at the venue has increased. This coupled with longer licensing hours, as a result of the Licensing Act 1988, has enabled enriched turnover especially in high density and tourist locations.

Concepts and competition

There are many more operators in this sector compared to the early 1970s although the locations in which they are found are very widespread in comparison. In addition, certain locations are in less demand nowadays, a prime example being the established retail locations in provincial and suburban towns, especially in the best locations. In this particular location it is estimated that there has been a drop in demand of approximately 80% from caterers although a far higher increase from A2 users. However, the number of concepts in operation is generally greatly higher than in the early 1970s and the incidence of counter service and take away as well as drive-through units has increased dramatically.

In summary, over the last twenty five years, in the most important expansion period that the catering sector has seen, there have been fundamental changes to the basic criteria relating to catering property.

Planning has become more restrictive and difficult to obtain, demand has increased with the number of operators in the sector, the number of locations in which those operators seek premises has expanded, as has the range of concepts, whereas landlords are now more than happy to have caterers as tenants.

The result of this mixture of changes is the production of a strong demand for a wide range of units and the creation of a complex multilevelled property sector deserving very special and careful treatment by the valuer.

Various types of restaurant

The UK marketplace in restaurants can be identified by the following specific areas of operation. These areas of operation have the following differing criteria:

1. Operators.
2. Average sizes.
3. Rental and premium values.
4. Planning, licencing and statutory requirements.

Prime locations in provincial and suburban shopping centres

Surprisingly, demand has dropped dramatically for this type of location. Over the last 20 years, there has been an 80% decrease in the number of operators seeking representation in this location. Most are leading international brands. The effects of the Town and Country Development Order 1988, have produced a great demand from the A2 sector (in the form of Building Societies, Banks, Employment Agencies and Estate Agencies) for the acquisition of existing A3 users in the high streets across the UK. This demand includes basement and first floor restaurants in and around the best positions from betting offices and employment agencies. As a result, not only has there been a slowing in demand from operators but there has been a taking up of existing units by the A2 sector. At the end of the 1960s the average size of unit taken in the high street was between 1,500 and 2,000 sq.ft but nowadays approaching 5,000 sq.ft is more desirable.

The valuer may consider that these locations are among the most valuable in the country. Certainly in the most sought after shopping centres, this may be the case, but it is dangerous to make general assumptions. The shortage of demand requires the valuer to seek support from the fact that there are still major operators who will take a unit in a particular centre to create a "marketplace". Such an operator could include the A2 bidder.

Most major suburban and provincial centres, although not necessarily the medium sized or smaller centres, do demonstrate what is known as the "crater effect". In essence, it can be proved that restaurants have moved outwards from prime city centre positions to the periphery and destination locations and that there are fewer restaurants in the prime locations compared to say 10 or 15 years ago. It is as if a bomb has landed in the middle of the centre and spread the restaurants accordingly. This argument must be borne in mind when uplift for catering use is suggested.

Valuers should almost without reservation utilise a zoning method in an identical way to retail zoning for the purposes of assessing rental value. It is not often that the restaurant value is higher than the retail value, but it is not unusual to have a dual use or even a triple use with A1 and A2 use amalgamated in leases of such properties.

It is not necessarily the case either that A2 use has a higher value in rental terms or for that matter on a capital basis than A1 or A3 use. The Planning Authorities do tend to be restrictive but consent is often obtained on Appeal. The Unitary Development Plans seem generally to indicate that the local authorities' attitude to restricting A3 consent in prime shopping locations will continue.

The valuer should be aware of extreme planning constraints on A3 use as, depending upon the overall demand for operators for the centre, this may have an effect on rental or premium values but this is not the general rule.

As far as drinks licensing is concerned their existence does not normally have any major bearing on value for these types of properties, unless the property represents a major restaurant/bar or public house venue.

Periphery and destination locations in provincial and suburban shopping centres

It is to this location that many operators have moved over the last decade. There has been a definite migration from the prime city centre position – often only a matter of 50–100 yards away to the periphery of the shopping centre or to locations close to travel termini, cinemas, theatres, leisure and recreational and social centres. These positions are normally prominent, easily accessible with excellent parking facilities, and the added security of being close to well lit and used areas of the city or town in contrast to the shopping centre in the evening. Quite often, there is excellent car parking, servicing and access.

Mostly, the traditional prime shopping location is far quieter than the periphery where opening hours are dramatically different with restaurants being able to serve breakfast, lunches, and an evening meal.

The number of operators in this sector is far higher than in the prime location. Accordingly there are a greater number of operators who could alternatively take the premises. A2 operators do not tend to compete as strongly with the A3 operator in this location as they might in the prime position.

Planning consent is normally easier to obtain in this position. Sizes tend to be in excess of 2,500 sq.ft. and often up to 5,000–6,000 sq.ft. There is a mixture of approach to rental value in this location. One can utilise a zoning code in predominantly retail pitches, but caterers have been known to pay in excess of retail levels in these locations, but normally only in very bullish markets. Premium values for restaurants in this location have never been as high as desirable units in prime retail locations. The overall rental basis normally applies for non-retail pitches or exceptionally large units.

During the 1980s there was an increase in destination venues, ie restaurants in very secondary and obscure positions, depending upon the generation of their own goodwill to draw trade from the surrounding areas. These tend to be larger than average, heavily licensed premises and are valued on an overall rental basis. The impact of licensing for liquor, music and dancing and public entertainment both in respect of the periphery and destination locations, is far higher than in the prime position, and may figure in the approach to value.

Generally, planning consent is slightly easier to obtain in these locations than in the prime position. Unitary Development Plans are now indicating that local planning authorities view this location preferentially.

Shopping developments and food courts

Developers of the older shopping developments in town centres tended to locate restaurants out on a limb in secondary malls. Developers now identify that the public need good catering facilities to enable them to stay for a longer period within the development. Progressively, developers are placing restaurants, especially so-called fast food units, in locations which benefit from trading within the development and also from external trading, thus offering longer hours to the tenants.

Larger catering units have emerged during the last decade in such developments, as developers appreciate that restaurants are very important to the customers visiting a scheme.

The approach to value for these type of restaurants tends to be on a zoning basis in line with retail practice within the scheme. There may be the necessity to apply the overall code, but these would be exceptions and related mainly to units in excess of 4,000 sq.ft which are still unusual in such schemes.

There are developments now which have a dominating use of turnover leases and of course these would have their own formula for review, although normally based on a percentage of open market value. The valuer will find a wide range of operators in such schemes, normally the same national brands, but also some local chains. The opportunity of alternative use for A2 is limited in such schemes. The impact of liquor and entertainment licences is nominal in these schemes unless they are very large units with the potential for high turnover. The planning authorities generally tend to be a little more lenient.

Premium values have tended to be a little subdued in these schemes unless the scheme is very much in demand. Rental values are normally on a par with retail rents without uplift unless the location is exceptional and competition is limited.

Mainly during the last 15 years, although there were several earlier examples, food courts have evolved within shopping developments.

This concept is based on a central public seating area servicing customers for a variety of small counter service catering units of different concepts surrounding the seating area. There are normally between six and ten such operations. They may be owned by the headlessee of the food court and run by them, or the headlessee may operate a few such units and sublicence or sublet the remainder. Tenure can be either on the basis of market rental, turnover percentage, or a mixture of both. The valuer should be accurately aware of the outgoings relating to such establishments from the headlessee's point of view or from the subtenant's point of view. When valuing a headleasehold interest, especially, the valuer should be careful to be aware of who might be in the market to purchase as there is a limited range of operators and the less successful food courts may not be easily assignable. Generally the approach to value either on a rental or capital basis is directed at the profit/turnover actual or potential. This is an ever changing field and the valuer should be particularly careful to be in touch with current criteria and concepts. The importance of brands within the foodcourt is paramount, as is location.

Tertiary or home delivery location
The valuer should recognise the secondary and tertiary positions as being specialised catering locations. At the beginning of the 1980s, Pizzaland International, a subsidiary of United Biscuits at the time, acquired the Perfect Pizza chain, a small home delivery and take away pizza concept, probably the first of its kind in the UK with about 20 branches of which half were company owned and the rest franchised. A dynamic expansion programme ensued, with the chain now being over 150 units, and several other operators joined the race, including Dominos and Pizza Hut. As a result, the secondary and tertiary positions attracted a demand from these operators far in excess of retail demand, and certainly until the late 1980s, retail rents bore little or no comparison to the A3 bid, either on a rental or premium basis. Those levels of rental and premiums have subdued subsequently, but the valuer must be aware that A3 units in these locations are worthy of special attention and investigation. There is certainly an abundance of these units, many of which will not show growth for a long time because they were so over-rented originally, whilst others may show some increase in excess of retail values of adjoining premises. The valuer should be careful not to value in accordance with the levels established in the late 1980s.

The code of rental valuation is normally zoning.

The sector is dominated by franchisees with very few company owned stores now being opened. The valuer should be careful to check whether the user clause in the franchisee's leases is restricted to the specific franchise use and to value accordingly.

Planning tends to be less of a problem. Average size is about 1,000 sq.ft gross and there are quite a few operators, although in recent years some degree of assimilation has taken place as operators have either gone out of business or have been acquired by the larger groups.

Roadside

This heading covers the entire spectrum of roadside users including trunk road operators such as Little Chef and Happy Eater, TGIF-type operations, Pizza Hut, Kentucky Fried Chicken, McDonald's and also the brewery owned operations, public houses and steak bars. Currently, this is probably the most important area of expansion in the UK as far as the restaurant sector is concerned. It has great potential for additional growth and is probably the main location into which most caterers are looking to expand.

Sites range in size from 0.2 acre to approximately one acre as a general rule and may be drive-through or drive-to operations, of freestanding sites, or linked to a leisure, retail park or other important venues.

Module size can be anything from 1,500 sq.ft to 10,000 sq.ft but most modules are between 3,000 and 6,000 sq.ft.

Car parking is an important factor as is access from trunk roads. Planning consents are more long winded with the Police and the Highways Authorities playing a major part in consultation and decision making. The likelihood of local residential petitioning and objection is also stronger in such applications.

Transactions in this sector tended to be freehold or long lease-hold acquisitions but straightforward lettings are now commonplace and are on an overall basis related to the buildings only. Rent reviews can be one of numerous permutations, often with an alternative value to consider. An example would be the "market value of the premise or the value of a B2 unit on the same Estate with an uplift of 15%". Other bases can relate to a Zone A figure in a nearby town suitably adjusted or to a percentage of turnover together with a base rent.

The marketplace is fast expanding and as it matures so a more solid foundation of market values has appeared and rent reviews and rental valuations will be more straightforward. The premium market is one of great fluctuation and the valuer should take care to consider the merits of location, competition, accessibility and potential very carefully before reaching a conclusion.

The impact of liquor and entertainment licensing in this sector is very widespread. Most fast food operators do not have any benefit of such licences but steak houses and public houses obviously do have benefit and, depending on the basis of tenure and many other aspects, the valuer must carefully take licensing into consideration.

Included in this section are motorway service areas, a very interesting and fast growing part of the marketplace. The Government has indicated that operators may now acquire sites on motorways at much closer intervals and there is therefore dynamic expansion in this area. This is a specialised area of valuation but the valuer should obviously consider the impact of such legislation when evaluating existing or new sites close to motorways.

Central London core

The Central London core comprises many different sub-markets which do not necessarily overlap and before evidence from any of these sub-markets is utilised for another, the valuer should consider the various valuation elements that relate to those properties and see if there is any interrelation or common bond other than the fact that they are both restaurants.

The marketplace is multilevelled and the range of operators in this general area is very wide and varied. The impact of liquor, music and dancing and entertainment licensing is highly important in terms of value, both for rent review and premiums.

The sub-markets can be briefly described as follows:

Central London tourist – high turnover positions
Central London prime shopping locations – such as Oxford Street, Bond Street, Kensington High Street and Knightsbridge
Mayfair and St James
Covent Garden
Chelsea
Kensington
Bayswater
The City of London
Midtown.

There are other subcentres such as Chinatown, Notting Hill/Holland Park, Islington, Camden, Bloomsbury and the evolving South Bank developments.

Certain of these areas are now predominantly being treated as one code or another, ie. zoning or overall rental valuation. For example, Mayfair and St James tend to adopt the overall approach generally, but there is still a mixture of zoning especially in retail streets. Soho has a mixture of both codes whereas Kensington, Chelsea and Knightsbridge in their retail positions are mostly zoned.

The City of London is probably the only area which almost universally adopts an overall basis unless one is dealing with a dedicated retail style module in a shopping thoroughfare. The confusions that lie within the overall approach are quite dramatic. Some valuers are approaching the analysis of comparables on a straightforward overall basis, whether the unit is on basement, first or ground floor or a mixture. Some are applying half value to basements and first floors. Others are applying gross internal and other net internals. The valuer may even come across rentals per seat or cover, rents per table, and numerous other concoctions. However, the approach to valuing appears to be polarising around gross internal net of WCs with some valuers still adopting a half value on basement and first floor levels, whereas others are applying an overall base of value to all levels.

Some valuers may consider placing different rates on various parts of the restaurant such as the kitchen, ancillary storage, staff areas and restaurant area. If comparable properties are on the same basis then so be it but generally this can be a dangerous approach to rental valuation. The main exception to that rule is that where there are major structural problems in terms of the layout of the premises and specific areas cannot be used for anything other than ancillary purposes. In that event there should be a downgrading in terms of rental value for those areas especially if they are in excess of the degree of space required by a normal operator.

As an important rule the valuer should accordingly investigate the comparables to ensure that he is comparing like with like especially in respect of structural layout.

The valuer should also be aware that prime retail does not necessarily mean prime catering positions. Quite often, a caterer will not be able to survive in a retail position in Central London.

Conversely, some forms of catering are able to survive very well in obscure positions in Central London. This ability to attract trade from elsewhere was identified in the case of *My Kinda Town Ltd* v *Castlebrook Properties Ltd* (1986), where the Court considered that the arbitrator had properly utilised evidence of so called "destination restaurants" located well away from the subject premises but they were in obscure positions.

The valuer should be wary of utilising a wide range of properties to value the subject premises in such circumstances. The valuer should first seek similar properties in the general area and in the absence of good support in this respect, seek further support from comparables of similar sized units in locations of similar personality and trading potential. It is very dangerous to apply evidence of a dissimilar size, significance and potential.

Size is highly important in the Central London Core. The bigger the unit the more potential for turnover and normally higher profit margins. However, the valuer should be very wary of comparing small units with large and vice versa as they are completely different market places.

There are numerous operators for different types of properties in the Central London core as well as there being the widest range of concepts in the UK. In comparison with other parts of the UK, premium and rental values, in comparison to other parts of the UK have traditionally been far higher although subdued currently. The Planning Authorities have always strongly resisted changes to A3 use and their current proposals in the Unitary Development Plan for Westminster indicate that their policy is continuing with a vengeance.

All in all, a very difficult area in which to value and one which will need specialist attention for success.

Generics

A new type of restaurant of a very large size has been appearing throughout the Central London core and may well do so in important provincial cities. This restaurant known as a "generic restaurant" is represented by such operators as Hard Rock Cafe, Planet Hollywood, The Fashion Cafe and numerous other new ventures and concepts coming from America, the Far East and Europe. These restaurants are seeking units of at least 10,000 sq.ft and sometimes as high as 70,000 sq.ft but most of them polarising around 20,000 sq.ft. They require prime locations, normally in the middle of the entertainment or tourist centre, such as Coventry Street and Leicester Square. Most of these operators are seeking representation only in the capital cities within a particular country and they are very specialised creatures indeed to value both on a rental and capital basis. Quite a few of the transactions evolving in this particular marketplace involve a turnover related payment or joint venture with landlords. The valuer is advised to be exceptionally careful unless they are immersed in this market.

Restaurants in tourist and special locations

This sector includes major tourist, leisure, entertainment and financial centres which have associated restaurant units. The tendency here is for purpose built units to be provided by developers often fitted out partially or totally by the landlord. They are subject to peculiar leases in comparison with normal catering units often with turnover rents, high landlords contribution, wide ranging service charges and with extensive licensing; all in all very difficult units to value. The valuer should be aware of the complete range of income and cost potential and endeavour to effect a residual rental value in order to reach a conclusion as to market rental value. Capital value of course leads from the basis of capitalised, actual and potential profit.

There are a number of operators seeking representation in or close to such venues throughout the United Kingdom and demand tends to be quite high.

In general, a wide ranging and difficult area for valuers to consider.

Traditional restaurants

The classic traditional restaurants in the city and town centre include old inns or taverns with good catering facilities or restaurants established often at basement or first floor level. They are mostly subject to the overall approach or a rental worked back from turnover and profits. Most of these restaurants are found close to the prime position and are not influenced by the rents sustained in that location.

Their value is highly influenced by their adaptability for alternative use to A2 and if they lack potential in this respect then their values can be greatly diminished, except as going concerns. The zoning code may possibly apply to these properties depending upon their proximity to the retail pitch and their physical layout.

Other influences on the A3 sector to be considered by any valuer include:

Public houses This marketplace is closely related to restaurants and increasingly public house operators are competing in all locations of the A3 sector. Led by Wetherspoons in the early 1980s and now followed by a wide range of small and large operators including some important public companies, the bids from the public house often will outgun the restaurant bid. Accordingly, premises with the potential for or having a Justices Full On-Licence will receive a superior bid in premium and possibly capital terms from the public house operator.

Due to the Town and Country Planning (Use Classes) Order 1987, public houses can automatically take over restaurants and vice versa without applying for planning permission.

Sandwich bars and coffee shops The valuer should be aware that these units do not necessarily have A3 consent, nor indeed do they require such consent. Nevertheless, the marketplace from such operators is highly active with such brands as Pret á Manger leading the way in terms of very high turnover units, mainly in prime city centre locations. Some of these units do have A3 consent and qualify as restaurants, but in general, the valuer can apply the same rules of valuation of restaurants to these units, as they are very close cousins.

A2 users Building societies, banks and other operators within this planning use are able to acquire restaurants and obtain change of use without planning consent being necessary. This has led to some very high bids since the Town & Country Planning General Development Order came into effect in 1988 from A2 operators for restaurants in prime locations. The valuer should be wary of valuing on the higher basis unless there is true demand from the A2 operators as many have now satisfied their requirements in prime locations. Equally, the valuer should be aware of the potential for a higher restaurant value as a result of A2 interest.

Factors affecting value

The valuer should be aware of the following matters when approaching a valuation either on a rental or capital basis. Some may appear straightforward but they equally may have important effects on value.

Access, servicing and car parking
Restaurants have deliveries and collections of far greater frequency than normal retail shops. Foodstuffs and cleaning materials may be delivered on several occasions from different suppliers throughout

the day, whereas collections of refuse can take place as often as three times in a day, especially in prime locations.

If there is rear servicing, especially vehicular servicing then there is no problem in this respect. Alternatively, if servicing is from the front of the premises and especially if there are severe parking and loading restrictions, then this can be a problem for a restaurant and may necessitate servicing through the restaurant itself, sometimes over quite long distances. In severe cases, this problem should be borne in mind by the valuer.

Normally car parking is only found on site in roadside locations or in some cases on the periphery. If a restaurant, other than in those areas has the benefit of extensive car parking, then this is a considerable advantage. However, the ability for customers to park in streets nearby without restrictions throughout the day and evening should be investigated. If there are severe restrictions this may have a detrimental effect upon trade.

The valuer should enquire of the Highways Authority as to their intention regarding important routes near to the restaurant and investigate future proposals which may effect access for loading and for customers, car parking, diversions away from the site, etc.

Alienation

The valuer should carefully consider the provisions of the lease in respect of alienation. Most leases provide that the landlord should not unreasonably withhold consent for an assignment or subletting of the whole of the demised premises.

Subletting of part would be advantageous for very large premises, especially over two or more floors. A discount in value should be attributable to this element of the alienation provision in most circumstances. The range of discounts of course depends on the particular circumstances of the case.

Quite a few restaurants are not actually sold but are licensed under a management or franchise agreement and a restriction against parting with possession may, in certain circumstances cause hardship to the tenant and be worthy of a reduction in rental value. Equally, and especially in the context of a capital valuation, the valuer should verify that there is no restriction on charging the asset which obviously could have a dire effect.

Some leases contain preemption clauses whereby the landlord has an option to purchase the lease from the tenant in the event of an assignment being proposed. The landlord would usually have a period of 4 weeks in which to make a decision to match the price offered. With a retail unit this is not necessarily problematic, but with an A3 use a bid is likely to include fixtures and fittings, goodwill and possibly stock at valuation. In addition, leased hired and rented items may well be included in the transaction agreement. Most landlords would not be interested in acquiring more than the leasehold interest under their preemption clause and therefore unless the clause refers to a global figure for the restaurant, this would be a clause which would have a very serious effect upon value for any purposes, especially that of charging for the assets.

Alterations

Most leases permit non-structural and internal alterations but have absolute restrictions against structural alterations. Where the land-lord has far reaching powers of restriction, eg the internal layout of the restaurant, non-structural partitioning, style and location of the drinks bar, etc then this may be worthy of reduction in value. It is important that the valuer identifies any benefit of value relating to alterations and to whom such benefit accrues.

Obligations of tenants to carry out works, for example to satisfy statutory requirements, or a Schedule of Condition, should of course be reflected in any capital and possibly rental valuation. Equally, an obligation to reinstate at the end of a term possibly in respect of an adjoining premises, will also play its part.

Competition for sites

The valuer should be aware of the likely range of bidders in the market place. There are locations such as in prime provincial and suburban retail locations and certain roadside positions, and indeed home delivery and food court locations where the range of operators likely to take the subject premises restaurant, may already be represented. Accordingly, the valuer must ask the question as to whether it is likely that the market would produce competitive bidding for the site. This implication is applicable to capital or rental values.

When approaching rental values for the purposes of rent reviews, in normal circumstances, the valuer should consider that the existing tenant may be a bidder in the market place, but place whatever weight he feels appropriate upon the fact that there may not be any other or only a limited number of likely bidders. Accordingly, if a major group makes an exceptional bid for a restaurant in a particular centre, it does not necessarily follow that similar bids will reflect the same level of rental or indeed capital value. The valuer is advised to seriously consider this aspect when utilising comparable evidence of this nature for their purposes.

Concessions

The valuer should consider any concessions that have been granted to the tenant in respect of rent free periods, rising rentals, capital contributions, reverse premiums, leaseback arrangements, capped rents or any other hidden benefits which may relate to the rental value to be attributed to the subject premises or indeed to comparable properties for the purposes of a rental valuation and possibly capital valuation.

Rent free period There are differing schools of thought as to the treatment of rent free periods. Some consider that it is normal, even in the best markets, to have rent free periods of up to three months upon the granting of a new lease on a restaurant. The philosophy behind rent free periods of this type are that it is inequitable for the tenant to have to pay rental outgoings while he is unable to trade during the course of carrying out works on the premises to enable it to open to the public. The question therefore, is whether the valuer should actually take this initial period of rent free concession into account when carrying out a valuation.

It is, however, not often disputed that any rent free period beyond the normal three month initial period should be taken into account. Again, there are different views as to how the rent free period should be treated. Some would take it over the entire length of the lease, others would take it to the first rent review period of say five years. It would seem logical, however, to treat this type of concession over a ten year period which is the normal period for depreciating assets within most companies.

Some valuers simply divide by the number of years without any adjustment. Others apply the annual equivalent of the total rent free period over ten years and discount by an appropriate percentage per annum, normally around 10% currently. The Years' Purchase for 10 years at 10% on this basis would be 6.145.

Neither basis is totally satisfactory, but possibly the latter basis does not lay the valuer open for as much criticism as the first, and certainly in the circumstances of cross examination at an arbitration hearing, etc, the valuer would have been seen to have been as fair as possible.

Rising rentals The approach to rising rentals can be on the basis of averaging the rentals over the full period to the first review, or by applying the Present Value of £1 at an appropriate percentage normally 10% currently, to each of the surplus rental increments over and above the first years passing rental.

These capitalised rental increments are added to the base rent for period up until rent review and then divided by five to give the equivalent annual rental.

Of course, the intentions of the parties may well be that the market value of the premises is fairly represented in the last year of the rising rental mechanism. If this is the case, the deficiencies in the earlier years would of course be representative of rent free period and the market value should have deducted from it the gross rent free period deductions divided by the annual equivalent appropriately deferred for each year.

If the market value is attributable in the centre of the mechanism, then the valuer must be wary of the possibility that earlier discounts are being outweighed by later benefits to the landlord.

Capital contributions It is not uncommon for landlords to contribute capital to tenants for the duration of a restaurant unit.

The treatment of such concession for valuation purposes again is a matter of choice. An annual equivalent can be assessed over a five, ten or twenty year period, or more if the lease is longer, depending upon the valuers viewpoint. Most would consider that certainly with a capital contribution of this nature the normal corporate approach of writing off most assets over a ten year period would be appropriate.

Another approach to the treatment of the capital would be the true benefit to the tenant in the "real world". The tenants would undoubtedly have to either borrow the money or utilise their own money, either of which would attract some degree of interest charge, either from the bank or equivalent interest loss from the tenants point of view. There would also have to be some undertaking to repay this capital to the bank or to refit after ten years or so. Possibly that type of assessment is more in tune with the reality of the situation and an average of those payments over say a ten-year period to include interest and capital repayments can sometimes be an interesting and possibly more realistic exercise.

The valuer should wherever possible recognise the attitude and logic of the operator who will in reality be purchasing or renting the site in the market place. It is not sufficient to simply apply valuation science when valuing restaurants. The restaurateur uses a completely different table calculation than those utilised by the valuer!

Other types of concessions There are often other concessions within a transaction which are not immediately apparent. The surrender of leases and the granting of longer terms can be very advantageous for a restaurant tenant. The capital value of a restaurant or a going concern can increase dramatically as a result of the lengthening of a short lease. Indeed, the practice of some public companies in recent years has been to extend their leases in excess of 25 years which have an advantage in terms of amortization of capital costs and in turn this increases net profit.

Change in the terms of a new lease to permit an extended user, certain beneficial alterations, changes in the repairing and service charge covenants, etc, can all play their part in having an effect on value.

In addition, changes in the tenant's ability to licence his premises will have an effect upon profitability and indirectly upon rental value and indeed capital value. The consent of a landlord permitting a music and dancing licence may well enable the tenant to make a great deal more money from the establishment and these sort of changes must be taken into account.

Other types of concessions take the form of reverse premiums unrelated to works being carried out or other matters; trade arrangements whereby there is a tie or obligation to purchase certain goods from the landlords who may be brewers or wholesalers of food goods; capped rents; lease-back arrangements etc.

Concessions directly relating to works of improvement to the premises The valuer must thoroughly investigate to whom the benefit falls in works of improvement to the premises carried out within the budget of a capital or rental concession. The reader is referred to the section on the tranches of fixtures and fittings and equipment which relate to restaurants. If any concession relates specifically to such works then the valuer must ascertain accurately as to whether the landlord or the tenant benefits from the rentalisation of these matters at review. If the landlord benefits then obviously the period of the lease over which this initial benefit is to be considered is foreshortened to the first rent review date. If the tenant benefits, then the approach to the write off period is far more extensive.

External seating

Increasingly, local authorities are granting licences for external trading where appropriate. Certainly in good tourist locations restaurants are benefiting from additional trade in good weather in this manner. The arrangement is subject to an annual licence fee and is revocable at the end of the period by the local authority should they so desire. However, the potential to trade in these circumstances certainly attracts additional rental value over and above the licence fee.

Fixtures and fittings and hinterland equipment

Restaurants contain a great deal of plant equipment and fixtures and fittings in comparison to a retail shop. They are a mixture of factory, storage and retail. There are basically three tranches of fixtures and fittings and equipment in any restaurant.

1. The initial fitting out from shell and capped off services to a condition whereby the unit is ready for the installation of trade fixtures. These works would include walls, ceiling and floor linings, partitioning, statutory works including those relating to means of escape, toilets, shopfront and facia, staff areas, fire and security alarms, air conditioning, heating, ventilation, gas, electricity and water plant and equipment. These types of works are likely to last throughout the length of an average lease of say 20 years except for maintenance, repair or possibly some replacement of the air conditioning plant. Much of this element of works would probably pass to the benefit of the landlords under the lease.
2. The next tranche of works carried out by the tenant would relate to fixed and heavy equipment and fixtures such as the kitchen equipment, bars and other custom made fixtures within the restaurant, fitted lighting, joinery and embellishments, etc. These are not items which would pass to the landlords.
3. The final elements under this heading are the movable items of equipment and fixtures including cutlery, crockery, pictures, pots, pans, electrical equipment, and all other trade items and chattels which are not fixed including badged and labelled goods. It is exceptionally rare if any of these items pass to the landlords.

The valuer should establish at the earliest stage as to the ownership of all the contents of the restaurant, whether fixed or otherwise. It is possible for leasing arrangements to be entered into for a completely fitted out restaurant.

Normally there are several items of leased or rented equipment and these should be accounted for in any valuation, especially in an assignment of the lease or a sale of the business.

The quality of fixtures and fittings must also be taken into account. Ironically, the resale value of such items, even a short period after they have been installed, is nominal compared to the cost price. However, if a new tenant and indeed a hypothetical tenant or a purchaser of the restaurant or the business can make good use by continuing in the same style, then the value of such items need not be written down dramatically. In these circumstances some degree of the replacement value comes into play dependent upon the age and efficiency of the items in question.

The tenant at rent review may well be saddled with the need to deal with a rent review mechanism which directs him to pay a rent on the basis of the premises being "fit for immediate occupation and use" or a similar description. Precedents would seem to indicate that this would require the valuer simply to assume that the property was free of defect but it would not be necessary to ignore any concession for a rent free period or otherwise from which the hypothetical tenant might benefit at the date of review for a letting in the open market and no more.

However, there are times when the phrase "fully fitted fit for immediate use and occupation", is likely to be more onerous from the tenant's point of view. In this case, certainly all the benefit of value under points 1 and 2 above could be rentalised for the benefit of the landlord.

These are general guidelines and each case must be considered on its merits. If in doubt as to the extent of fixtures and fittings and equipment that should be involved the valuer is advised to consult with a solicitor.

The valuer is advised to refer to the following cases amongst others which, dependent upon the circumstances, may be relevant to his/her valuation:

Cornwall Coast Country Club v *Cardgrange Ltd* [1987]
    1 EGLR 146
Orchid Lodge (UK) Ltd v *Extel Computing Ltd* [1991]
    2 EGLR 116
Iceland Frozen Foods plc v *Starlight Investments Ltd* [1992]
    1 EGLR 126

Pontsarn Investments Ltd v *Kansallis-Osake-Pankki* [1992]
     1 EGLR 148
London & Leeds Estates Ltd v *Paribas Ltd* [1993] 2 EGLR 149

Forfeiture

The valuer should look carefully at the forfeiture provisions in respect of re-entry and the alienation provisions in respect of charging as these may have a bearing upon his valuation. In addition, it is prudent to consider what other charges may be registered against the asset on the charge register.

Goodwill

Goodwill can be identified in several ways:

The goodwill relating to the site of the premises There is no doubt that there are certain sites which in themselves attract goodwill. Typical examples would be catering establishments close to major tourist locations such as Madame Tussauds, The Tower of London, Windsor Castle, etc. In addition, there are sites which are the venues of very famous restaurants which if they were to become vacant would in themselves have some residue of goodwill. At the lower end of the scale, even prominent traditional restaurant sites in provincial and suburban shopping centres will be recognised by the local populace as being a venue where they can eat and where they would seek a meal and try out the new operator.

The identification of value in relation to this type of goodwill is particularly hard to ascertain, but if the valuer feels exceptional value might be attributable on this basis, then this should be borne in mind, certainly for rental purposes and possibly for capital purposes.

The goodwill relating to a single business and premises (personal goodwill) This type of goodwill is that which will enable the tenant or purchaser of a business to be assured of being able to continue to trade at the same level on the assumption that all other standards are maintained. It is the ingredient within the formula of the value of the going concern which is probably the most important.

Accordingly, if a business is trading at moderate levels, the value of goodwill is nominal and possibly non-existent. The valuer must bear in mind the period that the business has been established and also observe the growth of turnover and profitability in order to assess the quality of goodwill. For example if turnover has been decreasing dramatically over a three year period from previously much higher levels, then goodwill may well be on the wane and unworthy of great value. On the other hand, a steady increase in turnover will indicate that goodwill is flourishing.

The valuer should be wary of goodwill established over a short period and in particular, of goodwill relating to a particular personality associated with a restaurant, unless that personality is to remain with the restaurant for a worthwhile commercial period under a binding agreement. This has always been a major problem in the valuation of traditional high class restaurants with chef patron owners or restaurants which relate strongly to a show business, sporting or culinary personality. It is not often that the capitalisation of goodwill is carried out independently of the capitalisation of the business as a separate asset. There are formulae for assessing the value of goodwill but in today's market place, most businesses are acquired on the basis of a P/E of net profit pre-tax or post tax with adjustments for major assets or liabilities with further reflection by an additional upgrading of capital value for such matters as exceptionally strong goodwill or potential for the further expansion and growth of the business.

The goodwill relating to the brand name locally, nationally or internationally The brand name of single restaurants can have the potential for expansion into other locations in the locality or nationally, or indeed internationally.

At the various stages of this expansion, the value of such potential and benefit should be identified and assessed by the valuer. For example, a particular fish and chip shop may produce a module of shopfitting and design coupled with a product which is so exceptional that others could easily be built around the concept. The valuer may be asked to consider the value of the business on the existing site and should accordingly take into account the potential of expansion either by company owned sites or possibly by franchising.

When approaching the value of an established brand, the valuer should consider the age of the brand, the possible need for refurbishment of existing units, the need for redesign, the potential expansion of branches and the potential for the upgrading of the quality of goodwill, etc.

The valuation of goodwill relating to the medium to larger sized groups is considered by many to be more within the expertise of accountants and stockbrokers than valuers, as many corporate matters are attached to the calculations of value of the goodwill and indeed other assets and liabilities relating to this size of group.

Values tend to lean further towards the corporate purchasing power of major groups and their own particular P/Es than to the market place within which restaurateurs operate.

Hours of opening

The local authority or the landlords may impose restrictive opening hours and indeed may restrict the restaurant from opening on specific days, normally Sunday. In such circumstances if this restriction is considered onerous then an adjustment must be made. Some leases also have an obligation to keep open at certain hours and again depending upon the circumstances if this is uneconomic from the tenants point of view a reflection in rental value must be made.

Insurance

The normal insuring responsibilities are attached to most restaurant leases, but in assessing values one should be wary of exceptional premium costs for certain types of restaurants which are considered a higher fire risk than normal.

Layout size and occupancy

This is a most important aspect of any caterers appraisal of a new or existing unit.

There is no ideal size for a restaurant property. Sizes may differ depending upon the location and concept adopted for the purpose of the restaurant. Ideal sizes have been described under the Section of "Various Types of Restaurants" earlier in this chapter. However, the valuer should be aware that adjustments must be made for any restaurant which is either too small or too large. There is no automatic rule that there should be discount for quantum or uplift for comparably small units (as is the normal approach for retail valuation). The rule as far as restaurants are concerned is that if the size is ideal for the concept and the location then maximum value should be applied.

The restaurateur will look at a site and wish to maximise the potential business derived from the restaurant. It is a cardinal sin to have a restaurant operating successfully and not have sufficient space in which to seat customers during peak trading periods. A reasonable analogy would be that of a rocket with a payload. It takes the same size rocket albeit with some degree of additional fuel to lift a much larger payload. The same principles of economies of scale apply to restaurants. The additional cost of shopfitting after the initial expense is proportionally far less and the same applies to other outgoings, as an example larger restaurants tend to be more efficiently run by a relatively smaller number of staff.

Accordingly, maximising size is one of the requirements of most operators in whatever location they are seeking restaurants. This aspect must be borne in mind by the valuer.

The caterer's philosophy regarding layout is fairly wide ranging. Again concept and location plays an important part in their ideology. For example a fast food operator in a prime position would want to have a fairly regularly shaped unit with ancillary areas possibly at basement or first floor level easily accessible and serviced. A wine bar operator may well make do with a limited frontage and an extensive basement in the same position.

In Central London the variations on this theme are numerous with operators being quite happy to take limited frontages with extensive rear areas or to possibly trade on several floors if they are able to get into the right location and ultimately benefit from sufficient trading area.

Inefficiency of layout will be a disadvantage. A narrow long restaurant may have problems in terms of layout and seating as well as "the length of run" from the kitchen to the trading area.

The permutations of possible layouts and the difficulties and the advantages relating to them are almost unending and the valuer is advised to approach such problems logically and commercially with the viewpoint of the caterer before making any adjustments. The question of frontage to depth ratio does apply to restaurants in certain locations and for certain types of concepts ideally suited to those locations.

As far as "quantum discount" is concerned, as stated previously, this theory does not necessarily apply and in many cases where there is high demand for large units and possibly planning resistance additional rent may be paid over and above market value.

External seating also plays its part nowadays with local authorities granting licences for this purpose and some value can be attributed in this respect.

Occupancy is a major factor in the equation of profitability for the caterer. There are different occupancy requirements for different types of concepts. A high class restaurant would be 1 person to 3 sq.m and a more popular restaurant may be closer to 1 person per sq m or less. These requirements are directly related to the possibility of a higher spend in the higher class restaurant and vice versa. Higher occupancy does not necessarily mean higher rental value as one must bear in mind the relevance of location, and many other factors before reaching a conclusion.

These are very wide ranging subjects and of the greatest importance in terms of restaurant valuations – possibly the most important aspect of the subject. The naive valuer may consider that comparing one restaurant with another is sufficient in itself but unless one has a grasp of the commercial implications of the varying sizes, layouts and occupancies of restaurant premises and the problems of trading in such units especially on various levels, the correct approach to value cannot be achieved.

The valuer is advised to treat this entire subject logically and realistically from the caterers point of view as well as from the property viewpoint.

Length of lease

The valuer should carefully consider the length of the lease underlying the valuation. The impact on rental or capital value can be considerable.

1. Most operators write down assets over a period of ten years and therefore a foreshortened lease would not make such provisions acceptable to the Inland Revenue and as a result artificially higher depreciation costs would be incurred.
2. The policy of most operators is not to acquire leases of less than 10 years duration and many will not consider less than 15 to 25 years.
3. Most restaurants take at least three years to reach maximum profitability and a lease of less than 10 years does not make the exercise of starting up from new viable.
4. Most banks are unwilling to charge against a leasehold interest of less than 10 years, or would certainly wish to discount the value dramatically.

For all these reasons and many others, the rental value of a lease of say less than 10 years is affected and the valuer should adjust accordingly. The appropriate discount varies, but should be in touch with reality and the logic of the operator.

For example, if under the terms of the rent review, one is enabled to value for a term of say five years unexpired and the basis of value is on the assumption of full vacant possession, it may not be a matter of simply discounting by a small percentage. The question might be asked which caterer would take on a five year lease on a restaurant which may cost several hundred thousand pounds to fit and still pay a market rental value?

When valuing on a capital basis, again it is not a matter of discounting from the normal. It really is more practical to consider whether there was a purchaser in the market place who would pay to purchase a short lease. In these circumstances, the valuer should be able to gain confirmation in some form that the landlords would extend the lease, possibly giving an undertaking to do so. The attitude of the landlord is obviously an important part of the preparation of a capital value in these circumstances.

Location

This subject has been dealt with elsewhere in this chapter. The valuer should be aware of the different locations for restaurants and the problems and indeed advantages to be gained in those locations. The valuer should investigate the general area to establish the possible sources of turnover, over and above passer-by traffic for the restaurant and in this way be aware of the fullest potential of value. The best retail pitch is not necessarily the best restaurant pitch. Prominence, accessibility, car parking, servicing, visibility and security are very important factors to be borne in mind in the question of location.

Means of escape

Investigations must be made as to whether the premises satisfy current statutory and bye-law requirements in respect of means of escape.

The premises may well have a fire certificate but there are quite a few restaurants which do not have the benefit of such certification or have older certificates and have continued to trade in that manner for many years. However, it is quite normal nowadays for the fire officer to visit premises which have just been sold and require them to be brought up to date. Such costs can be quite extensive and may involve the provision of new lobbies, corridors, staircases, fire doors, various types of cladding, and equipment to the appropriate standards. Loss of floor space may result.

Accordingly, the valuer should be fully aware of the possibility of such circumstances and make the necessary enquiries.

In respect of areas which may be suitable for subletting, and form part of the calculations for rental valuation, the valuer should ensure that those areas would be passed fit for occupation by the fire officer and that they are capable of being utilised for the user under the terms of the lease and possibly even in planning terms. For example it is quite possible that the fire officer would not permit a basement to be used for music and dancing or to benefit from a drinks licence because the means of escape provisions cannot be satisfied to his standards.

The valuer should if at all possible inspect all documents relating to means of escape routes. The tenant will have an obligation to provide such routes, often to adjoining premises requiring specific agreements being reached with neighbours. The terms of such agreements may be on a short term basis whereas the asset being valued may be freehold or long leasehold. If the premises are able to be shut down by the fire authorities because a suitable means of the escape is not available, then this has a detrimental, possibly disastrous effect upon the asset.

Licensing

The potential benefits of various types of licencing should be identified by the valuer.

Justices full on licences come in various forms. In the most basic form, the standard so called "restaurant licence" relates to customers purchasing alcoholic drink accompanied by a meal during normal licensing hours, between 11.00 am and 11.30 pm.

A Section 68 Supper Hours Certificate permits the serving of drink until 12.30 am and a Special Hours Certificate under Section 77 goes through normally until 2 am, although in Central London and other major City Centres licences can be granted to as late as 5.00 am or 6.00 am. The licencing authorities can restrict these types of licences into certain days, on a regular or one off basis and conditions of trading depend upon what other licences are held.

As licences become less conditional so they become more valuable. Licences permitting the sale of alcoholic drink to customers not partaking of a meal are becoming more easily available, especially in Central London and major provincial towns, with the impact of value really being directed at the hours relating to such licences. There are various forms of these licences including those restricting the sale of draft beer or limiting the sale to a couple of types of lager, and others permitting solely the sale of wine under a wine bar licence, and at the other end of the sector, a public house licence permitting the sale of all types of alcoholic beverages, again with conditions relating to opening times, etc adding to value.

The extension of licencing hours has not been as imposing as first anticipated. It is only in locations such as high density tourist and entertainment locations that additional benefit of turnover is achievable and therefore drinks licences have additional value.

In recent years, licences have been easier to obtain and indeed the protection and transfer of existing licences has also become less problematic.

Accordingly, the valuer is advised not to place too much value on the aspect of a drinks licence unless it has exceptional potential and advantage to the tenant.

The benefit of such licences can of course be taken into account for capital valuations but may not be taken into account fully for rental valuation in most circumstances as the licence does not run with the property.

Other licences obtained by application to the local authority include Music and Dancing Licences which can be highly advantageous and profitable in certain locations. Again, conditions attached are of great relevance. Opening hours, occupancy, etc, all play their part in affecting the desirability of the licence and indeed its profitability. For example, a Music and Dancing Licence may be subject to a compulsory admission fee or to pre-registration. These will have a depressing effect upon value.

Public Entertainment Licences permitting live entertainment can be advantageous. Again, there may be severe restrictions which will have an effect upon value.

The valuer must of course make the fullest investigations of the local authority and the licensing authority as to the nature of all licences attached to the premises, including the current validity, their expiration date, any possible objections to renewal, any history of problems with the licencing, local or police authorities, etc.

The valuer should also be aware of any trade ties or restrictions on the sale of alcohol. These would have normally been imposed by previous owners, possibly a brewer or the body or institution in opposition to the sale of alcohol.

Within many leases, there are also clauses whereby the tenant must undertake to maintain, protect, transfer and insure licences. These all, in their varying forms, may have an impact upon value.

Noise and disturbance

Most leases have restrictions upon levels of noise and although this does not often play a major part in valuation, there could be occurrences which will have an effect. The author recalls such an event when a major restaurant underneath a very important central London theatre was subject to such a clause and one Sunday afternoon a well known spiritualist was holding a seance in front of a packed house and asked the normal questions as to whether "anybody was there?" The silence was broken by the noise of "*Jumping Jack Flash*" coming from the restaurant below. A Section 146 notice followed. The costs of insulation and monitoring were quite extensive for the restaurant.

Obligations under the lease including landlords licences

Where landlords have obligations to insure, carry out works of repair maintenance and replacement, permit quiet enjoyment, etc, then these are normal matters found within the lease and have no bearing upon valuation. It is when these obligations do not exist that problems may arise which may have an effect upon value. The valuer should be wary especially of a lack of obligation on behalf of the landlord to carry out works of repair to the building. This can have a major detrimental effect upon the appearance of a restaurant and the standards required by the operator for his establishment.

The valuer should consider all additional documentation relating to landlords consent for alterations, drinks licence, variations of the lease, improvements and any other aspects which may have an effect upon value.

In most leases the landlord will undertake not to permit a letting within his nearby ownership of property to a tenant in competition. In the absence of this clause and in suitable circumstances a discount should be sought at rent review. However, it does not necessarily mean that competition affects trade and therefore rental values could in fact be enhanced by competition. The valuer should approach this aspect carefully and logically.

Planning and highway matters

The valuer is advised to make enquiries of the planning and highway departments at the local authority office and if necessary at County level to ascertain the implications of planning consents which have been obtained or indeed which have not been obtained in respect of the subject premises in order to ensure that they comply in every way.

In addition, enquiries should be made of the Highways Authority in respect of roadworks which may affect the property in terms of trading potential in the future covering such aspects as diversions of a temporary or a permanent nature, car parking restrictions and proposals etc.

Refuse provisions

Many local authorities, especially within city centres such as the City of Westminster have very strict regulations regarding the storage, treatment and disposal of refuse and waste products from restaurants. The undertakings of the tenant to satisfy such requirements can be costly, time consuming and disruptive. For example if there is no rear vehicular access for servicing, there may be a need to provide an area within the establishment for the storage of refuse and means for its compaction or removal, possibly through the restaurant, to the front of the premises for collection at certain times of the day. In Central London for example there are two and sometimes three collections of refuse from restaurants, as the general policy is that refuse should not be left on the streets for collection as there is a severe vagrant problem in this respect. Internal storage in this manner may also lead to problems with vermin and other health related matters.

Extreme difficulties relating to refuse should be borne in mind by the valuer, especially in terms of its impact upon net lettable area for rental valuation purposes.

Rent reviews, disregards

It is assumed that the valuer has a working knowledge of rent review practice and generally the approach to this subject is very similar to that of other types of properties subject to rent review.

Most rent review "disregards" follow Section 34 Paragraph a, b, c and d of the Landlord and Tenant Act 1954 Part II, namely:

1. *Any effect on rent of the fact that the tenant has or his predecessors in title have been in occupation of the Holding.* It is generally accepted that this disregard prohibits the lessor from seeking advantage from the fact that the tenant may be a special

bidder at rent review. In the absence of this particular disregard obviously there will be considerable advantage gained by the lessor at review and the valuer should take note. The extent of advantage would much depend upon the viability of the tenants business, however.

2. *Any goodwill attached to the holding by reason of the carrying on thereat of the business of the tenant (whether by him or by a predecessor of his in that business).* The valuer will obviously be aware of the implications of the absence of this particular disregard. However even if the disregard applies the valuer can still consider the adherent goodwill running with the property. In many cases this aspect will have no relevance but there are sites which are traditionally known as important restaurant venues and as such have goodwill of their own. A prime example would be the old Post Office Tower Restaurant.

3. *Any effect of rent of any improvement carried out by the tenant or a predecessor in title of his otherwise than in pursuant of an obligation to an immediate Landlord.* This disregard is self-explanatory and the Valuer is directed to the more detailed description of the impact of "Fixtures and Fittings and Hinterland Equipment".

4. *In the case of holding comprising licensed premises, any addition to its value attributable to the licence, if it appears to the Court that having regard to the terms of the current tenancy and any other relevant circumstances the benefit of the licence belongs to the tenant.* This particular paragraph is often omitted from a lease and a lessor could have regard to its relevance. It is a particularly hard one to take into account but certainly the value of a licence on a property which has a very high liquor turnover in a location where such licences are not easily obtained may well prove to be advantageous in the circumstances. One to bear in mind for the valuer.

Other aspects of the rent review mechanism include the basis upon which the hypothetical term of years is to be assessed which can have great bearing upon value and which is referred to separately under "Length of Lease" elsewhere in this chapter.

There is no room in this chapter for an extensive discussion upon rent review procedures and third party referrals and the valuer is advised to seek guidance in alternative publications to that extent.

Repair

The direct effect of disrepair upon the capital or rental valuation should be obvious to the valuer. In the context of rent review valuations, onerous repairing covenants obviously have a bearing upon value as do those with less liability than normal.

The impact of a schedule of dilapidations when valuing for the acquisition of a restaurant which needs refitting may not be as onerous as the valuer may originally anticipate. Certainly, the extent of the works that go into the creation of a restaurant are far more than those which may relate to say a retail unit and a proportion of the schedule may already be covered by the works anticipated.

In addition, the valuation should take into account the impact of an onerous service charge or for that matter one which is advantageous. Quite often, restaurants are located beneath large buildings, the outgoings in relation to their owner occupancy are disproportionately expensive and this may have a bearing upon value. Sometimes, to the advantage of the tenant outgoings such as heating, hot water and air conditioning costs can be beneficially low if facilities are shared with the occupiers of the main building.

Rights of way

The valuer should investigate that the property has the benefit of rights of way for the purposes of servicing, means of escape, refuse and access to plant and equipment etc. Easements should also be verified in respect of such matters.

Signage

Signage should be carefully considered by the valuer. This can take the following form:

- signage at facia level
- signage on columns including space suitable for menus
- signage for posters and hand-written signs on windows
- display and signage on pavements outside the premises
- signage at upper levels

Very few restaurants have the benefit of all these types of signage and display, but where there is a restriction imposed either by the landlord or by the local authorities then that should be taken into account in rental and capital terms where appropriate.

The valuer should also make enquiries that the appropriate planning consents have been obtained for signage and indeed landlords' consents.

Statutes and bye-laws

Restaurants are affected by numerous statutes and regulations, the most important of those which have to be considered in respect of such premises are as follows:

Food Safety Act 1990
Local Authority Food Hygiene Regulations
Offices Shops & Railways Premises Act 1963
Chronically Sick and Disabled Persons Act 1970
Joint Circular 1970 no.12 issued by the Department of Health and Social Security as further amended
Building Act 1984 and Building Regulations 1985 as further amended
Health & Safety at Work etc. Act 1974
The Licensing Acts
The Disability Discrimination Act

The valuer must be certain that the premises qualify in respect of all these matters and should enquire of the local authority as to any notices which may have been served in respect of environmental, hygiene, health and employment matters, etc. If any such matters should arise then if they are of fundamental importance the valuation should be adjusted accordingly.

More recently, the valuer should be aware of the provisions of the Food Safety Act 1990 and its subsequent enactments, particularly in respect of the obligation of most caterers to register their compliance with the local authority. Failure to do so may lead to severe penalties but also possibly to closure in extreme cases.

Uplift in rental value for catering use

Since the Town and Country Planning (Use Classes) Order 1972 came into operation separating restaurants from what was known as Class I Retail Use, and subsequently the Town and Country Planning General Development Order 1988 which permitted direct change of use to A2 and thence A1 from A3 but not in reverse, many valuers have considered that A3 consent implies an automatic uplift in rental value over and above A1 consent. This is a very dangerous stance to adopt and one which the valuer should consider very carefully. The majority of restaurants actually do not attract an uplift against A1 retail use and indeed there are many examples of A3 values being less than A1 use value.

In prime retail positions in suburban and provincial locations it is not unusual for retailers to pay more money than the A3 operator and if anything, especially in the more popular town centres, there has been a definite trend of caterers leaving the town centre to go to the periphery and destination locations.

The rent review valuer may prove this point by comparing Street Traders Plans of say 20 years ago, if these are available, or possibly 10 or 15 years ago may suffice, with Street Traders Plans of today's date. In town centres the trend of movement of catering premises and the replacement by A1 and A2 users is most definite. This is known as the "crater effect", so called because it is as if a bomb has hit the centre of the town and spread the restaurants to the edge of the town onto the periphery and destination locations.

In locations where there is high density tourist or entertainment trade there is a strong possibility of uplift for A3 use in rental terms and indeed premium values will be demonstrated at higher levels than A1 premium values. The valuer, however, should not assume that an automatic uplift of any percentage should be applied across the board for A3 consent.

User clause
There are numerous variations of user clauses which may have different affect upon value. Examples are as follows:

1. *An absolute user clause.* The valuer may come across the user clause which restricts the premises solely to that of the restaurant of a specific type. This user may be prefixed by the word licensed, thus allowing for the sale of drink. The restriction to a specific type of restaurant is onerous and worthy of a discount, normally in the region of 10%, but possibly more if the type of restaurant is of an unusual variety. One often comes across this type of user clause in franchise leases, where the franchisee undertakes to operate the restaurant under the name and style of the franchiser. Both for capital and rental valuations, this type of restriction is worthy of major discount. If a restaurant may not be licensed, then such a restriction is also worthy of a discount.
2. A user clause of less impact would be where the use is restricted to A3 consent or to specific types of A3 uses, such as a

restaurant, a public house, a wine bar, etc. In certain circumstances, a discount would not be appropriate, especially in very popular locations where there is excellent A3 trade, but the valuer should consider applying a discount in most circumstances. An absolute restriction to A3 use does not necessarily imply discount unless there is dominating retail value in excess of A3 value in the locality.

3. A user clause as above but with the addendum that the landlord's written consent must be obtained and cannot unreasonably be withheld, would normally render the user clause fairly harmless from the tenants point of view and therefore not worthy of discount for valuation purposes. A clause which includes not only A3 consent, but possibly other advantageous users such as D2 or permits music and dancing and public entertainment in that those areas where such a use could be highly valuable, should be adjusted accordingly.

    Under most leases, the landlords make the proviso that no warranties are given as to use. Circumstances can arise whereby planning consent has not been obtained for the user under the lease and wherever possible, the valuer should endeavour to assess rental value on the basis that the user clause with the benefit of planning consent must be worth more than the user clause with the promise of planning consent and a discount applied accordingly.

4. The valuer will also come across user clauses which include alternative users, normally A1 and more increasingly A2 (due to the effects of the Town and Country Planning General Development Order 1988 after which so many A2 operators acquired restaurants for their own particular use). Again the valuer should beware of the pitfall of assuming that any particular use has dominating value based simply upon hearsay. Such facts should be verified properly before a conclusion is reached and certainly substantiated fully for the purposes of a third party representation at rent review.

    The valuer should not jump to conclusions as to the capital value of restaurants especially for the purposes of selling in the market place based upon the assumption that A2 operators may pay more than an A3 user, or vice versa.

Value added tax
The valuer must take into account the impact of value added tax should this apply.

Rental valuations

Background
Traditionally restaurants were closely aligned to the traditional method of retail valuation for retail purposes being mainly zoning with larger units being valued on an overall basis where appropriate.

With the development of the restaurant market place over the last 20 years, there now can be no doubt that restaurants, although having many of the characteristics of a retail shop and indeed often trading immediately adjoining, are to a great extent subject to a totally different approach to value.

For the purposes of open market rental valuation or for rent review purposes the valuer has available three basic methods of achieving his aims:

1. The zoning method.
2. The overall method.
3. The turnover or profits method.

The valuer should be wary of interrelating these methods and in addition, the valuer should recognise that none of these methods are able to be applied universally.

The question is where does one draw the line and adopt one particular method and not another? By utilising the locations of the various types of restaurants as a base, the valuer may be guided by the following comments as to the method to be adopted but these are only "guidelines" and local valuation practice may well dictate one particular method or another.

Prime locations in provincial and suburban shopping centres
Within these areas a zoning method normally dominates. The exception would be very large units normally well in excess of 4,000 sq ft and even then most valuers would still try to adopt a zoning basis in the absence of direct comparables of large units demonstrating an overall analysis. It is not common practice to utilise a turnover or profits method for deriving market rental.

Periphery and destination locations in provincial and suburban shopping centres
In this particular location a zoning method or an overall method can be adopted. There is a tendency to come across quite large units in this particular location and unless the local

method dictates, the valuer is advised to utilise the overall method especially for properties with a trading area of over 2,000 sq.ft. If the site is secluded it is possible to adopt a profit or turnover method although the valuer is advised to utilise comparable evidence wherever possible rather than to use this method.

Shopping developments and food courts The zoning method normally dominates in this particular sector. Larger units can be approached on an overall basis but again much depends upon the local practice.

The head lease of food courts may normally be valued on a profits or turnover basis unless otherwise dictated within the terms of the lease. The single units would normally have their own mechanism for review but otherwise a turnover or profits basis is recommended.

Tertiary or home delivery locations This particular location is almost without exception zoned. The local approach maybe on an overall basis for a particular parade of shops but this would be the exception. The profits or turnover method is very unlikely to be utilised.

The roadside market For the purposes of valuing open market rentals, overall rates are applied often from locations outside the immediate vicinity. The roadside market is evolving in a similar way to that of the retail warehouse market whereby rents can be compared between various towns. In these early days of the market's development the mixture of rent review "equations" is fairly wide. Examples would be rentals based upon retail warehousing values appropriately adjusted, relationship to nearby retail rents again with adjustments, Retail Price Index adjustments and hypothetical calculations based upon an alternative use for the site and even an alternative hypothetical building description.

Turnover and profit methods can be adopted for this sector although this is a very difficult approach and would be quite dangerous for most valuers without expertise in the sector.

Central London core This is a multi-levelled market place. Generally, zoning, overall and profit/turnover methods may be adopted in specific areas and sometimes a mixture of all of these methods are seen in one particular thoroughfare or area.

During the last decade we have seen more stability in the approach to rental valuation with local practice now being more clearly defined.

Most retail dominated thoroughfares such as Oxford Street, Brompton Road, Bond Street, Regent Street and Edgware Road are valued utilising the zoning method unless the unit is particular large or has physical peculiarities such as very limited frontage or dominating trading levels at first floor or basement.

The overall method is normally applied to areas or thoroughfares where there is a dominating restaurant presence including most thoroughfares in Soho, Covent Garden, Smithfield and the City of London.

Properties which have peculiar shapes or dominating trading areas either at first floor or basement levels should also be approached with the overall method. Equally, very large properties or those off the beaten track outside of the main retail areas would also be valued with the overall method.

The valuer is advised to carefully consider the method to be adopted within the Central London core. A prime example is Soho, where with the exception of Old Compton Street, parts of Wardour Street and Shaftesbury Avenue the restaurants within that general area are valued with the overall method. In the thoroughfares mentioned, a zoning basis is normally adopted. Within Soho Village itself retail units as against A3 units are zoned. This can be confusing for the naive valuer and investigation is imperative.

There are many such examples of the zoning and overall method resting side by side and it is not safe to interrelate the evidence between the two locations even though they are adjoining.

The increasing incidence of generic restaurants of between 10,000 and 30,000 sq.ft in Central London currently and getting bigger all the time, requires a very special approach to rental valuation incorporating classic overall calculations, but also incorporating assessment of turnover, not only from food and drink, but also merchandising and other aspects. These deals do not tend to be straightforward and specialised attention is required.

Restaurants in tourist and special locations Normally the overall method is adopted but where there are exceptional difficulties in obtaining comparables or where a property has tremendous potential for high turnover and profits the valuer is recommended to derive an appropriate value from an assessment of turnover and profits. In this latter respect, if the valuer does not have the experience to assess appropriate turnover figures and other components for the equation for deriving the correct answer from the profit and loss accounts the services of an accountant would be recommended.

Traditional restaurants Unless the restaurant is very close to a retail pitch and has great similarity to adjoining shop premises it is best to utilise the overall method using comparables of other nearby restaurants of a similar type. In the absence of such evidence a profit/turnover method would be appropriate.

Zoning – relevant matters

The valuer is assumed to have a basic understanding of the zoning method and its application to the valuation of retail premises. There are not many major differences in the approach to valuation of restaurants utilising this method. Normally 6 m zones would be utilised unless the local practice differs.

Ancillary areas could be anything between 1/6th and 1/10th Zone A unless there is excellent trading potential or a major disadvantage in terms of access, ceiling height etc. The valuers should be wary of the occurrence of a small ground floor and a much larger trading basement. Adjustments would have to be made in this respect not only to the value of the ground floor but more importantly the uplift in relation to the basement.

If the user is restricted to A3 use only the possibilities for deductions for means of escape or statutory provisions are far greater. Much depends upon the description under the rent review provisions in this respect.

Certainly, if there are major structural divisions which restrict the utilisation of specific areas for any other purposes than ancillary, storage, staff, plant and equipment, etc and certainly if such uses are in excess of those required by the operator then further deductions could be made.

Whether utilising the zoning or overall method other advantages can be gained by consideration of additional trading potential. In this respect, external seating can often be a major bonus to a restaurant. Such seating is dependent upon local authority annual licensing but if the potential is there then obviously this would have some degree of rental value over and above the rental for restaurant without such benefit. The valuer should of course bear in mind that the benefit of trading is seasonally restricted.

Equally, whether utilising zoning or an overall basis the valuer must consider and apply the matters raised earlier under the section titled factors affecting value and apply them accordingly where appropriate.

The valuer should also consider whether the frontage/depth ratio is such that an end allowance should be made. For example there may be a restaurant in say Kings Road with a 120 ft frontage and a depth of say 60 ft. The difficulties of trading within such a property in terms of layout, staffing, security, etc is reflected in an end allowance and possibly up to 15% should be applied and indeed has been applied in similar circumstances. There are no general rules and the valuer must investigate each case on its merits.

Overall – relevant matters
The overall approach is seen by many valuers as a short cut. It is highly dangerous to analyse all restaurants on an overall basis whatever their size, location and use.

If the valuer insists upon utilising the overall method for rental valuations purposes then it is imperative that the valuer considers the effect and inter-relationship of the following factors when ascertaining whether properties are comparable.

Size and layout
Location
Licensing
Demand and competition
Planning difficulties in specific areas
Use and concept
Fitting out costs
Trading potential

For example, it will be exceptionally dangerous to compare a 1,000 sq.ft unit with a 5,000 sq.ft unit on an overall basis. The logic is of course that a caterer wishing to take a 5,000 sq.ft unit just would not even consider a smaller unit and vice versa. Equally, a caterer wanting a say, St Annes Square in Manchester would not consider the same unit in Deansgate.

Investigate the basis of analysis utilised for various comparable properties. "Compare like with like."

No specific method has been adopted for the valuation of various parts of a restaurant when utilising the overall method. Some valuers apply one single rate over all levels and uses within a restaurant. Others apply half value in basement and first floor levels or others might apply a mixture of these approaches or put lower rentals on specific areas of use such as kitchen storage, staff plant and equipment.

Be careful as to the basis upon which comparable areas have been measured. Enquire as to whether comparable properties have been assessed on a gross internal or net internal basis. Common practice currently is to adopt a gross internal basis with a deduction for WCs only and statutory works.

The valuer may come across the phrase "destination restaurants" which is derived from the case of *My Kinda Town Ltd* v *Castlebrook Properties Ltd* (1986). This case related to an application to set aside the decision of an arbitrator. In the process of the Arbitration, other comparable properties outside of the general area of the subject premises (which was a large restaurant behind Brompton Road in a retail "backwater"), were considered. The Judge upheld that such evidence could be considered and as a result it has become almost common practice for destination restaurants to be compared with each other even though such restaurants are within different locations, often several miles apart.

The valuer should be wary of utilisation of such evidence. The basic rules of interrelationship, as set out previously in this section, must apply. Most importantly, the valuer must consider the comparability of size and potential for trading as well as the fashionability comparative and demand for the restaurant location in general.

The valuer should also be wary of utilising the analysis of premium transactions in relation to restaurant rents. They do not de-value comfortably. Premiums are a manifestation of matters outside the realms of profit rent capitalisation in the traditional manner. They relate to commercial economics from the caterers point of view which may cover such matters as the cannibalisation of existing plant and equipment, the time saved in not having to obtain planning consent, landlords consent and statutory and local authority consents etc, anticipated potential of the purchaser's own trading levels and numerous other factors which are not able to be broken down into rental terms. The tax position of the purchaser also plays a major part.

Profit and turnover method and turnover leases

There are occasions when the valuer will not be able to depend upon comparable evidence of other restaurant lettings. Examples of such occurrences would be establishments in the countryside in secluded locations, properties of a unique personality or character in town centres and restaurants which depend upon a particular venue for income such as the Tower of London or Madame Tussauds etc.

In these events, the valuer cannot depend upon the zoning or overall methods of valuations and is left to depend upon derivation of rental value from the assessment of actual or estimated profit and turnover.

In reality, this method almost to the exclusion of any others is that adopted by most operators in assessing rental value and indeed their own rental bid in the market place. To this extent, it is probably the purest form of rental valuation. Rental value is a very close relation to turnover potential and indeed to profit. They are directly linked and it is only that relationship which is of interest to the operator. One would rarely, if at all, hear a restaurateur make an offer at say £20 per sq.ft overall or £55 per sq.ft of Zone A when looking at a site. Their first questions are "What turnover can I produce?" "What is the potential of the site?"

Of course the valuer is often fettered by the constraints of the rent review provisions under a lease and as often is the case, those provisions do not entitle the valuer to consider the occupation of the tenants nor his profit or goodwill. The valuer in those circumstances has to look at the site with vacant possession. This does not preclude some sort of assessment of possible turnover and profit and thereafter rental value but the arbitrator or independent expert is not likely to take much heed of such hypothesis if he has the benefit of other comparable evidence.

So how does one go about assessing the turnover potential of a particular site which is of course the starting point of any calculation of this nature? The answer is with great caution and an even greater degree of imagination! Firstly, it is imperative that the valuer has a good grasp of the potential income and outgoings in relation to similar restaurants in similar locations. Again the maxim of "comparing like with like" must apply. The comparison must also relate to size, location, concept, licensing, trading hours etc. Having got several examples of profit and loss accounts of other establishments which are directly comparable, the valuer should be able to ascertain the normal range of outgoings and percentages which apply to a properly run business.

Traditionally there have been "rule of thumb" percentages applied to turnover, normally around 10% as being representative of rental value. This is not necessary to the case because the more successful restaurants would have lower rental percentages due to their higher than normal turnovers.

A calculation of gross turnover net of VAT but inclusive of service is a very difficult figure to ascertain accurately. Obviously different types of restaurant concepts will produce different trading levels and the valuer should ascertain what is the most likely use of the premises and then adopt the appropriate turnover level thereafter. With experience, the figure comes quickly to mind for the valuer but its components are very straightforward, it is a calculation as follows:

$$\text{Covers} \times \text{sittings} \times \text{net spend} \times \text{days.}$$

Covers are of course the number of seats within the restaurant. The density of occupation depends upon the concept. A very high class restaurant might have one seat per 3 sq.m whilst a Brasserie Bar may be closer to one seat per sq m or less.

The number of sittings is a far harder matter to assess. A very popular restaurant may turn its seats up to 10 or 15 times in a day, especially if there is a low spend and a small menu range. A high class restaurant may only see a turn around in seats of 2 or 2.5 times.

Spend is self-explanatory and is the average cost per head of a meal exclusive of VAT but inclusive of service charge. There may be different spends at different times of the day as some restaurants have differing menus for breakfast, lunch and evening.

The number of days that the unit trades is self-explanatory.

The next part of the equation is food cost or inversely gross profit and this can range between 75% and 50% depending upon the class of establishment and the expertise of the operator in food and liqueur purchasing. Popular catering tends to be around 25–30%, higher class establishments closer to 35% and 40% although it is quite possible to see figures of less than that for well run operations.

Staff costs should be between 20% and 25% normally again depending upon the class of the establishment. Obviously a higher class restaurant needs more experienced and well trained chefs and serving staff.

Staff wages would normally include distribution of service charges entirely or certainly a proportion of them. The valuer should enquire whether a "tronc" system is in place, usually with a "tronc master" who collects and distributes service charges and tips in agreed proportions to all staff. This payment from the establishment to the tronc master may well be separately audited and taxed. Obviously, if the wage cost does not include an allowance for the tronc, then turnover and profit/loss must be adjusted.

The valuer should be wary of exceptional items of expenditure which are not directly related to the "on-site business". These would be Head Office expenses, consultancy fees, exceptional professional fees, motor costs and all the other add-ons which can be attributed to a particular business and which do not have any particular relevance to the day to day running of that business.

Whether one deducts depreciation interest costs is dependent upon the circumstances of the transaction involved. If a landlord has contributed a major part of the fitting out costs then obviously these factors do not figure greatly. If the hypothetical tenant is obliged to fit out the establishment then these costs must be taken into account fully.

Depreciation tends to be over 10 years although it is not unusual to see examples of anything between 1 and 5 years. Obviously the avoidance of profit is sometimes advantageous and writing off capital costs over a year or two can subdue profits dramatically.

The rule generally is to impose logical and commercial circumstances to your example by taking normal and most likely figures and implanting them within the formula. Having carried out this exercise, the valuer will be left with one figure outstanding in the equation, namely rent.

This is not a very safe process of valuation because as there are so many imponderables the exercise tends to be too nebulous to be totally accurate, but it is certainly more accurate than any other alternative method in the circumstances of there being no comparable evidence available.

If the valuer is preparing a case for submission to an arbitrator the use of trading accounts in comparing other properties is admissible evidence. There are leading cases in this respect, namely:

Harewood Hotels Ltd v *Harris* [1958] 1 All ER 104; [1957] 170 EG 77
WJ Barton Ltd v *Long Acre Securities Ltd* [1982] 1 WLR 398; 1982
    1 All ER 465
Cornwall Coast Country Club v *Cardgrange Ltd* [1987] 1 EGLR 146;
    (1987) 282 EG 1664
Electricity Supply Nominees Ltd v *London Clubs Ltd* [1988] 2 EGLR
    152; [1988] 2 EG 71
ARC Ltd v *Schofield* [1990] 2 EGLR 52; [1990] 38 EG 113

Most rent review provisions would preclude the valuer seeking an Order of Discovery at arbitration in respect of the Trading Accounts of the establishment but the valuer can indicate the quality of comparable properties by utilising Trading Accounts for those properties which in turn can indicate the potential of the subject premises.

Turnover leases The market is demonstrating progressively a liking for turnover based leases. These will become far more common practice and the valuer may well come across them for the purposes of the valuation in the near future.

The essence of the arrangement is that the landlord will accept a lower base rental normally geared to 50/75% of market rental value. In addition or in substitution the tenant will pay a percentage of turnover, normally between 5% and 15% depending upon the circumstances of the agreement. Within the agreement the landlord would normally contribute some degree of capital towards partially fitting out or even fit out the establishment entirely. The higher the contribution the greater the turnover percentage normally.

Within the circumstances of a major contribution it is not unusual to find that the lease is contracted outside of the provisions of the Landlord and Tenant Act 1954 Part II in respect of matters of compensation and security of tenure.

The base rent is paid quarterly in advance and there is a refund or top-up assessment at the end of the trading year, depending upon the turnover of the establishment. The base rent is the minimum figure that is payable to the landlord. The base rent is normally reviewed annually usually to the turnover rent level of the previous year.

These types of lease incur additional costs in terms of auditing and reporting but can be of great benefit to the tenant as their rent relates directly to their turnover and profitability.

From the landlord's point of view the monitoring of turnover can be a problem but this process has become far more sophisticated and much has been learnt from the American market where such arrangements are commonplace.

The valuer should be aware that in most instances security of tenure is not available but equally, potential for profit can be enhanced.

Capital valuations

The components of value

Fixtures and fittings These are usually purchased for cash and remain in the balance sheet adjusted annually to take into account capital allowance relief, permitted by the Finance Act provisions. This allowance is permitted against written down values so that by the fifth year there really is a nominal provision against fixtures and fittings. This capital allowance relief is highly important in terms of valuation because from the vendor's point of view, if the asset has been written down and a higher value has been attributed he is going to have to pay substantial tax in the form of capital gains and possible income tax. The purchaser on the other hand will want to have a fairly high value for fixtures and fittings because he can gain the relief described earlier.

In practice fixtures and fittings really have a nominal value in terms of resale in the open market. Once they are taken outside the premises, they have a very low comparative value whatever their age and condition. They may have far more value *in situ* if the purchaser has some use for them within his own operation. Alternatively they tend to be of no consequence, although they may be of great tax importance in the context of apportionment of a sale price. Branded items, ie with the name of the restaurant on them are not of any importance unless the business is sold as a going concern. Leased and rented items have to be identified.

Some restaurants contain very valuable fixtures and fittings, silverware and antiques and these should be valued by experts.

Much depends upon the type of valuation being carried out by the valuer. If the valuation is for a funding source such as a bank then they may want to know the true value for resale purposes of all assets including fixtures and fittings and the net book value will have no relevance, whereas for balance sheet purposes they may have. Certainly if valuing for acquisition or sale the value attributed if utilised for apportionment could be fundamental.

Goodwill As described earlier there are several types of goodwill to consider. There is the goodwill relating to the business, but also the goodwill relating to the trading name and there is the goodwill relating to the property.

Brand names and trade marks are eminently saleable. Excellent trade names have been sold for anything between £50,000 and £100,000 in the restaurant market.

Goodwill in tax terms has different effects for the vendor and the purchaser. The vendor can gain rollover relief against goodwill as long as he invests in a similar type of business within the time permitted by the Inland Revenue. The purchaser of goodwill cannot offset the cost against tax but he can sell it again. The base value is increased annually by indexation, the revenue having allocated 1982 as the base from which indexation commences.

The valuation of goodwill is a very difficult exercise for the valuer to undertake and is exceptionally hard to define unless there are very high traditional profits.

Leasehold or freehold interest The vendor can benefit from rollover relief, but leases are particularly complicated because of the need to reinvest into a lease certainly as long if not longer than the lease you have sold. There are other fairly complicated aspects which also relate and the valuer should seek advice if he is not sure.

From the purchaser's point of view the Revenue looks on leases as diminishing assets and when they are sold the Revenue will have written off the value of the lease over the period up until the next rent review until the leasehold value basically evaporates. Accordingly the taxation implications when a lease is sold that has been totally or partially discounted can be punishing as far as capital gains tax is concerned. Unfortunately leases cannot be depreciated against profit.

A vendor would quite obviously prefer to have the apportionment of a sale mainly in favour of goodwill or leasehold interest with fixtures and fittings being the last thing he wants in terms of value. The purchaser would obviously require the opposite with fixtures and fittings being at the top, goodwill second, and leasehold interest third. Normally in the open market a deal is done to this extent and the values attributable to various assets which make up the whole restaurant value are fairly artificial for that reason alone.

Stock When dealing with stock, care should be taken that you do get the right stock values from the vendor, that they are not inflated and of course they should be based upon net cost value not on retail value. The incidence of VAT is also an important aspect if appropriate. There are very specialised valuers for stock, but most importantly the implications of liquor value are the strongest and here there are some very big gains to be had in certain circumstances and specialist advice is absolutely necessary.

Licensing It is important to ensure that your valuation takes into account the ability to transfer licences or certainly an assumption that there is an undertaking in any contract to fully support the transfer of the licences especially Justices full on, Music and Dancing &

Entertainment Licences, and as part and parcel of the valuation the valuer should investigate this aspect. Some licences have very large values and play a very important part in the profitability of the business. This is an important aspect.

Tax losses If the assets of the company are being valued, the suggestion may be that a tax loss runs with the corporation. Be careful about assessing the value of the tax loss. Many accountants discount tax losses entirely. The Revenue are very strict indeed in the application of tax losses and you basically have to have a duplication of the acquired business if there is to be any chance of utilising the benefits of the loss for another companies profits, to the extent that it is almost impossible to gain benefit and the value of the tax loss must be discounted down to nil or very nominal value.

These are basically the component assets of most restaurants and at times you may be requested to value them independently of each other. Some banks for example ask the valuer to give an assessment of the value of fixtures and fittings independently of the lease or the lease by itself, although not often the goodwill of the business. This is a very dangerous exercise as it is not possible to just sell off these assets in the real commercial world and get any reasonable value. The general rule, and it is in the interests of the fundor and the fundee to make this point, is that the whole in respect of the restaurant is certainly worth much more than the individual parts and it is a viewpoint that you should insist upon maintaining if at all possible.

Other aspects to consider before casting your valuation have been covered in the Section headed "Factors Affecting Value" earlier in this chapter. All of these matters should be considered in-depth where appropriate.

Restaurants with vacant possession

Freehold values are fairly straightforward. If you have a vacant restaurant and it is a freehold then the owner/occupier will normally pay slightly less than what would appear to be the investment value. Not many operators wish to buy freeholds and normally they are funded simultaneously or as soon as possible after completion. Some of the major groups do own their own freeholds but they really are the exception in most parts of the market place.

The main exceptions are the roadside sector, where freehold purchases have to be considered regularly because of the lack of good funding sources for the time being. In addition the traditional or classic restaurants in the City Centre also changes hands as freeholds fairly regularly. This is a different market place based upon the residential market with houses being used as collateral.

If the equipment and fixtures and fittings in the restaurant are of good class then the valuer may place a little bit of overage on the freehold price. The basis of assessment is the standard method of capitalisation of market rent by years' purchase to perpetuity at the appropriate yield.

Leasehold properties are an entirely different matter. The normal calculation of leasehold value by applying the appropriate multiplier in the form of years' purchase suitably adjusted for tax and sinking fund, to a profit rent does not apply to a calculation of value for leasehold restaurants.

This traditional approach to leasehold value plays absolutely no part unless the leasehold interest is of such substance that it dominates the restaurant value. The length of such a lease would have to be well in excess of 20 years without break or rent review, albeit at a fairly low rental in comparison to market value, to stand a chance of dominating and superseding the restaurant value. This brings us to the most important maxim to be considered by the restaurant valuer. "One must value the purchaser and not the property." This means in simple terms that you must look at the market place in general, the likely demand and range of operators who might want the property and be aware of the plateau of price that is likely to be achieved from that fraternity.

Basically, the catering market operates in a very similar way to the stock market. There are bands of value which go up and down depending on the market circumstances and operators pay premiums within those bands at the appropriate time. In essence, they are paying what is physiologically acceptable to their fraternity. In Central London we have seen those bands move up from a £100,000 just over ten years ago as being the normal price that people would be paying for these sort of restaurants right the way up to over £1m at the end of 1989. This does not mean that the entire market pays those prices but those who are active have to seriously consider doing so and up until the beginning of 1990 were already paying such figures. There has been a slip in that market by dramatic amounts but there are still very substantial premiums paid in the Central London core. It does not seem to matter either that properties are rack rented. Often a recently reviewed or renewed lease or indeed a lease which has only just been taken in the open market is sold on for a major premium. The question of capitalised profit rent just does not apply.

In essence, the restaurant purchaser carries out a form of residual valuation based upon their estimated turnover and breaking down to a minimum net return on capital. Within that equation will be implanted the maximum premium that they can afford to pay after taking into consideration fitting out costs and possibly those elements of the existing building which they can cannibalise for their purposes.

In a highly competitive market where expansion is important especially for the large corporations the payment of premiums is simply a commercial equation relating to their business and in most cases their anticipated level of business. In essence, therefore, the caterer is actually paying for his own potential in many cases especially in a bull market. Most purchasers in the vacant restaurant market will not be in the slightest bit interested in the previous occupier's trading accounts.

Some logic to the caterer's viewpoint in making bids for vacant leasehold restaurants is that in purchasing a unit they will have the benefit in many instances of the hinterland equipment such as plant, trunking, ventilation and all the other pieces of equipment which are quite expensive when they are installed originally and still have a great deal of life left. Also this would save a great deal of time in terms of gaining landlords' consent for all sorts of rights and easements relating to trunking, rights of way, means of escape etc. The purchaser will also have bye-law and statutory consent in terms of hygiene, means of escape, licensing etc.

A great deal of risk is taken out of the situation accordingly especially in relation to planning and a great deal of time and money is saved in the process.

These premiums do not stand up to any analysis for distillation of profit rent.

Conversely caterers are not prepared to "fund" major premiums for equally excessive rentals and accordingly their philosophy applies simply to premiums.

The business value

When looking at company accounts in support of a valuation the initial aspect to consider is the standard and quality of the auditors and information given to you. Most accountants are very fine professionals whatever their size but accounts prepared by an obscure accountant may not be as credible as a more established accountant. One must consider the nature and stature of the vendor and his circumstances of sale. Basically, is the vendor someone to be trusted and is there a less than authentic reason for his selling? In this respect the date of preparation of accounts is often quite interesting. Hastily prepared accounts although undoubtedly in most cases quite bona fide, should be approached with some degree of extra caution and the reason for the delay ascertained.

The source and quality of turnover is very important. Is trade seasonal or are there other special circumstances affecting turnover?

From the turnover one can derive the gross profit. This would classically reflect a food cost of between 27% and 35%. If it is more than this amount, depending upon the style of operation which is being valued, you are probably facing an understated profit and if it is less then you are undoubtedly facing an inflated profit. A vendor will surprisingly wish to verbally, although not in writing, point out the former but tend not to discuss the latter at all!

The turnover or gross profit can be adjusted in several ways. Transfers and additions of cash by the vendor inflate or deflate gross turnover as do such changes as private deals with suppliers and so on. The general rule is that you ought to look closely at the food cost and if you have a major difference on say an average of 30% food cost then further scrutiny is necessary.

Other key percentages have been considered earlier in the discussion of profits/turnover method of rents.

Light, heat, telephone, insurance, motor expenses, accounting, cleaning, laundry, credit card commission, repairs and renewals, etc, all have approximate percentage costs for each different sector of the market and may have to be considered in reaching the correct adjusted net profit.

It is normally important for most purchasers to look at profit in relation to turnover in order to calculate capital value. Some look at turnover and utilise a simple multiplier in order to get to capital value and this is more in line with the classic public house valuation approach. In restaurants it is not such a good guideline. Profit and turnover ratios have a use in displaying the creditability and potential of a business and certainly most professional operators would be able to ascertain the scope of possible improvement by looking at that ratio. Indeed in this latter respect a seasoned valuer would also be looking to capitalise the possible potential of improving trade and profit.

The most important ratio is profit to capital costs and in today's marketplace pre-tax and pre-finance, most operators would be looking for a 25%/30% return on capital costs. This will enable them to have a repayment plan deriving capital and interest out of profit, which is a criterion currently demanded by most funding sources.

Other points to look out for are head office expenses and administrative costs and other miscellaneous outgoings, such as directors' remuneration. Another is consultancy fees for the directors or for an associated company.

All these items can be added back in or discounted depending upon the circumstances of the purchaser and they will have an effect on the bottom line, that is pre-tax profit.

Depreciation practice is also an area to watch. A company may depreciate over 1 to 10 years against profit, obviously a short depreciation period will have a substantial effect on profit and vice versa.

Other items that the valuer should look at are undisclosed liabilities – these are very important in terms of valuation of a business. Certainly indemnities, warranties and retentions play a big part in such matters as VAT, wages, PAYE, National Insurance, Corporation Tax, Statutory Fines and other types of obligations. These unforeseen costs materially affect the ultimate yield on capital and must be identified and provided for in a valuation.

The same applies to employment, redundancies and holiday pay entitlements and other hidden accruals.

The valuer should also look closely at the assets which are shown on the balance sheet – have they been overstated or overvalued? Are they necessary for the business?

In terms of dealing with a major freehold or leasehold asset, the general rule is not to double count. The purchaser cannot pay for a business and pay an additional price for the freehold. Many naive vendors would like this to be taken into account.

The approach to the valuation of these assets within the scope of the business should be quite straightforward and it makes practical sense to adopt the attitude of the hypothetical or likely purchaser. For example if a freehold restaurant was worth £1m and the business to which it is attached is making £160,000 net profit the funding costs of repayment of capital and interest would swamp the net profit to such a degree that a major loss would be incurred. In these circumstances, the valuer should look at the vacant possession value of the freehold together with any other important asset values including goodwill, fixtures and fittings and stock. The value of the business as such would be very nominal and totally superseded by the dominating value of the freehold or long leasehold interest. Another approach to this problem could be the assumption that the freehold would be funded. Assumption is the operative word as there is no guarantee that that would be the case and equally no guarantee that a purchaser would acquire an asset of this nature dependent upon the need to arrange a leaseback.

Following the above example, assuming the rental value to be £100,000 p.a. exclusive to achieve a leaseback for the £1m freehold asset, this would leave a net profit pre-tax for the business after rental of £60,000 p.a. and then this would be capitalised accordingly.

The problems arise when in the above example the net profit was traditionally say less than £100,000 p.a. pre-tax. The valuer would then revert to the basic asset values.

A further asset to be considered is the potential of the business, after all most businesses are being sold because they are tired or need capital injection or possibly the intervention of a large corporation to exploit their promise. How the valuer deals with this added benefit to the purchaser of realising this potential is a difficult question to answer. Basically, one must go back to the old maxim of valuing the likely purchaser and to seeing what he can bring to the party in terms of stimulating the business.

As an example, if one had a group which was ailing and they wanted to purchase a trading brand which had great potential for exploitation in the purchaser's units there has to be some added potential or marriage value. Alternatively, one could consider a purchaser who had major advantages by the acquisition of a business which when assimilated would have its administrative costs reduced and its buying power increased. Again there is some degree of potential which has some value in this package.

Unless there is an identifiable profit element to derive from the hypothetical purchaser's point of view the process is very much one of rounding up. On the other hand of course the reverse can apply and if one is aware of the potential of loss of trade then the normally applied capital value would have to be subdued.

And so the valuer will ultimately get to the stage whereby having considered all the aspects mentioned previously in this chapter, he has the accounts before him properly investigated and it is time to value the business.

The classic approach is basically to reflect the value of the net trading entities in the balance sheet together with other intangible assets which may be included such as goodwill. Whether or not the goodwill is included in the balance sheet the business would be valued as a going concern in the open market to reflect its overall potential earning capacity and therefore there may be a value higher or lower than a balance sheet figure.

In practice, one starts by capitalising the net profits of the company and making adjustments for all matters that have been mentioned so far in this chapter. The most important figure to consider is the true net profit pre-tax. The multiplier that is applied to the adjusted net profit varies depending upon several factors.

Of relevance in this respect is the calibre of the net profit being produced. If this net profit has little potential for improvement and is of small stature then the multiplier, years purchase for pretax or P/E for post-tax profits is normally directly in line with a commercial return on capital. Accordingly, if you were valuing a fish and chip shop in Scunthorpe and it was producing £30,000 net profit pre-tax and finance you are not likely to value at more than about 2½ times the net profit. After a repayment plan and interest provision, and by the time some tax has been paid as well as directors' remuneration, some profit is left and the purchasers would have somewhere to live above the shop.

However, if profits increase in stature so the year's purchase and P/E increases dramatically. Restaurant profits become far more interesting once they start approaching £100,000 pretax and at this level, the smaller catering groups would be interested in acquiring property in the region of 3.5/4.5 times pre-tax profits currently. This figure will change depending upon market conditions. The author hastens to add here that the potential is highly important in the scheme of things. If the restaurant has got potential available then the higher levels of year's purchase and P/E are achievable. If the restaurant is completely exploited in terms of its potential then it starts becoming of less interest unless there is a good brand name attached which can be utilised elsewhere.

In excess of £100,000 net profit and certainly once you start to value one of the smaller sized groups the year's purchase and P/E increases dramatically because the public companies come into play and depending upon the size of the group, the potential, the branding element etc, one can see dramatically increased net profits even in the current market place.

The public companies certainly in the market leading up to 1990 and in recent months played a game of buying net profits on a P/E dramatically less than that applied to their own P/Es in the stock markets but higher than applied in the private sector of the restaurant market. As a result, pure net profit was purchased and capitalised at far higher levels than the acquisition price once it became part of the public company's annual figures.

The maxim of valuing the purchaser certainly relates far more to the large portfolio acquisitions. All sorts of reasons can apply to the value attributed to the large group including the opportunities to quickly expand an existing group, potential for franchising, better purchasing power, better utilisation of existing management and so on. The reasons and angles are numerous and various. This is an exceptionally difficult valuation for all but very experienced valuers.

Branding and franchising also play their part in the valuation of restaurants. It is exceptionally hard to place a value on these elements or indeed give an indication of how to value within a chapter of this nature. Basically, a brand name can generate goodwill all on its own and in doing so, profits can be dramatically enhanced by conversion of new units to the brand name. The purchaser will know its value better than any other person involved in the transaction. However, if you are valuing an existing brand you have to look carefully at the goodwill that is related to that brand, consider whether it has further potential to be exploited or whether indeed it has franchising potential. Only by knowing the circumstances of revenue and the saleability of the franchise can figures be obtained which enable you to provide a value relating to the situation.

When valuing master franchises the valuer must consider any contractual obligation to expand, the costs of such expansions, the status of the franchiser, the contract under which the franchise is held and the potential for sub-franchising both nationally and internationally. All these matters basically bring the value outside of the realms of straightforward restaurant valuation and into corporate valuation.

The comments under this particular section do not in any way comprehensively cover what is a major subject with many more facets than have been described above. The valuer is advised to seek more detailed advice in the event of any reservations as to the approach to value. The valuer should be aware that undervaluing can be just as disastrous for a restaurateur as overvaluing can be for the fundor, especially in the current financial climate.

Restaurant Red Book valuations

Following publication of the RICS Appraisal and Valuation Manual which effectively amalgamates and revises the former Statements of Asset Valuation Practice and Guidance Notes (the Red Book) and the Manual of Valuation Guidance Notes (the White Book) – the valuers main reference point for guidance in valuing restaurants will be Guidance Note 9 entitled "Valuation of Restaurants". This section is now completed and will effectively be an extension of Guidance Note 7 which deals with "Trading – Related Valuations and Goodwill". As with SAVP 12 of the old Red Book, Guidance Note 7 deals with the *valuation of property fully equipped as an operational entity and valued having regard to trading potential.*

Restaurants can normally be valued therefore, on the basis existing use value. The Valuer should be careful to emphasise when valuing in accordance with Guidance Notes 7 and 9, that the property is looked at as an operational entity.

Restaurants can normally be valued therefore on the basis of open market value for the existing use. The valuers should be careful to emphasise, when valuing in accordance with SAVP 12, that he is looking at the property *as an operational entity.*

Restaurants fall into the category of properties which invariably change hands in the open market at prices based directly on trading potential. The purest form of valuation under this code will be a global figure to include fixtures, fittings, furniture, stock and goodwill, but the code is flexible and the exact form of valuation may be varied in accordance with instructing client's wishes. It is common to find for example that the valuer is not required to include stock. The valuer may also be asked to ignore goodwill which has been created in the business by the present owner and which may be transferable to other properties in the event of the subject property being sold, but in preparing a valuation on this basis, the valuer may still be able to take into account the value which is reflected in trading potential which runs with the property. The valuer must be careful to differentiate between the two.

Commonly, the valuer may be asked by an instructing lender to prepare a valuation on a "bricks and mortar" basis, which supposedly represents the open market value of the land and buildings element of the trading entity. Such a valuation poses problems for the valuer for two reasons.

1. Firstly, restaurants, especially those held on a leasehold basis, are rarely sold in the open market denuded of fixtures and fittings

and therefore there will be limited comparable evidence upon the required basis.

2. The valuer may be required to value a restaurant which is already fully fitted and equipped and operational and remain so even in the event of default.

The "bricks and mortar" basis of valuation is therefore usually an artificial exercise which has little relevance to market practice and more importantly the valuation on this basis may not actually be of any assistance either to the borrower or the lender because it does not relate to a price realisable on sale. In such circumstances, the valuer may be able to persuade his client that it would be more appropriate to value the restaurant with the benefit of all trading assets.

The "bricks and mortar" basis of valuation may be appropriate for valuing high street fast food restaurants, where the value lies in the property and the occupier's fixtures and fittings are highly personal and unlikely to be of interest to a potential purchaser. In fact, the best bidders for such sites are often A2 users.

There may still be a need, however, to provide a valuation which the lender can rely upon in the event of default, ie when as a result of failure to pay interest and/or capital, the property is to be placed on the market at the insistence of the lender. This is often referred to as a "forced sale valuation", although this was a term which the former Red Book declared invalid and one which should not be used under any circumstances. Under the new Valuation Manual, a "forced sale valuation" is dealt with by Practise Statement 4.7, which is the estimated restricted realisation price for the existing use (ERRPEU), as an operational entity valued having regard to trading potential.

A valuation in the event of default is still an open market valuation which may reflect trading potential and also other trading assets of the business such as fixtures, fittings and equipment. Furthermore the business may also be open for trade but the key distinction between this and a full valuation will be the proviso that the vendor has imposed an undue time constraint for securing completion of the disposal and the accounts or trading records may not be available to a potential purchaser. The client may also make further stipulations on the ERRPEU basis in terms of the extent of the inventory remaining and the degree of permanence of existing licences, consents, certificates or permits.

Clearly the time scale will be a key factor in determining the price obtainable and then will commonly stipulate between two and six months. Subject to market conditions prevailing at the date of valuation, a six month period may be ample time to find a purchaser and complete the sale and in such circumstances the valuation in the event of default would not be as unduly difficult as the valuation of the same restaurants without the time constraints.

Whatever the nature of the valuation required it is imperative for the valuer to state his assumptions from a source of information especially in relation to trading records and most importantly the valuer should be careful to stipulate exactly the basis upon which his valuation is prepared. The words "open market valuation of the leasehold interest for the existing use as a restaurant" are rarely sufficient. One final comment in respect of restaurant valuations in accordance with the Valuation Manual. Quite often within the restaurant fraternity, information is not up to date or readily available and the valuer may be asked to provide the valuation without the opportunity to carry out adequate inspections or without definitive information which would normally be available in carrying out a formal valuation. Guidance notes 7.8.3 of the valuation manual deals with this problem and should be carefully considered and utilised by the valuer in such circumstances.

© David Coffer, 1996

INDEX

D